MW00561196

The Pearl Harbor Secret

The Pearl Harbor Secret

WHY ROOSEVELT UNDERMINED THE U.S. NAVY

Sewall Menzel

Foreword by Tobias R. Philbin

PRAEGER®

An Imprint of ABC-CLIO, LLC

Santa Barbara, California • Denver, Colorado

Library of Congress Cataloging-in-Publication Data
Names: Menzel, Sewall H. (Sewall Hamm), 1942- author.
Title: The Pearl Harbor secret : why Roosevelt undermined the U.S. Navy /
  Sewall Menzel ; foreword by Tobias R. Philbin.
Description: Santa Barbara, California : Praeger, [2020] | Includes bibliographical
  references and index.
Identifiers: LCCN 2019047790 (print) | LCCN 2019047791 (ebook) |
  ISBN 9781440875854 (cloth) | ISBN 9781440875861 (ebook)
Subjects: LCSH: Roosevelt, Franklin D. (Franklin Delano), 1882-1945. |
  Pearl Harbor (Hawaii), Attack on, 1941. | World War, 1939–1945–Naval operations,
  American. | Strategy–History–20th century.
Classification: LCC D767.92 .M46 2020 (print) | LCC D767.92 (ebook) |
  DDC 940.54/26693–dc23
LC record available at https://lccn.loc.gov/2019047790
LC ebook record available at https://lccn.loc.gov/2019047791

ISBN: 978-1-4408-7585-4 (print)
       978-1-4408-7586-1 (ebook)

24 23 22 21 20   1 2 3 4 5

This book is also available as an eBook.

Praeger
An Imprint of ABC-CLIO, LLC

ABC-CLIO, LLC
147 Castilian Drive
Santa Barbara, California 93117
www.abc-clio.com

This book is printed on acid-free paper ∞

Manufactured in the United States of America

To Those Who Served

In politics, nothing happens by accident. If it happens, you can bet it was planned that way.

—*Franklin Delano Roosevelt*

It's a Goddamned mousetrap!

—*Admiral James O. Richardson*

(describing Pearl Harbor and its narrow channel that only would allow one ship to pass through at a time)

The enemy was Hitler and Japan had given us an opportunity.

—*Harry Hopkins, secretary of commerce under FDR*

(White House cabinet meeting discussion the evening of December 7, 1941)

Contents

Photo essay appears following page 142

Foreword

Historian Sewall Menzel illuminates and reminds us of the not well-known pivotal crisis of the last century, involving the imperative to defeat the nuclear bomb threat that Nazi Germany represented to the United States and the other democracies of our global civilization. In so doing he lays out the communication about the existential Nazi threat portrayed by Albert Einstein to President Franklin D. Roosevelt (FDR) in late September 1939. Delivered in a letter that stated the Germans were in the process of very likely acquiring a nuclear weapons capability that would enable them to literally blow the USA off the face of the earth caught Roosevelt's attention: the survival of America was at stake. And FDR took action!

He had two courses of action open to him: first, to immediately engage the American scientific community in its own top-secret project of acquiring an atomic bomb and second, to directly confront and defeat Nazi Germany militarily through outright invasion. FDR decided to do both! But it would not be easy, as there was no money available at that time for the scientific community to fully gear up. In addition, 80 percent of Americans did not, under any circumstances, want to become engaged in another ground war in Europe as had happened a little more than two decades before in 1917. The horrendous American losses on the Western Front in just six months of brutal fighting, combined with the rise of the dictators (Stalin, Mussolini, and Hitler) as a result of the Great War, brought on bitter recriminations that continuously plagued the American antiwar psyche. How to get around this problem vexed the president tremendously.

As time went on the dynamics of world politics played into FDR's hands. The Japanese in late 1940 offered Nazi Germany a military alliance against the United States. A cocky Adolf Hitler, who had just conquered Western Europe, jumped at the opportunity, little knowing that he had given the American president an unexpected opportunity. This enabled FDR to develop over time a baiting strategy to bring about a confrontation with Japan that would lead directly to a confrontation and war with Nazi Germany. To bring this about was Franklin Roosevelt's driving imperative from that moment on, as Menzel succinctly brings out in so much vivid detail. FDR needed an overt act and Japan would provide it, paving the way for a Nazi declaration of war on the United States just four days after the December 7, 1941, attack on America's Pacific Fleet at Pearl Harbor.

Dr. Menzel also tells the incredible story of the U.S. and Allied direction-finding stations and their breaking of the Imperial Japanese Navy's (IJN's) key, highly complex operational codes. Some 22 American, British, and Dutch radio intercept stations arrayed across the Pacific, combined with their radio direction capabilities referred to as the "splendid arrangement," enabled Washington to virtually track the Japanese Pearl Harbor Strike Force right down to the very moment when it launched its avalanche of bombs and torpedoes against Adm. Husband Kimmel's unsuspecting fleet in Hawaii. Unsuspecting in Hawaii perhaps, but not in Washington, which was alerted as to what was about to befall Kimmel by its highly effective splendid arrangement. The system worked and Menzel brings this all out in meticulously researched, vivid detail. We all, Menzel included, owe a debt to Robert Stinnett whose tenacious pursuit of the Crane Files in Indiana under the Freedom of Information Act forced Washington to release thousands of the documents, which "spilled the beans" in illuminating what the politics of Pearl Harbor was all about.

Based on five years of research in the national archives in Maryland, New York, Washington, and California, Menzel carefully unwinds the complex web of truth and falsehood by omission and commission of a half century of cover-up for reasons of state. He literally connected the proverbial "dots," which have brought out the complexity and immensity of the Pearl Harbor overt act, placing it in its appropriate context of a baited trap and road to war with Nazi Germany. The American commanders at Pearl

Harbor were deprived of the critical intelligence they needed to locate, divine its intensions, and even ambush the IJN's strike force as it made its approach into its launching sites just 230 miles north of Pearl Harbor. But it should be noted that had not Nazi Germany been baited into declaring war on the United States, the policy, strategy and resource allocations needed for victory in the world's first nuclear arms race would not have been possible.

As someone who has both studied and practiced strategic warning for nearly 20 years in both National and Defense Warning staffs during the cold war, the Pearl Harbor issue was indeed a well-kept secret. In digging it out, Menzel, following in the footsteps of Stinnett, has broken vitally important new ground. *The Pearl Harbor Secret* is a benchmark for scholarship in the history of crisis and the nature and use of strategic warning. It is also a model of persistence in the historian's craft.

Tobias R. Philbin, PhD
Commander U.S. Naval Reserve (Ret.); Intelligence Officer at the National Geo-Spatial Intelligence Agency (Ret.); Warning Officer and Analyst, National Intelligence Council and Defense Intelligence Agency (Ret.); Adjunct Professor, University of Maryland Graduate School of Management and Technology
Lexington, Virginia, 2019

Author of books on naval history and strategy:
Battle of Dogger Bank: The First Dreadnought Engagement 1915,
The Lure of Neptune: German-Soviet Naval Collaboration
1919–1941, Admiral von Hipper: The Inconvenient Hero

Acknowledgments

I would be remiss if I did not acknowledge the assistance of many archivists and librarians whose able support enabled this work to come to fruition. First and foremost is Nathaniel S. Patch, archives specialist with the National Archives and Research Administration (NARA), Archives II, Reference Section, Textual Archives Services Division, who guided me over a series of weeklong visits through the labyrinth of a haphazard and convoluted filing system that constitutes hundreds, if not thousands, of Hollinger storage boxes that house the estimated half-million or more documents of one sort or another that deal with the years leading up to the outbreak of World War II in the Pacific. With his assistance I was able to screen through and find the key documents and pages that verified that the Imperial Japanese Navy had broken its own radio listening silence midway through its maneuvering toward Pearl Harbor during the first few days of December 1941—a critical event that was noted by a number of radio monitoring and intercept sources and duly reported to Office of Naval Intelligence in

Washington, DC. Patch also helped me locate the all-important, original translations of the ONI's decoded "Bomb Plot" messages referred to in the Pearl Harbor Attack Hearings.

Archivists Kathleen Crosman, Susan H. Karren, and Patty McNamee of NARA's Pacific Alaska Region archive in Seattle guided me over a period of a week, gleaning key pieces of information that I was otherwise unaware of about the 13th Naval District's contributions to and operations of the West Coast Communications Intelligence Network (WCCI). At the NARA Pacific Region San Bruno archive near San Francisco, archivist Robert Glass helped me screen through one of the most disorganized archival systems I have ever encountered, involving a mix of hundreds of Hollinger boxes and cardboard cartons, some of which provided important insights into the organization and functions of the 14th Naval District in Hawaii and the 12th Naval District's operations in San Francisco, which included a number of the commercial radio and cable communications companies operating in support of Naval Intelligence. The Laguna Niguel (now Riverside), California, archive has an excellent file on Adm. Kimmel's Plan 2M-1, as well as other reports and orders from Washington, DC, that impacted on the 1941 situation in the Pacific.

A frequently overlooked but also important NARA facility is the Franklin D. Roosevelt Library at Hyde Park, which provided me with numerous insights into Roosevelt's modus operandi and related features of his ad hoc style of foreign policy management. In addition, the key letter from Albert Einstein to Roosevelt in late 1939 was made available to me for purposes of this book. I also want to recognize the able support of Erma Fink, senior librarian at the Dudley Knox Library of the Naval Post Graduate School in Monterey, California, for permitting me to examine the 14th Naval District's Combat Intelligence Center (formerly HYPO) daily Communication Intelligence Summaries (CIS), Part III, which provided an insight into the spectacular progress made in the breaking of the Imperial Japanese Navy's operational Code Book D (5-Number or JN-25) that enabled the outnumbered U.S. Navy to win the decisive Battle of Midway in mid-1942. This book would not have been complete without the dedicated efforts on the part of the Broward County Library's Special Research Librarian Amy Miller, who not only obtained valuable and otherwise obscure technical books and studies on radio operations and radio direction finding from numerous other libraries around the country but also obtained on loan the complete microfiche film rendition of Secretary of War Henry Stimson's personal typewritten diary, which was invaluable in understanding President Roosevelt's 1941 overt act strategy in regards to Japan in the Pacific.

In addition, through the efforts of Grady Lewis, editor of *Cryptolog*, the official publication of the Naval Cryptologic Veterans Association, I was able to obtain back issues of the journal that provided insights into the operations and functioning of all the navy's official signal intercept and radio direction finding (tracking) stations operating as part of the "splendid arrangement" in the Pacific. I also want to recognize the able assistance provided to me by a former military attaché friend of mine from our Bolivia days, Richard Montalvo, who greatly aided my initial foray into the complicated world of the national archives at Laguna Niguel, California. I want to thank Padraic (Pat) Carlin at Praeger, whose guidelines for putting the master manuscript together made this book better; Tessa Somberg, Michelle Scott, Kristen Beach, and Robin Tutt at ABC-CLIO; Nicholle Robertson and Kristine Hunt at BookComp, Inc., for their invaluable assistance; Toby Philbin for his prolific and thoughtful comments throughout the manuscript; and Silverander Design Firm for the cover.

Finally, this book would not have come to fruition without the advice and editorial expertise of Jan Kardys and Barbara Ellis-Uchino at Black Hawk Literary Agency, Stephen B. Ellis for gratis proofreading, and Tak Uchino for formatting and creating superb prepublication copies of *The Pearl Harbor Secret*.

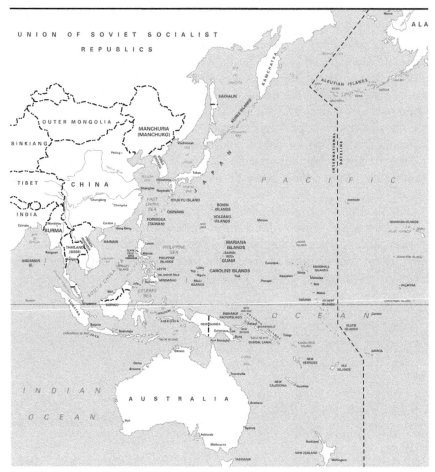

The Western Pacific. (United States Military Academy Department of History)

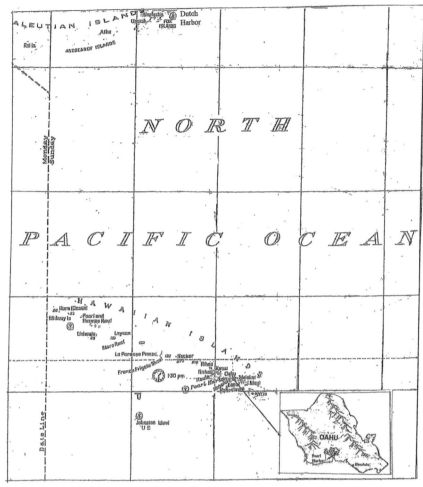

North Pacific Ocean. (National Archives)

Introduction

Of all the battles and all the wars, one might ask, "Why yet another book about Pearl Harbor?" One might think that by the 21st century, the issue has been so thoroughly worked over that it ought to just go away. Ninety minutes that history refuses to forget. It remains a contentious issue and there is a reason for this.

The crux of this book, about great power politics, is an examination of the inherent conflict that exists between the moral duty of a national leader to protect citizens' lives on the one hand and the duty to defend the vital national interest of survival on the other. Stated in an another way: What happens when a president finds himself in a quandary, trying to save lives in the long run, but having to expend them in the short term in order to protect the survival of the nation as a free, democratic state? This is what happened to President Franklin D. Roosevelt.

Alerted in 1939 by the free world's top scientific minds, including Albert Einstein, Roosevelt was put on notice that Nazi Germany was working on the development of an extraordinarily destructive weapon. The end goal of this sinister enterprise was to produce a nuclear chain reaction of incredible power—the atomic bomb! The president instantly grasped the horrific significance of Hitler's new threat, but his hands were tied by a population struggling to survive the Great Depression. After "the war to end all wars" had failed to do so, the vast majority of Americans were not interested in seeing America involve itself in another of Europe's seemingly perpetual wars for an ever illusive peace.

If Hitler's scientists were successful, the survival of the United States would be placed in jeopardy. Preventing the German scientific community from achieving Hitler's aim of quite literally blowing the United States and England off the map became an all-consuming, driving imperative for Roosevelt. In order to prevent this, Roosevelt would have to defeat Germany militarily, overthrow its Nazi government, and neutralize its scientific resources for making an A-bomb. The alternative would be to use his own scientific community and resources to develop America's own atomic weapon first. Roosevelt opted to do both.

A major obstacle in this effort would be the winning over of not only the American people but also the U.S. House of Representatives; only they can declare war and Congress was not interested. All this led to Roosevelt's most important command decision of World War II, some two years *before* the United States formally entered the war.

From the president's perspective, Pearl Harbor and the events leading up to the outbreak of war in the Pacific were not about war with Japan per se; they were about war with Adolf Hitler's Nazi Germany. The road to war in Europe would have to lead through the Pacific.

The question is: *Why?* With some of the finest intelligence available in military history, with almost certain knowledge that war was at hand, and with capabilities available that offered a defense against precisely the type of attack that was executed by the Imperial Japanese Navy (IJN) on the morning of December 7, 1941, how was it possible for Pearl Harbor to occur?[1]

The above question begs further ones: Did U.S. Navy cryptographers crack the Japanese naval operations codes prior to the Pearl Harbor attack? Was the U.S. Navy aware that the Japanese Strike Force warships broke radio listening silence in the North Pacific as they began their final approach runs to their attack positions north of Pearl Harbor? Where were the Pacific Fleet's most important battle weapons—its aircraft carriers—at the time of the attack?

Americans have been told about the U.S. military's cryptographic success in cracking the pre–Pearl Harbor Japanese diplomatic codes (PURPLE), but little if anything has been officially acknowledged about breaking the IJN's operational naval code, known as JN-25, but referred to in 1940 and

1941 as "Code Book D" and the "5-Number Code." Did this really matter? Unknown to most Americans is the fact that the U.S. Navy could actually identify and track the IJN's key warships, the aircraft carriers and battleships, via a complicated radio direction finding system, by homing in on the sending ship's radio transmitter each time it sent a signal. Could the Japanese have worked around this situation to keep their movements secret?

For the half-century after the end of World War II, the U.S. Navy locked up the vast majority of hundreds of thousands of pages of documentation dealing with U.S and Japanese command decision-making operations in secure storage vaults in Crane, Indiana, including signal intelligence decoded message intercepts and tracking reports concerning Pearl Harbor.[2] For about as many years, the National Security Agency (NSA) also refused to release key documents under its control, even going to the extent to deny the existence of the U.S. Navy's capability to break portions of the IJN's operational code throughout 1941.

This control was so complete, and the secret of the success of the U.S. military's breaking of a significant number of Japan's military codes was so well kept, that even the nine official government investigations during the 1940s into the attack on Pearl Harbor were not aware of the existence of these documents.

This book could not have been written without extensive use of once-secret documents. Thanks to Robert Stinnett and his persistent use of the Freedom of Information Act, the U.S. Naval Security Group Command, the primary custodian of the "Crane Files," began to dribble the documents out in small batches, beginning in the mid-1980s until the winter of 1993–1994, when a large quantity of files was released to the National Archives and Research Administration at its College Park, Maryland, Archives II. Other releases in smaller quantities have continued to take place since the late 1990s to the present. I was able to take advantage of these releases as part of a five-year research effort in the U.S. National Archives. This and a meticulous study of diaries, memoirs, and official testimonies rendered at key Pearl Harbor hearings drove this book forward and contributed to its most important revelations.

In late 1940, there was a debate as to whether Pearl Harbor should be developed into a major U.S. Navy base for a forward-deployed fleet in Hawaii. Roosevelt was determined to do it, but the U.S. Fleet commander, Adm. James Richardson, resisted; he called the island of Oahu and its Pearl Harbor port "a God-damned mousetrap!" After an acrimonious encounter with the president, Richardson's objections were dismissed. Worse, he found himself relieved of duty and then retired from the naval service. His replacement on February 1, 1941, was Adm. Husband E. Kimmel, newly promoted by Roosevelt himself over 46 senior admirals.

SEALED SECRET

NAVY DEPARTMENT

Phone Ext, No, Op-12. Br. 2992		Addressees	Message Precedence
From Chief of Naval Operations	To.	CinCaf	Priority
Released by:		CinCpac	
		Com11	Routine
Date November 24, 1941.		Com12	
		Com13 Com15	Deferred
TOR Code Room			Priority
Decoded by		Spenavo London	Routine
		CinClant.	
Paraphased by			Deferred

Indicate by asterisk addressees for which mail delivery is satisfactory

2 4 7 0 0 1 CR0443

Unless otherwise designated this dispatch will be transmitted with DEFERRED precedence.

Originator fill in date and time for DEFERRED and MAIL DELIVERY.

Date   Time   GCT

TEXT Cincaf, Cincpac, Coms Eleven Twelve, Thirteen, and Fifteen Info action Spenavo London and Cinclant for info xx CHANCES OF FAVORABLE OUTCOME OF NEGOTIATIONS WITH JAPAN VERY DOUBTFUL X THIS SITUATION COUPLED WITH STATEMENTS OF JAPANESE GOVERNMENT AND MOVEMENTS THEIR NAVAL AND MILITARY FORCES INDICATE IN OUR OPINION THAT A SURPRISE AGGRESSIVE MOVEMENT IN ANY DIRECTION INCLUDING ATTACK ON PHILIPPINES OR GUAM IS A POSSIBILITY X CHIEF OF STAFF HAS SEEN THIS DISPATCH CONCURS AND REQUESTS ACTION ADEES TO INFORM SENIOR ARMY OFFICERS THEIR AREAS X UTMOST SECRECY NECESSARY IN ORDER NOT TO COMMUNI-CATE AN ALREADY TENSE SITUATION OR PRECIPITATE JAPANESE ACTION X GUAM WILL BE INFORMED SEPARATELY

SECRET

Copy to WPD, War Dept) and to Op-12 but no other distribution.

Make original only. Deliver to Communication Watch Officer in person. (Sec Art. 7614) Navy Regulations.)

TOP SECRET

This November 24, 1941, message to Adm. Kimmel from the office of the Chief of Naval Operations causes the Pacific Fleet to terminate its reconnaissance in force in the North Pacific. (NARA, Archive II [CNO Files])

Kimmel trained his fleet, especially his aircraft carriers, unmercifully. Ten months after he took command, in late November 1941, the aggressive admiral took part of his battle-ready Pacific Fleet some 250 miles north of Pearl Harbor, conducting a reconnaissance in force in the North Pacific. All hands were manning their battle stations. The training mission: find the Imperial Japanese Navy and defeat it on the approaches into Pearl Harbor.

But destiny did not favor Kimmel. He was abruptly ordered to return the fleet to Pearl Harbor, his battle reconnaissance aborted. Eleven days later, his men would face an avalanche of bombs and torpedoes launched from a transpacific Imperial Japanese Navy Strike Force located in exactly the same area where he had just been operating. What had gone wrong and why is the subject of *The Pearl Harbor Secret*.

When Tokyo and Berlin formally entered into a late-1940 military alliance, Washington had certain economic leverages over Japan, which the Roosevelt administration exploited to develop a foreign policy strategy for a war against Japan; this would also lead to war against Germany. These key levers, or vulnerabilities, involved the substantial Japanese financial assets in the United States and the Japanese military's overwhelming dependence on American petroleum, iron ore, and steel exports for supporting its military adventures in Asia, particularly China.

These vulnerabilities constituted a *key center of gravity* over which Tokyo had little or no control. Karl von Clausewitz defined it as "the hub of all power and movement on which everything depends."[3]

Roosevelt's strategy adeptly exploited the Japanese psyche of "death before dishonor." National honor was now at stake. Washington's demands forced Tokyo's leaders to strike first. Commenting on this situation in his diary entry 11 days before Pearl Harbor, Secretary of War Stimson stated, "The question was how we should maneuver them [the Japanese] into the position of firing the first shot without allowing too much danger to ourselves. It was a difficult proposition."[4] As Roosevelt himself said, "In politics, nothing happens by accident. If it happens, you can bet it was planned that way."

The attack's first wave came roaring out of the sky at 7:48 a.m. It was a lopsided victory: the United States lost a total of 3,581 killed and wounded. The Japanese lost a total of 64 killed and one taken prisoner. Pearl Harbor should not have happened.

President Roosevelt was an astute political strategist who accomplished his goal of forcing a reluctant America to come to grips with and defeat the tyrannical Adolf Hitler and his Nazi atomic bomb program—a program that threatened the existence of Western society.

Abbreviations

2M1	surprise ambush attack strategy (Kimmel)
ABD	American-British-Dutch
ABDA	American-British-Dutch-Australian Command
AD	IJN Flag Cipher/Administrative Code
AE	U.S. Navy radio intercept/RDF station at Sitka, Alaska
AF	U.S. Navy radio intercept station at Midway Island
AN-1	IJN operational code (aka 5-Number, 5-Num, or JN-25B)
B	*see* BAKER
BAKER	U.S. Navy signals intelligence intercept/RDF tracking station B (Libugon, Guam)

CAST	U.S. Navy signals intelligence and RDF intercept processing center (Corregidor Island, Philippines)
CAXM	U.S. Navy aerial and surface (ocean) surveillance radar
CETYH	U.S. Navy coded radio circuit for intelligence and operational directives
CIBHK	Combined Intelligence Bureau, Hong Kong (British)
CIC	Combat Intelligence Center
CINCAF	Commander-in-Chief Asiatic Fleet
CINCPAC	Commander-in-Chief Pacific Fleet
CIS	Communications Intelligence Summary (HYPO/ FRUPAC)
CIU	Combat Intelligence Unit (HYPO), Pearl Harbor
CNO	Chief of Naval Operations (OPNAV)
COIC	Combined Operations and Intelligence Center (British)
COM-11	Communications Unit, 11th Naval District, San Diego, California (aka: Station ITEM)
COM-12	Communications Unit, 12th Naval District, San Francisco, California (aka: Station FOX)
COM-13	Communications Unit, 13th Naval District, Seattle, Washington (aka: Station SAIL)
COM-14	Communications Unit, 14th Naval District, Honolulu, Hawaii (aka: Station HYPO); (aka: Station CAST)
Combined Fleet	total operational fleet of the Imperial Japanese Navy (IJN)
COMINT	communications intelligence
COMSUM	Communications Intelligence Summary (ex: Station HYPO)
COPEK	U.S. Navy coded radio circuit for Hawaii, the Philippines, and Washington, DC
COSMO	U.S. Navy coded radio circuit
DCO	District Communications Officer
DIO	District Intelligence Officer
DNC	Director of Naval Communications (OP-20)
DNI/DOI	Director of Naval Intelligence
ECM	Electronic Cipher Machine (U.S. Navy)
ENIGMA	German Encoding Machine (Army–Navy–Air Force)

FAF	First Air Fleet or IJN Pearl Harbor Strike Force (Kido Butai)
FBI	Federal Bureau of Investigation
FDR	Franklin Delano Roosevelt
FECB	Far East Combined Bureau, Singapore (British intelligence)
FOX	U.S. Navy RDF site, Farallon Islands, California
FRUMEL	Fleet Radio Unit Melbourne (USN intelligence)
FRUPAC	Fleet Radio Unit Pacific (USN intelligence)
G-2	U.S. Army Intelligence/Director of Military Intelligence
GUPID	U.S. Navy coded radio circuit for radio intelligence reporting and exchange of communications data
H	Station H: radio intercept station at Heeia, Oahu, Hawaii
HF	high-frequency radio signals, 3–30 MHz (short wave); long-range radio transmissions (sky-wave propagation)
HF/DF	high-frequency direction finder
HYPO	Station H: U.S. Navy signals intelligence and RDF processing center (Pearl Harbor, Hawaii)
IBM	International Business Machines (Type 405 Tabulator)
IJA	Imperial Japanese Army
IJN	Imperial Japanese Navy
ITEM	U.S. Navy radio intercept/RDF station at Imperial Beach, California
J-19	Japanese consular code
JICPOA	Joint Intelligence Center Pacific Ocean Area
JN-25B	IJN operational fleet code (aka: 5-Number/Code Book D)
KAMER 14	Dutch radio intercept/RDF plotting and code-breaking center in Batavia, Dutch East Indies
Kana	Romanized phonetic form of Japanese language to enable messages to be sent via Morse code transmission systems (aka katakana)
KING	U.S. Navy signals and RDF intercept station at Dutch Harbor, Alaska

LF	low frequency radio signals, 30–300 kHz (long wave); used for surface-wave to ships and submarines
M	Station M, Cheltenham, Maryland (also thought to be generic symbol assigned by OP-20-G to Mackay Radio & Telegraph)
MAGIC	decrypted intelligence derived from Japanese radio signals
MF	medium-frequency radio signals, 300–3,000 kHz
MS-5	Army radio intercept station in Hawaii
ND	naval district
NEGAT	alternate name for OP-20-G
NEI	Netherlands East Indies (aka Dutch East Indies)
NGS	Naval General Staff (Japanese)
ONC	Office of Naval Communications (OP-20)
ONI	Office of Naval Intelligence (OP-16 Navy: Washington, DC)
OPNAV	Office of the Chief of Naval Operations (Stark)
OP-12	Office of Naval Plans and Operations (Turner), War Plans
OP-16	Office of Naval Intelligence (Wilkinson)
OP-16-F	ONI–Foreign Intelligence Division (Heard)
OP-16-F-2	ONI–Foreign Intelligence Division Far East (McCollum)
OP-20	Office of Naval Communications (Noyes)
OP-20-G	U.S. Navy signal intelligence and RDF processing center (Washington, DC) code-named Security Section
OP-20-GI	OP-20-G's radio intelligence analysis section
OP-20-GX	OP-20-G's radio direction finding (RDF) plotting facility
OP-20-GY	OP-20-G's code-breaking/message-decoding facility
OP-20-GZ	OP-20-G's translation and dissemination facility
OP-38	Office of Ship Movements (Brainard)
ORANGE	codename referring to Japan (ex: War Plan Orange)
OTRG	On the Roof Gang
PAK-2	U.S. intelligence designation for Japanese Consular Code

PBY	U.S. Navy flying boat (amphibious airplane)
PHLO	Pearl Harbor Liaison Office (archival records)
PURPLE	nomenclature for Japanese Diplomatic Cipher Machine
Q Team	British radio intercept station (Stonecutters Island, Hong Kong)
Rainbow Plans	U.S. color-coded war plans for war with Japan (Orange) etc.
RCA	Radio Corporation of America
RDF	radio direction finding
RED BOOK	IJN operational code in use 1930s
RI	radio intelligence
RIP	registered intelligence publication
RN	Royal Navy (British)
Romaji	Roman letter format of kana code Japanese ideographs
Room 40	British intelligence
SAIL	U.S. Navy intercept station and RDF plotting center, Bainbridge Island, Washington
SECNAV	Secretary of the Navy
SIGINT	signal(s) intelligence
SIS	Signal Intelligence Service (U.S. Army Signal Corps)
Station AE	U.S. Navy radio intercept/RDF station at Sitka, Alaska
Station AF	U.S. Navy radio intercept/RDF station at Midway Island
Station B	see BAKER
Station C	see CAST
Station FIVE	Army radio intercept station, Honolulu, Hawaii
Station I	see ITEM
Station M	main U.S. Navy radio intercept center and message receiving facility at Cheltenham, Maryland
Station S	see SAIL
Station T	see TARE
Station TWO	Army radio intercept station, Presidio of San Francisco
Station US	receiving station for all electronically transmitted radio intercept and RDF reports to OP-20-G in Washington, DC (also called NEGAT)

Station X	MacKay Radio & Telegraph, and Press and Globe Wireless commercial communications centers in the San Francisco area that had radio direction finding, as well as cable message receiving and sending capabilities (the "X" was a generic code symbol assigned by OP-20-G to identify them)
Station Y	British intelligence radio intercept
T/A	traffic analysis (signals)
TARE	U.S. Navy radio intercept/RDF station at Point St. George, Crescent City, California
TESTM	U.S. Navy coded radio circuit for transmission of IJN RDF bearings and call signs
TINA	radio intelligence frequency identification system
TWX	radio telephone transmitter
ULTRA	radio signal decoded intelligence system
USAAFE	U.S. Army Air Force Far East
USAFFE	U.S. Army Forces Far East
USMC	U.S. Marine Corps
USN	U.S. Navy
VICTOR	U.S. Navy signals intercept/RDF station, Vaitogi, American Samoa
WCCI	West Coast Communications Intelligence Network
WPL-46	U.S. Navy war plan against Japan for the Pacific Ocean
WPO	War Plan Orange (U.S. Navy plan for war against Japan)

1

Rising Sun in the Pacific

The year 1853 altered the course of Japan's destiny and that of the entire world. Ships belching black smoke, but not on fire, was a sight never before seen in Japanese waters. When Commodore Matthew C. Perry's American squadron of four ships-of-war, with some 100 guns and more than 500 men, sailed into Edo Bay to deliver a letter from U.S. President Millard Fillmore, it was a psychological shock of the first order. The Tokugawa Shogunate took notice.

Perry's cannons awed the shogunate. The realization of how technologically obsolete its society was, in conjunction with a conviction that it was time for a major change in its foreign affairs, served to propel Japan's leaders forward. To help set the course that same year: the law prohibiting the construction of oceangoing ships was abrogated. Perry had opened the proverbial door and Japan—the Land of the Rising Sun, as Japanese called their country—charged on through, challenging the United States 90 years later for dominance of the Pacific Ocean.[1]

When the feudal lords in Edo (renamed Tokyo in 1868) allowed Perry to open up Japan's islands to foreign trade, the immediate result was the collapse of the feudal system and the reorganization of the government into a centralized monarchy. The nobles of the samurai warrior caste were now forced to give up their way of internal war, turning their military bent outward to embrace the new mandate of nationalist expansion. While they put away their treasured samurai swords, their Bushido warrior spirit and ideology continued to animate Japanese society as a whole into the 20th century, stressing honor and the way of the warrior for both civilian and military leaders alike.

For the Japanese, it was honor above all else and selfless devotion to the emperor that held their minds in a complete psychological embrace, culminating in the real national concept of *death before dishonor*. The possibility of failure and its resulting humiliation were not acceptable under any circumstances. In terms of Japan's military mindset, these concepts were so strongly held that it was better to seek a glorious death in the service of the emperor than face the humiliation of defeat. While the Bushido spirit would drive Japan's imperial ambitions forward, it would also eliminate the possibility of seeking out alternate solutions in a flexible manner, accepting reverses and even defeat in one area in order to attain more important goals in other areas. This inflexible mindset would ultimately undermine Japan's national security interests in Asia as it approached the late 1941 outbreak of World War II in the Pacific.[2]

By July 1859, a formalized trade was established between Japan and the United States; Yokohama became America's commercial door. On the military side of an emerging modern Japan, Holland had already been contracted to furnish warships, as well as to provide various books and studies from Europe on military and naval operations and strategy. The Dutch also gave instructions in modern seamanship, and by 1860, a Japanese warship crossed the Pacific for the first time.[3]

But it was to the British that the shogun turned to receive instruction in the art of maritime warfare. Work on organizing a navy went forward, and by 1866, the first steam warship was constructed in Japan's fledgling naval yards. An intervening civil war (the Meiji Revolution and Meiji Restoration in 1868) was a major transformation. This revolution was due in large part to the determination of the Japanese elite to avoid the humiliation of being dominated and colonized by the Americans and Europeans, as was happening in other parts of Asia. National interest, in which wealth and strength worked hand-in-hand, would now enable Japan to compete with the outside world.[4] The educational system was revamped and expanded, a modern banking system was put in place, and experts from Britain's

Royal Navy were brought to Edo to provide advice on the creation of a modern navy. The next eight years saw steel-hulled vessels, all produced in England, entering the Japanese fleet.

Paralleling this were the Prussians, who assisted in the modernization of the Japanese army. An indigenous armaments industry was created and Japanese officers were sent abroad to study at various Western military and naval schools. Over time, a railroad network, telegraph system, and shipping lines were also created to foster the infrastructure needed to assist in the development of heavy industry, involving iron, steel, and shipbuilding. The Japanese had quickly realized that economic and military/naval power worked in tandem.[5] To attain their goal, the Japanese would need markets and raw materials from the rest of Asia.

Throughout this time training in seamanship, gunnery, and torpedo practice was ongoing, and by 1878 the Japanese-built cruiser *Seiki* was observed in European waters flying the Rising Sun flag. The shipyards at Kure, Maizuru, Sasebo, and Yokosuka came on line and combined to produce just enough steam warships with cannons in twin turrets to ensure a victorious naval war with China in 1894, whereby Japan was able to gain control of Korea and Formosa. This success whetted Japan's imperial appetite, and further battleships and cruisers were ordered from Europe to enhance the firepower of the fleet.[6]

Shortly thereafter, two Americans came on the scene, and their expertise added to the ever-expanding Japanese Navy. Alfred Thayer Mahan's book *The Influence of Sea Power upon History 1660–1783* impacted Japan's navy much in the same way it did the U.S. Navy, synergizing thought on the importance of sea power as a means to enhance economic interests and promote imperial ambitions. Mahan's theories emphasized the imperative of commercial expansion through the command of the sea to gain overseas markets. Seizing and protecting colonies were part and parcel of the raison d'être that a nation needed a large and powerful navy. By 1896, Mahan's book had been translated into Japanese and Japan's navy became a mirror image of the U.S. Navy with its emphasis on battleships, command of the sea, and annihilating your enemy's fleet in one decisive battle.[7]

As the higher echelons of the Japanese Navy began to read Mahan's book, another American arrived in the Pacific to demonstrate Mahan's basic thesis. U.S. Navy Commodore George Dewey, in command of America's Asiatic Squadron and under orders from President William McKinley, massed his ships in Hong Kong during the spring of 1898 and then moved directly into the Spanish Philippines' Manila Bay. There he engaged Spain's fleet and, within a few hours of opening fire, had sunk all seven of that country's warships. The successful engagement has been described as "the most one-sided victory in the annals of naval warfare." Not a single

American sailor lost his life to Spanish gunnery. Big guns had defeated little guns. More importantly, it was a decisive battle in that Spain lost its Philippine colony, all 7,083 islands. Implementing its vision of Manifest Destiny, the United States had now projected its power some 8,000 miles across the Pacific; this would ultimately support the American Open Door Policy for China. If Mahan had provided the sea power theory, it was Dewey who had provided the object lesson for the Japanese Navy.[8]

Not fully appreciated at the time were the long-term strategic consequences of the acquisition of the Philippines, which placed the now imperial United States on a collision course with imperial Japan. Acting on Manifest Destiny had its advantages but also costs, which would play out with the onset of war in the Pacific in 1941.

As a result of its successful war with China in 1894–1895, Japan began to look outward in terms of empire building. By 1903, a period of six years, Japan had built 3,150 steamers, while its shortages in steel required 1,267 steam-propelled vessels to be purchased abroad. Thus a total of 4,417 steamships of all sizes were now added to its merchant marine.[9] During this time the Japanese Navy was also busy building ships so that, by the outbreak of the Russo-Japanese War in 1904, it had a battle fleet of 6 battleships, 52 cruisers, and 99 destroyers and torpedo boats.

The Russo-Japanese War was defined by a couple of signature events. The first was the surprise attack in February 1904 on China's Russian-controlled Dairen coastal city of Port Arthur, *without a Japanese declaration of war in advance.* This had come about as a result of failed negotiations on the part of Japan to get Russia to withdraw from Manchuria. The Japanese responded to this humiliating diplomatic failure by conducting a surprise night destroyer attack on the Russian fleet located at Port Arthur. The Japanese Navy then blockaded the port for months. The second event was the decisive victory in the Tsushima Strait in May 1905, which saw Adm. Togo Heihachiro's battle squadron outmaneuver and then annihilate the entire Russian Baltic Fleet of some 27 ships in one decisive battle.

In an effort to lift the blockade at Port Arthur, the main Russian battle fleet left its Baltic Sea ports in late 1904, sailing for some seven months in order to reach the Strait of Tsushima and mass its ships with those at Russia's Vladivostok naval base before confronting Japan in open battle. The Battle of the Tsushima Strait took place between the tip of the Korean peninsula and the Japanese island of Kyushu, where Japan's British-built battleships and torpedo boats carried the day at sea, while its German-produced Krupp artillery won the army's battle on land.

This astounding Japanese victory over imperial Russia caught the world's attention. It was the first time in modern history that an Asian country had defeated a European power in war. For the Japanese people it proved the samurai spirit of military honor, discipline, fortitude, and courage. These military successes enhanced the Japanese people's patriotism.[10] Japan's naval success was duly noted on the other side of the Pacific in Portsmouth, New Hampshire, where President Theodore Roosevelt intentionally involved himself in the mediation of the Russo-Japanese peace treaty, ending the war.

At the turn of the century, Akiyama Saneyuki, who became known as the father of Japanese naval strategy, was a naval attaché in Washington, DC, and then a military observer aboard Rear Adm. W. T. Sampson's flying squadron flagship in July 1898 as Sampson engaged the Spanish fleet in the Battle of Santiago de Cuba and then blockaded Havana Harbor. Akiyama became the senior strategy instructor at the Japanese Navy War College. So impressed was Adm. Togo with Akiyama that he used him as an advisor during the Battle of Tsushima Strait.

The other Japanese naval thinker of note was Sato Tetsutaro, who had been a student in London in 1899. Sato argued that, as a priority of national security, Japan's navy ought to prevent American naval power along its coasts. Since the U.S. Navy was Japan's potential number one enemy (Russia was number two), this gave Japan a major focus for the first part of the 20th century.[11]

At this point in time, the fickle finger of historical fate intervened. As the guns of August 1914 began to roar on the Western Front in Europe, Britain requested on August 7 (three days after the British entered the war in Europe) that Japan help provide assistance in tracking down and destroying German raiding ships operating in and around Chinese waters. Sixteen days later, on August 23, Japan formally declared war on Germany. With Germany largely distracted in continental Europe, it was impossible for the country to protect its vast colonial island holdings in the Pacific Ocean. They were ripe for the picking, and Japan did just that. By the end of October, the Japanese Navy had seized Germany's Caroline, Mariana, and Marshall Islands in the South Pacific with little resistance.

Japan now had a far-flung empire in the Pacific, extending eastward from the Philippines and northward from New Guinea, an area approximately the size of the continental United States. Its navy would now be titled the Imperial Japanese Navy (IJN), taking on all the responsibilities that this distinction implies. The Mandates, as these islands would become known, generally lay athwart America's sea lines of communications to the Philippines. If some of these were developed into forward naval bases, they could sufficiently enhance the power of the IJN to the degree that Japan would now have a strategic balancing factor to offset America's own bases in the Philippines. This point was not lost on Tokyo's leaders.

One other noteworthy event concerning the IJN in 1914 was its seaplane-launched aerial bombing attack in September against German land targets in the Tsingtao Peninsula of China's Shantung Province. The IJN's seaplane carrier *Wakamiya*, which carried out the operation, was a converted Russian transport ship, captured in 1905. It carried four seaplanes and made 49 attacks, dropping some 190 bombs. Not possibly appreciated at the time by the great powers of England and the United States was the fact that the IJN had begun to enter the age of aerial naval warfare. The *Wakamiya* would be further modified so that by 1920, it became the IJN's first regular aircraft carrier.

Japan's operations in the Pacific during World War I continued: Tokyo's Imperial Marines assisted the British in suppressing a 1915 mutiny by Indian troops against English colonial rule. The year 1917 found Japan's Rear Adm. Kozo Sato and his Second Special Squadron of some 17 ships, including a cruiser, escorting British troop transports throughout the Mediterranean Sea. An estimated 700,000 British soldiers on some 788 transports, involving 348 escort sorties from Malta, were shuttled from place to place in the various war theaters.

As a reward for this service to the British war effort, London recognized Japan's territorial gains in Shantung and its seizure of German territories north of the equator. At British insistence, the 1919 Paris Peace Conference formally recognized the transfer to Japan of Germany's former Pacific colonies. Called the South Pacific Mandate or just Mandates, the Caroline, Mariana, and Marshall islands (except Guam, which was a U.S. possession), along with islands in the vicinity of the Bismarck Archipelago north of Australia, were now legally in Japanese hands. With both Formosa and Korea under its control, as well as the Mandates, Japan had now achieved de facto imperial status in the Pacific.

The only flaw in this process that otherwise so benefited Japan was the rejection of its bid to include a racial equality clause as part of the Treaty of Versailles. This was perceived by Tokyo as a serious slap in the face to Japanese pride and prestige and would not be forgotten. This was especially so because, 13 years earlier in 1906, there had been a bout of anti-Japanese hysteria in California, the unreasonable fear that a resurgent Asia under Japanese leadership would overrun Western civilization. The San Francisco school board mandated that all nisei (first-generation Japanese American children) in the city would have to attend school in Chinatown. The crisis receded, but the antagonism and resentment of the two above events remained deep seated in the Japanese psyche.

Japan gained a permanent seat on the Council of the League of Nations (the United States never joined the League of Nations) and was now emerging from World War I as a recognized player in the game of international politics. By 1919, articulate Japanese thinkers were beginning to advance ideas about an East Asian "co-prosperity sphere" of interest. Japan's own manifest destiny was beginning to make its mark.[12]

During the period of the 1914–1918 war, Japan's economy had expanded considerably, as it filled orders for war material for its European allies. It was an economic boom like none other up to that time in modern Japanese history, and the country became far more industrialized and technologically advanced than ever before. The nation's industry not only grew but also diversified, increasing its exports and rapidly transforming Japan from its status as a debtor country into that of a creditor nation.

From 1913 to 1918, Japan's exports tripled, or more. Heavy industry, principally iron and steel, contributed to shipbuilding and an evolving capability in cement and textile production. Shipbuilding escalated dramatically, launching 650,000 tons in 1919 compared to just 85,000 tons in 1914. In terms of industrial and manufacturing production indices, by 1920 Imperial Japan's production outpaced that of both France and Italy combined. As Paul Kennedy pointed out, "For the Japanese, economic power and military/naval power went hand in hand."[13]

Japanese animosity toward the United States was reinforced when the U.S. Congress passed the 1924 Exclusion Act, barring Japanese from emigrating to the United States. To many in Japan, it was the blatant racism of 1906 and 1919 all over again. This event took place immediately following the considerable turmoil of postwar years, which saw Japan suffer an unexpected economic recession. Those were gloomy times, with cries for change and political parties opposing the government beginning to emerge. The issues involved corruption within the government and the stagnant economy, which saw farmers on the verge of starvation and many thousands of city workers losing their jobs. All said and done, Japan was passing through hard times at the beginning of the 1920s, and protestors were making their voices heard.

John Toland concluded from his demographic studies of Japan that the population explosion taking place was producing about 1 million people a year, causing the nation's population to rise to nearly 60 million—far too many for the national economy to absorb. A downturn in the world's economy further aggravated the situation, with the Tokyo stock market collapsing in March 1920.[14] Tokyo's solution to the problem of feeding its population and the turmoil associated with soaring rice prices, which had provoked a number of riots, was to subsidize rice cultivation in Korea and Formosa. Another initiative to try to ameliorate the socioeconomic and political problems was to improve trade relations with America and Europe, which saw Japan's leaders embrace the U.S. initiative to confer in Washington over naval matters.[15]

The IJN was struggling to maintain a reasonable ratio of relative battleship strengths between itself and the U.S. Navy. When the Washington Conference of 1921–1922 was convened in response to the clamor for peace after 1918, this appeared to be an opportunity to further IJN interests. In Washington, the IJN found itself dealing with the American and British navies, who were advocating a 10-year hiatus in capital shipbuilding programs. This idea was embraced by all, and each nation pledged not to fund or authorize more building programs. A ratio system was promulgated of 5:5:3 in battleship tonnage for the United States, England, and Japan respectively. The Japanese grudgingly accepted this ratio, which was, in part, offset by a clause in the agreement that said that the United States and Britain would maintain the status quo in terms of fortifications and bases in the Pacific.

This set the pace for the next five disarmament conferences, all of which reconfirmed the ratios. American aid in the form of $11.6 million was sent to help some 2 million Japanese made homeless by a 1923 earthquake; the new relationship with Tokyo reduced tension. Even so, over the next decade, Tokyo began to feel seriously constrained by the League of Nations in its foreign policy dealings with China. In 1934 Japan quit the League. This made sense to the Japanese government and its senior naval staff, which had become disenchanted with the soon-to-expire (1936) Washington Naval Treaty. That year, Japan opted out of the treaty and began its unrestricted effort to build more and bigger ships.[16]

To give an idea of the impact of the above on Japan, one just has to look at its defense expenditures from 1930 to 1938 compared to those of the United States. Japan's expenditure in 1930 was some $218 million, while the United States spent $699 million. By 1938 Japan's expenditures had boomed to $1.74 billion, while depression-ravaged America now lagged behind at $1.13 billion. In other words, in a startling reverse, Japan was now spending some 50 percent more than the United States on defense. In order to do this, Tokyo had to borrow recklessly—all in support of its armed services.[17]

The Japanese armed services were taking up 70 percent of their government's expenditures, an amount far greater than any one of Japan's competitors. But what was Japan spending its money on? The IJN, which had been restricted by the Washington Treaty to its 60 percent ratio relative to the U.S. and British navies, secretly built well beyond the treaty's limits. By the early 1930s, its cruisers typically displaced upwards of 14,000 tons rather than the 8,000-ton limit of the treaty. By 1938, while it already had 10 existing battleships, the IJN was laying down the keels of the *Yamato*-class battleships, including the *Yamato* and *Musashi*, each of which would have 18.1-inch guns and displace upwards of 72,000 tons, rendering them too big to pass through the Panama Canal. The 18.1-inch guns would be the largest caliber of naval artillery ever mounted in a warship and represented the epitome of Japanese naval engineering.[18] Big guns and big ships were at the forefront of Japan's strategic planning.

But this was not all. After the end of World War I and on into the early 1920s, the IJN Naval General Staff had taken note of Brig. Gen. William (Billy) Mitchell's successful aerial bombings and sinkings of surrendered

German World War I battleships. IJN commander Isoroku Yamamoto, while a student at Harvard, noted the advent of the airplane. This, and the fact that at the end of the war in 1918, the British Royal Navy had completed the world's first aircraft carrier, fascinated him. It was the beginning of a long love affair with military aviation, which Yamamoto would pursue with gusto. The IJN's Naval General Staff also noted the long-range solo flight by Charles Lindbergh from New York to Paris across the Atlantic in 1927. That same year, the *Akagi* aircraft carrier conducted sea trials.

Capt. Yamamoto took command of the *Akagi* carrier in 1928. He held the view that supremacy in modern sea battles would be based on the aircraft carrier. Yamamoto, a trained aviator, would become head of the Technical Division of the Aeronautics Department and by 1933 would be given command of the IJN's First Carrier Division, which included the *Akagi* as his flagship. At his insistence, Japan also built two new carriers, the 30,000-ton, 34-knot *Shokaku* and *Zuikaku*, more modern and faster than the converted battleships *Akagi* and *Kaga*.[19] Thus, naval aviation was in the process of finding its niche in the development of Japan's military power. By the end of the 1930s the IJN would have 10 aircraft carriers, a naval air service of some 3,000 planes, and about 3,500 pilots.[20] It had come a long way since the seaplane carrier *Wakamiya* launched its 1914 attack against the Germans in China.

Yamamoto himself seems to have despised the big guns–big ships syndrome of the IJN, arguing that no battleship should be considered unsinkable, because an airplane could drop a bomb or launch a torpedo that could destroy the targeted vessel before it could ever fire its guns. Inevitably, battleships and especially the super-battleships of the Yamato-class would become "white elephants." In 1937, in a discussion about how to destroy a battleship, Yamamoto said, "Torpedo planes can do it!" Citing an old Japanese proverb, he went on to say, "The fiercest serpent may be overcome by a swarm of ants." Yamamoto was thinking big for his time and only four years away from demonstrating that a swarm of dive and torpedo bombers could devastate a battleship fleet.[21]

By 1939, Yamamoto would be in command of the IJN's Combined Fleet. What is interesting about the battleship versus aircraft duel in the IJN was the lack of realization that airpower had revolutionized naval warfare. The *Yamato* and the *Musashi* displaced some 144,000 tons of irreplaceable steel. Had the steel for just these two battleships been devoted to the building of aircraft carriers, by 1941, the IJN would have been able to increase the size of its carrier fleet by 40 percent, from 10 to 14. Unfortunately for Japan, building battleships was a misallocation of the precious steel resources; aircraft carriers would become the dominant factor in naval warfare. The IJN's decision to give equal priority to the construction of both battleships and aircraft carriers was a strategic blunder of the first degree. No battleship in the IJN or the U.S. Navy would ever fight it out between themselves on the high seas of the Pacific.

Paralleling the IJN's extensive buildup in ships and planes during the 1930s was Japan's army. It would ultimately reach more than 1 million men in 51 active combat divisions and 133 air squadrons, consisting of some 2,000 attack aircraft. All these were supported by another 2 million trained reserves.[22]

As part of its army-navy aviation development program, Japan used a strategy to jump-start its race for superior technology. According to Hiroyuki Agawa: "Whenever an interesting aircraft was produced abroad, it would be purchased and dismantled for thorough study. Foreign manufacturers were known to remark sarcastically that they would be grateful if, for once, Japan would buy several at a time rather than just one."[23] The strategy worked. Japan's aviation industry would evolve to a point where it could produce its own domestically made aircraft. Examples were the formidable Zero fighter (officially the type-0 carrier-based attack plane), the type-94 reconnaissance seaplane, the type-96 land-based attack plane, and the type-97 carrier-based attack plane, among others. Japan's shipbuilding industry had come to fruition, producing the world's third-largest merchant marine.[24]

It is worthwhile to comment on the organization and command structure of the Japanese government and the role of the emperor. The government was dual headed in that there was one military head and one civilian head. These two divisions were nominally headed by Emperor Hirohito, who, under the Meiji Constitution, was the commander-in-chief of the Armed Forces. He held plenary power, and all state decisions needed his sanction. By tradition, once his civilian cabinet and the military leaders had agreed on a policy, he was not allowed to withhold his approval. His position was that of a person *above politics.* He was the representative of the people, and every Japanese, without exception, was expected to serve him unto death.

For the Japanese people, the emperor was a god. No matter how high or how low one's station in life, each person felt a family kinship to the emperor—for Japan considered itself one family. Each child was taught the concept of *kodo,* the Imperial Way. In essence, this was the basis for Japanese morality called *on,* the obligation to serve the emperor and one's parents. Without an emperor, there was no nation, just as without parents, there was no family.[25]

Hirohito's status as emperor led to an imbalance of power below him, favoring the heads of the army and the navy; this, in turn, led to problems in decision making. Paul Kennedy's assessment of the situation indicates that decisions were often "rendered erratic and, at times, incoherent by clashes between various factions, by civil-military disputes, and by assassinations."[26] That the army and the navy did not always coordinate their interests and operations did not help. If the navy was anticipating a possible war with either the United States or Britain (or both), the army's focus was exclusively on the Asian continent (China and Manchuria) and the threat that the Soviet Union appeared to pose to Japan's interests in the region. With the army being the more influential of the two in Japanese politics, as well as inside the Imperial General Headquarters, its views usually prevailed.

The army, being unconditionally imbued with the Bushido spirit, prided itself on its ultranationalist militancy. For Japan's military, the Bushido spirit represented a unique Japanese esprit de corps. Both officers and men exhibited a fanatical zeal, which would be demonstrated time and again on the battlefield. Nothing was impossible—it was simply mind over matter. As Paul Kennedy points out, "While other armies merely talked of fighting to the last man, Japanese soldiers took the phrase literally, and did so."[27] Throughout the 1930s, the army became the dominant service in terms of influencing Japan's foreign policy action for the region.

The IJA's militancy came to the fore in September 1931. Japan invaded China's northern province of Manchuria without the permission of Japan's Foreign Ministry, under the pretext of avenging the death of a Japanese army officer as well as putting down local civil disorders. The army had cleverly staged an incident alleging the sabotage of the Japanese-owned South Manchurian Railway by anti-Japanese militants and even Chinese army troops. The result was the invasion and then occupation of Mukden and a number of other cities in Manchuria, to be followed several months later in 1932 by the complete subjugation of the region. Manchuria, now known as the puppet state of Manchukuo, became part of Imperial Japan.

The timing for this was fortuitous, because the United States was becoming distracted by its ever-deepening economic depression; the GNP dropped from $98.4 billion in 1929 to about $44 billion just three years later. With some 15 million people out of work and no end in sight, America's foreign policy under both Hoover and Roosevelt had become more insular than ever.[28] Even the seizure, over time, of Shanghai with its large international population and worldwide commercial interests did not attract the attention it should have. Despite this being another move by the Japanese military toward the conquest of the Asian mainland and the closing of the Open Door to China, U.S. President Herbert Hoover said he would fight for the continental United States but not Asia.[29]

American interests in the region were not strong. The League of Nations, of which Japan was still a member, did nothing. The British and French, who were its principal members, had no effective means for either preventing or taking action against Japan's aggression in northern China. Simply put, Manchuria was not of sufficient national interest to warrant any kind of retaliatory action. Nazi Germany's military rearmament in the mid-1930s served as a further brake on these European democracies, circumscribing their foreign policy interests in the Western Pacific.[30] Japan's success in Manchuria now led it to undertake other military adventures in Asia, and its imperial ambitions broadened considerably.

With the League of Nations not interested and the United States bogged down in its eighth year of a severe economic depression, 1937 saw the IJA take further action against China. To provide a check on Soviet interests in northern China, the IJA took advantage of an incident involving an exchange of fire in July between Chinese and Japanese troops at the Marco Polo Bridge.

In Tokyo, inflammatory rhetoric was substituted for well-thought-out strategic calculations to actually go to war. Claiming that the *prestige* of the Empire of Japan was at stake, the Marco Polo Bridge Incident was used as a pretext to wage all-out war on China. As a result, a large-scale invasion of China from Manchuria and a series of coastal landings were undertaken in the vicinity of Shanghai. This so-called punitive expedition was expected to be a relatively quick and easy three-month operation with the Chinese suing for peace, as had been the case in Manchuria—but it was not.

By the end of the year, the Imperial General Headquarters had poured well over 700,000 troops into China, striking along two axes of advance: the first along a general line from Manchuria toward Peking and to points northwest, and a second along a line from Shanghai through Nanking to Wuhan to the west. Chiang Kai-shek, the Kuomintang's nationalist leader, refused to surrender and retreated across endless mountains and ridge-lines, including the nation's capital at Nanking, carrying out a dogged resistance that would last for eight years. The IJA was thoroughly bogged down in China. Unwittingly, it had taken the first of a number of steps toward war with the United States.[31]

The IJA's appalling display of brutality in 1937 in what became known as the Rape of Nanking, Japanese soldiers rampaged through the city, conducting an orgy of murder, rape, and looting that shocked the civilized world and was recorded in vivid cinematic and printed detail by the international news media, including the *New York Times* and *Life* and *Time* magazines.

It was one thing to conquer a territory, but it was another to administer and garrison it. The cost of the war by 1938 was debilitating Tokyo's funds at a rate of $5 million a day, and defense spending was continuing to rise to the point that Japan was forced to introduce rationing. The IJA called for total mobilization, claiming that an efficient war economy was the only way Japan could protect itself. In the face of the powerful IJA, the Diet voted for total mobilization in March 1938. The Japanese people were now subjected to a clever psychological operation intended to reinforce their xenophobia and Bushido spirit, and then prepare them mentally to support a new Imperial Way aimed at Japanese control of all East Asia.[32]

In its first application the Imperial Way was being depicted as a crusade in East Asia, with the nation's honor at stake. Joseph J. Rochefort, who studied Japanese and lived in Japan for a number of years as part of his U.S. Navy intelligence training during the 1930s, asked a Japanese entrepreneur why it was that Japan had involved itself in a land war with China, knowing that it could not defeat the Chinese in the long run. The Japanese businessman replied: "That's right. Our honor has become involved in this. . . . When honor is involved, we don't care about anything else."[33] This statement provided an acute insight into the implacable hold that the Bushido spirit had on the Japanese mindset. And the IJA continued to drive on into the Chinese quagmire of endless mountain ranges and Chiang Kai-shek's stubborn defense.

Inside America, despite having "one-third of a nation ill-housed, ill-clad, ill-nourished," as Roosevelt put it on January 20, 1937, in his second Inaugural Address, and endless breadlines as part of a renewed slump in its economy, Washington was beginning to take serious note of Japan's activities in East Asia. The bombing of the *Panay* in the Yangtze River early that December, in which three Americans and one Italian national were killed as it was in the process of evacuating the U.S. Embassy staff from the besieged capital of Nanking, caused the Roosevelt administration to denounce Japan's aggression. While Japan made an official apology and provided indemnity payments for the Americans killed, Washington put an embargo in place in June 1938 against the export of aeronautical equipment and parts to Japan. In July 1940, aviation fuel and crude oil would also be added.[34]

This embargo reinforced Japan's perception of hypocrites. The Japanese wondered how it could be considered acceptable for England and Holland to occupy India, Hong Kong, Singapore, Malaya, and the East Indies and for the United States to occupy the Philippines and Hawaii, but a crime for Japan to follow their example. As John Toland pointed out in his 1970 book, *The Rising Sun: The Decline and Fall of the Japanese Empire, 1936–1945*, the Japanese also wondered why it was perfectly all right on the part of America to have grabbed up so much of its lands from Native Americans by "trickery, liquor and massacre" and then turn around in outrage and castigate Japan for doing essentially the same thing in China.

As a result, in November 1937, Tokyo signed an anti-Comintern (anti-Communist International) Pact with Nazi Germany.[35] But Japan had other significant problems to deal with. The Japanese military operations had gotten bogged down in inconclusive fighting in China, and things were going not well along the Russo-Manchurian border. During the summer of 1938, the IJA received a serious drubbing from the Red Army along the border. A year later on the plains of Nomonhan along the Manchurian–Outer

Mongolian border, Soviet Lt. Gen. Georgi Zhulov's forces carried out a coordinated armor (500 tanks), infantry, artillery, and air-supported double envelopment (encirclement) of the IJA, inflicting a devastating defeat, including more than 50,000 IJA casualties. This demonstrated clearly that suicidal samurai bravery was no match for the technologically superior armaments and competent generalship of the Red Army. For the "Strike North" elements of the IJA, which had dominated Japanese strategic thinking, this thoroughly dashed their hopes for an expansion into the Soviet Union's eastern territories. Now the "Strike South" elements of the IJN would come into ascendancy.

While the setback in the north drove Japan closer to an alliance with Germany and Italy, the Soviet Union's Joseph Stalin made a prophetic observation in a letter to Chiang Kai-shek: "Japan has lost her balance . . . and is hurling herself recklessly . . . against Soviet Russia. . . . this is a sign of Japanese weakness and her conduct may unite all others [Britain and the United States] against her."[36] Ironically, in August 1939, Stalin signed a peace pact with his greatest adversary, Nazi Germany's Adolf Hitler. A month later the two dictatorships were carving up a hapless Poland and thus beginning what would become World War II.

To hide its humiliating defeat by the Soviets, Tokyo kept the IJA's losses a secret from its people and then directed the seizure of the southern Chinese island of Hainan in February 1939. This action now gave Japan a military presence along the sea routes running from Hong Kong to Singapore. Early in 1940, Tokyo announced the annexation of the Spratly Islands, an archipelago of nearly 750 reefs, inlets, atolls, cays, and islands lying some 700 miles southwest of Manila, between the southern Philippines and Indochina. The islands, while not particularly impressive, straddled the shipping lanes around Indochina and offered the potential advantages of docks and airfields for operations against the Philippines and the Dutch East Indies.

On May 10, 1940, another dynamic was thrown into the equation: Hitler's Wehrmacht launched a full-scale Blitzkrieg attack on France and the Low Countries. With Holland and France overrun and capitulating to Germany, the strategic situation in Europe changed dramatically, which impacted the colonial possessions of the Dutch East Indies (also called Netherlands East Indies) and French Indochina. Japan's military leaders were elated. With Holland and France defeated and Britain fighting for its survival, an excellent opportunity had now blossomed on the Southeast Asian scene in favor of Tokyo's imperial interests.[37]

Because the IJA largely felt that Chiang Kai-shek's forces were only able to keep up their successful defensive operations due to the constant movements of materials and supplies flowing into China via Burma and French Indochina, now was the time to take action. Action meant military operations in the Southwest Pacific to isolate China and even, if needed, to seize the oil and other raw materials of Southeast Asia and the Dutch East Indies. The IJA naval operations required additional resources in order to preserve Japan's economic security and continue the war. Overnight, the war with China was suddenly now a viable option.

At the end of July 1940, Prince Konoye formed a new cabinet: Yosuke Matsuoka became foreign minister and the army's Lt. Gen. Hideki Tojo became war minister. National fervor, taking advantage of the chaotic situation in Southeast Asia, now became national policy, with militants thundering the slogan "Don't miss the bus!" By September 22, 1940, Japan was on the "bus" and had convinced the besieged French government in French Indochina's Hanoi to permit the establishment of Japanese airbases and IJA bases, as well as the movement of troops into the northern part of the colony along the Vietnam-Chinese border. This partial takeover of French Indochina not only allowed the IJA a jumping-off place for future attacks on China, it also made the rice fields of the Mekong Delta available to the hard-pressed Japanese war economy. It could not have come at a better time: crop failures in Korea during 1940 would force Japan to import rice from both French Indochina and Thailand.[38]

On September 27, 1940, the long-anticipated Tripartite Pact with Germany and Italy was successfully concluded in Berlin, giving Japan a feeling that it was not alone. While this appeared to both the Americans and the British as an example of Japanese duplicity, Foreign Minister Matsuoka argued that the pact "would force the United States to act more prudently in carrying out her plans against Japan." Matsuoka said that the pact would prevent war between Japan and the United States and, if Germany ended up fighting America, Japan would not necessarily be obligated to enter into the fray.[39]

But Adm. Yamamoto was suspicious of the pact; Japan might inadvertently be taking on another powerful enemy in the form of the United States, in addition to China. Based on his years in America—studying at Harvard, serving as a naval attaché in Washington, and working on the post–World War I Washington Naval Treaty—Yamamoto concluded that "a war between Japan and the United States would be a major calamity for the world, and for Japan . . . an extremely perilous matter for the nation."[40]

Complicating the issue in Yamamoto's mind was what the United States would do. What about the Philippines? To deal with all these fronts simultaneously would conceivably lead Japan to a state of imperial overstretch, especially since the war with China was to be sustained along with a credible defense against the Soviet Union on the Manchurian frontier.[41]

Obtaining economic security through the domination of Southeast Asia was at the core of Japanese strategic planning. Despite some four years in laboring to win the war in China and become self-reliant, Japan was becoming more and more dependent on outside powers for critical material resources. As local fuel supplies became exhausted by the end of 1939, Tokyo found itself having to import more and more crude oil and refined petroleum products such as aviation gasoline from both the United States (30 million barrels or 75 percent of its needs) and the Netherlands' Dutch East Indies (NEI) (10 million barrels).[42] By the end of 1938, the United States was furnishing about 75 percent of Japan's scrap metal imports, or over a million tons, that would become high-quality steel. Copper was also imported from the United States: 93 percent or 105,000 tons was used to supplement Japan's own production of 90,000 tons. By 1938 Japan had grown largely dependent on America for 60 percent of its imports of machine tools.[43]

Both the United States and the NEI were key players in sustaining Japan's war economy. If for some reason these supplies should be embargoed or otherwise cut off, Japan's war effort would grind to a halt and the IJA and IJN would essentially become paralyzed, placing in jeopardy the homeland's security and even sovereignty. Japan was vulnerable to pressure from other nations, especially that of the United States. How to get around this situation and out from under economic dependence on the United States was a vexing problem. Confrontation with the United States would undoubtedly mean an economic embargo and the strangling of Japan.

On January 26, 1940, the Treaty of Commerce and Navigation of 1911 between Japan and the United States lapsed, removing all legal obstacles to instituting restrictions. In July, Washington announced that all exports of aviation fuel and high-grade scrap iron and steel would be placed under federal license and control. Two months later, in September, in response to Japanese military moves into northern French Indochina, Roosevelt announced that an embargo on scrap iron and steel was now in effect against Japan. The United States was implementing a far stricter policy, which might well lead to war in the Pacific.

Having observed the highly successful tactical operations carried out by the IJN's aircraft carriers during the spring 1940 fleet maneuvers, Yamamoto began to formulate a dramatic plan. Achieving a decisive victory through a surprise blow against the enemy had been ingrained in the Japanese character since the last century. Now, in one sudden crushing blow, the American fleet at Pearl Harbor would have to be so crippled by Japanese naval aviation that Japan could seize all of Southeast Asia and its valuable petroleum resources. Taking the NEI would offset any embargo the United States could possibly bring to bear against Japan. It was an intriguing idea.

The Naval General Staff war games that took place in late 1940 were led by Yamamoto himself; he had been promoted to full admiral and given the operational command of the IJN. The map exercises indicated that an attack on French and Dutch possessions in the Southwest Pacific would bring both the British and the Americans into the war. The IJN saw that the situation indicated that the Netherlands, Britain, and the United States were essentially inseparable. In December 1940, as Yamamoto was contemplating the pros and cons of an attack directly on Pearl Harbor, the General Staff in Tokyo directed several of the IJA's divisions in China to begin training for operations in tropical regions. A special staff, known as the Formosan Army Research Department, was constituted to collect information on geography and the impact of tropical conditions on military operations in Southeast Asia. This was contingency planning at its best and an omen for the future.[44] Diplomatic pressure would continue to be placed on the Dutch to supply more oil, rubber, and tin to Japan. Oil had become a Japanese obsession.

Tokyo had not given up on Dutch cooperation, and in the autumn of 1940 a special delegation went to Batavia, the capital of the NEI, arriving on September 12. What the Japanese wanted was unrestricted access to the raw materials of the region, especially the oil owned by the Dutch, British, and American companies (Royal Dutch Shell and Standard Oil of New Jersey, among others). The focus was on aviation-grade crude oil, other traditional crude oils, aviation gasoline (87 octane and higher), and related petroleum products. This amounted to a little over 3 million metric tons or some 22 million barrels and represented about 50 percent of the NEI's total production. The Dutch countered with an offer of about half that amount, about 10 percent of the aviation-grade crude oil (840,000 barrels) and a little over 10 percent of the 87-octane aviation gasoline (221,000 barrels) requested. The Japanese delegation accepted what they could get.[45] Despite this setback, Japan did not give up, and diplomatic overtures would continue well into 1941.

By February 1941, Adm. Yamamoto turned over the general concept of an operation for an attack on Pearl Harbor to the IJN's Cdr. Minoru Genda, an expert in mass, long-range fighter operations in China. After studying the intended operation, Genda concurred that it was feasible. An operational preemptive strike plan (Operation Kuroshima) was developed. Japanese naval intelligence was ordered to collect as much data as possible about Hawaii and the U.S. Pacific Fleet. A special naval intelligence observer was to be sent to Honolulu to learn as much as he could about the exact positions and comings and goings of the various American fleet units.

The success of the plan was based on two assumptions: first, that the U.S. Pacific Fleet would be anchored at Pearl Harbor at the moment of the attack, and second, that the carrier striking force carrying out the attack could be maneuvered halfway across the Pacific Ocean without being detected.[46] This would protect the element of surprise in a preemptive strike battle.

Also of interest to the IJN, as initial planning ideas were debated, was the successful aerial torpedo-bomber attack launched by the British aircraft carrier *Illustrious* against the Italian Navy's battleships at Taranto on November 11, 1940. Three out of four of Italy's most powerful warships had been sunk, dealing the Italians a devastating blow in the Mediterranean Sea.[47] The technique of aerial torpedo attack was something that Japanese naval aviation had been practicing for some time. Taranto reinforced the IJN's attitude on the effectiveness of aerial torpedo attacks. On April 10, 1941, the IJN created its new First Air Fleet (FAF), massing a significant portion of its 10 aircraft carriers under one distinct command. The FAF, as U.S. Navy intelligence would often refer to it, would become the core element of the Japanese Pearl Harbor Strike Force.

The situation in the Western Pacific began to clarify. In April 1941, Matsuoka convinced Joseph Stalin to sign a neutrality pact with Japan. Both parties celebrated: Stalin, because he did not have to worry about a Japanese stab in the back in Siberian Russia if war broke out with Nazi Germany, and Matsuoka, because Japan could now operate freely without having to worry about its own "stab in the back" from Stalin.[48] Even better, the IJN now had the freedom to focus on its southern strategy of military conquest of southern China and French Indochina, British Hong Kong, Malaya, and Singapore, and finally the grandest prize of them all—the Dutch East Indies. The Greater East Asia Co-Prosperity Sphere, as Tokyo called its imperial goal, was about to become a reality. Japanese self-sufficiency was now on the horizon.

In the event of war with American, British, and Dutch for control of the Pacific, Japan's 1941 strategy was a policy of conquest, consolidation, and then defense. The first phase involved a preemptive surprise strike on Pearl Harbor to neutralize the U.S. Pacific Fleet, while other IJA and IJN forces occupied Southeast Asia, the NEI, and then the Philippine, Wake, Guam, and Bismarck Islands. The second phase was the establishment of a defensive perimeter running from the Marshall Islands south through the Gilberts and then west and through the Solomon Islands, New Guinea, and the NEI. This would establish a three-tier barrier defense system based on the Marshall, Mariana, and Caroline Islands, Formosa, and the Philippines. The third or final phase was the interception and destruction of any intruding naval forces that attempted to penetrate this three-tiered system of defense.[49]

With several barrier systems in place, the overall concept envisioned a great battle with the U.S. Navy off the coast of Japan. It was an ambitious scheme that the Japanese hoped would replicate their victory over the imperial Russian Fleet in the Strait of Tsushima.[50]

Ironically, the rise of Japan over a period of just 90 years to challenge the United States for control of the Pacific had been the consequence of America's own successful efforts at coercing the Japanese into joining the modern world of the 1850s.

2

War Plan Orange and the Evolution of U.S. Naval Intelligence in the Pacific

If 1853 was a momentous year in Japanese history, 1898 was equally so for the United States. Manifest Destiny, a messianic concept for spreading the blessings of America's civilization that providence had bestowed upon the United States for the benefit of mankind as a whole, bit hard into the American psyche. For some, this meant assuming Rudyard Kipling's "white man's burden" to rescue backward people from darkness. For others, it meant an economic opportunity by which the United States could then command both sides of the Pacific. This, it was compellingly argued, would establish an American dominance over the entire Pacific that was destined to be the focus of the world's future commerce in the 20th century.[1]

Commodore George Dewey's crushing defeat of Spain's fleet in Manila Bay signaled a new dawn for Washington in the Western Pacific. This enabled the United States to enforce its "sovereignty" over the some 7,083 islands in the Philippine archipelago. As a result of quashed ambitions for independence, an insurgency broke out against the American occupation, which lasted some 10 years and involved upwards of some 160,000 U.S. troops. The Americans practiced their traditional form of counterinsurgency or "pacification," which succinctly meant repression as opposed to winning hearts and minds. A common refrain of the American soldiers was: "We'll civilize 'em with a Krag!" (the Krag-Jorgensen U.S. Army rifle). Approximately 250,000 Filipino civilians lost their lives, compared to 4,500 American deaths.[2]

The United States soon acquired the Pacific island territories of Hawaii, Midway, Guam, Wake, and Samoa.[3] These were stirring events for Americans and John Philip Sousa, America's high-spirited music master, celebrated the tenor of the times with military marches: "Hands Across the Sea" (1899) and "Invincible Eagle" (1901). But it was the acquisition of the Philippines that would propel the United States into a collision course with Japan. In fact, at the turn of the century, the United States found itself involved in China as part of its Open Door Policy and a commitment of some 2,500 troops in support of an international army to put down the Boxer Rebellion.

But it was the emphasis on sea power that energized the U.S. policy. Easy victories in the war against Spain justified Adm. Mahan's arguments that great powers needed large navies and lots of colonies. This strengthened the positions of various agricultural and industrial groups in the United States who were urging for more and more secure markets overseas. Mahan contended, in his *The Influence of Seapower upon History* (1890), that the United States should "compete aggressively for world trade, build a large merchant marine, acquire colonies for raw materials, markets and naval bases, and construct a modern battleship fleet." The objective was to enable the U.S. Navy to use its power to promote U.S. economic development, as well as keep the nation's mercantile sea lanes open and secure in peace or war.[4]

In light of Mahan's naval doctrine, President Theodore Roosevelt initiated the U.S. Navy's shift from a traditional harbor defense posture to a modern battleship fleet by increasing the number of battleships from 11 in 1898 to 36 by 1913. The United States was now a naval power to be reckoned with; the Great White Fleet's world cruise of 1907 emphasized the point.

Teddy Roosevelt, impressed by Japan's defeat of imperial Russia's high seas fleet in 1905, encouraged the U.S. Navy to develop a transpacific contingency plan to protect U.S. interests in Asia from possible Japanese imperial intentions. Roosevelt and other officials were well aware that Japan's enhanced battle fleet could threaten the Philippines, and perhaps the Territory of Hawaii, where the Japanese population outnumbered the native Hawaiians by a ratio of two to one.[5]

WAR PLAN ORANGE

On Roosevelt's orders, the U.S. Naval War College undertook a study called War Plan Orange (also called Plan Orange or just Orange). This would evolve over the years into a series of contingency war plans, pitting the U.S. Navy against the Japanese Navy for control of the Pacific. How otherwise could America defend its new Pacific empire, stretching from Hawaii to the Philippines and even as far south as Samoa? The dominant assumption for this planning was that Japan, now a naval power itself, would attack American possessions in the Pacific to satisfy its appetite for land and raw material.[6]

War Plan Orange was more of an operational naval campaign plan than anything else. Examining the defensive enigma presented by the Philippines, located about 7,000 miles away from the continental United States with a myriad of some 3,000 islands (estimated in 1910) and hundreds of distinct ethnic and linguistic groups, the U.S. Army declared that it was impossible to defend the archipelago; thus the burden of fighting a successful defense of American interests against Japan in the Western Pacific would have to fall upon the U.S. Navy.

Plan Orange, during the period of 1907–1914, anticipated that Japan might use its navy to attack and seize the Philippines and even Guam, along with raids against Midway Island and Hawaii's Oahu. According to the plan, the U.S. Navy would react to the Japanese challenge by marshalling its forces (battleships and supply vessels) along the West Coast of the United States and then proceed to move its battle fleet from San Francisco across the Pacific via Hawaii, Midway, and Guam, to establish a forward operating base at Manila Bay in the Philippines. If this happened, the U.S. Fleet would move north to engage in decisive battle with the Japanese Navy in the vicinity of the Ryukyu Islands, lying just to the south of Japan's main islands.

After the defeat of the Japanese Navy, the U.S. Navy would then establish a blockade to strangle Japan, starving it of food, fuel, and raw materials until it surrendered. This strategy of unlimited economic war to enable Washington to impose its will upon Tokyo was in reality a siege scenario, based on the experiences of Adm. Dewey and a number of his contemporaries who had served during the American Civil War and seen firsthand the success of the U.S. Navy's Anaconda Plan in bottling up the Confederacy.[7]

At the turn of the 20th century, the United States was now the leading industrial nation in the world, followed by Britain, Germany, France, Russia, Austria-Hungary, Italy, and finally Japan, in descending order.[8] Parallel to the rise of the United States, two revolutionary technologies came into play: the ability to transmit messages by radio (called *wireless* or *wireless telegraphy* at the time) and the ability to pinpoint the location of a radio transmitter through its own signals.

On December 12, 1901, Guglielmo Marconi startled the world when he created the first radio signals in the form of "dots" in Morse code, heard across the Atlantic Ocean from England to Newfoundland, a distance of more than 1,800 nautical miles. Within a year, shore-to-ship communications had taken place.[9] By 1907, Ettore Bellini and Alessandro Tosi had developed a type of radio direction finder (misnamed during its early years as a "radio compass"), using a looped antenna to orient the radio transmitter of interest.[10]

Military organizations around the world, on both land and sea, became interested in radio, as it facilitated rapid communications and the coordination of fleet units over long distances. On the high seas, this was a revolutionary event, enabling naval control at all levels of tactical, operational, and strategic command. It was quickly discovered that naval personnel could listen to their enemy's signals and obtain what would be called *signals intelligence* by "intercepting" (monitoring and copying) radio transmissions. By using multiple radio direction finding (RDF) stations, positions of enemy radio transmitters could be located with considerable precision, whether they were in the air, on land, or out at sea.

Radio telegraphy was perfected rapidly, and by 1912 major flagged shipping lines as well as the world's navies began to install signal transmission systems on their primary ships. The British White Star Line's *Titanic* was one of these. It was found that during the day, ranges of 250 nautical miles were the norm, but that signaling at night was even better, due to the not fully understood phenomenon of ionosphere "skip" propagation, which tended to extend the signal transmission ranges out to some 2,000 miles.[11]

Continuous radio communications contact from ships to shore stations and the ability to use RDF to locate ships in distress at sea clearly indicated the value of this new communications phenomenon. But the birth of modern signals intelligence—SIGINT as it would be called—came about because of World War I. This event and its ramifications at war's end would have major impacts on both the U.S. Navy and its Japanese counterpart in the Pacific.

As the guns of August were blasting away along the Western Front in 1914, a small group of French cryptographers were intercepting and reading German military radio communications ("traffic"). Soon, intercept stations were set up along France's eastern frontier. Simple traffic analysis of the German radio call signs gave the French high command the complete order of battle for the German army, as well as up-to-the-minute tactical intelligence for immediate exploitation on the battlefield.[12] Their successes at radio intercept significantly enabled the French army to defeat the Germans in the Battle of the Marne in September 1914. Throughout the war the French would continue to make use of radio intercept and cryptanalysis, as well as RDF systems against the Germans.

In 1917, as the United States began to battle the German submarines (U-boats) in the Atlantic and prepare to project its million-man American Expeditionary Force into France, there was an urgent call by both the army and the navy for amateur radio operators. Several thousand of these amateurs underwent training. Their great advantage was that they already knew Morse code and were familiar with the radio transmitters and receivers from their own personal experience going back, in some cases, almost 10 years. They served in key communications positions for the duration of the war. They were the experts in this new field of radio communication.[13]

One of these amateurs, Charles Apgar, served the U.S. Secret Service in 1914–1915, intercepting coded German commercial radio traffic inside the United States at Sayville, Long Island, beginning as early as several days before the actual outbreak of the war. With his inventive mind, he developed a radio-receiving and cylinder-recording apparatus.[14] During this time, the Army Signal Corps was also keenly involved in radio and radio intercept operations, especially for its forces involved in its 1916 Mexico campaigns. By 1918, a chain of about a dozen intercept stations was functioning along the border with Mexico.[15]

During World War I, however, it was the British who took the lead in SIGINT operations, with great success. The British Admiralty established the highly secret Room 40, with some 50 officers selected because of their knowledge of German and because they were some of the "best brains" of their generation. While one group toiled away at breaking ("solving") the German cipher, or secret writing, and radio transmission codes, a second group devoted its work to studying German radio call signs (each radio transmitter used an identifying number-letter-word code) as an aid to determining specific military units and naval ships, and still another group maintained huge charts of the Atlantic approaches, plotting the radio direction findings and decoded radio intercept locations of German U-boats.

This latter group enabled the British to route merchant marine convoys around the lurking enemy submarines or to attack them directly. For their part, the German military set up a series of radio transmitters and a weather station to broadcast directives and reports. These messages were now intercepted and analyzed at Room 40.[16] The Royal Navy Radio Intercept Service established its own series of intercept stations called Y stations, using Marconi radio receivers and RDF equipment and antennas, around the periphery of the British Isles facing the Atlantic approaches, the English Channel, and the North Sea.[17] In 1915 and 1916, the system began to pay large dividends.

The German High Seas Fleet commenced raiding operations along Britain's eastern coast in December 1914 and hoped to repeat these operations again in early 1915 by disrupting the British fishing fleet working in the

North Sea area of Dogger Bank, about halfway between the British Isles and the Baltic Sea. During this time, the German naval forces were exploiting their relatively new aerial technology, in the form of dirigibles or Zeppelins (cigar-shaped, motorized, propeller-driven balloons), to act as scouting forces for their battleships and cruisers at sea.

Room 40 found that, while these reconnaissance aircraft were equipped with excellent radios, it was fairly easy to intercept their radio messages and reports, and also to track them through RDF. Quite often, a Zeppelin operator would miss part of a naval radio message and request that parts of it be retransmitted, often in clear text. The British Admiralty was informed of German intentions, and the German raiding efforts were foiled.[18]

In 1916, Berlin developed a strategy that could break the British naval blockade of Germany and allow the German merchant marine free access to the Atlantic. The imperial German High Seas Fleet intended to lure the British Grand Fleet into a decisive battle in the North Sea. Winning such a battle would break the British stranglehold over the German economy. As the Germans massed their fleet in the Baltic Sea, the first hint that something was afoot came from French RDF stations, using Bellini-Tosi radio direction finders. These stations were plotting Zeppelin reconnaissance flight positions and routes coming out of the German bases in the Baltic Sea. The French concluded that a major fleet operation was underway.

Room 40, which had obtained a copy of the main German naval code book from the Russians, was in the process of intercepting and decrypting the German fleet's operational signals directing the beginning of its sortie from the Baltic Sea through the Kattegat and Skagerrak straits into the North Sea. Armed with this precious intelligence advantage, the British Grand Fleet met the Germans in the North Sea and fought the Battle of Jutland, involving some 250 warships, off the coast of Denmark on May 31 and June 1, 1916.[19] While the results were inconclusive and both sides would claim a tactical victory, the British did defeat the German effort to break the former's blockade. This was a strategic victory for the British in that they were able to maintain their own crippling blockade of Germany for the duration of the war, ultimately contributing to decisive results in 1918.

One of the most decisive SIGINT operations in the war came about in 1917, when the British Wireless Intercept Service, operating in support of MI-6 and Admiralty Room 40, recorded and then decoded the Nauen–Sayville–Mexico City radio-telegram, known to history as the Zimmermann Telegram of March 3, 1917. Deciphered by the Admiralty code breakers and then passed on to Washington, the telegram, in conjunction with a formally announced campaign of unrestricted U-boat warfare in the Atlantic, precipitated America's entry into the war on the side of the British and French against the Central Powers.

In the Zimmermann Telegram, Germany offered Mexico the chance to regain Texas, Arizona, and New Mexico. The German strategy was to tie up the American forces along the Rio Grande River in a war with Mexico so that the U.S. Army would not be able to deploy soldiers to the Western Front in France.[20] But the Germans had committed a major blunder of strategic proportions. The news of the intercepted telegram's contents broke on the American public as a shocking example of German perfidy.

The administration of President Woodrow Wilson, in a major turn-about from its declared posture of international neutrality, promptly focused on defeating Germany. Congress declared war on Germany on April 6. In an all-out effort from April 1917 to November 1918, the United States would send a million-man American Expeditionary Force (AEF) across the Atlantic and into the trenches on the Western Front, helping to turn the tide and decisively defeat Germany in 18 months.

By June 1917, the War Department had formally established a crypto-graphic office called the Cipher Bureau, under the auspices of Herbert O. Yardley, a former State Department telegrapher who had become inter-ested in the construction of ciphers. Yardley's organization, consisting in part of lexicographers and mathematicians, would grow from a mere 3 persons to some 150 with a budget of $100,000. Known as MI-8 and later as the American Black Chamber, this effort attacked German crypto-code systems, which were broken entirely by a laborious hand process. Surpris-ingly, the U.S. Navy made no attempt to undertake cryptographic work to decipher the German naval codes during the period of 1917–1918.[21]

During 1917, the Navy Radio Research Laboratory at Austin, Texas, did develop the highly effective SE 995 destroyer direction finder. Besides a number of medium-frequency RDF stations along the Atlantic coast for tracking German submarines, the SE 995s were fitted to all navy destroy-ers along the Atlantic seaboard, plus for those operating from a base at Brest, France, on the Bay of Biscay. Brest was the port where most of the logistical support for the AEF entered France. Logically, the Germans con-centrated their U-boats in the Bay of Biscay in an effort to sever this key line of communication for the Allies.

Adm. Henry Wilson, the commander of the U.S. Navy in the Bay of Bis-cay, directed that several land-based RDF stations be established to cover the bay. While these stations were being constructed and brought into operation, the U.S. Navy's destroyer captains began to form hunter-killer groups, to better use their new RDF capabilities and successfully track and attack U-boats. Greatly helping matters was the propensity of the U-boat commanders, unaware of the RDF technology, to continuously use their radios, thus facilitating the U.S. Navy's tracking efforts.[22]

While U.S. naval intelligence was far behind the British Admiralty's Room 40 in cryptanalysis, it was aware of that organization's contributions to winning the war. By the end of World War I, the U.S. Navy had entered the radio technology age. It was now able to instantaneously communicate with and command and control not only individual warships but large groups of warships, greatly facilitating naval maneuvers and tactics at sea. The parallel development of RDF now gave the U.S. Navy an asset for locating ship and submarine radio transmitters far out at sea. The use of identifying radio call signs further enhanced the navy's intelligence-gathering capabilities.

The U.S. Army Signal Corps' efforts, especially in the field of RDF operations, was impressive. By November 1918, more than a dozen army radio intercept stations and some eight RDF stations were operating along the Western Front in support of the AEF. The Signal Corps' five principal radio intercept stations "took a total of 72,688 messages and 232,977 calls." Some 20 RDF stations in operation during this time took 177,913 bearings on German army radio transmitters.[23] What the navy would do with this newfound SIGINT knowledge and capabilities after the war would depend upon the U.S. Naval War College's evaluation of potential foreign naval security threats to the United States.

The end of World War I saw significant changes in the strategic relationships between the great powers of the world. Entire empires were now turned topsy-turvy; the Russian, German, and Austrian empires no longer existed. The Imperial German Navy and its vaunted U-boat force no longer existed. The British and the French, along with the Japanese, scrambled to pick up the pieces of the former German Empire in Africa and the Pacific. By the Versailles Treaty, the Japanese were awarded control over the Caroline and Marshall Islands, as well as the German island possession of New Britain and its valuable port of Rabaul. These island possessions in the Central Pacific now became known as the Mandates; Japan now outflanked the Philippines.

By 1919, Japan began to look outward from its new ocean empire to create an East Asian "co-prosperity sphere." Japan was producing 650,000 tons of steel, compared to 85,000 tons just five years earlier.[24] The balance of power in the Western Pacific was in upheaval.

Now that the German Navy was no longer a threat in the Atlantic, the U.S. Navy could once again focus on what it perceived to be the primary threat to American interests in the Pacific—the Imperial Japanese Navy. In late 1919, Rear Adm. Robert E. Coontz, now promoted to chief of naval operations (CNO), saw Japan as America's primary adversary in the Pacific. He transferred the U.S. Fleet through the Panama Canal to the Pacific coast of the United States, and refocused the navy on planning for the possibility of war in the Pacific. The Naval War College continued to refine War Plan Orange.

An outright invasion of Japan was out of the question. An Army War College analysis depicted Japan as "almost invulnerable" to an amphibious land invasion, due to the ferocity of the Imperial Army and the general lack of suitable roads and bridges to support heavy equipment in the generally mountainous countryside. A land war was hardly an inspiring proposition. In 1928, the Naval War College developed its own full war scenario: an up-to-two-year campaign for a naval war that would result in victory against the Japanese.[25]

NAVAL INTELLIGENCE

If the United States had to fight the IJN, the Naval War College had to know all about the enemy's capabilities, both technical and physical, as well as Tokyo's intentions. Orange's focus on war with Japan now gave the U.S. Naval Intelligence Service (a different entity from the War College) its own parallel mission. World War I had vividly demonstrated that there was nothing quite like intercepting (monitoring) the "messenger," whether it was a human courier or an invisible radio signal wave. The huge advantage of radio intelligence was that it was "timely, pertinent, and reliable, and cost-effective." This meant that the breaking of an enemy's codes and ciphers had now taken on the aspect of being a vital intelligence function and key element in support of future naval operations.[26]

American intelligence operations against Japan got their start from an army initiative in favor of the Yardley's Black Chamber team, which was relocated to New York City in 1919 to begin a concerted effort on Japanese diplomatic message traffic between Tokyo and Washington, DC. Yardley's code-breaking organization (MI-8) found that Tokyo's communications relied on American commercial cable systems, such as Western Union, to a large degree.

Since Japanese writing relies on some 10,000 ideographs that stand for words and combined words, these were not adaptable to telegraphic transmission technology. To work around this, Tokyo used their katakana characters, an alphabet system of 48 characters developed about 950 CE to facilitate reading. Each katakana represents a syllable in the Japanese language. The katakana characters can be used to spell out the sounds of the ideographs. They could then be converted to Roman letters that could be printed out on Western typewriters for use by commercial telegraph offices. These became known as *romaji*. In turn, the *romanji* were converted to straightforward dot-and-dash-style Morse code. The complexities of the Japanese language would now become its Achilles' heel in terms of codes and ciphers.

A corps of typists helped Yardley compile the katakana letter groups on three-by-five index cards, totaling some 10,000 entries. From 1917 to 1929, the Black Chamber solved over 45,000 cryptograms in its efforts to successfully break and read Japan's secret codes. This success gave the

American negotiators at the Washington Naval Conference of 1921–1922 a significant advantage over the Japanese and was instrumental in getting Japan to accept the adverse 3-to-5 ratio of battleships, meaning that Japan would only have 9 battleships to 15 for the United States. When Yardley published his memoirs in 1931 (*The American Black Chamber*), a major scandal erupted in Japan, and the Japanese, now aware that the Americans were reading their most secret messages, changed their codes.[27]

In 1920, at the direction of President Wilson, Secretary of the Treasury Carter Glass arranged to have a secret fund of $100,000 deposited in a bank and credited to the account of the director of naval intelligence. This money, called a *slush fund*, was not accountable to Congress or even the comptroller general. It became the needed seed money that enabled the Research Desk of the Navy's Code and Signal Section (future OP-20-G) to begin to conduct actual intelligence-gathering activities. One of these activities included getting a copy of the IJN's secret naval operations code book, published in 1918.

In 1922 or so, the FBI assisted the navy in carrying out a number of undercover operations ("black bag jobs"), which consisted of a series of break-ins, involving picking the door locks and a combination safe in the Japanese consulate in New York City, and then photographing each page of their code book. As a result, the IJN's operations code was now in the U.S. Navy's hands.[28]

It was also about this time, in 1924, that the Code and Signal Section of the U.S. Naval Communications Service was reorganized and renamed OP-20-G. Located in Room 2646 in the Navy Department's offices on Constitution Avenue in Washington, DC, its head was Lt. Laurence F. Safford, USN, who was fascinated by mathematics and mechanical coding machines. As a cover for its true purposes, it was called the Research Office or Research Desk. Located next door in the Munitions Building was the army's Signal Intelligence Service (SIS) under the auspices of William Friedman, a recognized genius in code breaking.

Under the navy's organization of the day, Safford and his code breakers were part of the Division of Naval Communications (DNC). Their final product, the English translations of the intercepted messages from the broken IJN codes by the U.S. Navy's first onshore radio intercept facility (Station A) at the American consulate in Shanghai, were forwarded to the director of Naval Intelligence. While this radio intelligence organization operated under the auspices of the DNC, its product was to be used by the Office of Naval Intelligence (ONI). In 1925, Safford's Research Desk was composed of one officer, two enlisted radiomen, and four civilians—a total of seven people.[29]

Safford had a number of problems to solve. He needed personnel who were trained to copy down Japanese cipher messages with their kana characters, others who could take the kana characters and convert them into readable Japanese, and finally personnel who could translate the Japanese into English. To work around the problem of receiving and transcribing the kana texts from Morse code, Safford designed a special typewriter that could print out in kana.

To get the typewriter into production, Safford contacted John Underwood of the Underwood Typewriter Company in November 1924 with his specifications. Underwood understood the importance of the navy's work and, just two weeks later, responded with four prototype copies of the Underwood Code Machine. These were produced by John Underwood and Charles Joerissen for Safford as the initial forerunners of what would become known as Radio Intelligence Publication 5 (RIP-5).

The RIP-5's keyboard, costing the navy $85 each, was the same as the regular typewriters used by navy, except that the face of each key had printed the *romanji* (Romanized) Japanese kana characters and the corresponding Morse code dot-dash combination, instead of the normal Roman lettering. Upon hearing the Japanese cipher message being transmitted in Morse code, the monitoring signal intercept operator would merely press the key of the relevant Morse dot-dash combination, which printed out the related kana character. Using both upper- and lowercase shift keying, the Japanese kana characters were now readily readable, along with the Arabic number keys that both systems used. The sailors who manned the headsets of the radio receivers and typed out the Morse code–kana combinations were an essential human component for the success of the intercept system.[30]

The RIP-5's partial mechanization of Safford's operation would become a core element in breaking Japanese codes from that time on. The $100,000 fund paid for the purchase of 40 Japanese (RIP-5) typewriters, their maintenance, and the cost of preparing the special dies for the type heads. Japanese dictionaries, grammars, and a variety of other publications useful in instructing students in Japanese were also utilized. Not forgotten were the "special bonuses" or bribes and other expenses associated with the photographing of the IJN's operational code. Sometime in 1931, the balance of the fund, about $65,000, was turned back over to the treasurer of the United States.[31]

Under the navy's Radio Intelligence Publication (RIP) system, each RIP was considered a secret document and contained decryption information on Japanese radio and cryptographic procedures. The broken 1918 Japanese naval code was, for example, produced as RIP 2. By 1941, when Safford's operation was beginning to break into the IJN's operations code of the day, known as the 5-Num code, information on this code was published as RIP 73 and RIP 80.[32]

The problem of finding code breakers was another issue. Here again, Safford was holding a lucky hand. By chance, Agnes Meyer Driscoll, 31, a former yeoman (petty officer) in the Naval Reserve, had rejoined the navy after completing earlier service in World War I. (Secretary of the Navy Josephus Daniels said these women were yeomen and were not to be called "yeomanettes.") Having trained in military cryptography, she became involved in the development of electronic cipher machines, which brought her to Safford's attention in 1924. He hired her on the spot and she went on to become the navy's unsung master cryptologist. By the end of 1941, she had solved (broken) every important IJN code system.

Known as Miss Aggie or Madam X, Driscoll was a woman working in what was a man's world and had become part of the inner circle of the Code and Cipher Section, called *cryppies*. She not only did the key work involving the solving of the IJN codes and ciphers but also trained the majority of the navy's leading cryptanalysts in World War II, starting with Ens. Joseph N. Wenger, the first officer cryptanalysis "short course" graduate in 1926. Her importance to OP-20-G also stemmed in the fact that, unlike her naval service counterparts, she did not rotate out of position every few years for sea duty and thus provided critical organizational continuity throughout the 1930s and into the 1940s.[33]

Another key person who worked with Safford on the research desk was Lt. Joseph J. Rochefort. Both Rochefort and Safford learned their basic code-breaking skills under the guidance of Driscoll. Safford also initially obtained the assistance of Dr. B. C. Haworth who, along with his wife as key Japanese translators, would spend the next four years working out the translations of the photographed IJN operations code. Since the translations ended up in two volumes in red buckram McBee binders, they became known as the Red Book.[34] In 1926, when Safford was ordered back to sea to maintain his qualifications as a naval officer, Rochefort took his place.

The terms *cipher* and *code* are not always clearly understood. A cipher scrambles the plaintext message by replacing letters with other letters in a pattern to conceal the message. A code makes the change idea for idea, replacing the plaintext message with other words to also conceal the meaning of a message. A cryptogram is something written in code or cipher. The word *cryptology* generally includes protecting one's own communications (signals security) *and* acquiring information from radio signals by breaking the enemy's codes (decrypting and otherwise nullifying the enemy's signal security). *Cryptography* is the process of enciphering (encoding) and/or deciphering (decoding) messages prepared in secret writing or code. A cryptographer or cryptanalyst is an expert in reading encrypted messages.[35]

Quite often, simple coded messages were further disguised or scrambled by adding an additional random number or "additive" to produce a multistage code. Any message with an additive could be considered to be enciphered (encrypted). Both the sender and the receiver of a message would have to work from identical lists of additives and codebooks for the system to work. The recovery or reconstruction of the plaintext of a message by a cryptanalyst required that the additives be stripped away as part of the process of deciphering. Generally speaking, mathematical techniques could be used to help identify the frequency of letter and character usage. Comparing many messages often led to understanding enough of the commonalities of the code groups, numerical units, and characters sufficiently so that the code breaker could make logical deductions as to meaning.

Another aspect of the process involved utilizing a *crib*. A crib was a *guessed* plain-language text of a message that could be matched up with whatever ciphertext (scrambled letters) had been previously broken to fill in "blank spots" in the text. Working in combination, the two functions served as an aid in determining the full text of a message, as well as helping to break down the Japanese kana code and its super-encipherments added in later years.[36]

In 1928, Rochefort organized a series of four-month classes to instruct navy and marine corps radio operators how to quickly and accurately receive IJN message traffic on their RIP-5 typewriters. Located in a special concrete blockhouse-style classroom on top of the Navy Building in Washington, DC, the first class commenced on October 1. The graduating classes became known as the On the Roof Gang (OTRG) or "roofers." By the end of 1941, the 176 enlisted navy and marine corps radio operator graduates would form the key personnel ("ears") of a chain of radio intercept stations around the Pacific. As trained personnel became available, stations were added in Heeia on Oahu (Hawaii), Bainbridge Island (Washington State), Guam (Marianas), Mariveles (Philippines), and Shanghai (China). People such as Arthur H. McCollum, Joseph Rochefort, Joseph N. Wenger, Thomas Huckins, and Dwane Whitlock, among others, would hone their cultural and language skills in Japan and then go on to become key players in radio intelligence operations against the IJN.[37]

While Safford and Rochefort struggled to bring on line a formidable radio intercept capability for the navy, other developments concerning the understanding of radio wave propagation were taking place. These would have a dramatic impact on radio signal intercept operations in the future. Some years after the turn of the 20th century, Marconi was having considerable success with long distance radio reception. The scientific community attributed this to an electrically conductive layer in the earth's atmosphere.

This ionized layer would be recognized, in 1931, as the ionosphere. Marconi's 1924 experiments indicated that short-wave signal transmissions could pass over a certain path one part of the day and over a different path on the other side of the earth during another part of the day. Distance traveled by radio signals appeared to depend upon daylight and nighttime conditions involving this invisible ionosphere layer. The power of the radio transmitter would determine the distance traveled by radio waves. By 1925, it was concluded that there were both ground or direct radio signal waves and also simultaneously reflected sky waves. These reflected waves were thought to take place among multistructured atmospheric layers at heights from about 40 to 120 miles above the earth's surface.[38]

Two types of radio signals became important. The first was *shortwave* signals, which generally travel the farthest due to the phenomenon caused by the ionosphere. In this case the ionosphere acts much like a mirror, reflecting the propagated radio waves back to the earth's surface, which in turn reflect or bounce the waves back into the atmosphere, whereby the process repeats itself numerous times. This means that shortwave signals can be heard off and on over extremely long distances and even around the world. For naval signals intelligence, this enabled an intercept station to monitor and intercept a radio signal over long distances not intended by the sender. Even low power shortwave signals were vulnerable to intercept under these conditions. The second was *longwave* signals; these were not affected by the ionosphere and generally traveled shorter distances.[39]

For Safford and Rochefort, it was the IJN's 1918 secret operations code in the form of the stolen Red Book that became the primary focus of the Research Desk of the Code and Signal Section. This book contained a total of some 100,000 expressions in the form of five-digit numbers, Roman letters, and three-character kana groups. It was the kana code groups that were exploited. Agnes Driscoll made the first break into the code in 1926, brick by brick formulating the solution to the ciphers as they were brought into play by the Japanese, until the code was finally discontinued on November 30, 1930. Fourteen distinct cipher systems were used with the Red Book, but with Driscoll leading the attack, all were solved.

This initial effort enabled the Research Desk to become familiar with IJN message forms, phraseology, and subject matter. Equally important, it gave Naval Intelligence valuable information about Japan's war plans, providing information about future conquests of Manchuria, China, and the Dutch East Indies. In the case of China, even the smallest towns were of interest to the Japanese and were given place names in Chinese, kana, and English equivalents. Ship name lists were also included by country.[40] With this experience, the Research Desk was in a better position to tackle the IJN and its Grand Maneuvers of 1930. When Safford returned from sea duty to once again take over the helm of the Code and Signal Section, Rochefort rotated out to Japan in the summer of 1929 for language training.[41]

The first indicator that the IJN was involved in a major fleet deployment and war maneuvers came on May 18, 1930, from the radio intercept station at Guam (Station B or BAKER). BAKER had been in operation since 1929, with a complement of nine personnel. Intercept radio receiver apparatus and an array of antennas had been installed at what was at that time the U.S. Navy's largest facility of this nature. An experienced intercept operator, Chief Radioman (CRM) Lyon, had arrived from duty at the Shanghai intercept station and another eight men had been trained at the Intercept Operators' School at the Navy Department. They took note of the sudden increase in radio traffic on May 18 and the higher percentage of coded messages on the IJN's radio circuits—something was up! Using a 24-hour round-the-clock radio watch system, spare receivers were manned as IJN traffic increased in volume, reaching a crescendo toward the end of the maneuvers on June 13. Once the recorded transmissions reached the Navy Department (flown by airplane), the Research Desk went to work.[42]

A new IJN's cipher system of daily keys was supposed to conceal the maneuver scenario, which had a number of phases and which would serve as a rehearsal for a future war with the U.S. Navy.[43] The IJN continued to use the Red Book, which the Research Desk had in hand. Driscoll again led the way with the first break, which enabled each of the daily keys to be solved without much difficulty. Every intercepted message was decrypted and translated to maximize the training value for the Research Desk. This was the first time that U.S. naval communications and intelligence officers had taken on a real-world signal code and cipher system of a potential enemy navy from start to finish.

The IJN's order of battle and campaign strategy for its Combined Fleet was also revealed through the radio intercepts. Specifically, while the IJN's Third Fleet blockaded China's coast, the Fourth Fleet would form and operate as the Philippine Expeditionary Force, which had assembled in the vicinity of Formosa. In turn, through night torpedo attacks, the Second Fleet would bait and decimate the U.S. Fleet in the area of Japan's Inland Sea. A worn-out U.S. Fleet would then receive the final coup de grâce from the IJN's First Fleet striking force, which would attack by surprise from a concealed position within the Inland Sea.

It was also noted that the use of the radio had solved the IJN's age-old problem of how to coordinate and control widely scattered forces at sea. No longer was the IJN relying on signal flags, blinker lights, and messenger vessels for relaying orders. The Japanese naval communications system was now in the process of being spread throughout the Japanese Empire and its Mandate islands, using a combination of shore-based stations in conjunction with those with the various fleets. The IJN's Combined Fleet was now operating as a single entity under its commander-in-chief and was confident that it could defeat the U.S. Navy in a war for control of the Western Pacific.[44]

The IJN did not know it, but U.S. Navy signals intelligence was actually far ahead of its War Plan Orange adversary, and in a moment of exultation in early 1931, the director of naval communications (DCI) advised the secretary of the navy, "The U.S. Navy has at the present moment as complete an ascendancy over the Japanese Navy in the matter of radio intelligence as the British Navy had over the German Navy during the World War."[45]

The DCI's comments did not reveal the full story of the lessons learned from the IJN's Grand Maneuvers of 1930. For one thing, Safford noted that the Division of Naval Communications' inability to continuously track the various IJN fleet units made it difficult to exploit traffic analysis to locate key warship locations in a timely manner. This clearly indicated the need for a specific strategic RDF network to function as part of the radio intelligence organization. This network would have to operate outside the Coast Guard's maritime system of navigational direction finder stations to assist merchant vessels. The IJN's fleet maneuvers showed that Guam would undoubtedly be a target for occupation almost immediately from the onset of the war, but it was pointless to potentially sacrifice an advanced crypto capability on a vulnerable island relatively close to Japan. Serious thinking was begun on the establishment of major intercept stations in Hawaii and Manila, which would also serve as strategic RDF sites. The Asiatic Decrypting Unit, at that time consisting of one officer in the Philippines, was to be given priority for the creation of a serious decrypting capability, followed by Hawaii.[46]

An intercept operator using kana code could determine from whom a message was sent. This was a *call sign*, identifying which radio transmitter was sending the signal. The way the person hit the keys varied; this became known as the *fist* and was as distinctive as handwriting. This identified the particular ship or land unit. If an intelligence analyst added the various frequencies, the transmission routines followed, and the idiosyncrasies of the radio transmitters and their individual operators, he could derive enough information to make an accurate identification of the source station without even decoding and translating the basic message. This, plus an effective RDF capability, identified the precise location of the sending station and often the receiving station.[47]

It was crucial to determine the high-priority messages (operational orders), important originators (fleet commanders), and their key addresses (fleet headquarters, aircraft carriers, battleships, and submarines) from the more routine transmissions of less important ships—in other words, "skimming off the cream" of what really counted.[48] The U.S. Navy still had some catching up to do, compared to the British and others.

IBM

As the IJN's combined fleet maneuvers of 1930 were taking place, International Business Machines (IBM) tabulating machinery was integrated into the Research Desk's efforts to solve ciphers and reconstruct codes. This mechanization greatly speeded up the process of achieving solutions.[49] This could not have come about at a better time for the United States, since the IJN discontinued its old 1918 Naval Code and implemented a new one in 1930. The new code consisted of first an enciphered code, which had to be stripped off in order to reconstruct the basic code. Again, Driscoll came to the fore, solving and reconstructing as required. Safford called this "the most difficult cryptanalytic task ever performed up to that date and possibly the most brilliant," because there was no equivalent to the Red Book, as had been the case for the previous IJN naval code.[50] This edition of the IJN's Secret Code became known as the Blue Book (due to the color of its binder). It would remain in effect from December 1, 1930, to October 31, 1938.

Edwin Layton, who was assigned as a translator in the Code and Signal Section (OP-20-G), observed Agnes Driscoll at work solving the new IJN code system. This required her to strip away the two-tier layer of protective enciphers, before solving the meanings of the code. She was, in fact, the first person to recognize that a new code had been instituted by the IJN. Lt. Thomas Dyer had been working on the code under the assumption that it was part of the Red Book's three-kana system, but Driscoll realized that it was actually a four-kana system. It was not an easy task to deal with the some 85,000 code groups of the new code. Driscoll worked full time on this before turning it over to Thomas Dyer. Dyer spent five months working full time on the problem, integrating IBM tabulating systems to take up much of the burden.[51]

The IBM punch card tabulating machines were crucial to Safford's operation. The machines had their origin in Herman Hollerith's invention of the electric tabulating system in 1889. After building a series of the systems to assist the U.S. Census Office to successfully complete the 1890 census in only one year (the 1880 census had taken eight years), Hollerith developed an automatic card-feed mechanism and keypunches. Flexibility was built into the system (early programming), so that it could do many business-related functions. Other companies merged with Hollerith to form a corporation in 1924. Under Thomas J. Watson, the company was renamed International Business Machines of America or IBM.

By 1934, IBM's Type 405 Alphabetic Accounting Machine could tabulate 150 punch cards per minute, or tabulate and print 80 cards per minute, making it possible to print complete reports from the data punched into the accounting machine cards. Not only could the Type 405 machine list both alphabetical and numerical details, it could print out *any desired arrangement of data* entered into the cards. This was revolutionary. An intelligence analyst could now mesh distinct RDF bearings by the various intercept stations, dates of intercept, radio frequencies, and IJN radio transmitter call signs. This included the identification of even a specific ship.[52]

Dyer and his immediate superior, Lt. Joseph Wenger, saw the tremendous potential for the Type 405 and convinced the navy's Bureau of Ships to invest $5,000 to rent IBM equipment and hire two key-punch operators.[53] The involvement of IBM equipment enabled Safford's 1935 organization to recover 144,354 code values, compared to 12,167 code values in 1930, representing a 1,200 percent increase in output.[54]

In the case of the Japanese *romanji* lettering, causal and accidental repetitions of characters or letter combinations facilitated the breaking down of the encipherment of plaintext and superimposed ciphertexts. Some letters (O, I, K, U, S) appeared with considerable frequency. This deductive pattern enabled the U.S. Navy's Japanese language experts to fill in missing letters and complete the "solution."[55] In 1941, similar IBM tabulating equipment would be sent to Manila (Corregidor Island) and Hawaii (Pearl Harbor).

An immediate return on these efforts was an intercepted and decrypted IJN message concerning the battleship *Nagato*'s sea trials, which stated that the ship had a maximum speed of at least 26 knots, or as fast as Japan's *Kongo*-class battle cruisers. This meant that the IJN had now eclipsed the expected 24 knots that were in blueprint planning for the next generation of U.S. Navy battleships. The navy upgraded its battleship propulsion plant systems to obtain at least a 27-knot speed, one more than the *Kongo*-class ships. Both the *North Carolina*- and *South Dakota*-class benefited from the upgrade, as did the *Iowa*-class of fast battleships.[56] Safford's efforts were now starting to pay dividends for War Plan Orange.

The IJN conducted major combined fleet maneuvers in 1933. By this time, the U.S. Navy had learned a great deal about IJN communications procedures and systems and had begun enhancing its SIGINT capabilities in the Far East. A small component of self-trained radiomen stationed in Shanghai in the mid-1920s supported this effort by using their radio receivers to intercept IJN communications traffic.

This ad hoc intercept station was formally recognized in 1924, but by 1929, the group was phased out, leaving Lt. Joseph Wenger, who had been attached by OP-20-G to the Asiatic Fleet's staff, operating out of Manila. Another radio intercept station had been founded in Peking under the auspices of the U.S. Marine detachment on legation guard duty. It, too, was moved, going to Shanghai, where it served as the Fleet Intelligence Unit attached to the 4th Marines on into 1937.[57] The navy now had radio intercept stations in China, the Philippines (Asiatic Fleet), Guam, and Hawaii with which to spy on the IJN.

With one officer and 30 men involved with radio intelligence operations scattered out among the four widely separated stations in the Pacific, U.S. Naval Intelligence was better organized than ever to monitor IJN communications. The IJN was well enough informed of the U.S. Navy's capabilities to use radio jamming from time to time or to send powerful signals on key frequencies in order to create what Safford called an "obliterative interference."

While the Japanese countermeasures were somewhat effective, they did not inhibit the navy's radio intelligence effort directed at the IJN. Several experiments were conducted among the various intercept stations, using intercept "spot analysis" or the recovery of immediately important information, traffic analysis without decryption, and full decryption of messages to verify the accuracy of traffic analysis, as well as an analysis of the IJN's maneuvers based on the message traffic. The Research Desk would spend up to three years comparing and contrasting the results of these efforts.[58]

The IJN's 1933 maneuvers were of the same magnitude and pattern of the 1930 Grand Maneuvers. The 1933 maneuvers covered four phases, lasting from May 17 to August 25: mobilization (two months), strategic operations (one month), tactical operations (five days), and finally a critique and fleet review by the emperor himself. The mobilization phase saw the creation of a full fleet (Fourth Fleet) from mostly older vessels that were being modernized. In the strategic phase, a second fleet (Third Fleet) conducted a blockade of China, while two others (First and Second Fleets) escorted troop transports and protected the amphibious operations of the Combined Landing Force (Japanese army and Marine troops) out in Japan's Mandates. This represented a strategic deployment to confront the U.S. fleet as it initiated its counterattack in the Central Pacific.

Last, the tactical phase of the maneuvers was undertaken with the First and Second Fleets representing the U.S. Navy. These two BLUE fleets attempted to attack Japan while the defending RED or Fourth Fleet, representing the mass of the Combined Fleet, waited in forward positions at the Bonin Islands. The "final battle" took place on August 18. Three years later in 1936, Japan actually would begin landing operations along the coast of China.[59] As was the case in the 1930 maneuvers, there were some lessons learned that came out of the exercise.

By June 1933, Guam's intercept Station BAKER was able to give a comprehensive and "extraordinarily accurate picture" of the makeup and up-to-date order of battle of the IJN's forces. A key point was the discovery that the IJN was able to rapidly take ships that were in reserve and put them into active service in support of the Combined Fleet's operations.

Station BAKER found that seaplanes were flown as far as Saipan in the Mandates. This meant that naval aviation was becoming a major component of the IJN's operations. Another aspect of the maneuvers was that the Japanese were beginning to use RDF with high-frequency direction finders operating from newly established air bases in Chichi Jima, Iwo Jima, Saipan, and Pagan of the Bonin and Mariana Islands.[60]

As the large volume of radio intercept data from the 1933 maneuvers was being digested as useful intelligence data, a number of additional lessons were revealed. Traffic analysis had been particularly successful in providing an accurate picture of the 1933 maneuvers, without the need for formal decryption. This resulted in a secret letter, March 7, 1937 (CF283), from Adm. Frank B. Upham, commander-in-chief Asiatic Fleet (CINCAF), to his chief of naval operations (CNO), recommending the establishment of an enhanced radio intercept and decrypting center in the vicinity of Manila Bay.

Adm. Upham's recommendation included all radio intercept stations be equipped with high-frequency, long-range RDF equipment suitable for the tracking of the IJN. He requested sufficient personnel: trained intercept operators, including two cryptanalysts, one translator, and two specialists for the analysis of intercepted material. Upham wanted an intercept capability so efficient that it could prevent a surprise attack as well as provide timely targeting information on primary IJN warships. These initiatives were implemented and gradually expanded so that by the time of the attack at Pearl Harbor on December 7, 1941, the Asiatic Radio Intelligence Unit would consist of nine officers and 61 enlisted personnel, functioning in a bombproof tunnel on the island of Corregidor in Manila Bay.[61]

Naval War College (NWC) strategists, having received U.S. Navy intelligence inputs from the 1930 and 1933 IJN maneuvers, revamped War Plan Orange to reflect the IJN's strategy for a war with the United States. This all took place from the end of 1933 to the middle of 1937. Of special note during this period was the Japanese withdrawal from the League of Nations in September 1934 and its announcement that within a period of two years it would abrogate the arms treaties it had entered into, including the Washington Naval Treaty of 1922.

NWC planners now had to take this new aspect of the IJN's strategy—Japanese interest in using its Mandates as part of a coordinated defense against the U.S. Fleet—into consideration. The navy's traditional plan for deep strike operations aimed at Japan was modified over the next few years to a more gradualist, island-hopping campaign through the Mandates. An advantage of this scenario was that it would allow sufficient time to review the actual war situation and develop flexible and more appropriate courses of action to deal with Japanese moves in the Pacific. This now became a basic consideration, if not a component, of all U.S. Navy campaign planning. The IJN's maneuvers of the early 1930s portended ill omens in the Pacific, and the U.S. Navy began preparing in earnest.[62]

From 1935 to 1937, Safford recognized that the complexities of radio intelligence collection in the Navy Department required comprehensive organization involving several functioning levels. The first was the organization of a principal decrypting unit, which would serve as a model for the others, to be located in Washington, DC. It encompassed a main analysis, administrative, and coordination center. Each major geographical area (two identified in the Pacific) would have its own analytical center, called a *second echelon processing center.* The individual radio intercept stations (signals and RDF) at their respective points of intercept were considered *first echelon* processing activities. In all cases, Safford considered it critical that the system be provided with fast and secure communications capabilities, which could exchange intelligence and technical information not only among all the elements in the several levels but also with the Army's Signals Intelligence Service (SIS) and even the Coast Guard.

In Washington, the Code and Signal Section (OP-20-G) was renamed the Communications Security Group (but still designated as OP-20-G) in March 1935 and divided into five distinct key but subordinate elements: OP-20-GC, Cryptographic Section; -GS, Communications Security; -GX, Radio Intercept and Tracking (RDF); -GY, Cryptanalytic Section; and finally -GZ, Translation Section. Safford's communications intelligence organization now consisted of 11 officers, 88 enlisted, and 10 civilians, a total of 109 personnel, compared to 7 total personnel in 1925.[63]

Advanced intercept and decrypting units were set up in Manila by 1932 and at the Pearl Harbor naval base by 1936. The extensive evolving network of radio intercept and "strategic" high-frequency RDF stations, running the length and breadth of the Pacific generally to the north of the equator, required some form of rapid communications in order to send critical pieces of IJN SIGINT information and radio signal bearings in a timely manner. *Speed* was essential.[64]

A RDF bearing or azimuth from a navy intercept station out toward the targeted transmitting station would be worthless unless transmitted to Manila, Pearl Harbor, or Washington within a period of 24 hours. Extremely important in this transmission process were the radio intercept stations' transmissions of code solution data, radio call sign identifications, and recorded IJN signal intercept messages, either in their original or decrypted forms. There was also a need for the continuous exchange of crypto data between Washington, Manila, and Pearl Harbor.

The traditional forms of communication by sea up until the mid-1930s had been on military and commercial ships and the island-hopping transpacific Pan American Clipper flights. Only once in a while, coded and non-coded radio messages were used to transmit SIGINT information. Laurance

Safford was well aware that the navy's communications system then in existence was totally unsatisfactory and needed to be modernized to meet SIGINT requirements.

A veritable dynamo in innovative thinking, Safford delved into the development of communications equipment to enhance OP-20-G's operations. During the late 1920s and throughout the 1930s, Safford was awarded seven patents:

1. Start-Stop Teleprinter

2. Scrambler AFSAX-500/AFSAJ-700

3. Synchronous Magnetic Teleprinter Scrambler—useable with Teletype AN/FGC-5, UGC-1, UGC-3, and Rixon AN/TCC-35

4. Single Output Coding System Improvement of AFSAX-500/AFSAJ-700

5. Cryptographic Telegraphy Programming System Programmer for Wozencroft Interactive Coding System (WICS)

6. Commercial TTY Scrambler Improvement over Western Union's TELEKRYPTON

7. Narrowband Analog Message Privacy System (WISPR II)[65]

Safford was contributing to a revolution in communications technology. Coinciding with this effort, the Naval Research Laboratory produced the world's first fledgling radar equipment in 1934 and was also involved in the production of high-frequency radio projects. In 1936, Bell Telephone Laboratories and the Massachusetts Institute of Technology were both involved with the transmission of ultra-high-frequency radio waves, and the Radio Corporation of America (RCA) demonstrated the operation of a two-way radio relay system.[66]

ECM

It was the electronic cipher machine (ECM) that became the workhorse of U.S. naval communications. Originally promoted through the innovative work of U.S. Army cryptologists Frank B. Rowlett and William F. Friedman, the ECM was a major improvement over the single-stepping rotor cipher machine for encoding radio transmissions. The ECM featured an invention called the *stepping maze*, which not only moved keying rotors to random locations for each message but also enabled each rotor to provide between one and four output signals. Ultimately, the machine would have up to three bands of five rotors each that, when used in selective series, could encipher and scramble every letter and number of plaintext into a different character of ciphertext. The action of two of the banks controlled the "stepping" of the third.

Only a similar machine at a receiving station could unscramble and make the decode.

Shown initially in 1935 to OP-20-G's Joseph Wenger, it caught Safford's attention. Safford was Friedman's counterpart in the navy's cryptographic community. The machine became the Electronic Cipher Machine Mark II (ECM Mark II), was further modified, and later codenamed SIGABA under a joint army-navy production project in 1941. In 1941, in addition to the ECM Mark II, the IJN signals intercepts and technical data were encoded in the navy's CETYH, COPEK, and GUPID cipher systems and transmitted over the navy's various radio networks. A further TESTM message system was used to transmit RDF data.[67] As the navy integrated state-of-the-art communications systems into its intelligence operations, it also focused on its RDF capabilities.

While the navy was advanced in medium- or intermediate-frequency direction finding (IFDF), it was not until 1937 that the Naval Research Laboratory designed and constructed a reliable high-frequency direction finder (HFDF) system. Production took place at the Naval Gun Factory, with the DT-1 and DT-2 HFDFs being sent to Manila, Guam, Midway, Oahu, Dutch Harbor, Sitka, Samoa, and Canal Zone radio intercept sites, along with the California coast intercept sites at Point Arguello, Farallon Islands, Point Saint George, and San Diego, and Bainbridge Island in Washington. By 1939, the strategic HFDF stations were successfully tracking the IJN's warships and merchant marine vessels as far away as the Western Pacific.[68]

Each station plotted its own RDF bearing, taken on an IJN radio transmitter on shore or at sea. To ensure accuracy, all RDF bearings were plotted on great circle nautical charts, not Mercator projections. Mercator flat projection maps tended to significantly distort RDF plots and ship locations the closer the subject was to the North Pole. The great circle charts followed the circumference of the earth's surface and were therefore well suited for both tracking and intersecting corresponding RDF bearings from the various intercepts, establishing accurately the shortest distance between any two points on that surface.[69]

Primary radio intercept and decode stations, such as OP-20-GX in Washington, in Manila, and in Oahu all used great circle tracking charts for the Pacific Ocean and IBM Type 405 tabulators and the Type 075 sorter composite file and map locator system for all IJN warships and merchant marine vessels. Each RDF bearing and related identification data was punched into cards for the purpose of quick retrieval.

War Plan Orange planners had noted that the string of central atolls running from Hawaii's Oahu northwestward toward Japan, the Wake and Midway islands, could serve as suitable "sentinels" for Pearl Harbor. With forward aerial reconnaissance bases and radio intercept and RDF tracking stations gradually constituted from the mid-1930s onward, the IJN's primary aircraft carrier approaches to the eastern part of the North Pacific were covered except one. That came from the immediate due north directly to Oahu.[70] This was a recognized vulnerability; the establishment of an RDF site at Dutch Harbor in the Aleutian Islands could not have come at a better time, closing the gap.

In 1936, the IJN delayed and finally cancelled its grand fleet maneuvers, only to reconstruct them through a real war scenario with the execution of an all-out attack on China in July 1937. Soon, the northern provinces and many of the Chinese seaports were overrun by the Imperial Japanese Army's invasion of upwards of a million men. Roosevelt advocated an international "quarantine" against the Japanese, but the U.S. public, still mired in the stubborn Depression of some eight years, was hardly interested in a war on the other side of the Pacific. Congress, however, as part of an effort to create badly needed jobs, authorized the expenditure of funds to expand the navy.

With war now a fact in Asia and the IJN involved, the Central Pacific campaign planning portion of War Plan Orange went through another iteration of changes. The navy's OP-12 (operations), now working with a joint army-navy board, decided in mid-1937 that the U.S. transpacific attack should initially seize eight of the Marshall and Caroline Islands before moving on Truk Island.[71] So there the matter rested.

The navy began its new SIGINT capability during 1924–1925 and found that its study of encoded Japanese cipher systems would be good training for its fledgling group of cryptographers. The army's SIS began to get interested in the same field. As a result, there was an interchange between the two services concerning the technical features and even translations of Tokyo's diplomatic cipher. The army took over the breaking of the diplomatic ciphers, leaving the navy free to focus on the IJN's code systems.

During the winter of 1935–1936, a new Japanese diplomatic signals code system based on machine-cryptography was brought into service by Japan's Foreign Office. This was due to Herbert Yardley's 1931 book, *The American Black Chamber*, which disclosed America's ability to break Japanese codes. Correctly identified as a machine-centered cipher system by SIS, this new system, a Roman-typewriter cipher machine, was called the Type A Cipher Machine by the Japanese. This machine was code-named RED by the U.S. Army and became the focus of William Friedman, who became SIS chief cryptanalyst in 1921.

Another burglary of the Alban Towers apartment of Japan's naval attaché in Washington greatly facilitated the solving of RED's ciphers. This enabled Jack Holtwick, a naval intelligence officer, to build a duplicate equivalent. This was the first electromechanical cipher machine of a foreign power to be broken by U.S. Army and Navy cryptanalysts, and it proved to be of immense value due to the large amount of message traffic it carried over the years.[72]

Although the Japanese were unaware of the break-ins, they were not satisfied with their diplomatic code machine and replaced it. This was called the Type B Cipher Machine or Alphabetical Typewriter 97—the infamous PURPLE machine. This new machine used a new cipher key each day and was based on the RED machine, but with the difference that there were now six banks (levels) of some 25 electrical stepping switches, similar to those found in telephone exchanges, on the coding wheels that could be flicked to one side or another before enciphering began. The system could encipher in English and *romanji*, as well as Roman-letter code texts.

The problem for the cryptanalysts was, in part, reconstructing the wiring and switches of the coding wheels. Since PURPLE used the same input-output units as RED and the same basic plug-board arrangement, a remaining problem was to determine which key was to be used for the first day. The Japanese shuffled the initial keys in order to form the equivalents for the next nine days, in a 10-day pattern. Lt. Francis Raven figured this out.[73] What the Japanese did not realize was that the RED machine had already been broken by the Americans and that some of its encryption weaknesses had been inadvertently repeated in the new PURPLE machine.

During 1939–1940, William Friedman, supported by IBM's Type 405 tabulating machines, directed a SIS team made up of electrical engineers, accounting machine experts, and Japanese linguists that again broke Tokyo's diplomatic code. The team also built a series of duplicate analog machine copies of PURPLE to be used to decipher messages. SIS personnel Larry Clark and Leo Rosen, assisted by the navy's Francis Raven, reproduced the electromechanical stepping-switch device, one of the machine's key components. They also found that for coding purposes, the Japanese divided each month into three 10-day periods, making minor predictable changes for each first day encountered. They noted that there was a cipher within a cipher that had to be unraveled. These and other weaknesses of the system enabled U.S. intelligence to read the Japanese Foreign Office's most secret dispatches to and from its embassies around the world. These were being fully intercepted, decoded, translated, and read simultaneously in Washington, DC, as they were in Tokyo.

Priority for reading the decoded diplomatic traffic from PURPLE became so high that the army and navy alternated daily decrypting, decoding, and translating efforts. The navy took the odd days and the army the even days. Friedman's effort was considered by Safford and others to be a "masterpiece of cryptanalysis." Friedman, mentally exhausted, suffered a nervous breakdown and was hospitalized in 1941. The Naval Gun Factory produced a small number of compatible PURPLE machines for distribution in Washington,

London, and key overseas sites. While the information from this radio signal intercept effort was code-named MAGIC by its American users, the overseas distribution of the PURPLE machines would become a controversial issue of considerable importance.[74]

In May 1939, as war clouds gathered in Europe, the U.S. Army and Navy agreed to develop five joint contingency plans for conducting multinational wars between what was now billed as the AXIS coalition (Germany, Japan, and Italy) and the United States. Called Rainbow Plans, these replaced War Plan Orange. While two of the plans provided for the defense of the Western Hemisphere, the navy had its own ideas and used the old War Plan Orange as a basis for its two drafts of Joint Rainbow Plans. These postulated a coalition war, which would include the British and the Dutch, against Japan in the Pacific. By July 1939, the Joint Board was ordered by Roosevelt himself to report directly to him, rather than to the civilian military secretaries.

As the war in Europe commenced in September 1939, uppermost in the planners' and the president's minds was the possibility that the United States could find itself alone in a hostile world and, if so, it might have to protect the western Atlantic approaches and the eastern Pacific approaches to the United States as well as the Panama Canal that linked them. The Joint Board concluded that the navy would protect Hawaii and Alaska. The Philippines were now written off as being too difficult to protect. Once the situation clarified itself in the Atlantic (the German Navy was considered "paltry" in comparison to its IJN counterpart), the navy would commence Phase II of its transpacific offensive and, using its Marine Corps assets, would proceed to conquer the Marshalls, Carolines, and even the Marianas, as a prelude to an advance on Japan. This plan became known as Rainbow 5.[75]

On June 1, 1939, the IJN completely changed its fleet operations code, introducing a new cryptographic message system, which included a distinctly different enciphered system of codes. Safford pitted some of his best brain power—Agnes Driscoll, Lt. Prescott Currier, and others—against the new code. Driscoll recognized that the code had similarities to one originally used by the U.S. government during the Spanish-American War, an older four-digit "S" code, stolen by the U.S. Navy from the Japanese consulate in New York, which helped serve as a crib to better understand the new code. These messages were being decoded as early as October 1940. The recovery of the encipherment keys and additives took a great deal of time and was far more labor intensive than OP-20-G could ever have imagined.[76]

This new code, referred to in a letter of May 5, 1941, from the commandant, Sixteenth Naval District, Cavite, Philippine Islands, to the navy's chief of naval operations as the "five numeral code," a five-digit, two-part, super-enciphered code, was called the 5-Number Code. It was soon short-ened to the 5-Num Code or AN-1 Code by OP-20-G.[77] The Japanese named it Code Book D (*Agon-sho* D), which was more appropriate because it really was a book system and not a machine cipher. Driscoll's decrypting team (OP-20-GY) wrote two full analyses of the 5-Num Code and had them issued as OP-20-G's Radio Intelligence Publications (RIPs) 73 and 80 in March and July 1941 respectively. By mid-1942, the 5-Num Code was renamed JN-25 by the Division of Naval Communications as part of a system for formally cataloging all of the Japanese signal code systems.[78]

The IJN radio operators were provided with an instruction manual and two books for implementing the cryptosystem itself: a book of codes and a book of super-encipherment additive tables. The basic book consisted of some 30,000 five-digit code groups that represented the Japanese phonetic kana characters, words, numbers, place names, and related items alpha-betically arranged for encoding. Much like a dictionary, groups of five numbers each were substituted for a Japanese word, name, or place ren-dered in alphabetical order. A second part was arranged in numbers-to-word order for decoding.

The additive book, several hundred pages in length, provided the "key" or specific page number of the book, which had 100 random numbers in 10 rows of 10 numbers each. These random numbers were changed about every five months, so that by the first week in December 1941, some eight additive books had been introduced. This offered the sender the selection from an additional 30,000 five-digit numbers at will.

To break into the basic code, Driscoll and Currier had to break through the additive encipherment first. From June 1, 1939, through November 30, 1940, the Japanese utilized five additives, categorized as A-1 to A-5. Since the 5-Num Code (JN-25) was used extensively as the IJN's principal opera-tional code, OP-20-G had to deal with thousands of intercepted radio mes-sages. The IBM Type 405 machine could strip out the key additive, then print the base code groups of the message. It would then search against tables of already identified code groups, comparing the code groups with those stored in its card memory deck and printing out whichever group made the match.[79]

On December 1, 1940, the IJN introduced a second version of the code, called Baker by Safford's people (noted as JN-25B later on). The Japanese super-enciphered the Baker version with additives B-5 through B-8, cor-responding to occasional add-on changes every two, three, or even six months (December 1, 1940; February 1, August 1, and December 4, 1941). The 5-Num Code was a never-ending challenge for OP-20-G.[80]

Toward the end of 1940, the Navy Department's Office of the Chief of Naval Operations acknowledged that its OP-20-G was addressing five major Japanese naval cryptographic systems relating to the IJN:

1. Administrative Code

2. Merchant Ship Code

3. Material Code

4. Operations Code (5-Num Code)

5. Intelligence Code

Events would prove that the IJN Operations and Merchant Ship codes were the most important.[81]

The U.S. Navy's OP-20-G had come a long way since the early 1920s. Its radio intelligence and RDF activities had provided knowledge of the organization and operations of the IJN, including the various fleets, squadrons, and divisions. It was noted that the IJN would form temporary taskforces, or naval combat groups, consisting of units and divisions, to perform special missions.

Traffic analysis gathered on units and ships communicating with each other often provided clues as to the composition of the task force and the nature and magnitude of the mission(s). RDF intersection data also provided information on the approximate locations of key ships and their task forces. This highly classified, top-secret intelligence-gathering process was called ULTRA, and each individual who served in Naval Intelligence had to sign an agreement (security oath) that he or she would not disclose any information concerning his or her work in communications intelligence.[82] In October 1939, Safford's section was redesignated as the Communications Security Section (still OP-20-G); a title to mask its actual work in SIGINT.

During the period between 1928 and 1941, 176 enlisted radio operators (150 navy seamen and 26 marines) were trained to intercept and analyze foreign radio communications. OP-20-G's personnel for conducting the navy's SIGINT effort jumped from 543 in January 1941 to 738 personnel by early December: 448 for the Atlantic and 290 for the Pacific. Safford's operation had approximately 145 RIP-5s targeted against the IJN.

The navy's On the Roof Gang in Washington formed the backbone of 22 radio intelligence intercept and direction finding (RDF) stations, operating in a network that included the United States, Canada, Britain, and the Dutch East Indies throughout the Pacific Ocean. Their mission was to determine the IJN's operational organization, its intentions, what it was doing, and where it was sailing. Adm. Harold R. Stark, chief of naval operations (CNO) in Washington, DC, called this network, the three-tiered intelligence-gathering system in the Pacific, the "splendid arrangement."[83]

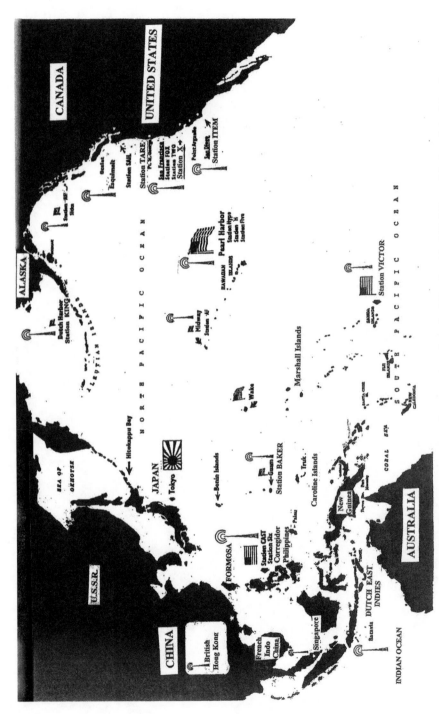

The U.S. Navy's "Splendid Arrangement" in the Pacific, 1941. (Unclassified/Declassified Holdings, National Archives)

3

The U.S. Navy's "Splendid Arrangement" in the Pacific

By 1941, the U.S. Navy in the Pacific had one of the most stellar radio intelligence and signal intercept systems in the world. It was the creation of one man: Cdr. Laurance F. Safford, known as the "father of U.S. naval cryptology." His brain and imaginative thinking enabled it to all come together: state-of-the-art navy technologies and outstanding cryptologists such as Agnes Meyer Driscoll, Joseph Rochefort, and Joseph Wenger.

OPNAV

This signal intercept system was under the control of OP-20-G (Office of Chief of Naval Operations, OPNAV, 20th Division of the Office of Naval Communications, G Section: Communications Security Section). Further code-named Station NEGAT, it was second to none in code-breaking capability. Safford continued to build upon the successes of OP-20-G throughout the 1930s, expanding the network of radio intelligence field stations. Two of these, along with OP-20-G, were capable of not only intercepting (copying), decoding, and translating IJN signal messages to a considerable degree, but also using key tracking information from radio direction finding (RDF) stations in order to plot and locate complete fleets and even individual ships, ascertaining their intentions via their maritime movements.

The system, arrayed around the Pacific Ocean's rim and across its center axis in what amounted to several tiers, encompassed the West Coast of North America from Sitka, Alaska, to the southern coast of California; the North Pacific from Dutch Harbor, Alaska, straight south through the Hawaiian Islands to Samoa in the South Pacific; and finally in the west, from the Philippine Islands through Hong Kong and Singapore and on into the Dutch East Indies. Dutch Harbor, approximately 2,250 miles due north of Pearl Harbor, was a remote, desolate place located on Amaknak Island in Unalaska Bay (part of the Aleutian Islands chain that extends some 800 miles out to the west of Anchorage, then the Territory of Alaska).

Safford had astutely realized that atmospheric conditions during the day or night caused radio signals to skip and bounce over the Pacific Ocean's surface. To overcome the possibility of an intercept station missing an important message due to this skip effect, Safford built into the system a redundancy of intercept station activities. Redundancy also meant that RDF stations could take a compass azimuth and home in on the IJN's radio transmitters from multiple directions, to ensure that accurate bearings would crisscross and therefore pinpoint the IJN's ship-borne and shore-based radio transmitters—Adm. Stark's "splendid arrangement."[1]

The entire enterprise was controlled by Safford from his OP-20-G office, hidden away in the bureaucratic maze of the Naval Communications Division in Washington. Safford's efforts, combined with the radio intercepts of Japanese code PURPLE diplomatic radio transmissions, provided insights into what Japan was going to do. This opened the Roosevelt administration's eyes and started them thinking about what policy positions the United States should take.

OP-20-G's reports went up the chain of command to Roosevelt himself. A key point in this chain was that although Safford's organization was at the fulcrum of the U.S. Navy's signal intelligence collection effort in the Pacific, all its collected information was forwarded through the Office of Naval Intelligence to Adm. Stark, chief of naval operations (CNO), who would decide what to do with it.[2]

By 1941, Roosevelt was served by what became known as his War Cabinet, made up of the senior civilian armed service and diplomatic cabinet members, as well as the military and naval chiefs of the day:

President and Commander-in-Chief:	Franklin D. Roosevelt
Secretary of State:	Cordell Hull
Secretary of War:	Henry L. Stimson
Secretary of the Navy:	Frank Knox
Chief of Staff, U.S. Army:	Gen. George C. Marshall
Chief of Naval Operations:	Adm. Harold R. Stark

All important decisions about American foreign policy and related military (army) and naval (navy) policy and strategies for 1941 would be finalized and then promulgated by the War Cabinet, which was led by the president himself. In terms of policy and strategy dealing with the IJN during 1941, Stark and his assistant CNO, Rear Adm. Royal E. Ingersoll, were served by bureaucratic layers; the mix inevitably creating its own challenges. Each one of these, like OP-20-G, had its own distinct, office code identifier under the control of the Office of the Chief of Naval Operations:

War Plans Division (OP-12): Directed by Rear Adm. Richmond Kelly Turner

War Information Room (OP-12): Directed by Rear Adm. F. T. Leighton

Ship Movements Division (OP-38): Directed by Rear Adm. R. M. Brainard

Intelligence Division or Office of Naval Intelligence (ONI or OP-16): Directed at the beginning of 1941 by Rear Adm. W. S. Anderson, then Capt. A. G. Kirk until mid-October, and finally by Capt. Theodore S. Wilkinson through to the end of 1941

Foreign Branch (OP-16-F): Directed by Capt. W. A. Heard

Far Eastern Section (OP-16-F-2): Directed by Cdr. Arthur H. McCollum

Communications Division (OP-20): Directed by Rear Adm. Leigh Noyes

Communications Security Section (OP-20-G): Directed by Cdr. Safford; besides its subordinate sections, such as OP-20-GA for administrative purposes and OP-20-GS for Communications Security, Safford's OP-20-G was composed of the following four key signal intelligence-related sub-branches during 1941:

OP-20-GI: Radio Intelligence: directed by Cdr. Safford

OP-20-GX: Radio Direction Finding (RDF): directed by Lt. Cdr. G. W. Welker

OP-20-GY: Cryptanalysis, including OP-20-GYP (special JEEP component): directed by Lt. Cdr. L. W. Parke

OP-20-GZ: Translation and Dissemination: directed by Cdr. Alwin D. Kramer (Kramer, attached to OP-16-F-2, served on special loan to OP-20-G)

By January 1941, OP-20-G was composed of some 60 personnel, both military and civilian.[3]

Stark controlled his intelligence operations through ONI, called Station US, the Navy Headquarters located at 18th Street and Constitution Avenue in northwest Washington. (Station US was used interchangeably with Station NEGAT [OP-20-G], which sometimes caused confusion.) Stark, without any real experience in senior fleet command, was selected by Roosevelt in July 1939, when he was a rear admiral, over the heads of some 50 more senior admirals. Stark's promotion as CNO on August 1 was accepted because he was well-known and liked.[4] Stark was faced with serious organizational and jurisdictional challenges involving his Intelligence Division and the War Plans Division.

The Office of Naval Intelligence (ONI or OP-16) and the Office of Naval Communications (OP-20), as major divisions of the Navy Department, shared joint responsibility for handling communications intelligence. OP-20 was responsible for the mechanics of radio signals interception, RDF and traffic analysis, cryptanalysis (involving decryption) and translation. OP-16's Foreign Branch (OP-16-F) worked with the information derived from OP-20-G, analyzing this information and formulating conclusions about the IJN's capabilities, plans, and intentions, and the locations and movements of its naval forces. Rear Adm. Noyes called the end product, incorporating information from OP-16-F as well as its Domestic Branch (espionage and subversive activities analysis), "finished information."

The melding of information from myriad sources, including naval attaché reports from various U.S. embassies around the Pacific, and the continuous PURPLE intercepts of diplomatic signals traffic to and from Tokyo and its Japanese embassies, not only in Washington but also in Berlin, Moscow, and other countries around the world, was important in terms of gaining a complete picture of Japan's political and military intentions. Also included were reports from the army, the FBI, the Federal Communications Commission, Pan American Airways (which ran a passenger clipper service across the Pacific), and even commercial steamship lines.

Stark maintained a 24-hour intelligence and communication watch, to support the CNO and the two major fleet commands at Hawaii (Pearl Harbor) and the Philippines (Manila Bay). Each fleet commander was supported by his own staff, which included intelligence and radio intelligence personnel involved with intercept, decode, translation, and RDF operations.[5]

Intelligence and related information deemed important was passed from the ONI's Foreign Branch directly to the CNO and even Roosevelt at the White House. Urgent reports were made orally, due to their possible immediate impact on the military situation in the Pacific. Usually, a daily Japanese summary went to the director of naval intelligence (DNI) from

Cdr. McCollum, the head of the Far East Section (OP-16-F-2), and was then relayed to Stark.

The three primary processing centers for communications intelligence received by the splendid arrangement in the Pacific were:

Station HYPO (Pearl Harbor Naval Yard, Oahu, Hawaii)

Station CAST (Corregidor, Philippines)

Station NEGAT/US or OP-20-G as part of the Office of Chief of Naval Operations, Communications Division OP-20, Washington, DC

While all three were staffed with top-notch cryptanalysts and Japanese translators, the entire system depended on input from its radio intercept monitoring and radio direction finding (RDF) stations, which fed their top-secret electronic reports directly into the processing centers via coded ECM radio messages or radio teletype systems. The lower-priority intercepts were sent by mail. However, *all* information of any importance flowed into OP-20-G and the Office of Naval Intelligence (ONI) and from there on up the chain of command and even into the hands of Franklin D. Roosevelt himself.

A weekly report of known and estimated positions of all foreign fleets (Japanese, German, and Italian in the main), including their operational organizations, was also produced for the CNO and the War Plans Division (OP-12). This information was provided in written reports and posted on nautical charts and maps in OP-12's War Information Room. Stark would require a "comparative strength table" by types of ships of all the world's fleets. There were also daily summaries of State Department dispatches and even a special daily bulletin for FDR's naval aide, Capt. John Beardall, who would relay pertinent information to Roosevelt. In 1941, the responsibility for the final evaluation of the enemy's intentions was given to the War Plans Division under Adm. Richmond Turner and not ONI.[6]

OP-16-F-2

Cdr. McCollum of OP-16-F-2 played a pivotal role as part of ONI. His duties included evaluating all forms of intelligence received concerning the Far East, correlating them, and advising the DNI—and through him, the CNO (Stark)—on political developments in the Far East, plus all forms of information concerning the IJN and its state of preparations for war in the Pacific. McCollum was assisted by commanders Hartwell C. Davis and Alwin Kramer, Lt. Cdr. Ethelbert Watts, and Lt. Col. Rodney A. Boone, USMC.

McCollum, born in Japan and speaking Japanese before he could speak English, had a keen insight into Japanese culture and psyche. He was singled out by the navy not only to learn to read and speak Japanese at a higher level but also to fully immerse himself in Japanese culture. Having completed the language course in 1926, he served as an assistant naval attaché in Tokyo; this included supervising the U.S. Navy's Japanese language training program for budding intelligence officers such as Lt. Cdrs. Edwin Layton and Joseph Rochefort, among others. McCollum worked in OP-16-F-2 during the early 1930s and then returned to the organization in late 1939 as an expert on Japanese culture, thinking, and military affairs. He had frequent access to Roosevelt himself.[7]

McCollum's office received naval attaché and ambassadorial reports from Japan and China, observers' reports from all the major ports in the Far East, and reports from the commanders-in-chief (CINCs) of the Asiatic (Philippines) and Pacific (Hawaii) Fleets. In addition to these, there were radio intelligence reports involving decryption of Japanese coded dispatches such as PURPLE (diplomatic) and J-19/PA-K2 (consular codes from Hawaii and others), radio traffic analysis and RDF bearings, and plots from not only OP-20-G but also its two other principal processing centers located in the Philippines and Hawaii. OP-16-F-2 also received reports from the State Department's own network of consular posts throughout the Far East.

These posts, located in Japan's port cities of Yokohama, Kobe, Nagasaki, and Moji, and then south along the Asiatic coastline from China into the area of French Indochina (Hanoi), and other navy observation posts at Bangkok (Siam-Thailand) and Batavia, Medan, and Sandakan on the Makassar Strait (all part of the Dutch East Indies), proved useful for information and tracking purposes. The Mitsubishi and Kawasaki shipbuilding yards at Kobe were an important focus of naval intelligence interest; these were reported on by local U.S. consuls.

The reports from these posts were integrated into the worldwide system of surveillance. They were then plotted on both ONI and War Plans charts and maps for a specific reason—it was thought that if Japan began to seriously prepare for war in the Pacific, Tokyo would probably withdraw its most important merchant shipping to prevent it from being seized in North and South American ports. Tracking Japanese merchant ship movements would, in the advent of war involving the United States, give the U.S. Navy the opportunity to target and destroy critical shipping and supplies headed for Japan. McCollum's office maintained its own map room, with charts of the Pacific pinned to its walls, depicting IJN fleet locations. This analytical mission was delineated in 1941 in a classified publication known as ONI 19. In his Veterans Oral History Project interview, McCollum specifically noted two of the articles:

> Article 107B. The value of intelligence depends on its reaching the person who can use it in time to serve its purpose.

Article 201A. Foreign Intelligence. The collection of all classes of pertinent information concerning foreign countries, especially that affecting Naval and maritime matters, with particular attention to the strength, disposition, and probable intentions of possible enemy naval forces.[8]

A key feature of ONI's mandate—which OP-16-F-2 had to carry out as part of its function of being an integral part of the Naval Intelligence Division—was supposed to be the *evaluation of the enemy's probable intent*; in this case, the IJN and its commanders. F-2 produced a Far East Section weekly report, about what McCollum and his staff of experts thought was going to take place in the Pacific in terms of the IJN's order of battle, locations, movements, and intentions, as well as strategic thinking within Japan itself.

The ONI directed F-2 to undertake "strategic cognizance"; this included the Dutch East Indies, India, Ceylon, and the British and French possessions in the Pacific, involving Malaysia, Singapore, and Indochina. This report was issued every two weeks or so.

When McCollum received intelligence information considered so serious as to impact directly on U.S. Navy affairs, he would, himself, bring it to the attention of both the DOI and the CNO. Sometimes, reports of this nature were forwarded through Beardall, who was located adjacent to the Oval Office. McCollum's F-2 was a busy and knowledgeable enterprise, supporting the Navy Department and its important commands afloat.[9] At least that was the intention of the Division of Naval Intelligence. Bureaucratic politics intervened to dictate otherwise.

Capt. Turner became head of the War Plans Division (OP-12) in 1940 and was promoted to rear admiral in 1941. As the head of OP-12, he was subordinate only to Stark. Apart from his earlier Naval War College experience as a student, and then in 1935–1938 as the head of its naval strategy faculty (War Plan Orange, etc.), Turner's only other experience dealing with Japan had been in command of the heavy cruiser *Astoria*, which had made a diplomatic visit to Japan in 1939. A hard-driving, hard-bitten, no-nonsense sort of a man with a "stormy temper, overbearing ego, and celebrated bouts with the bottle," Turner took a dislike of Naval Intelligence officers in general and the Naval Intelligence Division in particular.[10]

Turner ran a tight ship. His War Plans Division had the mission of not only performing operational and strategic war planning but also coordinating the conduct of naval operations and actual war fighting, which included issuing operations orders to the fleets and monitoring their locations, movements, and activities with the commanders of the Atlantic, Pacific, and Asiatic Fleets, who would be conducting the actual tactical naval battles.[11]

OP-38's Ship Movements Division became the de facto command and control center. Its general functions involved the publication of the Operating Force Plan, the assignment of ships and vessels to the various fleets and naval districts, ports, and the formulation of schedules for the maintenance and training. In addition to being responsible for U.S. Naval operations in the Far East, Atlantic, and Mediterranean, Turner arrogated to himself the principal function of ONI—the estimating of enemy intentions. This touched off an intense internecine struggle between Naval Intelligence and Naval Operations over who would have the definitive say over the evaluation of intelligence information, confusing the navy's prescribed intelligence system and undermining its efforts to accomplish its mission.[12]

During the latter part of 1941, Turner aggressively took the bull by the horns and began issuing his own version of intelligence estimates. Rear Adm. Frank Leighton's War Information Room, with its maps and charts maintained for the purpose of plotting and keeping track of all combatant ships afloat around the world, was commandeered by the War Plans and the Ship Movements Divisions. Data concerning Japanese warships and merchant and passenger shipping locations, normally maintained by ONI, were now also part of Turner's War Room; Turner was in the driver's seat for both operations *and* intelligence functions.[13]

It became more and more apparent to McCollum that he was the "odd man out" and only considered a "contact man from ONI," relegated to the provision of intelligence information data. McCollum was now without formal authority or permission to draw conclusions and make estimates based on the information he was obtaining, which had been his principal function. F-2 could now only send information to the War Plans Division itself and *none* to the U.S. fleet commanders, unless specifically approved by Turner.[14]

In September 1941, ONI's Capt. Kirk brought this situation to Stark's attention, complaining that Turner was operating in a manner contrary to the Naval Intelligence Manual (approved by Stark himself). Kirk became outraged when Stark sided with Turner. Not only that, but Stark relieved Kirk of his duties in mid-October, reassigning him to another part of the navy. Kirk's replacement was Capt. Theodore Wilkinson, who would serve out the rest of a frustrating 1941 as the new director of OP-16.

Stark's actions implied that ONI was apparently incompetent in terms of analytical work, allowing Turner to take full advantage of the unusual state of affairs by setting up his own Intelligence Section within War Plans. This section consisted of three officers without any intelligence experience. In his Veterans Oral History Project interview given after World War II, McCollum stated the new situation succinctly: "This put ONI in the unenviable position of being blamed for anything that went wrong in the estimates without the benefit of any knowledge whatsoever of what estimates were being sent out to our major Commanders-in-Chief." Even the assistant CNO, Rear Adm. Royal Ingersoll, remained mute, unwilling to stand up for what was right in terms of confronting Turner and correcting the obvious jurisdictional injustice taking place.[15]

Stark's kowtowing to Turner and his incredibly unprofessional decision to not allow his premier intelligence organization to accomplish its analytical mission on behalf of navy interests would have grave consequences. What should have been incisive F-2 intelligence estimates with thoroughly vetted conclusions by ONI became mere assumptions and otherwise not well-thought-out opinions rendered by Turner's War Plans office. A case in point: earlier in the year McCollum had dispatched an intelligence estimate up the chain of command and out to the Asiatic and Pacific Fleet commanders, predicting a formal invasion of French Indochina by the Japanese within a month or so of the date of the dispatch. Turner, without the knowledge of ONI, issued his own contradicting dispatch, stating that he was convinced that the Japanese were going to invade Siberia.

When McCollum pointed out the contradictory nature of Turner's report to Stark, Stark, at the height of hypocrisy, explained that while he agreed it was a function of ONI, according to the Manual, to address Japanese intentions, he thought that in the interest of "coordination," Turner ought to be in charge. As it turned out, McCollum, the intelligence professional, was correct; Turner, the intelligence neophyte, was wrong. ONI was being excluded from knowing the content of Turner's orders issued to the various fleets—a case of "the right hand not knowing what the left hand is doing."[16] The integrity of ONI, and especially OP-16-F-2, was compromised, resulting in an uncoordinated and disjointed state of affairs, which would plague both McCollum and Safford, his OP-20-G counterpart.

OP-20-G (NEGAT) (WASHINGTON, DC)

NEGAT (referred to as Station US and also Station M, which gets confusing since the naval communications center at Cheltenham, Maryland, was referred to as Station M) was focused on Japan. All information received by Safford's section was provided in reports to Lt. Cdr. Alwin D. Kramer, who then relayed them to F-2 and other interested parties. OP-20-G's mission concerned the monitoring and interception of IJN radio signal messages, their decryption and translation into English, RDF operations, and communications intelligence derived from an analysis of the radio signals, transmitters, and related call signs. This information was then analyzed by F-2 as to the plans, operations (locations and movement), and intentions of the IJN, with comparative analysis over a period of time.

Additional OP-20-G missions involved Safford in the formulation and provision of the navy's own codes and ciphers on the one hand and the supervision of the navy's communications security efforts on the other. By December 1941, the core component of Safford's communications intelligence personnel focused on Japan numbered more than 150 persons, of which a quarter were officers and civilians and the remainder crypto clerks of one sort or another.[17]

OP-20-GX (WASHINGTON, DC)

OP-20-GX (Radio Direction Finding—RDF) directed by Lt. Cdr. George W. Welker, generally received its radio signal bearing reports from three distinct networks:

1. The West Coast Strategic High-Frequency (HF) Direction Finder Net, headquartered in Seattle, Washington. Consisting of 10 RDF stations (seven naval and three commercial), it ran from Sitka, Alaska, south along the Canadian and western U.S. continental coastline to San Diego.

2. The Mid-Pacific Strategic High-Frequency Direction Finder Net, headquartered in Pearl Harbor and Honolulu. Consisting of four distinct naval RDF stations, it ran from Dutch Harbor, Alaska, south through the mid-Pacific, picking up Midway Island, Lualualei (Oahu), Hawaii, and American Samoa.

3. The Western Pacific High-Frequency Direction Finder Net headquartered in Corregidor, Philippine Islands, consisting of Guam and Corregidor as U.S. Navy stations to the north, and British-controlled Hong Kong and Singapore and Dutch Batavia as part of the Dutch East Indies to the south.

The concept of the "net" system was based on the realization that, while one station might not always be able to make out the radio call sign of a transmitter, it could gain a directional fix or bearing to it, identifying its frequency. It could then contact one or more other stations in the net to take their respective bearings and call sign identification on the same radio signal contact frequency. Each signal bearing plot was called a *case* by the RDF operators. The net control station received the various plots and performed the intersections on a nautical chart to ascertain the transmitter's location and identity.

This was done in a timely manner, and the information was transmitted to the various fleet intelligence officers and/or Station NEGAT's GX section at the Navy Department in Washington, where central plotting was also conducted. GX's RDF plots of key IJN warships were then sent to

OP-16-F-2, OP-12's War Information Room, and OP-38's Ship Movements Division for immediate posting and analysis.

Upwards of a hundred radio signal receivers of various types focused on the key radio frequencies utilized by the IJN communications system. Stations with high concentrations of receivers were Corregidor (Philippine Islands) with 25, Bainbridge Island (Washington) with 13, Heeia (Hawaii) with 21, and Libugon (Guam) with 9. In January 1941, GX consisted of one officer, three enlisted men, and one civilian stenographer. Given the small number of personnel assigned to this section, it had more than enough work to do to keep up with the RDF plotting inputs from its several networks and sometimes even individual stations themselves.[18]

OP-20-GY CRYPTANALYSIS (WASHINGTON, DC)

OP-20-GY Cryptanalysis, directed by Lt. Cdr. Lee W. Parke, had a complement of some 70 military and civilian personnel. They were involved with decrypting and decoding all IJN radio signal traffic, which had been monitored, transcribed, and forwarded via ECM Mark II radio, wire cable, radio-teletype, and sometimes airmail from the several naval intercept networks covering the Pacific. The IJN's principal operational or fleet 5-Num Code was top priority for GY's cryptographers. Additionally, there was a focus on the Japanese Merchant Marine or Shin Code (Code Book S), the Yobidashi Fugo or radio call sign code for each category of commercial ships. Lastly, there was focus on Japan's naval Ship Movement Code (SM) utilized by warships, merchant marine vessels, and individuals to report their departures, destinations, and arrivals. These were the most important and principal key code systems of interest to Safford's OP-20-G.[19]

On the diplomatic side, Japan's cipher machine–transmitted diplomatic messages were also intercepted, decoded, and then read, using four army- and navy-produced analog PURPLE machines; these focused on the traffic sent from Tokyo, Berlin, and Washington, DC. The Japanese utilized their PURPLE encoding machines at their consulates in such places as Bangkok, Batavia, Manila, and Singapore, but *not* Honolulu. The end result of the process of decoded and translated messages into English by any means was called MAGIC.

At the same time, other Japanese diplomatic code systems, such as the PA-K2 code, LA code, and the key J-19 code were addressed and exploited. J-19 was the code normally used by the Japanese consul in Honolulu to send reports to Tokyo in Morse code via RCA Wireless and Mackay Radio & Telegraph in San Francisco. Naval intelligence officers photographed the messages at the commercial transmission companies' offices in San

Francisco. These were then dispatched by airmail to Station NEGAT's GY section for decoding. Tokyo also used a makeshift "hidden word code" in which key concepts were geographic names and places.

Station M at Cheltenham, Maryland, was the navy's primary communications center; it received and forwarded all types of signal communications involving both the navy and the army. The army's own Signal Intelligence Service (SIS) was located at the Army Headquarters in the Munitions Building on the corner of 20th Street and Constitution Avenue.[20]

Personnel assigned to work in OP-20-GY and related branches were recruited from universities and colleges such as the University of California, Chicago, Harvard, Temple, Virginia, and Yale, among others. Many of these men became reserve officers; others became civil service employees on special duty.[21] Besides Agnes Meyer Driscoll, who had been with OP-20-G from its inception, Dorothy Edgers, Fred Woodrough, Phil Cate, and Albert Pelletier (Japanese translators) and John Lietwiler, Lee Parke, Prescott Currier, and Robert Weeks (cryptanalysts) served on GY's team of all-star radio intelligence experts. Assistance was further provided to both of Safford's GX and GY processing units through the use of the latest technologies available from the commercial sector inside the United States.

Historian John Prados reports that Safford had some 16 IBM tabulating systems, operated by nine naval personnel eight hours a day in the "machine room." IBM's frequency counters, card sorters, and keypunches had been used by commercial American businesses since before World War I; now they would come to the rescue of modern U.S naval cryptology.[22]

IBM

The IBM 405 Alphabetical Accounting Machine contributed to code breaking in two revolutionary ways. First, it could identify the frequency with which a letter, word, or expression appeared in radio signal traffic, or even in ordinary language; the more signals intercepted, the more identifications and relationships could be made. Whether Japanese codes were in two-, three-, four-, or even five-kana letter/number groups and appeared in scores of thousands of code groups, it did not matter. As each intercepted message code was punched into a card, a database was built up, and as the bits and pieces of the database were decrypted, the decoding effort became faster and faster. The IBM machines linked the Registered Intelligence Publication (RIP-5) kana typewriter that Safford had invented to its machine card-sorter and keypunch equipment.

Second, the machines could "attack" and break down a Japanese code fairly quickly. This speeded up the decryption process by dozens, if not hundreds of times. Instead of years to break codes, now it could be done in months. The On the Roof Gang intercept operators in training would sometimes spend several afternoons a week keypunching newly received IJN messages recorded by the navy intercept stations arrayed around the Pacific, or use the card sorters to identify items of interest for GY's officer cryptanalysts.[23] A Type 077 Collator equipped with a collator counting device was so effective that it enabled GY to accomplish in a matter of a few hours what would have taken several days.[24]

Station NEGAT's use of the IBM machines throughout the 1930s enabled it to reach full operating capacity in 1941 in the mechanization of radio intelligence signal analysis capabilities. This enabled the genius of people like Agnes Meyer Driscoll to penetrate Japan's naval and diplomatic code systems and produce decryption solutions. Driscoll understood the machines and was able to use them to quickly get to the essence of a decoding problem, sort out its essential components, and solve it.[25] In addition to OP-20-G's IBM systems, Safford directed that the 14th Naval District (Hawaii) and the 16th Naval District (Philippines) have a full complement of IBM tabulating machines, a mirror reflection of NEGAT's own setup.

OP-20-GI RADIO INTELLIGENCE (WASHINGTON, DC)

OP-20-GI Radio Intelligence, under Safford's direct control, produced a series of reports known as Radio Intelligence Publications (RIPs). These were passed on to those with a "need to know" in the Naval Intelligence and Communications Divisions. These consisted of what GY had garnered from breaking the various Japanese naval and diplomatic codes, as well as other technical details important for radio intercept and RDF operations.

In minutes, GI could use its Type 405 machine to generate complete multiple call sign identifications and listings by date and related RDF plots. Between the mechanization of the cryptanalytical processes and the work of GY and GZ, based on inputs from the splendid arrangement in the Pacific, OP-20-G could with considerable accuracy identify and locate key warships and determine to a large extent the intentions of the IJN in the Pacific.

OP-20-GZ TRANSLATION AND DISSEMINATION (WASHINGTON, DC)

When Cdr. Kramer was named director of OP-20-GZ Translation and Dissemination in 1940, he already had extensive credentials, having studied in Japan for three years in the early 1930s and then having two tours of duty with ONI. GZ's primary intelligence function involved the translating from Japanese into English of all decrypted radio signal traffic obtained from intercepts and then delivering them to the ONI.

Normally, 14 copies of each translation of a decryption were prepared. Seven went to the Department of the Army (Stimson, Marshall, the General Staff, and the SIS) and seven went to the Navy Department (Knox, Stark, and the navy staff), including Roosevelt and Secretary of State Cordell Hull. Since the volume of translated traffic could run as high as 130 messages a day, a brief summary of the important or urgent messages was included, and key messages were singled out and highlighted for senior officials.[26]

Kramer's staff was three U.S. Civil Service employees, Phil Cate, Dorothy Edgars, and Fred Woodrough, all of whom had been born and raised in Japan, growing up with Japanese as their first language. Several other civilian translators were carried on ONI's rolls; this made a total of seven people available to accomplish the translation mission. Kramer personally checked each message for importance before having it translated. In this case he was acting as a filter in the name of the director of naval intelligence and more directly for the head of the Far East Section (F-2). Priority was given to the most difficult of the IJN codes, such as the 5-Num system, since they would probably have the most important radio intelligence information.[27]

While Kramer would personally carry the message folders (often referred to as "books") around to the various recipients, such as the CNO, the secretary of the navy, and others, he also made the extra effort to interpret the significance of the highlighted contents for the readers.[28] Toward the end of November and the beginning of December 1941, as America descended into war, Kramer did everything possible to make rapid deliveries of urgent, critical messages.

Additional factors in the success of the navy's communications intelligence network were its own specialized electronic signal transmission systems, which were utilized for important intelligence traffic, radio, radio telephone, radio teletype, cable, and commercial and military telephone systems. The advent of radio teletype eliminated the need for the laborious Morse cable code systems, enabling the army and navy intelligence systems to operate by installing the required equipment at each end of the sending/receiving stations. For example, at Station SAIL on Bainbridge Island near Seattle, an intercepted message could be punched into a teletype tape. After the NEGAT phone number was dialed on the typewriter exchange and the connection made, the tape was fed into the transmitter, which would then pull the tape through its system at a rate of 60 words per minute. A page printer beside the desk of the GY watch officer would produce both an original and carbon copy on yellow and pink teletype paper, much like a city newsroom would receive information over its wire-service ticker tape machine. OP-20-G could now rapidly send, receive, and control the handling of intercepted signals and RDF data in large quantities from around the Pacific.

ECM

The navy's secure communications service used a transmitting instrument called the Electronic Cipher Machine (ECM) Mark I. The army's Frank Rowlett had originated the idea. This highly secure cipher machine used a series of five rotors—of some 10 available—to key the machine's encoding capability. Although similar in some respects to the Japanese PURPLE (diplomatic) machine and the German ENIGMA (military) machine, this was far different in operation.[29] This system and its specialized circuits contributed immensely to the rapid flow of signals intelligence data and intercepts.

The OP-20-G maintained several special ECM circuits to further this end. One of these used the code word COPEK, which was a code designator for dispatches of material forwarded in a crypto channel having to do with all aspects of the decryption process. This might involve technical and personnel-related issues, IJN code and cipher changes, and even the retransmission of complete IJN- and Tokyo-related messages. Exchanges were only made in that channel between the three processing stations: OP-20-G in Washington, Station HYPO at Pearl Harbor, and Station CAST at Corregidor. An example would be any local intercepts that related to an IJN code, such the 5-Num system. It was assumed that signals communications intelligence officers at those stations would analyze the incoming COPEK message, supplement it with their own decrypting efforts, and then bring it to the attention of senior commanders. The main body of each message transmitted in this special circuit was headed with the code word COPEK.[30]

Electronic correspondence specifically involving the exchange of RDF bearings and ship radio call signs also took place between stations CAST, HYPO, SAIL, and NEGAT. The special circuit for this type of transmission was called TESTM or simply TEST. The coded TESTM dispatches could only be decoded at CAST, HYPO, and NEGAT. One can find the initials of the radio intelligence intercept officer (or yeoman, as sometimes was the case) responsible for the preparation of the message; for example, "TAH" for Thomas Huckins at Station HYPO.

Other special radio circuit systems known as CETYH (intelligence and operational directives) and GUPID (textual radio intelligence reporting and exchange of communications data) connected McCollum's OP-16-F-2 with the 12th Naval District (Adm. John Greenslade, commander of the

Western Sea Frontier and commandant of the 12th Naval District, among others), and provided additional information gleaned from RDF and other IJN radio intelligence intercepts.

STATION M (MARYLAND)

While all these assets were available to Safford's OP-20-G, there was still another one of interest: Station M at Cheltenham, Maryland. It was one of the U.S. Navy's largest radio-receiving intercept stations in support of its communications intelligence operations against Japan, as well as Germany and Italy. It had not only a teletype TWX transmitter in its Intercept Receiving Room but also the famed RIP-5 typewriter capable of typing out the Roman-letter equivalents of Japanese characters. It functioned on behalf of Station NEGAT throughout 1941, most importantly during the period of November 25 to December 7. Since during the winter months receiving conditions tended to be relatively good on all frequencies, Station M on the East Coast of the United States was acknowledged as having the best chance to intercept Tokyo's PURPLE-encoded radio broadcasts. It always operated in conjunction with stations such as SAIL at Bainbridge Island, Washington.

OP-20-G dictated orders to M via teletype, indicating specific Japanese stations, broadcasting in voice as well as Japanese Morse and International Morse codes, and were often monitored 24 hours a day. Important diplomatic traffic back and forth between Tokyo and the embassy in Washington were intercepted, transcribed on Boehme high-speed tape, and forwarded to OP-20-GY.[31]

While Safford's 20 years of evolutionary work had given his Washington, DC, enterprise considerable communication intelligence intercept and decoding capabilities, in reality, everything depended on the navy's radio intercepts in the Pacific. In total, the 17 U.S. (13 navy and 4 army), 10 British (including 3 Canadian), and 2 Dutch radio intercept monitoring and RDF stations were the key to OP-20-G. The reports, going into the army and navy cryptographic centers in Washington, DC, served as the "eyes and ears" of this elaborate setup. During the 1920s and 1930s, a radio direction finder was usually referred to as a *radio compass* station, since the bearings were literally taken from a pedestal-mounted compass that would indicate the "null" point's azimuth (exact bearing) taken in the direction of the targeted radio transmitter's signal.

Beginning on July 1, 1941, in accordance with the navy's updated War Plan Orange (now called War Plan/WPL-46), Stark divided the western coast of the United States into two geographic areas called *frontiers*. The Northern Naval Coastal Frontier was assigned to the commanders of the

12th and 13th Naval Districts at San Francisco and Seattle. The Southern Naval Coastal Frontier was assigned to the commander of the 11th Naval District in the vicinity of Los Angeles. These two districts were set up to "gather information only" and report to ONI in Washington, DC. The 13th Naval District, responsible for the general functioning of the network, monitored and maintained the facilities located within the confines of the 11th and 12th Naval Districts, as well as its own, running from the Canadian border to the southernmost part of California.[32]

WEST COAST COMMUNICATIONS INTELLIGENCE NET (WCCI)

The primary signals intelligence intercept and RDF monitoring system for the West Coast was the West Coast Strategic Net and the West Coast Communications Intelligence Network (WCCI). It stretched from Sitka, Alaska, south to San Diego, California. Net Control for the entire WCCI setup was Station SAIL on Bainbridge Island, which, in turn, received its operational mission and instructions from OP-20-G through the headquarters of the 13th Naval District at Seattle, Washington. Each district was responsible for part of the defense of the U.S. Western Coastal Frontier, as well as their part of the WCCI.

On October 31, 1941, the WCCI, 13th Naval District, sent detailed instructions to its entire RDF network. In large part, this codified the earlier missions and operations already in place, emphasizing that all entities, including *commercial stations*, were to carry out intercept and RDF functions.

The basic mission for the WCCI was to perfect efficiency in the obtaining of maximum communication intelligence of the enemy through the operation of a high-frequency direction finder organization. In order to comply with this mission, all stations with four or more men were to maintain a 24-hour watch. All radio signal bearings being taken were logged with the radio frequency used by the transmitter, time, peculiarities of the signals transmitted, and, if possible, "an exact transcript of the message on which the bearing was taken." First and foremost in importance were the radio transmitter call signs and their signal bearing taken from the RDF station. The navy felt that operators would develop a "feel" or "sense" from the nature of the signals monitored and intercepted, which would help them make better and quicker IJN transmitter station identifications. It was expected that the information obtained would indicate the type of ship and/or the fleet units involved. IJN operator peculiarities (radio fingerprinting) were also considered important in making an accurate identification.[33]

Watch Standing at each station was given great importance. Radio signal intercept and RDF operators were exhorted to use every available spare minute searching for new targets: "Do not depend on Net Control to always inform you when to take a bearing. An overall time of 5 seconds on the air. Report the bearing taken exactly as you see it. A copying speed of 18 words per minute with no errors. . . . A single letter error could easily indicate an entirely different type of vessel." All RDF radiomen were trained in kana code. All station information reported was to be in accordance with Greenwich Civil time.[34]

While the 13th Naval District was firmly in control and directing the general operating procedures of the WCCI, it was Stark in Washington, advised by OP-20-G, who gave the WCCI its Pacific Ocean mission focus. On April 2, 1941, Rear Adm. Royal E. Ingersoll, acting in Stark's name, gave the commandant of the 13th Naval District, Rear Adm. Charles S. Freeman, his primary mission concerning the operations of the West Coast Strategic Direction Finder Net: "[The net was] hereby assigned the task of locating and tracking all Japanese merchant vessels in the eastern part of the Pacific Ocean." It was a straightforward mission. Ingersoll ordered ONI to issue a weekly report to the California coast districts as to the number of Japanese merchantmen ("targets") afloat and their expected locations.[35]

A September 8, 1941, memorandum from Capt. W. P. Gaddis, the 12th Naval District Operations Officer, indicated that the Japanese (often referred to as "Orange" from the War Plan Orange days) merchant ship identifications and movements were being maintained in the District's "Confidential Orange Merchant Ship notebook." High priority was the tracking of Japanese oil tankers leaving the West Coast with petroleum shipments. Reports also came in from the 14th Naval District (COM 14, Hawaii), Cheltenham (Maryland), Station KING at Dutch Harbor (Alaska), and the 11th Naval District as examples.[36]

The navy, concerned about the confusing array of station names and places, clarified the matter. In April 1941, the 11th Naval District published a list of alphabetical codes for identifying stations. Examples include A = AFIRM, B = BAKER, C = CAST, D = DOG, E = EASY, F = FOX, G = GEORGE, H = HYPO, I = ITEM, K = KING, M = MIKE, N = NEGAT, S = SAIL, T = TARE, V = VICTOR.[37]

Station S—SAIL (Washington State)

Known as the Bainbridge Island Radio Intelligence Unit, Station SAIL was located in the army's old Fort Ward post exchange building. Positioned at the southwest end of the island on a high bluff overlooking

Seattle's Puget Sound, the fort had been taken over by the navy toward the end of the 1930s as an appropriate site for its West Coast radio signals intercept and RDF training schools. These, it was thought, could now take advantage of the outstanding reception provided by the skip and bounce phenomenon that affected radio waves radiating out from the Western Pacific and Japan proper. The radio school was housed in the army's now converted former brig (jail).

Primitive, bleak, and almost barren, except for scattered pine trees and rolling hills, the island was home to a small rural community of some 3,000 residents, including 227 Japanese Americans who had been migrating to the area since the 1880s. Access to Seattle was by ferry boat, which came in handy for bringing in supplies and otherwise transporting women over to the city hospital in order to give birth. A U.S. Marine detachment provided security against intruders.

The navy's radio intercept and RDF Station SAIL was led by Cdr. B. C. Purrington, had two important missions in support of the splendid arrangement. The first was running the Naval Reserve Radio School at Fort Ward, beginning in late 1940. Purrington was the officer-in-charge (OIC). Classes of up to 40 students would report in for four months of training in radio signal intercept and RDF operations. The school was equipped with a complement of 10 special Kana typewriters (RIP-5s) and one audio oscillator to measure radio signal vibrations, as one would do with an oscilloscope.[38]

The second mission of the school was operating the radio intelligence and RDF tracking center or Station S (SAIL), commanded by Cdr. D. F. Gravel, located in what had been Fort Ward's Post Exchange building. The most efficient RDF station operating unit consisted of nine officers and eight operators. Four men were dedicated for the RDF watch and the other four men focused on a continuous independent receiver watch. Knowing that the RDF operator might miss a signal, the receiver watch would serve as a backup, hearing the signal and then notifying the RDF operator on duty to take the bearing.[39]

Station SAIL plotted daily RDF position fixes on separate charts; one chart often denoted as a "case" was prepared for each merchant vessel located. A card index file for each report was also prepared and arranged alphabetically by radio call sign for further comparison. A formal Plotting Center kept track of all Japanese merchant shipping monitored and located by RDF fixes. Besides identification, determining a merchant ship's direction of movement was a primary goal.

Stations such as those at Point St. George (Station T or TARE) and Imperial Beach (Station I or ITEM) sent their RDF reports directly to SAIL's Plotting Center by TWX. Farallon Islands utilized the RCA's communications office at San Francisco for rapid transmission. Each station in the Net conducted its own radio search and took bearings on the pre-scribed schedule of frequencies as directed by SAIL.

Each week, a summary of the bearings tabulated by the navy's Ship Movements Division was forwarded to the commandants of the 11th, 12th, and 13th Naval Districts, plus the 14th District in Hawaii. This summary included the names of the Japanese merchant vessels and their radio call signs; all this was based on the inputs from the stations in the WCCI involving the bearings, the estimated targeted transmitter's intersected RDF position in the Pacific, and finally any remarks concerning the vessel's direction of movement.[40]

The mission of identifying and tracking Japanese merchant shipping was taken so seriously that the earlier commander-in-chief of the Pacific Fleet, Adm. J. O. Richardson, personally requested on January 14, 1941, that the 12th Naval District in San Francisco provide him tracking data. Richard-son saw that the forward position of his fleet located in the Hawaiian Islands now gave him, in the event of war, an ideal position from which to sortie out and interdict Japanese merchant shipping. He began contingency planning for the possibility of intercepting Japan's commercial vessels attempting to cross the Pacific. To do this he needed to anticipate the trav-eled routes and have an idea as to the types of ships and their speeds. Rich-ardson requested route charts and up-to-date ship movement information to enable anticipated intercept planning to proceed with some precision.[41]

Besides RDF work, Station S was also responsible for radio signals inter-cept operations. To accomplish this during peak radio traffic periods, the station utilized an array of technical equipment.

SAIL also utilized landline systems involving a teletypewriter unit and a Western Union leased loop serving various sites, including the Alaska Communications Service in Seattle. In turn and on behalf of the Naval Communications Division's Leigh Noyes, the CNO mandated in March 1941 that a TWX teletype wire service with a transmission rate of 60 words per minute between the 13th Naval District and the Department's OP-20-G be established for the rapid transmission of messages "distin-guished by a five-numeral group [5-Num Code]," special "war warnings," three specific "five-letter" groups, which mixed their consonant and vowel orders, and "messages of an unusual nature . . . of sufficient importance to warrant immediate attention."[42]

Esquimalt—Gordon Head—Ocelot (Vancouver)

Canada had three radio signal intercept and high-frequency RDF sta-tions on its west coast: Esquimalt, Gordon Head, and Ocelot. These stations reported any information concerning Japan's merchant and warship movements to the British radio intelligence system; they also reported to the Commandant 13th Naval District (Station SAIL) via teletype direct from Esquimalt (the Canadian RDF plotting center for all bearings taken in the Pacific). These three RDF stations were located on Vancouver Island in western British Columbia.[43]

During 1941, the establishment of direct teletypewriter communication and radio telephone with a voice transmitter and speech scrambling device and associated equipment was accomplished between the 13th Naval District Headquarters in Seattle and the Canadian naval headquarters at H.M.C. Dockyard, Esquimalt.[44] The 13th Naval District relayed the Canadian signal intercepts on to OP-20-G in Washington, DC.

Station AE (Alaska)

Another radio signal monitoring and intercept station, known by its station code AE, was located in the center of Japonski Island, near the Naval Air Station at Sitka, Alaska. Originally settled by Russian explorers in the 1740s, Sitka was nestled among forbidding, snow-laced mountains, which were part of the Baranof Islands group. Being colocated with a PBY Catalina sea plane reconnaissance base was the one advantage Station AE had in its otherwise fog-shrouded, dreary existence. Communication with the site was accomplished primarily by naval radio, infrequent ship visits, and now and then PBY flights bringing in mail and other supplies.

This bleak site was operating as part of the WCCI net and reported directly to its Net Control Station (SAIL) at Bainbridge Island. In his monthly report covering the period of November 1941, Radioman-in-Charge J. R. Tate indicated that 184 bearings for that month were taken on Japanese merchant vessels in the Pacific (this was part of the 633 bearings total taken by AE for 1941).[45]

The 12th Naval District (San Francisco)

The 12th Naval District (COM 12) operated under the command of Vice Adm. John W. Greenslade. Its headquarters, operating 24 hours a day, seven days a week, was located in downtown San Francisco at 717 Market Street on the sixth and seventh floors of the Kamm Building. Greenslade's responsibility included command of the Western Sea Frontier, extending westward across the Pacific to approximately the international dateline (the Panama Sea Frontier covered points south of California). He held a third position, that of the Naval Convoy director for *all* American-controlled shipping moving westward across the Pacific to Hawaii, Australia, and the Far East.

Two of Greenslade's key offices were those of communications, under the command of District Communications Officer (DCO) Cdr. Frank Venzel, and intelligence, under the command of District Intelligence Officer (DIO) Capt. Richard P. McCullough. McCullough not only sent RDF bearings to Station SAIL's plotting room, which used Tracking Chart #1, but also maintained contact with Station NEGAT (US) in Washington, DC, by sending high-priority intercept data and reports via the GUPID communications system circuit. McCullough was so well acquainted with Roosevelt that he freely contacted the White House directly concerning matters of importance. McCullough's staff, including Lt. Cdr. Preston Allen, Lt. Ellsworth Hosmer of the radio intelligence section, Seaman First Class Robert Ogg, and Seaman William Thompson, would play a key part in the events leading up to the war in the Pacific.

Hosmer, formerly a communications engineer with AT&T, had a close professional working relationship with the Globe Wireless and Press Wireless companies. Press Wireless ran a commercial RDF site located 10 miles to the south at Point Montara west of Belmont, California. Ogg had studied celestial navigation and how radio transmission wave propagation was affected by electromagnetic storms and atmospheric ionization at Stanford University prior to joining the navy. An avid sailor, he had completed the navy's correspondence course on celestial navigation and was familiar with plotting techniques for radio signal tracking on great circle sailing charts. These abilities would prove critical during the days immediately leading up to the IJN's December 7, 1941, attack on Pearl Harbor.

Thompson had completed the navy's Basic Cryptanalysis Course, involving training in the Japanese kana telegraphic Morse transcription code, and was supported by Cdr. Lawrence, a Japanese language translator on the DIO's staff. Using a radio Dictaphone recorder, Hosmer, Ogg, and Thompson frequently teamed up to perform wiretaps and bugging of hotel rooms frequented by Japanese officials. Lesser known but also important individuals were ensigns William Barkan and Charles Black, who specifically contacted Japanese merchant ships (called *maru*), purchased copies of their Merchant Marine Code books, and even bugged the Japanese consulate in San Francisco. (The word *maru* has a special meaning in Japanese folklore: "circle," which means that commercial ships complete their respective trips much like circles, always returning to their loved ones back home. The word also signifies good luck in terms of dealing with the perils of the high seas. This contrasts to a warship in the IJN, which goes in harm's way and risks not even completing the circle.)

The 12th Naval District's intelligence personnel numbered about 30, of all grades.[46] Of particular interest is the role played by the 12th Naval District's signal intercept and RDF stations and their commercial counterparts. Frank Venzel was in administrative charge of these stations, under the operational control of SAIL at Bainbridge and OP-20-G in Washington, DC. The army operated its own Station TWO, located at Fort Winfield Scott at the Presidio, San Francisco, which monitored and then relayed Japanese low-grade diplomatic radio and nonnaval radio intercepts to the Signal Intelligence Service (SIS) in Washington, DC.[47]

Station T—TARE (California)

Located on Point Saint George at the westernmost part of California and northwest of Crescent City, TARE was a lonely, remote site. Lashed by high winds and foaming waves from high seas that pummeled its shoreline day and night, it was considered one of the least sought-after assignments. It was a bleak, cold, generally miserable place. Even the required provision of food and water was a challenge for the navy's logistical support services. The site had been chosen because there was practically no deviational shift in its RDF bearings.

Housed in the top floor of the west end of a building, the RDF system was equipped with a Model DT High-Frequency Direction Finder unit. Its 24-hour monitoring and RDF capability was maintained by three rotating shifts made up of three chief radiomen and 11 signal/RDF operators. A teletypewriter TWX service to the 12th Naval District provided TARE with rapid reporting capability.[48]

Station FOX (Farallon Islands, California)

Barren and rocky, the Farallon Islands sported a RDF tracking facility on top of a hill overlooking San Francisco Bay. Supplies and potable water loaded in cargo nets were provided weekly by a lighthouse tender, using winches and hoists. Sea lions and seals were the only amusement the sailors at this site had.

Located 27 miles outside of San Francisco's Golden Gate in the Farallon Islands, FOX covered the approaches into San Francisco Bay. Three chief radiomen and 12 radio intercept/RDF operators manned this station, operating in three rotating shifts, 24 hours a day, supported by one DT Direction Finder.[49] While Stations FOX and TARE were the 12th Naval District's signal intelligence mainstays in support of OP-20-G, there were also a number of commercial stations, all operating under the generic code symbol X, that made significant inputs into the WCCI, as well as OP-20-G's splendid arrangement in the Pacific.

Station X (California)

Station X was a generic term, used by OP-20-G to identify, as a group, the assortment of commercial radio-telephone-wireless-cable stations. One of these was the Radio Corporation of America (RCA), located at the fishing village of Marshall, 60 miles to the north of San Francisco. Tokyo Radio communicated with RCA's Station KPH, using radio telegraphy. RCA's wireless circuit connected its San Francisco station with its offices on South King Street, Honolulu; this circuit allowed the Japanese consulate in Honolulu to use its J-19, PA-K2, and LA codes to send and receive messages to and from its home office in Tokyo.[50]

Mackay Radio & Telegraph at Half Moon Bay, near Palo Alto, about 30 miles south of San Francisco, served as a communications hub for the United States. Japanese diplomatic cable traffic destined for Japan's Washington embassy was sent via New York through Mackay's headquarters office located at 67 Broad Street, New York.[51] During 1941, Mackay's president and chairman was none other than U.S. Navy (Ret.) Adm. Luke McNamee, who had distinguished himself over a 42-year career serving as commander battle force, naval governor of Guam, director of the Office of ONI, and finally president of the Naval War College, retiring in 1934. With his extensive experience, McNamee placed Mackay Radio & Telegraph's services at the disposal of ONI.[52]

This meant complete access by ONI and OP-20-G to the transoceanic radiotelegraph circuit, which was utilized by the Japanese consulate in Honolulu to send cable messages via San Francisco to Tokyo and vice versa. Mackay also provided the navy with an additional radio signal intercept monitoring and RDF capability, sending its RDF bearing reports to Station HYPO via the 14th Naval District in Honolulu. One of Mackay Radio's main focus targets was the IJN's *Akagi* aircraft carrier.[53]

There were several other stations that carried Japanese commercial and diplomatic communications. American Telephone and Telegraph (AT&T) transmitted voice telephone to and from Tokyo and Washington; Globe and Press Wireless performed similar functions, relaying messages for American merchant marine vessels. Globe Wireless, with offices at 141 Battery Street and the Robert Dollar Building at 311 California Street in San Francisco, operated a receiving station at Point Reyes National Seashore Park, 20 miles north of the city. Press Wireless, with offices at the Taft Building at Hollywood and Vine in Los Angeles, operated another receiving station at Belmont, 10 miles south of San Francisco. While both these stations had a RDF capability, Globe Wireless also intercepted J-19 diplomatic code from Honolulu intended for Tokyo and IJN intelligence.[54]

In Southern California, the 11th Naval District, commanded by Rear Adm. W. S. Holmes, was located at San Diego and rounded out the WCCI's efforts in California. Its two RDF stations were located at Imperial Beach (ITEM) and Point Arguello and networked with Station SAIL to the north. Apart from tracking Japanese merchant ships and IJN warships, the 11th Naval District ran an undercover organization to keep track of what was going on within the Japanese community of Southern California. Communications between the 11th Naval District and the WCCI were maintained via teletype.[55]

Station I—ITEM (San Diego)

Originally a summer retreat located in part of the Tijuana estuary to the south of San Diego, ITEM was located on the beach in a wooden, two-story octagonal building; its RDF system was positioned on the second floor. Barren, flat, and featureless sandy beaches vulnerable to flooding, as well as seashells and seaweed, formed the setting for this naval intelligence site. Chief Radioman H. F. Kane ran the station.

Station I, or ITEM, was a Naval Medium- and High-Frequency RDF operation staffed during the latter part of 1941 by a dozen radio intercept specialists and several chief radiomen to man its three direction finders.[56]

Each Japanese radio transmitter emitted a distinct sound, due to its tube technology construction. This sound, called a *signature*, could be recorded by a camera and an oscilloscope. It was then compared to other transmitter sounds to determine if it was the same or a completely different transmitter. Station ITEM had an oscilloscope. Since no two transmitters were alike, an oscilloscope could display a transmitter's radio wave patterns. It was then possible to photograph the image. Even changes made to the transmitter's radio call signs would make no difference, as the distinctive radio wave patterns would make the identification. The process became known as radio fingerprinting (RFP).

This technology helped immeasurably in rapidly identifying changes in call signs for IJN ships of interest. This station had TINA, a radio intelligence frequency identification system, utilizing an ink tape recorder that could take down a radio operator's hand-keyed Morse sending style. The inked tapes of the Morse-keyed messages could clearly identify operators by making their respective keying styles that much more identifiable. The two technologies together greatly facilitated IJN ship identifications.[57]

Point Arguello (California)

High on a bluff overlooking the Pacific Ocean, U.S. Navy Radio Station Point Arguello, 150 miles north of San Diego, was a relatively isolated RDF station. It had received a model DP Intermediate Frequency Direction

Finder in 1937, and by mid-1940, two intermediate-high-frequency receivers and one low-frequency receiver would fill it out. Personnel consisted of one chief radioman, CRM H. T. Knudsen, and four RDF specialists.[58] The navy's WCCI intelligence effort was now firmly focused on Japan's merchant marine in the Pacific.

MID-PACIFIC STRATEGIC HIGH-FREQUENCY DIRECTION FINDER NET

Operating under the auspices of the Commandant 14th Naval District at Honolulu, Territory of Hawaii, the Mid-Pacific High-Frequency RDF Net generally ran from north to south, bisecting the Pacific in terms of its radio intelligence and RDF coverage. The central Control Station H sites were Heeia, Lualualei, and Wahiawa (RDF) sites on Oahu Island; three other key RDF stations in the net included Dutch Harbor Station K (KING) in Alaska in the north; Station V (VICTOR) located at Vaitogi, Samoa, in the south; and Station AF at Midway Island to the west. Coded radio dispatch provided the means for transmitting key data to and from the 14th Naval District and its subordinate Combat Intelligence Center (HYPO) to Stations AF, KING, and VICTOR.

In theory, the Control Station's signal intercept and RDF stations searched for IJN radio transmissions and then broadcast the targeted frequencies to the outlying RDF stations, so that they, in turn, could immediately take bearings on the targeted transmitter. In reality, this would only work if the length of the IJN radio broadcast lasted for more than 15 seconds.

RDF operators on duty had to be able to catch the "flash" from the Control Station, tune in on the IJN frequency, and then take the bearing. This meant that two operators had to be on watch continuously just to successfully home in on an IJN radio signal. All bearings taken were then immediately forwarded by encrypted radio dispatch. The RDF stations learned which frequencies tended to be used by the IJN during various times of the day or night. Knowing these times enabled an outlying RDF watch team to be on the alert for short-duration IJN broadcasts.[59]

INTELLIGENCE AND NAVAL BASE DEFENSE (PEARL HARBOR)

In 1941, Rear Adm. Claude C. Bloch was responsible for the Navy Yard at Pearl Harbor and the entrance and egress of all navy ships, their berthing, control, and movement within the Pearl Harbor Naval Base, including security patrols and dredging. He was also responsible for the base's oil storage tanks, machine shops, roads, housing, and the provision of food and clothing for the sailors of the U.S. Pacific Fleet. Finally, he was responsible for the close-in naval defense, extending out 150 miles in all directions from Pearl Harbor. He had a full plate.

This was accomplished in conjunction with the army's Lt. Gen. Short, who was responsible for the actual air, ground, and close-in sea defense of the Pearl Harbor base itself: both its shore establishments and the Hawaiian Naval Coastal Sea Frontier, the outlying territorial waters extending out around the Hawaiian Islands for 150 miles into the Pacific. Both Bloch and Short were concerned with the possibility of Japanese espionage, so much so that Bloch had his intelligence officer, Capt. Irving Mayfield, conduct counterespionage activities with Short's own intelligence officers and Robert L. Shivers, the FBI's lead agent in Honolulu.

Short also had under his command SIS Station FIVE, located in the vicinity of his headquarters at Fort Shaftner. FIVE only monitored, intercepted, and transcribed the Japanese consul's diplomatic signals traffic (J-19, etc.), promptly sending information on to its SIS receiving station in Cheltenham, Maryland, without informing either Bloch or Short.

In terms of Pearl Harbor's outer or long-range defense, Adm. Kimmel and his Pacific Fleet were responsible for all areas extending beyond the 150-mile limit. Bloch also commanded Kimmel's Task Force 4.

Bloch's 20 key staff officers coordinated and controlled the daily functions and operations at Pearl Harbor; he also had 12 port captains for the Hawaiian Islands and other outlying regions, including Midway and Wake Island. There were also critical naval air stations and wartime staff positions at the 14th Naval District headquarters, involving intelligence and war plans. The intelligence positions operated at the direction of the Navy Department in Washington.[60]

Bloch's headquarters were located inside the Young Hotel in Honolulu; by late July 1941, the intelligence section alone occupied the entire sixth floor and was made up of 65 persons, double its complement of June 1940. This was a deliberate pattern across the board, clearly a war indicator. Included were Capt. Irving Mayfield, the District Intelligence Officer (DIO), and his deputy, Lt. Cdr. George Pease. There were Japanese linguists and translators, such as Lt. Denzel Carr and Lt. Yale Maxon; cryptanalysts, such as Prescott Currier; cryptographic clerks; and radiomen and yeomen.

One of Bloch's missions was to conduct domestic intelligence and counterespionage operations to protect the Hawaiian Islands against attack. Bloch found that an increase of just five cryptographic clerks enabled his cryptanalytic unit to triple its output. The district's radio intercept station at Heeia had 21 enlisted personnel, including three chief radiomen, 16 signal radio intercept and RDF specialists, plus two cooks. In contrast, the district's Direction Finder Station at Lualualei (later moved to Wahiawa) had one chief radioman and three RDF operators.[61] These two stations directly supplied information to Kimmel.

As OP-20-GY in Washington began to mechanize its signal intelligence operations, it encouraged the 14th Naval District to do the same thing. Beginning in July 1937, the Naval District received a full complement of IBM Automatic Alphabetical Tabulator Accounting Machines. Modifications and updated items of equipment were constantly being requested as they became available on the commercial market.[62]

In addition to the IBM tabulating equipment, the 14th Naval District had an oscilloscope. A study demonstrated that navy radios were "less vulnerable to identification by camera-oscillograph" than those of the IJN. Camera technology had improved to the point where "photographic work" was important enough so that on December 2, 1941, Rear Adm. Noyes requested an increase in the number of photographers. They were to "be of unquestioned loyalty and integrity."[63]

Signal intercept equipment also figured in the 14th Naval District's upgrades. In mid-1940, the 28-foot arms for Heeia's DT-2 direction finder were put in place, providing a much better signal pick-up of lower IJN radio frequencies than the 12-foot arms. A DY direction finder was also sent to Samoa at the southern extension of the Mid-Pacific RDF Net. Additionally, it was determined that to be effective at Heeia, it was necessary to have a minimum 15-man watch in order for each man to operate a series of signal receivers covering up to 30 frequencies in various spectrums.

To ensure that there was a minimum of RDF bearing divergences when focusing on IJN radio frequencies, frequency meters were issued to all RDF stations in order to keep "the direction finders continuously and accurately calibrated." An IBM Type 405 Alphabetical Accounting Machine was given to the Heeia Radio Station, separating it from the IBM machine section at Pearl Harbor.[64]

Both the 14th Naval District (Station H) and its Combat Intelligence Unit (CIU), known as Station HYPO (Station H and HYPO terminologies were often utilized interchangeably), used a series of navy communications systems to send and receive radio intelligence information. The district employed sending equipment such as the Boehme 4-E Series B Automatic Keying Head, with keying speeds of up to 500 words per minute. The TBC and TAL transmitters could produce keying speeds of up to 1,000 words per minute.

In the late 1930s, Safford recognized the ECM Mark II cipher machine as having tremendous communications potential; the machine became known as the Army-Navy ECM Mark II. The Pacific Fleet's communications and security officers were responsible for their own ECM machine, which had a special set of rotors and code wheels designed only for messages being sent to and from Adm. Kimmel as CINC Pacific Fleet.[65] With Safford's avid support, the machine began functioning as a primary cipher and cryptographic system for the two services on August 1, 1941.[66]

HYPO (HONOLULU)

Cdr. Joseph J. Rochefort arrived at Pearl Harbor on June 2, 1941, and reported to Bloch at the 14th Naval District's new building and headquarters, relocated from its former downtown Honolulu location to the naval shipyard at Pearl Harbor. As the new officer-in-charge (OIC) of Station HYPO, Rochefort had been personally selected by Safford to upgrade HYPO, not only because of his unique background as an expert in the Japanese language and culture, but also because he had cryptanalyst training under both Safford and Driscoll. By the time of his assignment to HYPO, Rochefort had served nine years in signal intelligence–related assignments. He was an accomplished intelligence officer, professional in every sense of the word.

In the spring of 1941, Safford came to the conclusion that HYPO could offer a great deal more as a full-blown radio signals intercept and decryption processing center. This would include both the RDF signals tracking function and the actual decoding of IJN's 5-Num Code radio messages. To accomplish this, the 14th Naval District capabilities were improved to place it on a par with OP-20-G's operations in Washington. The station would now provide the Pacific Fleet with quicker, better, and more independent access to signals intelligence than could be provided by the politics-driven Navy Department.[67] Spending money was critical to success; Japan had to be taking note of this.

To get Rochefort's operation off to a running start, Safford authorized him to hand-pick key intelligence officers for his HYPO group. Taking full advantage of the offer, Rochefort selected the best officers in the signal intelligence code-breaking business: Lt. Cdrs. Thomas Dyer, Jasper Holmes, Thomas Huckins, W. A. ("Ham") Wright, and Lt. Jack Williams. Rochefort considered his team of experts "the best communications intelligence organization that this world has ever seen." Safford himself would corroborate that, stating, "The best we had, as far as experience and all-around skill" were concerned.[68]

Almost all these personnel, with the exception of Holmes, would serve with Rochefort from mid-1941 on to the end of the year. For operational purposes, Rochefort divided HYPO into three sections:

1. The **Crypto [decoding] Section** (GY) headed by Lt. Cdr. Thomas H. Dyer and supported by Lt. Cdrs. R. W. Brandt, J. S. Holtwick, and W. A. Wright, all of whom were experts in decode recoveries. This core

group was backed up by Ens. Werner's four chief yeoman cryptologists: CY Conant, CY Rorie, CY Johnson, and CY Woodward. To be complete, the effort required translation of the decodes from Japanese into English. To do this, Lt. Cdr. T. Fullinwider was placed in charge of translations, assisted by Capt. Alva B. Lasswell (USMC) and Lt. Finnegan and Lt. Farnsly Woodward.

2. The **Radio Section** (GX), headed by Lt. Cdr. Thomas A. Huckins and assisted by Lt. Cdr. H. C. Moore, plotted and tracked and analyzed all RDF radio bearings and related intelligence data inputs. Lt. J. A. Williams and two other radio traffic analysis specialists, CRM Hopkins and CRM Willis, also supported this effort. Later, Lt. W. J. Holmes would be integrated into the section from Bloch's Station H, bringing with him his chart desk, plotting equipment, and a portfolio of Pacific Ocean great circle charts.

3. The **Statistical Section,** headed by Lt. Cdr. J. S. Holtwick Jr., was in charge of IBM statistical tabulating as his primary function, as well as related analytical operations. He was assisted by Lt. P. P. Leigh and CY F. C. Golian for the actual overseeing and indexing of radio intelligence data cards by the IBM machines. Upwards of 11 other yeoman ensured that the equipment was functional and operating in accordance with the needs of Rochefort's HYPO operation.[69]

In an August 15 memorandum directed to the 14th Naval District's Operations, Intelligence, War Plans, and Communications Offices, Bloch delineated the functions and missions of the now titled Combat Intelligence Unit (CIU) under Rochefort. Part of the mission of the CIU was to "maintain a master plot" of U.S. merchant shipping and naval vessels in the Pacific, excluding those inside Pearl Harbor and its immediate surrounding areas. The other part of the CIU's mission was to plot all Japanese merchant shipping in the Pacific, as well as the Japanese IJN fleet units.

The 14th Naval District's Operations Section maintained its own master nautical chart plot of U.S. merchant shipping and naval vessels within the Hawaii Coastal Zone, and Japanese merchant shipping and naval units within the Hawaii Coastal Frontier. Bloch specifically directed that his man, Lt. W. J. Holmes, be attached to the CIU to assist Rochefort with RDF bearings and chart plotting. Others, such as Ens. Wallace and a yeoman, would be attached to the 14th District's Operations Section to maintain its own set of parallel plots to those of the CIU.[70]

Inferred from this memorandum was that Rochefort's CIU and the District Operations Section would keep Adm. Kimmel and his Pacific Fleet operations and intelligence staff officers up-to-date in regard to the daily chart plots by means of an overlay system, using tracing paper with a copy of the master plot forwarded to Kimmel's own intelligence center each morning. Kimmel and his intelligence officer, Cdr. Edwin Layton, were wholly dependent on the 14th Naval District and its CIU (HYPO) for operational combat intelligence concerning the IJN.[71]

Rochefort required absolute security from intruders and so placed HYPO in the underground basement of the new wing of the 14th Naval District's headquarters building, which finally completed its movement from Honolulu to the Pearl Harbor Naval Base in August 1941. In reality, his mission and related specific tasks came not only from Bloch but also, and more importantly, from OP-20-G. Rochefort's CIU focused primarily on obtaining signal intelligence data and information, passing it on via coded ECM radio channels to Adm. Thomas Hart, the CINC of the Asiatic Fleet (Philippines), and to Adm. Kimmel, the CINC of the Pacific Fleet at Pearl Harbor.

Now that a secure place had been made available to maintain RDF plots, the CIU became the plotting center for the 14th Naval District. An overlay system for actually copying down the plots on tracing paper was developed. Each morning, a copy was forwarded to Cdr. Layton, the CINCPAC intelligence officer. Layton had worked with Agnes Driscoll on the signals communication intercept and decoding system, which made him a key player.[72]

With the basement air conditioning system set at 74 degrees, a number of the 42 personnel that made up HYPO's complement were putting in upwards of 80 hours of work a week in this dungeon-like environment during the late summer of 1941. Using radio call sign analysis and RDF intersectional plots, Lt. Wilfred Holmes was in charge of preparing the charts and tracing paper overlays, which could then be placed on Layton's own charts for briefing Kimmel on the IJN's capital warship locations.[73]

The RDF bearings that Holmes plotted came from stations scattered throughout the splendid arrangement and not just the Mid-Pacific Net in itself. An IBM printout report for August 1–24, 1941, prepared by Station H's Statistical Section on IJN radio call signs and RDF bearings, is an interesting perspective as to how well FDR's plan was working and which stations were providing what inputs to the HYPO RDF plotting center. The following stations specifically took bearings during the reporting period on the IJN's top-of-the-line *Akagi* aircraft carrier, which was using radio call sign 8E YU:

Stations VICTOR in Samoa and Mackay Radio & Telegraph (Station "X") at Half Moon Bay, California, *each* took 30 bearings on the *Akagi*;

Station KING at Dutch Harbor took 8 bearings;

Station BAKER at Guam Island took 5 bearings;

Station TARE at Point St. George, California, took 2 bearings;

Stations CAST in the Philippines and Station H at Heeia, Hawaii, took one apiece.[74]

STATION H (OAHU)

Since H's intercept station at Heeia typically processed about 40 intercepts an hour, this meant that the 10 radio intelligence operators on duty per shift were kept busy monitoring IJN radio broadcasts. Working as quickly and accurately as possible, each operator, using his two radio (RAS) receivers covering selected frequencies, copied down the details of the broadcast on his two RIP-5 typewriters. One of the operator's RIP-5s was used to copy verbatim the actual kana-coded message, and the other was used to prepare the operator's log, recording circuit chatter, IJN transmitter, and operator peculiarities. Finally the operator added his own personal comments about the intercepted signal. Station H had 65 personnel assigned to perform its function as a radio intercept monitoring station working on behalf of Rochefort's CIU at Station HYPO.

Station H Chief Radioman (CRM) Homer Kisner was in charge of the station's intercept facilities. Each morning, after reviewing and highlighting the most important items in each of the three 8-hour-watch supervisors' intercept results, Kisner added his own comments or key pieces of information. He would then drive 15 miles over the Oahu Pali highway, hand carrying what was called the "day's take," and personally deliver the bundle to Rochefort.[75] There was no secure radio teletype communication system in place, so he also had to hand-carry the RDF reports to HYPO at Pearl Harbor.[76]

STATION K—KING (ALASKA)

Station K, the Dutch Harbor RDF site in Alaska, was code-named KING. Located in the eastern Aleutian Islands some 900 miles southwest of Anchorage, Dutch Harbor suffered vicious, swirling winds, known as *williwaws*, throughout the year. Dressed in multiple layers of clothing, the sailors manning the RDF intercept site suffered the bitterly cold, foggy weather all year long. With the navy having designated the harbor as a major PBY seaplane reconnaissance base and the army having provided portions of an infantry regiment to defend the base, life at KING was nothing short of miserable. Fortunately for the handful of personnel assigned to KING, for security purposes, it was located near the navy's Dutch Harbor Air Station and the army's Fort Mears.

The RDF facility was installed in a round brick building called the "barrel." That the building was solidly built helped, because of its need to withstand the frequent 100-mile-per-hour winds typical for that part of the Aleutians. Operating space inside the facility was about 15 feet in diameter. In order to operate the arms of the DT model detector, it was necessary to physically rotate the system in a circle around a pivot to finally capture the bearing.[77]

The primary mission of KING was to take high-frequency direction finding bearings against the IJN's radios on land and at sea. Assignments included the IJN's Combined Fleet; unit commanders; submarines; aircraft; the Mandate Fleet (Caroline and Marshall Islands area); the North, Central, and South China Fleets; and Japanese commercial merchant vessels. This was a complicated mission, even though in January 1941 there were only five men working the station.

R. J. Fox, the radioman-in-charge and Station KING's leader, was responsible for the performance of the other four radiomen assigned to the station. His equipment was the bare minimum, but it did include an electric space heater. Since KING did not have a RIP-5 typewriter, all IJN call signs had to be copied by hand. The men took bearings on various assigned frequencies, encoded the bearings, and delivered them to the "general service radio station," where they were transmitted to Rochefort's HYPO in Hawaii.

Fox's men developed a "garble table" for analyzing radio call signs to better determine if the transmitter being targeted by RDF represented an IJN warship or just a Japanese merchant marine vessel. RDF bearing reports were sent electronically to HYPO. Hard copy correspondence, such as monthly reports, went by airmail to Seattle and on to Hawaii.[78]

STATION V—VICTOR (SAMOA)

Protected by coral reefs, rocky beaches, and high, craggy, mountain-like cliffs, the island had inhospitable shores—a perfect place for the southernmost RDF tracking outpost. Located five miles to the southwest of Pago Pago in the South Pacific, it suffered from the 200 inches of incessant tropical rainfall that poured down each year and 100-mile-per-hour winds in the form of typhoons, which would all too frequently lash the island. If this didn't round out its climactic and geographical natural defenses, there was always the 500-man marine infantry battalion that manned concrete bunker-like defenses, located primarily in the vicinity of Pago Pago's vulnerable open-water harbor beaches.

Located some 2,500 miles to the south of Pearl Harbor on the site of an abandoned Pan American Airways station, Station V, or VICTOR, was officially known as the U.S. Naval Communications Supplementary Activity. Despite its considerable distance from Pearl Harbor, Station VICTOR had been enhanced to the point that it could play a significant role. Positioned at Vaitogi on the south coast of the island of Tutuila, Samoa, it was connected to the U.S. Naval Station 13 miles away by road and a Morse telegraphic cable landline.

Initially, the DT high-frequency direction finder in use at the beginning of 1941 sat on a platform six feet off the ground. Its 12-foot arms extended out from each side to hold the required dipoles. Bearings were taken by the aural null method, rotating the entire unit as necessary 360 degrees. The operator literally walked the unit around in a circle. One time, a typhoon took place the first week of March, causing operations to shut down for a day.

The navy recognized VICTOR's importance, and by late April 1941 a newer model DY-1 direction finder had been installed and was operating as a replacement to the now dismantled DT unit. Three 70-foot cigar-shaped antenna masts were constructed about 350 feet away from the DY-1 unit to provide the antenna support for its two Model RAS-1 receivers and the newly provided ECM Mark II cipher machine. By June, VICTOR was transmitting daily reports to Hawaii via Tutuila's radio transmitter.[79]

During the period from August 20 to September 20, 1941, the Vaitogi Station logged bearings on 188 IJN radio call signs. By August, the personnel allowance for VICTOR had gone from four to nine: one radioman-in-charge (RMC), five first-class radiomen (RM1), and three second-class radiomen (RM2). VICTOR's RMC R. F. Mundy reported directly to HYPO at the 14th Naval District headquarters.[80]

STATION AF (MIDWAY ISLAND)

Midway Island lies about 1,300 miles to the west of Pearl Harbor. Even though its wide lagoon was too shallow to be a suitable harbor, in 1903 the navy still took it over for use as a cable repeater station. As the years passed, Pan Am established an airfield on the island, and a two-loop radio direction finder for its flights. The ONI in Washington saw Midway as a potentially valuable RDF station; in 1941, Station AF was located in the vicinity of Pan Am's landing field.

AF's radio intelligence operators were able to have a two-story octagonal building constructed to house their model DT direction finder. Positioned on the second floor, it operated throughout 1941, taking bearings on both Japanese warships and merchant marine vessels. Toward the end of 1941, a four-section RDF watch around the clock was established, with the men off duty sleeping on the first floor. All DT bearings taken were recorded in a log, and the next morning, CRM K. B. Selch, using a five-wheel ECM encoding machine, would encode the RDF bearing data and send it on to Pearl Harbor via the navy's special TESTM circuit.[81]

With Station KING to the north and Station VICTOR to the south, Midway's Station AF completed the 14th Naval District's Mid-Pacific Network of RDF stations. *All* stations by mid-1941 could not only conduct efficient RDF operations but also communicate rapidly and securely with their plotting center at Pearl Harbor. With hard work and considerable foresight, Safford and his OP-20-G staff had fashioned HYPO's mid-Pacific radio intelligence network into a key cog. Unfortunately, although well-equipped and manned with some of the best crypto signal intelligence brains in the navy, HYPO's contribution to the U.S. Navy intelligence-gathering effort in the Pacific during the latter part of 1941 would be severely marginalized, due to politics far beyond its control.

WESTERN PACIFIC HIGH-FREQUENCY DIRECTION FINDING NET

Station C—CAST (Corregidor, Philippines)

Station C (CAST) at Corregidor Island was one of OP-20-G's three principal crypto processing centers for the navy's North Pacific Ocean signal communications intelligence effort against Japan and was the fulcrum of the Navy Department's Western Pacific High-Frequency Direction Finding Net. The Net was in reality a trinational communications intelligence effort, involving the British Far Eastern Combined Bureau (FECB) in Singapore, and the Dutch Army's Kamer 14 intercept station at Batavia in the Netherlands East Indies. The British and the Dutch exchanged intelligence data and intercepts with CAST, as well as forwarded information through their own liaison officers assigned for that purpose in Washington, DC. Their involvement was critical.

Guam Island, to the east of the Philippines, completed the American portion of the Net, with CAST reporting the important inputs it received and processed to OP-20-G at Station NEGAT. With an evolving concern about Japan's IJN expansion and its development of aircraft carriers toward the end of the 1920s, the possibility of a naval threat to the Philippines became a significant concern of the navy's War Plan Orange.

In a May 13, 1929, letter to the commander-in-chief Asiatic Fleet (CINCAF), the navy's CNO pointed out, "The peculiar situation of the Asiatic Fleet renders it most important in the development of a radio intelligence service." CINCAF was further given the mission to work out the establishment of a radio intelligence intercept organization for the Philippines, "as he may see fit."[82]

By early March 1930, Olongapo in the Bataan Peninsula was selected as a radio intercept site. The site was expanded and developed, but, as time went on, experiments with other sites such as Mariveles, Sangley Point, and the Cavite Naval Base were conducted. Finally, the island of Corregidor, known to the army as Fort Mills (one of five islands guarding the entrance to Manila Bay), became the primary focus of CINCAF's signal intelligence effort in the late 1930s. Lying some two miles from the southern tip of the Bataan peninsula and dividing the mouth of Manila Bay into two distinct channels, the 1,735-acre Corregidor Island was to become the center of an immense construction project, beginning in 1939.[83]

Construction at Corregidor (called the "Rock" by those stationed there) involved a series of tunnels drilled into the hard rock hillsides. In July 1940 a tunnel called Project DOG was begun, with a completion date estimated in June 1941. By late August 1939, the tunnels then under construction were code-worded as Projects AFIRM (radio intelligence), BAKER (the RDF site), and CAST (the offices and quarters of the personnel assigned to Station C).

Project QUEEN, the main tunnel of the entire complex, running some 1,400 feet in length and 30 feet in width, with an additional five laterals of reinforced concrete, was completed in August 1941. Used by both the army and the navy, QUEEN had a DT high-frequency direction finder, consisting of two Type RAS search receivers, a typewriter, a LM frequency meter, and an electronic cipher machine (ECM). Waterproofing, drainage, electrical power, sanitary facilities, special splinter-proof doors, and ventilation were included. It became officially known as the Malinta Tunnel complex, housing the U.S. Army headquarters of Lt. Gen. Douglas MacArthur (CINC United States Army Forces Far East—USAFFE), the U.S. Philippine Administration, a hospital, various quartermaster supplies, and the navy's principal radio transmitters.

Station CAST lost no time in taking over tunnel AFIRM. By the first week in December 1941, CAST had a total of 10 officers and 62 enlisted personnel performing communications intelligence duties there. Of these, seven officers and 19 men were doing decryption work. Lt. Lietwiler was now the officer-in-charge (OIC), supported by the former OIC Lt. Rudolph J. Fabian and eight other officers, half of whom were crypto intelligence experts, with the others being Japanese language translators.[84]

By 1940, CAST's mission became more narrowly focused; its top priority now was breaking the new IJN operations cipher system (the 5-Num Code). Throughout the construction on Corregidor, CAST was busy with an assortment of missions on behalf of Adm. Thomas Hart. CAST's general mission since April 1939 had been one of obtaining all types of signals intelligence information by decrypting IJN messages and conducting related radio direction finding and traffic analysis. The problem was not so much one of difficulty, even though the task involved the recovery of some 4,000 key words or phrases (which were changed every four months) and the solution of a new transposition form every 10 days; it was more one of quantity and time in terms of the number of cryptographic personnel that could be dedicated to the project. It was an all-consuming effort for one man, Fabian, who had to be able to recognize the "key" or known word (numeral) for starting each message in order to solve the crypto problem.

Increasing the number of cryptographic clerks would considerably enhance the output of CAST. This resulted in an ongoing battle between CAST and OP-20-G. During the spring of 1941, Rear Adm. Ingersoll, the assistant CNO, authorized Ens. Laurence MacKallor to transport a complete PURPLE diplomatic decode machine and OP-20-GY's latest up-to-date or current solutions for the 5-Num Code to CAST. MacKallor arrived in late March 1941 to set up the systems.[85]

Station CAST's Tunnel AFIRM, dedicated to radio signal intercept and decode operations, was located just south of Kindley Field in the eastern quarter of Corregidor Island, about a mile east of the Malinta Tunnel complex in the west-central part of the island. A short distance to the east of CAST was sited its Model DY high-frequency direction finder (HFDF) and further out to the southeast, along the southern bend in the configuration of the island at Monkey Point, was the Model DT HFDF system.[86]

The unit's mission was studying the enemy fleets' organizations and communications and determining their intentions in order to avoid a surprise attack, as well as to maintain an order of battle of the various IJN fleets. Adm. Hart took a special interest in CAST. He was particularly interested in the IJN's order of battle or fleet organizations and main warship locations and PURPLE, the decoding machine for Japanese diplomatic radio traffic.

The Asiatic Fleet of just three cruisers, a handful of destroyers, and 23 submarines had been issued the PURPLE machine, but the U.S. Pacific Fleet at Hawaii, which was easily five times larger and 10 times more powerful, including aircraft carriers and battleships, had not.[87]

In June 1941, Cdr. Safford informed CAST that the United States expected to hold Manilla Bay as a base for operations against Japan at the start of the war. The 42 navy personnel at Corregidor's Fort Mills were increased to 72. It was quickly becoming apparent that CAST's Corregidor capabilities were being upgraded to wartime standards.

In mid-May 1941, the navy communications system at Corregidor had eight transmitters (models TAB, TAD, TAF, TBA, TBB, and TCC) with frequency ranges of upwards of 26,000 kHz and kilowatt powers running up to 5 kW. There were 26 radio receivers and a complete IBM system.[88] A significant communications upgrade was made in a July 3, 1941, letter from Safford to Fabian, directing him to begin using his ECM Mark II.

Of special note, in June 1941 Station CAST was directed by Stark, as a top priority, to solve the IJN's primary operations 5-Num Code. While this was to occupy CAST's crypto personnel full time, the PURPLE machine decoding mission continued against Tokyo's diplomatic traffic, particularly the Tokyo-Washington, DC, and Tokyo-Berlin circuits. Therefore, a continuous exchange of information was maintained with OP-20-GY; the latest 5-Num Code break in points or "keys" were sent by coded radio instructions as decoding updates.

In September, to ensure that CAST kept its eye on the ball, Ingersoll had Lietweiler, one of the navy's top cryptologists, moved from OP-20-G to CAST, replacing Lt. Fabian as OIC. (Fabian stayed on as an assistant.) Lietweiler brought with him a crypto decoding device known as the JEEP IV (GYP-4), developed by Lt. Lee W. Parke of OP-20-GY for solving the random number components of Code Book D's Table 7 (5-Number) system.

CAST now used another key piece of equipment to enhance its efficiency—the IBM Type 405 alphabetical tabulator and its related components. Senior Yeoman V. Knutson ran the installation. Maintenance was performed by a representative of the Watson Business Machine Company, an IBM affiliate, in Manila. An oscilloscope and its camera were also moved to CAST's Tunnel AFIRM.[89]

But what was Tunnel AFIRM all about? Station CAST conducted its cryptology and intercept operations against the IJN from Tunnel AFIRM, which was carved from solid rock and located 40 feet underground. The shape of the tunnel was actually in the form of a T, with the upper or larger crossbar at the top of the staff and a smaller crossbar forming the base of the T. Besides a main entrance, there was at least one, and possibly two, emergency exits.

The radioman-in-charge sat at the top center of the T intersection facing the staff. To his right, along a wall encompassing about half of the upper crossbar, sat six or seven signal intercept operators with their RIP-5 typewriters. On the opposite wall from them sat the watch chief, who supervised their work. So as not to waste space, the remaining part of the watch chief's side was dedicated to receivers, ink tape recorders, and what was known as the "antenna panel." In the space provided by the other half of the large crossbar, where the main entrance was located, were the 16th Naval District's COM 16 communications personnel, plus working areas, an airlock door system, and then the air conditioning pumps and filters, generators, the power control board, a blast shield, and the main gate.

Half a dozen cryptologists and their desks occupied one wall of the trunk of the T along with the officer-in-charge and his assistant. Eight traffic analysts and Japanese linguists, along with the crypto chief, were on the opposite wall. Taking up the wall space of the smaller crossbar was a radio transmitter, teletype communications coding equipment, a PURPLE machine, a radio signal photo analysis setup with the oscilloscope and camera, and finally the IBM statistical machine room used for tabulating and correlating RDF and 5-Num Code data. The setup, officially known as "Tunnel AFIRM, Kindley Field, Monkey Point, Corregidor, Philippine Islands," had 63 personnel, organized into three rotating shifts, operating around the clock.[90]

Station B—BAKER (Guam)

The island of Guam, almost by default, became a key link in the navy's West Pacific Net. Guam was caught up in America's late-19th-century fascination with Manifest Destiny, falling into Washington's imperial orbit as a result of its capture, along with the Philippines Islands, in 1898. As part of the Treaty of Paris, Guam, a rectangular-shaped island of some 225 square miles, was ceded to the United States and then placed under the control of the Navy Department.

Lying at the southern end of the Marianas Islands and 1,400 miles from Japan's Yokohama Harbor, Guam appeared to be an ideal location from which to spy on the Japanese. Once a week, Pan American's "China Clipper" flights connected it to Honolulu and Manila. For the sailors of Station B at the site of the Libugon Hill Naval Radio Station, it was an idyllic tropical setting: palm trees, old Spanish forts, beaches, and rickshaw taxis pulled by carabao cows.

Naval Intelligence became interested in the island as a radio intercept site in 1929. Guam's intelligence successes during the IJN's fleet maneuvers of 1929 and 1930 cemented its position as an important signal intercept station. With a population just over 21,000 and located 1,500 miles to the east of the Philippines, 3,400 miles from Honolulu, and 5,100 miles from San Francisco, it was to become one of the early mainstays of OP-20-G's signal intelligence operations in the Pacific.

CAST had a major RDF problem. Their bearings taken against IJN warships along the east coast of the Japanese islands were the same identical azimuth, making it impossible to specifically target the precise location of the radio signal. For this reason, it was absolutely critical to have another RDF site, to provide the cross-bearing to find the exact location of a ship. Therefore Station BAKER was brought into play. By the late 1930s, BAKER was established at Libugon, Guam, located facing the sea on a low plateau in the northwest quarter of the somewhat rectangular, sock-shaped island.

In conjunction with CAST, BAKER's location offered the RDF not only net shorter distances but also fewer differences in longitude and allowed bearing lines to generally cut at favorable, almost 90-degree angles for accurate plotting.[91]

During 1941, eight personnel under the leadership of the radioman-in-charge CRM J. W. Pearson and then later on in September CRM D. W. Barnum manned the station. The RDF components, consisting of DY and DT HFDF model RDF units and located on a knoll a quarter mile from the main station, were effective, taking 632 bearings, an average of about 29 bearings per day, during the period of August 24 to September 15. Of these, 362 were taken on merchant marine and other ships, and 270 were taken on "secret calls" or the IJN's main fleet.

Besides a Model TCC-1 transmitter to provide direct communications with the Asiatic Tracking Net control station at Corregidor, three antennas supported the communications transmission system: a rhombic directional antenna oriented toward Corregidor, another of the same type oriented on Oahu in the Hawaiian Islands, and one vertical radiating antenna for general transmissions. Eight RIP-5 Kana typewriters served the signal intercept operators at BAKER, who maintained a four-section watch.[92]

BAKER's five major intercept missions monitored the IJN radio circuit between Tokyo's Navy Headquarters and the Sasebo Naval Base, the principal circuits into and out of the IJN's outposts in the Caroline and Marshall Islands, IJN fleet exercises and movements, high-speed Boehme (ink-paper tape) recording and transcribing of the Tokyo-Berlin diplomatic traffic, and finally RDF line bearings on signals transmitted from major units (aircraft carriers, battleships, and cruisers) operating in and around the home waters of the IJN.

The results of RDF intercepts and daily traffic analyses were sent via coded radio (TESTM) reports on a daily basis to Station CAST. More lengthy reports were forwarded weekly to CAST in Manila via the Pan Am Clipper flight. Monthly reports, along with the more bulky bundles of intercept traffic, were sent by whatever navy transport was available.[93]

While Guam appeared to be a superbly located island for signal intelligence data-gathering purposes, it was also vulnerable. It had figured in early War Plan Orange strategic planning around 1914, whereby it was considered for upgrading into a "naval base of the first order." At that time, plans were even made for the dredging of a copious major harbor. By October 17, 1941, with war looming on the horizon, the last of Guam's military dependents were evacuated from the relatively defenseless island.[94]

Throughout 1941, Station BAKER provided valuable signal intelligence RDF inputs for the navy's Western Pacific Net. The British and Dutch also maintained comprehensive signals intelligence networks to points south of the Philippines, which were also linked to CAST as part of the splendid arrangement.

BRITISH FAR EASTERN COMBINED BUREAU (FECB)

Beginning in the mid-1920s, the British began to use their Commonwealth territories of Hong Kong and Singapore for radio intelligence operations focused on the Japanese in the Pacific.

British Q Team (Hong Kong)

In the mid-1930s, a cryptanalysis unit on China's coast was formed at the naval dockyard on Victoria Island in Hong Kong, with an affiliated

RDF station at nearby Stonecutters Island. This was the Combined Intelligence Bureau Hong Kong, known as Q Team. This office became the Far Eastern Combined Bureau (FECB). Some 29 personnel worked on rotating shifts 24 hours a day at Stonecutters, and another 17 operated from the HMS *Tamar.*

Beginning with the Sino-Japanese War in the 1930s, there was a surge in Japan's military and naval radio traffic, and the FECB's primary mission became focused on maintaining an up-to-date analysis of the disposition of the IJN. Additionally, there was a focus on intercepting and breaking Japanese diplomatic and naval codes. In the late summer of 1938, due to Hong Kong's relative vulnerability to a potential IJN attack, most of the FECB operation was moved to Kranji and the Selatar Naval Base in Singapore.[95]

British Y Intelligence Section (Singapore)

The Royal Navy thought that Singapore should be its mainstay of intelligence operations in the Pacific. The British intelligence buildup at the Royal Navy's fortified Selatar base in Singapore began in earnest when the British government's Code & Cipher School (GCCS) at its Bletchley Park naval intelligence center decided to focus on the German Navy's Enigma ciphers. As a result, in 1940, 40 British personnel (Hut 7) were transferred from London to Singapore. Under the command of Capt. (RN) K. L. Harkness, the director of the FECB, Hut 7 focused on breaking the Japanese cryptographic systems. Air Vice-Marshall Sir Robert Brooke-Popham, the British commander-in-chief Far East, was directly supported by the FECB; the Selatar code-breaking organization became known as Y Intelligence Section.

The FECB's Direction Finding (D/F) Intelligence Section was the reporting hub or center for all RDF bearings taken from an assortment of direction finding stations scattered about the south-central Pacific and even the Indian Ocean. Y ran a plotting center in the War Room of the Naval Headquarters at Selatar. Some 10 officers formed the plotting staff, assisted by several civilians. Y Section traffic analyses involved radio call sign identifications and high-speed movie cameras to capture IJN transmitter signal patterns revealed by oscilloscope pictures. In addition to RDF stations in Australia, India, and New Zealand, key stations reporting to FECB's plotting centers were Stonecutters Island (Hong Kong), Penang Island (Malaya), Kuching (British North Borneo), Bukit Gombak (Singapore), Kranji (Singapore), Naura Island (northeast of Australia in the south-central Pacific), and even Esquimalt (Canada). All stations used the proven and highly reliable Adcock direction finder systems.[96]

In November 1940, Stark directed Hart, as CINCAF, to conduct an interchange of intelligence information with the FECB concerning the Far

East. This included not only updates on the IJN's order of battle and location data but also the key crypto systems necessary for breaking the 5-Num Code, among others. McCollum termed these "joint cryptographic systems." An American naval intelligence liaison officer was stationed at the British naval headquarters in Singapore (FECB), and his British counterpart was stationed in Manila (Station CAST).

By March 1941, coded radio communications channels and procedures for the transmission of "urgent" and "important" signal intelligence information were put in place between Singapore and Corregidor. The exchange of important diplomatic and consular information with not only CINCAF in the Philippines but also the Navy Department in Washington was part of the agreement.[97]

McCollum was impressed with what he saw at the British Admiralty during a visit to London in 1941. He noted that the Royal Navy's headquarters operated what they called a Combined Operations and Intelligence Center (COIC), whereby an operations officer at the commander rank level was assisted by a naval intelligence officer of similar rank. The COIC's mission was to filter and evaluate on the spot, immediately, all intelligence that came in of a tactical nature.

What greatly impressed McCollum was how the British used the same COIC setup in Alexandria, Egypt, to make the intelligence analysis and then take the initiative to coordinate tactical operations. Information available in London was also available to Alexandria and vice versa. Everything was exchanged, analyzed, "digested," and made available to the CINC Mediterranean Fleet. The FECB at the Selatar Naval Base in Singapore was operating in much the same manner.[98] By 1941, the British and Dutch were both formally integrated into the intercept system.

THE NETHERLANDS (DUTCH) EAST INDIES (NEI)

The Netherlands (Dutch) East Indies (NEI) were Holland's supremely valuable colonial possession in the Pacific, consisting of more than 60 million people and extending 2,275 miles (roughly the equivalent of the straight line distance from New York to Los Angeles). They controlled a third of the world's rubber and a fifth of its oil. Tokyo knew that the NEI was an immense reservoir of raw materials, including oil, tin, bauxite, rubber, and manganese, as well as rice. The Royal Dutch Shell's oil interests in the islands of Borneo, Java, and Sumatra dominated the colony's export industry.

In 1940–1941, the NEI found itself enmeshed in an ever-evolving negative state of regional power politics, over which it had little control. With the German invasion of Holland in May 1940, the NEI was largely left to its own devices. The Dutch government was in exile in London. Due to the Nazi occupation of the Dutch homeland, a number of Netherlands banks and shipping companies moved their headquarters overseas to Batavia (NEI's capital city).

Tokyo's aggressive moves into French Indochina during the fall of 1940 were unsettling to both Adm. Conrad Lambert Helfrich, the Gov. Gen. of the NEI, and Lt. Gen. Hein Ter Poorten, the commander of the Royal Dutch East Indies Army of only some 35,000 personnel, headquartered at Bandoeng on the island of Java.[99] These Dutch soldiers were responsible for defending a territory as large as the continental United States. This included 10 major islands.

Using a combination of diplomatic maneuvering and the brute force of the Imperial Japanese Army, Tokyo intimidated the Vichy French government sufficiently to cause it to agree to an open occupation of its Southeast Asian colony, French Indochina. Into this power vacuum, Japan's army and air force poured an armada of planes and troops. The Japanese military now had a forward operational staging base that potentially threatened both British and Dutch interests in the region.

Washington responded by threatening Tokyo with sanctions on oil, to be imposed if Japan did not withdraw from French territory. As the sanctions began to take serious effect in 1941, it became obvious that Japan, now bogged down in a never-ending war in China, would be forced to turn to the NEI to make up its oil shortfall. How to protect the Dutch-controlled oil fields and rubber plantations scattered over the islands of Borneo, Celebes, Ceram, Java, Sarawak, and Sumatra became a serious problem for Lt. Gen. Ter Poorten. Dutch military had not been sleeping when it came to determining strategic threats and understanding the capabilities and intentions of their potential enemies in the Pacific.

Kamer 14 (Java)

The constantly expanding IJN constituted the primary transpacific invasion threat to the NEI. It became imperative for Batavia's military leaders to engage in a serious signal intelligence intercept effort focused not only on Japan's diplomatic circuits but also the IJN. The Dutch codebreaking center, the army's Kamer 14, was located at the Bandoeng-Batavia Technical College in Java. Cryptanalysts such as Lt. Col. J. A. Verkuyl, Capt. J. W. Henning, and Lt. W. van der Beek focused on Japanese diplomatic cable traffic passing between Japan's consulate in Batavia and its Ministry of Foreign Affairs in Tokyo.

The Dutch government controlled the local telegraph office at its main post office, so it was easy to obtain copies of each message sent out. Besides decoding the Japanese consular code (J-19) and its related Red Code, the cryptanalysts also made serious progress in breaking the IJN's 5-Num Code. The British were impressed enough with Kamer 14's work that in January 1941, they began a gradual exchange of decrypt data and information. A similar signals crypto data and intelligence exchange was taking place between the Kamer 14 and the American CINCAF in the Philippines. This was made possible through a special rapid and secure telecommunications ECM radio link.[100]

Kamer 14 ran two high-frequency direction finders at Randja Ekek and Timor Sundepang. Two other radio reception stations were located at Rantjaokek east of Bandoeng and Kobajoran southwest of Batavia, part of a radio intercept network extending to other islands of the NEI. Of the 51 functioning radio transmitters, two primary sets were located at Malabar and Tegallegah; these connected the NEI radio system with other parts of the world.[101]

Signal intercept and intelligence information was sent to the Free Dutch Government-in-Exile in London via coded cable, as well as to the FECB at Singapore. Kamer 14 established a system of both military and naval liaison officers to ensure that its radio intelligence was forwarded not only to CAST at Corregidor, but also to naval intelligence in Washington.

The U.S. Army assigned a military attaché, Lt. Col. Elliot Thorpe, to Batavia, along with his U.S. Navy attaché comrade-in-arms, Lt. Cdr. Slawson. Their mission was to report promptly via coded ECM naval dispatches any information from the Dutch concerning the IJN's operations and Japanese intentions to Washington, DC. Kamer 14 arranged to have the Royal Netherlands Navy send Cdr. H. D. Linder and Lt. Cdr. Wisden to CINCAF in the Philippines to maintain contact with Adm. Hart and CAST.[102]

Dutch Attachés

To make sure that there was close coordination between Kamer 14 and the U.S. Navy's intelligence operations in Washington, the Dutch Navy's Capt. Johan Everhard Meijer Ranneft and his Dutch Army counterpart, Col. Weijerman, were assigned as attachés to pass on key signals intelligence and RDF bearings concerning the IJN (which had been picked up by Kamer 14) to OP-20-G. Of course, a reciprocal exchange was also expected.

Ranneft, born in Semaray, Java, in 1886, was a naval radio signal communications expert who, as the former director of Dutch Naval Communications and a naval attaché on duty in Washington, DC, since 1938, had an "open door" in terms of access to McCollum and ONI's signal intelligence and RDF plots. Ranneft solidified his friendship with the U.S. Navy in 1940 by assisting in the clandestine acquisition of the engineering blueprints for the Swedish Bofors 40mm, Mark 3 antiaircraft gun system, which ultimately became the mainstay of the U.S. Navy's shipboard air defense systems throughout World War II.[103]

During September 1940, Japanese diplomats demanded that Batavia formalize an oil contract to provide some 3 million metric tons annually to Japan, along with a fixed delivery schedule. Batavia refused, claiming that only the oil companies themselves could negotiate sales. By October 16, a PURPLE signal's intercept indicated that Tokyo's rebuffed Foreign Office was now advocating a deeper and more sinister intention: seizing the Dutch East Indies.

McCollum summarized the details for Roosevelt in an October 16 memorandum, "Japanese Plans to Seize the Dutch East Indies." But the Japanese were not done, by any means. A PURPLE intercept of October 25 disclosed the Japanese strategy: leasing a piece of property disguised as a commercial "technical base" and turning it into a Trojan Horse forward operating base for a presumed commando operation to seize the government. A few days later, on October 30, McCollum provided a copy of the dispatch to Ranneft, who passed it on to the Dutch Government-in-Exile in London. The proposed lease was promptly rejected.[104]

As a consequence of what was going on, Ranneft was drawn even closer to the United States, depending on ONI to keep him apprised of Tokyo's diplomatic and militant intentions. With the close ties now established by Washington and Batavia via their communications networks and liaison officers, the North Pacific was complete.

This constituted the most prolific and comprehensive intelligence-gathering operation ever conducted by the U.S. Navy up until that time. Upwards of 30 radio intelligence intercept and processing stations now ringed and bisected the North Pacific, focusing in an integrated manner on Japan's diplomatic and naval-related signals and code systems. Capable of processing thousands of signal intercepts, crypto decoding information, radio direction finder bearings, radio identification call signs, and peculiar radio transmitter emission characteristics, the U.S. Navy's communications intelligence system was second to none.[105]

On the eve of war in 1941, while the splendid arrangement would be the product of considerable insightful thinking and outright brilliance on the part of Cdr. Safford and many others at OP-20-G and ONI, it contained a serious flaw that would place America in jeopardy.

4

Roosevelt's Driving Imperative

In politics, nothing happens by accident; if it happens, you can bet it was planned that way.

—*Franklin D. Roosevelt*

By the 1930s Franklin D. Roosevelt, due to his experiences as assistant secretary of the navy during World War I and then as governor of New York, had developed a consummate understanding of America, particularly in terms of two of its most important national interests: the nation's economic health and its national security. If these were not properly protected when threatened, the survival of the nation could well be placed in jeopardy. They were essential elements to the life of the nation, what one would call *vital* interests.

As he assumed the presidency in early 1933, Roosevelt found himself confronting two major challenges to these interests. The vexing and most immediate one was the dire economic situation facing the United States, the Great Depression, which he had inherited from the administration of President Herbert Hoover. The second challenge, although not initially recognized as such, would involve the rise of Adolf Hitler's Nazi Germany during the early 1930s and its conquest of much of Europe by 1941.

The first challenge, the Great Depression, would work itself out over the next eight years as America girded itself for and then entered into World War II. The second and infinitely more dangerous challenge would become apparent toward the end of 1939 as Hitler's Nazi Germany expanded into Poland as a key initial step in its military conquest of much of Europe. In coping with these extreme situations, Roosevelt's inner Machiavellian personality and adroit capabilities as a politician would come into play. In so doing, as one of his later biographers would so aptly characterize him, he strategically became both the "lion and the fox."[1]

Roosevelt was a *lion*, prescient and practical as he forcefully dealt with the threat that jeopardized the survival of the United States. At the same time, his leadership was full of guile and deception, a *fox* slyly and subtly exploiting and manipulating political forces and economic situations to accomplish his ends.[2] It was the aggression of Imperial Japan on the other side of the Pacific Ocean that would ultimately enable him to attain his goal. It is in this context that his decisions and political maneuverings would play out in the run-up to the outbreak of the war for the Americans on December 7, 1941.

Roosevelt's immediate challenge in taking office was the Great Depression, which had seen America's gross domestic product (GNP) drop dramatically from $98.4 billion in 1929 to slightly less than half that amount by 1933. By that time 15 million Americans were out of work, and the value of manufactured goods was less than a quarter of what it had been in 1929. Concurrently, American exports had fallen in value from $5.24 billion to $1.61 billion, constituting a drop of about 70 percent. That this was an immensely serious situation was highlighted by American wheat exports, which had slumped to a paltry $5 million compared to the $200 million sent overseas some years earlier. Worse, $541 million in auto exports in 1929 had fallen to $76 million during the 1932 election year. This was all part of the general collapse of world trade, which contributed immensely to America's dismal economic situation. High unemployment contributed to social unrest in the form of riots, strikes, and other protests routinely taking place, adding pressure to the situation.[3]

Americans felt that the sacrifices they had made in the Great War, "the war to end all wars," had been in vain. The huge victory parades of 1919 and the great homecoming celebrations with entire American Expeditionary Force (AEF) divisions marching down New York's Fifth Avenue were now forgotten. In their place was the realization that old dynasties had tumbled and entire empires had disintegrated, destabilizing Europe and making it vulnerable to political changes no one had foreseen. Out of this chaos, new nations had now been formed; dictators such as Adolf Hitler of Nazi Germany, Benito Mussolini of Fascist Italy, and Joseph Stalin of the Soviet Union were being touted as the future of Europe, in stark contrast to the apparent failings of capitalism in America.

American casualties of the last five months before the armistice of November 1918, when the AEF suffered something on the order of 50,000 battle deaths and several times that number wounded, were not forgotten. The figures signified that during this relatively short period of time, roughly 15 percent of the AEF's million-man army had become casualties. Thousands more were maimed and gassed; survivors now languished in Veterans Administration hospitals throughout the land. Americans were disillusioned by the failure of their idealized commitment to "make the world safe for democracy." They embraced isolationism as a solution to protect the nation from another European debacle.

If war, from the point of view of Americans, entailed death, destruction, horror, and the wasteful futility of it all, on the other side of the Pacific there was a different perspective. In the Japanese psyche, war involved struggle, force, and heroism; these were important and enduring features of life and the Bushido spirit of fighting for honorable ends.[4] At the end of World War I, when the League of Nations awarded Japan, by mandate, the former German colonies of the Caroline and Marshall Islands (east of the Philippines in the Central Pacific), there began to develop a feeling in Tokyo that Japan's true destiny lay in dominating all of East Asia.

This idea would gradually transform itself into a concept of Japanese Manifest Destiny. This would clash with Washington's attempts to maintain the American position, the Far Eastern Open Door Policy, in the Philippines. Their geographic location was viewed as an advantageous springboard into China. China's xenophobia, expressed by its Nationalist Party's antiforeign ideology, exacerbated the situation during the 1920s. Initially directed against all foreigners, it was narrowed dramatically to focus on Japan. This included a boycott of Japanese goods pouring through its Open Door treaty ports during the summer of 1931.[5]

In September 1931 the now simmering impulses of Japan's military boiled over in response, and the army seized Manchuria, the northernmost province of China, roughly one-sixth the size of the continental United States. Four months later, in early 1932, in a follow-up naval operation, the Imperial Japanese Navy (IJN) occupied China's international port of Shanghai.[6] These incidents brought condemnation down upon Japan from the League of Nations, of which the United States was not a member. But other than words, the League took no action. This generated unrestrained Japanese hostility. Japan abruptly withdrew from the League in early 1933.

Joseph Rochefort, then serving on official U.S. Navy duty in Japan, questioned a prominent Japanese business executive as to why the two conquests had taken place in the face of the League's mandate to seek peaceful solutions to territorial disputes. The response was a rationale in defense of Japan's nationalism: "Our honor has become involved in this. . . . When honor is involved, we don't care about anything else!"[7] It was a statement of Japanese attitudes, boldly laying out their plans for the future.

Secretary of State Henry L. Stimson, serving President Hoover, condemned the Japanese actions as a form of closing the free commercial Open Door in China to America. The Japanese were intent on undermining Sino-American commerce. Stimson aggressively challenged the Japanese by announcing his Stimson Doctrine: nonrecognition of Tokyo's activities in both Manchuria and Shanghai. While well intentioned, the initiative failed for the most part, as Hoover was fearful that further action might involve the United States in unwanted military entanglements on the other side of the Pacific. Hoover tersely commented on "the folly of getting into war with Japan on this subject."[8] It was now becoming obvious the United States was as ineffective as the League of Nations in preventing aggression in Asia.[9]

But Japan was not finished. By January 1934, one year into the first Roosevelt administration, U.S. Ambassador Joseph C. Grew was reporting that Tokyo believed that preserving peace in Asia genuinely meant a complete Japanese dominance of the region. Japan's leaders could point to a historical trend, indicating that the earlier successful Sino-Japanese and Russo-Japanese wars, the acquisition of the mandated Caroline and Marshall Islands, and the recent seizing of Manchuria were merely extensions of the irresistible flow of its own Manifest Destiny.[10]

In April 1934, the Japanese Foreign Office, with Ambassador Grew present, formally announced its own equivalent of a Monroe Doctrine by promulgating the "Amau Statement." This repudiated the right of any nation other than Japan to determine the "political relations" and military security policies for the sake of peace in the Far East.[11] It was a declaration of Tokyo's right to protect its newly perceived national security interests in the region. There was now a distinct probability of direct confrontation in the region between the Japanese and not only the Americans but also the English and the Dutch.

Germany, too, had been busy during these years, with German Chancellor Adolf Hitler withdrawing simultaneously in 1933 from both the League of Nations and the Geneva Disarmament Conference. By early 1935, Hitler, now ruling as an absolute dictator, announced the re-creation of the German Air Force (Luftwaffe) and the introduction of conscription for the new German Army (Wehrmacht). In August 1935, realizing that the militarists were on the ascendancy in both Germany and Japan and that multinational wars in Europe were once again a possibility, the U.S. Congress passed the Neutrality Act, which declared a general embargo on trading in arms, munitions, and war materials with any and all parties in any war.

Still another Neutrality Act of the same nature was passed in February 1936, further forbidding all loans or credits to all belligerents. These were the shields to protect the United States from becoming involved in another foreign war. At the time of this legislation, the worldwide depression and its problems of massive unemployment served to continue the economic disruption of the entire liberal-capitalist system. This caused many Americans to question the viability of democracy and the free capitalist system.

During the early part of the 1930s in Japan, economically cautious conservatives were displaced by nationalists and militarists. Making the situation worse, the IJA had gotten heavily involved in politics, even creating a revolutionary political movement along the lines of the Nazis in Germany; this movement was able to gain a controlling influence inside the government. This contrasted considerably with the IJN, which continued to remain loyal to civilian power in the Meiji tradition. In the end, the Japanese Navy was outmaneuvered by the army; the army would dominate politics in Tokyo for the next decade.[12]

In 1936, the militarists in Tokyo flexed their political muscles by forbidding the U.S. Navy to visit any of Japan's mandated islands.[13] By August Tokyo was promulgating a strategic vision for Japan encompassing the acquisition of naval supremacy in the Western Pacific, military superiority over the Soviet military in Northeast Asia, and a political hegemony over China. It was an ambitious program and reflected the Japanese adoption of an Asiatic Monroe Doctrine.[14]

During this time, the U.S. Congress, spurred on by Rep. Carl Vinson of the House Naval Affairs Committee, concluded that new naval construction would both reduce the general unemployment and strengthen the U.S. Navy. A long-range naval construction program was formulated and funded in 1937, with the goal of building 129 warships of various sizes, including three aircraft carriers: the *Enterprise*, *Yorktown*, and *Wasp*. U.S. defense spending for that year approximated a little over $1 billion.[15]

At the end of 1936, with militarists now in power in both Germany and Japan, and Roosevelt having won reelection for a second term, the Gallup Poll's interviews found that 62 percent of Americans felt that the United States could "stay out of another general European war."[16] Some months later, in May, the Neutrality Act of 1937 was passed by Congress, prohibiting American ships from transporting personnel and war materials to belligerents. An exception was made to America's neutrality by the administration with a "cash and carry" provision for the sale of materials and supplies to belligerents in Europe, which would be permitted as long as the recipients paid immediately in cash and arranged for their own transportation.

In Roosevelt's second term, his New Deal, with its massive program for economic reform and social welfare, began to unfold at the beginning of 1937, while an earlier event in China, just two months before, would form the catalyst for another Sino-Japanese war in Asia, this one lasting some eight years. Northern Chinese warlords became convinced that Chiang Kai-shek, the leader of the Nationalist Guomindang government, was following an erroneous strategy of first trying to crush Mao Zedong's Chinese Communists and only then focusing on the perceived Japanese threat to China. While the details of Chinese politics are not within the scope of this book, suffice it to say that Chiang was kidnapped by the warlords, placed under house arrest in Xi'an, and ultimately compelled to accept the concept of forming a united front with Mao's Communists. This "Xi'an incident" and Chiang's adoption of a more forceful and focused military posture against Japan's attempts to dominate China aroused a sense of national unity among the Chinese people.[17]

This new situation in early 1937 brought about considerable consternation in Tokyo, since Chiang Kai-shek consistently rejected its demands for outright submission. This gained China time to prepare their armies for the long war that was sure to come. The decision by Japan to conduct a war of chastisement on the one hand and a war of political annihilation on the other against China in mid-1937 was to be a fundamental fulfillment of its imperial ambition to impose its ideology of the Imperial Way on the Chinese. By the end of 1937, the IJA, with its seemingly invincible samurai spirit, had scored major victories in Shanghai and captured the Chinese capital of Nanking. The activities, now called the Great Patriotic Endeavor, forced Tokyo to decree the total mobilization of all of Japan's economic and manpower resources.[18] All Japanese were now expected to embrace and support the war effort, no matter what the cost.

The seizure of Nanking in late 1937, the gutting of the city by fire, the massacring of thousands of male civilians of military age, the raping of women and girls, the bayoneting and cutting off of heads of captured prisoners, and the slaughtering of upwards of some 200,000 civilians—the barbaric brutality that took place in China's capital did not win friends around the world.[19]

In 1938, *Life* magazine ran articles on January 10 and May 16 titled "A Week of Hell in Nanking" and "Rape of Nanking," respectively. On December 18, 1937, and again on January 9, 1938, *New York Times* correspondent Tillman Durdin, under a special dateline "Nanking," reported in full page articles the details of the "wholesale looting, the violation of women, the murder of civilians" as part and parcel of the atrocities.[20]

Movie newsreels in the United States, providing horrific pictures of the indiscriminate bombing and carnage, had a highly inflammatory effect on the public; prominent Americans began demanding a boycott of Japanese products. Labor unions also wanted boycotts, and longshoremen refused to handle Japanese goods at American docks. Others called for an embargo on all cotton, petroleum products, machine tools, and scrap iron sales to Japan. Investors were furious that Tokyo was not only approving the seizing of American coastal shipping and products at dockside in Shanghai but also cutting off American commercial and oil companies from their markets in China.

When Nanking fell to the Japanese, an American ship, the *Panay* (a former Chinese river-traffic boat), was bombed while trying to evacuate Chinese and American civilians. Although Tokyo apologized and promised indemnities for the four killed, there followed a series of Japanese aerial bombings of other clearly marked American missionary buildings, schools, and even the Standard Oil Company's properties on Hainan Island, this time without any apologies.[21] Whatever goodwill Japan had within the United States was now being rapidly eroded. By October 1937, a Gallup Poll reported that 59 percent of Americans sided with China and only 1 percent with Japan.[22] An incensed U.S. Ambassador Grew interpreted Japan's actions as a deliberate shutting down of the Open Door Policy with America in China.[23]

Secretary of State Cordell Hull, with Roosevelt's approval, cancelled any further issuing of licenses for the export of aircraft that could be used by any nation's military to attack civilian populations. Obviously, Japan was the intended target.[24] The horrendous breaches of military discipline and morality on the part of the IJA in China were so brazen that Roosevelt even toyed with the idea of implementing a joint British-American long-range naval blockade of Japanese merchant marine traffic passing in the vicinity of Singapore, the Dutch East Indies, and as far away as Australia, as well as America's own West Coast region. In January 1938, U.S Navy Capt. Royal K. Ingersoll was sent to London to explore and coordinate the plan, but the idea fell on deaf ears in Whitehall and was never implemented. Other planning with the British Admiralty staff would involve the Rainbow series of contingency war plans, entertaining the possibility of war in both the Atlantic and the Pacific.[25]

An earlier series of polls, conducted December 30, 1937, and January 4, 1938, indicated a significant change in attitude on the part of an incensed American public: 74 percent now said they wanted a "larger navy," 69 percent said they wanted a "bigger army," and 80 percent said they wanted a "bigger air force."[26] In part this was the result of various newsreels on the events taking place in Nanking, as well as news reports in the *New York Times*, *Chicago Daily News*, and Associated Press among others.[27] A buildup along these lines was not long in coming.

The 1938 Naval Expansion Act proposed by the House Naval Affairs Committee under Rep. Vinson in May sought to expand the U.S. Navy by

25 percent, increasing its size by several aircraft carriers, to join the five already on duty, along with some additional cruisers, destroyers, and submarines. In an action known as the Navy Second to None Act, Congress added a total of 69 more ships to the navy's fleet. The Act included the construction of some 3,000 war planes. This would be funded by a defense expenditure for the year of about $1.3 billion.[28]

While war raged on in China, and Tokyo placed Japan on a "total war" mobilization,[29] events were also taking place in Europe, with Hitler's Germany annexing Austria in March 1938 in violation of his earlier pledge to refrain from such action. This was followed in September 1938 when Hitler demanded control of the German-speaking portions of Czechoslovakia's Sudetenland. The possibility of general war in Europe now loomed on the horizon. British Prime Minister Neville Chamberlain rushed to Munich to confer with Hitler, in the hopes of avoiding war. The result of the effort was that Great Britain and France assured Germany that they would not fight for Czechoslovakia and further agreed to Hitler's demand that he be allowed to take over the Sudetenland. Six months later, in March 1939, Germany would, in violation of the agreement at Munich, make an unresisted occupation of the rest of Czechoslovakia.

These events, and the blatant initial stages of Jewish persecution in what would become known as the Holocaust, worried Roosevelt considerably in terms of what appeared to be evolving into an ominous future for Europe; but economic difficulties inside the United States seriously circumscribed his ability to take action. Despite massive federal expenditures, the Great Depression lingered on, with unemployment actually increasing from 14 percent in 1937 to 19 percent in 1938.[30] What was not clearly understood in Japan and Germany at this time was that despite the negative effects of the Great Depression, America's actual iron and steel production was higher (about 29 million tons) than Germany's roughly 23 million tons and four times that of Japan's 7 million tons. If military strength can be determined by indicators of industrial productivity, as historian Paul Kennedy suggests, then the United States was still the strongest power in the world by the end of the 1930s.[31]

During the last half of 1939, the IJA now found itself hopelessly bogged down in the vast mountainous hinterlands of China, expending large numbers of lives and much equipment in a campaign involving almost a million men; it had become a quagmire, leading Tokyo nowhere. The Chinese doggedly fought on, trading space for time, evoking widespread sympathy for the Chinese on the part of Americans.

A May Gallup Poll asked, "In the present fight between Japan and China, with which side do you sympathize?" A full 74 percent of Americans sympathized with China, while only 2 percent sympathized with Japan. While the United States actually had at best only modest economic interests in China, lobbying groups such as United China Relief depicted China in a valiant and overmatched fight against Japan, "holding the western ram-parts for us and for the democratic way of life in the world."[32]

And Europe? On September 1, 1939, Hitler's Wehrmacht tank columns smashed into western Poland. The Luftwaffe dominated the air over the battlefields. Within 24 days, Poland ceased to exist as a nation. Hitler's tanks had seized the western two-thirds, and the Molotov-Ribbentrop Pact in August between Germany and the Soviet Union permitted Stalin's armies to conquer the eastern third. Two days later, protesting the attack on Poland and not deterred by the fact that they were not capable of placing a single soldier on Polish soil, Britain and France declared war on Germany.

The shock of this new war in Europe resonated all the way to the White House. Reaction from Washington was not long in coming. On September 5, Roosevelt, in coordination with the chief of naval operations (CNO) Adm. Harold Stark, announced the formation of a "neutrality patrol" to be carried out by the U.S. Navy in the Atlantic. Its stated purpose was to keep the European war out of the Western Hemisphere by patrolling a hemi-spheric safety zone of sorts in both oceans around the Americas south of Canada (confirmed by the Declaration of Panama on October 3). This first war-related task was not exactly neutral. In actuality, the president pro-posed to accomplish this mission by having the navy report and track bel-ligerent aircraft and surface ships within the "safety belt," which varied in width from 300 to 1,000 miles. German ships were tracked and their posi-tions reported in plain English by American ships.[33] This did give the Royal Navy a definite advantage and placed the German Kriegsmarine (navy) at a disadvantage.[34] One way or another, the U.S. Navy was now involved in the initial stages of an evolving, undeclared war in the Atlantic.

On September 8, 1939, just seven days after the German invasion of Poland, Roosevelt declared a state of "limited national emergency" for the United States, increasing naval enlisted strength from some 110,000 to 145,000 personnel.[35] Yet, answers to a Gallup Poll released on September 18 suggested a more sobering perspective by Americans. In answer to the ques-tion "Should we send our army and navy abroad to fight Germany?" 84 per-cent responded "No" as opposed to some 16 percent who responded "Yes."[36] But another, far more important event with far-reaching consequences for Roosevelt, the United States, and even the world, took place some weeks later in Washington. And it involved Adolf Hitler's Nazi Germany.

ALBERT EINSTEIN

Albert Einstein, a German-born physicist and refugee from Nazi perse-cution and now living in America, had written a letter to Franklin Roosevelt dated August 2, 1939.

The letter did not reach the president's hands until October 11, some 10 weeks after Einstein had signed it. This letter, which arrived after Hitler's startling conquest of Poland, would dramatically change how Roosevelt viewed Adolf Hitler, Nazi Germany, and the ever-evolving events that were yet to take place in Europe during 1940 and 1941.

Einstein's comments not only changed Roosevelt's perspective on the importance of the war in Europe but also provided him with a driving imperative to deal with this new and totally unforeseen threat that could actually place in jeopardy the survival of the United States of America and its way of life as a nation. To confront this now dire situation and vital national interest as he now saw it would require all Roosevelt's political abilities as a both a lion and a fox. But what was of such great importance?

The essence of the issue involved an understanding of Einstein's theory of relativity—introduced in 1905—which theorized that mass and energy were equivalents of sorts and that a small amount of mass could result in a massive quantity of energy. It took many years before it was possible to determine that the components of atoms were important in this regard. The proton and the electron had been identified by 1930; and in 1932, James Chadwick, an English scientist, discovered the neutron or third necessary component, revolutionizing the field of nuclear research. It was now understood that protons and neutrons formed the mass or nucleus and that electrons orbited the nucleus, much like planets orbiting the sun.

Another scientist, Hungarian-born Leo Szilard—who also had escaped the Nazis in the early 1930s by fleeing to England and then to the United States—concluded that a chain reaction of the several components could be brought about to liberate enough energy to form an atomic bomb. His late 1930s work at Columbia University convinced Szilard that atomic bombs could actually be built. By the summer of 1939, he was deeply disturbed by the lack of American interest in this regard. Since atomic bombs were theoretically possible, he thought that Nazi Germany's scientists at the Kaiser Wilhelm Institute just might gain an unbeatable lead in developing them. It troubled Szilard that Germany had stopped the sale of uranium ore from occupied Czechoslovakia to other countries in order to proceed with its own research. Szilard thought Roosevelt ought to be apprised of the potential Nazi threat. But how should one go about doing this?[37]

Szilard astutely recognized that someone other than himself with considerable acclaim, a recognized expert in the field, ought to make the approach to the White House. If Albert Einstein could be persuaded to do the speaking, the president would most likely listen to Szilard's theory about an atomic bomb. Visiting Einstein in his Long Island cottage on July 16, 1939, Szilard and another Hungarian-born physicist, Eugene Wigner, laid out their proposal. Szilard explained that a chain reaction could be produced in uranium that had been layered with graphite, allowing the neutrons to be released in order to create nuclear fission. Einstein was impressed. They explained that German physicists had somehow split a uranium atom and might be in a position to actually develop atomic weapons.

A draft letter to be presented to Roosevelt was drawn up. Over the next few days, more drafts were created. Two weeks later, during a visit to the great physicist's cottage, Szilard introduced Einstein to Edward Teller, another Hungarian-born refugee and also a theoretical physicist. The final draft of the August 2 letter was composed, typed out, and signed by Einstein. Still, with Einstein being so humble, there remained the problem of who should actually make the approach and deliver the letter to Roosevelt. After considerable confusion and attempts to determine a suitable presidential contact, Alexander Sachs was contacted. He agreed and finally made the delivery in the afternoon of October 11.[38]

Sachs was ushered into the Oval Office carrying Einstein's letter, along with a memo from Szilard, plus his own personally written summary. Roosevelt greeted Sachs warmly, saying, "Alex, what are you up to?" Over a friendly glass of brandy and after passing Einstein's letter to the president, Sachs summarized the situation in layman's terms. In essence, he was warning the president that the Nazis were working on the problem of harnessing atomic energy into a military weapon in the form of an air-delivered bomb. If Hitler and his Nazis could manufacture a usable bomb of this nature, they could conquer Europe and then focus on the rest of the world.

After listening, Roosevelt, who had mentally captured the implications of what Sachs's comments and Einstein's letter were telling him, said, "Alex, what you are after is to see that the Nazis don't blow us up!" Sachs replied with a single word: "Precisely!" At that point, the president summoned his secretary, retired Maj. Gen. Edwin ("Pa") Watson, exclaiming: "Pa, this requires action!" The lion in Roosevelt had come to the fore.[39] It was Roosevelt's most important command and foreign policy decision; it would determine the outcome of World War II and form the nucleus of his driving imperative to stop Hitler at all costs.

But time was of the essence. That same evening, an ad hoc committee known as the Advisory Committee on Uranium was set up to begin some introductory research efforts. Present were the Hungarian triumvirate of nuclear physicists, Szilard, Wigner, and Teller, who would launch the effort. Poorly funded by bureaucrats who were not given enough information to appreciate or even understand the significance of what the top-secret project was about, progress was slow. In March 1940, Szilard went to Princeton, and, at his urging, Einstein wrote and signed a second letter to the president, laying out the facts: work on uranium was being conducted in

Albert Einstein
Old Grove Rd.
Nassau Point
Peconic, Long Island

August 2nd, 1939

F.D. Roosevelt,
President of the United States,
White House
Washington, D.C.

Sir:

Some recent work by E.Fermi and L. Szilard, which has been communicated to me in manuscript, leads me to expect that the element uranium may be turned into a new and important source of energy in the immediate future. Certain aspects of the situation which has arisen seem to call for watchfulness and, if necessary, quick action on the part of the Administration. I believe therefore that it is my duty to bring to your attention the following facts and recommendations:

In the course of the last four months it has been made probable - through the work of Joliot in France as well as Fermi and Szilard in America - that it may become possible to set up a nuclear chain reaction in a large mass of uranium,by which vast amounts of power and large quantities of new radium-like elements would be generated. Now it appears almost certain that this could be achieved in the immediate future.

This new phenomenon would also lead to the construction of bombs, and it is conceivable - though much less certain - that extremely powerful bombs of a new type may thus be constructed. A single bomb of this type, carried by boat and exploded in a port, might very well destroy the whole port together with some of the surrounding territory. However, such bombs might very well prove to be too heavy for transportation by air.

Letter from Albert Einstein to President Roosevelt, August 2, 1939. (President's Secretary's Files, Franklin D. Roosevelt Presidential Library and Museum)

The United States has only very poor ores of uranium in moderate quantities. There is some good ore in Canada and the former Czechoslovakia, while the most important source of uranium is Belgian Congo.

In view of this situation you may think it desirable to have some permanent contact maintained between the Administration and the group of physicists working on chain reactions in America. One possible way of achieving this might be for you to entrust with this task a person who has your confidence and who could perhaps serve in an inofficial capacity. His task might comprise the following:

a) to approach Government Departments, keep them informed of the further development, and put forward recommendations for Government action, giving particular attention to the problem of securing a supply of uranium ore for the United States;

b) to speed up the experimental work, which is at present being carried on within the limits of the budgets of University laboratories, by providing funds, if such funds be required, through his contacts with private persons who are willing to make contributions for this cause, and perhaps also by obtaining the co-operation of industrial laboratories which have the necessary equipment.

I understand that Germany has actually stopped the sale of uranium from the Czechoslovakian mines which she has taken over. That she should have taken such early action might perhaps be understood on the ground that the son of the German Under-Secretary of State, von Weizsäcker, is attached to the Kaiser-Wilhelm-Institut in Berlin where some of the American work on uranium is now being repeated.

Yours very truly,

A. Einstein

(Albert Einstein)

Letter from Albert Einstein to President Roosevelt, August 2, 1939. (President's Secretary's Files, Franklin D. Roosevelt Presidential Library and Museum)

Berlin, and the Nazis were making progress in producing chain reactions of a huge explosive potential. And it was good that he did, since by the summer of 1940, Germany had not only gained control of large uranium deposits in Czechoslovakia but also a Norwegian heavy water factory that could be used for controlling chain reactions. Sensing the urgency of the situation, Roosevelt intervened to move the project forward. He placed Brig. Gen. Sherman Miles in charge of yet another committee.[40]

Aiding in the effort was Vannevar Bush, the head of the Carnegie Institution in Washington, DC, who in June 1940 had urged the president to create the National Defense Research Committee (NDRC). Roosevelt also established the Office of Scientific Research and Development (OSRD) by executive order on June 28. Funding allocated for the NDRC reached more than $6 million by the end of June 1941.[41] Bush, both an engineer and mathematician, became the director of the OSRD; the primary goal was to develop atomic fission by mobilizing the scientific resources of the nation.[42] V. F. Weisskopf of Austria and Enrico Fermi of Italy, among many, would soon be heard in the halls of nuclear science at such places as Hanford, Los Alamos, Oak Ridge, and the University of Chicago.

By early October 1941, Roosevelt authorized an all-out research effort aimed at the goal of producing an atomic bomb. Funding for the project would be provided to whatever extent was required to achieve success.[43] The Manhattan Project was formally launched on December 6, 1941, under the direction of Army Maj. Gen. Leslie R. Groves, then commanding the Manhattan Engineer District.[44] Roosevelt's decision had charted the course that would ultimately lead to the building of the atomic bomb— history's deadliest military force at that time.

Meanwhile, what had been happening in Europe? Despite the blockade established by the British to economically isolate Germany after its invasion of Poland, the results of the Nazi conquest in the east were providential for Hitler. The Hitler-Stalin Pact guaranteed that a constant flow of raw materials were sent to Germany.[45] The Wehrmacht had successfully tested its battle doctrine, known as the Blitzkrieg. A confident Hitler now sought to exploit his battle-tested army by turning the tables on the British and French. In May–June 1940, the Wehrmacht tore apart Holland, Belgium, Luxembourg, and France in rapid succession, forcing the evacuation of the defeated British Expeditionary Force from Dunkirk. Nazi Germany now ruled Western Europe from Norway to the Spanish Pyrenees.

May 29, 1940, the Gallup Poll released a survey: "Do you think the United States should declare war on Germany and send our army and navy to fight abroad?" The overwhelming response was a 93 percent "No."[46] In England, Winston Churchill replaced a discredited Neville Chamberlain as Britain's prime minister. On May 15, Churchill sent Roosevelt a startling request for among other things: a "loan of forty or fifty of your older destroyers; . . . several hundred of the latest types of aircraft" and permission to purchase steel from the United States.[47] As the days passed, Churchill intimated that failure to support his request might force Britain to turn the Royal Fleet over to the Germans as part of a bargain for survival.[48] If the shockingly rapid defeat of France did not stir the American president, Churchill's pleas for help most surely did.

Over the next several months, Britain and the United States worked out a 99-year leasing pact: destroyers for naval and air bases (Newfoundland, Bermuda, Bahamas, Jamaica, St. Lucia, Trinidad, and British Guiana). Roosevelt lost no time in requesting Congress pass legislation to further expand the navy, over and above that which had been authorized in 1938. Here, his experience as assistant secretary of the navy in World War I came to the fore. During that war he had supervised the navy's civilian personnel and construction yards, worked out estimates of supplies needed for the war and the production capacity of plants, all the while eliminating red tape and inefficient middlemen, to increase the flow of supplies for the navy's expanding construction effort.[49]

The Naval Expansion Act of 1940 was signed into law on June 15. Two days later, CNO Adm. Stark requested Congress to authorize $4 billion for the navy, to increase the combat fleet by 70 percent—an additional 257 ships, including 18 aircraft carriers, and 15,000 aircraft over and above that which had been approved in 1938. Called the Two-Ocean Naval Expansion Act, it was approved on July 19; the navy would now surge forward in construction, awarding contracts for 210 new ships, including 12 aircraft carriers and 7 battleships, to be able to defend both the Atlantic and the Pacific Ocean coastal regions.[50]

This seemingly incredible expansion of the navy might on the surface appear to be rather absurd, given the fact that the United States was still in the throes of the Great Depression and unemployment was around 10 million in 1939. However, by the end of the 1930s, the key fact about the American economy was that it was significantly underutilizing in its manufacturing capacity. Even so, the United States in 1938 produced 26.4 million tons of steel, well ahead of Germany's 20.7 million tons, the Soviet Union's 16.5 million tons, and Japan's 6 million tons. While the steel industries of Germany, Japan, and the Soviet Union were working at full capacity, *two-thirds* of the American steel plants were idle.

The doubling of the navy's combat fleet would now begin to jump-start the American economy. In August, Congress passed the first peacetime Selective Service and Training Act, which established an army of some 1 million men and authorized the calling up of the Army Reserves and National Guard for active duty, further reducing the jobless rate.[51]

A May 22 Gallup Poll found that 90 percent of Americans would support an increase in the U.S. Armed Forces.[52] All these initiatives now complemented Gen. George Marshall's earlier, Roosevelt-approved actions on behalf of the English war effort, providing half a million U.S. Army .30 caliber rifles left over from World War I, as well as some 900 French 75 model field guns, thousands of machine guns, and related stocks of ammunition.[53] In early September, it was announced that the British would get 50 of the navy's World War I–type destroyers. The destroyers-for-bases deal gave Churchill what he wanted most: an alliance.

On the other side of the world, the successful German conquests of Holland and France had provided new opportunities for Japan and had whetted Japan's appetite for expansion into Southeast Asia. Back in July 1939, in reaction to the continued Japanese presence and aggression in China, Hull had notified Tokyo that the Treaty of 1911, dealing with economic trade with Japan, would terminate on January 26, 1940. If the Treaty were to lapse, Japan would be vulnerable to any economic pressure that the United States desired to place upon it. That September 1939, as war commenced in Europe, Ambassador Grew stressed in conversations with Roosevelt that U.S. sanctions against Japan might lead to war. He further emphasized that an embargo placed on oil exports to Japan would probably cause the Japanese to make a thrust into the Dutch East Indies to obtain replacement petroleum resources.[54] In an attempt to further solidify their control of conquered Chinese territories, the following March (1940), the Japanese established their "New Central Government of China" at Nanking. Chiang Kai-Shek, in turn, merely retreated westward ever deeper into the mountains, reestablishing his own seat of government at Chunking.

With the defeat of the Dutch and French—the colonial powers in Southeast Asia—in Europe and the distraction of the British in terms of protecting their British East Indies possessions, it was obvious to both Japanese economic and military planners that a bounty of raw materials such as oil, iron ore, scrap iron, nickel ore, bauxite, manganese ore, chrome ore, rubber, and tin were now there for anyone willing to make the move. Japan hoped to obtain a million metric tons of oil from the Dutch East Indies.[55] Losing no time in exploiting the situation, that summer of 1940 Tokyo announced the formation of its Greater East Asia Co-Prosperity Sphere. It was a euphemism for the establishment of its soon-to-be economic and political hegemony in the region.[56]

A U.S. naval attaché cable dispatched from Tokyo reported on Premier Konoye's August 2 statement that "Japan's fundamental policy is to establish perpetual world peace in accordance with the great spirit of the foundation of the Empire." Another attaché report described Konoye's perspective on the Imperial Way, *Kodo*, as the new order to be attained in Greater East Asia. First would come the "settlement of the China affair," and second, there would take place the advancement of the "national fortune."[57] McCollum, an expert on Japanese culture, commented:

The Japanese have been great mystics. You have *Kodo*—the Imperial Way, *Hakko Ichiu* means eight directions of the world under the Imperial sway, that's Chinese for one unity. In other words, the entire world under Japanese domination.[58]

While this added another problem on British Prime Minister Churchill's full plate, he was in no position to deal with it. Neither could the now-conquered French Vichy government; on September 23, Japan had taken over northern Indochina with the intention of cutting off all supplies currently moving through the region to Chiang Kai-shek. Japan was also pressuring the British to close down the Burma Road as part of Tokyo's strategy to isolate the Chinese.

On September 27, 1940, Japan, duly impressed by Germany's military successes in conquering Europe, and with the apparent intention of intimidating the United States, entered into the Tripartite Pact with Germany and Italy. Ironically this military alliance now linked Japan with Roosevelt's de facto primary enemy, Nazi Germany. It also meant that Germany had linked itself to Japan with a promise to come to the latter's aid in the event that Japan should find itself at war with a third party such as the United States.[59]

This linkage now provided Roosevelt with the opportunity to get at Nazi Germany by exploiting the alliance against itself in the form of a trap. If Japan could be baited into going to war against the United States, Nazi Germany would, by obligation, have to declare war on the United States—thus springing the trap. In so doing, the United States could now directly face off against its deadliest enemy.

Roosevelt took the new Rome-Berlin-Tokyo AXIS as a potential design for war. Thoroughly incensed, he called the pact an "unholy alliance" with the ultimate aim of trying to "dominate and enslave the entire human race."[60] His reaction took the form of showing his displeasure through a series of economic sanctions, which in the main meant placing a ban on the export of scrap iron and steel to Japan. The White House made an announcement in late September, indicating that all scrap export licenses would be revoked in mid-October and new ones would only be issued for Great Britain and other destinations in the Western Hemisphere. Also included in the embargo were shipments of high-octane gasoline, fuel oil, aircraft parts and engines, and certain minerals and chemicals.[61] A short time later, iron ore, pig iron, copper, and brass would be added to the embargo. This was in reaction to an ONI intelligence report, dated October 16, 1940, which stated that the Japanese had plans to seize the Dutch East Indies.[62] It was sent to the CNO and forwarded to Roosevelt two days later.

The summer of 1940 found Churchill attempting to mobilize the British Empire for a life-or-death war against Nazi Germany. Albeit for the moment, his industrial plant could outbuild that of Hitler's in both aircraft and tank production, Churchill would badly need the logistical support of the United States over the long run if he was to win the war. Additionally, even though the Royal Navy was overwhelmingly superior in combatant capital ship surface craft compared to Hitler's Kriegsmarine, the German U-boat submarine service was now so rapidly increasing in strength and improving its attack capabilities that it would soon offset the Royal Navy advantage and severely challenge Britain's antisubmarine efforts in the Atlantic.[63]

In early August, Hitler unleashed his Luftwaffe against England in an aerial campaign involving a 2,500-plane attack, lasting some two months. Hitler's mission was to take control of the air over England as a prelude to a cross-Channel attack by the Wehrmacht against the British Isles. The Royal Air Force (RAF) doggedly held its own, shooting down two Luftwaffe planes to the RAF's one. Barges, ferries, and other ships earmarked for the invasion of the British Isles were being assembled along the Belgian and French coastal areas in preparation for Hitler's Operation Sea Lion, but by mid-October, the Luftwaffe's planes had been driven out of the sky by day. The invasion had failed, and Hitler's orders shifted to the destruction of London and other English cities.

Throughout the winter and spring of 1941, the German planes bombed only at night, taking out their revenge against civilian targets. In spite of causing significant civilian casualties and property damage, the Germans lost the Battle of Britain. There would be no invasion. The inspiring and stout British defense against superior odds impressed Americans and Roosevelt alike.

Breckenridge Long, a friend and confidant of Roosevelt, noted in his War Diary on September 14, 1940, that Secretary of State Hull and Ambassador Grew agreed about the Japanese situation in the Far East: the only way to deal with the Japanese was through a show of force. FDR's "administration has made up its mind to deal firmly with Japan and that no steps will be spared and that those steps may even lead to war."[64] Roosevelt's hardened thinking was beginning to permeate the higher echelons of American government. One of these was McCollum.

As an officer in Naval Intelligence, McCollum had a unique background, unlike any other military intelligence officer involved with the political-military affairs of Japan. Born in 1898 in Nagasaki to Southern Baptist missionary parents, he was speaking Japanese before he could speak English. He became one of the navy's primary experts in Japanese affairs. As an assistant naval attaché at the American Embassy in Tokyo in 1928, he taught Japanese to a number of naval officers, including Joseph J. Rochefort, Edward Layton, and Ethelbert Watts (Watts became an assistant to McCollum at F-2 in 1941).[65]

From 1922 to 1925 McCollum intensively studied Japan's language, as well as its history and culture. He became acquainted with Nagano Osami and Isoroko Yamamoto, both of whom became key admirals in the IJN. Crown Prince Hirohito even invited McCollum to teach the young Crown Prince the latest American Roaring Twenties dances, including the Charleston.[66]

Significantly, it was McCollum's understanding of the Japanese psyche, the sense of cultural uniqueness, the traditions of emperor worship and veneration of the state, and the samurai ethos of military honor and valor, with its emphasis on discipline and fortitude, that set McCollum apart from others.[67] He understood that these values had produced a culture that was at once fiercely patriotic and undeterred by sacrifices in the name of national honor and interest and also unwilling to accept any form of failure or defeat ("death before dishonor") in the pursuit of its strategic goals. National humiliation was unacceptable.

By late 1940, McCollum, as the head of F-2, realized that Japan was so driven by the urge for imperial power that its leaders' intentions to expand were a natural reflection of the nation's fundamental cultural imperatives. While Japan's aggressiveness might appear to be a strength out of proportion to the other countries and territories in the Western Pacific, it had a hidden, serious vulnerability: Japan was unprepared to face an equal adversary.

In late 1940, army cryptanalysts broke Japan's most sophisticated diplomatic code through the use of an army-developed PURPLE Code machine. The product of this operation was called MAGIC in Washington. The nature of McCollum's work meant that he was a recipient of not only the English translations of IJN signal intercepts in the Pacific but also military attaché reports, American Embassy reports of a diplomatic and economic nature, public media, and even the army-navy English translations of the PURPLE intercept system's highly classified Japanese diplomatic traffic between Tokyo and its various embassies throughout the world.

Of particular interest to McCollum were the reports from Dutch sources regarding the September 12 visit of a Japanese trade delegation to Batavia in the Netherlands East Indies. The delegation was forthright. Japan wanted the Dutch to increase their annual oil exports to Japan from the current 570,000 tons (10 million barrels) to some 3,750,000 tons (60 million barrels) or about 100 percent of the total Dutch East Indies production capacity. The end result of the negotiations was that Batavia agreed to deliver 1.8 million tons of petroleum products or about 40 percent of what Japan was obtaining from the United States (4.5 million tons).[68] That previous January, *Life* magazine had published a five-page article on the Dutch East Indies, informing its readers about Batavia's export capacity as well as the fact that the United States was selling 30 million barrels of oil annually to Japan.[69]

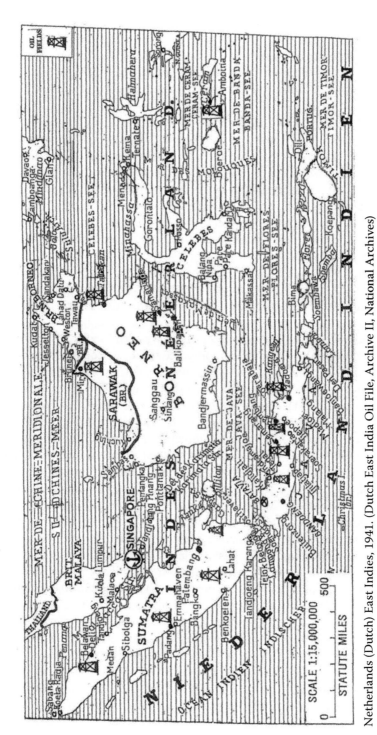

Netherlands (Dutch) East Indies, 1941. (Dutch East India Oil File, Archive II, National Archives)

At this point, Japan's war machine in China badly needed Dutch oil, along with the high octane aviation gasoline produced by Royal Dutch Shell and the American-owned Standard Oil of New Jersey. If Japan lost its American oil import market, it would have nowhere to turn, except to the Netherlands (Dutch) East Indies. If this effort also failed, then its war effort in China would be placed in jeopardy, probably grinding to a humiliating halt. Of the NEI's some 20,000 islands, only Java (Rembang, Madoera, Samarang, and Soerabaya oil fields), Sumatra (Belawan, Laanfket, Padang, Palembanga, and Pertak oil fields), Borneo (Balikpapan, Kotai, Samarinda, and Tarakan oil fields), Celebes, and New Guinea (Ceram oil field) were of interest to the Japanese—all because of their prolific oil fields, as well as rubber, tin, rice, tea, quinine, tobacco, sugar, and sulfur.[70] These fields extended over an area as large as the continental United States.

All this was not lost on McCollum. As the navy's premier intelligence expert on the Japanese, he had gained the respect of those who appreciated his weekly intelligence reports, with their insights into the thinking of Japan's key leaders. That September 1940, as Hitler's Luftwaffe pummeled the British Isles, McCollum was well aware of the Roosevelt administration's frustration in its attempts to arouse Americans to face the reality of what was obviously becoming an evolving Nazi menace. Working at both the strategic and operational levels of intelligence gave McCollum access to the Oval Office unlike any other midgrade naval officer. Uniquely aware of the ramifications of the Tripartite Pact, and with war in the Pacific between Japan and the United States already a distinct possibility, McCollum sensed the need for someone to create a strategy that would enable the president to deal with both the singularly important Nazi threat in Europe and the aggressive Japanese in the Far East. He took it upon himself to offer a solution in a strategic concept paper.

The navy's War Plans Division's War Plan Orange had now evolved into the Rainbow series of war plans. Both Orange and Rainbow were fundamentally strategies geared to taking advantage of Japan's vulnerability to an economic blockade. By 1940, McCollum knew that while Japan produced enough food, its industrial plant and war-making efforts were dependent on access to iron ore, steel, and oil.[71] McCollum was well versed in War Plan Orange and developed an innovative strategy to bring about a policy endgame in the Pacific.

McCollum laid out his strategy in a five-page memorandum under the dual letterheads of the Office of the Chief of Naval Operations and Office of Naval Intelligence (OP-16, F-2). It was titled "Estimate of the Situation in the Pacific and Recommendations for Action by the United States." Using his comprehensive understanding of the Japan's economic vulnerabilities, psyche, and attitudes toward the United States, McCollum produced a well-thought-out, brilliant plan to goad Tokyo into committing an overt act of war against the United States. Dated October 7, 1940, the memo was intended to be distributed, at a minimum, to CNO Adm. Stark and Rear Adm. Walter Stratton Anderson, the veteran director of ONI.

The chain of command had to be followed; it led from Anderson through Stark directly to Roosevelt himself. Considering that both admirals had the ear of the president on a frequent if not daily basis and that McCollum himself was one of the key staff officers and briefers for diplomatic and military messages, as well as F-2 intelligence summaries and reports going directly to the president's naval aide at the White House, McCollum undoubtedly presumed that his memo would make it into the president's hands. As part of McCollum's work, he was also responsible for overseeing the routing of special, analytical communications intelligence reports to the Oval Office.[72] (See Appendix A, this volume.)

After a brief analysis of the global military situation, including that Germany and Italy had been seriously attempting to "foster a continuation of American indifference to the outcome of the struggle in Europe," McCollum noted that they had failed in this endeavor. The United States, he stated, was now more and more becoming "a full-fledged ally of the British Empire" to the degree that now Germany and Italy had embarked upon a "policy of developing threats to U.S. security in other spheres of the world." Germany and Italy had "concluded a military alliance with Japan directed against the United States." The "three totalitarian powers" were prepared to make war on the United States "should she come to the assistance of England or should she forcibly interfere with Japan's aims in the Orient." This deep understanding of the real significance of Tripartite Pact led McCollum to conclude that "once the British Empire is gone the power of Japan-Germany and Italy is to be directed against the United States." Whether deliberately intended or not, this appreciation of the situation coincided with how Roosevelt viewed the Nazi menace.

Gallup polls released earlier on June 9 and July 7, 1940, indicated that while Americans under the age of 45 would overwhelmingly (86 percent) be willing to fight if the United States were attacked, otherwise they would overwhelmingly (86 percent) vote to stay out of a war in Europe.[73] McCollum concluded that domestic American political opinion would similarly remain adamant against declaring war against Japan unless there was "more ado." In this case "ado," as McCollum termed it, meant creating a series of actions so humiliating and troublesome to Japan's leaders that they would lash out militantly against the United States, thus presenting the American people with a fait accompli in the form of an overt act of war, forcing the United States to react.

To achieve this, McCollum laid out eight specific actions on page 4 as a "course of action":

1. Make an arrangement with Britain for the use of British bases in the Pacific, particularly Singapore.

2. Make an arrangement with Holland for the use of base facilities and acquisition of supplies in the Dutch East Indies.

3. Give all possible aid to the Chinese Government of Chiang-Kai-Shek.

4. Send a division of long-range heavy cruisers to the Orient, Philippines, or Singapore.

5. Send two divisions of submarines to the Orient.

6. Keep the main strength of the U.S. Fleet now in the Pacific in the vicinity of the Hawaiian Islands.

7. Insist that the Dutch refuse to grant Japanese demands for undue economic concessions, particularly oil.

8. Completely embargo all U.S. trade with Japan, in collaboration with a similar embargo imposed by the British Empire.

As part of his conclusion, McCollum stated, "If by these means Japan could be led to commit an overt act of war, so much the better." His Action H was on the mark. Indeed, this was a stellar Machiavellian strategy of the first degree that would appeal to Roosevelt's own foxlike psyche. The next year would see the president actually implementing in innovative ways all of McCollum's recommended actions.

A Gallup Poll on October 28 asked, "Do you think our Government should forbid the sale of arms, airplanes, gasoline and other war materials to Japan?" Some 90 percent of Americans responded with a resounding "Yes."[74]

Coincidentally, on October 8, the day after McCollum's memorandum (also known as the "8-Action Memorandum" or simply the "McCollum Memo") began working its way up through the chain of command, Roosevelt met with his commander-in-chief U.S. Fleet (CINCUS), Adm. James O. ("Joe") Richardson. While the admiral had in mind to sound out the president about some issues that were of great concern to him, at the same time Roosevelt had in his own mind a similar interest. As a former undersecretary of the Navy, he understood clearly what he wanted from his highest ranking naval officers.

One reason the meeting took place was the fact that earlier, in the spring of 1940, the president had ordered the navy's U.S. Fleet, then on training exercises in the vicinity of the Hawaiian Islands, to remain in the Islands (McCollum's Action F was already in play). While the objective of the move was allegedly to have a "deterrent effect" on the Japanese doings in the East Indies, this essentially moved the fleet out of its extensive permanent basing areas in California and into the Pearl Harbor cul-de-sac formed by the island of Oahu.[75]

Adm. Richardson did not like the idea, vividly describing the Pearl Harbor naval base as "a Goddamned mousetrap." Richardson considered that his fleet could not only better train and maintain a higher state of readiness while in its California bases but also better defend the West Coast of the United States. The fleet's forward posting to Hawaii without its logistical supply ships essentially neutralized its offensive, transpacific striking capability. Earlier, Adm. Stark had made the same points but had been overruled by Roosevelt, and in this case, Richardson would be, too. While Roosevelt's CINCUS was interested in the operational and tactical effectiveness and safety of his fleet, the president was interested in a far higher strategic level of politics.[76]

As the conversation continued, the president mentioned that an idea of his was to provoke the Japanese into making a "mistake" by placing a U.S. Navy ship in harm's way. He then went on to say, "Sooner or later the Japanese would commit an overt act against the United States and the nation would be willing to enter the war."[77] Angered by Roosevelt's apparent insensitivity to the safety of the navy men and warships in the Pacific, an exasperated Richardson exclaimed, "Mr. President, senior officers of the Navy do not have the trust and confidence in the civilian leadership of this country that is essential for the successful prosecution of a war in the Pacific."[78] The discussion finally ended with a pained Roosevelt declaring, "Joe, you just don't understand."[79]

From Roosevelt's perspective, not only was Adm. Richardson not a team player in the sense that he would not do the president's bidding without an obstinate confrontation, but now he had bluntly insulted the president to his face. Slightly less than four months later, after Roosevelt had been reelected to an unprecedented third term in November 1940 and duly sworn in, in January 1941, Joe Richardson found himself relieved of his U.S. Fleet command on February 1, 1941; his showdown with his commander-in-chief had backfired.

In early November 1940, apparently synergized by McCollum's 8-Point Memorandum, Adm. Stark had come up with his own appreciation of America's national situation, dated November 12, 1940. In this "Plan Dog," as his 26-page memorandum to Secretary of War Stimson became known, Stark discounted the Pacific as a primary focus for the United States and advocated a Germany-first focus. The survival of England and its Royal Navy were paramount.[80] Roosevelt reacted to the CNO's memorandum in dramatic fashion. On December 29, in one of his famous radio Fireside Chats, he spoke of the United States becoming the "Arsenal of Democracy," proposing what would become the Lend-Lease program to aid England in its struggle to survive against the threat of Nazi invasion. Portraying the world as divided between good and evil, the president spoke of the situation being "an emergency as serious as war itself."[81]

Albeit that he had promised American voters before his reelection "that American boys were not going to be sent into foreign wars," Roosevelt's initiative was generally on good ground. In October, 83 percent of Americans wanted to "stay out" of a war against Germany and Italy. By November 18, responding to the question, "If it appears that England will be defeated by Germany and Italy unless the United States supplies her with more food and war materials, would you be in favor of giving more help to England?" an overwhelming 90 percent responded "Yes."[82]

Things were not going well for the British. Under constant Luftwaffe bombardment, a distressed Churchill wrote Roosevelt a letter dated December 8, 1940, from his 10 Downing Street office. Churchill laid out the case that monthly shipping losses from German U-boats were now so substantial that the continued "diminution" would be fatal to England's survival. The situation was becoming more and more desperate each day. In essence, the Royal Navy was currently taxed beyond its capabilities and only the intervention of the U.S. Navy could tip the scales and propel the British onto a winning curve against the U-boat peril.[83]

Two days later, Roosevelt requested that Congress pass the Lend-Lease Act, which would enable the British to borrow the ships and weapons needed to fight Germany and then return them at the end of the emergency.[84] In March, both houses of Congress had passed the bill, allowing Roosevelt to sell, lend, or give war materials to nations his administration wanted to support.

In early January, Roosevelt sent his close confidant and alter ego, Harry Hopkins, as his personal emissary to England to confer with Winston Churchill. Knowing that Churchill needed to be reassured and buoyed up in terms of where America stood in his struggle to confront the Nazi onslaught in the air and on the sea in the face of a possible cross-Channel invasion, Roosevelt gave Hopkins explicit instructions. At Whitehall, Hopkins explained to Churchill that while America was not in the war, she was marching beside England. He went on to say about Roosevelt's attitude toward England:

> The president is determined that we shall win the war together. Make no mistake about it. . . . He has sent me here to tell you that at all costs and by all means he will carry through, no matter what happens to him—there is no thing he will not do so far as he has the human power.[85]

In his memoirs, Churchill summarized Hopkins's statements by saying that the "cause" would now be "the defeat, ruin and slaughter of Hitler, to the exclusion of all other purposes, loyalties or aims."[86] Winston Churchill had now become aware of Franklin Roosevelt's driving imperative to bring down Nazi Germany as the number one priority of his administration's foreign policy.

Another interesting development took place in late January 1941 involving an American Embassy diplomatic report out of Tokyo. A member of Ambassador Grew's diplomatic office staff had been approached by a senior member of the Peruvian embassy, who provided an insightful report on future Japanese military contingency planning. Received by Secretary of State Cordell Hull on January 27, 1941, the ambassador's telegram stated:

MY PERUVIAN COLLEAGUE TOLD A MEMBER OF MY STAFF THAT HE HAD HEARD FROM MANY SOURCES INCLUDING A JAPANESE SOURCE THAT JAPANESE MILITARY FORCES PLANNED IN THE EVENT OF TROUBLE WITH THE UNITED STATES, TO ATTEMPT A SURPRISE ATTACK ON PEARL HARBOR USING ALL OF THEIR MILITARY FACILITIES. HE ADDED THAT ALTHOUGH THE PROJECT SEEMED FANTASTIC THE FACT THAT HE HAD HEARD IT FROM MANY SOURCES PROMPTED HIM TO PASS THE INFORMATION. GREW[87]

Secretary Hull distributed copies of Grew's cable to Army Intelligence (G-2) and ONI. ONI then passed the information on to Arthur McCollum at F-2 to get his appraisal.

This now placed McCollum in a quandary. His own 8-Action strategy paper, written just a few months earlier, called for the basing of the U.S. Fleet at Pearl Harbor (Action F) as part of the overall plan to antagonize and otherwise goad the Japanese into lashing out at the United States militarily with an overt act. Whether the Japanese lashing out took place against the Philippines, Midway, Wake, and Hawaiian Islands, or even the West Coast of the United States, was immaterial. What counted was that it took place. Rather than substantiate the possibility that such an attack could take place at Hawaii sometime in the distant future, McCollum pointedly quashed the idea; on February 1, 1941, he sent an analysis to the newly designated commander-in-chief Pacific Fleet, Adm. Husband E. Kimmel, which contradicted and thoroughly downplayed the importance of Grew's cable. McCollum's analysis succinctly stated, "The Division of Naval Intelligence places no credence in these rumors." He further went on to say that "based on known data regarding the present disposition and employment of Japanese naval and army forces, no move against Pearl Harbor appears imminent or planned for the foreseeable future."[88]

What is amazing about McCollum's analysis is that it completely ignored the multisource aspect of Ambassador Grew's report. The minimum that should have taken place was for McCollum to reply back through Hull to Grew and request verification and details on the various Peruvian sources before sending out his own analysis to Kimmel.[89] That would have been the professional approach to the situation. Instead, McCollum adhered to his 8-point strategy; by so doing, he did a great disservice to the Pacific Fleet by lulling Adm. Kimmel and his staff into a false sense of security in terms of the possibility of a Japanese transpacific naval attack taking place against Pearl Harbor. Was this an inexcusable and unprofessional lapse on his part, suggesting serious implications in terms of his loyalty, or was it done in service to Roosevelt's Machiavellian plot? Ironically, in early December 1941, during the last couple of hours prior to the actual attack on Pearl Harbor, McCollum would undergo a complete change of heart on the issue, actually trying to have Adm. Kimmel alerted to an imminent transpacific naval attack on his fleet at Pearl Harbor.

With Harry Hopkins still in England, Roosevelt agreed to the need for secret staff talks between American, British, and Canadian war planners, to deal with global war strategy and lesser regional planning. The initial meeting, known as ABC-1, took place on January 29, 1941, and resulted in the future Allies embracing a Germany-first strategy for winning the war, since Germany was the predominant member of the AXIS powers. Roosevelt's driving imperative apart, the planners were unable to agree on details involving the Pacific.[90]

On February 1, a complete restructuring of the navy's principal operational forces took place. Roosevelt embraced and then approved the concept of a two-ocean navy, dissolving the old U.S. Fleet and creating the Atlantic Fleet and the Pacific Fleet in its place. The Atlantic Fleet was to be commanded by Adm. Ernest J. King (CINCLANT) and the Pacific Fleet by newly promoted Adm. Husband E. Kimmel (CINCPAC), who had been hand-picked by the president himself over the heads of 46 senior admirals.[91] The Asiatic Fleet, commanded by Adm. Thomas Hart (CINCAF) and based in the Philippines, was left in place.

Two months later, on March 27, the ABC-1 Staff Agreement was promulgated. This planned for "full-fledged war co-operation when and if AXIS aggression forced the United States into the war." King's Atlantic Fleet was directed to take on a convoy escort mission in support of Lend-Lease shipping and supplies going to England.[92] The Rainbow 5 contingency plan was designated to deal with the anticipated global war situation involving both the Atlantic and the Pacific. The navy's OP-12 developed a supporting plan, focused on the Pacific and called WPL-46 (Navy Basic War Plan, Rainbow 5, aka WPL-46/WP Pac-46, dated May 26, 1941).[93]

In April, the Dutch, who were gravely concerned about their own vulnerability to Japanese military actions against the NEI, were also included in the planning in what was now called the ABDA (American-British-Dutch-Australian) Staff Agreement, which took place in Singapore. Fundamentally, the agreement stipulated that American military action would take place in the event of the Japanese striking British or Dutch territory. A Gallup survey taken a month earlier had asked, "Do you think the United

States should try to keep Japan from seizing the Dutch East Indies and Singapore?" The "Yes" response was 56 percent.[94] This response was probably due primarily to the flurry of articles in the American media about the Dutch East Indies and its valuable oil resources, rated at around 60 million barrels in the South Pacific.

Shortly after Adm. Kimmel took command of CINCPAC on February 1, 1941, a curious meeting took place 10 days later at the White House. Involved were Roosevelt; Secretary of War Stimson; Secretary of the Navy Frank Knox; Gen. George Marshall, army chief of staff; and Adm. Harold Stark, chief of naval operations (CNO). Roosevelt was apparently contemplating McCollum's Action D, which involved sending a division of long-range heavy cruisers to the Far East; he wanted to sound out his senior military officials as to what they thought of this idea. The president's own thoughts centered on deploying navy cruisers on patrols into the Northwest, Central, and South Pacific regions, to create confusion among the Japanese and perhaps bring about an incident with the IJN. These provocations, called "pop-up" cruises by the president, were to be deliberately carried out by small task forces within or adjacent to Japanese territorial waters.

Adm. Stark, as CNO, would now have to execute these unusual types of missions. When Stark warned Roosevelt that the cruises "will precipitate hostilities rather than prevent them," he was brushed off by the president, who cavalierly retorted: "I just want them to keep popping up here and there and keep the Japs guessing. I don't mind losing one or two cruisers, but do not take a chance on losing five or six." As such, the concept was perfectly in line with his thoughts, expressed some four months earlier to Adm. Richardson about sacrificing a navy ship and that "sooner or later the Japanese would commit an overt act against the United States and the nation would be willing to go to war."[95]

When Kimmel heard about the proposed cruises, he wrote to Stark on February 18, complaining that they were "most ill-advised." He further stated, "I believe that we should be prepared for war when we make this move."[96] But orders are orders, especially presidential ones. Between March and July, several naval detachments tailored as task forces were sent out on three distinct occasions into Japanese waters.

Historian Robert Stinnett thoroughly researched and documented those several deployments. The first took place March 15–21, 1941, and involved a task force of four navy cruisers (*Brooklyn*, *Chicago*, *Portland*, and *Savannah*) and a squadron of 12 destroyers, which deployed into the Central and South Pacific in the vicinity of the Japanese Mandates. Newspaper dispatches more than anything else revealed the American presence.[97] The second, in July and August, involving the USS *Northampton* and USS *Salt Lake City*, provided for an American pop-up presence again in the Central and South

Pacific in areas adjacent to the eastern Japanese Mandates.[98] The third and more provocative cruise took place in late July and early August, when a similar-sized task force actually swept into the Bungo Strait, which separates the Japanese islands of Kyushu and Shikoku, just to the south of Hiroshima. This area was noted by Stinnett as being an operational training area for the IJN. The chances of contact were high. The incursion did catch the IJN's attention, as it reported the apparent sighting of two cruisers on the night of July 31. No shots were fired, and the American cruisers disappeared behind a ship-generated smokescreen.[99]

The Bungo Strait patrol was exceedingly dangerous business, and the navy commanders in charge had undoubtedly figured out the real purpose of this most unusual mission: by taking the Japanese by surprise with an audacious incursion at night, the cruiser commanders involved had been able to conduct their mission without losing a single man or ship, thereby avoiding an overt act. However, since in Roosevelt's mind, it was not supposed to end that way, pop-ups would continue; the last known cruise of this nature would be personally directed by the president to take place just before the attack on Pearl Harbor.

Out in the Western Pacific and the Philippine Islands, Adm. Hart was the commander-in-chief of the Asiatic Fleet (CINCAF). His land-based senior partner was Douglas MacArthur, the former chief of staff of the army. After serving as military advisor to the Philippine president Manuel Quezon since the mid-1930s, he was appointed as the commander-in-chief of the American Army Forces Far East. Hart arrived in October 1940, and after reviewing the situation, reported his observations to the navy's CNO, Adm. Stark, suggesting that the Japanese might bypass the Philippines in order to seize the British and Dutch possessions to the south. Four months later, on February 7, 1941, Hart was informed that U.S. war planners believed that Japan would attack the Philippines, making war inevitable.[100]

Adm. Hart could feel somewhat relieved in that Japan was now four years into intensive warfare in China, with over a million men thoroughly bogged down and no end in sight. The United States had helped out by providing a $25 million loan in September 1940 to Generalissimo Chiang Kai-shek, to help bolster his defense of central China.[101] Further actions would take place to favor China; on April 15, 1941, Roosevelt issued an executive order that authorized army, navy, and marine corps officers to fly and fight in China on a voluntary basis.[102] Over the next several months, 100 volunteer pilots—known as the American Volunteer Group (AVG) or simply the Flying Tigers—were hired by the Chinese government. In addition, 181 ground personnel to service 100 P-40 Warhawk fighters would be deployed, first to Burma and then on into China.[103]

That April, Japan and the Soviet Union formally signed a neutrality treaty, agreeing to respect each other's territorial integrity and inviolability and to remain neutral if the other became an object of military action by a third power. This, Tokyo hoped, would deter the Soviets from considering any expansion into East Asia, allowing Japan to focus its Manchuria-based military forces on its intended expansion efforts to points south.[104]

Over in the Atlantic, things were seemingly going better. An ONI report dated March 27 indicated that as of mid-March 1941, the British shipping situation was now beginning to hold its own. While some 5,323,733 tons of shipping had been sunk or otherwise lost, the losses had been replaced by more than 6,690,000 tons of new construction, captures, purchases, and allied and neutral ships on charter or in British service.[105] Using his Plan Dog as a justification, Stark now transferred the aircraft carrier *Yorktown* and three battleships from Kimmel's Pacific Fleet to the Atlantic, where the powerful Royal Navy's surface fleet was actually concentrated against a comparatively smaller German Kriegsmarine, which did not have an operational aircraft carrier. The transfer made no sense, since the Royal Navy had eight aircraft carriers (two in the British Isles, two in the Eastern Mediterranean, two in the Western Mediterranean, one in the North Atlantic, and one in the South Atlantic) and nine battleships (located in either the British Isles or in the North Atlantic on convoy duty).[106] The move diminished the Pacific Fleet's long-range striking power, while keeping the remainder of the fleet in the relatively vulnerable position that the now-relieved Adm. Richardson had warned about.

In Europe, Hitler continued to march. At the end of April, he unleashed Gen. Erwin Rommel's Afrika Korps against a British army equivalent in Libya. This began a seesaw campaign in the desert, lasting some two years, over who would control North Africa, the Middle Eastern approaches into both the Suez Canal and the region's oilfields. More importantly, on April 6, the Wehrmacht attacked Yugoslavia and Greece; in 18 days, both countries had surrendered, consolidating Hitler's control of central Europe and completely driving the British off the continent. These events and a naval incident, involving the sinking of an American merchant ship *Robin Moor* en route from New York to Cape Town on May 21 by a German U-boat operating outside the blockade zone, brought things to a head.

The White House responded with Roosevelt's May 27 proclamation of an "Unlimited National Emergency," which essentially placed America on a de facto war footing in the Atlantic, demanding that military and civilian defense interests be readied to "repel any and all acts or threats of aggression directed toward any part of the Western Hemisphere." All citizens were exhorted to place the needs of the nation as a first priority and set aside their lesser differences on behalf of national defense. Each community was to do its part for "maximum productive effort and minimum of waste and unnecessary frictions." It was a rallying cry and a plea to the people to rise to the occasion "to the end that we may mobilize and have ready for instant defensive use all of the physical powers, all of the moral strength and all of the material resources of this nation."[107]

In Europe, almost on cue, Adolf Hitler, now brimming with confidence and maniacal ego, made one of his major strategic blunders. Breaking his erstwhile alliance with Russia's Joseph Stalin on June 22, he ordered his 3-million-man Wehrmacht to invade the Soviet Union along a 2,000-mile-wide front, from the White Sea in the north to the Black Sea in the south. While impressive in terms of numbers on paper, the German army was not properly equipped or prepared in any sense of the word for the long, drawn-out struggle that lay ahead. Hitler had now committed Germany to fighting a war on three major fronts (British Isles, Africa, and Russia), something he had vowed would never happen. The invasion of Russia reinforced Roosevelt's perception that Hitler, with his insatiable appetite for conquest, was the number one threat to U.S. national security. Even with all these developments, a Gallup Poll released June 29 indicated that 76 percent of Americans wanted to stay out of war.[108]

The military services were not far behind in supporting Roosevelt's proclamation. In his annual report to the president for the fiscal year, U.S. Navy Secretary Knox noted that as of June 30, the navy had 697 vessels under construction, including 12 fleet aircraft carriers, or more carriers than the IJN had.[109] There were also some 15,000 planes of all types programmed for construction in 1941, to flesh out the naval aviation expansion program.[110] On July 1, 1941, Gen. George Marshall reported in his biennial analysis of the state of the armed forces that the army had "increased eightfold [since July 1, 1939] and consists of approximately 1,400,000 men."[111]Although not officially at war, no matter what the anti-war mood of the country was, Roosevelt's military was on the march.

With the PURPLE Code machine intercept operation now in full swing, Roosevelt was able to read firsthand the MAGIC messages being sent via Japan's highest level diplomatic code. A similar machine also served Winston Churchill. Japan's diplomatic and military leaders had no idea that the code had been broken and that their embassy reports from all over the world, as well as Tokyo's decisions and promulgations of political policies, were now being read by America's key leaders every day. Over the next half year, hundreds of PURPLE messages would be intercepted, decoded, translated, reviewed, and analyzed by Roosevelt and his Secretaries of State, War (Army), and Navy, as well as their key operations and intelligence staffs.

PURPLE was continuously bearing fruit and producing key pieces of information essential to understanding Tokyo's intentions, policies, and political-military strategies for its Far Eastern operations. Besides Tokyo and its Washington, DC, embassy, other users were the Japanese embassies and consulates in Berlin, London, Rome, Ankara, Berne, Mexico City,

Bangkok, Hong Kong, Hanoi, Singapore, Manila, and Batavia. That April, intercepts revealed that Japanese Foreign Minister Yosuke Matsuoka had told Hitler that "sooner or later a war with the United States would be unavoidable" and that "this conflict would happen sooner rather than later." In turn, Hitler had promised that "Germany would conduct a most energetic fight against America."[112]

An intercept from Tokyo to its Berlin embassy on July 2, 1941, indicated Japan's intent to move forward toward "establishing the Greater East Asia Sphere of Co-prosperity, regardless of how the world situation may change." It further reiterated its "endeavor" to finish the war in China and at the same time to "take measures with a view to advancing southward" in order to secure the resources necessary to guarantee Japan's ability to continue its war effort. Another part of the same message stated that in order to bring down the regime of Chiang Kai-Shek, measures would be taken by applying pressure from the south, involving French Indochina and Thailand, in an effort to further isolate China from international aid.[113] While the war in China would remain a top priority for Japan, another priority, now considered equally as important, would be carried out in terms of capturing the highly vulnerable British and Dutch possessions to the south.

Twelve days later, on July 14, another intercept of considerable importance to Roosevelt revealed that Japan was undergoing a general mobilization in order "to put an end to Anglo-American" efforts to thwart Japan's expansion southward. The immediate Japanese object was to "occupy French Indochina peacefully but if resistance is offered, we will crush it by force." The message went on to say that the Netherlands Indies would be given an ultimatum, but if that did not work, then it, too, would be seized by force. British Singapore was also on the agenda for seizure, with the IJN playing the principal role. Having commented on the missions of the dozen or so IJA divisions that would be involved in the various invasions, the message summed up Tokyo's intentions: "We will once and for all crush Anglo-American military power and their ability to assist in any schemes against us."[114] It was a statement of Japan's intention to go to war against not only the British and the Dutch, but also the United States in the Pacific. Tokyo was now embarking on a course of action that would produce the "mistake" or "overt act" that Roosevelt had talked about with Adm. Richardson eight months earlier.

The situation now gave Roosevelt two obvious choices: one would be to do nothing and let events take their course; the other would be to do as McCollum suggested in his Actions G and H, to create "more ado" in order to obtain an full-blown overt act, which could then be exploited politically in order to propel the United States into war. A PURPLE intercept dated July 21, from the Japanese Embassy in Washington to Tokyo, reported on

Acting Secretary of State Welles's conversation with Kaname Wakasugi, the Japanese Embassy's first minister. It stated that Welles had said that any Japanese advances into the southern portion of French Indochina would be taken by Washington as a violation of the spirit of the then ongoing Japanese-U.S. conversations toward maintaining peace in the Pacific.[115]

Two days later, Tokyo replied: any steps taken by the United States, including "the freezing of assets," could create "an exceedingly critical situation." Additional comments on July 24 stated that should a freeze be put into effect on Japanese funds inside the United States, it would "hasten the development of the worst [war] situation."[116] During the first week of June 1941, Japan's reported assets inside the United States amounted to about $160 million, of which $104 million were in bank deposits and another $12 million in mostly U.S. government paper securities. Once Hitler had launched his June 22 invasion of the Soviet Union, Japanese trade with Germany terminated, as the Trans-Siberian Railway route, delivering such items as machine tools, was shut down to all German trade.[117]

Now isolated from Europe, Japan's only medium of international exchange was the U.S. dollar. It was vulnerable to financial sanctions. On a positive note for Japan, the German attack against Russia now served as a distraction to Stalin, reducing Tokyo's fears of any possibility of a Soviet stab in the back with an attack into Manchuria. As such, Tokyo began to look south in earnest, toward the easy pickings of Southeast Asia. If Japan could take the southern part of French Indochina, both the British naval base at Singapore and portions of the Dutch East Indies would be within range of its land-based bombers. Also of some importance was the fact that Indochina had vital tin and rubber utilized for the American industrial plant. This would now be cut off and diverted to Japan for its own industrial effort.

Beginning in early July 1941, Japanese military planners decided to occupy southern Indochina, as indicated by the intercepted PURPLE-originated diplomatic message traffic read in Washington. McCollum's OP-16-F-2 duly noted Japan's July 1 worldwide recall of its merchant marine shipping. This recall pointed toward something important taking place in the near future. Some four days later, under Roosevelt's orders, Japan's merchant marine shipping was denied transit rights through the Panama Canal. This meant that the ships now had to return to Japan via the lengthy, roundabout Straits of Magellan, a hardship adding thousands of miles and weeks to their voyage.[118]

The Departments of Commerce and Treasury took a special interest in this and followed the Japanese merchant marine shipping recall. Their own sources indicated that all Japanese vessels had been ordered to be in Pacific waters by August 1, 1941, and that all principal officials of the Mitsui and Mitsubishi shipping companies had been ordered to proceed to

Japan not later than mid-July. All Japanese shipping along the Atlantic and Gulf coasts of North America were further ordered to transit the Panama Canal no later than July 22. Treasury noted that there had been no sailings from Japan for the east coast ports of either North or South America since June 24.

The implications of the drawing in of its merchant marine fleet were that Japan feared some of its ships would be in unfriendly ports at the outbreak of war and that this situation must be avoided at all costs. The U.S. Customs officials in Honolulu, San Francisco, and Seattle were reporting that Japan's merchant marine vessels were in the process of repatriating Japanese nationals as rapidly as possible. Fuel tankers were picking up their last shipments of fuel from New York, New Orleans, San Francisco, Los Angeles, San Diego, Seattle, Portland, and Honolulu. It was estimated that by September, Japan's trade with the United States would be terminated.[119]

Rear Adm. Richmond Kelley Turner, chief of the Naval War Plans Division, predicted that an oil embargo on all U.S. petroleum exports to Japan would cause Tokyo to attack and seize British Borneo, Malaya, and the Dutch East Indies oil fields, drawing the United States into war. This echoed the sentiments of the secretary of the interior and Roosevelt's designated petroleum coordinator, Harold Ickes, who wrote in a 1941 memo to the president that previous spring: "To embargo oil to Japan would be as popular a move in all parts of the country as you could make. There might develop . . . a situation as would make it not only possible but easy to get into the war in an effective way." On Friday, July 25, some of the larger Japanese oil tankers hastily departed the United States with their cargos, totaling 770,000 barrels of crude and diesel oil.[120]

From the beginning of 1941, the Treasury Department Under Secretary Henry Morgenthau had been tracking U.S. exports of petroleum products to Japan. Morgenthau's secretary, Herbert E. Gaston, was sending weekly reports directly to Roosevelt himself, detailing gas, oil, crude oil (high octane), gasoline, and lubricating oils. Total quantities ran from a high of 773,000 barrels during the week of January 4 to some 508,000 barrels during the week of July 26. As the embargo took hold, exports dropped off rapidly to as little as 3,000 barrels the week of August 2, with none being reported the following week.[121] Roosevelt was thinking of a complete freeze of Japanese financial assets inside the United States.

The occupation of southern French Indochina on July 24 by some 40,000 Japanese troops triggered the next action against Japan's economy. Within 48 hours, Roosevelt, citing his previously released May 27 declaration of an unlimited national emergency and Section 5(b) of the Trading with the Enemy Act, issued an executive order to totally freeze Japanese assets in America, bringing all financial and import-export transactions under the control of the U.S. government.

Earlier, in the middle of July, 43 U.S. tankers had been moving oil to England. Despite the fact that there were no gasoline shortages on the East Coast of the United States, on July 24, Roosevelt, in a clever ruse, informed the American public that gasoline shortages and sales to Japan were linked. He went on to explain that oil going to Japan meant that "we are helping Japan in what looks like an act of aggression."[122]

The oil embargo by Britain, Holland, and the United States, added to the freeze of financial assets and took a toll, both physically and psychologically, on the Japanese leaders. Acting Secretary of State Welles reported in a July 24 memorandum about a conversation with Japanese Ambassador Nomura in Washington, DC: Nomura told him that Japan was in a critical economic situation in terms of "procuring raw materials, particularly food supplies from abroad." Welles stated that "Japan was now importing a million tons of rice a year from Indochina." To alleviate its food crisis, Tokyo saw occupying southern Indochina as a logical step, to gain control of the Mekong Delta's rice-growing region.[123]

Roosevelt's Executive Order 8832, signed on July 26, for a total embargo of Japan was a calculated plan to break Tokyo financially. While Japan did have ample liquid dollar assets and gold reserves exceeding $200 million in U.S. banks or enough to purchase four years of U.S. oil alone, at the stroke of a pen, Washington had rendered those assets illiquid.[124] Edward S. Miller, in *Bankrupting the Enemy*, says: "The U.S. freeze presented Japan with three choices: suffer economic impoverishment, accede to American demands to yield its territorial conquests, or go to war against the United States and its allies. Unfortunately, Japan chose the latter."[125]

As the financial freeze began on August 1, Welles directed that all customs officials at U.S. ports revoke Japanese oil export licenses. This meant that the Japanese would have to obtain a license for each American-produced product and then another license to unfreeze sufficient dollars to pay it off. Tokyo tried to end-run the freeze and license revocations by bartering commodities, such as silk for gasoline and diesel oil but to no avail. By mid-August it was obvious that the freeze was unbreakable.[126]

Both the Export Control Administration (ECA) and ONI had made oil vulnerability studies of Japan's situation in the Pacific. ONI suggested that Japan, even under emergency restrictions and severe rationing of its people, would have enough oil in its inventory to enable it to fight two years against the United States and its allies. The ECA took a far more conservative and more correct position, estimating that Japan's stocks were only sufficient for six months of extended warfare. Both agreed in the end that an efficient embargo would force Tokyo to seize the oil-rich Dutch East Indies to make up the oil shortfall.[127] Japan's shortage of steel was as critical as oil. Simply put, Tokyo did not have enough steel to build both warships and maintain its economic plant infrastructure.[128]

Roosevelt had now cut Japan off from its international funding, oil, iron ore, and steel—the combination of vital commodities that it needed for its war machine. Tokyo was now in an economic hammerlock with Roosevelt controlling *all* the levers. If it could not resolve the situation diplomatically, Japan would have nowhere to turn except war. But the price of war would be high. The United States had nearly twice the population of Japan and 17 times the national income even in a time of the Great Depression and produced five times the amount of steel and 80 times as many motor vehicles each year. The U.S. overall industrial potential was seven times larger than Japan's. To go to war against the United States was to unleash the fury of a gigantic tiger against oneself.

Japan was now facing an all-encompassing economic disaster, put in place by the foxlike Roosevelt. As Paul Kennedy summed up the situation, "Unable to go back, the Japanese military leaders prepared to plunge forward into an unknown Armageddon of their own doing."[129] As such, they would now try a dual-track strategy: they would prepare to simultaneously move south, all the while pursuing diplomatic approaches to work their way out of their impending economic debacle.

To address the situation that July, Premier Konoye reshuffled his cabinet for the third time. A U.S. intelligence report from Tokyo dated July 29 indicated that of some 16 key ministers in the Konoye cabinet, seven were top-ranking IJA and IJN generals and admirals. In two critical positions, Adm. Teijiro Toyoda became the foreign minister and Lt. Gen. Tojo continued on in his position as war minister. The report went on to say that the IJA was in the process of mobilizing an additional 750,000 men as part of its preparations to cope with the future "opportunities [missions]" that might come its way.[130]

As Tokyo struggled to resolve what it saw as a diplomatic impasse over the financial freeze imposed upon it by Washington, its demands for financial relief and licenses to purchase oil led nowhere. Whenever points were raised to settle their differences with the United States, there was always the main sticking point of China. Washington insisted that Japan withdraw forthwith from China proper and further recognize Chiang Kai-Shek and his nation as an independent and sovereign entity. For Tokyo, the "China Incident" revolved around Washington recognizing Japan's "legitimate interests" or conquests already accomplished on mainland Asia. For Japan to withdraw from China after four long years of war and significant economic sacrifice and suffering on the part of its people would be tantamount to an unparalleled national humiliation, which, of course, was unacceptable.[131] Thus the diplomatic efforts to resolve the embargo in Japan's favor remained at loggerheads. Tokyo's Foreign Ministry stated its case in a July 31 PURPLE message intercept:

Commercial and economic relations between Japan and third countries, led by England and the United States, are gradually becoming so horribly strained that we cannot endure it much longer. Our Empire, to save its life, must take measures to secure the raw materials of the South Seas. Our Empire must immediately take steps to break asunder this ever-strengthening chain of encirclement [by] England and the United States.[132]

Japan's seemingly endless war in China continued to be a tremendous drain on its national resources, specifically causing Japan's air force to consume large amounts of fuel. While its own domestic oil production per year was approximately 400,000 tons, its annual oil consumption rate was 5 million tons, or 2,920,000 barrels (the American Petroleum Institute's formula to convert metric tons of crude oil to barrels is to multiply the number of metric tons by 7.3 barrels). The net effect was that Japan's estimated fuel storage capacity of some 10 million tons was being rapidly depleted. Despite Tokyo's emergency mobilization orders for homeland factories to reduce fuel consumption by 37 percent, shipping oil consumption by 15 percent, and automobile gasoline consumption by 65 percent, it was not enough.[133]

The American oil embargo of July 26, 1941, was now in place. Three days later, the Dutch East Indies suddenly suspended its late 1940 agreement to deliver 1.8 million tons of oil annually to Japan. Tokyo now found itself locked into a commercial corner with no escape. The Dutch further placed all their monetary and commercial dealings with Japan on a special permit basis, much like the United States. To show his good faith and follow Roosevelt's lead, Churchill likewise directed the British Commonwealth of Nations worldwide to freeze all Japanese assets under their control.[134] Roosevelt, with his astute understanding of politics and his reading of the intercepted PURPLE message traffic, undoubtedly saw that the economic stranglehold embracing Japan would lead to some form of an overt act against one or more of the ABD allies in the Pacific. He was not wrong.

Tokyo reacted to the embargos in a definitive manner. While it continued its recall of all of Japan's merchant marine shipping to their home ports, with a deadline of being west of the Panama Canal by August 1, well over a half-million men were being conscripted into the armed forces. All of the IJN's warships, supporting vessels, and military aviation were recalled from their forward-deployed bases in and around China. These were all steps that one would expect from a maritime nation marshalling its resources and mobilizing for war.[135] An OPNAV August 14 update for CINCAF, CINCPAC, CINCLANT, as well as the 14th–16th Naval Districts, reported:

ORANGE [JAPAN] SHIPS FORMERLY IN NORTH ATLANTIC RETURNING JAPAN VIA [STRAITS OF] MAGELLAN, 4 TANKERS ONLY

VESSELS ON PACIFIC COAST. JAPANESE RAPIDLY COMPLETING
WITHDRAWAL FROM WORLD SHIPPING ROUTES. RESUMPTION OF
SHIPPING SERVICES INDEFINITE RESULT OF USA, BRITISH AND
DUTCH PRESSURE THROUGH REFUSAL OF TRANSIT OF PANAMA
CANAL, EXPORT CONTROL RESTRICTIONS, REFUSAL OF BUNKER-
ING AND PORT FACILITIES AND FUNDFREEZING.[136]

Another report from ONI, after mentioning that two of Japan's tankers
had left the United States empty, went on to say that both the British and
the Canadians had closed their ports to Japanese ships. In the Dutch East
Indies, Batavia had "stopped . . . the issuing of licenses for shipment of
exports to Japan" and that Japanese citizens were "leaving India, Australia,
New Zealand, Singapore, and Hong Kong."[137] Joseph Rochefort, a former
student of Japanese language and culture under Arthur McCollum during
the late 1920s in Japan, commented on the overall situation: "We cut off
their money, their fuel and trade. We were just tightening the screws on
the Japanese. They could see no way of getting out except going to war."[138]

Exactly two weeks after the economic embargos had been put in place
against Japan, Roosevelt met his British counterpart, Prime Minister Winston Churchill, on August 9, 1941, in Placentia Bay in Newfoundland for
what would become known as the Atlantic Conference. It was the first time
the two had met in person, and their meeting took place on Roosevelt's U.S.
Navy heavy cruiser *Augusta*. Roosevelt's staff, consisting of admirals Stark
and Turner and Gen. Marshall, conferred with Churchill's Adm. Dudley
Pound and Gen. Sir John Dill.

Out of this conference, the Atlantic Charter was promulgated as a "joint
declaration" of common moral and political principles, which pledged "the
final destruction of Nazi tyranny." The Conference's greater significance
came from the behind-the-scene discussions that took place. The British
were led to believe that the United States would build up its Far Eastern
forces with additional ships and planes based in the Philippines, to deter
the Japanese. The British agreed to send a squadron of modern aircraft
carriers and battleships to Singapore. This, it was presumed, would ensure
adequate protection for the Netherlands (Dutch) East Indies.[139] Sumner
Welles, who was acting as the secretary of state for Roosevelt, proposed an
initiative that basically said that the United States should be prepared to
repel any Japanese thrust directed against the Soviet Union, the Dutch
East Indies, or any of the British possessions in the South Pacific region.
Roosevelt and Churchill were in agreement with what was a de facto
Anglo-American alliance against Japan.[140]

Stanley Weintraub noted in his comments on the Atlantic Conference
that Harry Hopkins had observed "that in the last analysis the enemy was
Hitler and that he could never be defeated without force of arms; that
sooner or later we were bound to be in the war and that Japan was giving

us an opportunity." Weintraub further noted the comments of British Lt. Gen. Henry Pownall of the Imperial General Staff, who observed in his own notes that President Roosevelt

> was *all* for coming into the war, and as soon as possible . . . but he said he would never declare war; he wishes to provoke it. He wants to create an incident that brings war about, being no doubt sure that he will then be fully supported by the people.[141]

The August 24 *New York Times* headline said: CHURCHILL WARNS JAP-ANESE TO 'STOP' OR FACE BRITISH-AMERICAN COALITION.

Two days after the Atlantic Conference, an August 16 PURPLE Inter-cept (#703, Part 2 of 4) from the Japanese Embassy to Tokyo's Foreign Office found Japan's Ambassador Nomura reporting, "I understand the British believe that if they could only have a Japanese-American war started at the back door, there would be a good prospect of getting the United States to participate in the European war."[142] Just a few days prior to Nomura's August 16 report, a 13th Naval District (Seattle) letter report, titled "Present Conditions in Japan," was forwarded to the director of naval intelligence on August 11. It stated:

> Present oil reserves will permit Japan to wage war for one year. The cumula-tive effect of the Chinese war is a definite war weariness. Everything which people use, eat, and wear is rationed. The fact that there is now practically no foreign exchange may drive Japan to desperation.[143]

On August 17, shortly after his meeting with Churchill off Newfound-land, Roosevelt and Hull both met with Ambassador Nomura in Washing-ton, DC. On August 19, Stimson recorded in his diary what Hull had told him about the meeting. While Nomura very much wanted Roosevelt to meet with the Japanese prime minister, Crown Prince Konoye, Secretary Hull openly refused the invitation, and Roosevelt seconded Hull, pointing out Japan's provocative actions in French Indochina and Thailand. Finally, according to Stimson's notes, Roosevelt terminated the conversation by stating that any Japanese intrusion into Thailand would be considered by the United States as a threat to its own national security and that would "make it necessary to take any steps within its power to preserve its secu-rity and safety." A line had been drawn in Southeast Asia.[144]

Some days before that, on August 9, Stimson had made a diary entry whereby he pointedly criticized the Japanese negotiations as "a pure blind," as they had "already made up their minds to a policy of going south through Indo-China and Thailand."[145] A Gallup Poll conducted during the week of August 21–26 asked, "Should the United States take steps now to keep Japan from becoming more powerful, even if it meant risking a war with Japan?" A strong 70 percent of Americans replied with a "Yes" answer.[146]

On September 1, the U.S. Navy began to assume more responsibility in the Western Atlantic for the provision of merchant ship convoy security for all shipping en route to the British Isles. Two days later, CNO Stark authorized the Atlantic Fleet to "destroy" any and all German Kriegsmarine warships that threatened American or Icelandic flagged vessels. The U.S. Navy was now sailing the Atlantic under "battle conditions."[147] Only an overt incident now remained to take place.

This was not long in coming. On September 4, a situation came about whereby the U.S. Navy destroyer *Greer*, which was headed for Iceland, was informed by a British plane that a U-boat lay in her path some miles ahead. The *Greer* not only made sonar sound contact with the German submarine but also tracked the sub for some hours, passing the target's location off to a British plane, which then ran a depth charge attack against the submarine. The U-boat commander reciprocated, firing a torpedo at *Greer*, and, in turn, her commander counterattacked with his own depth charges. While neither side scored any hits, it was the first formal battle action in the Atlantic for the U.S. Navy in World War II.[148]

Despite the fact that Roosevelt tried to turn the incident into a true "overt act," he accomplished little along this line. The incident was just not convincing enough to the American public at large. On the other side of the Atlantic, Hitler gave his U-boat commanders explicit orders to avoid any further engagements with the U.S. Navy.[149]

On September 11, Roosevelt now ordered the navy to "shoot on sight." The U.S. Atlantic Fleet was in a de facto shooting war with Nazi Germany as part of its convoy escort missions.[150] A little over a month would pass before the next incidents would take place. On October 16–17, the U.S. destroyer *Kearny* was caught up a pitched battle between some British and Canadian warships and German U-boats. The *Kearny* was actually hit by a torpedo, losing 11 sailors, but not sinking.[151] Taking advantage of what now appeared to be a genuine overt act, Roosevelt tried to arouse the American people, exhorting them that America had "been attacked. The . . . *Kearny* is not just a navy ship. She belongs to every man, woman, and child in this Nation. . . . Hitler's torpedo was directed at every American!" A Gallup Poll conducted earlier and released on October 3 had asked Americans the question, "In general, do you approve or disapprove of having the United States Navy shoot at German submarines or warships on sight?" Almost two-thirds (62 percent) of Americans now approved of the policy.[152]

On October 31, two weeks after the Kearny episode, another navy destroyer, the *Reuben James*, was hit by a U-boat torpedo and sunk in the Atlantic, with the loss of 115 sailors. The sinking of the *Reuben James* represented the first U.S. Navy vessel to be lost to enemy action in World War II. The net result of the *Reuben James* sinking was that on the one hand,

Congress repealed most of the provisions of the Neutrality Acts in mid-November, allowing American merchant vessels to be armed and to carry any cargoes they wanted to belligerent nations, but on the other hand, navy recruiting actually plummeted 15 percent.[153] The strategy to create an overt act with Germany in the Atlantic did not appear to be fully achieving its intended goal in terms of arousing the American people.

A NEW WAR PLAN

Toward the end of 1941, an obscure army lieutenant colonel named Albert C. Wedemeyer, working in Gen. Marshall's War Plans Division of the War Department's General Staff, was putting the finishing touches on a special project after four months' work—the Victory Program. Because of his studies as a student at the German War College during the late 1930s, he was considered by Marshall and others to be the most up-to-date and knowledgeable officer in the U.S. Army in terms of understanding the Wehrmacht's thinking and war fighting concepts at the operational and strategic levels. Hand-picked by Marshall, he had been given the mission to formulate an overall strategic, contingency war plan for the United States, involving the full mobilization of the nation's wealth, manpower, and industrial capacity for the defeat of Germany, Italy, and even Japan. It was to be a blueprint for total war unlike any other in American history, placing under arms some 13.5 million personnel, of which 9 million would be allocated to the army and another 3 million to the navy.[154]

The Victory Program was not an easy one to develop. Wedemeyer had to balance America's manpower requirements to enable the nation to operate effectively and efficiently in a wartime economy at home and still have sufficient strength within the military services to win the war overseas. Additionally, he had to mesh America's productive capacity and manufacturing genius to meet the myriad equipment requirements involving the program. This meant coordinating the training, equipment, armaments, vehicles, planes, shipping, and thousands of other items that had to be produced at the right time and sent to the right place. Hundreds, if not thousands, of agencies involved in the war effort had to be able to function in a coherent and logical manner.

Wedemeyer was assisted in this effort by the navy's multibillion-dollar expansion program, which was constructing some 100 aircraft carriers of various types and sizes over the next several years.[155] While the navy's Rainbow 5/War Plan 46, put in place in late May 1941, had helped immeasurably, Wedemeyer had to also think of amphibious landing operations and all the related amphibious assault craft and vessels needed to transport and support the army for the anticipated formal invasion of Europe.[156]

In accordance with Roosevelt's policy, the principal thrust of the Victory Program was geared to accomplish the military defeat first and foremost of Hitler's Nazi Germany.[157]

In late September, the Victory Program was submitted to Marshall at the War Department for review. Implementation of the program began almost immediately. After Pearl Harbor, the United States would be producing one ship a day and one aircraft every five minutes![158] Wedemeyer's planning could not have come at a better time; the mobilization of some 13 million personnel to serve in the armed forces and another 9 million to work in the myriad factories needed to provision the U.S. Army, Navy, Marine Corps, and Coast Guard now solved the problem of unemployment caused by the Great Depression.

A few days after Wedemeyer submitted his Victory Program to the Army General Staff, Ambassador Grew in Tokyo submitted his observations on Japanese psychology in a September 29 report to Secretary of State Hull in Washington. Grew had spent a decade in Japan, carrying out the basic three functions of an ambassador: to represent the United States and explain its policies in an amicable manner, to observe and report on all aspects of Japan's domestic and international relations activities and thinking, and to solve problems involving Washington's interests in the region. The stalemate in negotiations was frustrating to this consummate diplomat so well versed in the Japanese language and culture. Grew had spent enormous time and energy in attempting to bring about a peaceful solution to the problem. Now time was running out.

Grew's insightful report could be taken as a venting of his frustrations on the issue. Japanese psychology, he reported, was

> fundamentally unlike that of any Western nation. The abnormal sensitiveness of Japan and the abnormal effects of loss of face causes one to be "discredited," resulting in a revulsion which can lead to anti-American feeling, leading to "unbridled acts."[159]

By "unbridled acts" he meant a lashing out at the United States. Roosevelt himself was well aware of the importance of face to the Japanese. Indeed, the adoption of a policy that would not allow some sort of face-saving solution would be tantamount to guaranteeing war.[160] In fact, Japan was preparing to lash out at the United States. And at least one of the targets was the U.S. Navy's Pacific Fleet, located at its Pearl Harbor base in Hawaii.

On September 24, 1941, Tokyo sent a cable message (#83) in its low-grade diplomatic J-19 code to its consulate in Honolulu, requesting that a location grid be prepared, to include five areas (A through E), depicting the layout of the Pacific Fleet's docking arrangements at its base. Specific position of warships and aircraft carriers at anchor and tied up at their respective wharves, buoys, and docks were to be reported each week. If there were two or more vessels alongside the same wharf, this was considered important. The message was intercepted at Station SAIL as part of the navy's radio signal intercept and tracking system in the Pacific; the message was decoded and translated on October 9.[161]

On September 29, five days after receiving the directive from Tokyo, the Honolulu consulate sent Tokyo their reply (#178) in the J-19 code. They carefully crafted a set of coded symbols (KS, KT, FV, FG, and an A and B special differentiation) to designate the location of the Pacific Fleet's vessels (see Appendix B, this volume). That same day, this message was photographed at Mackay Radio & Telegraph by naval intelligence officials from Washington, fully decoded and translated by October 10.[162]

The "bomb plot" messages, as they were called, were a dead giveaway about Japanese intentions; no other U.S. Navy installation was reported on in such a determined manner over the following weeks. Given Pearl Harbor's configuration and location, reports detailing exact ship locations by target grid could only be useful to aircraft-carrier-borne aerial bombers and torpedo planes. When Capt. Allan G. Kirk, then director of naval intelligence, pressed Rear Adm. Turner to inform Hawaii and Adm. Kimmel as to what was going on in the messages, he was at first ignored and then relieved of his position on October 15.[163] No report was ever sent to Kimmel about the J-19 bomb plot intercepts.

When Roosevelt was informed of the two intercepts concerning Pearl Harbor, he invited David Sarnoff, the founder and president of RCA, to come to the White House on October 14 to discuss how RCA might be able to play a role. RCA did have a downtown Honolulu office. Although Sarnoff spent over a week in Honolulu, supposedly at the president's behest, to coordinate the provision of the RCA's intercepts of the Japanese consulate's messages to and from Tokyo to U.S. Naval Intelligence at the 14th Naval District, nothing happened. At Pearl Harbor Joseph Rochefort's Station HYPO had the capability to decode the J-19 messages, but it was never used. Kimmel, as the CINCPAC, should have been informed about the ongoing espionage effort targeting his Pacific Fleet.[164] Kimmel was never even told about Sarnoff's mission as it pertained to the IJN's naval intelligence espionage efforts taking place on his doorstep.[165]

In mid-October, when Tokyo's moderate Konoye government found itself unable to arrange a meeting with Roosevelt to work around the American embargos arrayed against Japan, it fell from power. Gen. Tojo's more militant group used its leverage to gain control of the Tokyo government, with Tojo in charge. That same day, the navy's CNO Stark in Washington released a message to all three of his main fleets:

> The resignation of the Japanese Cabinet has created a grave situation. Since the US and Britain are held responsible by Japan for her present desperate

situation there is also a possibility that Japan may attack these two powers. Take due precautions including such preparatory deployments as will not disclose strategic intention nor constitute provocative actions against Japan.[166]

This constituted the *first* directive to the Asiatic and Pacific Fleets *not* to take any actions that the Japanese could consider "provocative." Compared to the elusive pop-up cruises intended to create a deliberate provocation, it signified a major shift in policy. In an October 22 reply to Adm. Stark, Adm. Kimmel at Pearl Harbor reminded him that his own Pacific Fleet's contingency war planning put "a premium on aircraft operations from carriers. We have only three. One of them is occupied part-time in training activities at San Diego."[167] The implication by Kimmel was that under the circumstances it was probably a good idea to consider building up the aircraft carrier strength of his fleet. Unfortunately for him, he was not privy to the strategic thinking going on at the highest levels in Washington. Stark ignored Kimmel, striving to maintain the current status quo in terms of American naval strengths in the Atlantic and Pacific.[168]

As the Konoye Cabinet fell in mid-October, the Office of Naval Intelligence in Washington released one of its intelligence summaries:

> The Japanese press has adopted a violently anti-American tone. The Japanese are particularly incensed at the Netherlands East Indies for permitting shipments of vital war materials to Russia. Army maneuvers are being held in Indo-China.[169]

Another ONI report commented on the resignation of Prince Konoye's cabinet:

> Lieutenant-General Tojo, Konoye's Minister of War, formed a new cabinet in which he holds the posts of Premier, Minister of War, and Minister of Home Affairs.... Tojo has thus concentrated enormous powers in his own hands, far more than any Premier of modern times. He is jingoistic and anti-foreign.... He has strong pro-Axis leanings.[170]

It was against this backdrop, on October 15, that Hidenari Terasaki, the second secretary of the Japanese Embassy in Washington, was invited to the home of Rear Adm. Richmond Turner. During their conversation, as revealed by an October 16 PURPLE intercept (#959, Part 2 of 2) of a message from Ambassador Nomura in Washington to his Tokyo Foreign Office, Terasaki commented to Turner, "Once a Japanese is in a corner, he will forget all interest in life and death and fight back with fury." He then went on to say: "If we [Japan] do not achieve what we are trying to do, it may come to that. Now if you Americans would only extend your hand in friendship to us a little, you could have our lasting amity; otherwise we may turn out to be permanent enemies."[171] These comments only reinforced what Turner and even Roosevelt already knew: Japan was in the corner.

Secretary of War Stimson committed to his diary for Thursday, October 16, 1941, some comments about a conference he attended between Roosevelt; secretaries Hull, Knox, and himself; Gen. Marshall; Adm. Stark; and Harry Hopkins. The discussion took about two hours and dealt with the crisis inside Japan and the new cabinet, which was expected to be much more anti-American. In summing up the situation, he wrote, "So we face the delicate question of the diplomatic fencing to be done to be sure that Japan was put into the wrong and made the first bad move—overt move."[172] Stimson had captured the essence of the Roosevelt policy to see that Japan fired the first opening shot in anger against the United States.

It was an extension of the earlier overt act policy, which had not succeeded in arousing the American public sufficiently to enter the war. If Americans had not become incensed over the recent German attacks on the destroyers *Greer* and *Kearney* as well as the sinking of the *Reuben James* with heavy loss of life, then a radically different approach would have to be implemented. This would fulfill Roosevelt's driving imperative, synergized by the Einstein letter in accordance with Szilard's warning about the atomic bomb, to enter the war to defeat Nazi Germany as rapidly as possible.

Apparently now aware of Roosevelt's foreign policy strategy, Harold Ickes, the secretary of the interior and a significant player in the financial embargo against Japan just a few months earlier, reflected on the new policy thrust, noting in his diary on October 18: "For a long time I have believed that our best entrance into the war would be by way of Japan. . . . And, of course, if we go to war against Japan, it will inevitably lead us to war against Germany."[173] Ickes had come full circle in his understanding of the full implications of the overt act strategy as a back door to war.

Ickes's appraisal of the situation in the Pacific was answered on November 5 by a key Japanese imperial conference meeting held by Tojo, his cabinet, and senior military officials. References to this meeting taking place had been made as early as November 2 in PURPLE message traffic intercepted and translated by army and navy intelligence personnel in Washington. In essence, the Japanese leaders in Tokyo had resolved to continue the pursuit of negotiations in the faint hope that the United States just might accommodate the Japanese expansion in China. If diplomacy failed and there was no tangible agreement by the United States in favor of Japan by November 25, Japan would then go to war, beginning in early December. A November 5 PURPLE intercept from the Tokyo foreign office to Ambassador Nomura reiterated the importance of concluding all negotiations with Washington by November 25.[174]

In his memoirs, Cordell Hull, America's senior diplomat and secretary of state, after considering the various intercepted PURPLE messages, concluded, "Japan had already set in motion the wheels of her war machine and she had decided not to stop short of war with the United States if, by November 25, we had not agreed to her demands."[175] Ironically, that November 3, Grew sent a cable to Hull in which he stated:

JAPANESE FULLY CAPABLE OF RUSHING HEADLONG INTO A SUI-CIDAL STRUGGLE WITH THE UNITED STATES (ECLIPSES AMERICAN STANDARDS OF LOGIC)[176]

Concerned about the different options the Japanese might have in mind for opening a war of conquest in British Malaya or the Dutch East Indies, Stimson noted in his diary on November 7 that Roosevelt called his cabinet together to poll their ideas as to whether he would receive American popular support "if it became necessary to strike at Japan in case she should attack England in Malaya or the Dutch in the East Indies. The Cabinet was unanimous in the feeling that the country would support such a move."[177] That same day, Stark wrote to his Asiatic Fleet commander, Adm. Hart: "The Navy is already in the war in the Atlantic, but the country doesn't seem to realize it. Apathy, to the point of opposition is evident in a considerable section of the press. . . . Whether the country knows it or not, we are at war."[178]

On November 15, the Tokyo Foreign Office reaffirmed to its Ambassador Nomura that the deadline of November 25 was "an absolutely immovable one."[179] Something imminent was about to happen in the Pacific. With a northern war against the Soviet Union improbable and southern operations inevitable, the Japanese preparations for operations in Southeast Asia ploughed ahead.

Roosevelt's strategy for accomplishing his driving imperative had apparently now come full circle. Economically speaking, he had the Japanese boxed into a corner without any apparent solution. As a last resort, by its way of thinking, Tokyo could only avoid national humiliation and the loss of its huge investment of lives, treasure, and equipment in the ongoing conquest of China by striking out at the United States and its allies in the Pacific. The Japanese could only rely on their Tripartite Pact alliance with Nazi Germany and Fascist Italy in Europe. Would this now become America's proverbial "back door" for participation in the war in Europe to bring about the defeat of Nazi Germany? One way or another, the main burden of Japan's new war effort would fall mainly upon the Imperial Japanese Navy.

As a result of considerable foresight over the previous 10 years, America's first line of defense in the Pacific to protect its national interests against any transoceanic war effort on the part of Japan in 1941 would rest to a considerable degree on the success of the U.S. Navy's own splendid arrangement for the region. How well this actually accomplished its mission was soon to be tested.

Roosevelt knew what was going on. This should have been the perfect time for the Roosevelt administration to reappraise Japanese intentions in the Pacific and its own strategy in terms of the navy's forward-based Pacific Fleet. The opportunity to coordinate the reinforcement of the fleet at Pearl Harbor in a timely manner with two or more aircraft carriers out of the Atlantic Fleet to set up a meeting engagement, if not ambush, in the near North Pacific was there, but again, nothing happened. Roosevelt was wedded to his game plan, which called for an "overt act," and nothing was going to be allowed to disturb it.

President Franklin D. Roosevelt. A full two years before the United States entered World War II, President Roosevelt was alerted by Albert Einstein that Adolph Hitler's Nazi scientists were working on an atomic bomb. Roosevelt became caught up in a driving imperative to enter the war at all costs, to thwart the Nazi effort; this was Roosevelt's most important foreign policy command decision of the war. (Franklin D. Roosevelt Presidential Library and Museum)

Chancellor Adolph Hitler. As he pressed his Nazi atomic bomb program forward in the fall of 1940, a cocky Hitler entered into a military alliance with Japan against the United States. It would prove a fateful decision. (Photos.com)

Albert Einstein (left) and Leo Szilard. Two of the world's foremost nuclear scientists, Einstein and Szilard discuss their letter of August 2, 1939, to President Franklin D. Roosevelt, alerting him to Nazi Germany's secret atomic bomb developments. (Franklin D. Roosevelt Presidential Library and Museum)

Adm. James O. Richardson. In late 1940, commander of the U.S. Fleet, Adm. Richardson, challenged President Roosevelt's policy to have the fleet stationed at Pearl Harbor, Oahu, Hawaii. In a meeting with Roosevelt, Richardson called the harbor "a Goddamned mousetrap!" A few months later, Richardson was fired and was retired from the U.S. Navy. (NH 865, U.S. Naval History and Heritage Command)

Adm. Husband E. Kimmel. Two weeks before the attack on Pearl Harbor, commander-in-chief of the U.S. Fleet Adm. Kimmel maneuvered his warships into the North Pacific to search for and attack the Japanese Strike Force, only to be abruptly called back to Pearl Harbor. (NH 48589, U.S. Naval History and Heritage Command)

Lt. Gen. Walter Short. In 1941, the U.S. Army commander in charge of the defense of Hawaii was Lt. Gen. Short. He followed orders to the letter to protect the U.S. base at Pearl Harbor against Japanese sabotage. (National Archives)

Adm. Thomas Hart. Commander in chief of the U.S. Asiatic Fleet, Adm. Hart was unwittingly caught up in President Roosevelt's overt act strategy involving the Philippines. (NH 49271-KN, Oil Painting. Naval History and Heritage Command)

Lt. Cdr. Arthur McCollum. As the U.S. Navy's foremost expert on Japanese culture and psyche, Lt. Cdr. McCollum wrote an 8-point action memorandum which synergized President Roosevelt's thinking for bringing a reluctant United States into the war. (Courtesy of Rear Adm. Arthur H. McCollum, USN (Ret.), 1969. NH 68797, Naval History and Heritage Command)

Adm. Harold R. Stark. In 1941, chief of Naval Operations Adm. Stark promulgated and protected President Roosevelt's secret overt act strategy up to and including its spectacular fruition on December 7, 1941, at Pearl Harbor. (Courtesy of the Stark Collection. NH 93432, Naval History and Heritage Command)

Cdr. Laurence F. Safford. Cdr. Safford's early work in the development of signal intelligence operations in the Pacific earned him the title of "Father of U.S. Navy Cryptology." (Parker, Frederick D. *Pearl Harbor Revisited: United States Navy Communications Intelligence, 1924–1941.* Fort George G. Meade, MD: National Security Agency, Center for Cryptologic History, 1994, 3)

Agness Meyer Driscoll. In 1941, the U.S. Navy's foremost cryptographer, Agness Meyer Driscoll, the solver of the Imperial Japanese Navy's main operational 5-Number Code, was relegated to futilely working on the German Naval Enigma Code. (National Security Agency)

President Franklin D. Roosevelt (left) and British prime minister Winston Churchill, both seated, attended their first joint wartime conference off the coast of Newfoundland, Canada, on August 9–12, 1941, four months prior to the Declaration of War by the U.S. House of Representatives. Roosevelt formed a de facto alliance with Great Britain, known as the Atlantic Charter, pledging "the final destruction of the Nazi tyranny." (Library of Congress)

Lt. Cdr. Joseph J. Rochefort. During the six months leading up to the attack on Pearl Harbor, the commander of Pearl Harbor's HYPO intercept and code-breaking operations, Lt. Cdr. Rochefort, and his team of experts were relegated to solving unimportant secondary Japanese codes of no consequence. (Courtesy of Captain R. Pineau, USNR. NH 84826, Naval History and Heritage Command)

Dutch attaché Johan Ranneft. On December 2, 1941, and again on December 6, Dutch naval attaché Johan Ranneft was at the U.S. Naval Headquarters in Washington, DC, where he was shown the progress of the Imperial Japanese Navy as they moved steadily eastward across the Pacific. Probable destination: Pearl Harbor. (Anefo/London Collection. Access number 2.24.01.04. Danish National Archives)

Adm. Isoroku Yamamoto. As the premier strategist for the Imperial Japanese Navy, Adm. Isoroku Yamamoto formulated Japan's 1941–1942 transpacific strategy, including the December 7, 1941, attack on Pearl Harbor. (Papers of Takagi Kiyohisa, #118. National Diet Library)

Vice Adm. Chuichi Nagumo. Two weeks after Adm. Kimmel was ordered to cut short maneuvers in the North Pacific and return his fleet to base at Pearl Harbor, Adm. Chuichi Nagumo led his Imperial Japanese Navy First Air Fleet Strike Force into the same area and launched the devastating December 7, 1941, attack against Kimmel's Pacific Fleet. (NH 63423, U.S. Naval History and Heritage Command)

5

Tracking the Imperial Japanese Navy in the Pacific

Unknown to the Japanese, the United States, Britain, and the Netherlands were using multiple interlocking intelligence technologies, including traffic analysis and ship fingerprinting, to identify specific IJN warships and supporting vessels. There has been much discussion by scholars over the last several decades as to *how much* message text from the Imperial Japanese Navy's key operations code (Code Book D, 5-Number Code, or JN-25B) was actually being read by the processing centers.

By 1941, the U.S. Naval Operations Communications Division in Washington, OP-20-G, was tracking the IJN around and throughout the Pacific, increasing its strength from 543 officers, enlisted, and civilian personnel in January of that year to 730 by December 7.[1] It was part of an intelligence effort second to none that supported President Roosevelt.

U.S. INTELLIGENCE 1941

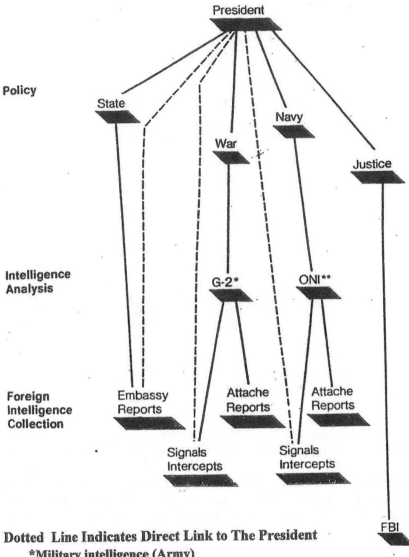

Dotted Line Indicates Direct Link to The President
  *Military intelligence (Army)
  **Office of Naval Intelligence

Intelligence Flow Chart, 1941. (Intelligence Files 1941, Archive II, National Archives)

TECHNIQUES

The success of signals intelligence was very much dependent on the conditions under which the various radio frequencies were used in actual practice. The Navy found that frequency, distance, time of day or night, and the location of the radio transmission's path all had an impact on the success of signal intercept operations against the IJN. The transmission of radio waves between the Japanese transmitting and receiving stations involved an understanding of how a ground signal wave moved in comparison to a sky wave, which was reflected off the various conducting layers in the upper atmosphere. This sky wave phenomenon is dominant for all signal transmissions except short distances, reflecting off the layers of ionized air created by the solar radiation effects from the sun at some 30 to 300 miles above the earth's surface. Radio wave transmissions in the Pacific were particularly affected by this situation.

Besides ionosphere impacts on radio waves, two other factors involving distance, or signal range, were important; they involved the actual power of the radio transmitter and its antenna design. Sky wave distances could be predicted in accordance with diurnal, seasonal, and year-to-year variations in the ionosphere and the levels of radio frequency involved. The maximum ionization density of a layer determined the maximum frequency that could be reflected from the layer. Since ordinary radio transmissions tended to send their waves obliquely, a maximum usable radio frequency could be predicted for a given distance. The National Bureau of Standards made these kinds of predictions each month.[2]

What became important for OP-20-G was the refraction or bending of radio signals as they coursed into or were reflected off the ionized layers of the atmosphere. The uneven bouncing effect, back and forth, of the signals between the ionosphere and the earth's surface often created silent zones in which no radio signal transmissions could be received. After the radio signal *ground wave* moving along the earth's surface had completed its passage, the *sky wave* phenomena now began as a result of the waves' own reflections off the ionized layers in the upper atmosphere. The silent zone created was commonly described as the "skip zone." This was often quite large at night but might even disappear completely during the day.

For long-range transmissions, distances reaching out to 2,500 miles or more, the nighttime period was usually preferred, because the sky waves descended back to the earth's surface, bypassing the skip zone. This was important for high-frequency waves reflecting off the ionosphere, which could be heard up to thousands of miles away and even well beyond the intended receiving station's antenna. An example of this was Tokyo's diplomatic radio transmissions, which could not always be readily heard on the West Coast of the United States (a skip zone) but were usually heard by the Japanese Embassy in Washington, DC. This signal was picked up as well by the U.S. Navy's intercept Station M at Cheltenham, Maryland.

Sometimes violent eruptions or sunspots on the part of the sun facing the earth would create ionosphere storms, causing abnormal radio conditions and contributing to inordinate skipping and bouncing of the radio waves. The effects could also be noted during unusually rough seas, if not violent storms, which occurred in the North Pacific due to the sun's solar action. This tended to be particularly severe in northern latitudes, decreasing in intensity toward the equator. The return to normal radio signal transmitting conditions would often take several days and largely depended on the latitude and severity of the storm's effects.[3]

The IJN's complete inability to control the skip phenomenon in the North Pacific, which allowed its signals to be unintentionally projected over long distances and then received in unlikely places, would play favorably into OP-20-G's hands in no small way.

Monthly reports of more than 200 pages in length were normally produced by each processing station in Hawaii and the Philippines. They summarized the intercepts, naval movement reports, supervisor watch reports, RDF bearing data, routine and special (secret) call signs and addresses, and equipment status reports. Each month, reports also prepared based on the IBM tabulating cards and termed "statistical section call lists" or words to that effect. They listed current IJN radio call sign system (HYOOs 8, 9, or 10) and any associated RDF bearings by date of the various IJN main fleet vessels and other shipping interests. Numbering up to 500 pages (up to several thousand items, arranged chronologically in accordance with each ship's radio call sign), these were utilized for reference at the issuing processing station and also forwarded to the other processing stations.[4]

Although the IJN had a code system called the Kaigun Ango, consisting of 29 separate naval codes, Vice Adm. Ingersoll, the Office of the Chief of Naval Operations, acknowledged that there were only five basic IJN cryptographic code systems in frequent usage at the beginning of 1941: an Administrative Code, a Merchant Ship Code, a Material Code, an Operations Code, and an Intelligence Code.

The **Administrative Code,** the AD Code (often wrongly called the Admiralty Code) was seldom used after 1940; and even though code book and cipher keys (RIP 54-A, RIP 54-B, and RIP 69) were held by the commandants of the 14th and 16th Naval Districts, no important messages appear to have been sent in this code.

The **Material Code** tended to deal with ship characteristics, construction, tonnages, speeds, and other related information that was not considered to be a high-priority operational interest, thus relegating this code to one of the lowest of priorities of interest.

The **Intelligence Code** was evaluated as being of "least importance," due to its concern about activities other than the IJN, and was therefore neglected in favor of other higher priority IJN code systems.[5]

The **Merchant Ship**, or IJN S Code, was described as "99 percent readable," although the cipher was changed quarterly. It was valuable because it was used by both merchant and fishing vessels in communication with their home ports, plus IJN activities. A RIP 68 had been published and was in use at the 13th, 14th, and 16th Naval Districts as part of their intercept and tracking efforts. Additional "solutions" or cipher decodes were handled by the Navy Department and further distributed back to those districts in the Pacific. OP-20-GY had been breaking this code with no problem for years.[6]

The **Operations Code** was the most important challenge. An additive key cipher was employed with this code, and although the method of decipherment was well defined, the process was a laborious one requiring from an hour to sometimes several days for each message. Even though a decoding machine was being developed to aid in the decipherment of the codes, only a few code values had been determined. Ingersoll estimated that it would not be until roughly mid-1941 that the code could be read to any extent.[7] The IJN first introduced this new, numerical operational code on June 1, 1939, and called it Code Book D. OP-20-G personnel referred to this two-part code in a variety of ways: AN, AN-1, 5-Number, 5-Num Code, five digit, JN-25 (after December 7, 1941), Code Book D, or even the Operations Code.

To use the IJN's Code Book D, the 5-Num Code, required the transmitting radio station to use two books. One book was an *actual* code book and the other was the *additive* code book. Breaking this superencrypted code meant first stripping away the superencryption, the additive cipher, to reveal the basic code and then breaking the code itself—a two-step process. While the basic code used five-digit numbers, each divisible by three, it ended up having some 33,000 numbers, each one of which had its own special meaning in terms of a word, phrase, or number (a name of a ship, specific commander, location, date and time, etc.).

Leading the attack on breaking the code was Agnes Meyer Driscoll, the navy's foremost authority on Japanese naval codes. Known as "Madam X" by Laurence Safford and "Miss Aggie" to her colleagues, Driscoll was familiar with the IJN's Red and Blue Book Codes, having cracked each code and its related additive encryption system. Her work in January 1940 revealed that in the case of Code Book D, each message contained a "key." The challenge was to find the keys and their additive tables. And here is where the IBM punch card systems could rapidly match additive group differences.[8]

By the summer of 1940, enough additives had been recovered to enable Driscoll, Al Pelletier, Alwin Kramer, Phil Cate, Fred Woodrough, and

Dorothy Edgers to begin breaking the code itself.[9] Fairly good progress was made, and by September, the first decrypts finally became available. As part of a January 1941 trip to Britain's Bletchley Park made by Lt. Robert Weeks, Ens. Prescott Currier and Ens. Leo Rosen, and Abraham Sinkov, OP-20-G gave the British Government Code & Ciphers School (GC&CS) some 2,000 recovered solutions taken from Code Book D from September 1940 to January 1941. Two PURPLE diplomatic decoding machines were also provided.[10]

The meeting with the British reaffirmed that there would now be a full exchange of cryptographic systems and cryptanalytical techniques as they pertained to the diplomatic, military, naval, and air services of both Germany and Japan. Unfortunately for the Americans, the British GCCS reneged on sharing a copy of their latest captured model of the German Naval Enigma encoding system; this created major problems for OP-20-GY in its own decrypting operations against the Nazi Kriegsmarine in the Atlantic.[11]

In Hawaii, Thomas Dyer and others from Station HYPO were begging for a chance to take a crack at the 5-Num Code, but were initially rejected.[12] While endeavoring to send more crypto-clerks to Corregidor, Cdr. Safford of OP-20-G at Station NEGAT, apparently following orders, told HYPO's cryptographers to ignore the 5-Num Code and concentrate on the nearly defunct AD Code. This would shut CINCPAC out of the intelligence loop. In January, Safford changed his mind, announcing that HYPO would join NEGAT in the decryption effort in place of CAST. It made sense, since the OP-20-G's naval intelligence group at Pearl Harbor was programmed to receive some of the navy's best cryptographers and a corps of seven top-notch Japanese language translators.[13] On April 24, Safford once again changed his mind. Reasoning that CAST was better positioned immediately to the south of Japan and its major naval bases to intercept operational messages, he now directed it to continue its work on the 5-Num Code. All raw intercepts of the 5-Num Code collected by HYPO would be bundled up and sent via airmail to OP-20-G for actual decoding.[14]

Instead of massing OP-20-G's brainpower, a dozen or more brilliant code breakers working together in a cohesive manner to rapidly bring about up-to-date solutions to Code Book D and its additives, Safford did the exact opposite. With storm warnings ever increasing on the Pacific's horizon, he had now seriously fragmented OP-20-G's effort to attack the 5-Num Code. Was this by accident or design?

While Station CAST's cryptanalysts on Corregidor were able to effect a solid liaison with the British Far East Combined Bureau (FECB) at Singapore and freely trade solutions back and forth to help crack the 5-Num Code, Station HYPO's cryptanalysts were left dangling in the dark, literally twiddling their thumbs for lack of substantive messages of any value to work on. None of the messages they actually worked on provided any decrypted information as to what the IJN's main warships were doing. Even the AD Code, which was never wholly solved for lack of message traffic, essentially remained an enigma.

If Safford thought that CAST was geographically well placed to receive IJN signals, HYPO certainly also was, receiving some 1,000 IJN intercepted messages per day. These were, as standard operating procedures in Hawaii mandated, generally bundled up and forwarded to OP-20-GY in Washington by Pan American Clipper airplane and even sometimes by boat, for decryption and translation.[15]

Not having the advantage of a U.S. Government stolen code book, as was the case with the Merchant Marine Code, all 5-Num decodes and translations were being done through laborious cryptanalysis. Helping matters for the Americans was the "garble" system in use by the Japanese to verify the accuracy of their Five Number coded messages, whereby the sum of all five digits in each code word group had to be divisible by three. This did provide for a crosscheck, but it also limited the number of different code words that could be used in what formed the some 33,000 five-digit groups.[16]

This meant that while the basic Code Book D generally remained the same, OP-20-GY would have to deal with breaking every one of the newly associated additives. This was no small feat, but it could be done, with enough manpower, time, and proper focus. The more brainpower the better. Alas, for the U.S. Navy in 1941 this was not to be.

Even Agnes Driscoll had problems. Following her successful initial break into Code Book D and her earlier work on the Red and Blue Codes, she was taken off the 5-Num decryption effort and reassigned by Safford in October 1940 to begin working on solving the German Navy's Enigma Code. The problem here was that the British had been working for some time on this German electromechanical, cipher-machine-based naval code, which differed significantly from Germany's Army and Air Force Enigma codes. While Bletchley Park had successfully replicated the German Army and Air Force Enigmas with the aid of an actual machine smuggled out of Poland, the Naval Enigma remained a major problem. Based on a series of up to eight distinct rotor settings that were changed every few months, the machine, looking much like a regular typewriter, was impossible to break, let alone replicate.[17]

By salvaging Enigma machines from sunken German submarines and captured surface vessels, the GCCS at Bletchley Park could continue to break the Enigma naval cipher. It was not until the capture of the U-110's Naval Enigma machine, as well as its code books and ciphers, that Alan Turing and his Bletchley Park code breakers could begin to crack the code. This changed the course of the war in the Atlantic.[18]

The Royal Navy successfully captured and salvaged working Enigma Naval cipher machines (such as the U-505 submarine capture intact in the Atlantic by the U.S. Navy in mid-1944). The failure of the German submarine campaign to isolate the British Isles from shipping would be a critical element in the defeat of Nazi Germany.

Unaware that she needed to have an actual Nazi Naval Enigma machine in order to arrive at a decode solution, Driscoll laboriously toiled away throughout 1941 and for some time thereafter in the futile effort to solve what OP-20-GY hoped would be the "cribs," or breaks into the German Naval Enigma's superb crypto system. By December 1941, the navy was focusing over 50 percent, 448 of its total of 738 personnel, on the intercept-decode effort in the Atlantic; the remainder focused on the Pacific.[19]

Madam X's incredible expertise and time could have been far better spent on solving the latest 5-Number IJN Code Book D (called Ango Sho in Japanese) system with its additive 7 version. This system, in effect from July 1, 1941, to December 4, 1941, would ultimately be used to organize and dispatch Japan's primary IJN aircraft carrier attack force against Pearl Harbor, Hawaii, on that fateful day, December 7.

The stereotyped pattern of military text meant that a small number of recoveries, in the realm of 2,000–5,000, could enable a code-breaking team to read a message well enough to make sufficient sense of Japanese intentions. Using a worksheet of rows of the five-digit numbers and searching for the "key" or entry-point number that determined the sequence of the actual code, a roadmap could be identified for making an "informed judgment" about the rest of the coded message. Indexed code groups went into the IBM printouts with actual meanings (called "values") provided by the translators for each number group.[20]

Assisting in the effort were the navy's directional antennas, focused on the IJN's key transmitters, diversity receivers to overcome the fading of signals, and recorders for copying high-speed automatic transmissions. Of course, all this also depended on the navy's highly trained intercept operators and their experienced supervisors.[21] At the end of each intercept report, each navy intercept operator affixed his two- or three-code letter initials.

Station CAST, now directed to lead the attack on the current IJN Code Book D, "took the bull by the horns," losing no time in enhancing its mutual 5-Number code-breaking relationship with the British FECB at the latter's Seletar naval base in Singapore. The British responded in early March 1941 by forwarding via cable to CAST their own exploitation of the Five Numeral system: some 500 code book value solutions, about 4,000 "subtractor groups" (additives), 500 worksheets with the code cipher removed, and 290 indicator subtractors for secret message numbers. On March 5, Adm. Thomas Hart, commander-in-chief, U.S. Asiatic Fleet, forwarded this important news to the navy's CNO Stark, via a secret radio dispatch.[22]

That same day, Rudolf J. Fabian, officer in charge of CAST, sent a packet to Safford's OP-20-GY that included 44 photographic negatives of the IJN's "Five numeral book [5-Num]—subtractors" and 12 photographic negatives of its "Five numeral code book and instructions," as well as one photographic negative of "Indicator subtractor tables."[23] Many of the IJN's pattern messages, using the same general vocabulary over and over again, could often be read with as few as 1,500 decoded meanings. CAST was making progress!

The Japanese also used different types of diplomatic communications codes for messages between Japan's foreign ministry in Tokyo and its embassies and consulates around the world, including Honolulu. The Tokyo-Washington link was top priority by both U.S. Army and Navy code breakers. The other major code-breaking focus of ONI in Washington, DC, involved MAGIC, the PURPLE Machine decryption system. Each diplomatic message intercepted from Tokyo was promptly decrypted and prepared for translation. While messages in relatively minor diplomatic code systems were often merely glanced at, those in PURPLE were decrypted and translated immediately.

The Diplomatic Section of the Navy Department's decrypting unit (OP-20-GY) considered this effort so important that by February 1941 it maintained 23 personnel on 24-hour standing watches, seven days a week. Once an intercept operator had received an encrypted message, it was transcribed and processed by the PURPLE machine. This involved setting the stepped levers in the correct sequence and running the message through the machine, which stripped off the encryption and produced Japanese text in Roman kana-text letters. Both the army and navy Japanese language officers then translated the message into English.

These teams were organized into four sections: one officer and three experienced petty officers, as well as other personnel including three translators on duty. They verified and solved, as necessary, the key settings for each day's take, producing 14 copies of each message. As time went on, the army and navy shared the work, the navy taking the odd days and the army the even days. By 11 a.m., each day, Kramer, head of the Translation Section (OP-20-GZ), would segregate, cross-reference, and then brief the most important PURPLE messages to the senior members of the navy, before they went on up the chain of command to Roosevelt himself.[24]

By the beginning of December 1941, OP-20-G was diverting 30 percent of its intercept, 12 percent of its decrypting, and 50 percent of its Japanese translation effort to Japan's diplomatic codes. The best coverage of the PURPLE Berlin-Tokyo circuit was received at Corregidor, which would then reencipher the messages and forward them in its Electronic Cipher

Machine's (ECM) KOPEK (also COPEK) crypto channel system reserved for technical aspects of decryption. The Tokyo-Washington traffic was monitored at both Bainbridge Island's Station SAIL and San Francisco, where transcriptions were recorded and then sent via Bell Telephone Teletype to Cheltenham's Station M. In Hawaii, Station HYPO continued to send its recorded but not decrypted or translated signals traffic to Washington via airmail and sometimes ECM.[25] PURPLE or MAGIC machines were now in place only at Station M in Cheltenham, Corregidor's CAST in the Philippines, and at Britain's Bletchley Park.

What is amazing is that Hawaii's 14th Naval District's HYPO had been denied a PURPLE decoding machine by Art McCollum, with the excuse that the machine's signals' traffic was diplomatic in nature and involved technical "matters of security" and was therefore not important to Adm. Kimmel's military mission of defending America's West Coast. Safford used the patently false excuse that there was a "shortage" of Japanese translators at HYPO and therefore it was "undesirable for the Hawaiian Decrypting Unit to handle diplomatic messages."

As a result, Adm. Husband E. Kimmel, the relatively new commander-in-chief of America's principal battle fleet in the Pacific, was now denied knowledge of what the IJN was doing. His primary code-breaking and message-processing center, HYPO, was now completely cut off from *any* ability to decode not only IJN operational message traffic but also Japan's diplomatic traffic.[26] Kimmel was now kept in the dark with no reliable code-breaking resources at his disposal that could shed light on the IJN's or Tokyo's intentions!

Another diplomatic code also figured in ONI's Japanese intelligence intercept operations. This one was a second-tier consular code system known as J-19 by the Americans, but as Tsu by the Japanese. Diplomatic text was transmitted using regular Roman letters and *not* in the kana code system. OP-20-GY decrypted the J-19 messages through cryptographic analysis, which meant that the code had to be broken anew each day to recover its key, but this was readily done over and over again. The navy was assisted in this effort through its "back-door" (breaking, entering, and photographing) espionage operations against Japanese diplomatic offices in Washington and New York, which enabled OP-20-GY to stay current with Tokyo's latest J-19 diplomatic and even the Merchant Marine Codes. With this advantage, both radio and cable intercepts were accomplished in Washington.

Some cable messages were photographed by naval intelligence personnel as they passed through the commercial RCA and British-owned Mackay Radio & Telegraph companies in San Francisco. Diplomatic radio messages from Tokyo back and forth to its consulates were intercepted and transcribed in the Philippines, Hawaii, and California. Mackay and RCA permitted U.S. naval intelligence officials to photograph Japanese Honolulu consulate's diplomatic traffic. During 1941, Mackay was responsible for March, May, July, September, and November; RCA covered April, June, August, October, and December. Globe Wireless also participated on April 2 and 30, and October 17 and 29.[27]

At HYPO, even though Cdr. Rochefort's signals center processing unit had qualified personnel who could decode J-19, the messages collected by the Army's Station FIVE at Fort Shafter were merely bundled up and forwarded by airmail to Washington. No effort was made by Station FIVE to inform either Rochefort or Maj. Gen. Short's G-2 (intelligence) about the J-19 intercepts.[28] Once again, HYPO's talented team of highly trained cryptographers was cut out of the code-breaking picture, which would have serious repercussions in early December 1941.

TRAFFIC ANALYSIS

Since the early 1930s, experience had shown that a great deal of information could be gleaned just from the headings of messages. Therefore, in addition to code breaking, there was radio traffic analysis (TA), being done by the navy's radio intelligence personnel.

Ship identification could be ascertained from a knowledge of the radio call sign system and noting which stations tended to be senders ("chickens") and which stations tended to be receivers ("eggs"). This often allowed a complete reconstruction of the radio signal networks themselves, leading to further identification of the fleet involved and giving the code breaker an idea of what the message sender was communicating.

Supply ships in the form of tankers (what the navy often calls the "train") could also be a dead giveaway: who was the tanker talking to? Movements and operations of Japanese naval forces were often revealed inadvertently as they announced a change from one communications zone to another (north to south and vice versa). Increased radio activity and/or ship movement reports over and above the norm also implied impending operations.[29] Code breakers and traffic analysts needed to interact constantly, exchanging interpretations and deductions as to what the message traffic really meant or otherwise implied as to what was going on.

RFP

A key component of TA was *radio fingerprinting* (RFP). Navy communications intercept operators discovered that the IJN's radio transmitters gave off peculiar or unique operating sounds and that a radio transmitter's operators had their own peculiar sending characteristics. These, over time, would allow an alert operator to identify a transmitter by its characteristic noise pattern. In part this was due to the construction of the Japanese transmitters themselves and their somewhat antiquated tube technology. Compared to the German naval transmitters, which were standardized in terms of design, construction, circuitry, and components, the IJN's were completely the opposite, allowing the American naval radio intercept operators to recognize the inconsistencies in transmission sounds.

Once an IJN transmitter was identified with a certain ship, it made no difference as to whether the ship's signal operator changed its radio identification call sign or whether the message was encrypted in a complex code. Most IJN transmitters were bolted to a table in each ship's signals station, which made it difficult to practice radio deception by switching out transmitters.

To aid in pattern matching to identify a specific radio transmitter and ship, the U.S. Navy used oscilloscopes. The oscilloscope allowed the operator to conduct visual pattern matching on a fluorescent screen of the actual radio wave being emitted. The intercepted radio signal was displayed on the oscilloscope and photographed to reveal its wave form.[30] The identification came from variances in wave consistency. The photograph was then compared to photographs of other known radio transmitters' wave patterns to make the corresponding identification or identify a previously unknown transmitter (ship or land-based headquarters). Voltage modulations, as well as relay breaks, buildup, and decay times and other electrical or mechanical faults were also contributing characteristics to signal transmitter identification. Station CAST, as an example, maintained a special working area at Corregidor for conducting "radio photo signal analysis," which received its wave form photos taken by its high-speed camera and electron oscilloscope. Even if Japanese radio operators were changed out for periods of time, the wave form of the signal gave away the identification of the sending radio station and its ship.

RFP also concerned itself with how signal transmitter operators struck their Morse code (kana) keys as they made their dots and dashes. A unique "fist," or distinctive way of thumbing the transmitter's sending key, could often reveal from which ship the signal had been received. No two operators transmitted in exactly the same way. A particular palm "swing" was so pronounced that it could be recognized as if it were the sender's voice. The speed of transmission could also be a recognition giveaway, especially if the station employed high-speed automatic keying. High-speed manual transmissions usually came from shore stations (headquarters) or flagships.[31]

TINA

TINA was a linking identification technique. Its purpose was to assist visually in recognizing an individual operator's sending characteristics (the fist or swing) in relation to a "perfect" Morse signal. Its paper-tape rendering of abnormally long or short dots, dashes, and pauses due to a sending operator's peculiar key stroke were printed out and compared to a special logarithmic scale on a "TINA ruler." This operated much like a form of handwriting comparison, thus indicating the operator's keying style and further identifying the ship. Similar in function to the serpentina fire alarm reporting box tape system used during the late 1930s and early 1940s, it was generally used concurrently with RDF tracking data and oscilloscopes. Station CAST maintained a special work area for its ink tape recorders, which were noted as a "transcribing unit" and listed as part of its equipment inventory.[32]

Each radio intercept operator maintained a worksheet on which all key data concerning the intercepted signal was logged in. Fourteen distinct pieces of information and a space for comments formed the main body of the worksheet. Each item had its own distinct block or space:

Sending station's radio identification call sign

Radio frequency on which the signal was heard

Time of transmission

Date of transmission

Radio call sign "addresses" identifying to whom the message was being sent

Times the transmitter was heard calling

Calls heard in conjunction with the types of message traffic sent

Radio station serial number

Originator's own serial number

Signal strength

Quality of sender

Morse keying speed

Zone/traffic time

Operator's peculiarities

Transmitter characteristics

Additional comments[33]

All intercepted Japanese-originated message traffic was recorded by the navy in Tokyo time. For instance, November 25 in Hawaii is November 26 in Japan, because the International Date Line is in the mid-Pacific. In other words, America's day begins in Guam. The IJN's policy was to always use Tokyo time, even when a warship was located in another part of the world (much like the U.S. Navy's radio dispatches, which are normally recorded in Greenwich Civil Time).

A radio dispatch number (NR), kept for record keeping purposes by the IJN sending station, was always included in the heading of the message and usually found on the intercept operator log sheets as well. While radio station call signs changed now and then, the IJN's tendency to maintain the numerical message sequences made the comparative identification of the new sending station that much easier. Additionally, the Secret Message Series (SMS) reference numbers usually preceded the text of the main body and were not only a chronological numerical record of the sending person's own messages but also a convenient method by which the U.S. Navy's own intercept operators, code breakers, and traffic analysts could identify the sender of the message. Each IJN commander or ship had its own distinct SMS number series, running from 1 to 999; it would be repeated for the next series of messages.

Helping the U.S. Navy's major message processing centers in identifying Japanese ships and fleet units were the variety of methods and errors the IJN's signal transmitter operators made. Always useful in tipping the IJN's intentions were the Code Movement Reports, which were routinely transmitted as standard operating procedure by its warships, but then intercepted across the Pacific by many of the navy's stations. Usually broadcast in a simple code, they indicated the ship's departure from a certain port for a new destination. When IJN ships moved from place to place, they often changed time zones (based on latitude). This in itself gave away that it was a ship in movement and its probable general direction.

The quality of the sending station's transmissions could also help in establishing what level of command was involved. "Good" quality usually indicated a major shore station or major flagship. Sometimes the IJN used "collective calls" to make contact with its fleet units by type of ships. In the case of forces afloat, the flagship was usually the directing station; on shore, it was the ground headquarters of the senior station. If two or more stations responded back to the sender, the identification of one often revealed the others as a group. When Japan's Emperor Hirohito sent out an imperial order or directive to his IJN commands, the signal was called an "Imperial Rescript."

Sometimes intercept operators could sort out call signs by the frequencies they were transmitted on. At other times an IJN operator would make a revealing mistake, such as when a new system of call signs came into being and he inadvertently used the old call, caught his error, and then retransmitted with the new call sign designator. If an IJN sending station had doubts about the receiving station's ability to successfully hear the message, it would sometimes send the same message several times and even sign off with its own call sign when no answer was received. This was called "sending in blind," and it gave a U.S. Navy radio intercept operator many more chances to transcribe the message. Of course all IJN radio operators were told not to stereotype their messages, but this was often impossible to do, especially with the externally formatted headings and addresses.[34] Radio signals were susceptible to compromise in many different ways, and traffic analysis (TA) played a major role in exploiting the situation.

Each navy monitor station, as well as the major processing centers, had a copy of the latest IJN radio call sign list (also referred to as a "call list"). This was the bedrock of ship identification. The IJN's RCS system was carefully crafted in what was called its Yobidashi Fugo (Radio Call Sign Table). It was systematically changed every few months; the changes became known as HYOOs or editions (always called "list" or "table"). For example, HYOO 8 or Yobidashi Fugo Hyoo Hachi (Radio Call Sign Table Eight) went into effect on August 1 and terminated on October 31, 1941. The next, HYOO 9, went into effect on September 20 for the month of November and then was replaced again on December 1, 1941, by HYOO 10, which was used until March 1942.

Each U.S. intercept station maintained its own master RCS index, which was updated informally by hand on a constant basis. At the principal processing centers of CAST, HYPO, and NEGAT, this was done both informally and also generally weekly on a more formal basis via IBM printouts, which listed all the radio call signs of the entire IJN chronologically by number and alphabetically by letter. These were then usually further integrated with RDF data for appropriate identification and tracking of each ship, as well as actual ship identifications. By the fall of 1941, both the radio intercept and RDF intercept stations copied the Japanese Morse code in its *romanji* kana form and regular Morse code for all numbers. Robert Stinnett found in his study of IJN radio call signs that in September 1941 the secret (tactical) calls of HYOO 8 were not changed and remained in effect up to December 8, 1941 (Tokyo date/time). Undoubtedly this was to ensure that, as Japan went to war with the United States, all the IJN's fleet units' radio networks were operating on clearly understood secret wartime codes.[35]

Cdr. Safford at OP-20-G required each of his intercept stations worldwide to issue monthly reports, which generally contained some key call signs and RDF data. Once an IJN fleet and its associated ships had been identified, this information would be constantly cross-referenced and updated for quick reference as needed.[36] Intercept operators found that while HA MU 5 might signify the IJN's South China Fleet, HA MU 55 signified the commander-in-chief, South China Fleet. Sometimes just a single kana and a number represented an aircraft. The HYOOs were one of the critical keys to the U.S. Navy's successful exploitation of its splendid arrangement in the Pacific, a secret weapon contributing to identifying and locating Japan's warships through their radio transmission call signs.

IBM

All this information, including that of the intercept operators' registration of every single IJN message monitored and then transcribed on their RIP-5 typewriters and worksheets, would have been hopelessly confusing and impossible to work with if it had not been for the adroit use of the IBM tabulator machines that supported all of the navy's key processing centers.[37] HYPO's Joseph Rochefort said that the IBM tabulator machines were a core element in his signal intelligence operations. They were the closest thing the navy had at that time that could be compared to the modern computer systems of today.

The IBM machines, often managed and maintained by cryptologic clerks, yeomen, and IBM-trained civilian technicians under special contract, were usually located in a special room, processing data from up to a thousand messages per day. By January 1941, OP-20-GZ was using 16 machines alone, operated eight hours a day by nine men. The RIP-5 kana typewriters and the IBM card sorters and keypunch equipment all operated in a synergistic manner. The card sorters were particularly important to identify information items of interest to the officer cryptanalysts on duty. For code breaking, the keypunch machines enabled one to identify the frequency with which certain letters, words, and even expressions appeared in coded radio traffic or in plain Japanese. These could then match specific code groups to related letters and words as was the case, and it could all be done with considerable speed.[38]

A tremendous number of IBM punch cards were utilized. Rochefort estimated that his operation used 2 to 3 million cards per month! By merely assembling the cards, HYPO could "pick out any group or two or three groups, or half-a-dozen groups . . . in a message." By running the cards through the collators and then the tabulators, the technicians working the system could then print out the forms that helped to break the coded messages. The data derived from one message would normally require the use of up to 70 cards. A message with 100 words or code groups might even require as many as 200 key-punched cards. Once processed via the collator or tabulator, the key data could be recalled almost instantly. The data then went into enough books so that each translator and cryptanalyst would have his own book to work with. It was a uniform process followed by CAST, HYPO, and OP-20-GY at NEGAT. The punch cards themselves were stored in boxes to be readily available as needed.[39]

The IBM tabulating machine system was fairly complex and involved the integrated use of up to as many as a dozen distinct machines. All messages to be deciphered were marked, to avoid wasting time and possible duplication. If two or more messages were intercepted, they were compared, and the best copy marked for deciphering. Cards typically sorted

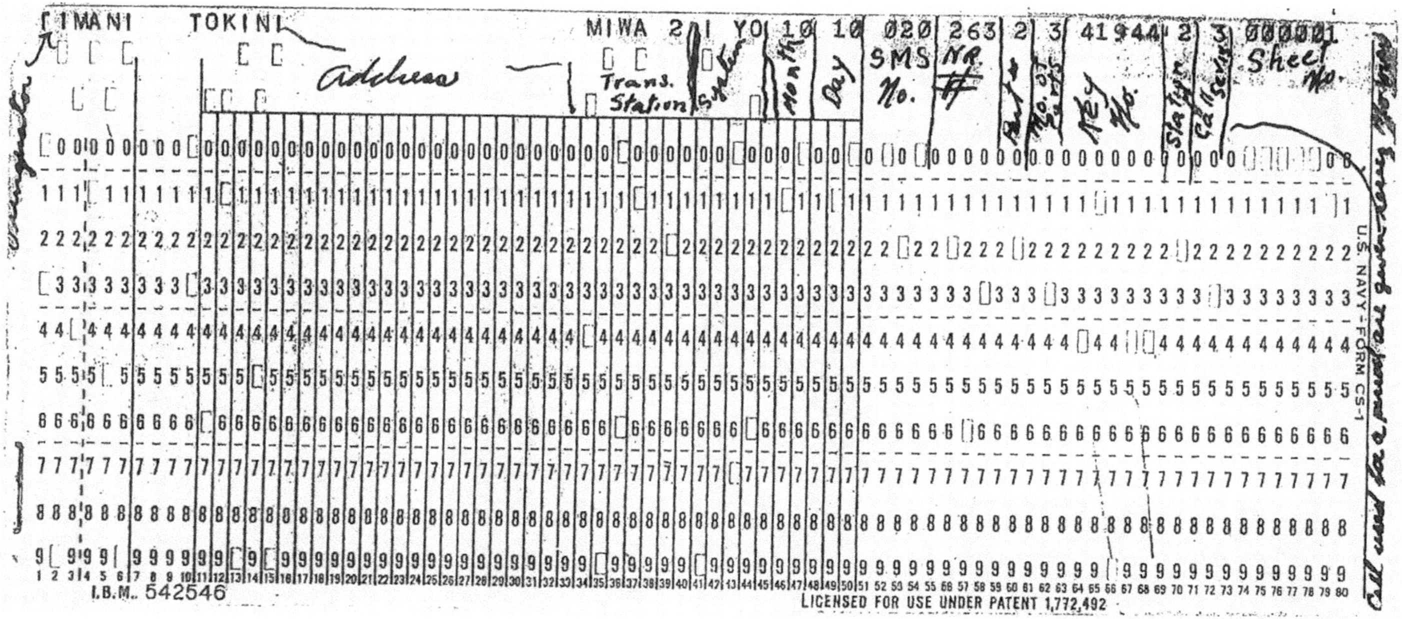

Example IBM punch card. (IBM File, Archives II, National Archives)

IBM printout reference room. (naval district unknown). (IBM File, Archives II, National Archives)

out both the headings and endings of IJN messages. Cards containing keys and ciphers of the message text were sent to a relay conversion unit, which converted the key and cipher to code, which was then punched by a technician into a reproducer machine. Information was stored from each card and repeated cipher groups were identified.

Another machine unit could be used to assist in the location of the messages with a given set of recovered additives, recognizing the frequent code groups in the code system. This also helped the cryptanalyst to correlate and to test the message code group of interest against several thousand messages. Intercepted messages taken down on teletype tape could also be transferred or punched directly into cards. This deciphering process enabled the cards to be punched with meanings to permit messages to be readable in clear text.

The collating portion of the IBM system allowed code and other data files to be merged together, allowing sequence checking, matching, counting, and sorting to take place. Fed by cards into a sorter machine at the rate of 400 per minute, the sorter automatically arranged the cards in alphabetical or numerical order. The tabulating printer was the final step in the process; it printed the information from the cards in an organized manner on the actual paper printouts. Controlled by a special plug board, the information from the cards could be listed in any desired position on the printout.[40]

RDF—RADIO DIRECTION FINDING

OP-20-GX maintained 16 radio direction finding (RDF) stations in the Pacific. The British Admiralty had 20 of its own stations in the British Isles alone and a further 69 covering the rest of the world throughout the British Empire. Of these, 17 stations from Britain's greater worldwide network were arrayed against the IJN, supporting the FECB at Singapore.

Traffic analysis (TA) operations would not have been as complete or as valuable if RDF had not been incorporated into the navy's intelligence-gathering system. RDF might have been able to stand alone as a reliable intelligence-gathering tool against the IJN, but its full value became apparent when linked to TA techniques such as radio fingerprinting's use of oscilloscopes, TINA, radio call sign identification, IBM machine operations, and just good common sense on the part of the intercept operators about what they were hearing day after day and night after night from the IJN's signals networks. If one could not break the enemy's naval codes, as was the case with Station HYPO in Hawaii, then RDF and TA became credible alternatives to ascertain what Adm. Yamamoto's order of battle, plans, and intentions were. While a message heading could reveal the composition of an IJN fleet, RDF could pinpoint its actual location and even direction or pattern of movement.

As a radio signal tracking method, RDF depended on locating radio stations through the use of specially constructed receiving antennae that could rotate 360 degrees in conjunction with a compass, using zero degrees or true north as its baseline for measurement.

Since the earth is shaped somewhat like an egg, the direction of travel of electromagnetic waves toward the receiving RDF station could be measured by comparing their reverse azimuth angle to that of true north. The RDF station's own bearing back toward the transmitting station was known as the *true bearing* and was what was actually plotted on the "case chart." The corresponding coded data were then sent by ECM radio to the principal processing stations' (CAST, HYPO, or OP-20-GX) own tracking sections for more precise, triangulated bearing plots. In this regard, the accuracy of RDF bearings or azimuths was important.

An Imperial Beach (Station ITEM) report of July 17, 1941, stated that bearings taken on intermediate and high frequencies over distances of

2,000 miles were "approximately the same." Other data indicated that bearing accuracy varied between 1 degree for strong signals and 5 degrees for weak signals. Both IJN low- and high-frequency transmitters operating from 500 to 1,000 watts had their signals ranging out to as far as 12,000 miles. On a great circle sailing chart for the North Pacific, the actual straight-line distances for signal interception averaged between 1,300 and 4,700 miles (Tokyo, Corregidor, Guam, Oahu, Dutch Harbor, etc.).[41]

With the right equipment, a naval intercept operator at an RDF station could hear a ship's broadcast and within a few seconds take a bearing or fix on the signal. The Model DY-2 Radio Direction Finder, with its 28-foot-long operating arm and 16-foot dipoles operating on a range of 2.5 to 30 megacycles, was standard throughout the North Pacific.[42] While the RDF station could only make a single directional azimuth toward the transmitting station, it required two or more other RDF stations to obtain the necessary multiple bearings and thus obtain a intersection location. Three triangulated bearings from as many RDF stations were ideal, because they gave a more reliable plot or intersect point on a nautical chart.

Since the bearings were taken on signals often traversing thousands of miles of the earth's surface, the triangular intersection or fix looked much like a "cocked hat." Assuming that the position fix of the targeted transmitter was at the center of the "triangle," making a more or less equidistant fix from the three crossing points, the bearing's plot position could then be considered reasonably accurate by an RDF processing center. Great circle sailing charts, *not* Mercator map projections, were the only reliable method of plotting RDF bearings, since they followed a straight line and were therefore the shortest distance between any two points on the earth's curved surface. A Mercator map is a *flat projection* on a plane of the curved, egg-shaped surface of the earth. As such, it causes extreme distortion in terms of actual navigation, and attempts to plot accurate RDF bearings and intersections are impossible.

Because the Pacific Ocean was so large, the navy generally had to break that geographic area into a series of sailing charts—all keyed to the true North Pole. Each RDF site's own individual IJN ship bearing was placed on a separate 8 × 10-inch horizontal chart by the operator who took the bearing at the intercepting station. When filled out, the chart, often overprinted with a compass rose (showing true north) to facilitate drawing the bearing, was now called a "case." The targeted ship's radio call sign (HYOO identifier) and the initial(s) of the RDF operator were also shown on the case chart. The intercept operator evaluated the reliability of the bearing. Each RDF operator, like his contemporary radio signal intercept operators, was trained in basic Japanese kana to facilitate IJN call sign identification.[43]

Central plotting of RDF data taken on the IJN was generally accomplished at OP-20-GX in Washington and HYPO at Pearl Harbor. CAST, in the Philippines, also used traffic analysis, call sign recovery, and RDF to locate and identify IJN fleet units in the South China Sea, near Palao and also the Mandated Islands. Oscilloscopes could also be used to flatten down their wave projections into a horizontal line when the receiving station's antenna was aimed precisely along the bearing. The operator then shifted his gauge from the scope to the tabletop in front of him to obtain the bearing actual data.[44] After receiving the various inputs of RDF intercept station bearing data on a daily basis over the navy's special TESTM code circuit, the processing stations' plotting centers would then note the location of each of the individual RDF stations and further make their own intersecting plots on a suitable and usually much larger great circle sailing chart, approximately 4 x 6 feet in size or even larger.

Using each intercept station's true north and zero degree reference base bearing from an overprinted compass rose for each station, the bearing lines were then drawn. The ideal situation was to receive bearing line data that intersected at right angles (90 degrees). Using a plotting scale or temp plate, the various azimuths were then struck off in an attempt to achieve at least a fix, if not "cocked hat" configuration. Keeping track of the dates and times of the fixes and the related radio call signs of the IJN's most important capital ships, along with oscilloscope and TINA matches, gave CAST, HYPO, and OP-20-GX a reasonably good idea of Yamamoto's current operational activity. Sometimes the positions of Japanese merchant and naval shipping could be determined by their sending of weather and other administrative plain language signals that included the ship's respective position.[45] By May 1941, OP-20-G and the British Admiralty were even exchanging RDF tracking data on German U-boat submarines in the Atlantic.[46]

STATION CAST TRACKS THE IJN

Station CAST, now designated as the lead code-breaking focal point for dealing with the IJN's operational Code Book D, forged ahead and by early December 1941 was beefed up to 78 personnel: 9 officers and 19 cryptoclerks for code-breaking purposes, and 50 radio and RDF intercept personnel (including Station BAKER's 8 personnel at Guam). It had a full complement of IBM equipment: a Type 405 alphabetical tabulator, a Type 075 sorter, a Type 035 card puncher, and a Type 513 reproducing gang punch. Other equipment included the transfer of 10 RIP-5 Typewriters from the commandant of the 14th Naval District in Hawaii to the commandant of the 16th Naval District in the Philippines.[47]

By May 11, 1941, CAST had made sufficient breaks into the IJN's HYOO 8 radio call system that it was able to identify the *Akagi* aircraft carrier's radio call sign as HA MI 9 and even RDF its location in the vicinity of the Sasebo Naval Base on Kyushu Island.[48]

During the previous month, April, the War Department had decided to defend outright the Philippines. Gen. Douglas MacArthur was recalled to active duty as the commander of U.S. Army Forces in the Far East (USAFFE), receiving top priority for modern weapons such as the B-17 heavy bomber. His war plan for the defense of the Philippines was authorized in late November by the Joint Board in Washington, DC, and included the intention to carry out B-17 strikes against all Philippine-oriented attacking forces and their bases, but not Japan itself.

CAST also received a copy of the PURPLE machine from OP-20-G, which now provided decrypts of the Japanese Foreign Office's most secret diplomatic traffic to both Adm. Hart and Gen. MacArthur. Diplomatic circuits covered were typically Tokyo–Berlin–Tokyo, Tokyo–Moscow–Tokyo, Tokyo–Rome–Tokyo, and Tokyo–Batavia–Tokyo. The consular circuit was typically Tokyo–Honolulu–Tokyo. The military circuits were: fleet commanders and major air groups, commander-in-chief South China Force, major shore stations and the Tokyo broadcast channel to all major military commands.[49] The Japanese were taking a notable interest in the Philippine defenses, reporting that there were 460 planes and 1,300 pilots on hand, along with 10,000 U.S. Army troops and some 130,000 Philippine Army soldiers.[50]

Traffic analysis (TA) at CAST revealed the IJN's communication plan, which led to an understanding of how the current Japanese Navy was organized in terms of its order of battle for its entire fleet. By mid-June, Lt. Fabian, CAST's commander, had begun to discover the details of a new IJN carrier command. This was in considerable part due to the insights and efforts of Lt. Jefferson Dennis, who brought together the station's TA activity and meshed it with its 5-Num decoding effort to produce a daily written summary on the activities and locations of various Japanese ships and aircraft, as deduced from their communications patterns.[51]

On August 30, Fabian wrote to Safford at OP-20-G that his replacement, Lt. John Lietwiler, an expert in Code Book D decoding (learned from Agnes Driscoll), had arrived on station and was taking over as the officer-in-charge (OIC) of CAST. With the IJN's changes to its newest operational code version, Code Book D, Additive 7, CAST was just barely reading the current IJN 5-Num message traffic (the British FECB in Singapore was having the same problem). But TA techniques were producing valuable information on radio call signs, enabling all sections to trade their findings and form a special intelligence data correlating center with Dennis in charge.

Fabian had visited the FECB at Singapore and was impressed with their methodology: integrating radio intercepts and decoded messages with all forms of traffic analysis, as well as RDF. With CAST and FECB exchanging cipher and code information as well as IJN RDF bearings and movements through a highly secure British radio system called COSMO, Fabian realized that CAST was on the right track. Contrasted to this was OP-20-G with its internally compartmentalized system of signal intelligence operations, which was not taking full advantage of the assets available to it. Fabian pointedly criticized Safford for allowing his OP-20-GY to work on the old 5-Number cipher period, instead of concentrating fully on the IJN's new operational Code Book D and its additive 7 in support of CAST's efforts.[52]

October 1941 was a very good month for CAST. Lt. J. M. Hess arrived with a copy of Lee Parke's OP-20-GY Jeep IV crypto machine (mentioned by Ingersoll in his memo of October 4, 1940) that could automatically decode the additive/subtractive columnar Table 7 of the IJN's 5-Number operational code. Lietwiler was impressed; the machine revealed that there were only about 500 relevant keys, which now enabled his code breakers to break down the coded additives more quickly. This was helpful in accomplishing the needed mathematical solutions for the various indicator subtractors.[53]

That same month, Lt. Dennis and Lt. Rufus Taylor put together an IJN fleet organization report based entirely upon TA. Addressed to OPNAV (Station NEGAT) via Adm. Hart, the CINCAF Intelligence Officer Lt. Cdr. Redfield Mason endorsed the report, indicating that it revealed that the IJN had taken up a wartime posture! A month later, another report was sent out informing OPNAV that some 250 merchant marine ships had been conscripted into the IJN, with a major portion of them located along the Straits of Taiwan and points south.[54] Since CAST had been tracking the IJN's buildup of warships in the South China Sea off the coast of French Indochina, it could accomplish this fairly easily.

CAST was placing a major emphasis on tracking via TA and RDF what was now identified as the Commander Carriers and the Air Squadrons of the Combined Fleet, operating off of the aircraft carriers *Akagi, Kaga, Zuikaku, Shokaku, Soryu,* and *Hiryu*—all of which would constitute the IJN's December 7, 1941, Pearl Harbor Strike Force.[55]

A CAST monthly report for the entire month of October 1941 contains 44 pages of radio call signs and RDF bearings that show the gradual shifting from administrative (two kana + number) to tactical battle formation (number + two kana) radio call signs. All of the above aircraft carriers were identified:

Akagi	HA MI 9 and 8 YU NA
Kaga	HO MO 1 and 7 RI RO
Zuikaku	1 KI RA
Hiryu	9 RU SI
Soryu	8 HO RE
Shokaku	RO TA 6 and 7 MU TO

The *Akagi* had some 12 bearings taken against it, the *Hiryu* 25 bearings taken, the *Soryu* 16 bearings, and the *Kaga* 31 bearings. These six aircraft

Secret—

C

CAVITE   TEST

12-5-41

S1511 Bearings 12 hours 4th: YoKoØ TaHa 8
NeNo1 at 2, KaNe1 at 348, YuKe3 at 92,
SuKa4 at 258, HeFu4 at 80, MeTe6 at 110,
NiRa9 at 358, 8YuNa at 30

DECLASSIFIED
Authority 003012
By EC NARA Date 5/17/11

```
JKIUT ZASMI NEXXB EARIN GSTWE LVEHO URSEO URTEX XYOKO
YOKOZ EROXT AHATA HAEIG HTXNE NONEN OONEA TTWOX KANEK ANEON
EATTH REEFO RTYEI GHTXD UKEYU KETHR EEATN IOETY TWOXS UKASU
KAFOU RATTW OFIFT YEIGH TXHEF UHEFU FOURA TEIGH TYXME TEMET
ESIXA TONEO NEZER OXNIR ANIRA NINEA TTHRE EFIFT YEIGH TXEIG
HTYUN AYUNA ATTHI RTGZX BEARI NGSXX RTGBN HUJMN  C 05 1511
```

TESTM call signs. (Philippines [CAST] File, Archives II, National Archives)

carriers were grouped under the command of the First Air Fleet (FAF), also known as the Air Ron Combined Fleet (2 NO KO), which had 10 bearings taken against it. The IJN's Combined Fleet (7 NI SI and 6 O SU) command headquarters had 9 bearings taken, and the Flagship of the South China Fleet (HA ME 8 and SI WI 5) had some 64 bearings taken against it.[56]

Little by little, traffic analysis and RDF were making the identifications and determining the organization of the IJN's primary battle fleets. The most prominent fleet that should have stood out as part of the IJN's reorganization for battle was the "Striking Force" and "Advanced Expeditionary Force," terms used for the identification of the First Air Fleet (FAF), which would ultimately carry out the attack on Pearl Harbor. These two terms showed up in the October 13, 1941, message traffic heading involving a Combined Fleet dispatch.[57]

A typical CAST encrypted TESTM radio call sign and RDF bearings report of 1200 hours, December 4, sent to OP-20-G and HYPO at Pearl Harbor from Tunnel AFIRM, Corregidor in clear text, along with the encrypted TESTM style (note that 8 YUNA is the call sign for the *Akagi* aircraft carrier):[58]

TESTM CALL SIGN AND RDF BEARINGS DISPATCH

CAST was also assisted in its RDF and TA efforts by its own organizational link to Station B or BAKER at Libugon, Guam, to the British FECB at Singapore, and to the Dutch Kamer 14 station at Bandoeng, Java, Netherlands East Indies. Station BAKER's RDF tracking station at Guam, located some 1500 miles to the east of the Philippines, gave CAST its badly needed additional bearings with just enough of a right (90 degree) angle to obtain a fairly reliable fix in the IJN's ships. The complete lack of BAKER's RDF reports for 1941 at NARA Archives II (College Park) forces one to rely on an earlier April 27 to May 31, 1941, radio call sign report to gain some idea of what Station B was doing. During that time, the station took down some 193 radio call signs, about six per day.[59]

In addition to its crypto attack on Code Book D, radio fingerprinting, and the use of oscilloscopes to identify IJN radio call signs, for triangulated bearings CAST relied on the British-Singapore-based FECB and its Station Y system consisting of a RDF substation network of upwards of some 17 distinct stations, including

Stonecutters Island (Hong Kong)

Bukit Gombak and Kanji (Singapore)

Esquimalt (Canada)

Bombay (India)

Auckland and Waipapakauri (New Zealand)

Darwin (Australia)

Fiji

Complicating the situation for the British was the fact that an actual movement of an IJN ship, say from Ariake Bay to Amoy (780 miles), would only cause a RDF bearing change of 7 degrees at Stonecutters, 3 degrees at Kranji, and 9 degrees at Auckland. Any bearing of 3 degrees or less was suspected as a possible error and would have to be confirmed by another station. FECB's RDF reports not only went out by coded radio dispatch immediately to CAST and via the American naval observer assigned to Singapore but also directly to the British deputy director of Military Intelligence in London, who passed on the Far East dispatches to the assistant U.S. military attaché, Col. Greenwell.[60]

Under the direction of Capt. J. W. Henning, Kamer 14 at the Bandung Technical College in Java was also making a break into Code Book D's five-digit IJN fleet system. Kamer 14 passed its intelligence intercepts to the FECB and also passed key intercepts and RDF reports to CAST via its Royal Netherlands Navy Cdr. H. D. Lander and Lt. Cdr. Wisden, attached to Adm. Hart in Manila.[61]

On November 16, John Lietwiler wrote a letter to his counterpart, Lee Parke at OP-20-GY, which offered a frank insight into CAST's signal intelligence operations: "The novelty has worn off the Jeep IV now and it is seldom in use. We have pretty well proved that it takes longer to set up ten groups and run the check by machine than do it by hand." Noting that he had 10 personnel working on Code Book D, Table 7 and only one Jeep IV, he went on to say that CAST's method of cryptanalysis attack had changed:

> Using 400 high frequency groups we have compiled a table of 24,000 differences. Two days ago I saw MYERS [Albert E. Myers Jr.] walk right across the first 20 columns of a sheet using this method almost exclusively. We are reading enough current traffic to keep two translators busy, i.e., with their code recovery efforts etc. included.

In his letter, Lietwiler went on to castigate Parke, much as Fabian had rebuked Safford earlier, saying: "I certainly wish you could see your way clear to drop the ancient history [outdated 5-Number Code editions] side of this cipher and work with us on each current system as it comes up." Apparently Parke wanted Lietweiler's CAST to also focus completely on the outdated Table 6, previously in effect from February 1 to July 31, 1941. Despite the fact that Safford, head of OP-20-G, had seen and initialed ("LES") receipt of the letter, nothing changed.[62]

This begs the question as to why Safford and Dennis would want to delay, if not stall, CAST as the navy's primary decryption attack on the 5-Number Code, Table 7, which was the precise code that the IJN was using at that time to organize, prepare, and marshal its fleets for impending battle operations against the United States in the Pacific. In a SRH-406 study ("Pre-Pearl Harbor Japanese Naval Dispatches") of some 26,581 coded messages transmitted during the period of September and December 1941, the vast majority, 23,778, were in the Code Book D (5-Number Code) cipher. This represented almost 90 percent of the IJN's message traffic.[63]

What this really meant was that a capable but much understrength Station CAST was not only inundated but also probably overwhelmed to a large extent by the sheer numbers of 5-Num messages being dispatched each day by the IJN. In contrast to CAST's crypto operation, OP-20-GY under Parke's supervision was expending its precious expertise and time working on outdated Table 6 message traffic, all the while Station HYPO's handpicked Crypto Section under Rochefort was frittering away its valuable talent and time on codes of an inconsequential nature. The full burden of decrypting the current Code Book D, Table 7, as the IJN made its final preparations for going to war, had fallen on Station CAST at Corregidor.

Things were coming to a head in the Far East. In early November, per the ABC-1 Agreement of early 1941, the British Royal Navy's Adm. Sir Thomas Phillips was appointed to take command of the British Far Eastern Fleet. This fleet included the battleship *Prince of Wales* and the battle cruiser *Repulse*, which were to be based at Singapore. In the Philippines, Adm. Thomas C. Hart noted the dispatch of large numbers of Japanese army troop-carrying ships moving south along the coasts of Indochina and China in November 1941. His principal fighting command consisted of 1 heavy and 2 light cruisers, 13 destroyers, and 23 large fleet-type submarines, as well as 28 PBY seaplanes for long-range reconnaissance patrolling.

The stark reality of Hart's situation, which reflected CAST's order of battle for the IJN, was that the Asiatic Fleet could potentially find itself up against Japan's 10 aircraft carriers, 10 battleships, 18 heavy cruisers, 18 light cruisers, 113 destroyers, 63 submarines, and hundreds of land-based bombers and fighters from nearby Formosa and even Japanese-occupied French Indochina. Even with Gen. MacArthur's 35 B-17 bombers and 107 fighter planes, Hart didn't stand a chance of winning in a major confrontation.

Under Adm. Stark's Plan Dog, based on the ABC Conference about Rainbow 5 (War Plan 46), the major surface ships of the Asiatic Fleet were, in the event of war, to move south to reinforce the British in the vicinity of Singapore. The seemingly very effective submarines, on the other hand, were to remain based in Manila and then be utilized to repulse any Japanese seaborne assault against the Philippines.[64]

WCCI—WEST COAST COMMUNICATIONS INTELLIGENCE NET

This tracking of Japan's petroleum purchases and supplies, beginning in early 1940, was of considerable interest to ONI and Station SAIL's West Coast Communications Intelligence (WCCI) network and its affiliated commercial radio facilities of Mackay Radio & Telegraph (MRT), RCA, and Globe Wireless, all of which were brought into play to track Japan's 2,500 merchant ships.[65] Earlier, in May, 1941, Cdr. R. P. McCullough of the 12th Naval District in San Francisco had worked out an arrangement with a U.S. Customs Service agent, George Muller; Muller would board a Japanese merchant ship (*maru*) and confiscate its code books. The SM or S Code Book was photographed in its entirety and the film passed on to OP-20-G. Other thefts of related codebooks took place at Japan's San Francisco consulate, which enabled OP-20-G to maintain its currency in the SM Code.[66]

Japan's merchant marine was "very well equipped with fast passenger liners, fast cargo liners and express tankers with great endurance." It was estimated that some 90 percent of the merchant fleet could be converted to "war duties" in the event of a transpacific war. Express tankers were those rated at 16 knots or better and capable of maintaining the pace of the IJNs fast-moving aircraft carriers and battleships.[67] In January 1941 Adm. J. O. Richardson, commander-in-chief of the U.S. fleet at Pearl Harbor, envisioning an interdiction campaign, had requested a chart from the 12th Naval District showing merchant routes and the average number of ships along each route. Richardson understood Japan's logistical vulnerability and was planning to attack it in the event of war.[68]

As Roosevelt's embargo against Japan was announced on July 3, 1941, the CNO sent out a formal dispatch for action to the navy's Asiatic, Pacific, and Atlantic Fleets, stating that Japan had ordered all of its merchant vessels in the Atlantic to be west of the Panama Canal by August 1, 1941. Movement of Japanese flagged shipping outward was noted as having been suspended.[69] This now alerted OP-20-G's West Coast Strategic High-Frequency Direction Finder (RDF) Net to be prepared to intensify its tracking of the Japanese merchant marine. An earlier OPNAV (OP-12) dispatch of April 5 had directed:

TASK OF TRACKING ALL JAP MERCHANT SHIPS IN EASTERN PACIFIC ASSIGNED COMMANDANT THIRTEEN BY OPNAV SERIAL 45020 NOW IN MAIL X COM FOURTEEN HEREBY ASSIGNED SIMILAR PROJECT FOR MID PACIFIC AREA WEST OF HAWAIIAN ISLANDS AND TO ASSIST WHEN REQUESTED BY COM SIXTEEN IN TAKING BEARINGS ON MANDATE FORCE.[70]

It appeared, as a rational contingency for war with the United States, that Tokyo was now calling home its entire merchant marine fleet. Joseph Rochefort at HYPO considered Japan's decision to withdraw all of its merchant shipping from around the Pacific as an obvious prelude to the outbreak of war. During July 12 to 25, 1941, HYPO and the 14th Naval District maintained a Japanese merchant ship tracking chart for the North Pacific that plotted the positions of 43 ships traveling the northern route from the American West Coast back to Japan.[71]

Tracking of the progress of Japan's merchant marine took on a major emphasis on the part of the Office of Naval Intelligence (ONI) in Washington. ONI was tracking Japanese *maru* in the North Pacific, Pacific Coast (West Coast USA), West Coast of South America, North Atlantic, South Atlantic, Indian Ocean, China Seas, and the Antipodes (Australia and New Zealand). Recorded ONI tracking data included the name of the vessel, departure port and date, location (northing and easting), destination, speed, and route. Tankers and passenger vessels were singled out and highlighted.

Japan's merchant marine shipping, blocked from their scheduled Panama Canal transits by Roosevelt's orders, were now being diverted to Rio de Janeiro, Brazil, for passage through the treacherous Magellan Straits into the Pacific Ocean. From July 9 to 30, anywhere from 135 to 152 vessels were being tracked by ONI.[72] Assisting significantly in ONI's efforts was the fact that OP-20-GY had broken the merchant marine SM Code and its radio call sign code, HYPO. Albert Pelletier Jr. commented: "We were reading ninety percent of the messages."[73] Each *maru* unwittingly contributed to the ONI's tracking effort by providing standard routine radio transmissions at 8 a.m. and 8 p.m. each day, denoting their current locations. This would continue throughout the war.[74]

A report from the communications officer at the 13th ND's headquarters in Seattle noted in November 1941: "We took bearings on 364 different Japanese vessels during August, 232 during September, and 147 during October." He went on to say that the WCCI had mimeographed various stenciled tracking charts with compass roses so that each bearing taken from a distinct RDF station could be recorded on a separate sheet of paper. A properly "plotted" radio fix at Bainbridge would be several radio bearings taken simultaneously with a "good intersection point."[75]

Station S or SAIL received Japanese merchant vessel reports (called "Orange movement reports") from ONI, the 13th Naval District, as well as hourly RDF reports sent by teletype/TWX from navy stations at Imperial Beach, Point Arguello, Point St. George, and Farallon Island in California, British-owned Mackay Radio in the vicinity of San Francisco, and the Canadian stations of Esquimalt and Ucluelet on Vancouver Island. These were then entered into a card index file and arranged alphabetically by radio call sign for reference with RDF tracking bearings.

All plots were maintained by the Central Control & Plotting Officer on master plotting charts (Types 5401 and 5405) that were updated hourly as required. A weekly summary plot chart was then prepared on a type Plotting Chart 1401 (aka Tracking Chart 1) and forwarded to the director of naval intelligence and the director of war plans for use in their Ship Movements Division's chart room. By the last several weeks, November 19 and 26, and December 3, the number of Japanese merchant marine *maru* reported still at sea numbered seven, four, and five respectively. The Western Hemisphere's waters were now essentially free of the *maru*.[76]

Besides RDF bearings, Station SAIL frequently received single and multiple radio signal intercepts from a single *maru* from Stations CAST and HYPO, indicating its specific location by longitude and latitude. These, along with SAIL's own RDF bearings and intercept work on the *maru* from the WCCI, were passed on to OPNAV in a single TWX message via the Naval Communication Service. One way or another, all information was entered on cards and appropriate charts. Since the *maru* typically transmitted their locations twice a day, this greatly facilitated their tracking by the WCCI.[77]

STATION HYPO—THE EYES AND EARS OF THE PACIFIC FLEET

At this point, HYPO was supposed to be the most important element in the defense of Pearl Harbor. Cdr. Joseph John Rochefort, the new officer-in-charge of the Combat Intelligence Unit (CIU) at Pearl Harbor, reported in to Adm. Bloch's 14th Naval District headquarters on May 15, 1941. He was unaware that things of considerable importance had been taking place on the far side of the Pacific.

Just before Christmas 1940, the IJN's Adm. Isoroku Yamamoto, thinking about Japan's political interests and the possibility of having to go to war with the U.S. Navy, brought up the idea of a surprise attack on the Pacific Fleet at Pearl Harbor. Knowing that Japan's Marshall Islands' shore-based bombers were out of range of Hawaii (4,000 miles round trip) and clearly inspired by the successful raid earlier that year of British carrier-launched torpedo bombers against the Italian battleships at Taranto, Italy, Yamamoto now created his own plan, which would overcome the overwhelming obstacle of distance between Japan and Hawaii. It would enable the IJN to attack and cripple the U.S. Pacific Fleet at Pearl Harbor, simultaneously capturing the resources of the oil-rich Dutch East Indies.

The core IJN fleet elements for carrying out Yamamoto's "Operation Hawaii" would ultimately compose the flagship aircraft carrier *Akagi*, along with its five sister carriers: *Kaga, Hiryu, Soryu, Zuikaku*, and *Shokaku*. Cdr. Minoru Genda, a veteran fighter pilot and experienced staff planner in long-range aerial attack operations in China, who had studied the Taranto operation in some detail while he was a naval attaché in London just before returning to Japan, seconded Yamamoto's plan as eminently feasible.[78] It was against this plan and its ardent IJN promoters that Joseph Rochefort and his key CIU staff would unknowingly have to pit their special intelligence efforts, constantly knowing the locations of the IJN's aircraft carriers. This would provide the best information about the intended movements of its main striking forces.[79]

If an effective intelligence operation is the first line of defense of a military organization, then Cdr. Rochefort's operation was supposed to be exactly that. In his *Oral History*, he stated that, as an intelligence officer, his primary task was to be able to tell "his superior, today, what the Japanese are going to do tomorrow. This is his job. If he doesn't do this, then he's failed. This is his number one job and only job."[80]

This was completely in line with what Rochefort was supposed to do when he was assigned under special orders to report directly to Adm. Kimmel, the commander-in-charge of the Pacific Fleet. He was now the "exclusive intermediary between the Pacific Fleet Commander and the Navy's cryptologic organization" at Hawaii. As such, every decrypt, every translation and every traffic analysis report, involving scores of thousands of man-hours of effort, were represented by Rochefort himself as the only visible mouthpiece of his highly secret and nearly invisible organization known as HYPO.[81]

HYPO's own radio intercept and RDF elements, which made significant contributions to its operation, involved two distinct stations. At Station H, located at Heeia, 12 miles to the north of Pearl Harbor on the windward side of the island of Oahu, were 47 radio intercept operators, manning their RIP-5 typewriters and operating in three eight-hour shifts. They used an RCA siphon recorder system that marked dots and dashes on paper tape moved by tape pullers. The RDF station at Lualualei, a small coastal town some 25 miles west of Pearl Harbor and manned by 17 radiomen, spent its time day and night searching out the IJN's radio transmitters. Its men manned the DT and CXK direction finder systems, with each one focused on at least five frequencies throughout their respective frequency assignments. Much like Station H, their bearings taken for the previous 24 hours were delivered each day to Rochefort's HYPO office, to be plotted in the HYPO chart room by Lt. Cdr. Wilfred J. Holmes.[82]

As mentioned earlier, Station CAST, after considerable indecision on the part of Safford at ONI, had been given the mission of breaking the IJN's operational code (Code Book D or the 5-Number Code). On the other hand HYPO, which had some of the navy's foremost 5-Num Code breakers, including a Lt. (j.g.) A. O. Prescott of OP-20-G, who was slated to arrive on station later on in the summer of 1941, was *refocused exclusively* on the unimportant "admiral's system" or AD Code.

Since the decision had taken place *before* Rochefort had taken over the CIU, it was a fait accompli. This was reaffirmed in an early May order from OP-20-G. Rochefort's CIU was also denied the transposition ciphers or current entry keys for breaking the Japanese J-19 cipher utilized in the secret diplomatic communications between Tokyo and its consulate at Honolulu. The only comfort Rochefort would initially have was that HYPO and the Pacific Fleet's formally assigned Intelligence Officer, Cdr. Edwin Layton, were being sent selected portions of the translations of diplomatic signal intercept traffic from the PURPLE system, which otherwise would have been unknown to them. This lasted until mid-July, when ONI's translated PURPLE inputs for Hawaii came to an abrupt halt.[83]

Succinctly put, Adm. Kimmel and his army counterpart for the defense of Pearl Harbor, Lt. Gen. Walter Short, were now at the mercy of their respective headquarters in Washington for critical intelligence feedback as to what was going on in the Pacific. HYPO, as a result, now found itself completely short-circuited and dependent on Stations CAST and NEGAT for all of its decoded signal intelligence about Japanese intentions and IJN fleet movements derived from PURPLE, Code Book D (5-Num Code), and the Japanese J-19 Consular Code. As one author, Clay Blair, would state it: "All the high-price talent at Hypo was, in effect, wasted."[84]

Despite these limitations, Rochefort now concentrated HYPO's efforts on traffic analysis (TA). Here, he was served by two of the best traffic analysts, Lt. Cdr. Thomas A. Huckins and Lt. John A. Williams. Rochefort himself was a sort of "crypto-linguist-analyst." When Homer Kisner, Station H's chief radioman, would bring over the prioritized, transcribed radio intercept messages from the previous 24 hours, Huckins and Williams would go to work, examining the headings, called the "externals." Desperate for concrete intelligence information, everything about an IJN message, short of decrypting it, was studied. Particularly of interest was the command relationship between the sending ship and the receiving ship(s). This and the RDF fixes provided movement tracking and order of battle identification for the IJN's fleet units.

Once anything of value had been gleaned from the IJN call signs, the intercepts were then delivered to Tommy Dyer, Jack Holtwick, and Ham Wright. Their expert eyes scanned each sheet for possible errors and repetitions that might be helpful in the TA effort. A row of IBM tabulating machines assisted in distilling additional key information. Once enough progress had been made in any code breaking that could be accomplished, Japanese linguists such as Alva Lasswell and Joseph Finnegan would make the translations. But HYPO had *not* been provided the essential crypto keys required to make a break into the IJN's operational, 5-Number Code.[85]

During the spring months of 1941, the Japanese consolidated their position in French Indochina, establishing forward operating bases in the northern part of the peninsula for operations against China. If Adm. Yamamoto and the IJN were now becoming concerned about future transoceanic naval operations in both the Western and Eastern Pacific, the Imperial Japanese Army was still obsessed with its war in China and would continue to be during the run-up to the expansion of the war into the Pacific. In Washington, ONI knew that the IJN had approximately 230 warships, most of which were under Yamamoto's powerful Combined Fleet command.[86] How and where they were actually being utilized was always the big question, and radio intelligence intercepts were being relied on to accurately uncover the IJN's operations.

Referring to TA and RDF operations by Com 14 and HYPO, June 4, 1941, OPNAV sent a dispatch (042257) to the Asiatic and Pacific Fleets indicating its concern over the fact that there were intense Japanese activities taking place in the Marshall and Caroline Islands some 2,000 miles to the southwest of Hawaii:

A TOTAL OF ABOUT FORTY SURFACE VESSELS AND TWELVE SUB-MARINES HAVE BEEN OPERATING IN THIS AREA THAT A CONSIDERABLE FORCE OF LANDPLANE BOMBERS HAVE BEEN LOCATED AT SAIPAN AND THAT AIRFIELDS CAPABLE OF HANDLING LONG RANGE LANDPLANE BOMBERS HAVE BEEN CONSRUCTED AT POINTS IN THE EASTERN MANDATES AND THAT SEVERAL ISLANDS IN THIS AREA HAVE BEEN GARRISONED.[87]

The dispatch went on to state that OPNAV (ONI) wanted a major intelligence focus maintained on this region in the Pacific and that the Department of the Navy wanted to be "kept continuously informed on this subject." There was no doubt that this was a clear mission statement for the Pacific Fleet and the 14th Naval District's HYPO in regard to the buildup of a potential Japanese threat to the Pacific Fleet in Hawaii. HYPO and Adm. Kimmel reacted appropriately, maintaining a major focus on the Japanese Mandates the remainder of 1941.[88]

A month later, Roosevelt announced his July 3, 1941, anti-Japanese economic and financial embargos. As the Japanese merchant marine was now called back home en masse, OPNAV included the 14th Naval District (COM 14) in its announced tracking missions of the various cargo, passenger, and tanker ships. One of the last PURPLE diplomatic intercepts that the CNO sent to Kimmel in mid-July indicated that the Japanese had decided to establish air and naval bases in French Indochina, even if it meant the use of force.[89]

This message intercept, combined with Japan's massive recall of its worldwide shipping, undoubtedly caused Rochefort to see the totality of these moves as a prelude to possible war with the United States. With the situation in the Pacific and Southeast Asia starting to deteriorate, Rochefort put HYPO on a full wartime footing, beginning July 16. It was a prudent decision. Added to around-the-clock shifts, a daily traffic analysis radio intelligence summary, usually written by Thomas Huckins and based principally on the Heeia site's radio monitoring intercept reports and related RDF bearings, was now provided to Kimmel via his fleet intelligence officer, Cdr. Layton.

Besides tracking Japanese merchant marine movements westward across the Pacific, the IJN's warships were also monitored. Specifically noted were the late July movements of the aircraft carriers *Soryu* and *Hiryu* from Japan's Inland Sea to the South China Sea off the coast of French

Indochina, some 2,000 miles to the south in support of Tokyo's ultimatum to the French Vichy government to allow full IJA occupation of the region. A crisis was looming.

Both Bloch and Kimmel began launching long-range aerial patrols some 500 miles out to the west-southwest toward the Marshall Islands. Even Lt. Gen. Short, commanding the U.S. Army forces in Hawaii and responsible for its ground and aerial defense, got into the act, placing his troops on alert against possible sabotage by Hawaii's Japanese population. A July 29 report from Capt. Irving Mayfield, the 14th Naval District's intelligence officer, added some fuel to the excitement of the moment. Mayfield's information was based on a U.S. military attaché report from some five weeks earlier (dated June 17, 1941) out of Mexico that detailed a "reported plan to concentrate small Japanese submarines off Molokai [Hawaii] for attack on Fleet in Pearl Harbor."[90]

Layton, in his memoirs, noted Kimmel's concern. Kimmel, in a July 26 letter to CNO Stark, stressed the "importance of keeping the commander-in-chief [Pacific Fleet] advised of department policies and decisions, and changes of policies and decisions to meet changes in the international situation." The day before, July 25, a letter from Stark reached Kimmel indicating that Roosevelt was considering sending an aircraft carrier loaded with planes to the Soviet Union's Asiatic ports. Kimmel's immediate response was one of incredulity. He challenged Stark, suggesting that any such action would jeopardize one of his most important carriers and that to ensure the success of the mission would actually require the entire presence of his now diminished Pacific Fleet (the carrier *Wasp* having been transferred to the Atlantic Fleet that spring).

This was understandable, given that the principal Soviet Asian port was Vladivostok, which was located just some 400 air miles away and within easy land-based bomber range from Japan. Kimmel went on to say that "in the tense situation it would be tantamount to initiation of a Japanese-American war." Not knowing, but possibly suspecting that Roosevelt's ongoing "pop-up cruises" here and there, as well as this proposed mission, were in actuality an effort to instigate some sort of bellicose incident leading to open hostilities between Japan and the United States, Kimmel sensed that something out of the ordinary was now taking place. In his concluding remarks to Stark, Kimmel confided: "If for reasons of political expediency, it has been determined to force the Japan to fire the first shot, let us choose a method that will be more advantageous to ourselves."[91]

The situation on the other side of the Pacific intensified. Roosevelt announced his National Emergency Declaration of August 5. In turn, in Hawaii, base commander Rear Adm. Claude C. Bloch became concerned about the navy's intelligence coverage of the IJN's fleet units and the Japanese merchant marine shipping in the Pacific. Uneasy over what he perceived as a confusing portrayal of American and Japanese ship movements in general, Bloch took action to resolve the problem as he saw it. In an August 15 memorandum to key elements of his district, including Cdr. Rochefort, Bloch laid out a definitive series of RDF intelligence plotting missions for his headquarters and HYPO alike.

After directing that Rochefort would remain designated as officer-in-charge, Bloch ordered that RDF plotting would be accomplished in two formats. First, Rochefort's CIU or HYPO would "maintain a master plot" of not only U.S. merchant shipping and naval fleet units throughout the Pacific but also Japanese fleet units and merchant marine shipping operating in that ocean. Second, the Operations Section of the District War Plans Office would maintain its own distinct plot of all U.S. merchant and naval vessels within the Hawaii Coastal Frontier, which radiated out some several hundred miles around Hawaii. This section was also to maintain a plot of all Japanese merchant shipping and naval units within that same coastal frontier.

To ensure a steady flow of information, the CIU was tasked with providing the Operations Section with the positions of all Japanese and American ships located in the Pacific on at least a daily basis. So this would in fact come about, Bloch directed that his own 14th Naval District's Lt. W. Jasper Holmes would be attached to the CIU. To make sure that the correct information reached the Operations Section, an ensign named Wallace and a yeoman would be attached to the Operations Section to maintain their own specific, separate plotting board.[92]

With HYPO's missions more clearly defined, Holmes now plunged into his new assignment, located in the center of the basement of the 14th Naval District. Both he and Lt. Cdr. Thomas Huckins, as well as Huckins's cohort, Lt. John Williams, would operate as a team. Holmes's desks, filing boxes, plotting equipment, and a plotting table covered with charts and maps were set up next to those belonging to Huckins. All information coming in from the various analysts passed through their hands, enabling HYPO to function in a very efficient manner. The thousand or so messages coming in, as well as scores of RDF bearings and radio call sign identifications of Japan's ships of all types, provided key data, which were then entered on the plotting charts, IBM cards, and otherwise filed in boxes for quick reference.

So TA was the name of the game and HYPO conducted it extremely well. Exploiting Japan's required daily weather reports from each merchant marine ship, radiomen Anthony Ethier and William Livingston plotted each ship's location. Tankers were a high priority, and their movements were tracked accordingly. If space ran out on the plotting table, then wall charts were employed. A chart overlay on tracing paper of all IJN and merchant marine ship positions was provided each morning by Huckins and Williams to Layton at his office at the Pacific Fleet's headquarters.[93]

While HYPO did plot the movements of the Japanese merchant marine's *maru* making their way back to their home ports, Huckins and Williams focused on the IJN's main fleets and their capital ships. The aircraft carrier *Akagi*, as Adm. Nagumo's command flagship, became a warship of keen interest and one of the highest priorities for tracking.

A case in point is the Station H (HYPO) Statistical Section's IBM-produced "Call List" dated August 31, 1941; it included not only the current Japanese HYOO 8's assigned radio call signs for the IJN's combat vessels but also their identified radio frequencies and RDF bearings taken from around the Pacific. In the case of the *Akagi* (call signs HA MI 9 or 8 E YU), it was noted that during the period of August 1–24, the carrier transmitted every day except one (August 3). A total of 45 RDF bearings (denoted as "BRG") were taken against *Akagi* from an array of stations ringing the Pacific:

V   (VICTOR at Vaitogi, American Samoa)

X   (Mackay Radio & Telegraph at Half Moon Bay, California)

K   (KING at Dutch Harbor, Alaska)

T   (TARE at Point St. George, California)

H   (HEEIA in Hawaii)

B   (BAKER in Guam)

C   (CAST at Corregidor, Philippines)

Of the seven distinct RDF stations tracking the *Akagi*, Station X (Mackay Radio & Telegraph in San Francisco) did the brunt of the work, taking bearings on the IJN carrier 17 times.[94] This is a typical IBM printout of the *Akagi* 8E YU listing.

The abundant RDF bearing angles came from around the entire North Pacific. By plotting them on their large great circle sailing chart, Huckins and Williams determined the approximate location of the *Akagi* and its direction of movement. For example, on August 5, with the *Akagi* transmitting on a radio frequency of 6,775 kilocycles, Station TARE took a bearing on the carrier's radio signal at 278 degrees from Point St. George. Station KING beamed in on the carrier along a bearing of 270 degrees from Dutch Harbor. Station VICTOR at Vaitogi picked up the *Akagi*'s radio that same day on 5,900 kilocycles and a bearing of 310 degrees. Using a circle chart and a plastic 360-degree circular plotting compass to measure the several bearings from their respective stations' north pole zero/360-degree measuring point, it was not difficult to get a triangular fix ("cocked hat") for the crossing points, neatly locating the *Akagi* in the vicinity of Kyushu, Japan.[95]

On August 9, Station X, monitoring the 5,900-kilocycle frequency of the *Akagi* (8 E YU call sign), intercepted and took a bearing of 295 degrees.

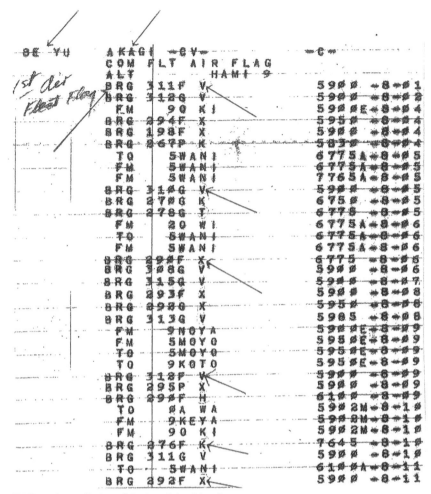

8E YU radio call sign. (National Archives)

Some three days later it took another bearing, this time at 291 degrees on the same frequency, indicating that *Akagi* had moved some four degrees further south.[96] At any given moment, Huckins and Williams could call on HYPO's IBM Statistical Section of 12 persons, run by Lt. Cdr. J. S. Holtwick and Lt. P. P. Leigh, to produce the latest tracking information on any ship identified by name and/or radio call sign in the IJN. This served as a cross-check for the data they were receiving from the externals of the message intercepts and RDF bearing data input sent in from the TESTM (ECM) system.[97]

The Statistical Section operated in conjunction with Huckins's six-man Radio Section (TA and RDF plotting), both operated under Rochefort,

HYPO's officer-in-charge. Rochefort was also in charge of the Crypto Section (message decoding), which included Lt. Cdrs. Thomas Dyer, R. W. Brandt, and W. A. Wright, as well as five other highly trained crypto system personnel. Lt. Cdr. Fullinwider and Marine Capt. A. B. Lasswell were the Japanese language translators. Two administrative personnel filled out the section's structure. Rochefort was proud of his HYPO group: "The best we [Naval Intelligence] had as far as experience and all-around skill was . . . at Pearl Harbor."[98]

By September 23, 1941, HYPO's TA, in conjunction with RDF bearings from the splendid arrangement and TESTM reports from CAST, enabled Huckins to use the Statistical Section's IBM capabilities to produce a partial order of battle on the IJN. The printout, called the Radio Organization List, focused on the key elements of Yamamoto's Combined Fleet. One of the divisions noted was the FLEET AIR—CARDIVs—three divisions of massed aircraft carriers as one major fleet unit:

CARDIV 1: including carrier *Akagi* and carrier *Kaga*

CARDIV 2: including carriers *Hiryu* and *Soryu*

CARDIV 4: including carriers *Zuikako* and *Shokaku*

The *Akagi* was tracked 12 times during September 6–24 by Stations X (Mackay Radio & Telegraph), B, C, V, and K. It was also tracked a second time in the same report 16 times, September 22–30 using *a different call sign.*

Always of interest to Huckins and Williams were the movement patterns of the IJN's various capital ships. These generally took some days to figure out through the analysis of the various call signs and RDF fixes, but a pattern would usually appear. This was all reflected in Rochefort's HYPO daily summaries for September 5 and 9, which were passed on to Kimmel, informing the admiral that the IJN was reorganizing and creating new aircraft carrier task forces. In fact, the September 24 summary stated that radio frequencies were being changed and that secret new call signs were now coming into use.[99]

Layton, Kimmel's intelligence officer, who was in constant touch with Rochefort by secure telephone, took note of the various intercepts and RDF fixes on the IJN's capital ships, submarines, and even merchant marine vessels, putting them together on his own location map, charting their up-to-date positions, as well as possible intended future movements. His daily briefings for the CINCPAC at 8:15 a.m. each morning were frequently attended by Kimmel's chief of staff and other senior plans and operations officers and, as the opportunity presented itself, the key aircraft carrier (task force) commanders. At these briefings, Kimmel encouraged a frank exchange of ideas and opinions. Kimmel met with his army counterpart Gen. Short at least twice a week and often sometimes with their staffs to exchange observations.[100]

Rochefort recognized the IJN's requisitioning of Japan's merchant marine fleet was a major step toward Japan completing its final preparations for war. This and the reorganization of the IJN's fleets on a more viable operational war footing caused Rochefort to take an unprecedented step on October 8: he placed his entire radio intelligence network on what he called an "eight-day" week. The eighth day was accomplished by adding a "scoop watch" to the now intensified effort on the part of the WCCI and other naval intercept stations in the Central and South Pacific, as well as Alaska, to go all out in terms of locating all categories of Japanese naval vessels.

Rochefort's top priorities included the flagships of the IJN, its aircraft carriers, battleships, submarines, and now the oil tankers and supply ships, which would be critical in the support of any transpacific amphibious invasion or attack forces undergoing long-range movements. Fuel tankers were key logistical tip-offs to the whereabouts of the IJN's primary warships. Since tankers often reported their locations by latitude and longitude several times a day (8:00 a.m., noon, and 4:00 p.m.) in the katakana Morse code system, tracking was made that much easier.[101] HYPO, as the Pacific Fleet's eyes and ears, was using its own IJN radio intercepts, TA and RDF, in an intensified effort to ascertain the whereabouts of the IJN's fleet units. The Japanese were using a more traditional means to track the U.S. Pacific Fleet inside its Pearl Harbor base at Hawaii.

THE IJN TARGETS PEARL HARBOR

From early January 1941 onwards, the Japanese consulate in Honolulu was sending messages to its home office in Tokyo. Using the J-series (J-18K8 or J-19) of enciphered Japanese diplomatic codes, a steady stream of reports as to the in-harbor strength of the Pacific Fleet poured forth. A March 10 report, photographed and finally translated by ONI in Washington on April 5, listed vessels observed, among others, inside Pearl Harbor: "Four battleships . . . five heavy cruisers . . . six light cruisers . . . *Yorktown* [aircraft carrier], 25 destroyers."[102]

Some weeks later, an IJN ensign named Takeo Yoshikawa arrived at the consulate. Using the cover name of Tadashi Morimura, he immediately began monitoring the locations of Kimmel's warships in the harbor, as well as those that had departed. He was trying to determine if a pattern of movement in terms of a time in and time out for each of the ships could be predicted. His job was relatively easy and he tended to blend in, since some 160,000 Japanese lived in Oahu. Often posing as a tourist and using taxies,

[*12*]   From: Tokyo (Toyoda)
To: Honolulu
September 24, 1941
J–19
#83
    Strictly secret.
    Henceforth, we would like to have you make reports concerning vessels along the following lines insofar as possible:
    1. The waters (of Pearl Harbor) are to be divided roughly into five sub-areas. (We have no objections to your abreviating as much as you like.)
    Area A. Waters between Ford Island and the Arsenal.
    Area B. Waters adjacent to the Island south and west of Ford Island. (This area is on the opposite side of the Island from Area A.)
    Area C. East Loch.
    Area D. Middle Loch.
    Area E. West Loch and the communicating water routes.
    2. With regard to warships and aircraft carriers, we would like to have you report on those at anchor, (these are not so important) tied up at wharves, buoys and in docks. (Designate types and classes briefly. If possible we would like to have you make mention of the fact when there are two or more vessels along side the same wharf.).

ARMY 23260   Trans. 10/9/41   (S)

Tokyo Report. (Pearl Harbor Attack. Hearings before the Joint Committee on the Investigation of the Pearl Harbor Attack. 79th Congress, 2nd Session, Part 12. Washington, D.C.: Government Printing Office, 1946, 261)

tourist buses, aircraft, and boats, he roamed the high ground around Pearl City to look down upon the array of ships in the harbor. Picture postcards and souvenir maps also helped to flesh out details for his reports.[103]

As Japanese contingency planning for a possible raid on Pearl Harbor progressed, there was a constant need by the IJN for more and more precise data as to the whereabouts of Kimmel's ships, especially aircraft carriers and battleships. Other key information needed for a transpacific voyage involved weather conditions between Japan and Hawaii. In Late October, Lt. Cdr. Suguru Suzuki, a seaplane pilot and air staff officer of the China Area Fleet, began monitoring the North Pacific's sea and air conditions along what was known as the "northern route" from Japan's Yokohama port to Hawaii.

Posing as the *Taiyo Maru*'s assistant purser, Suzuki noted the stormy weather and rough seas en route and the fact that there did not seem to be any vessels plying the route, which lay outside the normal sea lanes for merchant marine shipping in that part of the Pacific. While at anchor at the Lahaina dock, Suzuki verified the navy's dockside routines, estimated the thickness of the Army Air Corps' concrete hanger roofs at Hickam

Field, calculated both the ordnance requirements in terms of the quantity of bombs that would be required to neutralize the airfields, and the quantities of bombs and torpedoes needed to sink the U.S. Navy's aircraft carriers and battleships.

By mid-November, Suzuki would be aboard the *Akagi* at Hitokappu Bay in Japan's northern Kuril Islands to brief Adm. Nagumo and his staff and key leaders about the pending Pearl Harbor attack. These included Minoru Genda and a Cdr. Mitsuo Fuchida, who had been specifically designated to lead the first wave of the air attack.[104]

While Suzuki did provide key intelligence information that would be of considerable value to the IJN as it planned its air raid on Pearl Harbor, there was other essential information that was absolutely critical to the success of the operation. This would be accomplished by Takeo Yoshikawa, working out of the Japanese consulate general's office in Honolulu. His mission directive, in Tokyo message #83—which arrived in the J-19 code on September 24—stated that he was to report in detail the locations of the Pacific Fleet's ships in Pearl Harbor. Unknown to Kimmel, the message, monitored and further transcribed by Station SAIL (S), was translated by the army on October 9, 1941, and then passed to ONI. Kimmel never saw this or any other J-coded messages reporting on the Pacific Fleet's locations at Pearl Harbor.

While the above directive originated with the foreign minister of Japan, Adm. Teijiro Toyoda, and was addressed to the Japanese consulate at Honolulu, it was definitely intended to serve Adm. Yamamoto's purposes. It called for the establishment of a coordinate grid target layout of the navy's anchorages at Pearl Harbor. The harbor was to be divided into five areas to include Battleship Row (Area B). Knowing "where there are two or more vessels alongside the same wharf" meant that a combination of torpedoes *and* bombs would be required.[105]

Five days later, on September 29, Consul Nagao Kita sent a reply message via the Japanese Embassy in Washington, adding four additional location codes to expand the grid layout, to denote the repair dock at the Pearl Harbor Navy Yard (KS), the Navy Dock in the Navy Yard (KT), some moorings in the vicinity of Ford Island (FV), and two sides of Ford Island (FG) on the east and west (A and B respectively). Intercepted by Station X, this message, the bomb plot target grid layout, was translated by ONI on October 10, 1941.[106]

While the delays in decrypting and translation appear abnormal, they were undoubtedly due in large part to the top priority being given Japan's diplomatic PURPLE messages (see Appendix B, this volume, for original intercept translations) by both the army and the navy translators. While the messages had arrived in Washington in a sufficiently timely manner for proactive counteraction, Roosevelt's overt act strategy would put an unfortunate dynamic in play. This would lead to the events that would soon engulf Kimmel's Pacific Fleet at Pearl Harbor.

In what became known as the "Bomb Plot message," the location grids were sufficient to enable dive-bomber and torpedo bomber pilots with crude maps to clearly distinguish their targets. The details demanded were the *exact* locations of each ship by type in the harbor. It was these meticulous details that eclipsed all other previous IJN intelligence operations involving the positioning of the U.S. Navy's ships in the Pacific.[107]

IJN's naval intelligence was doing its job in support of Yamamoto's intended operations, exactly as expected. The revelation of the Bomb Plot message should have been top priority, vital intelligence information not only for Stark and McCollum at OP-16's F-2 in Washington, Hawaii's Rear Adm. Bloch of the 14th Naval District, Cdr. Rochefort at HYPO and Cdr. Layton, the Pacific Fleet's intelligence officer, and especially Kimmel himself. The Japanese intentions had now been revealed: a possible attack on the Pacific Fleet while at anchor at Pearl Harbor. This should have triggered an effort to reinforce the fleet and prepare it for an aggressive, proactive defense of its base in the Hawaiian Islands. But nothing happened.

In Washington, Lt. Cdr. Kramer, the officer-in-charge of the navy's OP-20-GZ translation section and responsible for distributing daily the translations of the intercepted diplomatic and IJN messages, highlighted the message as "interesting," adding a special note that read: "Tokyo directs special reports on the ships in Pearl Harbor which is divided into five areas for the purpose of showing exact locations."[108] This message and others went up the chain of command all the way to Roosevelt via his naval aide, Capt. John Beardall.[109]

Both Capt. Allan Kirk, director of Intelligence (OP-16), and Capt. Howard Bode, director of Foreign Intelligence (OP-16-F), strongly urged Rear Adm. Turner to immediately send a copy of the decoded and translated Tokyo J-19 consular cable message #83 to Kimmel. They saw this as a primary duty as intelligence officers in the service of a U.S. Navy on the verge of war in the Pacific. Undoubtedly, they did not mince words and were candid and to the point in pressing their demands that Kimmel be immediately notified.

Kirk and Bode were in good stead in that the navy's Basic War Plan— Rainbow 5 (WPL-46), promulgated May 26, 1941, specifically stipulated under its "Section 3. THE NAVAL INTELLIGENCE SERVICE" that ONI had two primary tasks:

Task 1: "DISSEMINATE . . . SUCH INFORMATION, PARTICULARLY CONCERNING THE ENEMY, ENEMY AGENTS AND SYMPA-THIZERS, AS WILL ASSIST AND FACILITATE THE EXECUTION

OF NAVY BASIC WAR PLAN—RAINBOW No. 5 AND THE PRO-
TECTION OF THE NAVAL ESTABLISHMENT;"

Task 2: "PREVENT THE TRANSMISSION OF INFORMATION OF MIL-
ITARY OR ECONOMIC VALUE TO THE ENEMY."[110]

Turner, as the director of the War Plans Division (OP-12) and an architect of WPL-46, was fully cognizant of this requirement, but chose to
ignore it. While both Kirk and Bode were experienced naval intelligence
officers, they were not privy to the politics of the evolving overt act strategy, as Turner was. When Kirk objected to withholding the intercepted
messages from Kimmel and Short, Turner not only rejected outright the
request, which was a *dereliction of his duty on his part*, but worse, he had
Kirk and Bode immediately reassigned to postings outside ONI.

During the period of October 10–20, Turner replaced Kirk with Capt.
Theodore Wilkinson, a relatively inexperienced intelligence officer, who
now became the third director of naval intelligence in less than one year.
Along with this, Safford of OP-20-G found his efforts to have Rochefort's
Station HYPO begin decrypting local consular traffic quashed by none
other than Rear Adm. Leigh Noyes, director of the OP-20 Communications Division.[111]

Rochefort had an expert cryptanalyst of J-19 message traffic, Farnsley
Woodward, on his HYPO staff. Had Woodward been provided with the
J-19 keys and cipher work already accomplished in OP-20-GY, he could
have made the critical difference that would have alerted Kimmel about
Japanese espionage interests at Pearl Harbor. Sadly, it was not to be. Saf-
ford had specifically denied Rochefort the keys for decoding J-19.[112]

The Army's Monitoring Station 5 (MS-5) at Fort Shaftner in the vicinity
of Honolulu was intercepting and transcribing the coded consular cable
messages and then forwarding them on to Gen. Marshall's headquarters in
Washington. Col. Rufus Bratton, chief of the Far East Section of the Army
Staff's G-2, concluded from the Bomb Plot message that it might be some
sort of a plan for an aerial attack. While his duty response should have
been to notify Gen. Short in Hawaii by coded message, he was derailed in
his efforts to do so by none other than Marshall himself.

However, Maj. Gen. Charles Willoughby, MacArthur's G-2 in Manila,
did receive this particular message through "back channel" sources, commenting: "coordinate grid is the classical method for pinpointing target
designation; our battleships had suddenly become targets."[113] Neither Kimmel nor Short would know of the existence of the Bomb Plot message until
several years *after* the Pearl Harbor attack.[114]

Ironically, while HYPO and Kimmel at Pearl Harbor were kept in the
dark, Station CAST intercepted and read the messages, in large part due to
Safford at OP-20-G, who was passing the J-19 keys for decoding on to

Lietwiler at Corregidor Island. Between Turner, Noyes, and Marshall, the stranglehold on key intelligence information for Kimmel continued.

Throughout October and November, the IJN's interest in the whereabouts and specific locations of the Pacific Fleet's ships intensified. On November 15, 18, 20, and 29, Tokyo directed its consulate in Honolulu to report in ever more detail and more frequently. Both RCA and Mackay Radio & Telegraph offices in California handled this radio telegraph cable traffic for the Japanese.

Beginning on November 15, Japan's Consul Kita was told by his Tokyo headquarters to make his "ships in harbor report" irregularly, but at the rate of twice a week. The previously agreed-upon symbols of the Bomb Plot message to denote ship locations were to be used for information detailing routes, speed, distances apart, and even nonmovement of ships inside the harbor. These critical reports from the Japanese consulate in Honolulu were passed on to Tokyo and then, in turn, to Adm. Nagumo.[115]

As Roosevelt received more and more translations of the J-19 messages to and from the Honolulu consulate and Tokyo, he took a significant enough personal interest in the intercepts to invite RCA president David Sarnoff to lunch at the White House on October 14. Apparently to ensure that he would have continuous access to the Honolulu Japanese consulate's reports, Roosevelt asked Sarnoff to allow U.S. Naval Intelligence to go into RCA's offices and copy the J-19 traffic.

Under this arrangement, Sarnoff made a special trip a few weeks later to Hawaii, spending nine days in Honolulu, to instruct his downtown office to make the cable traffic available to navy intelligence. Satisfied that he had complied with Roosevelt's wishes, he left Hawaii on November 14, exactly one month after his White House visit. Albeit Roosevelt undoubtedly profited from the arrangement by keeping up-to-date with ONI's monitored Japanese consulate cable traffic concerning the Pacific Fleet's specific Pearl Harbor ship locations, there is no indication that prior to the December 7 attack on Pearl Harbor that Adm. Kimmel or Maj. Gen. Short ever saw a single one of the espionage messages.[116]

THE IJN GIRDS FOR BATTLE IN THE PACIFIC

What had been a contingency plan for the attack on Pearl Harbor was now becoming an operational reality. On September 2, Yamamoto gathered together all his fleet commanders, their key staff officers and other officers from the Naval General Staff, the Naval Ministry, and the Combined Fleet, at the Naval War College just outside of Tokyo. He laid out a series of war games that would last for about a week, enabling the IJN's war planners to work out the details for conducting a surprise raid on Pearl

Harbor and to additionally determine the schedule of operations that would enable Japan to occupy Malaya, Burma, Thailand, the Dutch East Indies (Java, Sumatra, Celebes, Ambon, Dutch Borneo, and Timor), British North Borneo (Sarawak and Brunei), the Philippines, the Solomons, as well as other Central Pacific islands, including Hawaii, as part of a later phase. Some operations would take place simultaneously and others sequentially.

The transoceanic attack plan was on a scale never before seen in the Pacific, with the IJN supporting the movement of 11 IJA divisions, or upwards of 200,000 troops, plus supplies and equipment. Although he had expressed some serious reservations about the outcome of the intended war (as Gen. Robert E. Lee also had during the U.S. Civil War), Yamamoto pressed ahead, even threatening to resign as commander-in-chief of the Combined Fleet if the plans were not approved in accordance with his liking.

Earlier analyses had shown that the Pearl Harbor Strike Force or First Air Fleet (FAF), created around April 10, 1941, did not have enough onboard fuel to make the journey to Hawaii and return; therefore a train of fuel tankers would have to be incorporated into the attack force, slowing down somewhat its movement across the North Pacific. No commercial shipping traveled at latitude 40 degrees north during November and December due to the nature of the rough seas, which would probably guarantee the supreme element of surprise that the FAF needed. The air attacks against Pearl Harbor, using a combination of technically innovative shallow-draft torpedoes and air-delivered bombs, would be supported by a submarine blockade at the harbor's mouth.[117] This action, sometimes referred to as a screening maneuver or spoiling attack, would not only seriously cripple the U.S. Navy in the Pacific, but also effectively cut the navy's lines of communication and supply to the Orient and block U.S. Navy reinforcement of the Western Pacific region under Japanese attack.

Yamamoto stated the case quite pointedly: "The presence of the U.S. fleet in Hawaii is a dagger pointed at our throats. Should war be declared, the length and breadth of our southern operations would immediately be exposed to a serious threat on its flank." To prevent this from happening, Yamamoto utilized Kagoshima Bay on the southernmost end of Kyushu Island for the all-important training of the IJN's torpedo bombers. The planes practiced take-off and landing from their respective carriers, skimming in low over the bay's narrowly constricted waters and releasing torpedoes, sometimes up to four times a day. It was both a rigorous and thorough training, with each pilot making more than 50 flights. The First Air Fleet was being prepared to break the American "dagger."[118]

With its war plans now in place, the IJN's First Air Fleet set about rearming, retraining, and reequipping its aircraft carriers and their associated tankers for the intended transpacific raid. October was a big month for the FAF, with its ships and tankers located in and around the southernmost Japanese home island of Kyushu, all undertaking the required preparations. Stations CAST and HYPO intercepted and transcribed numerous messages in the IJN's Code Book D or 5-Number Code. But because HYPO was unable to decode these messages, it was CAST that took on the burden and responsibility to do the vast majority of the decoding and translation work.

Even so, a large number of Station CAST's and HYPO's 5-Number intercepts were bundled up and sent to OP-20-GY for cryptanalysis. The U.S. National Archive II at College Park, Maryland, has dealt with many of those that survived the end of the war and were then formally decoded and translated in January 1946.[119]

Using the 5-Number Code and the designated HYOO 8 radio call signs, the IJN's General Affairs Section (MA FU TI) coordinated much of the preattack preparations. By October 2, it was directing the FAF's chief of staff (RI TI 958) to order the commanders of Carrier Division 1 (RU A 66), Carrier Division 2 (WA HE 77), and Carrier Division 5 (U YU 33) to receive an allocation of 20 type Zero fighter planes to replenish the *Kaga*, *Hiryu*, *Soryu*, and *Zuikaku* throughout the month. An additional October 19 message from the Tokyo Aircraft Technical Arsenal (WI N KE) discussed the provision of "shipboard fighters and attack planes" that were to be distributed from the arsenal's storage areas.

October 3 and 7, bomb replenishment coordination was carried out with the Type-97 (dive-bomber): 32 for the *Hiryu* and as many as 54 for the *Kaga*. At the Yokosuka Navy Yard, aircraft carrier commanders were ordered to resupply *Akagi* (HA MI 99), *Shokaku* (RO TA 66), and *Soryu* (KO SI 00); and at Kure Navy Yard, *Zuikaku* (MO MU 00), *Kaga* (HO MO 11), and *Hiryu* (SE WA 99). Each aircraft carrier was a given special 5-Number Code, a five-digit identification number with the letter X before the number (e.g., *Akagi*: X28494).

An October 10 message from the Yokosuka Aviation Research Arsenal directed that "remodeling work" be undertaken for FAF torpedo planes on the *Akagi*, *Kaga*, and *Shokaku*. This meant fitting each torpedo plane with a special launching rack, for the shallow draft torpedoes; these, in turn, were fitted with special wooden stabilizer fins to permit aerial launches from low altitudes into shallow water. These technical modifications reflected Yamamoto's own personal perspective that an "unsuspecting" enemy fleet could be overwhelmed by a mass torpedo attack.[120]

During October, at least one of the FAF's aircraft carriers engaged in a series of "medium attack plane" bombing exercises against an unsuspecting American merchant marine vessel. Yamamoto responded to this potentially grave error in judgment by the pilots; on October 11, all

Combined Fleet elements were tersely ordered to ensure that "strict precautions" were to be taken to prevent a similar situation from happening again. Japan was still technically at peace and Yamamoto did not want to jeopardize diplomatic endeavors, let alone his cherished Pearl Harbor attack plan.[121]

Further 5-Number Code intercepts taken by HYPO and sent on to OP-20-GY in mid-October included a number of FAF messages dealing with the IJN's key fuel tankers. One of these, the *Kenyoo Maru*, was ordered to transfer fuel oil from the carrier *Kaga* and then to proceed to the Kure Naval Base, where special gear for refueling under tow would be installed. After that, she would receive some 750 drums of oil from the Kure military stores department in order to support the *Akagi*. The commanding officer of Carrier Division 2 (WA HE 77) reported the successful conduct of training in refueling while in movement at sea at a speed of 7 to 9 knots. The thrust of these messages indicated that the FAF's six carriers were being matched with their respective tankers for en route refueling. That could only mean that some sort of long-range operation was intended.[122]

During late October, CAST intercepted a number of IJN messages involving the FAF's preparations for war. The FAF's commander-in-chief, Nagumo, directed that Carrier Division 1 would conduct night exercises, to be followed a week later by carrier landing drills that would be conducted by shipboard attack bomber and fighter plane units from Carrier Divisions 1 and 2. Fresh water and fuel were also issues to be resolved, with each ship receiving upwards of 115 tons of water. Extra fuel was also planned for the FAF, and some 45,000 "18-liter tanks" and some 3,000 drums of fuel oil were to be procured. With the training and logistical operations going on, sometimes around the clock, Yamamoto realized that his FAF sailors would need a break, especially if they were to be in top form for the grueling first days of war ahead. His Combined Fleet operation order #5 directed that "all fleets will put in at nearest recreational port during the last 10 days of October and there will be 2 days liberty for all hands."[123]

An incomplete message (lacking the heading and externals of the first page) indicated that flying boats and land attack planes were being forward-positioned throughout the Mandate islands of Truk, Wotje, Saipan, Ruoto, and others in the Marshalls. This corroborated what Layton had noted in the late spring of 1941, when he briefed Kimmel about the Japanese buildup then going on, using detailed charts and maps of the larger mid-Pacific atolls.

Using multiple sources, such as U.S. submarines, Pan American Airways, and agent reports from merchant seamen in ports throughout the Far East, Layton now discovered that such places as Kwajalein and Jaluit in the Marshalls had been having their coral lagoons blasted out to form seaplane and submarine bases. Others, such as Ponape in the Carolines, now had radio transmission towers rising above their palm trees; Saipan in the Marianas had developed airfields capable of handling long-range bombers; and Truk, also in the Carolines, had an advanced deep-water anchorage sufficiently large enough to handle the entire IJN Combined Fleet.[124]

Earlier that month, an October 4 message from the IJN's Naval General Staff to all fleet commanders concluded with an intelligence report on the composition of the U.S. Fleet in Hawaii: 2 aircraft carriers, 6 battleships, 15 cruisers, 52 destroyers, and 28 submarines.[125] On November 1, the IJN changed all its radio call signs for its fleets and air units—HYOO 8 was obsolete; HYOO 9 was now in effect.[126]

Throughout October 1941, Kimmel maintained contact with his superior, Adm. Stark, the navy's CNO in Washington. In a letter dispatch of October 16, Stark informed Kimmel that there was a possibility that Japan would attack the United States and Great Britain. This letter was immediately followed by one dated October 17 in which Stark wrote, "Personally I do not believe the Japanese are going to sail into us and the message I sent you merely stated the 'possibility'." Kimmel interpreted "possible" to mean "not probable."[127]

During October, Kimmel ordered part of his submarine force to assume a wartime patrol off both Wake and Midway islands. Besides Wake, the islands of Johnston and Palmyra out to the southwest of Hawaii were reinforced with marines. Certain vessels of his fleet in West Coast ports were placed on 12-hour standby notice, six submarines were prepared and held in readiness to be sent to Japan's home island waters, and 12 PBY patrol planes were sent to Midway in order to conduct daily patrols out to 100 miles around the island.[128] But Kimmel was hardly finished. About a month later, in November, he would carry out his own independently conceived search for Japanese carriers in the near North Pacific that would shake up the navy's high command. This action resulted in Kimmel's isolation remaining a sacrosanct fact.[129] Back in Japan, things had become so desperate, due to the American embargo, that Japanese leaders had determined that if a diplomatic solution favorable to Tokyo could not be concluded in Washington, going to war with the United States was the only option.

For the first time in its daily Communications Intelligence Summary (CIS), on November 3, 1941, Rochefort's HYPO noted: "A WE address today broke down as ITIKOUKUU KANTAI. The literal reading of this as '1st Air Fleet' is correct [sic] it indicates an entirely new organization of the Naval Air Forces." The "WE WE" administrative cipher, as Layton termed it, was a useful source of information dealing with Japanese military engineering projects, which included the buildup in the Caroline and Marshall Islands. This had been a subject of focus for HYPO since the spring of 1941. HYPO now began to contribute concrete information about the IJN's new order of battle.[130]

Station CAST had identified the same First Air Fleet reorganization in its earlier September 23 IJN radio call sign order of battle report and had supposedly forwarded one of its copies to HYPO as well as OP-20-G. The HYPO CIU team was somewhat behind in terms of laying out the IJN's complete order of battle. This was understandable, since CAST had a significant advantage in that it was partially reading the Code Book D (5 Numeral Code). HYPO could not do this; following OP-20-G's orders, HYPO was not authorized to make the relevant decodes at all. But HYPO kept on working as best it could and, on November 5, noted in its daily COMSUM that two WE messages in kana code (not 5-Num Code) had been transmitted by Japan's Naval General Staff to the chief of staffs of the Combined Fleet and Submarine Force.[131] And these messages would be critical to future IJN operations in the Pacific.

On October 30, McCollum's OP-16-F-2 had already issued an intelligence report at ONI in Washington, concerning the "Organization of the Japanese Fleets." Noting that the aircraft carriers had been reorganized into a separate organization, the report further identified eight major fleet commands. One of these McCollum termed the "Carrier Fleet (Aircraft Carriers), consisting of 5 carrier divisions (Cardivs.): Cardiv 1: *Akagi* and *Kaga*; Cardiv 2: *Soryu* and *Hiryu*; Cardiv 4: *Zuikaku* and *Shokaku*" in one group, and the other carrier divisions (3 and 5) operating separately, for a total of 10 aircraft carriers.[132]

With the contingency planning for wartime operations completed and the diplomatic crisis between Japan and the United States still unresolved, Adm. Osami Nagano, the chief of the Naval General Staff, issued a directive on November 5 that was apparently transmitted by coded radio dispatch under the newly implemented HYOO 9 radio call sign/address system. (Some controversy still surrounds the issue as to whether the original encoded operational message was intercepted by CAST at Corregidor, or NEGAT in Washington, or was merely reconstructed from memory by IJN officials after the end of World War II.) The directive was issued to Adm. Yamamoto, the commander-in-chief of the IJN's Combined Fleet, stating:

1. In view of the fact that it is feared war has become unavoidable with the United States, Great Britain, and the Netherlands, and for the self preservation and future existence of the Empire, the various preparations for war operations will be completed by the first part of December.
2. The C in C of the Combined Fleet will effect the required preparations for war operations.[133]

That same day, a formally printed IJN Combined Fleet Top Secret Operations Order 1 was issued in 700 copies to all the various commands and ships that would be undertaking the first phase of the operations as part of the major thrust along the East Asian coast into the Dutch East Indies and South Pacific, including the supporting foray involving the special Strike Force moving across the North Pacific to attack Pearl Harbor.

Two days later, November 7, a second IJN Combined Fleet Top Secret Operation Order 2 was issued, in 600 copies. It indicated that "Y Day 8 December" (December 7 in Hawaii) was a key commencement date for all operations. While all the fleets would focus on Y Day as the date they were expected to be in their preinvasion/attack rendezvous points for the initiation of a coordinated effort throughout the Pacific, another follow-up order would be required to actually launch the attack.[134]

Extracts from Order 1 are pertinent on its page 7: "In the east the American Fleet will be destroyed and American lines of operation and supply lines to the Orient will be cut." On page 8: "The empire is expecting war to break out with the United States, Great Britain and the Netherlands." On page 13 a series of five task forces were delineated, including the "Striking Force (1st Air Fleet)," which "will operate against the American Fleet."[135]

That same day, November 7, Yamamoto issued a further executing order to the First Air Fleet: "The Task Force, keeping its movement strictly secret, shall assemble in Hitokappu Bay by November 22 for refueling." Hitokappu Bay was an inlet on Etorofu Island, part of the Kuril Islands group located to the north of Japan.[136] It is unknown whether CAST or HYPO intercepted these messages and/or passed them on to Station US (NEGAT) and ONI's OP-20-GY.

On November 18, 1941, the IJN's Naval General Staff sent a message to the chief of staff of the First Air Fleet, coordinating the pickup of an individual from "HITOKAPPU Bay," also known as Tankan Bay. Etorofu Island was one of the southernmost of the 16 Kuril Islands archipelago chain, some 800 sea miles north of Tokyo.

What is interesting about this message is that the IJN's Code Book D, seventh edition, did not have a Five Numeral Code cipher number that covered the word Hitokappu. Since there was no other way to indicate the geographic location, the word was spelled out and encrypted letter by letter in katakana form by the IJN signal dispatch writer preparing the message. The message was intercepted and transcribed at Station H that day at 1932 hours by Radioman Second Class A. C. Sheldon. The katakana coding of the name of the bay should have stood out and been easily recognized by Rochefort's HYPO, but it is unknown if anyone caught the name or, if so, passed it on to Kimmel or Layton.[137]

With his key orders now in effect, Yamamoto made sure that Nagumo's First Air Fleet continued "battle preparations" for the raid on Pearl Harbor. The FAF's staff directorate (RI TA 349) directed through a 5-Number Code message that special practice drills in "ambushing" would be carried out in the early morning each day, November 4–6, by 54 shipboard bomb-ers (torpedo bombers) in the vicinity of the Saeki Naval Base and then fol-lowed by 54 shipboard attack planes (dive-bombers).

The IJN's naval engineering command was ordered to speed up con-struction of a series of new forward operating bases at Truk, Palao, Pulap, Mortlock, and Mille Islands, involving land and sea plane installations (runways, seaplane ramps, plane shelters, etc.). These all had to be opera-tional by April 1942, some four full months in the future.[138] In terms of island base construction, Japanese war planners had concluded that shore-based aerial bombing squadrons would be able to operate from a chain of island bases within supporting distance of each other and thus prove invincible against most attackers.[139] How many 5-Num messages OP-20-GY were decoded and translated in a timely manner still remains a controversial issue, if not a mystery.

While the FAF was preparing for operations, things were picking up in French Indochina. McCollum's OP-16-F-2 issued a November 1 intelli-gence report ("Weekly Summary—Far East"), stating, among other things,

> The Japanese are moving reinforcements to Indo-China. . . . It is believed Tokyo intends to at least double the garrison. This would bring the Japanese forces in the colony to 100,000. Between 750 and 1000 Japanese troops are arriving daily at Haiphong. War materials, including light tanks and light artillery (75mm), are also being landed. A large air base is being established in northern Indo-China. . . . Premier Tojo stated that Japan stood at the cross roads of her destiny and must push forward to victory.[140]

As November wore on, Vice Adm. Nagumo, the IJN's commander of carriers (First Air Fleet–FAF) was targeted by RDF bearings from both CAST at Corregidor and BAKER at Guam. On November 9, a BAKER TESTM reported Nagumo using his call sign 2 NO KO at 328 degrees. Three days later, a CAST TESTM reported him using the same call sign along a bearing of 030 degrees, establishing an intersection fix just off the east coast of the Japanese island of Shikoku. On November 16, both BAKER and CAST reported that 2 NO KO was located slightly further north, but still off the coast of Shikoku Island.

Since the *Akagi* was Nagumo's flagship and a carrier, it was an RDF tar-get, singled out for special attention with BAKER TESTMs reporting RDF bearings of 329 degrees on November 11 and 330 degrees on November 14. CAST established the approximate fix on the 8 YU NA signal with its TESTM reported RDF bearing of 026 degrees on November 13, establish-ing that the carrier was located in the vicinity of Shikoku Island's southern coast. During this time, the aircraft carriers *Shokaku* (8 RO SA), *Hiryu* (9 RU SI), and *Kaga* (7 RI TI) were all picked up by RDF and located in the vicinity of Shikoku Island.[141]

Using a great circle sailing chart of the Northern Pacific as a plotting aide, the RDF bearings from BAKER and CAST were easy to establish and were important in terms of reliably tracking the IJN. This would change drastically over the following weeks as the IJN brought two new war measures into play: *radio deception* and *radio listening silence* (listening to radio signals' traffic but not responding).

On November 15, Yamamoto gave the Pearl Harbor attack plan his final approval. Undoubtedly he thought back to early February when he had commented: "If we have a war with the United States, we will have no hope of winning unless the U.S. fleet in Hawaiian waters can be destroyed." The next day, November 16, the IJN's Combined Fleet began to amass its FAF, converging throughout the next week on Hitokappu Bay. This was not the first time that Yamamoto had used the bay; two years earlier, his own fleet training exercises in that remote and stormy part of the northwest Pacific had enabled it to anchor for a time in this out-of-the-way, largely remote region.[142] As both an assembly and staging area, its remoteness provided ideal cover. There, the FAF would spend four days before heading out on November 26 in the direction of Pearl Harbor, some 3,000 miles away.

To cover his various operational fleet movements, Yamamoto used a series of deceptive measures, involving a combination of dummy or false radio message traffic, false radio transmitters to simulate key IJN warships, and more importantly, radio listening silence on the part of the ships actually in movement; if there was no radio signal to home in on, a ship could not be tracked by RDF measures. The dummy radio traffic was designed to load up the airways with such large amounts of message traffic that intercept operators would have trouble separating out the real from the false radio signals.

Often, previous broadcasts were repeated over and over again in an effort to camouflage and cover the legitimate, up-to-date messages that would now and then be intermingled with the barrages of false traffic. This was meant to cover the actual initiation of the intended IJN operations throughout the Pacific by maintaining a high enough intensity of message traffic to prevent U.S. Navy intercept operators from becoming suspicious that something unusual was taking place.[143] While effective at first, Rochefort's men at HYPO caught on to the deceptions.

The use of false radio transmitters was begun as early as November 16 and was conceived in a manner to give the U.S. Navy's radio direction finders the impression that a warship was still operating in one area when in reality it was actually in another, or even on the move. In order to conceal the movement of the FAF to Hitokappu Bay, a series of simulated key warship radio broadcasts were made. Using the radio call signs of the *Akagi, Kaga, Shokaku, Hiryu,* and *Zuikaku*, the IJN made random dummy radio signals to simulate the normal radio traffic that had been so typically occurring during the previous weeks.

The deception objective was to convince U.S. Naval Intelligence that the IJN's aircraft carriers were still training in the Kyushu and Inland Sea areas, all the while they were deploying to its forward transpacific launching point for an eventual attack on Pearl Harbor. Both Stations BAKER and CAST aimed their radio direction finders at what they thought were the legitimate transmitting stations, duly reporting the locations as indicated by their RDF systems and TA analysis.[144]

While BAKER and CAST may have fallen for the ruse, other intercept/RDF stations on the U.S. West Coast did not. The WCCI system was not duped, as Stations SAIL at Bainbridge and AE at Sitka both discovered the radio deception. The Station AE traffic chief, Radioman First Class Fred R. Thompson discovered that a radio transmitter at the Japanese naval air base at Kasumigaura in the vicinity of Tokyo was actually sending out messages to supposed IJN ships and then pretending to receive replies. Rochefort himself claimed: "It is awfully difficult to deceive a trained counter-communications intelligence organization."[145]

CAST's RDF operation at Corregidor, applying its bearings taken to a great circle sailing chart of the North Pacific, typically placed all the carriers along the bearing lines of 027 to 030 degrees. From early November on into early December 1941 the multiple bearings taken on the FAF's Strike Force carriers rarely changed, if ever.[146] A major problem for CAST in this situation was the unfortunate geographical fact that Hitokappu Bay's location in the southern Kurils and those of Shikoku and Kyushu Islands (Kure naval base) in southern Japan were all generally located along the same axis or magnetic compass line 027–030 degrees from Corregidor to Hitokappu Bay. This unusual circumstance by its nature created multiple, logical location possibilities for any RDF bearing emanating out of CAST along this line. Obtaining an accurate fix was an impossibility, unless Baker at Guam could get its own RDF cross-bearing on the subject transmitter.

Station BAKER's RDF facility typically took its bearings on the same radio transmitter signals that CAST took. Beginning in early November and continuing on through the end of the month and even on into early December, BAKER took the multiple cross-bearings that CAST needed to get for what it thought were accurate fixes. The bearings taken from Guam typically spanned a segment of 328 to 332 degrees and never changed, even after November 16 as the FAF gradually made its way north.[147] Therefore, the FAF was always located by BAKER and CAST in the vicinity of Japan, even after it began its move to Hitokappu Bay, some 800 miles further to the north, and then on across the North Pacific.

If the FAF's Strike Force ships had now and then broken radio listening silence, Baker should have been picking them up and plotting them on a great circle sailing chart in the range of 350 to 005 degrees. That BAKER remained focused on the area of Shikoku Island and the Kure Naval Base indicated that insofar as Station CAST went, the IJN's deception plan using false radio transmission had worked extremely well in concealing the FAF's movement to the southern Kurils.

There was only one exception. The November 22, 1941, 0800 hours, bearing taken by CAST's RDF station against a radio call sign (SA SO 2) was described in the TESTM report as identifying the *Kaga* aircraft carrier. CAST's bearing was 040 degrees or considerably out of the norm at that time. Unknown to CAST, this was perfectly logical, in that the IJN was infiltrating its FAF units in small groups at spaced intervals further out to the south and eastward of Tokyo Bay, in between the Hachijojima and Aogajima Islands, before routing them on north to their southern Kurils marshalling area, the trip taking roughly four days. The *Kaga* was one of the last ships in the FAF to make its rendezvous at Hitokappu Bay, arriving a day or so late.[148]

Over at HYPO, the RDF TESTMs sent by CAST were received by Huckins, the head of the RDF analytical section, who affixed his "TAH" initials to each copy. During the first half of November, Rochefort's own communications intelligence summaries corresponded to CAST's TESTM reports, reflecting his assumption that the carriers were still in and around their "home waters with most of them in port" or "are mostly in the Kure-Sasebo area with the exception of a few which are operating in the Kyushu area." His November 18 CIS report stated "No movement from home waters has been detected."[149]

Other Combined Fleet movements were more readily detected. Beginning in September and continuing on into November, it was noted that a major part of the IJN's forces were massing in the South China Sea to the south of Japan, and around November 20–21, a submarine squadron was noted as having arrived in the Marshall Islands.[150] In Washington on November 18, McCollum released his own estimate on the IJN's fleet locations, which reflected what CAST had been reporting: Japan's carriers were in the vicinity of Kyushu Island in southern Japan, specifically the Kure-Saeki naval bases.[151]

With no more PURPLE intercepts being received in Hawaii from either Washington, or Cavite, in the Philippines, or evidence that Pearl Harbor was in any way under threat, Layton, Kimmel's intelligence officer, began to focus more and more on what appeared to be the primary IJN areas of interest: the South China Sea in the Western Pacific and the Marshall Islands in the Central Pacific. From Layton's perspective, the IJN was organizing for a series of offensive moves against Malaya, the Dutch East Indies, the Philippines, and in and around the Mandates. HYPO's communications intercepts indicated that the IJN's Third Fleet appeared to be the main amphibious invasion force, since it was frequently reflected in communications with shore-based aerial unit commanders in Indochina.[152]

Even if the *Akagi* and the other IJN aircraft carriers were not being heard from as November wore on, Rochefort and Layton could feel comfortable in the fact that when the *Akagi* did come on the air, it would be readily identified. It had been noticed that even though the IJN practiced an element of concealment from time to time, they could not hide the Morse key sending "signatures" of certain shipboard telegraphers. In the case of the *Akagi*, its "ham-handed telegraphists," as Layton called them, were dead giveaways and easily identified by radio fingerprinting.

Even the change in radio call signs on November 1 had made no difference, as the IJN radio operators' "swing" or way they touched their respective radiotelegraph keys gave them away once more. Rochefort summed up HYPO's more real feelings around November 20: "There was great unease in all of our minds because of the lack of [IJN radio] traffic." The main force IJN carriers of the Combined Fleet appeared to have disappeared from the airwaves, at least for the moment.[153]

Just as the FAF was beginning its infiltration movements toward Hitokappu Bay, an unusual event took place thousands of miles to the east, in Washington, DC. With war clouds on the horizon and having read the PURPLE intercepts from Tokyo to Washington, as well as other official American military and naval intelligence reports and intercepts concerning Japanese intentions and preparations to go to war in the Pacific, a media-sensitive and prudent Gen. George C. Marshall called together the leading influential magazine and press officials of the day to his office for a special secret briefing on November 15. There were seven of them present; they included the major wire services represented by Edward Bomar of the Associated Press (AP), Lyle Wilson of the United Press (UP), and Harold Slater of the International News Service, as well as Charles Hurd of the *New York Times*, Bert Andrews of the *New York Herald Tribune*, Robert Sherrod of *Time* magazine, and Ernest K. Lindley of *Newsweek*. Marshall wanted these important news providers to have an overview of America's strategy, and to give them some insight into his own thinking in terms of Japan versus the United States in the Pacific. Only *Time* magazine's military correspondent, Robert Sherrod, made some notes of this important meeting and then passed them on to one of his editors.[154]

George Marshall was particularly worried that the press might get hold of and misinterpret or otherwise compromise key elements of the military strategy of the United States for the Pacific. To assure them that they were privy to what was really going on, the general stated, "The U.S. is at the brink of war with the Japanese." He added that America had an advantage over the Japanese: "We know what they know about us [PURPLE, etc.] and they don't know we know it." He then went on to explain some of the things the United States was doing in the Pacific, especially in terms of building up its strength in the Philippines.

Marshall specifically mentioned programmed increases in B-17 and B-24 bombers that could be used for long-range bombing attacks on Japanese cities in the form of a merciless assault, which would include fire-bombing Japan's most vulnerable urban areas. Other initiatives dealt with increases in various quantities of tanks, artillery, and even dive-bombers. The army's overall strength was said to be on the verge of reaching 2 million men under arms.

Marshall directed that under no circumstances should any of this information be leaked to the public. The only leaks would be official ones from Washington. While Sherrod's notes were fairly detailed, he did append them on August 29, 1945, adding a comment made by the general at the briefing. Perhaps reflecting on Adm. Nagano's November 5, 1941, message to Adm. Yamamoto, Gen. Marshall stated, "The danger period is the first ten days of December." The war would probably break out during the first 10 days of the next month.[155]

This was an amazing briefing, providing insight into the dynamics taking place in the Pacific. The reporters and attending officials maintained their secrecy; not a word leaked out! Yet this information, especially the disclosure that Japan would attack the United States during the first 10 days of December 1941, was so important that one might have thought that Marshall would have communicated it directly to not only his army commander in the Philippines, Gen. Douglas MacArthur, but also his army commander in Hawaii, Lt. Gen. Walter Short. Who really deserved to receive this critical, secret information: the media moguls or America's leading admirals and generals, such as Hart and Kimmel, or MacArthur and Short, all of whom would have to face the initial Japanese onslaught of the war on land, in the air, and at sea?

6

The Combined Fleet Prepares to Attack

Ever since taking command of the Pacific Fleet, Adm. Kimmel had trained his men and ships rigorously, carrying out fleet maneuver exercises each month for all the sailors and marines under his command. Kimmel divided his fleet into three distinct surface task forces: two of these at Pearl Harbor with one aircraft carrier and supporting cruisers and destroyers apiece, and the third, with its one aircraft carrier based in California, but otherwise with its battleships, cruisers, and destroyers located at Pearl Harbor. One or two of the task forces were always at sea, conducting training exercises, and the other(s) in port. On occasion, all three would be at sea, undergoing maneuvers, often against one another. As part of the fleet's November 1941 training schedule, an exercise in fleet tactics called Exercise 191 had been designated for the period of November 21–25, Thanksgiving weekend. It was to start that Friday and terminate the following Tuesday.

Whether it was Kimmel's intuition, his basic understanding of War Plan Orange, or his own earlier estimate of the situation (that the Japanese might open a war with the United States by way of a surprise attack on Pearl Harbor over a weekend), he deliberately focused this exercise on a point 300 miles due north of Oahu, where he thought the Japanese could logically launch an aircraft-carrier-based raid against Hawaii.

This was not without precedent; four years earlier, Vice Adm. Ernest King had conducted a surprise, simulated training raid on Pearl Harbor with his aircraft flying in from points due north of Hawaii. Additionally, a March 31, 1941, analysis of Pearl Harbor's vulnerabilities to surprise air attack written by Kimmel's own aerial operations expert, Rear Adm. Patrick Bellinger, pointed out "that the most likely and dangerous form of attack on Oahu would be an air attack" that could be conducted by aircraft carriers approaching within 300 miles of Oahu. The following day, April 1, an OPNAV coded electronic message to all naval district commanders stated in part:

EXPERIENCE SHOWS THE AXIS POWERS OFTEN BEGIN ACTIVITIES IN A PARTICULAR FIELD ON SATURDAYS AND SUNDAYS OR ON NATIONAL HOLIDAYS OF THE COUNTRY CONCERNED. TAKE STEPS ON SUCH DAYS TO SEE THAT PROPER WATCHES AND PRE-CAUTIONS ARE IN EFFECT.[1]

With the Mandates and the Marshall Islands fairly well covered and constantly under watch during 1941 through the efforts of his intelligence officers, Cdr. Rochefort and Cdr. Layton, Kimmel wisely chose to conduct a reconnaissance in the relatively ignored area to the north of Pearl Harbor. In essence, the admiral had recognized it as an intelligence gap in the Pearl Harbor defenses that needed to be covered, and he intended to do something about it. His confidence must have gone up when Adm. Stark, in one of his letters to Kimmel, stated, "I believe that, in all probability, the Pacific fleet can operate successfully and effectively even though decidedly weaker than the entire Japanese Fleet, which certainly can be concentrated in one area only with the greatest of difficulty."[2]

Normally, the Pacific Fleet conducted training exercises to the south or southwest of Hawaii. Made up of 83 warships, including the aircraft carriers *Enterprise*, *Lexington*, and *Saratoga*, and divided into three numbered task forces (One, Two, and Three), the Pacific Fleet was organized for battle as Kimmel envisioned he would fight it.[3]

On Friday, November 21, 1941, at 0600 hours, two of the three task forces on Exercise 191 now headed out of Pearl Harbor in seemingly the same direction the Pacific Fleet always followed, toward the east and then south, for traditional maneuver exercises. Once out of sight of its Pearl Harbor base, the fleet's direction of movement was dramatically shifted to a northerly direction. Kimmel wasn't taking any chances on an inadvertent disclosure of his intentions, and the fleet moved under conditions of radio listening silence. Only blinker lights and signal flags would be used to communicate until, or if, contact was actually made with any IJN warships.

Determined to seek out and find any Japanese forces approaching Pearl Harbor, the admiral's training exercise, described in his operation order as "training in war operations under realistically simulated war conditions," was in reality a full-blown, battle-ready reconnaissance in force, designed to seek out and make contact with an enemy at a point on the high seas in the North Pacific some 200 to 500 miles to the north of Oahu, aerial reconnaissance permitting.[4]

By coming at the IJN from out of the northeast, as was Battle Plan 2M1's basic circular maneuver concept, Kimmel intended to achieve surprise and quickly go into the attack from an unexpected direction before the enemy force could react. Once contact or a sighting had been made with the enemy, the rest of the Pacific Fleet, then held in reserve at Pearl Harbor and California, would sally forth to reinforce Kimmel and fight to the finish any Japanese ships encountered.

During Exercise 191, the White Forces (Task Force 1), with 25 warships and 54 aircraft, would defend Pearl Harbor. The Black Force (Task Force 3), with 11 warships, including the carrier *Lexington* with its complement of 72 aircraft, would perform the role of the raiding force, attempting to attack Pearl Harbor. By Saturday midnight, November 22, the White Forces were expected to be in position 400 miles north of Oahu, and the Black Forces were to be in position some 500 miles north of Oahu. Unaware of each other's presence, the two "enemies," now separated by some 100 miles, would commence "battle" the next day.[5]

All day Sunday, November 23, the Black and White Forces swept back and forth over the entire maneuver area as Kimmel practiced his Battle Plan 2M1. Despite the rolling and pitching of the high seas brought about by the North Pacific's storms that were typical of that time of year, the *Lexington*, having maneuvered in accordance with 2M1, was on location at 27 degrees, 29 minutes North, 156 degrees, 31 minutes West. It was the approximate site of the Prokofiev Seamount (25 degrees North, 157 degrees West) from which the IJN's First Air Fleet (FAF) would actually launch its deadly aerial attacks on Pearl Harbor, just two weeks to the day later![6]

The next afternoon, Monday, November 24, at about 1:30 Kimmel received an abrupt message from Rear Adm. Royal Ingersoll, Stark's assistant chief of naval operations. The highlights of the message read:

CHANCES OF FAVORABLE OUTCOME OF NEGOTIATIONS WITH JAPAN DOUBTFUL A SURPRISE AGGRESSIVE MOVEMENT IN ANY

DIRECTION INCLUDING ATTACK ON PHILIPPINES OR GUAM IS A POSSIBILITY UTMOST SECRECY NECESSARY IN ORDER NOT TO COMPLICATE AN ALREADY TENSE SITUATION OR PRECIPITATE JAPANESE ACTION.

Unaware of Washington's strategy in terms of goading the Japanese into firing the first shot, Kimmel suddenly found himself having to curtail his high-priority maneuver Exercise 191 by 15 hours. He obviously did not like this order, but, like a good sailor who had been trained since his Naval Academy days to follow his superior's orders, and especially those of the navy's CNO, he terminated his cherished reconnaissance in force around 3:30 p.m.

Everyone had to be in sync; even Hart, CINC Asiatic Fleet in the Philippines, received the same dispatch.[7] Yet, while Kimmel was reorganizing his ships in the North Pacific for their return to base at Pearl Harbor, Vice Adm. William "Bull" Halsey initiated what was intended to be a continuation to Exercise 191 under *his* own control. Halsey intended to launch his exercise on November 28. Utilizing both the aircraft carrier *Enterprise* (72 aircraft) and the battleship *Arizona* to form part of a 25-warship Task Force 2 (then still anchored at Pearl Harbor), this exercise was to last seven days and terminate on December 5.

As this had been coordinated in advance, it is apparent that Kimmel was planning to cover the next several weekends, rotating or otherwise exchanging one major task force of his fleet for another. It is possible, had Kimmel not received Ingersoll's order to terminate his own exercise on November 24, he might well have ordered the original Exercise 191 maneuver task forces back into the North Pacific after Halsey had completed his own exercise and reconnaissance in force. If he had, the Pacific Fleet would have continued to close the neglected intelligence gap involving the highly vulnerable northern approach routes into Pearl Harbor over the weekend of December 7, and probably even beyond.

But Halsey's exercise never left Pearl Harbor. It, too, was prematurely cancelled during the afternoon of November 26, this time by Adm. Stark himself, who had other plans in mind for Kimmel's Pacific Fleet.[8]

Unfortunately for Kimmel, Exercise 191 was the last time he would be freely allowed to command the Pacific Fleet on his own terms. Having overstepped his bounds by ordering what he intended to be a prolonged reconnaissance of points north of Pearl Harbor, he was now being reined in and essentially circumscribed from acting on his own initiative; further orders from Stark would soon indicate this de facto situation. The admiral could not know at that moment, but history's capriciousness would now only allow him no more than a mere 23 more days in command of the Pacific Fleet, and this only lasting until his premature relief from duty on December 17, 1941.

On November 25, in HYPO at Pearl Harbor, while elements of the Pacific Fleet were still in the North Pacific looking for the IJN, Rochefort's traffic analysts were reporting that a full carrier division (2 carriers) was located somewhere in the Mandates. While the Mandates are roughly 2,000 miles wide, running from the Carolines in the Western Pacific to the Marshalls in the Central Pacific, Kimmel now had to confront the possibility of an IJN carrier strike coming out of those islands against Hawaii, just some 2,500 miles away. The HYPO report conflicted with McCollum, who issued yet another Japanese fleet location estimate, reporting that all 10 of the IJN's aircraft carriers were still located in the vicinity of South Kyushu Island or the Kure naval base.

At that approximate moment in time, or around 0600 on November 26 (Tokyo time—November 25, Pearl Harbor time), the FAF, having completed its final preparations including refueling and now sailing under special orders from Yamamoto, CINC Combined IJN Fleet, weighed anchor in Hitokappu Bay and headed eastward across the North Pacific. At that same time, another IJN fleet-sized force of 30 submarines, moving in coordination with the FAF, made its way stealthily through the Central Pacific. The two groups together constituted what the IJN now called the Kido Butai or Strike Force, functioning under the command of Vice Adm. Nagumo. Their trip would take 11 eventful days—target: Pearl Harbor.[9]

As Kimmel was coordinating the return of his Pacific Fleet to its Pearl Harbor base on November 25, a key meeting took place that Tuesday at the White House between Roosevelt and his War Cabinet, as he liked to refer to it. Present were Henry L. Stimson (secretary of war), Cordell Hull (secretary of state), Frank Knox (secretary of the navy), Adm. Harold R. Stark (chief of naval operations), and Gen. George C. Marshall (chief of staff of the army). Stimson recorded key points and summaries of important conferences in his diary throughout 1941. Stimson noted:

> Starting around noon, the meeting lasted until nearly 1:30 p.m. Roosevelt's focus was entirely on America's relations with Japan. A recent PURPLE intercept of November 22 had extended the deadline to achieve a signed settlement favorable to Japanese interests between Tokyo and Washington to November 29. Tersely, the message stated: "The deadline absolutely cannot be changed. After that things are automatically going to happen."[10]

According to Stimson, Roosevelt was influenced by the specificity of the cable, with its date for action to take place, and Ambassador Grew's early November comment that Japan would even risk national suicide rather than give in to foreign pressure. Roosevelt mentioned that the Japanese were likely to attack the United States by surprise out in the Pacific by perhaps as early as the following Monday, December 1. What should be done was of paramount importance.

In spite of the risk involved in letting Japan fire the first shot, the War Cabinet knew that in order to have the support of the American people, it was important to ensure that the Japanese did exactly that. As was Stimson's custom, he summarized the key points and concepts discussed at the meeting: "The question was how we should maneuver them [the Japanese] into the position of firing the first shot without allowing too much danger to ourselves. It was a difficult proposition."[11]

It was a confirmation of the overt act strategy, which had been promulgated earlier that October, talked about numerous times, and was still much the policy in play.[12] Much of the maneuvering had already been accomplished economically and politically speaking, but there was still more to come.

That afternoon, when Stimson returned to the War Department, he received a G-2 intelligence report indicating that a Japanese military expedition had embarked with "30, 40, or 50 ships" from its Chinese ports and was now located to points south of Formosa. He duly informed Roosevelt and Hull. It was Hull who took action.[13]

Hull was aware that Japan had sent a special envoy, Saburo Kurusu, to join Nomura to try and convince the United States in one last attempt that the Japanese positions in regard to East Asia were the correct ones. A previous November 16 PURPLE intercept from Tokyo had stated, "the fate of our empire hangs by a slender thread of a few days, so please fight harder than you ever did before." Tokyo's position was that besides the lifting of the several economic and financial embargos imposed upon Japan, there was also the need to nullify the United States' own demand that Japan withdraw from China and, finally, to then get Washington to recognize the new Japanese sphere of influence covering Eastern Asia and the Southwest Pacific.[14]

After having come to the conclusion that Japan's ambassadors were merely fencing with him, and after coordinating with Roosevelt, Hull abandoned all thought of a truce with Tokyo. On November 26, he wrote out his own "Ten Point Note," a restatement of the earlier American positions and the equivalent of an official ultimatum from the United States to Japan. Nomura reported in a November 26 PURPLE message to Tokyo that the U.S. position included two key points, among others, that Japan would have to implement before it would be possible to reestablish its reciprocal trade treaty with America: "The complete evacuation of Japanese forces from China and all of French Indo-China" and that "Japan and the United states both definitely promise to support no regime in China but that of Chiang Kai-Shek." The diplomatic solution and reprieve from national humiliation so avidly sought by Tokyo had failed.[15]

While Hull was covering the diplomatic side of the first shot strategy, Stark was busy with the military side. Aware that Kimmel's Exercise 191 being conducted in the North Pacific was out of sync with the administration's overt act strategy, Stark gave his Pacific Fleet commander a mission that would circumscribe any further aggressive adventures outside the Hawaiian Islands. On November 26, the day after the Pacific Fleet had returned to its base at Pearl Harbor, Kimmel received a priority secret message from Stark stating that the army would station 25 pursuit fighter planes each at Midway and Wake Islands. The planes and their ground crews were to be uploaded and then transported to their destinations by aircraft carrier.

The planes would fly off the carriers' decks, and the rest of the forces were to be lowered into boats off to the side of their carriers and then landed at their island destinations. Complicating matters was the fact that in the case of Wake Island there were no harbor facilities at all. While all these forces would be quartered in tents with wooden floors, the navy would be responsible for supplying water, food, and other supplies such as spare parts, tools, ammunition, and fuel to support the planes for at least six weeks and probably longer. The hundreds of bombs would all need special additional handling, as well as revetments constructed. The Pacific Fleet would have to conduct the transfer of planes, personnel, and logistics so as not to interfere with a planned flight of B-17 bombers destined to fly to the Philippines via the islands. Kimmel was to confer with Short and reply back to Stark as soon as possible.[16] Seemingly simple enough on the surface, it was actually a complex mission that would be modified and changed over the next 10 days sufficiently to distract the admiral and his Pacific Fleet staff about what was going on operationally with Japan throughout the Pacific.

As Adm. Kimmel and his staff, in conjunction with Lt. Gen. Short and his staff, began to analyze the mission, a number of problems surfaced. First and foremost, Short's staff determined that using army P-40s for the defense of Midway and Wake made no sense, since the pursuit planes could not successfully operate more than 15 miles from land, due to the pilots' unfamiliarity with long-range navigation over water out of sight of land. This and the inability of that type of plane to land on a carrier made them practically useless for any further overseas expeditions of any kind.[17]

Kimmel did not like the mission as it was construed; with so many additional (up to 25) planes on board for passage, each carrier would become overly crowded and unable to operate; the carriers would not be prepared for war under these circumstances. It would take more than a week for the army to prepare its 50 pursuit planes to be put on the carriers. It would also require a flotilla of small boats to receive the cargos and personnel being lowered from the carriers and ferried to shore at their new stations.[18]

Washington's instruction to transfer up to half of Hawaii's P-40 fighters to Midway and Wake Islands was taken by Kimmel and his staff to mean that the senior army and navy staffs "did not consider hostile action [by the Japanese] on Pearl Harbor imminent or probable." Had not the November 24 message from OPNAV to CINCPAC and CINCAF specifically mentioned only the Philippines and Guam on the far side of the Pacific as possible targets? This message, and the fact that on October 17 Stark had stated in his letter to Kimmel, "Personally I do not believe the Japanese are going to sail into us," were reassurances that Hawaii was outside the immediate danger zone.[19]

What Kimmel did not realize was that he was, in fact, losing both of his primary offensive and defensive "fists" in terms of controlling his Pearl Harbor–based aircraft carriers for the defense of the Hawaiian Islands. Kimmel was able to convince Stark that it would be better to send properly trained Marine Corps pilots and planes based at Pearl Harbor, who could land and take off from aircraft carriers, out to the islands in order to wage a proper defense. In a November 28 message to Stark, Kimmel indicated his intention of sending 12 marine fighters that day to Wake Island on one carrier and then, on December 1, sending another 12 marine fighters on a second carrier to Midway.[20] And so the matter rested for the moment.

Having brought the diplomatic negotiations to an end with his ultimatum of November 26, that Japan would withdraw completely from China, Hull now informed Stimson, "I have washed my hands of it and its [*sic*] is now in the hands of you and Knox—the Army and the Navy!"[21]

Directed by Roosevelt to send out a war alert message to the various army commanders in the Pacific, Stimson went to work with members of Marshall's staff to draft a suitable message to go out under Marshall's signature. Stimson recounted that "The President himself . . . had now actually directed the sending of the message."[22] Incorporated into the beginning of the message of November 27 was the sentence:

NEGOTIATIONS WITH JAPAN APPEAR TO BE TERMINATED TO ALL PRACTICAL PURPOSES WITH ONLY THE BAREST POSSIBILITIES THAT THE JAPANESE GOVERNMENT MIGHT COME BACK AND OFFER TO CONTINUE.[23]

Lt. Gen. Short in Hawaii and Gen. MacArthur in the Philippines were also instructed in the Stimson (Marshall) message:

IF HOSTILITIES CANNOT, REPEAT CANNOT, BE AVOIDED THE UNITED STATES DESIRES THAT JAPAN COMMIT THE FIRST OVERT ACT.

Marshall, himself, later commented on this statement during the Pearl Harbor hearings that it "was a direct instruction from the President."[24] Maj. Gen. Leonard T. Gerow, a plans and operations staff officer, explained at a Pearl Harbor attack hearing that "the President had definitely stated that he wanted Japan to commit the first overt act."[25] As part of this directive, there was included the instruction that while commanders were not to jeopardize their defense, they should not take actions that might "ALARM CIVIL POPULATION OR DISCLOSE INTENT."[26]

In Hawaii, Short took the message seriously; he interpreted it to mean that all public utilities, reservoirs, bridges, and the like should be protected against possible sabotage by the some 160,000 Japanese living in the Hawaiian Islands. That night, army forces began going on the alert and deploying to their designated antisabotage positions.[27] While Short's actions were unknown to Marshall's staff, on November 28, Army Adj. Gen. Emory Adams, sent out a message under Marshall's name, specifying exactly what was expected to be done in Hawaii:

> CRITICAL SITUATION DEMANDS THAT ALL PRECAUTIONS BE TAKEN IMMEDIATELY AGAINST SUBVERSIVE ACTIVITIES. INITIATE FORTHWITH ALL ADDITIONAL MEASURES NECESSARY TO PROVIDE PROTECTION OF YOUR ESTABLISHMENTS, PROPERTY, AND EQUIPMENT AGAINST SABOTAGE MEASURES SHOULD BE CONFINED TO THOSE ESSENTIAL TO SECURITY, AVOIDING UNNECESSARY PUBLICITY AND ALARM.[28]

It now appeared to Short that he had taken precisely the actions that the War Department expected of him. He replied November 29 that "full precautions are being taken against subversive activities."[29] Now, with the army seemingly having placed its "house in order" in the Pacific, the navy proceeded to do the same.

Aware that Stimson was arranging to send out a war warning to the senior army commanders in the Pacific, Ingersoll composed a similar message to the one that the army had sent out on November 27. Using the same opening sentences, it stated in part:

> THIS DISPATCH IS TO BE CONSIDERED A WAR WARNING. NEGOTIATIONS WITH JAPAN LOOKING TOWARD STABILIZATION OF CONDITIONS IN THE PACIFIC HAVE CEASED AND AN AGGRESSIVE MOVE BY JAPAN IS EXPECTED WITHIN THE NEXT FEW DAYS. THE NUMBER AND EQUIPMENT OF JAPANESE TROOPS AND THE ORGANIZATION OF NAVAL TASK FORCES INDICATES AN AMPHIBIOUS EXPEDITION AGAINST EITHER THE PHILIPPINES OR KRA PENINSULA OR POSSIBLY BORNEO."[30]

Sent to both Kimmel in Hawaii and Hart in the Philippines, the message not only again focused on the Philippines but now also included the Kra Peninsula (Malay Peninsula) and Borneo, suggesting that the focus of all Japanese military operations were toward the periphery of the Southwest Pacific. But Ingersoll, just like Stimson, had made a serious mistake—Roosevelt had intended that *each one* of the senior army and navy

NAVAL MESSAGE   NAVY

PHONE EXTENSION NUMBER Op-12 Ext. 2092   ADDRESSEES

FROM Chief of Naval Operations

RELEASED BY NR Stark

DATE November 28, 1941

FOR ACTION

COM PNHCF
COM PSNCF

ROUTINE
DEFERRED

TOR CODEROOM _____

DECODED P: _____

PARAPHRASED BY _____

INFORMATION

CINCPAC
COM PHCF

PRIORITY
ROUTINE
DEFERRED

INDICATE BY ASTERISK ADDRESSEES FOR WHICH MAIL DELIVERY IS SATISFACTORY   CR 066

290110

UNLESS OTHERWISE DESIGNATED THIS DISPATCH WILL BE TRANSMITTED WITH DEFERRED PRECEDENCE.
ORIGINATOR FILL IN DATE AND TIME FOR DEFERRED AND MAIL DELIVERY

R N T V L   DATE   TIME   GCT

TEXT H o r z z

REFER TO MY 272358 X ARMY HAS SENT FOLLOWING TO COMMANDER WESTERN
DEFENSE COMMAND QUOTE NEGOTIATIONS WITH JAPAN APPEAR TO BE TERMINATED
TO ALL PRACTICAL PURPOSES WITH ONLY THE BAREST POSSIBILITIES THAT
THE JAPANESE GOVERNMENT MIGHT COME BACK AND OFFER TO CONTINUE X
JAPANESE FUTURE ACTION UNPREDICTABLE BUT HOSTILE ACTION POSSIBLE
AT ANY MOMENT X IF HOSTILITIES CANNOT REPEAT NOT BE AVOIDED THE
UNITED STATES DESIRES THAT JAPAN COMMIT THE FIRST OVERT ACT X THIS
POLICY SHOULD NOT REPEAT NOT BE CONSTRUED AS RESTRICTING YOU TO A
COURSE OF ACTION THAT MIGHT JEOPARDIZE YOUR DEFENSE X PRIOR TO
HOSTILE JAPANESE ACTION YOU ARE DIRECTED TO UNDERTAKE SUCH
RECONNAISSANCE AND OTHER MEASURES AS YOU DEEM NECESSARY BUT THESE
MEASURES SHOULD BE CARRIED OUT SO AS NOT REPEAT NOT TO ALARM CIVIL
POPULATION OR DISCLOSE INTENT X REPORT MEASURES TAKEN X A SEPARATE
MESSAGE IS BEING SENT TO YOU NINTH CORPS AREA RE SUBVERSIVE

TOP SECRET

(page one of two)

SEE ART. 76(4)
NAV REGS

MAKE ORIGINAL ONLY, DELIVER TO COMMUNICATION WATCH OFFICER IN PERSON

99999.

CNO Harold R. Stark's November 28, 1941, message laid out President Roosevelt's actual overt policy for Japan in the Pacific for the first time for Adm. Kimmel. (RG 38, Box 164 [CNO File], Archive II, National Archives)

NAVAL MESSAGE ( )   NAVY DEPARTMENT

			MESSAGE PRECEDENCE
PHONE EXTENSION NUMBER Op-12 Ext. 2992	ADDRESSEES		
FROM Chief of Naval Operations	FOR ACTION	COM PNNCF	PRIORITY
RELEASED BY		COM PSNCF	ROUTINE
DATE November 28, 1941			DEFERRED
FOR CODEROOM	INFORMATION	CINCPAC	PRIORITY
DECODED BY		COM PNCF	ROUTINE
PARAPHRASED BY			DEFERRED

INDICATE BY ASTERISK ADDRESSEES FOR WHICH MAIL DELIVERY IS SATISFACTORY

791011 00

UNLESS OTHERWISE DESIGNATED THIS DISPATCH WILL BE TRANSMITTED WITH DEFERRED PRECEDENCE.
ORIGINATOR FILL IN DATE AND TIME FOR DEFERRED AND MAIL DELIVERY

DATE	TIME	GCT

TEXT

CONT'D (Page two)

ACTIVITIES IN UNITED STATES X SHOULD HOSTILITIES OCCUR YOU WILL
CARRY OUT THE TASKS ASSIGNED IN RAINBOW FIVE SO FAR AS THEY PERTAIN
TO JAPAN X LIMIT DISSEMINATION OF THIS HIGHLY SECRET INFORMATION
TO MINIMUM ESSENTIAL OFFICERS X UNQUOTE XX WPL52 IS NOT APPLICABLE
TO PACIFIC AREA AND WILL NOT BE PLACED IN EFFECT IN THAT AREA
EXCEPT AS NOW IN FORCE IN SOUTHEAST PACIFIC SUB AREA AND PANAMA
NAVAL COASTAL FRONTIER X UNDERTAKE NO OFFENSIVE ACTION UNTIL JAPAN
HAS COMMITTED AN OVERT ACT X BE PREPARED TO CARRY OUT TASKS ASSIGNED
IN WPL46 SO FAR AS THEY APPLY TO JAPAN IN CASE HOSTILITIES OCCUR

Orig: Op 12
Copy to: Op 30, 38, WPD

TOP SECRET

SECRET

EIMUS
ECM25

(page two of two)

SEE ART 76(4)
NAV REGS

MAKE ORIGINAL ONLY, DELIVER TO COMMUNICATION WATCH OFFICER IN PERSON

The November 28, 1941, message also provided specific instructions for Adm. Kimmel about how he was to operate until the Japanese fired an opening first shot (overt act) against the United States in the Pacific: "Undertake no offensive action." (RG 38, Box 164 [CNO File], Archive II, National Archives) commanders in the Pacific clearly understood the intent of his foreign policy objective, which was to have the Japanese fire the opening first shot(s) whenever and wherever their operations might take place in the Pacific.

Remedial action was required. Stark, having been personally present at that key strategy session with Roosevelt on November 25, now took action with a second, clarifying message, dated November 28, to Hart and Kimmel. Similar to that of the previous day, it now added that, while being authorized to conduct reconnaissance and other like activities prior to hostile Japanese action, "these measures should be carried out so as not, repeat not, to alarm civil population or disclose intent." The two most important parts of the message and the reason it was being sent out stated:

IF HOSTILITIES CANNOT REPEAT NOT BE AVOIDED THE UNITED STATES DESIRES THAT JAPAN COMMIT THE FIRST OVERT ACT. UNDERTAKE NO OFFENSIVE ACTION UNTIL JAPAN HAS COMMITTED AN OVERT ACT.[31]

Because the message instructed both admirals to be prepared to carry out tasks assigned in War Plan-46, Kimmel took this to mean that he should begin preparing for an expedition against the Japanese Mandates, particularly the Marshalls, as they were relatively close (2,000 miles) to Pearl Harbor. The part of the message that directed that he conduct naval reconnaissance activities appeared to be contradictory, since just a few days earlier, Stark had terminated Kimmel's reconnaissance and instead, was now having him ship fighter planes to Midway and Wake islands.

Since Hawaii had not been mentioned in any of the messages as an apparent Japanese target—as opposed to the Philippines, which had been singled out on two distinct occasions—it would stand to reason that, even with the imminence of war between Japan and the United States, Hawaii for the moment was not going to be part of Japan's opening overt acts. An evaluation of the situation was made on a daily basis as Kimmel conferred over the next several days with his Pacific Fleet War Plans Officer, Capt. Charles H. McMorris. In the discussion on November 27 concerning the probability of a surprise air attack on Oahu, Lt. Gen. Short, who was also present, recalled McMorris, stating that there was no probability of an attack against Pearl Harbor.

To weigh in on the safe side, Kimmel immediately placed into effect a direct order for the entire Pacific Fleet to attack all IJN submarines located in and near the operating areas around Hawaii. Layton was also busy, producing a formal Pacific Fleet Intelligence Bulletin that day, which clearly depicted the organization of what he called the "Carrier Fleet (Cardivs)" into its five distinct divisions for a total of 10 aircraft carriers. The IJN's *Akagi* and the *Kaga* headed the list as "Cardiv1."[32]

Had Kimmel been aware of the intense Japanese espionage effort targeting Pearl Harbor, he undoubtedly would have had a completely different attitude as to what was going on in terms of the overt act strategy and his Pearl Harbor–based Pacific Fleet. Unknown to Kimmel, his warships and aircraft carriers were part of the IJN target grid system in preparation for an attack on Pearl Harbor.

At least 14 cable messages sent in the J-19 diplomatic code were exchanged during the period from September 24 to December 6, 1941, between Tokyo and its Honolulu consulate concerning the Pacific Fleet's warship locations and their movements. Tokyo also wanted reports of ships tied up at wharves, buoys, and docks. Included were to be special situations that found warships also docked side by side. And every cable had been intercepted, photographed, and then sent on to Washington for decoding and translation by ONI. None of this was sent to Kimmel.

A November 18 cable to Tokyo, intercepted and translated by the army, indicated precise reporting of the routines followed by the battleships and aircraft carriers. Destroyer course directions and formations upon entering the harbor were reported in detail, including maneuvering between specific buoys, numbers of changes of course direction, speeds, and the various elapsed times to perform a complete harbor entry. In answer to a Tokyo J-19 coded directive of December 2 to report "day by day" Pacific Fleet "warships, airplane carriers, and cruisers," its Honolulu consulate responded quickly, indicating that there were neither barrage balloons over the harbor nor torpedo nets present at the moorings of the battleships. One J-19 report sent to Tokyo from Honolulu stated that the Pacific Fleet never conducted training operations into the North Pacific, indicating that Kimmel's Exercise 191 had been successfully carried out in complete secrecy.[33]

The J-19 cable information received by Tokyo indicated that Japanese Honolulu consul Tadashi Morimura (IJN intelligence officer Takeo Yoshikawa) had done his work remarkably well. His detailed reports now enabled each attacking plane of the Pearl Harbor Strike Force to have its own specific target location map.[34] Kimmel had not received a single one of the translated cable intercepts, or any relevant information concerning the IJN's espionage efforts being carried out at his doorstep.

Despite the fact that David Sarnoff had coordinated making available copies of the Japanese consul's cable messages serviced by RCA Radio with Adm. Bloch of the 14th Naval District in Honolulu, none reached Rochefort until December 5, and, even then, these were not decoded until *after* the Japanese attack.[35] The PURPLE and MAGIC intelligence isolation of Kimmel that had been coordinated by Marshall and Stark that previous summer was still in effect.

Rear Adm. Turner, who had quashed efforts by ONI's Kirk and Bode to send the intercepted October (J-19) "bomb plot" cable to Kimmel, now went on to intimidate Theodore Wilkinson to the degree that all decryptions from ONI directed to CNO Adm. Stark or any other office would have to be cleared personally by Turner himself. As John Toland stated it, Turner had, in effect, become "the ultimate censor."[36] The end result of this was that Marshall, Stark, and Turner had effectively isolated Kimmel to the degree that the aggressive Pacific Fleet commander would not be able to unintentionally upset the overt act strategy as it played out. If Kimmel was not privy to what was about to happen to him at Pearl Harbor, the IJN's Strike Force certainly was.

Nagumo, in command of the Pearl Harbor Strike Force (called Kido Butai or Force Z, which copied Adm. Togo's own original code name during the latter's 1905 fleet battle against the Russian Imperial Navy), had received precise orders from Yamamoto.[37] On November 25 (just as Kimmel was withdrawing his Pearl Harbor–based fleet units from the North Pacific), Nagumo received a coded radio message from Yamamoto that stated in part:

> The task force, keeping its movement strictly secret . . . shall advance into Hawaiian waters, and upon the opening of hostilities shall attack the main force of the United States Fleet in Hawaii and deal it a mortal blow. The first air raid is planned for the dawn of X-day (exact date to be given by order later). Should the negotiations with the United States prove successful, the task force shall hold itself in readiness forthwith to return and reassemble.

A further radio message that same day had stated:

> The task force, keeping its movement strictly secret, shall leave Hitokappu Bay on the morning of 26 November and advance to 42 degrees North, 170 degrees East on the afternoon of 3 December and speedily complete refueling.[38]

This meant that Nagumo had to move his Strike Force out into the North Pacific to a holding position, where he would refuel and await the outcome of the negotiations then ongoing in Washington between Japan's Ambassadors Kurusu and Nomura and Hull of the State Department. Since a last-minute agreement was deemed a real possibility by Tokyo, Nagumo had no choice but to await further orders from Yamamoto. If given the go ahead, he would move by stealth into his attack position, some 250 miles north of Pearl Harbor and launch his 360 planes early in the morning of December 7. Orders would come by coded radio messages from the IJN's headquarters in Tokyo.

Nagumo's attack was to be synchronized with the movements of the IJN's Southern Force (Second Fleet), South Seas Force (Fourth Fleet), as well as others; all focused on the Dutch East Indies, Singapore, the Malay (Kra) Peninsula, and the Philippines, Guam, and Wake Islands. McCollum astutely pointed out that Yamamoto had essentially reversed or otherwise turned on its head the strategic concept under which the IJN had previously always operated: to "fight in waters contiguous to their home territory," which was a strategic defense mixed with a tactical offense. The transpacific operations now being undertaken to the east and south were innovatively long range in concept and operationally designed as a strategic offense to support Japanese imperial adventure and expansion.[39]

On November 26, the Strike Force, with 38 warships and logistical support vessels now completely refueled, weighed anchor from its rendezvous point inside the misty, cold Hitokappu Bay and began its long 3,100-mile journey to its anticipated attack position to points north of Pearl Harbor. This meant at least eight good sailing days, covering 400 miles per day, provided there were no disruptions due to any unexpected or adverse sea conditions. The FAF would travel at a speed of some 13 knots, the maximum speed that the tankers, the slowest ships in Nagumo's command could muster.

An advantage for Nagumo, however, was that his ships would be moving east along the line of subarctic currents, otherwise known as the North Pacific Drift, which facilitated eastward movement. The task force took up a box-shaped formation, with a destroyer screen some 18 miles wide in the lead. Six miles behind the lead screen was a five-mile-long file of cruisers and tankers, followed by another screen of destroyers, cruisers, and tankers some eight miles wide. Finally, massed together, were the six aircraft carriers, spaced some two miles apart in two parallel columns of three ships each. Taking up the rear were the two battleships and the remaining tankers. Two submarines were "on point," serving as an early warning element out in front of the 18-by-18-mile-square formation.[40]

The FAF's course was set so that it would proceed southeastward out of the Kurils at a 45-degree angle to a point of latitude at 43 degrees North. It would then move along this line over the next week until it finally began its surge southward toward Hawaii's Oahu Island. The route across the North Pacific was gauged according to the estimated 500-mile reconnaissance flying range of the navy's PBYs, which were based at Dutch Harbor, Alaska, to the north and at Pearl Harbor, Hawaii, in the south. The gap of some 400 miles between the two patrol plane ranges provided just enough space to allow the Strike Force to slip through undetected.[41]

Nagumo's Strike Force actually consisted of two major components:

1. The First Air Fleet (FAF), commanded directly by Nagumo himself, which consisted of six first-line attack aircraft carriers (*Akagi*, *Kaga*, *Hiryu*, *Soryu*, *Shokaku*, and *Zuikaku*), two fast battleships (*Hiei* and *Kirishima*), two heavy cruisers (*Tone* and *Chikuma*), one light cruiser (*Abukuma*), 16 destroyers, and eight other logistical or train (tanker) vessels.

2. The Advance Expeditionary Force was under the Command of Vice Adm. Mitsumi Shimizu, the IJN's Sixth Fleet commander-in-chief. This force, also called the "Shimizu Force" in some documents, was

composed of several cruisers, at least 20 I-class fleet submarines, including five midget submarines carried onboard, and six train vessels.

The I-class submarines, with a cruising range of 12,000 miles, and the midget submarines were the primary attack elements of the Shimizu Force. The midgets were actually two-man submarines that could operate underwater for a distance of 18 miles, far enough to be launched outside of Oahu Island without detection before making a follow-on attempted penetration of Pearl Harbor. Operating together, they would be known as the IJN's Special Naval Attack Unit. It was estimated by Rochefort's HYPO on November 26 that one-half of the Sixth Fleet's submarines were already in the Marshalls or en route toward Hawaii, moving directly from their bases around Japan.[42] Because the forces constituted two completely distinct attack organizations, or task forces, within the IJN, both aerial and undersea, their command and control for the Pearl Harbor raid was quite complex, requiring careful coordination by not only Nagumo, but also Yamamoto himself.

The big question for Nagumo was the weather. At that time of the year, winter, the North Pacific is typically fickle, only providing some seven days of calm waters as opposed to days of stormy weather.[43] Since Nagumo had to refuel certain of his ships several times en route to his forward attack position, this was a serious concern.[44] To accomplish its refueling operations, the FAF would depend on its eight *maru*, which were essentially commercial merchant vessels or tankers. The eight tankers were identified partly by their own radio call signs.[45]

All warships carried drums of extra fuel on their decks, taking advantage of all available space on board. To avoid any mishap that might cause a shortage of fuel for the Strike Force, one of the IJN's special naval tankers, the *Shiriya Maru*, an additional resupply backup was directed to proceed to a position 30-00 North, 154-20 East, arriving by December 3, and thereafter proceeding eastward along the 30-degree north latitude line at a speed of 7 knots. Its mission was to provide a refueling stop in the vicinity of Nagumo's post–Pearl Harbor attack assembly point, as Nagumo returned to Japanese waters.[46]

The fuel tankers were one of the critical keys to the success of Nagumo's mission. They provided the precious oil reserves required to move *all* the warships in one cohesive body to and from their designated attack position north of Pearl Harbor. It was a top priority to ensure that each tanker stay up with the main body of the task force as it moved along its designated route and provide the precious fuel whenever needed by the warships.

To accomplish the refueling, the tankers used two techniques. One was called the "alongside method," which meant that a tanker sailed *side by side* in the same direction and at the same speed, passing the oil through a flexible tube-like hose from the tanker into the warship's oil storage bunkers. The other was known as the "astern method," by which a tanker, using a towrope, would tow the warship behind her while moving at the same speed and on the same course.[47] Both techniques were tricky to execute, requiring not only expert seamanship but also relatively calm seas with only gentle ocean swells to be successful.

Yamamoto was nobody's fool. An experienced naval officer with considerable time at sea operating under extreme weather conditions, he appreciated what could potentially happen to Nagumo's Strike Force while crossing the unpredictable North Pacific. To resolve a situation of this nature, and to allow Nagumo and others some flexibility in dealing with the unexpected, the IJN's top operational admiral (KE RO 88) sent out a 5-Number Code message to his Combined Fleet designed to deal with his otherwise mandatory radio listening silence that had previously been specified for all warships in movement. It stated as an order:

1. Except in extreme emergency, the main force and its attached forces will cease communicating.
2. Other forces are at discretion of their respective commanders.
3. Supply ships, repair ships, hospital ships, etc., will report directly to parties concerned.[48]

The all-important proviso was "Except in extreme emergency." And that was exactly what Adm. Nagumo would be facing, some five days into his advance toward Pearl Harbor. One radioman, Second Class Jack Kaye (initials "JK" on the message time of intercept line) at Station H copied down and recorded the coded intercept.[49] Like all the other messages in the 5-Num Code, it was bundled up and sent to Washington, only to be finally decoded and translated in 1946! Whether Stations CAST or KING or even OP-20-GY made the same intercept is unknown.

One day into his movement across the North Pacific, Nagumo (SI WI 1) received a coded radio message from the chief, 1st Naval Section, Imperial Headquarters (MA YU RU) to make him aware that two Russian merchant ships, the *Uzbekistan* and the *Azerbaijan*, had left San Francisco, westbound, a little before mid-November, en route to the Soviet Union's Sea of Japan port of Vladivostok via the Kuril Islands.[50] This would normally take them some distance to the north of the Strike Force, which would continue to guarantee the latter's security. Otherwise, the North Pacific was now devoid of American shipping. And there was a reason for this.

With the declaration of a "national emergency" by Roosevelt on October 10, 1941, the Office of the CNO in Washington had gone to work. On October 16, the CNO issued a radio dispatch to all U.S. merchant ships in the Pacific. In essence, those merchant ships in the Western Pacific were instructed to proceed immediately to Manila, Singapore, or northern

Australian ports. Those in the North Pacific and points east were to proceed to Honolulu or a West Coast U.S. port. A day later, another CNO dispatch called on all "U.S. flag" transpacific shipping to use the Torres Strait, "keeping to the southward and well clear of Orange [Japanese] Mandates." (The Torres Strait comprises that narrow body of water between Papua New Guinea and the northern tip of Australia.) That same day, October 17, a formal letter went out from the CNO to all 16 naval district commandants and the naval coastal frontier commanders, involving all the Atlantic North and South, Caribbean, Pacific Northern, Pacific Southern, Panama, Hawaiian, Philippine, and finally even the CINCs U.S. Asiatic and Pacific Fleets, reaffirming the procedures to be used in the new routings of American flag and merchant vessels.[51]

On November 25, yet another OPNAV message released by Rear Adm. Ingersoll was sent out to the 12th Naval District for action and to CINCPAC and CINCAF, as well as the 14th and 16th Naval Districts for information to "ROUTE ALL TRANSPACIFIC SHIPPING THRU TORRES STRAITS [sic]." This diversion of *all* American commercial shipping out and away from the North Pacific essentially turned the area into what the army's head of intelligence, Maj. Gen. Sherman Miles, termed the "Vacant Sea."[52] Important to the overt act strategy, Rear Adm. Richmond Turner, chief of the navy's War Plans Division, authorized the diversion of marine traffic down into the South Pacific via the Torres Strait. The reason for this was to ensure that there would be no commercial traffic in the North Pacific that could interfere with any Japanese ships approaching the Hawaiian Islands. This meant that the North Pacific "would be clear of any traffic."[53] Turner called the track followed by the Strike Force the "composite great circle course," which was the official naval expression from whence the "vacant sea" concept was derived. It was the shortest and most logical distance from Japan to the Hawaiian Islands.

To reemphasize the policy and make sure that the North Pacific's great circle routing was not used and that all hands clearly understood that all further transpacific shipping had to be routed through the Torres Strait, Ingersoll's two messages from his OPNAV headquarters on November 18 and 25 to both admirals Hart and Kimmel reinforced the point. Both admirals were tasked to provide naval warship escorts for commercial ships, which for Kimmel was not only an additional burden but also an additional distraction from his immediate project of providing as quickly as possible the two dozen fighter planes that were to be sent by aircraft carrier to Midway and Wake islands.

The rerouting of all commercial shipping through the Torres Strait was also a burden on the American merchant vessels; their journey from Seattle and San Francisco to the Philippines was extended by an additional 4,000 miles.[54] Nagumo and his Pearl Harbor Strike force would be the immediate, primary beneficiaries of the policy; Kimmel and his Pacific Fleet would be the immediate, primary losers.

To assist the Strike Force as it churned its way across the North Pacific, the Naval Staff of the IJN's headquarters continued to send out weather updates throughout the last week of November. Whether these were particularly useful to Nagumo and his sailors is a moot point, since the waters of the great circle route were notorious for their ferociously bad weather, seemingly coming out of nowhere. The Strike Force was about to find this out first hand as it came face to face with the treacherous nature of the North Pacific.[55]

The Strike Force was on the move! Slipping out of Hitokappu Bay at 0600 hours on November 26 (Hawaii date line) in the midst of a raging snowstorm, and with all ships on radio listening silence, Nagumo's FAF ploughed into the North Pacific at 13 knots. As was expected, there were cold winds and now and then gusts of driving snow as the ships were buffeted by large swells from the rough waters. Despite the heavy wave action and gale-like winds, which caused considerable pitching with the smaller ships rolling up to 30 degrees from side to side, progress was being made on November 27 and even some refueling of destroyers took place. Two days later, the swells had subsided considerably and a relative calm, accompanied by a dense fog, now descended on the task force.

Sunday, November 30, started off well enough, but then Mother Nature rolled in a severe cold front, accompanied by high, rolling waves and a further dense fog that caused extreme problems in terms of visibility and command and control of the Strike Force's ships, which were maintaining radio listening silence. Over at HYPO in Hawaii, intercept Station H at Wahiawa was picking up some faint radio signals, which Rochefort reported in his Communications Intelligence Summary (CIS) for November 30: "The only tactical circuit heard today was with AKAGI and several MARUs [oil tankers]." Through radio fingerprinting, it was easy to identify the *Akagi.* Rochefort undoubtedly recognized that the use of a tactical radio circuit of this nature by the *Akagi* meant that some sort of a major operational maneuver was underway.[56] Normally, all important radio signal intercepts, taken by HYPO and noted in its CIS reports, also included the RDF bearings associated with the intercept. Surprisingly, beginning in mid-November 1941, Rochefort's CIS reporting discontinued including RDF reports, as had been the case without fail up until that time. The reason for this remains a mystery.

Why, after holding to Yamamoto's radio listening silence order so steadfastly, did the *Akagi* now break the radio silence and risk jeopardizing its security? What happened was that another huge storm, bigger than the one before, had unpredictably descended upon the Strike Force. The main energy source for this storm was apparently the solar energy radiated in bursts from the sun's surface, called solar storms. While the effect is negligible at the earth's equator, it increases in intensity to points northward and in this case impacted precisely the region where Nagumo and his sailors were frantically working to maintain formation. The storm roiled the North Pacific from November 30 until December 4, scattering the Strike Force's smaller vessels far and wide.

Destroyers pitched and rolled 47 degrees from one side to the other, signal flags shredded, and men were washed overboard. The combinations of driving rain, winds, huge swells, and intermittent fog meant that the tankers, in particular, were driven out of formation and lost visual contact with the rest of the Strike Force; even the traditional blinker light system used both day and night did not work. To avoid the pitching and rolling, some ships just "went with the flow" and modified their courses to ameliorate their dire situations.[57] The situation involving an inability to refuel the main warships of Kido Butai, which had been one of Nagumo's foremost concerns, was now a reality: only drastic action could solve the problem. And Nagumo took emergency action!

With his tankers obviously driven off course and out of sight over the horizon by the typhoon-like storm and the intermittent fog conditions, Nagumo ordered his own flagship *Akagi* to break radio listening silence in order to contact the tankers and serve as a homing beacon that they could use to guide them back into formation. It was a simple solution, but one difficult to carry out in the short term due to the raging storm still thrashing the tankers. The low-power transmissions that the *Akagi* made were only supposed to radiate out to a distance of about 100 miles, but solar effects from the sun's solar storms striking the ionosphere apparently produced a series of radio sky waves or "skip" propagations, which enabled Station H to pick them up that night, November 30.[58] But Station H was not the only station to monitor the *Akagi*'s homing beacon signals that night.

The luxury liner SS *Lurline* was one of the Matson Navigation Company's (215 Market Street, San Francisco, California) elite passenger ships. On a regular basis each month, it made a three- to four-day passage from Los Angeles and San Francisco to Honolulu. Having its official "issuance of clearance" rendered by the commandant, 12th Naval District, confirmed on November 19, it now prepared to deliver its full-capacity load of some 750 defense workers and civilian passengers to their Honolulu destination. Scheduled to leave Los Angeles November 29 and return to San Francisco December 10, it was a full 10-day round trip. For the ship and its crew, this particular voyage would prove eventful: Chief Radio Officer Rudy Asplund and First Assistant Radio Operator Leslie E. Grogan would make an astounding discovery out in the North Pacific.[59]

On November 30, the second night out, with the *Lurline* moving in a west-southwesterly direction toward Honolulu, Grogan noted in his signal log book entries during his 8 p.m. to midnight radio-watch, "The Japs are blasting away on the lower Marine Radio frequency—it is all in the Japanese code [probably katakana Morse code], and continues for several hours." He went on to say that the signals being monitored were sometimes strong and sometimes weak. By rotating his directional loop receiving antenna until a null was obtained by sound and even visually on its meter, he was able to obtain "good D.F. [radio direction finding bearings] on the 'main body' from the signals which he plotted out at a point located to the 'North and West of Honolulu'."[60]

Apparently, the signals were somewhat spread out. The next night, December 1, there was a repeat of the same barrage of signals that were again plotted the following night; December 2, there was yet another barrage, except that this time, the RDF plots or line-bearings were more closely grouped together but still out to the northwest. The *Lurline* was now approaching Hawaiian waters. Grogan thought, "The Japs must be bunched up, biding time."[61] But what had Asplund and Grogan discovered up in the North Pacific?

What they had stumbled upon, as they traversed their radio receiver's lower marine frequency bands on what they thought was going to be just another, perhaps boring and uneventful *Lurline* transit voyage, was none other than IJN Adm. Chuichi Nagumo's Pearl Harbor–bound Strike Force! By sheer chance, they had caught Nagumo at a most vulnerable moment, as he broke radio listening silence with the *Akagi*'s own transmitter. Using the *Akagi* as a radio beacon signal that his eight fuel tankers could home in on with their own shipboard RDF systems, Nagumo was now desperately working to bring these storm-blown vessels back into formation. Once he succeeded in doing this, over a period of the next two days and nights, the Strike Force was then held in position so he could not only conduct major refueling operations for all his warships and vessels but also await the much-anticipated signal from Yamamoto to continue the FAF's movement into its actual attack position north of Pearl Harbor.

Some of the Japanese signals may have actually been long-range, high-power transmissions, from Japan's naval shore stations, reaching out to IJN surface and submarine fleet elements throughout the Pacific as they also maneuvered into what would be their initial invasion positions. Grogan, himself, astutely concluded that "it's the Jap's Mobilization Battle Order." That was the night of December 1 (November 30, *Lurline* date/time) Adm. Osami Nagano, chief of the IJN's Naval General Staff, began transmitting a flurry of coded messages out to his major commands (CINC Combined Fleet and CINC China Area Fleet, etc.), announcing Japan's decision to declare war on the United States, the British Empire, and the Netherlands.

This was followed a day later by a coded message from Nagano to Yamamoto. Yamamoto then ordered his Strike Force commander, Nagumo, to commence a full-blown hostile attack on Pearl Harbor to commence on December 8 (Japan date/time, which is December 7 at Pearl Harbor, Hawaii date/time).

Grogan says he differentiated the IJN's systems of long-range radio "repeat-back" transmissions from those of the lower marine band frequency of 375 kilocycles, the latter of which his *Lurline* RDF picked up on for several successive nights during the voyage. And these pointed to something moving eastward out in the North Pacific! It is worth noting here that the 375-kilocycle low-power signals could only be received at night, whereas Tokyo was sending its own high-power signals in broad daylight. Nagumo's Strike Force was the only IJN force in the North Pacific.[62]

The Strike Force was moving toward the east, while the *Lurline* was moving generally westward, enabling the *Lurline*'s bearings and tracking to reflect the steady easterly crossing movement of Nagumo's IJN Strike Force as it moved toward its predesignated refueling position to the northwest of Oahu. Upon docking at Honolulu's Aloha Tower on Wednesday, December 3, both Asplund and Grogan went immediately to the Hotel Alexander Young building, where the 14th Naval District's Naval Intelligence Office was located. Meeting with Lt. Cdr. George Pease, they passed on to him copies of all the data they had meticulously compiled in the *Lurline*'s signal logbook with regard to the IJN's radio frequencies monitored, RDF bearings taken, and related intersection locations identified.

What exactly Pease did with the information is not clear, but one would have supposed that he informed his superior, Capt. Irving Mayfield, the District Intelligence Officer. Perhaps Pease and Mayfield thought that Asplund and Grogan, being merchant mariners, were nothing more than rank amateurs and did not know what they were talking about. Nothing could have been further from the truth. Grogan was a navy veteran of World War I who had been doing communications and RDF work with merchant marine shipping for at least 10 years. He was an expert in terms of taking RDF bearings on distant radio signals, both on land and at sea, as part of a commercial ship's navigation procedures.

With the possibility of a full-scale Pacific war in the offing and that past Sunday's November 30 *Honolulu Advertiser*'s blaring headline "Japanese May Strike over Weekend" in mind, the least that Mayfield and Pease could have done was pass the information with its RDF bearings on to Rochefort at the 14th Naval District's HYPO. There, a dedicated navy team of professional RDF analysts could have evaluated and even plotted the *Lurline*-sourced data.

Given that the mass of the IJN carriers had not been heard from for some days, disappearing as it were from the navy's intelligence "radar screen," and that only once during the period had Rochefort reported the *Akagi* in communication with its *maru* in his November 30 daily intelligence summary, the Asplund-Grogan input should have provided an intelligence windfall of the first order. This was not done and the information never reached Kimmel, who so badly needed it.[63] So where did the information go?

By December 5, the *Lurline* was once again at sea, making its way to its San Francisco destination. This was fortunate for the hundreds of navy dependents who were being shipped back to the safety of the continental United States, but it was far less fortunate for Mayfield and Pease, who undoubtedly realized after the attack took place that Apslund and Grogan had been correct in their estimate that there had been something ominous going on in the North Pacific.

When that realization set in, they undoubtedly were caught up with a serious case of anxiety, if not consternation. And no wonder—they had failed to report Apslund's and Grogan's critical information to Rear Adm. Claude Bloch, commander of the 14th Naval District, who was not only their superior but also responsible for the Pearl Harbor naval base's inner defense systems! This, in itself, was a serious breach of duty. Neither had they informed Rochefort at HYPO, nor Layton. It was Kimmel himself who needed to know this critical information, since it would be his Pacific Fleet that was the IJN's intended target.

Mayfield and Pease had blatantly violated the intelligence officer's credo: "Tell your commander today what the enemy is going to do tomorrow." This blunder, if not dereliction of duty, was embarrassing for the two navy officers as their naval careers were now much in jeopardy if anyone ever found out what had actually transpired. Yet, there was a way out of the situation and it lay at the *Lurline*'s next destination.

As the *Lurline*'s voyage proceeded, Grogan reported in his radio log on the night of December 5 that all was quiet out in the North Pacific: there were "no more Japs heard blasting away like before." By reporting the log's information to the 14th Naval District, he could be satisfied that he had done his duty. By the time the *Lurline* docked in San Francisco at 8 a.m. December 10, after completing its 2,400-mile return trip, there was a serious surprise waiting for them in the form of Lt. Cdr. Preston Allen of the navy's 12th Naval District Intelligence Office.

Apparently, Pease or Mayfield at the 14th Naval District in Honolulu *had* notified the 12th Naval District at San Francisco that the *Lurline*'s radio signal log was a hot intelligence item. Immediately after it docked, Allen boarded the *Lurline* and went directly to the radio room. There, on the basis that it was a war-related report, he demanded the right to take possession of the radio log covering the *Lurline*'s just-completed voyage. Apslund reminded him that the *Lurline* was still under the orders of the merchant marine and that, while they could not turn the log directly over to him, the master of the *Lurline*, their superior officer, could do so.

Since the original copy of the *Lurline*'s radio log with its RDF bearings data never reached the offices of the Matson Navigation Company and presumably remained in the hands of the navy, Grogan became suspicious that something strange was going on. He took it upon himself to write a reconstruction of the log as best he could remember it (his "Record for Posterity"), and this was submitted some days later in lieu of the *Lurline*'s formal Radio Log to the Matson Line's company office. Unfortunately, all the valuable RDF bearings were completely left out of Grogan's second version of the log. The *Lurline*'s arrival in Honolulu on December 3 was such an item of interest to the Japanese consulate that it sent cable #362, in the form of an "urgent report" to Tokyo. This cable was intercepted, photographed, decoded, and translated into English by ONI sometime prior to December 7.[64]

Tracking operations by the navy's WCCI focused on the North Pacific during the period of November 30 to December 4, 1941. A directive from ONI in Washington instructed all navy intercept facilities to be especially attentive to and focus as they could on the IJN's aircraft carriers.[65] At the 12th Naval District's District Intelligence Office (DIO), headed by Capt. Richard McCullough, the RDF plotting and evaluation of the radio signals concerning the Japanese were a top priority.

Lt. Ellsworth Hosmer served on McCullough's DIO staff in the Radio Intelligence Section, as did Seaman First Class Robert D. Ogg, an expert in electronics and marine navigation who was officially assigned as a special staff investigator. Hosmer worked at what could be called a key hub of the organization, receiving signal intelligence input from commercial radio and telephone firms around San Francisco. Sometime on or near December 2, Ogg was approached by Hosmer, who requested that he plot a series of radio direction bearings; Hosmer had received these from the Press and Globe Wireless companies. The signals were noted as being transmitted on completely new frequencies in the 4-megacycle range, which was a complete surprise to Hosmer, as well as the Press and Globe Wireless companies themselves. Hosmer wanted to ascertain where the source of the radio transmissions was located.

Since Ogg had considerable expertise in navigational aids, Hosmer thought that this could be put to good use by rendering the plots on a great circle chart. Over the next several days, a series of bearings taken by Globe and Press Wireless were plotted and their respective intersections (two bearings per plot) were noted on a nautical chart. The chart plots indicated that a Japanese naval unit of some sort was moving progressively across the North Pacific from west to east. These locations were then identified with pins on a Mercator wall map of the North Pacific. Ogg understood from conversations with others at the 12th Naval District that the signals had been transmitted on "odd frequencies" range as he termed it (a 4-megacycle range) and could not have come from Japan proper, since the time of intercept in the 4-megacycle range could only have emanated from the area where the multiple bearings crossed or otherwise intersected at night.

Hosmer took the RDF plots rendered on the chart and converted them into latitude and longitude grid locations. This location data was provided to McCullough, who then apparently forwarded the information on to the White House, as well as ONI. On December 7, *after* Nagumo's attack had taken place, Hosmer's office was directed to destroy all records of the various RDF bearings and related data that had been received and plotted.[66]

Some years later, Ogg re-created a nautical chart tracking of what he remembered had been plotted at the 12th Naval District's Intelligence Office during those first days of December 1941. The tracking approximates the exact track of Nagumo's Strike Force as it moved across the North Pacific.[67] What is important to remember is that the sun storms and other solar activity taking place over those several days generated immense quantities of ions that then bombarded the earth's atmosphere. These, in turn, tended to wreak havoc with radio transmissions throughout the Pacific. In the North Pacific, radio signals such as those sent by a low power transmitter from the *Akagi* could be unintentionally bounced by this phenomenon for distances of hundreds, if not thousands, of miles. This meant that not only Hosmer's 12th Naval District intercept stations but also all the rest of the WCCI, including the Mid-Pacific network, could potentially have picked up Nagumo's emergency homing signals.

Between Rochefort's November 30, 1941, HYPO report of the *Akagi* in communication with its *maru* and the Asplund-Grogan *Lurline* RDF report of what was going on in the North Pacific, something was up. Without realizing it, Ogg had opened Pandora's Box to reveal Nagumo's Strike Force presence in the North Pacific. In so doing, he provided a treasure trove of vital information to ONI in Washington.

OP-20-G's identification of the *Akagi*'s radio call signs (first by Rochefort at HYPO and then by Ogg at 12th Naval District) during that December 1 to 4, 1941, period was absolutely critical in discovering the whereabouts of Nagumo's FAF. Later, in 1942, OP-20-GT's office (formally GY-cryptanalysis or GX-direction finding) in Washington, DC, rendered a report called "JN Call List HYOO 10 (2 Kana Numeral Call) 1 December 1941 to 9 April 1942." On page 31 of the report (copy, author's file), in the section designated "Orange Service Calls," there is depicted the *Akagi*'s radio call sign: I MI 4 FLAG FIRST AIR FLEET CMD 12 / 1–4 Dec. 41.

I MI 4 was a new HYOO 10 call sign initiated December 1, 1941, the "FLAG" FIRST AIR FLEET meant that I MI 4 was Adm. Nagumo's command ship (the "flag" being the *Akagi*) and that the carrier's radio transmissions had been heard and recorded over the first four days of December 1941. Nowhere else is there another report of I MI 4 for December.

Another report on the *Akagi* appears in the section "Orange Secret Calls" by which radio identification call signs are listed numerically by their number and 2 kana coding. Here the *Akagi* again appears and is listed as 8 YU NA (ALT. HA MI 9) Akagi F/S 11/7 11/26 12/1 on Flt Air Net. This entry indicates the *Akagi*'s principal radio call sign (8 YU NA) that was intercepted was a replacement for an older call sign (HA MI 9), which was also associated with the carrier in previous months. The F/S is the "flag ship" abbreviation, and the dates rendered indicate when the carrier's transmissions were heard and recorded, not only on November 7 and 26, but also and most importantly on December 1, 1941. The phrasing of the remainder of the citation refers to the Fleet Air net, which is associated with "First Air Fleet." There are no other entries for this *Akagi*-related radio call sign for the first few days of December 1941.[68]

These listings are proof that Ogg's own 12th Naval District's commercially sourced radio intercept and RDF bearing reports, along with his own longitude-latitude grid computations, were not only dead accurate but were also sent to Washington, DC, where they were accepted as fully reliable by Safford's OP-20-GX in support of the navy's Office of Naval Intelligence (ONI). The splendid arrangement had worked!

Still, there is another, independent first-person corroborating source, providing compelling information. This source is Royal Netherlands Navy captain Johan E. M. Ranneft, who had been assigned as Holland's naval attaché in Washington, DC, since April 1938. Born in Semarang, Java, the Dutch East Indies, in 1886 and formerly the head of the Dutch Naval Radio Service in Amsterdam for some years prior to coming to Washington, he developed a close working professional relationship with key U.S. Naval Intelligence officers by the end of 1941. This was due to what was seen by ONI as his great accomplishment in surreptitiously obtaining and then turning over to the U.S. Navy the highly prized design blueprints and specifications for the Swedish Bofors firm's vaunted 40-mm automatic antiaircraft gun.

The fall of Holland in 1940 to the Nazis forced Queen Wilhelmina into exile in England. The Dutch government was now located in Batavia, Dutch East Indies. For Ranneft, the loss of his homeland to German occupation forces was a severe blow, cementing a close working relationship between him and hoped-for liberators of his country. ONI reciprocated and embraced the Dutchman with a certain zeal reserved only for important people.[69]

Ranneft was assisted in his efforts to support ONI by the Dutch army's radio signals intercept and radio direction finding unit, Kamer 14, located in Batavia, Java. Similar in setup to OP-20-G, it was staffed by some of the best Dutch cryptanalysts of the day, who were experts in breaking coded Japanese radio transmissions being sent out to the IJN's naval units throughout the west-central Pacific, as well as Tokyo's diplomatic radio traffic to its embassies in Southeast Asia. Each week, Ranneft visited ONI to drop off Kamer 14's forwarded decrypted intercepts, which he then translated from Dutch into English. In turn, he was allowed into ONI's inner sanctum, where he consulted with ONI's director, Capt. Theodore Wilkinson, as well as McCollum, the Far Eastern Section of the ONI's F-2 section head.

Ranneft kept a detailed diary of each day's visit, laying out his personal observations about what he saw and heard. His visit to ONI on December 2 caused him to make a diary entry (officially translated from the Dutch): "2–12–1941 Meeting at Navy Department, the location of 2 Japanese carriers leaving Japan with eastern course are pointed out to me on the map." Whether the map symbols were representing two distinct IJN aircraft carriers or two carrier divisions (two or more carriers in each division) on McCollum's chart/map is a moot point: the IJN was on the move in the North Pacific along an eastward track (*Oostelijke koers*).

More to the point is the ironic fact that, while a Dutch national, Capt. Ranneft was taken into the navy's fullest confidence and provided key information, indicating that an operational movement toward Hawaii had now commenced in the North Pacific, Adm. Husband E. Kimmel and his U.S. Navy Pacific Fleet, as America's defenders of the North Pacific approaches into California, were not.

The only message in regards to the IJN operations in the Pacific around this time was one on December 1 by the director of naval communications, Capt. Leigh Noyes, transmitted as OPNAV Secret 011400, *urgent* to CINCAF and Com 16 in the Philippines and *priority* to CINCPAC and Com 14 in Hawaii, indicating that the Japanese were planning a landing at Kota Bharu in Malaya.[70] All said and done, Yamamoto's Combined Fleet was now completing its final approaches to its various forward assembly positions prior to launching its carefully planned, well-coordinated, multifaceted attacks throughout the Pacific.

7

"The Cornered Mouse Bites the Cat"

The Overt Act Strategy Comes to Fruition

In early to mid-November 1941, the Japanese Imperial Army and Navy began to implement their final organizational movements for all-out war to control the Pacific. Gen. Tojo and his cabinet were trying to deal with what was a confrontational attitude on the part of Roosevelt and Hull. Roosevelt had made it clear that lifting the ever-tightening embargos would have to be based on Japan's complete withdrawal from China.

The Japanese people had endured five long years of war, involving severe sacrifices at home, as well as suffering some 360,000 military casualties on the Chinese battlefields.[1] The IJA had been severely mauled by the Soviet Union's Gen. Georgi Zhukov along the Manchurian border a couple of years earlier, but this humiliating defeat had been concealed from the Japanese people. November 29 was considered the last possible deadline by which an acceptable settlement with the United States could be accomplished ("After that, things are automatically going to happen").[2] Japan's die had been cast.

On November 23, Lt. Cdr. William Smedberg drove Japan's Ambassador Kichisaburo Nomura to a meeting with the navy's CNO, Adm. Harold Stark. Conversing for some two hours at Stark's home, Nomura was straightforward: if Washington did not relax its economic and trade sanctions, Tojo's military-dominated government would have no course but to go to war.[3]

Three days later, Hull handed Nomura his 10-point ultimatum, which included the demand that Japan withdraw from China. This was laid out in detail by Nomura in his PURPLE-encoded message #1189 to Tokyo. (All PURPLE messages were in their entirety intercepted, decoded, and translated within 24 hours of their being received by the army's and navy's signal intelligence services.[4]) On November 28, Tokyo responded with PURPLE message #844, declaring the Hull proposal "humiliating" and not viable "as a basis for negotiations." Tokyo now considered negotiations with Washington "de facto ruptured."

To alert his overseas embassies to the possibility of an emergency situation involving the cutting off of diplomatic relations, leading to the outbreak of war, on November 19 Tokyo transmitted a series of J-19 diplomatic cables formatted in the PA-K2 code. The cables established a series of coded signals that were to be embedded as *false* weather forecasts in the middle and at the end of the daily Japanese language short wave radio news broadcasts. They were:

(1) In case of a Japan–U.S. relations in danger: HIGASHI NO KAZEAME [East wind rain–]

(2) Japan–U.S.S.R. relations: KITA NO KAZE KUMORI [North wind cloudy]

(3) Japan–British relations: NISHI NO KAZE HARE [West wind clear]

Intercepted by Station SAIL at Bainbridge, Washington, and sent via teletype to ONI, this particular "winds setup code" was not actually decoded and translated until November 28.[5] *That* did catch Washington's attention.

Interestingly enough, on the next day, November 29, Tokyo received a coded PURPLE message (#1393) from its ambassador in Berlin, recounting the comments of Nazi foreign minister Joachim von Ribbentrop:

Should Japan become engaged in a war against the United States, Germany, of course, would join the war immediately. There is absolutely no possibility of Germany's entering into a separate peace with the United States under such circumstances. The Fuehrer [Hitler] is determined on that point.

While not translated and brought to Roosevelt's attention until December 1, it must have been satisfying to the president in terms of the results he was hoping for from his overt act strategy.[6]

The following day, while relaxing in Warm Springs, Georgia, Roosevelt became aware that Tokyo was further attempting to reassure itself that Germany and Italy would enter into any future war with the United States on the side of Japan, as part of their obligations under the Tripartite Pact of September 27, 1940. Both Germany and Italy had once again acknowledged the viability of the Pact.[7]

A December 1 Tokyo PURPLE message (#865) to its Washington embassy now mentioned that the deadline of November 29 for the resolution of negotiations had "come and gone." It went on to say that "to prevent the United States from becoming unduly suspicious" the Japanese envoys should continue negotiations in order to allay any suspicions of a hostile Japanese move. The two ambassadors would string Washington along until further ordered to do something else. Unfortunately for Tokyo, all its secret messages so carefully crafted, guarded, and coordinated via PURPLE were being translated within 24 hours of their transmission by Washington.

The Diplomatic Section of OP-20-G had been standing watch 24 hours a day, seven days a week since the beginning of February 1941. Every diplomatic message in PURPLE that could be intercepted by either the U.S. Army or Navy was promptly decrypted and typed error-free for translation into English. These diplomatic messages were the top-priority intelligence source in that they spelled out Tokyo's *real intentions* in terms of its dealings with the United States.[8]

Roosevelt abruptly terminated his stay in Warm Springs and returned to Washington. Another probable influencing factor in the president's decision to return quickly to the White House was a Saturday night November 29 FBI intercept, based on their special Japanese Embassy telephone wiretap in Washington, DC. Ambassador Kurusu was overheard in a transpacific plain language telephone call asking K. Yamamoto, the chief of the Foreign Affairs Office in Tokyo: "Tell me what zero hour is. Otherwise I won't be able to carry on diplomacy." The Tokyo-based voice (K. Yamamoto) replied: "Well then, I will tell you. Zero hour is December 8 [Tokyo date/time, but December 7 in Hawaii] at Pearl Harbor."[9] Here the FBI wiretap had identified not only a specific date but also a specific target for the initiation of war against the United States in the Pacific!

Over in the Philippines, Adm. Thomas Hart, commander-in-chief of the U.S. Asiatic Fleet, had been watching matters gradually evolve throughout 1941. When he first arrived in Manila, the defense plan for the Philippines envisioned his submarine flotilla engaging the Japanese, while his surface ships withdrew southward to reinforce the British and Dutch forces for the defense of Singapore and its Malay Barrier. All this appeared to have changed in January 1941, when it was deemed by OPNAV that it would be better to reinforce the Atlantic Fleet by bringing an aircraft carrier, a cruiser division, and a squadron of destroyers over from the Pacific Fleet. A month later still another change took place, and the plan was essentially reversed, embracing the original withdrawal plan, with the surface force once again reinforcing the British and the Dutch in the event of war. This was important, because by the spring of 1941, things began to appear alarming in terms of IJN movements southward along the coasts of China and French Indochina.

Fearing an imminent attack, Hart moved his naval forces and submarines from their relatively exposed position at Manila into the area of the southern Philippines. As it turned out, his fears were unfounded. When no attack took place, he returned his fleet to Manila Bay.[10]

In June, Army Lt. Gen. Douglas MacArthur took full personal command of both the U.S. Army and Philippine ground forces. Arguing for an aggressive defense of Luzon, he implemented his "stand and fight" policy, whereby upwards of 200,000 newly trained Filipino men, backed by an additional 50,000 U.S. Army troops and 100 long-range B-17 bombers ("Flying Fortresses"), would fight it out with any Japanese invaders. MacArthur's bravado was convincing enough that CNO Harold Stark made the decision to reinforce Hart with two additional divisions of submarines (12 submarines each), which would beef up the Asiatic Fleet to a total of 29 submarines, compared to the Pacific Fleet's 10 at Pearl Harbor.[11]

An intelligence report release by ONI, based on the American naval attaché in Tokyo, noted that there were *nine* Japanese air and naval bases within range of the Philippines. Predicting "widespread bombing raids in the Philippines for the purpose of effectively destroying, or severely limiting, the aviation and submarine defense forces," the report went on to say that Hainan, Formosa (Taiwan), and the western Mandates were the most logical points from which raids would be staged against Hart and MacArthur. Potentially arrayed against the Philippines from these three sectors would be some 360 planes, over half of which were judged to be bombers. Land-based Japanese air power was a threat that had to be taken seriously. In late October, Hart informed the Navy Department, in yet another strategy change, that he would keep his fleet together and fight the war from the Philippines.[12]

With the implementation of the economic embargos against Japan by Roosevelt that summer, the IJA and the IJN began to think in terms of immediate military operations and campaign planning to alleviate their ever-worsening situation. When Tojo became prime minister in mid-October 1941, he and his army and navy general staffs developed a strategy that envisioned the formal invasions of the Philippines, Hong Kong, Singapore, the Malay Peninsula, and the Dutch East Indies. Hart, himself, had received from Stark an October 16, 1941, message warning him that Japan might attack the United States and Britain and that he needed to "take due precautions including such preparatory deployments as will not disclose strategic intention nor constitute provocative actions against Japan."

ONI in Washington thought the campaign to carry out Japan's strategy in the Southwest Pacific would involve a double envelopment, or "pincers movement," whereby the largest Japanese invasion force would come down through the South China Sea west of the Philippines, and a smaller force would come out of the Palau area to the east of the Islands. The Philippines did not offer Japan any crucially important raw materials, but its strategic location as a thousand-mile-long archipelago in close proximity to and paralleling the primary seaborne invasion routes and lines of communication running from the Japan islands to Southeast Asia posed a serious threat.

The question for Japanese war planners was whether the American Pacific Fleet would make an attempt to reinforce the Philippines and then commence interdiction operations against the invading forces' vulnerable, logistical umbilical cord that would have to be defended. To prevent that situation from taking place, Adm. Yamamoto devised his plan (see map, 240) to take out the American aircraft carriers and cripple the Pacific Fleet to the degree that they could not possibly contemplate conducting a reinforcement of the Philippines, let alone undertaking further interdiction operations in the Western Pacific. To prevent the use of the Philippines as a naval base against the IJA's and IJN's operations, it was decided to formally invade the island of Luzon. Vice Adm. Nobutake Kondo's Southern Expeditionary Force would carry out the operation.[13]

Adm. Hart had 28 PBY-4 Catalina long-range, flying boat patrol aircraft and 15 other scout observation planes to physically track the IJN's movements in the South China Sea region.[14] The admiral's other primary source of information was in the form of Station CAST, the navy's Asiatic Radio Intelligence Unit. Comprising a total of 70 men (9 officers, 19 cryptoclerks, and 42 intercept operators) and located on Corregidor, it tracked Japanese ships of all types and intercepted and decoded not only portions of the IJN's operational (5-Number/JN-25) code system but also Japan's high level diplomatic code through its own PURPLE decoding machine

CAST's Duane Whitlock had homed in on Kondo's Southern Expeditionary Force at the end of October, indicating that it consisted of numerous troop transports, torpedo boats, submarines, and other small craft. The IJN's Third Fleet was the primary invasion force with specifically trained amphibious assault troops, supported by cruisers and destroyers. The IJN's 11th Air Fleet was made up of land-based attack aircraft that would operate from Taiwan, Hainan, and French Indochina as required in conjunction with the bomber and fighter squadrons of the remaining four of the IJN's 10 aircraft carriers.[15]

Besides his own intelligence assets reporting to him, on November 24, Hart began receiving a flurry of intelligence reports from Stark's OPNAV, indicating significant Japanese naval and troop movements into the Palau, South China Sea, and French Indochina areas, which indicated "that within a short time Japan may execute a surprise movement of aggression possibly even against the Philippines or Guam." An ONI Bulletin of November 26 further made the point, stating that 24,000 IJA troops had sailed from Woosung, China, with a large quantity of military equipment, including 184 landing boats loaded on five vessels. That same day, a COPEK-transmitted report from COM 14 in Honolulu indicated that IJA air forces were building up their equipment on Taiwan.[16] Both Hart and MacArthur now realized that things were coming to a head in the Western Pacific.

Much like Kimmel and Short over in Hawaii, both Hart and MacArthur in the Philippines had received the initial war warning reports from Marshall and Stark respectively on November 27, which included the Roosevelt administration's strategy for dealing with the initial outbreak of war with Japan in the Pacific. More importantly, on November 28, came the follow-up, directing them that "the United States desires that Japan commit the first overt act" and that they "undertake no offensive action until Japan has committed an overt act." This clearly enunciated the policy of the first shot strategy that they were ordered to follow. On November 28 and December 1, MacArthur replied to Marshall that "everything is in readiness for a successful defense" and that "all practical steps . . . being taken to protect all air and ground installations." Like Short in Hawaii, MacArthur was ordered to protect against local sabotage attempts.[17]

With Japan's army and navy on the move in the Western Pacific and pressure building up, as previously indicated by Stimson's earlier (November 26) Memorandum for the president, which indicated that some 50,000 troops were about to arrive in French Indochina to reinforce the 40,000 already there, action was required. Admirals Stark and Turner at OPNAV needed more precise information as to the flow of troop transports passing to the west of the Philippines en route to the region.

Accordingly, a directive, personally approved by Roosevelt himself, was sent out specifically to Adm. Hart, CINCAF, on November 30 for immediate action. In brief, the message stated that the Japanese were moving into position in order "to attack points" along the Kra (Malay) Isthmus and that CINCAF needed to cover, by aerial reconnaissance, the line between Manila and Camranh Bay (French Indochina). It was a clear mission for the PBYs to continuously track the invasion forces. The PBYs ascertained the destination of the Japanese expeditionary forces in a manner to not "appear to be attacking." They were allowed "to defend themselves if attacked."

In the meantime, the British Armed Forces, with 75,000 troops under the command of Lt. Gen. Arthur Percival, were beginning preparations to occupy a blocking position across the narrowest point of the Malay Peninsula at Singora (the Malay Barrier), well north of Singapore, as well as to conduct their own aerial reconnaissance of the Gulf of Siam to the east. All this was designed to protect the British naval base at Singapore with its three cruisers, six destroyers, and the soon-to-arrive battleship, *Prince of Wales*, and its supporting battle cruiser, *Repulse*, under the command of Vice Adm. Tom Phillips.[18] While the evidence pointed to the fact that the Japanese were intending to carry out a series of amphibious assault and invasion operations, exactly where they would all take place still remained an unknown.

Perhaps Roosevelt had a lingering worry that Japan's "overt act" might not take place against an American territory. While the president could seemingly rest assured from the PURPLE intercepts that the U.S. possessions in the Pacific, the Philippines, Guam, Wake, Midway, and the Hawaiian Islands, were the obvious American targets in the Pacific, suppose Japan bypassed or otherwise avoided a confrontational situation with America over these land areas and focused on the British and the Dutch? This lingering uncertainty in the president's mind had considerable basis in terms of the play out of his first shot strategy (overt incident = popular indignation = declaration of war).

Apparently, Roosevelt's worry was that, without a direct overt attack on the United States, the situation could appear confusing, causing Congress to not respond with a full-blown declaration of war against Japan. Even though Nazi Germany had reaffirmed the Tripartite Agreement, there still needed to be an event so obvious and damaging enough that it would directly involve the United States and Japan in outright war. This, in turn, would then trigger Germany's own agreed-upon declaration of war on America in support of Japan. Adhering to the ABD agreement in the event of a Japanese attack on either the British or the Dutch alone was in itself no guarantee of Congressional support.

Put another way, if there was *no* overt act on the part of Japan against the United States and *no* declaration of war by Congress, it would mean that Hitler would probably back away from making Germany's own declaration of war on the United States. A November 22 Gallup Poll indicated that 63 percent, or almost two-thirds of Americans, opposed Congress passing "a resolution declaring that a state of war exists between the United States and Germany." Frances Perkins, Roosevelt's secretary of labor, noted that the fretting president was burdened with a "terrible moral problem."[19]

Perkins was correct; Americans were simply not reacting to the German U-boat attacks in the North Atlantic as the president had hoped. How to get Japan to attack the United States with a clean-cut, clear act of war in such a way to solidify the American people's support behind a war remained Roosevelt's fundamental problem. There was no doubt in his mind that, one way or another, an overt act had to somehow take place, even if he had to manufacture one on his own.

Undoubtedly Roosevelt's experience as assistant secretary of the navy in World War I, where in 1917 the United States was using 50-foot and 100-foot patrol boats to conduct reconnaissance missions around the Atlantic, came to mind. He was also aware of the 1939 congressionally amended Merchant Marine Act of 1936 (Section 902), which stated, "President may proclaim that security of national defense makes it lawful to requisition or charter any vessel or watercraft owned by a citizen of the United States."[20]

THREE SMALL SHIPS

Reconnaissance or "pop-up" cruises, as they had previously been called, were the order of the day. Roosevelt conjured up a plan that would involve three small ships, which were to sail into the path of the Japanese fleet and its convoys moving south toward French Indochina and the Gulf of Siam. Call it what you may, it was a genuinely bizarre, desperate plan to obtain an overt act. Albeit Hart was already conducting an extensive reconnaissance of the Asian coastal regions with his Manila-based PBY planes; this was now irrelevant.

Adm. Stark was duly instructed by the president to get the mission underway. Assistant CNO Royal Ingersoll, who drew up portions of the plan and dispatched the presidential directive to that end, testified during the Pearl Harbor Attack Hearings that Roosevelt had in fact personally directed the deployment of the three vessels in the hopes that they would provide the overt act that he so much desired. If fired upon or otherwise attacked by the IJN, "it would have been an incident on which we could have declared war."[21]

On December 2, Hart received this unprecedented order from Stark:

PRESIDENT DIRECTS THAT THE FOLLOWING BE DONE AS SOON AS POSSIBLE. WITHIN TWO DAYS AFTER RECEIPT THIS DISPATCH CHARTER 3 SMALL VESSELS TO FORM A "DEFENSIVE INFORMA-TION PATROL." MINIMUM REQUIREMENTS TO ESTABLISH IDEN-TITY AS U. S. MEN-OF-WAR ARE COMMAND BY A NAVAL OFFICER AND TO MOUNT A SMALL GUN AND ONE MACHINE GUN WOULD SUFFICE. FILIPINO CREWS MAY BE EMPLOYED WITH MINIMUM NUMBER NAVAL RATINGS TO ACCOMPLISH PURPOSE TO OBSERVE AND REPORT BY RADIO JAPANESE MOVEMENTS IN WEST CHINA SEA AND GULF OF SIAM. ONE VESSEL TO BE STATIONED BETWEEN HAINAN AND HUE ONE VESSEL OFF THE INDO-CHINA COAST BETWEEN CAMRANH BAY AND CAPE ST. JACQUES AND ONE

VESSEL OFF POINT DE CAMU. USE OF ISABEL AUTHORIZED BY
PRESIDENT AS ONE OF THE THREE BUT NOT OTHER NAVAL VES-
SELS. REPORT MEASURES TAKEN TO CARRY OUT PRESIDENTS
VIEWS. AT SAME TIME INFORM ME AS TO WHAT RECONNAIS-
SANCE MEASURES ARE BEING REGULARLY PERFORMED AT SEA BY
BOTH ARMY AND NAVY WHETHER BY AIR SURFACE VESSELS OR
SUBMARINES AND YOUR OPINION AS TO THE EFFECTIVENESS OF
THESE LATTER MEASURES.[22]

In reality, Hart's aerial reconnaissance patrols were bringing back considerable detailed information as to the progress of the Japanese buildup
and ship movements, which he included in a report, indicating that a Japanese expedition had docked near Saigon in French Indochina. With this
information having been passed on to Washington, the mission appeared
extremely illogical. But Hart was a smart fellow and he had come to the
conclusion that the three ships represented nothing more than "bait" that
was to be sacrificed in order for the administration in Washington to
obtain a provocation by the Japanese.[23]

Of the several "small vessels" available to Hart, the USS *Isabel*, commanded by Lt. John Payne, was the CINCAF's officially assigned yacht and
considered a part of the navy, but the other two vessels, or better stated,
schooners, *Lanikai* and *Molly Moore*, would have to be modified and
declared "warships" in accordance with the presidential directive. As these
two vessels were being prepared, Hart instructed Lt. Payne to conduct "a
special reconnaissance mission off the coast of Indo-China . . . Utmost
secrecy was to be observed." The *Isabel*, painted white for easier detection
by the Japanese, was to operate under the guise of searching for a "lost PBY
plane." Payne was to fight as necessary and then to destroy the ship, rather
than let it fall into enemy hands. When Payne heard that he was to sink his
own ship, he concluded that the *Isabel*'s actual mission was to produce an
incident to get the United States into a war with Japan.[24]

The 67-ton auxiliary schooner *Lanikai* was to be commanded by Lt.
Kemp Tolley, who had received his own special orders from Hart on
December 4. Although Tolley would not actually leave Manila until after
the Japanese attack had taken place at Pearl Harbor, Lt. Payne's *Isabel* came
close to meeting its departure deadline and carried out a portion of its
intended mission.

On December 2, Hart's PBYs had noted some 50 ships, including some
cruisers and destroyers, at anchor in Camranh Bay. Early on the morning
of December 5, the *Isabel* found itself about 170 miles off the Indochina
coast. There, it encountered a Japanese seaplane, which intermittently
observed and followed its progress. As Payne approached to within 22
miles of the coast and then turned southward toward Camranh Bay, he
abruptly received orders to return to Manila immediately. Hart, upon

seeing that the Japanese were not about to take the bait and conduct an attack on the *Isabel*, had recalled Payne back to the Philippines. When Payne returned to Manila Bay and the *Isabel* dropped anchor at 8:22 a.m., he immediately went ashore to report to the CINCAF. Hart addressed him in a frank manner: "Well, I never thought I'd see you again!" Yet, when all was said and done, John Payne had done his duty.[25]

Cdr. McCollum, head of the Far East Section (OP-16-F-2) of the Division of Naval Intelligence, was in the center of the action in terms of intelligence input being received by the Office of Naval Intelligence. With all the activity going on in the Western Pacific and the IJN and the IJA moving into the French Indochina region, as well as key information coming in from diplomatic intelligence (PURPLE) sources indicating the ever-increasing imminence of war, McCollum and his two assistants, Lt. Cdr. Ethelbert Watts and Maj. (USMC) Rodney Boone, set up a 24-hour watch system to support ONI.

With only three personnel available, each person served an 8-hour overlapping shift to ensure that a knowledgeable expert on Japanese naval affairs was always available to the chain of command all the way up to Adm. Stark and even to Roosevelt himself. This availability meant that F-2 could receive, at a moment's notice, input from key personnel involved with cryptanalysis (OP-20-G) in the Office of Naval Communications, who were working 24 hours a day. Kramer was a key point of contact for F-2 at ONI; he served as a liaison officer and navy courier, providing constant input from OP-20's GX (direction finding), GY (cryptanalysis), and GZ (translation and dissemination) sections.

Kramer's primary mission was to segregate and cross-reference all key intercept messages that had been received at ONI and be prepared to brief and highlight the most important ones. Each day at 11 a.m., he would routinely show the file to directors Noyes (Communications), Wilkinson (Intelligence), McCollum (F-2), Turner (War Plans), and Ingersoll (Asst. CNO). Ingersoll would indicate the ones that were to be shown to Stark (CNO), Knox (Sec. Navy), and finally to Beardall (Naval Aide to FDR).[26]

McCollum's reports included a daily Japanese summary, a daily bulletin for Beardall, a weekly known and estimated disposition of all IJN warships, a fortnightly summary of the current Japanese national and naval situations, and sometimes even special reports and oral updates; these were avidly sought throughout the higher echelons of the navy's OPNAV headquarters. While all information was evaluated as to its credibility, implications, and the conclusions, the *final evaluation*—in the form of enemy *intentions*—was relegated to Rear Adm. Richmond Turner, the Navy War Plans Officer.[27]

Be that as it may, Arthur McCollum was now an increasingly frustrated man. Since proffering his 8-Point Memorandum in the fall of 1940—which had been largely executed in most respects by Roosevelt's strategy—he had analyzed and reported on the recall and reconfiguration of Japan's thousand-ship merchant marine into a naval auxiliary force in support of the IJN, including the exchange of diplomatic notes and messages (PURPLE) between Tokyo and its embassy in Washington. This had produced, over a period of months, an increasingly tense stalemate and finally the all-out mobilization of the IJN's invasion fleets now headed toward the South China Sea and the Gulf of Siam.

All this had culminated with a December 1 order from Tokyo to its embassies in London, Manila, Singapore, and Hong Kong to destroy their various cipher machines.[28] This mass destruction of critical communications equipment, including PURPLE machines, had never taken place before. It was an ill omen of impending war and a definite indication that the zero hour was near. (As Tokyo had said to its Washington ambassadors, "After that [November 29] things are automatically going to happen!")

McCollum and other elements of ONI had been "constantly sending out information" up the chain of command in Washington but had not seen any apparent reaction from the admirals in the navy's high command hierarchy. What concerned McCollum most was that there did not appear to be "any warning dispatches going out to anybody." In the latter part of November, he drafted a memorandum about what had been going on in the Far East. Both he and Wilkinson took it directly to the CNO Stark who immediately called a conference of his principal flag officers.

After detailing the Japanese preparations for war, including the forward deployment of some 95,000 troops into French Indochina alone, the IJN's formation of two major task forces to operate in the South China Sea area and the Mandates, and the evacuation over the previous 30 days of all Japanese residents, including women and children, from British India and Singapore, the Netherlands East Indies, the Philippines, Hong Kong, Australia, and even the United States, Canada, and South America, McCollum asked his superiors the key question: Had the Pacific Fleet and Asiatic Fleet had been warned?

Stark, Ingersoll, and Turner all assured McCollum that "adequate and ample" warnings had been sent out, but McCollum, himself, had not seen any! As the navy's leading authority and military expert on Japanese naval affairs and now visibly irritated, he created such a ruckus over the issue that Turner finally went to his office at War Plans and showed McCollum a copy of the war warning dispatch of November 27, sent to admirals Hart and Kimmel.[29] The dispatch actually shown to McCollum was one that had been sent out initially *in error* by Ingersoll, who had *excluded* the key first shot strategy information the president wanted passed on. McCollum did not fully understand the true context or intended meaning of the message, which was corrected the next day, November 28, and then retransmitted by Stark to his fleet admirals in the Pacific for action in terms of the first shot strategy's implementation.

As part of his effort on December 1, McCollum drafted a more complete analysis of the situation memorandum for Wilkinson and Turner for immediate transmission to the Pacific Fleet in Hawaii, laying out what McCollum considered to be the outstanding military and political moves made by Japan over the two previous months. McCollum, believing Station CAST's erroneous report of the IJN's aircraft carrier locations November 30—primarily due to the highly effective radio deception operations on the part of the Imperial Japanese Navy's General Headquarters, denoted all 10 of the IJN's carriers as still being located at the Kure and Kyushu naval bases in Japan's southern islands. The end result of McCollum's effort was that the dispatch was never sent out as intended and remained at OPNAV headquarters.[30]

On December 1, Capt. Wilkinson, as director of ONI, now echoed McCollum's information and observations and issued, under his own name, "Fortnightly Summary of the Current National Situation," whereby he summed up the Japanese naval situation by stating, "The current major capital ship strength remains in home waters, as well as the greater proportion of carriers."[31] Shortly thereafter, information did arrive at ONI and McCollum's own F-2, indicating that the IJN had a force of at least two aircraft carriers advancing eastward from Japan in the North Pacific. This new information was pointed out on a chart to the Dutch Naval Attaché, Johann Ranneft, during his visit to ONI on December 2.

Rear Adm. Turner had the final word on the dispatch of intelligence information out to the Asiatic and Pacific Fleets, and apparently not one word of McCollum's carefully crafted memorandum of December 1 was authorized in whole or in part for transmission to Adm. Hart or Adm. Kimmel.[32] Turner was not about to let himself be upstaged by McCollum. Later that same day, his office produced an information summary for CNO Stark and Roosevelt that contended that Japan was ready to undertake "major operations in the Indo-China-Thai Theater soon." Commenting on Japan's strategy, he wrote, "Should the main effort (on the continent) then evoke no reply from the U.S., the flank screen [Mandates] may become free for a descent on the East Coast of Borneo." Turner thought the OP-12 (War Plans) meant that the Japanese would "advance on an ambiguous (as far as the U.S. is concerned) objective and await developments."[33]

The fact that a previous PURPLE intercept had stated that "the deadline [November 29] cannot be changed" and added "After that, things are automatically going to happen" caused McCollum at F-2 to interpret these words to mean "that movements of forces at this time were already under way and they could not be changed. The forces would not be recalled. We knew that they were already underway at that time."[34] While Turner's analysis of what was going on was somewhat muddled, ONI's appreciation of the situation was right on target.

By December 3, intercepts were indicating that the Japanese Foreign Office had ordered its offices in London, Paris, Batavia, Singapore, Manila, Hong Kong, and Washington to begin destroying not only their own PURPLE but other code machines, code books, and confidential and secret papers. McCollum himself recommended that a special watch be placed immediately on the Japanese Embassy in Washington, which, it was found, was following Tokyo's orders and incinerating its documents. Embassies burning documents meant war was obviously coming on fast.

That same day, McCollum (ONI) and Safford (Naval Communications) each prepared and sent out coded messages to the American Naval attachés in Tokyo, Peking, Shanghai, and Bangkok to destroy all their codes and ciphers in preparation for their offices being evacuated or even seized. The code word to indicate that the destruction order had been carried out was "Gobbledygook." Both the Asiatic and Pacific Fleet commanders, as well as the commandants of the 14th and 16th Naval Districts received an "information" copy of the message.[35]

The Japanese preparations for war had come full circle. Tokyo had concluded that a diplomatic solution favorable to its interests in Asia was not possible. Because of the humiliating demand that Tokyo withdraw from China, as well as Roosevelt's series of gradually strangling embargo policies—which now found Japan's finances not only frozen but the nation also fully cut off from its strategically critical iron ore, steel, and oil resources—Tokyo now made the fatal decision to lash out at the United States, Britain, and the Netherlands rather than face national humiliation.

Tokyo promulgated its most important command decision of World War II. Approved by Emperor Hirohito, Prime Minister and Gen. Tojo, and Japan's Imperial Army and Navy General Headquarters, on December 2, 1941, Adm. Isoroku Yamamoto, using his YO WI 00 radio call sign, issued an all-points, top-secret order to his entire IJN Combined Fleet (call sign SE TU 7): "Attack on December 8!" The actual Code Book D, 5-Number-coded order transmitted at 1500 hours included a special prearranged series of words to convey the intended attack message: "Climb NIITAKAYAMA 1208, repeat 1208." While the wordage interpreted freely meant "attack on December 8," there was a special significance for the phrasing since Niitakayama was the highest mountain in Japan's empire. To climb that mountain meant that one was accomplishing one of the greatest feats to be undertaken. The "1208" signified the 12th month and 8th day of 1941 (Tokyo date/time), but more importantly for the United States it represented December 7, 1941 (Pearl Harbor date/time).[36]

Undoubtedly, Yamamoto's order was transmitted several times to ensure that all IJN commands were in receipt.

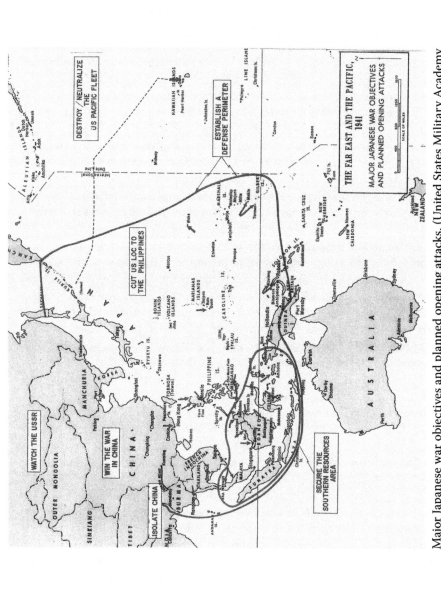

Major Japanese war objectives and planned opening attacks. (United States Military Academy Department of History)

Given the number of transmissions, it is reasonable to assume that the navy's intercept stations in the Pacific would also pick up the message.

In Hawaii, the HYPO-linked Station H's Radioman Second Class Joseph C. Howard intercepted Yamamoto's order. The transcribed message was placed into a pile with Howard's other messages at the side of his worktable. Picked up at the end of his midnight watch shift, they were integrated into the "batch" by the senior supervisor on duty and forwarded early that morning to Cdr. Rochefort's HYPO office for further processing.

This was a Yamamoto authored and transmitted message; Adm. Kimmel should have been briefed. Unfortunately for Kimmel, due to Cdr. Laurance Safford's 5-Number code-breaking cancellation order of the previous summer, *none* of HYPO's expert code breakers were authorized to work the IJN's operational Code Book D, 5-Number (JN-25) system. Those specially coded messages were merely bundled up and forwarded via airmail to Safford.

The HYPO handicap might have been significantly mitigated by Safford's own team of 5-Number, JN-25 code experts, but right to December 7, the cryptographers were dealing with messages that were generally a month old. This incredibly serious error in focus had been pointed out by CAST's Lt. John Lietwiler in a letter to his counterpart, Lt. Lee Parke at OP-20-GY. Nothing was done to correct the situation. Time was running out.

Another case in point was Agnes Driscoll, who was handicapped by not having on hand the necessary German Navy Enigma machine that was available to her British counterparts. For some six months, Driscoll, as OP-20-G's top Code Book D, 5-Number cryptanalyst, had been given a new focus, which caused her to divert her brain power and labor fruitlessly in an effort to break the U-boat-related Nazi Enigma Naval Code—a total waste of time that lead nowhere.

Simply put, even if Yamamoto's Combined Fleet attack order had arrived in Washington in time for decoding and translation, Safford's haphazard and fragmented organization of the navy's effort to decode the IJN's most important operational 5-Number Code would have been for naught. The only naval organization that would benefit immediately from Yamamoto's "climb Mt. Niitakayama" message was the IJN's Vice Adm. Chuichi Nagumo and his Pearl Harbor–bound Strike Force, which had been standing by in the North Pacific, awaiting that order.

Carefully calculated, Yamamoto's order had taken into full consideration the need for Nagumo to be able to arrive at his attack position north of Oahu on precisely the correct date. Now unleashed to continue their transpacific mission, Nagumo's six aircraft carriers and several hundred pilots would not only arrive at the correct time and place on December 7, but they would also release an avalanche of bombs, bullets, and torpedoes early that morning onto an unsuspecting Pacific Fleet at Pearl Harbor.[37]

With the November 29 deadline date (when things would "automatically begin to happen") having come and gone and Tokyo's J-19 coded November 19 (decoded and translated on November 28) "Winds alert" set-up message having been received, ONI's radio intelligence community immediately began making preparations to receive the "Winds Code" messages however and whenever they might be sent out. It was an all-encompassing effort.

Both CAST in the Philippines and HYPO's Heeia or Station H in Hawaii went on a special alert to monitor the Tokyo radio broadcasts 24 hours a day. Rochefort at HYPO ordered four of his best Japanese language–trained officers to go his Station H intercept monitoring operation on the other side of Oahu and stand a full 24-hour watch, listening for the expected Winds execute message. Station H monitored voice only, while CAST, in the Philippines, monitored both voice and Morse code. Station SAIL at Bainbridge Island was also directed by OP-20-GX to monitor Tokyo Morse code broadcasts, tracking some 15 distinct radio circuits simultaneously, of the Mackay and RCA radio stations between San Francisco and New York. This was in addition to its routine monitoring of the Tokyo–San Francisco radio telephone circuit.

Due to the radio wave propagation effect, or skip phenomenon over long distances, Safford believed that the navy's intercept Station M at Cheltenham, Maryland, actually had the best reception capability during the winter months on the East Coast. Press broadcasts sent in both kana code and English were covered. Even the Federal Communications Commission was incorporated into this ad hoc network, with its own monitor station at Portland, Oregon, placed on alert. In this case, Portland monitored exclusively for voice only.

On the western side of the Pacific, British Intelligence (Singapore), Dutch Intelligence (Java), and Australian Intelligence were also requested to be on the lookout for Winds radio traffic. With Tokyo having directed its London, Hong Kong, Singapore, and Manila embassies to destroy their respective code machines—but ordering Washington to maintain its own—ONI truly began to take a higher interest in the expected Winds messages.[38] It did not have long to wait.

DECEMBER 4

In the early hours of December 4, before dawn, Chief Warrant Officer Ralph Briggs, then on duty watch at the Naval Communications Station M at Cheltenham, began receiving the routine Japanese weather broadcast from Tokyo. Copying down the katakana Morse code on his RIP-5 Typewriter, he noted the phrase *Higashi no kazeame* ("East Wind Rain").

Checking his watch supervisor's 3 x 5 card classified instructions about the three types of Winds execute weather phrases to be looking for, he realized that *this* was actually one of the key Winds messages. Moments later, he placed the message on the TWX circuit, which was connected to a page printer next to the Navy Department's OP-20-GY (cryptanalysis) Watch Officer's desk. After that, he made two carbon copies and then an entry on his message intercept log sheet.

With the kana figures typed out and a handwritten translation he did himself, Lt. Cdr. Kramer (OP-20-GZ) exclaimed, "This is *it!*" Cdr. Safford viewed the message on yellow teletype paper. There was no doubt about it, it was the real McCoy. Kramer's underscored translations read, "War with England, including the invasion of Thailand and the capture of Malaya and the Dutch East Indies—War with the United States—Peace with Russia." Safford later commented, "There was a Winds Message. It meant War—and we knew it meant War!" A copy was sent by messenger to Capt. Leigh Noyes, the director of naval communications. While standard operating procedure mandated that distribution of the Winds message was the responsibility of the ONI, not Naval Communications, Noyes contacted the War Department and otherwise placed the gist of the message on the navy's MAGIC distribution list that included the Naval Aide to Roosevelt. The navy had now been given 72 hours' advance notice of Japan's planned attacks.[39]

On December 4, given that Guam, with all its codes and ciphers, was only 100 miles distant from Japanese-controlled Saipan, and fearing a possible surprise commando raid by the Japanese military, Station BAKER in Guam was directed by OPNAV to reduce its crypto materiel for "special intelligence" to a minimum. On the same day, Wake Island was also singled out for special destruction orders, and an OPNAV message went out under the signature of Asst. CNO Ingersoll to CINCAF directing that the island should be stripped of all classified documents "which in the hands of an enemy would be of disadvantage to the United States." But that was not all. The situation had become so serious that OPNAV also sent a message to its naval attaches in Tokyo, Bangkok, Peking, and Shanghai, directing that they, too, should destroy their key codes and registered publications. Upon execution, they were to respond back in plain language to OPNAV with the codeword "Boomerang."[40]

War was imminent. The navy was now clearing the decks and battening down its vulnerable ONI "hatches" throughout the Far East. Although ONI's Director, Capt. Theodore Wilkinson, also considered that war was imminent and expected that the Japanese would strike any day now, he never bothered to convey this "imminence" directly to either Kimmel himself or Kimmel's fleet intelligence officer, Lt. Cdr. Layton.[41]

Along with Station M's adept intercept of the Winds execute message, there were others that also received the same "East Wind Rain" weather message. Adm. Hart's CAST had received confirmation of receipt of the message from the British Far East Combined Bureau (FECB) in Singapore, which had also obtained an intercept from its Stonecutters Island, Hong Kong, station. The Dutch were also in the game with Col. J. A. Verkuyl, the commander of Kamer 14, informing Lt. Col. E. R. Thorpe, the American intelligence officer on duty in the Dutch East Indies, of what was happening. Thorpe turned the "East Wind Rain" intercept over to the State Department's consul general in Batavia for transmission to Cordell Hull in Washington, DC. The British Government's Code and Cypher School (GCCS) also received the Winds execute.

Finally, there was one other office that received the message: the Imperial Japanese Embassy in Washington, DC. The radio room of the naval attaché office at the embassy received the "*Higashi no kazeame* [East Wind Rain]" weather signal, repeated several times during the morning of December 4. Interviewed after the war by historian John Toland, who was fluent in Japanese, naval attachés Capt. Yuzuru Sanematsu and Lt. Cdr. Yoshimori Terai confirmed the receipt of the Winds execute.[42]

Cdr. Safford could be proud of the navy's intercept of the East Wind Rain message. It was a major intelligence coup. Japan's strategic military strategy had been unmasked, and the Roosevelt administration now had confirming proof that Japan was going to war not just against the British and the Dutch but also against the United States. And it was Safford's intercepts that had ferreted out Japan's hand—all the cards were now on the table. Safford had accomplished his mission and done his duty in the spirit of the intelligence officer's basic credo: "Tell your commander today what the enemy is going to do tomorrow."

Safford's 20 years of brilliant inventiveness and persistent efforts to set up a multinational intelligence network of 22 radio signals intercept and direction finding stations around and throughout the Pacific had paid off in spades. Of course, he didn't do it all alone. It was a team effort, involving both the army's development by Col. William Friedman of the PURPLE electronic cipher machine for breaking Japan's most important diplomatic codes and the navy's parallel breaking of the IJN's most important operational codes by Agnes Driscoll. And there were so many more, such as the On the Roof Gang and all the thousands of personnel that had manned the radio intercept and RDF systems and performed the mind-boggling cryptanalysis duties, manually or by machine, over the years to constantly break the Japanese diplomatic and military codes. They also had done their duty.

The Roosevelt administration knew what the Japanese were about to do, and Tokyo was unaware of this. Unfortunately for Safford, his apparent intelligence victory over the Japanese on behalf of navy interests would be relatively short lived. Unknown to Safford, another dynamic, involving strategic politics far above his level of work in OP-20-G, was very much in play.

While not knowing how or when Tokyo would formally announce its breaking of diplomatic relations with Washington, signifying that active hostilities were underway, but understanding that the East Wind Rain broadcast was tantamount to Japan's declaring war on the United States, Safford set about trying to take advantage of the intercept. First and foremost in his mind was to get word out to both fleet commanders in the Pacific. Knowing that as a communications officer he did not have the intelligence clout or prestige that McCollum held with the navy's high command, Safford coordinated with McCollum to try to exert pressure on Adm. Stark. While Safford prepared technical alert messages to the various exposed overseas intelligence and radio intercept stations in the Pacific with regard to the destruction of their respective cryptographic aids (sent out around 1500 hours Washington time on December 4), McCollum took several hours to draft a warning message of some 500 words, summarizing events in the Pacific since that past summer, laying out the immense Japanese buildup of military troop and naval forces in the South China Sea area, including fully translating and providing the significance and meaning of the Winds execute message.

McCollum understood this. He was trying to pass on the juxtaposition that Tokyo's November 29 deadline for completing an acceptable agreement with Washington and the idea that the receipt of the Winds (East Wind Rain) broadcast were tantamount to a Japanese declaration of war on the United States. All previous information received by ONI had been statements of intent, but this was now a statement of fact! Safford, who read the draft in its entirety, noted that the message ended with a terse statement: "War is imminent."

It was now apparent to Capt. Joseph R. Redman, assistant director of navy communications, and Col. Otis Sadtler, one of Gen. Marshall's key army staff communications officers, that the Winds message had been delivered *and* the change to the IJN's naval operations 5-Number Code (Additive 8 replacing Additive 7) had taken place in the middle of the week. It was only two days to Saturday and three to Sunday. In effect, war was descending upon the Americans and the British within the next 72 hours in the Pacific![43]

But McCollum was somewhat in a quandary. His earlier 8-Point Memorandum on how to aggravate the Japanese to the degree that they would lash out at the United States had served as one of the stimulants for the promulgation of Roosevelt's overt act strategy. With the IJN now advancing eastward across the North Pacific and Tokyo's acknowledgment of its decision to go to war against the United States, things were nicely coming to a head. McCollum, as the navy's most knowledgeable intelligence officer in terms of assessing and understanding Japan's politics and its struggle for power, wealth, and influence in the region and at the fulcrum of the navy's intelligence system dealing with the Pacific, was directly serving the interests of both Adm. Stark, chief of naval operations, and America's leader, President Roosevelt.

Still, McCollum did have an obligation to look out for the interests of the rest of the U.S. Navy in the Pacific, which in the main consisted of the two fighting fleets, large and small, commanded by Adm. Kimmel and Adm. Hart respectively. The Asiatic and Pacific Fleets were the cutting edge of America's defenses in the region. As such, the navy operated like a team, a large team, and, in order for the team to be eminently successful in defending America's interests in the Pacific, it needed to know what its enemies were doing. This meant that when all was said and done, McCollum had an obligation to keep the navy's Pacific Fleet commanders informed of the developing situation. It was a moral dilemma that would not go away. Yet, at this late moment in the warlike crescendo of events taking place throughout the Pacific and in Washington, DC, he apparently had undergone a change of heart in terms of his broader obligations.

Because of the OPNAV's standing operating procedure that subordinates were not allowed to release messages to their counterparts in the active fleets, McCollum had to coordinate the approval and release of his proposed message with his superiors, who included Wilkinson, the director of ONI, and the triumvirate of admirals Turner (War Plans), Ingersoll (Asst. CNO), and Stark (CNO). In accordance with procedure, Wilkinson took McCollum's lengthy message and, after approving it, showed it to Leigh Noyes, the director of naval communications.

Noyes read the message and commented, "I think it's an insult to the intelligence of the Commander-in-Chief [Kimmel]." Wilkinson replied, "I do not agree with you. Admiral Kimmel is a busy man and may not see the picture as clearly as you and I do. I think it only fair to the commander-in-chief that he be given this information and I am going to send it if I can get it released by the front office [Turner, Ingersoll, and Stark]." They were the gatekeepers who kept Kimmel in the dark.

Apparently, the message was then taken to Rear Adm. Ingersoll, who also then examined it. What McCollum would not know until sometime after the Pearl Harbor attack was that his carefully considered and crafted message was never sent out to the Pacific Fleet's Adm. Kimmel.

Kimmel's intelligence isolation remained complete. He was ignorant of not only the Winds execute message but also its potential implications for him and his Pacific Fleet. Now, with the overt act strategy still fully intact, only 72 hours remained until Vice Adm. Nagumo perpetrated his own special "overt act" on Hawaii.[44]

DECEMBER 5

On Friday, December 5, Roosevelt called for a cabinet meeting, a sort of "White House huddle" with himself as quarterback, calling the signals. The purpose of the meeting was to review the situation in the Pacific. The day of that meeting, OP-16 released a secret classified Memorandum for the president, laying out in detail the quantities of troops and aircraft as well as naval forces and transports involved in what was going to be a major series of operations against Singapore, the Dutch East Indies, and probably the Philippines.

The locations of the IJN's primary fleet units moving south had been known for some weeks but beginning in mid-November, ONI had temporarily lost track of the IJN's aircraft carriers. A combination of radio listening silence and radio deception practiced by Japanese naval authorities to deliberately confuse U.S. Navy intercept stations had been working fairly well. It was known as of December 2 that there were some aircraft carriers advancing east across the North Pacific. These had been pointed out to Dutch Capt. Ranneft by McCollum that same day. At the cabinet meeting, Secretary of the Navy Frank Knox, apparently updated by ONI's director Wilkinson that the IJN's aircraft carriers had been located, said to Roosevelt, "Well, you know, Mr. President, we know where the Japanese fleet is."

The president replied, "Yes, I know. I think we ought to tell everybody just how ticklish the situation is. We have information as Knox just mentioned. . . . Well, you tell them what it is, Frank." Somewhat excited, as anyone might have been under the circumstances of impending war, Knox blurted out, "Well, we have secret information that the Japanese fleet is out at sea. Our information is—"

Roosevelt abruptly cut him off, not only to prevent the technical aspects from being revealed but also to keep the navy's precise knowledge of the emerging IJN threat in the North Pacific a complete secret. Not all the cabinet had been included in the finer points of the first shot strategy, and it needed to be protected.[45]

DECEMBER 6

The next day, Saturday, December 6, at 1400 hours, Capt. Ranneft, the Dutch naval attaché, once again stopped by ONI at U.S Navy Headquarters in Washington. He noted in his diary for that day that the Navy Department appeared closed, except for ONI personnel, where "everyone" was present. There, he spoke to Wilkinson, McCollum, and Kramer about the situation in the Gulf of Siam and the South China Sea. Due to the classified nature of their information, he would not have dared to commit any of the details he picked up to his diary. Certainly for him, the situation in the Southwest Pacific must have appeared grim.

Considering his full access to ONI and the free exchange of intelligence information gleaned from Kamer 14's own radio intercepts and RDF operations against the Tokyo government and the IJN, Ranneft must have felt comforted as he listened to both McCollum's and Wilkinson's evaluations of the situation, knowing that they were dedicated allies. The Winds execute message, stating that Japan was going to war with not only the NEI but also the United States, meant that the Dutch and the Americans were both, proverbially speaking, "in the same boat."

If the IJN's Vice Adm. Nagumo was about to unleash an avalanche of bombs, bullets, and torpedoes against the U.S. Navy in Hawaii, this was relatively nothing in size compared to the series of invasions being contemplated by Tokyo for the Dutch East Indies for December 1941 and the early months of 1942. Japan's Southwest Pacific war plans, in execution, would constitute the greatest array of amphibious operations ever carried out as one coherent naval campaign up to that time in modern warfare. The Japanese would incorporate an innovative combination of amphibious and airborne forces, protected by strong aerial and surface warship elements of the IJN. According to the OP-16 Memorandum to the President, the Japanese had the capability of throwing some 100,000 men, 50 warships, and 30 transports at the Dutch East Indies alone, in order to seize all six of the territory's six principal islands and their oilfields.[46]

For Ranneft, information clarifying the reality of the situation facing the Dutch would be immensely useful to both the Netherlands foreign minister, Dr. Eelco van Kleffens, and to the commander of the Netherlands East Indies Army, Gen. Hein Ter Poorten, at Batavia. Ter Poorten had only some 35,000 men to defend an area the size of the continental United States against the IJA.

After contemplating Wilkinson's and McCollum's information concerning Dutch interests in the Southwest Pacific, Ranneft requested an update on the progress of the IJN's aircraft carriers moving eastward from Japan as of December 2. It was pointed out to him, on a chart, that the carriers had now moved to a position to the "west of Honolulu." Considering that map symbols are usually fairly good size (2 x 2 inches), "west of Honolulu" would place the carriers somewhere immediately north of Midway Island. On December 6, the IJN's Pearl Harbor Strike Force, having advanced two-thirds of the way across the North Pacific, now completed its precipitous southeastern turn and was in direct movement southward toward its attack position immediately to the north of Oahu (Honolulu). The map locations referred to by Ranneft were probably the same ones presented to Secretary of the Navy Frank Knox by ONI's Capt. Wilkinson. Ranneft's officially translated diary entry said: "None of us talk about a possible air attack on Honolulu. I myself don't even think about it because I believe that everyone in Honolulu is 100% on the alert, like everyone here at O.N.I. The atmosphere at O.N.I. is tense."[47] "Tense" was a good description of the ONI's atmosphere on that December 6 afternoon. But Ranneft's visit to ONI was not the only thing going on that Saturday.

On that day, December 6, at 1:05 a.m., U.S. Army Military Intelligence officer Lt. Lewis Brereton, on duty at the headquarters of the 1st Battalion, 37th Infantry, Station KING at Dutch Harbor, Aleutian Islands, Alaska, received an unexpected message from the Alaska Defense Command (ADC) headquarters at Fort Richardson (Anchorage):

RADIO REPORT: NAVY REPORTS JAP SHIPS 270 MILES SOUTH EAST OF DUTCH HARBOR

The ADC, under the command of Brig. Gen. Simon Bolivar Buckner Jr., had been given the mission to establish a defensive position, known as Fort Mears, to protect the Naval Air Station Dutch Harbor (some 105 personnel), which included Station KING. In addition to the 932-man infantry battalion, the defense force included artillery, antiaircraft and antitank guns, and other supporting units or a total of some 1,329 troops.[48]

Who exactly sent this message to the U.S. Army in Alaska remains a mystery. One or more stations involved with the Mid-Pacific or WCCI radio intercept networks could have taken bearings of some kind to indicate that there was indeed an IJN force in the North Pacific. Probably the actual bearings were taken two to three days earlier than the delivery date (December 6) to the 37th Infantry. "Southeast of Dutch Harbor" on a nautical chart would place Adm. Nagumo's Strike Force in its refueling position and about in line where it began its own southeasterly turn toward its attack position north of Pearl Harbor.

While straight-line distance (Chart #1500) between Dutch Harbor and Honolulu is 2,046 miles, the Japanese Strike Force was following a course along the 43rd parallel or about 800 miles south of and just outside the reconnaissance range of the Dutch-Harbor–based PBYs. While the location "250 miles southeast of Dutch Harbor" is seemingly too close to the Naval Air Station there, the error could have been due to a two-bearing intersection taken or an irregular, triangular, "cocked-hat" configuration that the RDF bearings quite often formed as they crisscrossed or otherwise intersected. The plotting station (SAIL or others) might have prudently interpreted the general longitude and latitude plot configuration of the bearings by "erring" on the side of security in terms of Dutch Harbor, thus safely compensating for any RDF bearing errors before transmitting the alert. Only then was the Fourth Army Headquarters at Presidio (San Francisco) presumably informed so it could then send out its own alert to its subordinate ADC at Fort Richardson.[49]

Chief Radioman-in-Charge Robert Fox, who headed Station KING, complained in his monthly "High Frequency Direction Finding Report for December 1941" that U.S. Army stations had received information that Japanese vessels were operating in the vicinity of Alaska and that information about the IJN was apparently picked up from radio bearings obtained by them. There was considerable merit in what Fox was reporting, since the U.S. Army did operate its own Station TWO from the headlands of San Francisco, Station FOUR in the Canal Zone (Panama), Station FIVE in Hawaii, and Station SIX in the Philippines. Any one or more of these stations could have passed information to the Fourth Army Headquarters. So there appears, in addition to the U.S. Navy report reaching the 37th Infantry, that there were multiple reports dealing with suspected threats to U.S. bases in Alaska coming from army intelligence channels during the first few days of December 1941.

It is also possible during that period, that the Fourth Army received from the 12th Naval District at San Francisco the longitude and latitude location plots of IJN ships in the North Pacific, based on RDF intersection bearing data that Robert Ogg had recorded over several days from Globe and Press Wireless. Ogg made his two-bearing intersections on a great circle chart for navigational purposes, which meant that, with a limited RDF baseline difference for the two stations, there could have been an intersection crossing error of as much as 200 to 500 miles. This might also have prompted the report "250 miles southeast of Dutch Harbor."

In an apparent reference to the 12th Naval District's RDF bearing plots sent into ONI, Safford stated at a post–Pearl Harbor congressional investigation, "We were insisting that Naval Intelligence keep out of the communications field of activity and disband the amateur intercept stations which various ambitious District Intelligence Officers had set up without authority from the Navy Department."[50]

The British FECB in Singapore had considered as part of its estimate of IJN operational intentions that, besides the conduct of amphibious assault operations against American, Dutch, and British possessions in the Western Pacific, there was also the distinct possibility of a surprise attack against the primary American fleet base at Pearl Harbor.

The Japanese were known for initiating military operations on a holiday, and the fact that the FECB had intercepted Yamamoto's "Climb Niitakayama 1208, repeat 1208" meant that a holiday attack scenario was a serious consideration. British intelligence further deduced that the IJN had dispatched a task force from the Kurils somewhere around November 26, the exact location of which was unknown. The conclusion was that an attack would likely take place on December 8. In Pearl Harbor, local time on the other side of the international dateline, this was Sunday, December 7.

Whether done deliberately or not, the U.S. Navy observer on station in Singapore, Capt. John. Creighton, was apparently *not* advised of the FECB's conclusions; there is no record of him having sent a message to Adm. Hart in this regard. Both the FECB at Singapore and CAST up in the Philippines had intercepted IJN signals that indicated major changes to the 5-numeral cipher (5-Number/Code Book 5) system then in use. It was obvious that the Japanese were taking no chances on their primary operational code being compromised.

The change from additive table system Number 7 to Number 8, however, was not that simple. The IJN's Office of Naval Communications quickly recognized that not all fleet units might have received Number 8 and therefore Number 7 would have to remain in use. The far-flung locations of so many amphibious task forces and warships, as well as submarines, made the distribution of the new coding tables complex, leading to the fact that in order to maintain continuity in the dozens of closely coordinated attack operations about to take place, messages would have to be sent in *both* the old and the new additive systems. The Japanese had compromised, for the short term, their operational code system! Even the routine change of radio call signs on December 1 did not particularly inhibit the identification of the principal IJN warships by astute U.S. traffic analysis and radio fingerprinting.[51]

In Canada, throughout 1941, Murton A. Seymour had been running a covert British and Canadian recruiting program to support the Royal Air Force in its defense of the British Isles against the German Luftwaffe. At a meeting he attended in Ottawa on December 1, he was informed that British Military Intelligence suspected that the Japanese were preparing to make a surprise attack on Pearl Harbor on December 8. (That date was undoubtedly a reflection of the FECB's decode of the Yamamoto's Climb Niitakayama 1208 message.) Seymour was directed to close down his recruiting program in the United States, since it was expected that the Americans would want all available pilots to return back under the control of the Army and Navy Departments.[52]

In Cairo, Egypt, at 10:00 a.m., Saturday, December 6, Col. Bonner Fellers, the U.S. Army liaison officer, was informed by British Royal Air Force Headquarters that the United States would be in the "war within 24 hours." Bonner concluded that, if the British knew about the attack, undoubtedly Washington would also know of it.

That same day, American ambassador John G. Winant in London sent a cable to Roosevelt, advising him, "Two parties seen off of Cambodia Point, sailing . . . westward toward Kra. 1st Group: 25 transports, 6 cruisers, 10 destroyers; 2nd group: 10 transports, 2 cruisers, 10 destroyers." The situation in the Western Pacific was now reaching a climax, as 6,600 miles to the west of Hawaii IJA Gen. Tomoyuki Yamashita's Twenty-Fifth Army bore down on the Thai and Malay coasts.[53]

As Ambassador Winant was making his December 6, 1941, report to Roosevelt from London, Hart, at his Asiatic Fleet headquarters in Manila, was rendering a similar report that day. His own scouting force of PBYs had sighted one IJN cruiser and 30 other ships anchored in Camranh Bay, French Indochina. These reports, and others, described Japanese intrigues in Malaya to try and get the British to cross its northern frontier into Thailand, and thus bring the Thai government into the war on the side of Japan. If this came about, it would facilitate Japan's efforts to establish forward-positioned air bases in the Kra Peninsula for operations against Malaya and Singapore. To Hart, it appeared that the Japanese were moving against the Kra Peninsula, or even Thailand. Hart, aware of the orders from OPNAV to Guam (Station BAKER) that it should destroy most of its secret and confidential communications matter as of December 4, and to "be prepared to destroy instantly in event of emergency all classified matter" still retained on the island, was feeling the mounting pressure of an inevitable war with Japan.[54]

At that time, British Adm. Tom Phillips, whose battleship *Prince of Wales* and battle cruiser *Repulse* had been based at Singapore as Britain's first line of naval defense in the Gulf of Siam and South China Sea, was working with Hart in Manila to coordinate American naval support on behalf of British interests. Things were becoming somewhat confusing for Hart, as he had received information from his U.S. Navy observer in Singapore, Capt. John Creighton, that the British were operating under the assumption that they would receive American armed support if the Japanese attacked any one or a combination of the territories of Thailand, the Netherlands East Indies, and Malaysia-Singapore.

Having received only vague instructions from Adm. Stark at OPNAV about what he should be doing in the evolving critical situation, Hart seized the initiative and, in the spirit of the ABD agreements in early 1941, ordered Destroyer Division 57 with its four destroyers to sail west from its station at Balikpapan, Dutch Borneo, to join the Royal Navy at Singapore. A part of the U.S. Navy in the Pacific was now operating under British command! With his coordination mission an apparent success and hostilities pending, Phillips flew back to Singapore. Four days later, Tom Phillips would find himself dead at the bottom of the South China Sea, a victim of Japanese naval air power.[55]

Prior to Tom Phillips's visit, Hart had received various intelligence reports of one sort or another over the previous several days. Some of these had come from OPNAV in Washington, DC, and others had come directly from his own intelligence-gathering assets in the form of CAST, as well as his 28 twin-engine PBY seaplanes. Hart's two PBY squadrons covered the approaches south of the Philippines into the Celebes Sea, the waters north of Borneo, and a zone that consisted of the coastal areas off French

Indochina, Hainan, and Formosa or that area fronting on the South China Sea. Hart now found himself potentially facing off against two major task forces west of the Philippines and another out in the Mandates.

While the forces in French Indochina had evolved into a strength of some 105,000 men, 250 land-based planes, and around 21 transports and 13 warships that were apparently focused on Malaya and Thailand across the Gulf of Siam, a more ominous threat were the forces assembled in the Hainan-Formosa area, consisting of some 95,000 men, 358 ground-based planes, and roughly 27 transports and 43 warships of various types. They and the Japanese forces building up forward staging areas at Palao, Saipan, Truk, and Kwajalein in the Mandates were the most likely threats to the Philippines. Intercepted IJN radio calls had identified the IJN's Fourth Fleet coordinating with these bases.[56]

While the reports appeared substantial, Hart was still beholden to CAST's December 5 RDF Cavite TEST report that, due to IJN radio deception efforts, erroneously maintained that the majority of the IJN's aircraft carriers were still located in Japan's southern home waters. It would only come to light after the initial attacks of December 7 and 8 that the other carriers reportedly identified, *Shoho* and *Ryujo*, were part of Vice Adm. Nobutake Kondo's Southern Force (Second Fleet).[57]

Other reports highlighted the fact that Japanese diplomatic and consular posts at Hong Kong, Singapore, Batavia, Manila, London, and Washington were being directed to "destroy most of their codes and ciphers at once and to burn all other important confidential and secret documents." Still another reported that no Japanese vessels located in the south were to leave for points north without permission. Japanese civilians were evacuating British and Dutch territories south of the Philippines. Parallel to this, Americans had been put on notice to leave Hong Kong. These reports, in conjunction with OPNAV's own communications destruction message to Guam and its COPEK priority message to CINCAF that Tokyo had ordered London, Hong Kong, Singapore, Manila, and Washington to destroy their respective diplomatic PURPLE machines, clearly meant that Japan was deadly serious and that war was just days, if not hours, away.[58]

Before Phillips had left for Singapore, he and Hart had drafted a formal plan for mutual action to deal with the Japanese threat in the Western Pacific. Albeit faced with overwhelming odds from the mass of Yamamoto's IJN Combined Fleet and the fact that the initiative at the outbreak of the war would surely rest with the Japanese, the two plucky admirals coauthored a plan by which the Royal Navy and the U.S. Navy would operate together in a coordinated manner under the principle of "mutual cooperation."

In essence, the two main British warships, or Battle Fleet, would operate from their Singapore base, supported by the already designated four destroyers of Hart's 57th Destroyer Division. Hart's three Asiatic Fleet cruisers (*Boise, Houston, Marblehead*) and two of Phillip's Royal Navy cruisers were now designated the Cruiser Striking Force. Along with four more of Hart's destroyers, Destroyer Division 58, this force would take up a station off the east coast of Dutch Borneo. At a later but not specified date, the Battle Fleet would be moved up to Manila, where it was expected to conduct offensive operations against the IJN. As to Hart's substantial force of 29 submarines based at Manila, the British-American plan had not one word to say. There is an old saying that *the proof is in the pudding*; unfortunately for both Hart and Phillips, their "pudding" would prove to be too meager to hold up in the crucible of war.[59]

Up in the North Pacific, Nagumo's Strike Force continued to churn eastward. Having endured successive days of heavy mist without a glimpse of the sun and having observed on December 5 an unknown merchant vessel of a third nation passing within sight of one of the north flank destroyer screens, his ships finally broke free from the inclement weather. With their refueling mission completed, that same day three of Nagumo's supporting oil tankers headed back to Japan's home waters. The next day, December 6 (Tokyo dateline), the remaining five tankers completed their refueling operations and also turned around westward en route back to home waters.

Now fully fueled and no longer plagued by the slow 13-knot speed of the tankers, Nagumo sped his Strike Force up to 26 knots, double its previous speed, and turned southward in the direction of Oahu. As night came on, under a full moon, a strong wind blew in from the northeast, causing the carriers to pitch and roll once again, often listing as much as 15 degrees. Weather in the North Pacific was a fickle element.[60]

Nagumo had anticipated the possibility of stormy weather disrupting preparations for his attack as the Strike Force carried out its approach run into its forward position north of Hawaii just before dawn on December 7. To make sure that all six of his aircraft carriers would be ready at zero hour to launch their shipboard fighters, bombers, and torpedo planes, throughout that Saturday, December 6, the planes were carefully brought up from their below deck storage areas to their respective flight decks. There, once armed, fully fueled, and in position for launching operations, they were then thoroughly lashed down with steel cables to prevent them from being blown overboard from slippery, shifting decks. Nagumo was counting on every one of his some 370 planes to carry out their carefully practiced attack missions; he could not afford a single mishap at this stage in the operation.[61]

To be kept up to date on the Pacific Fleet's ship locations at Pearl Harbor, Nagumo was continuously being fed coded radio reports from the chief of the 1st Bureau, IJN Naval General Staff. Based on the Japanese consulate's J-19 coded cable messages from Honolulu, which were then re-recoded as Code Book D, 5-Number transmissions, the Strike Force's commander learned that on that Saturday evening, there were no barrage balloons in and around Pearl Harbor, the battleships were not protected by torpedo-defense nets, and there did not appear to be any air patrols being carried out in the Hawaii Islands area. That was the good news.

The bad news was that both the carriers *Enterprise* and *Lexington* were outside the harbor. In fact, there were *no* carriers inside the harbor. Yamamoto and Nagumo had been expecting to catch not only the *Enterprise* and *Lexington* at their moorings but also the carriers *Hornet* and *Yorktown*. The whole fundamental operational premise of the Strike Force's intended attack was to decimate the U.S. Navy's most important striking power in the Pacific, the carrier forces, leaving Japan free to carry out its imperialistic ambitions.

Where the carriers were located, Nagumo could not be sure, but he would follow his orders and continue his mission, if for nothing else than to at least destroy the Pacific Fleet's battleships. The IJN's intelligence setup for the Pearl Harbor raid may have been good, but it obviously was not perfect. Both the *Hornet* and *Yorktown* were in the Atlantic, along America's East Coast, where the *Wasp* was also operating.

Yet, helping matters in Nagumo's case was another coded message that was received by the *Akagi* later that night, revealing that Honolulu was operating as normal and not under any kind of black-out conditions. Nagumo's staff communications officer, Lt. Cdr. Ono, had also been monitoring Hawaii via its local commercial radio stations and noted that there were no indications that the islands were aware of the Strike Force's approach, even as Vice Adm. Shimizu's Advance Force of 26 long-range submarines as well as the five mini-submarine Special Force had taken up their positions surrounding the Hawaiian Islands.[62]

For the past nine days, Adm. Kimmel and his staff had been working on the transfer of fighter planes to Midway and Wake Islands. OPNAV's transfer request had come immediately after the war-warning messages, causing a major diversion of staff attention on the part of both the army and navy in Hawaii. Confusing matters appreciably was CNO Stark's directive to conduct the transfer of the two groups of planes and their respective servicing ground crews using both Kimmel's aircraft carriers.

Since the U.S. Army Air Corps fighter planes had no real offensive capabilities against hostile surface craft or submarines, lacked navigational equipment and experience for flying over water beyond a range of 15 miles from land, and could not fly off or land on aircraft carriers (which made their transfer and recovery operations complicated), only marine fighters could efficiently accomplish the defense of the Midway and Wake Islands. In the end, after a dedicated nine-hour army-navy conference convened by

Kimmel, on November 27, the decision was made to dispatch Vice Adm. William Halsey and the carrier *Enterprise* with 12 marine fighters to Wake Island that next day.[63]

Halsey, as commander of Task Force 8, consisting of not only the *Enterprise* but also its three battleships, three modern heavy cruisers, and other warships, had to manage his November 28 departure from Pearl Harbor within the framework of not causing undue notice by the general public and making the movement appear as natural as possible. To accomplish this as surreptitiously as possible, he had the marine aircraft fly from Hawaii out to sea and only then land on board the *Enterprise*, out of sight of Hawaii. To maintain security, the marines had been told that they were going to sea for "two or three days' maneuvers." The plan worked, and Halsey then abruptly diverted his slow-moving obsolete battleships out to a traditional training exercise area.

As they disappeared over the horizon, Halsey began his movement west toward Wake. This now allowed *Enterprise* to move at 30 knots, instead of the battleships' 18 knots. At that point, he signaled Task Force 8 to prepare for combat. Warheads were now attached to all torpedoes, ammunition was ordered to be placed in all the various guns' ready racks, planes were armed with bombs, and aerial searches were conducted morning and afternoon out to distances of 300 miles. Specific orders directed all crews of all ships to regard any submarine observed as hostile and to attack it immediately. Any plane encountered in the air that was not known to be American was to be shot down. To that end, Halsey kept an intermittent combat air patrol over his ships throughout the day.[64] All this was taking place as the Japanese fleet was moving into attack its position.

On December 5, Task Force 12, under the command of Rear Adm. John Newton, had found itself bound for Midway with 18 marine fighter aircraft. Like Halsey the week before, he, too, believed he was going into harm's way and began a zigzag course with aerial scouts overhead to protect his carrier *Lexington* and its complement of three modern heavy cruisers and five destroyers. As Halsey had, Newton also had the marine fighters fly from Hawaii and land on his aircraft carrier out of sight at a far distance, so they would not cause undue suspicion as to what was going on. Once within 400 miles of Midway, Newton planned to launch the marine planes to continue the trip under the protection of patrol planes dispatched from Midway.

It reasonably appeared to Kimmel that OPNAV's order to transfer fighter aircraft from Hawaii to the outlying islands of Midway and Wake was a full confirmation for him, as well as his Pacific Fleet staff, that Washington did not see any imminent danger to Hawaii from a Japanese transpacific aerial attack. Sabotage was the only potential danger, and that had been highlighted and reinforced by Marshall in another message to Short, in Hawaii, reminding Short that internal civil "subversive activities may be expected." Knowing that antisabotage measures might alarm the civilian population at large, Short prudently grouped together his bomber and fighter planes under enhanced guard at their respective airfields to make them easier to protect.[65]

During the first week of December 1941, Cdr. Rochefort at HYPO maintained a perspective similar to that of Kimmel in terms of a potential IJN attack on Pearl Harbor but for different reasons. Rochefort was relying on his own analysis of November 26—sent to CNO Stark and the other U.S. Navy commands in the Pacific—in which he had noted the IJN's Second and Third Fleets' buildup in the Western Pacific at Taiwan's Bako and Takao naval bases and Hainan off the coast of southern China just to the northeast of French Indochina. He further noted the concentration of at least a third, or upwards of 20 subs, of the IJN's submarine force, a land-based aerial squadron, and a full carrier division in the Marshall Islands, as well as other IJN forces in Palau of the western Caroline Islands.

Rochefort's conclusion was that the IJN was about to begin a simultaneous, converging pincer-like invasion of both Malaya and the Dutch East Indies, with its main force attacking out of the South China Sea and its other force attacking from Palau into the area of Borneo. The presence of the IJN in the Carolines and Marshalls was considered to be a defensive screen, guarding the IJN's extended western flank against any intrusion by the Pacific Fleet based in Hawaii. All this was based on traffic analysis, RDF bearings, spurious transmitter sound emissions, and the solving and reading of the IJN's radio call signs that represented a significant portion of radio intelligence.[66] Inexplicably left out of this analysis was any follow-up to his November 30 HYPO signal intercept report of the *Akagi* communicating with its *maru* oil tankers.

While CAST took issue with Rochefort's HYPO over the division (two carriers) being located in the Marshalls, both stations agreed that the IJN was poised to carry out a major effort to points south in the form of a series of amphibious expeditions. Even CNO Stark's war warning pointedly mentioned Borneo, the Kra Isthmus, Thailand, and the Philippines. And Stark's own warning reflected the earlier January 1941 Rainbow 3 War Plan, in which the basic concept of a war with Japan anticipated an IJN attack on the Philippines, accompanied by attacks on either Malaya or Borneo, or even both.

A COPEK, urgent precedence December 1 message from OPNAV's Adm. Noyes to CINCAF (information to CINCPAC) discussing a Tokyo-sponsored plot to get the Thais to side with Japan against the British clearly kept Southeast Asia in the forefront as the top-priority Japanese focus. The December 1 change in the IJN's radio call signs, just a month after having carried out a previous change, also indicated that Japan was on the move, at least in the Southwest Pacific.

At HYPO, the sudden change in call signs initially confounded the traffic analysts, but just two days later some 200 of the most commonly used IJN transmitters and their new call signs were once again identified. Over a period of days, but primarily denoted by IBM statistical analysis of the IJN's radio traffic on November 21 and then again on December 4 and 6, Station H communications summaries concluded that "a movement of some sort involving a large portion of the Navy" (November 21) was taking place; "that the entire Navy is being instructed to be prepared for drastic action" (December 4); and that traffic volume indicated that the IJN was operating under a certain sense of military urgency (December 6).[67]

At the Pacific Fleet headquarters, Cdr. Layton was not taking any chances, either. While the island of Jaluit, in the western Marshall Islands, was just over 2,000 miles away, to the southwest of Oahu, it was close enough to be a threat but only if an IJN forward operating base was actually established there. By Layton's calculation, a fast-moving carrier attack force could make the trip from Jaluit to Oahu within five days. Supporting Layton was Rochefort's own Communications Intelligence Summary of November 25: "CinC. Fourth Fleet is still holding extensive communications with the Commander Submarine Fleet, the forces at Jaluit and Commander Carriers." So Jaluit now also became a top priority for a more intensive intelligence reconnaissance focus.

Earlier, in a December 2 intelligence update briefing for Adm. Kimmel, while Layton agreed with Rochefort's earlier analysis as to IJN strategy, placing four aircraft carriers of Divisions 3 and 4 in Formosan waters, Layton could not account for six of the remaining carriers, especially the *Akagi, Kaga, Soryu,* and *Hiryu.* Layton was challenged at this point by Kimmel, questioning, "Do you mean to say they could be rounding Diamond Head and you wouldn't know it?" But Kimmel was being facetious, as both knew from previous experience over the last half year, when IJN carrier locations had been intermittently uncertain from as many as 9 to 22 days at a time, due to either radio listening silence or nonuse of shipboard transmitters.[68]

Layton was undaunted. He knew that the marine fighter plane transfers to Midway and Wake Islands would enable the Pacific Fleet to conduct aerial reconnaissance out to the west of Hawaii. Even though each task force had been ordered to send out air patrols each morning and evening to cover the southern and western approaches to Oahu, it still wasn't enough. Kimmel ordered both Midway and Wake Islands to make PBY Catalina aerial scouting sweeps some 525 miles wide along each route. A PBY patrol wing left Ford Island at Pearl Harbor and refueled at Johnston Island to the southwest before heading up to the northwest en route to

Midway, producing a triangular reconnaissance zone out to the southwest and west of Oahu.

With a total of 81 PBYs on station and available for reconnaissance work at the end of November, but, with having to account for pilot and crew fatigue due to the 16-hour, 700-mile full-range sorties for each mission, this meant that only 30 planes could actually be available on a sustained basis for daily patrol operations at any given time. One had to be careful not to wear out the engines of the PBYs through overuse. This was considered particularly important, since each PBY had to be available to support the Pacific Fleet, which was expected to be ordered to sea in its entirety by Adm. Kimmel at the outbreak of hostilities. Each plane could only cover an 8-degree arc of the ocean approaches into Oahu. This meant that each day a significant portion of the 360-degree arc around Oahu would not be covered.

By December 6, Kimmel only had a total of 49 operational PBYs. Fortunately, Task Force 3, with Vice Adm. Wilson Brown in command, was covering the zone out to the southwest of Oahu. Brown left Hawaii with the cruiser *Indianapolis* and five destroyer minesweepers the same day as Halsey to conduct simulated bombardments and landing exercises at Johnston Island, some 700 miles southwest of Oahu.

On December 6, at Layton's recommendation, Kimmel requested of Stark that Kimmel himself be allowed to conduct a series of aerial photography missions over the Makin and Tarawa Islands in the Gilberts as an additional security measure. Apart from that, the 14th Naval District's (Adm. Bloch) own close-in surveillance of the immediate area around Pearl Harbor and Kimmel's standing order to bomb any IJN submarines encountered were the only remaining reconnaissance efforts in effect from the navy. Other close-in defense involved the army's six SCR-270B mobile radar units deployed around Oahu, to provide early warning out to roughly 150 miles.[69]

Kimmel and his staff acknowledged that submarines would most likely be the IJN's main form of any long-range attack against a protected base such as Pearl Harbor. Since the U.S. Navy's Bureau of Ordnance had concluded that torpedo planes could not be effectively employed in waters with a launch depth of less than 75 feet, as was the case of the relatively shallow waters of Pearl Harbor, the torpedo threat could only come from outside the base itself. No thought had been given to the possible use of midget submarines by the IJN.

In terms of Kimmel's own submarines, two were on patrol off Midway Island and two others reconnoitered the area around Wake Island. Remaining inside Pearl Harbor were eight World War I–era battleships at their moorings, two heavy cruisers, six light cruisers, eight destroyers, five submarines, seven ship tenders of various types, 12 mine layers, and various auxiliary and repair ships. With the local Hawaiian press talking about tensions building up around the Pacific, on December 5 a prudent Kimmel had directed his war-plans officer, Capt. Charles McMorris, to develop a special emergency action plan for the Pacific Fleet in the event that war broke out over the next 48 hours. The fleet aircraft carriers would remain outside Oahu and massed together with their fast-moving cruisers and destroyers to react to any unexpected situation.[70]

As matters stood on December 6, 1941, at Pearl Harbor, Halsey and the USS *Enterprise* had completed their transfer mission to Wake Island and were some 400 miles west of Oahu, returning back to Pearl Harbor. Newton and the USS *Lexington* were fast approaching to within 500 miles of Midway Island in order to complete their transfer of planes on December 7. The Pacific Fleet's third aircraft carrier, the *Saratoga*, with its complement of 80 aircraft,[71] was preparing to leave San Diego on December 8, bound for Pearl Harbor.

Kimmel was completely unaware of any of the PURPLE diplomatic intercepts dealing with the progress or status of negotiations with the Japanese, RDF plots based on intercepted IJN radio transmissions indicating a naval surface force in movement across the North Pacific, or the Japanese Honolulu consulate's highly detailed espionage efforts specifically targeting individual Pacific Fleet ships at their moorings. The key political-military intelligence information available to Roosevelt, CNO Adm. Stark, Asst. CNO Ingersoll, Navy Plans Officer Rear Adm. Turner, ONI Director Capt. Wilkinson, and their respective staffs as to the intentions and operations of Tokyo and the IJN in regards to Pearl Harbor had also been denied to Kimmel. Kimmel and his Pacific Fleet staff remained oblivious as to what was going on around them.

The diversion of Kimmel's attention away from what was soon to befall his fleet consisted of the apparent fixation of OPNAV on Japan's multiple southward moves into the South China Sea and French Indochina as forward staging areas for its invasion of British and Dutch possessions to points south, the vast distances that separated Japan's empire from Hawaiian waters, the natural feeling that the U.S. Navy was "invincible," and the assumption that the IJN would simply not dare to attack Pearl Harbor.[72]

So there the matter rested, or so it seemed, on December 6, with Kimmel and his staff wholly dependent on reading newspapers to find out what was going on in the Far East, all the while hoping to receive a timely alert from Washington as to where and how the actual outbreak of war in the Pacific might take place.[73]

Just eight days earlier, both he and Hart had received their instructions from CNO Stark to be sure that Japan was permitted to make an overt act before the Americans took any remedial offensive action. Kimmel would begin to fathom what his role was in terms of the first shot strategy only after the attack on Pearl Harbor had taken place. That his two key offensive battle fists or punches in the form of the *Enterprise* and the *Lexington* were not available to him meant he would now unknowingly face Nagumo's onslaught with both hands tied behind his back.

If there was a general calm and an ambience of complacency out in Hawaii, that was hardly the case in Washington; tensions during December 6 were about to crescendo to the highest levels imaginable. Secretary of War Stimson was very much feeling the buildup of the pressure, entering in his diary on December 6 his usual terse comments: "The news got worse and worse and the atmosphere indicated that something was going to happen. I was in frequent conference with Gen. Marshall and also Gen. Miles of G-2."

Stimson knew that the greatest burden in waiting to see what would happen in the Pacific rested with the U.S. Navy. With that apparently in mind, to keep the navy staff busy, if not distracted, that evening at 8 p.m. he ordered OPNAV to provide him, by the next day, December 7, at 10 a.m., a full "compilation of men of war" and their locations from the American, British, Dutch, Russian, and Japanese navies. This would automatically include not only both the Asiatic and Pacific Fleets in the Far East but also the Atlantic Fleet. This meant that Adm. Turner's newly established War Room would be working all night to compile the data for the army's secretary of war.[74]

With the East Wind Rain PURPLE message having been intercepted a couple of days earlier, announcing Japan's intention to go to war with the United States, the pressure was mounting at OPNAV to see how Tokyo would announce the actual outbreak of war. Given the vagaries of the wintertime skip phenomenon on transpacific radio transmissions, Safford of OP-20-G had planned carefully for this by having both Station S (SAIL) at Bainbridge on the U.S. Pacific coast and Station M at Cheltenham on the Atlantic side of the United States maintain a full intercept alert. Both stations covered the PURPLE diplomatic code frequencies utilized for the Tokyo-Washington circuits. Bainbridge would send its PURPLE intercepts to Washington by teletype. With intercept operations now arranged, the two military services took turns at translating the incoming traffic, the army taking the even-numbered days and the navy responsible for the odd-numbered days.[75] They did not have long to wait.

At 7:20 a.m., December 6, PURPLE intercept #901, known as the "pilot message" from Tokyo to Ambassador Nomura, arrived in Washington. The coded message stated that a special separate memorandum, responding formally to Hull's 10-point proposal of November 26, was to be issued in *English* as message #902. While this special memorandum was to arrive in 14 parts, most likely the next day, it was to be held in secrecy until yet another message arrived with special instructions as to the time of delivery of the entire #902. A little more than six hours later, between 11:49 a.m. and 02:51 p.m., the first 13 parts, all in English, arrived in Washington. It was the first time since the inception of the PURPLE system that a decode had come out in perfect English—no translation needed. These would be followed by part 14 at 7:00 a.m. the next day, December 7. SAIL at Bainbridge had captured all 14 parts and forwarded them by teletype to OP-20-G.[76]

By midafternoon of December 6, the intelligence services understood that the parts coming in via PURPLE were Tokyo's reply to Hull, indicating that all talks were now to be broken off and that the declaration of war and the actual breaking out of war might well coincide. History had shown that the Japanese had a penchant for timing the severance of diplomatic relations with that of a surprise attack on the enemy's fleet to announce the outbreak of hostilities. This had taken place at the opening of their war against China in 1895, at Port Arthur against Russia in 1904, and at Tsingtao against Germany in 1914.[77]

Lt. Cdr. Kramer, who served as the head of OP-20-G's translation section, was also ONI's official courier. Having prepared 14 copies of each decrypted translation, seven were then forwarded to the army and the other seven went to the navy—six going up the chain of command to include Roosevelt at the top, while the remaining seventh copy was retained on file. The White House, the secretary of the navy, the navy's CNO, the director of ONI (including F-2 Far East), the director of naval communications, and the director of naval war plans all received their personal copy.

It was Kramer who saw the importance of initially getting the first 13 parts into the hands of the president. Using his wife as his chauffeur, he arrived at the White House around 9:00 p.m. on the evening of December 6. He was received by assistant naval aide Lt. Lester Schulz, who had been alerted by his superior, Roosevelt's own primary naval aide Capt. John Beardall, that something important was to be delivered. Shortly after 9:30, Schulz was brought into the president's study, where he passed the intercepts into the hands of Roosevelt himself. Also in the room was the president's special confidant and former Secretary of Commerce Harry Hopkins. Having read the documents over, the president turned to Hopkins and exclaimed, "This means war!"

A few minutes later, Roosevelt attempted to reach Stark but was informed that he was at the theater. Apparently for fear of causing public alarm, the issue was set aside for the moment. Around 10 p.m., Kramer left the White House but was unsuccessful in contacting other high-ranking members of the chain of command.[78]

DECEMBER 7

By 3:10 a.m., early that morning of December 7, Station SAIL had monitored, copied, and forwarded by teletype to Washington the missing 14th part of the special message for Hull from Tokyo. At 4:37 a.m., SAIL intercepted the PURPLE-coded #907 message with the special delivery instructions fixing Ambassador Nomura's time of delivery to Secretary of State Hull at 1 p.m. that Sunday.

In Washington, DC, around 5:00 a.m., Lt. Francis Brotherhood picked the two messages off his WA 91 printer page machine, located beside the OP-20-GY Watch Officer's desk. Running the messages through the PURPLE machine, he noted that the 14th part of the memorandum was in English. The other message (#907) required Japanese translation, and this would take a little longer.

By 9:00 a.m., the 14-part message had been picked up by Kramer, who then delivered the entire memorandum to Stark at his office. The 14th part criticized the United States for conspiring with Great Britain to obstruct Japan's efforts to establish a new order in Asia. As part of its concluding paragraph, it further stated that due to the inflexible attitude of Washington, "it is impossible to reach an agreement through further negotiations." This was Japan's declaration of war against the United States.[79]

Having finally read through all 14 parts of the memorandum, Stark cried out, "My God! This means war! I must get word to Kimmel at once."

It is not known if this was intended for theatrical purposes to mollify Capt. Wilkinson and Cdr. McCollum, his key junior ONI staff members present in his office. Kramer then left and then returned some minutes later, around 10:30, with the formally decoded PURPLE #907 that stated, "Will the Ambassador please submit to the United States Government (if possible to the Secretary of State) our reply to the United States at 1:00 p.m. on the 7th, your time." It was obvious to all those present in Stark's office that 1:00 p.m. that Sunday afternoon in Washington was 7:30 in the morning in Hawaii. The implications were obvious: The Pacific Fleet was the target for Japan's opening, surprise salvo against the United States in the Pacific.

For McCollum the intended 1 p.m. timing of the declaration of war presentation in *English* to Secretary of State Hull and the fact that both he and Wilkinson had just the day before briefed the Dutch naval attaché, Johan Ranneft, as to the eastward movement of the IJN aircraft carriers across the North Pacific toward Hawaii, enabled him to quickly connect all the dots: What was happening was now all clear—the Japanese were synchronizing the timing of the delivery of their declaration of war with the attack on Pearl Harbor.

Both McCollum and Wilkinson discussed the time elements with Adm. Stark, who suddenly now did not appear to be perturbed at all. When advised to send a warning to Kimmel, Stark surprisingly replied, "No, I don't think any further warning is necessary." Pressed by Wilkinson a number of times as to whether the Pacific Fleet had actually been alerted, Stark responded that yes, it had. But McCollum and Wilkinson still had some doubts. Around 11 a.m., Wilkinson earnestly pressed Stark to pick up his telephone, with its transpacific naval command circuit, and call Kimmel directly.[80]

Eleven a.m. in Washington was 5:30 a.m. at Pearl Harbor. That meant there were only about two hours remaining to alert Kimmel about the anticipated attack so he, in turn, could give his sailors the general alert order: "Man your battle stations—man your battle stations!"

Timing was imperative. Every second counted, if the Pacific Fleet was to have some sort of fighting chance to defend itself. With even an hour's notice, all fleet weapons could be manned, ammunition uploaded into ready racks, bulkheads and hatches secured against fires, army P-40 War Hawk fighter planes ordered into the air to conduct an early dawn and sunrise reconnaissance around Oahu. There was a lot to do, and time was running out!

Stark, finally reacting to Wilkinson's urging, reached over to pick up his telephone as though he was going to call Kimmel. Instead, he tried to call Roosevelt at the White House, with no result. Stark made no effort to contact Kimmel at Pearl Harbor and, instead, referred the issue to the army's Gen. Marshall.[81]

While Stark was trying to decide whether or not he should contact Kimmel at Pearl Harbor, out in the North Pacific, Nagumo's Strike Force had finally reached its launch position some 200 miles north of Oahu. The North Pacific was a vacant sea, and his task force was the only one in it—at the right place and right time to launch its attack. Unknown to Nagumo was the fact that Kimmel had been maneuvering over this exact area some 10 days earlier, looking for elements of the IJN fleet. Even if Nagumo had known this, it would not have mattered to him in the least. What was important was that he had not been recalled by the Combined Fleet's Adm. Yamamoto, signifying that the Strike Force's mission was still a go.

This meant that Nagumo's attack would now lead Japan into battle against the United States, determining once and for all who would dominate the Pacific. It was 5:30 a.m. in the North Pacific. Nagumo's scout planes were making their reconnaissance flights to verify weather and flying conditions around Pearl Harbor. The remainder of the planes, armed and loaded with bombs and torpedoes, were waiting to be detached from their flight deck security cables and taxi into their launch positions.

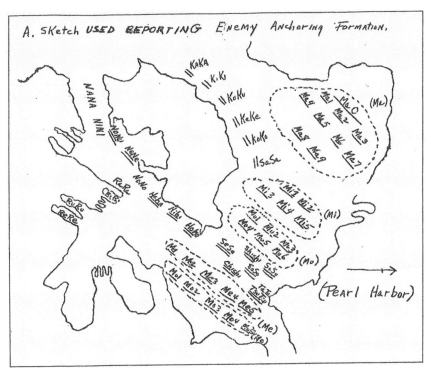

Pearl Harbor U.S. warship target location map. (Sketch recovered from Japanese plane shot down over Pearl Harbor on December 7, 1941. Pacific Fleet Intelligence Bulletin I-42, RG 38, Archives II, National Archives)

Each pilot was equipped with a special Pearl Harbor ship location map, based on data provided by Ens. Takeo Yoshikawa (cover name: Tadashi Morimura) of the Honolulu consulate. There were targets aplenty at Pearl Harbor with the Honolulu consulate now reporting 9 battleships, 7 cruisers, 19 destroyers, and 3 submarine tenders at their moorings or at the docks.[82] Well trained and having practiced their attack routines ad nauseam, the pilots of the 361 shipboard planes now began taking off the pitching and rolling decks into the early morning haze.[83]

For the IJN, it was victory or death; for Adm. Kimmel and his Pacific Fleet, it would be the first battle test of the U.S. Navy in World War II, and they would be found wanting.

Confirming PURPLE messages from Tokyo had arrived by 10:30 a.m. at OP-20-G over at OPNAV headquarters. One (#909) thanked Japan's two ambassadors for all their efforts in representing Tokyo's positions to Washington and the second (#910) ordered the complete destruction of the remaining embassy PURPLE machine and its related codes. This was to be expected, as an earlier November 15 PURPLE intercept had provided detailed instructions as to how to take apart, piece by piece, the electrical plug boards, toothed coding wheel, A-B-C-D gauge, switch, and other key items for the machine's functioning. Each piece would be demolished with a hammer or by pouring acid over it. Rear Adm. Royal Ingersoll, Asst. CNO and close confidant of Adm. Stark, commented, "The fact that we expected it would be war with the United States was indicated in the dispatch which told them to destroy their codes in Washington."[84]

Kramer was busy that December 7 morning. After delivering the declaration of war intercepts to CNO Stark, he headed over to the State Department at 11:00 a.m., where Hull had convened a special meeting. Arriving there, he immediately provided a complete copy of the memorandum and its delivery instructions to the Secretaries of State, War, and Navy. On Knox's copy, there was a note appended that stated that the time of delivery of the Japanese declaration of war at 1:00 p.m. in Washington was sunrise in Honolulu and nearly midnight in Manila. The implication of the timing meant a surprise air raid on Pearl Harbor in just a few hours.[85]

In the meantime, over at Army Headquarters, Marshall's staff and, in particular, Col. Rufus Bratton (Army G-2 intelligence courier and liaison officer to ONI) were desperately trying to contact Marshall to inform him about the part 14 declaration of war message and the 1 p.m. delivery time. Finally at 11:30, Bratton caught up with the general at his office. After reading through the entire 14-part message and its delivery instructions, Marshall was urged by Brig. Gen. Sherman Miles of Army G-2 (intelligence) that all the commands associated with the Pacific, including Hawaii and the Philippines, be informed immediately. Marshall telephoned Stark, who discounted the general's intention to send out another war warning as unnecessary. After Marshall hung up the phone, both Bratton and Miles insisted that some warning be issued.

As a result, Marshall then wrote out what he thought would be an appropriate but disingenuous message and called Stark a second time to inform him of the text. Stark, under continued pressure from McCollum and Wilkinson, not only then finally concurred but also offered Marshall the use of the navy's rapid, secure telephonic communications system (used worldwide to contact far distant commands). Capt. Noyes, director of naval communications, now stopped by and pointedly asked Stark, "Why don't they let us send it? I know I can send it and we'll have a definite confirmation in less than twenty minutes."

One navy system, called the "scrambler telephonic system," fragmented the words of the speaker into garbled sounds and then recomposed them at the receiver's end. Evolving since the 1920s, the technology was now at such a reliable state that even Roosevelt used the system to speak to

Winston Churchill. There were multiple means for contacting Kimmel and Short—not only the scrambler telephone but also the navy and FBI radio systems that could establish communications within 30 minutes.

Despite Stark's offer, Marshall elected to transmit the cable by RCA cable, the *slowest* electronic communications means available to the army: Western Union. Marshall's message stated:

JAPANESE ARE PRESENTING AT ONE PM EASTERN STANDARD TIME TODAY WHAT AMOUNTS TO AN ULTIMATUM ALSO THEY ARE UNDER ORDERS TO DESTROY THEIR CODE MACHINE IMME-DIATELY. JUST WHAT SIGNIFICANCE THE HOUR SET MAY HAVE WE DO NOT KNOW BUT BE ON ALERT ACCORDINGLY. INFORM NAVAL AUTHORITIES OF THIS COMMUNICATION

Marshall and Stark could now rest assured that they had done their "duty" in sending out the alert. Dispatched by Western Union at 12:17 p.m., the message was received by RCA in Honolulu at 7:33 a.m. Nagumo's first assault waves were beginning their attack. With the confusion of the moment due to the Japanese attack, the message did not arrive in the hands of Maj. Gen. Short and Adm. Kimmel until 2:58 p.m., some seven hours too late.

The message represented an astute study in obfuscation, ignoring and essentially negating McCollum's and Wilkinson's accurate appraisals that Pearl Harbor was about to be attacked within just a couple of hours.[86] McCollum summed up the atmosphere at 11 a.m. that Sunday, rationalizing the situation:

The general feeling was that everything had been done and all preparations had been made to minimize any damage that would be resulting. It was realized that with a surprise attack coming . . . that we were going to have to take it on the chin. The problem actually was one for people such as Admiral Kimmel and Admiral Hart to hope that they could minimize the extent of the blow, the extent of the damages. I don't know that Admiral Kimmel ever seemed to clearly understand that feature of it.[87]

Kimmel, under oath at the Navy Court hearing in 1944, testified:

Under my orders [November 28, 1941] to permit Japan to commit the first overt act, technically, I could not fire a shot at a Japanese Fleet until after they had first shot at us, and also, technically, had I sent out patrol planes armed, I would have had to wait until the enemy fired at these patrol planes or committed some other overt act before I could do anything more than protest.[88]

The overt act strategy was being protected all the way to its dramatic finale; Adm. E. Kimmel and his comrade in arms Lt. Gen. Walter Short were about to become the strategy's ultimate scapegoats.

WAR BREAKS OUT IN THE PACIFIC

The first indication of enemy action at Pearl Harbor that morning of December 7 came shortly after 7:00 a.m. when a destroyer at the harbor's entrance radioed that it had contacted a submarine and run a depth charge attack against it. This was the opening shot of World War II in the Pacific, but it went relatively unnoticed.

At 7:53 a.m., Nagumo's first wave of 183 fighters, bombers, and torpedo planes rolled into the attack. A second wave of 170 similar aircraft commenced its attack at 8:40. As it approached Midway Island at 8:22 a.m., Rear Adm. Newton's *Lexington* aircraft carrier received a message from Pearl Harbor: "Air raid on Pearl. This is no drill!" Newton aborted his marine aircraft delivery mission and prepared for outright war with the IJN.

At Pearl Harbor, the losses were catastrophic. Of the eight battleships present, five were sunk, the most famous being the USS *Arizona*, and three others were badly damaged. In total, 18 U.S. ships were sunk or damaged, including three other light cruisers, three destroyers, four smaller vessels, and a seaplane tender. In addition, 2,403 army, navy, marine, and civilian personnel were killed (2,008 navy, 218 army, 109 marines, 68 civilians; the USS *Arizona* lost 1,177 men) and hundreds more were badly injured and hospitalized.[89]

Yes, Kimmel did "take it on the chin"! And he did it, blinded, without key intelligence information and with both of his aircraft carriers, his primary battle fists, away from base as the bombs descended upon his unsuspecting fleet early that tropical sleepy Sunday morning.

In the Philippines, the overt act strategy had repercussions far beyond what anyone could have imagined. Both Adm. Thomas Hart and Gen. Douglas MacArthur were hamstrung by the same orders as Kimmel and Short: not to attack the Japanese unless attacked first. Marshall's War Department directive of late November to MacArthur clearly spelled it out: "If hostilities cannot be avoided the United States desires that Japan commit the first overt act." MacArthur's Army Air Corps would take the initial brunt of the Japanese aerial assaults around Manila. Even though MacArthur had received notice at 5:30 a.m. on December 8 that hostilities had begun with the Japanese attack at Pearl Harbor and he had been directed to execute the Rainbow 5 War Plan through retaliatory air strikes, he dithered and dithered and dithered.

Maj. Gen. Lewis Brereton, MacArthur's Air Corps commander, wanted to carry out a series of preemptive B-17 bomber air strikes at dawn against the Japanese air bases in Formosa. MacArthur refused to see Brereton and ignored Brereton's strident requests to launch his 35 B-17 heavy bombers. In this situation, every minute counted.

Six hours later, with no orders yet from MacArthur, Japan's Eleventh Air Fleet rolled in over central Luzon with 106 bombers and fighters, attacking Iba Field, and another 90 bombers and fighters attacked Clark Field, destroying more than 100 planes on the ground including a major portion of the B-17s. No U.S. Army Air Corps attacks would take place against Formosa, and the American losses sustained would place in jeopardy the defense of the Philippines. The Japanese seized the initiative in the Philippines and would never let go.[90]

Japan's formal invasion of the Philippines began just two days later; Gen. Masaharu Homma's Fourteenth Army initiated its amphibious landings in northern Luzon on December 10. Facing little or no aerial opposition, it took a little less than a month for Homma's forces to capture most of Luzon, and they were about to penetrate MacArthur's vaunted last resort bastion of defense, the Bataan Peninsula.

In Washington, Secretary of State Hull had planned to meet Japan's ambassadors at 1:00 p.m., but the appointment was postponed until 2:00. Just before 2:00, as Secretary of War Stimson sat down to have lunch, Roosevelt called him directly: "Have you heard the news? They have attacked Hawaii. They are now bombing Hawaii." Later on that evening, at an 8:30 full cabinet meeting, the president mentioned that the attack at Pearl Harbor was part of a concerted effort running over several or more weeks, involving Germany, and that he expected the possibility of war with Germany and Italy momentarily.

Harry Hopkins commented on the meeting, "The conference met in not too tense an atmosphere because . . . all of us believed that . . . the enemy was Hitler and that he could never be defeated without force of arms; that sooner or later we were bound to be in the war and that Japan had given us an opportunity."[91]

The next day, December 8, after a mere 40 minutes of debate, the House of Representatives, in a vote of 388 to 1, declared war on Japan. (Jeannette Rankin, D-Montana, was the only no vote, stating for the record that she believed Roosevelt had lured Japan to attack Pearl Harbor.) Roosevelt commented in a cable to Winston Churchill that same day: "Today all of us are in the same boat with you and the people of the Empire and it is a ship which will not and cannot be sunk." He was not wrong and just three days later, Hitler's Nazi Germany declared war on the United States.[92]

The news of the Japanese attack at Pearl Harbor, the U.S. declaration of war against Japan, and, in turn, the declaration of war by Nazi Germany on the United States caused Winston Churchill to celebrate the moment in his post–World War II memoirs:

No American will think it wrong of me if I proclaim that to have the United States at our side was to me the greatest joy. I knew the United States was in the war, up to the neck and in to the death. So we had won after all! England would live; Britain would live; the Commonwealth of nations and the Empire would live. How long the war would last or in what fashion it would end, no man could tell, nor did I at this moment care. We should not be wiped out. Our history would not come to an end. Hitler's fate was sealed Mussolini's fate was sealed. As for the Japanese, they would be ground to powder.[93]

"Ground to powder" ... little did Churchill realize that his prophecy would actually be realized to a large degree with the atomic bombings of Hiroshima and Nagasaki, Japan, a little over three and a half years later, in August 1945.

Harry Hopkins commented on the Japanese attack, "In spite of the disaster at Pearl Harbor ... it completely solidified the American people."[94] Americans were not only solidified against a hostile Japan but now also solidified on behalf of Roosevelt's crusade in Europe to defeat Nazi Germany. Although it would remain a national and international secret throughout World War II, Germany's atomic bomb development project would be quashed.

PEARL HARBOR AFTERMATH

By mid-December 1941, America, the most powerful industrial country in the world, found itself simultaneously at war against two of the world's great military powers, largely brought on by the Japanese attack at Pearl Harbor and Adolf Hitler's gratuitous declaration of war against the United States. Because of Roosevelt's driving imperative to stop the threat of the Nazi atomic bomb development program from coming to fruition, Germany would become America's primary adversary and first priority for defeat in World War II.

With his maniacal zeal, Hitler made three strategic blunders, dooming his Thousand-Year Reich after only 12 years. The first involved not following through his initial intention to invade the British Isles in early 1941. The cancellation of his Operation Sea Lion invasion plan that spring meant that three years later Britain would ultimately become the forward staging area and springboard for the Allies' successful invasion of Western Europe at the Normandy beaches in June 1944.

His second blunder was to invade Russia in June 1941, without having resolved his "British problem." Hitler totally underestimated the modernized military-industrial war capacity of the Soviet Union, as well as Joseph Stalin's ability to equip and mobilize up to 15 million Soviet soldiers to successfully face off against the invading Wehrmacht.

Hitler's third mistake, ill-considered and equally disastrous, was his decision taken during a moment of euphoria over the anticipated fall of

Moscow in early December 1941 to declare war on the United States. Albeit honoring the Tripartite Pact, Hitler not only now exposed himself to the full military-industrial potential of the United States as the "arsenal of democracy" (which just some 25 years earlier had tilted the balance of power against Germany during World War I), but also caused him to fight a war on several fronts instead of just one.[95]

For the Japanese, Adm. Nagumo's successful attack on Pearl Harbor appeared to be a spectacular victory. The Bushido and samurai spirits had salvaged national honor. Japan would now gain strategic military security as well as secure markets and raw material petroleum assets in the Dutch East Indies.[96] The Japanese mouse had lashed out to bite the American cat![97] And it did bite hard. But Pearl Harbor was only one bite in a war spanning the entire Pacific. In early 1941, Yamamoto had cautioned, "If we have war with the United States we will have no hope of winning unless the U.S. Fleet in Hawaiian waters can be destroyed."

None of Kimmel's aircraft carriers had been destroyed and all of the Pearl Harbor naval base's infrastructure, repair facilities, oil storage tanks, machine shops, dry docks, and related installations remained intact. Pearl Harbor would serve as a forward staging base and springboard for most of the U.S Navy's operations against the IJN. Even more importantly, it would serve as a rallying cry for the no longer isolationist American populace: "Remember Pearl Harbor." Roosevelt had achieved his goal.

The U.S. industrial potential that Yamamoto so greatly feared now produced 3 new fleet carriers, 3 light fleet carriers, and 15 escort carriers in 1942; in 1943: 5 fleet carriers, 6 light fleet carriers, and 25 escort carriers; and in 1944: 9 fleet carriers and 35 escort carriers—an incredible production rate. Japan produced less than 10 carriers over the same period of time.

In part, this phenomena can be explained by the fact that the IJN suffered from "battleship mentality," which saw it continue to invest its precious, dwindling materiel resources in iron ore and steel on the construction of the gigantic but obsolete Yamato-class battleships. The U.S. Navy's transpacific offensive maneuvers, based on massed aircraft carrier formations, destroyed the IJN's Combined Fleet.[98]

As for Roosevelt, after having been apprised by Albert Einstein in the fall of 1939 about Nazi Germany's atom bomb development, made his most important command decision of World War II. He took action. He really had only two choices. The first was to engage the American scientific community in an all-out effort to develop the bomb before the Nazis did. The Manhattan Project, which would see the advent of the atomic bomb and its use, ironically, against Japan not Germany. The second was to defeat Hitler in an all-out military effort in Europe. This was far more complex politically to pull off in the face of the antiwar feelings the American people. What turned the trick was the Tripartite Pact of Japan and Nazi Germany in the fall of 1940. Roosevelt was now able to brilliantly exploit this as part of his driving imperative to enter the war against the Nazi dictator.

Roosevelt astutely manipulated economic levers for U.S. control over iron ore and steel, petroleum, and financial investments and assets inside the United States. He demanded that Japan withdraw from China. Coupled to this demand were Washington's July 1941 trade embargos and the freezing of Japanese assets inside the United States. These now meant that Japan would have no choice but to strike out in search of raw material supplies, especially oil, in Southeast Asia's Dutch East Indies. To reach this end, Tokyo would have to deal not only with the American military bases in the Philippines but also those as far away as Hawaii. And it was there that the primary transoceanic naval threat to its contemplated offensive operations was located: Kimmel's U.S. Pacific Fleet.

Roosevelt was able to adroitly exploit in terms of his overt act strategy. Tokyo's recall of its entire merchant marine fleet was the first obvious step in Japan alleviating its precarious economic situation. This step and the recognition by Tokyo that only military force could decide Japan's fate became the fundamental driving issue over who was to actually dominate the Pacific. Would it be Japan or the United States?

During the fall of 1941, despite the sinking of a U.S. Navy destroyer by one of Hitler's U-boats, the American people still wanted to stay out of "Europe's war." This did not bode well for Roosevelt's driving imperative to enter the war against Germany. It was not so much creating an overt act, but more importantly it was about *who perpetrated* the act. Americans' xenophobic attitudes against the Japanese would be the key factor.

Beginning in October 1941, Tokyo was taking an unusual interest in the navy's Pearl Harbor–based fleet. Whether an overt act took place in Hawaii or in the Philippines or both was a moot point, as long as it took place. It was important that the senior commanders in Washington and in the Pacific at Honolulu and Manila were keenly aware that the president desired that Japan fire the first opening shot. Somebody, somewhere, would have to be sacrificed.

Adm. Kimmel and his U.S. Pacific Fleet were blacked out, beginning in late summer 1941, from receiving the key political-military intelligence information that would enable them to respond aggressively to a Japanese move coming in from the North Pacific. On December 7, 1941, Japan took the bait, first in Hawaii, and a few hours later, in the Philippines. But it was Pearl Harbor that brought the American people into the war.

Hitler's declaration of war against the United States in support of Japan's war efforts some four days later sealed Nazi Germany's fate. Roosevelt's foreign policy effort to destroy the Nazi atom bomb threat to America's national security and the nation's continued survival as a democracy was splendidly successful.

8

An Alternative Course of Action

Kimmel's Preemptive Ambush in the North Pacific

Roosevelt's overt act strategy worked amazingly well. Yet, did the devastation at Pearl Harbor have to happen? There was enough military and political intelligence available in Washington to warrant the formal dispatch of a reinforced U.S. Pacific Fleet into the near North Pacific to directly confront the Imperial Japanese Navy's own Strike Force in a surprise, decisive battle, as the FAF arrived into the vicinity of the Prokofiev Seamount to launch its attack on Pearl Harbor.

Intelligence intercepts of Tokyo's intentions to attack Pearl Harbor had been translated. The U.S. Pacific Fleet at the Pearl Harbor naval base was fully prepared, with battleships and aircraft carriers, to enable Adm. Husband E. Kimmel to engage the Japanese on the high seas of the North Pacific. A preemptive strike would have avoided the tragedy that took place at Pearl Harbor, with the costly defeat of the Pacific Fleet in its home port. This course of action would have better protected the American interests in the Pacific, *as well as providing an overt act incident with Japan*, which would have still propelled the United States into the war in Europe against Nazi Germany—Roosevelt's driving imperative. The high-priority 5-Num keys, dispatched from Washington two weeks before the attack on Pearl Harbor, had been sent by boat, the slowest possible transport means between California and Hawaii![1] They finally arrived in Honolulu after the attack.

FIGHTING OUTNUMBERED AND WINNING I: NIMITZ AT MIDWAY

The capabilities of Rochefort's superb HYPO team had been squandered, but now all this would change. On December 10, three days after the bombing of Pearl Harbor, Rochefort was directed by Safford's OP-20-G at the Navy Department to begin an all-out concentrated effort to decipher the 5-Number, Code Book D, IJN fleet operations code (later renamed JN-25).[2] HYPO would now become the navy's *lead* code-breaking team in this effort, all the while supported by Station CAST and OP-20-GY.

Rochefort and his HYPO team of radio intelligence code breakers and experts, including Thomas Dyer, Joseph Finnegan, Jasper Holmes, Alva B. Lasswell, and Wesley A. "Ham" Wright were the core of the code-breaking effort. Thomas Huckins, John Williams, and Jack Holtwick maintained their focus on traffic analysis and RDF plotting or ran the IBM machines.[3] On December 9, Rochefort's CIS, written two days after the attack on Pearl Harbor, provided a complete order of battle for the principal elements of the IJN's FAF (Striking Force): Carrier Division 1: *Akagi* (Flagship) and *Kaga*; Carrier Division 2: *Hiryu* and *Soryu*; and Carrier Division 4 ([*sic*]: 5): *Shokaku* and *Zuikaku*.[4]

HYPO's new focus would now combine its own talent with the now up-to-the-minute results of the laborious efforts of Ens. Prescott Currier's OP-20-GY cryptographers, including Agnes Driscoll, and Station CAST's own team led by Lt. John Lietwiler. Station CAST at Corregidor had broken into the new 5-Number Code on December 1, as well as the new additive books, tables, and related indicators that were issued by the IJN three days later.

On December 16, Safford directed Station CAST (Corregidor) to send its 5-Number Code subtractor and additive recoveries to HYPO via the navy's secure COPEK radio communications channel as part of the now highly focused joint effort to break down the IJN fleet's recently modified operational cryptographic system. OPNAV transferred six officers and 14 enlisted men experienced in decrypting the IJN fleet operations code to HYPO as reinforcements.[5]

This was to be an all-out effort with HYPO now finally becoming a full-fledged U.S. Navy intelligence processing center with a critical mission.

The meshing of HYPO's cryptanalysis brain power with that of OP-20-GY and Station CAST's would now produce spectacular results. By January 17, CAST had circulated, via COPEK channels, some 1,700 new additives, 950 new code group values, and 650 additional indicators. Rochefort, for the first time at HYPO, could now perform his most important intelligence task: tell the CINC Pacific Fleet today what the Japanese were planning to do tomorrow.[6]

On December 16 Adm. Kimmel was relieved of his duties as CINCPAC, retiring from the navy in early 1942. On December 17 Kimmel was replaced by Adm. Chester A. Nimitz, hand-picked by Roosevelt himself (skipping over the rank of vice admiral to become a full admiral), as the new commander-in-chief U.S. Pacific Fleet (CINCPACFLT, Pearl Harbor). On December 17 Lt. Gen. Short was also relieved of his command and ordered back to Washington. He retired from the army on February 28, 1942.

In early February 1942, with the Imperial Japanese Army's rapid advance through Luzon into the Bataan peninsula of the Philippines, OP-20-G made the decision to evacuate CAST's entire compliment of 74 radio intelligence personnel from Corregidor to Melbourne, Australia. They were transported by submarine. This took place in several increments on February 4, March 16, and April 8. Rudolf Fabian, one of the CAST leaders, was part of the first group, carrying out boxes of key equipment including RIP-5 typewriters, RDF gear, and the precious PURPLE machine as well as copies of all the keys and solutions derived from their 5-Number code-breaking efforts. It was fortunate that OP-20-G made its decision when it did. On April 9, some 78,000 American and Filipino troops in Bataan surrendered to the invading Japanese. On May 7, Corregidor's 10,000-man garrison also surrendered.[7]

During this time, HYPO was redesignated Fleet Radio Unit Pacific (FRUPAC). Top priority was given to identifying and tracking the IJN's carriers that were then playing hob with the Royal Dutch Navy and the American Asiatic Fleet in the Dutch East Indies and the British Royal Navy's Eastern Fleet off the coast of Ceylon in the Indian Ocean. Rochefort's team in Hawaii recovered and stripped additives from intercepted radio signals to the degree that enough plaintext was uncovered to reveal the basics of the IJN's operational messages.

On or about March 10, decoded IJN radio messages indicated that a Japanese Kawanishi flying boat was going to conduct a reconnaissance mission to analyze the American defenses at Midway Island. The plane was intercepted and shot down, but this gave Nimitz an indication of the IJN's interest in Midway. Other 5-Number decodes enabled FRUPAC to predict that the IJN would strike through the Coral Sea with the intention of invading and capturing Port Moresby on the south coast of New Guinea in early May. The accuracy of these predictions went a long way toward cementing Rochefort's credibility with Nimitz.

An additional helping hand was the January 20 sinking of the IJN submarine I-124 by an American naval force off Port Darwin, Australia, in only 40 feet of clear water. Navy divers recovered the key IJN operational code books, which facilitated immensely Rochefort's work on solving Code Book D's 5-Number groups.[8]

By early April, the Japanese were consolidating their new Greater East Asia Co-Prosperity Sphere. After the fall of Singapore, the Dutch East Indies, and the Philippines, Japan was now in the process of establishing a defensive perimeter extending out from the Kuril Islands southeastward through Guam, Wake, the Gilbert and Marshall Islands, westward along New Guinea's northern coast, and then onward through Borneo, Java, and Sumatra and up through the Malay Peninsula, which placed Tokyo's imperial frontier at the Indian border. Overstretched it was, but it was there.

As Adm. Yamamoto understood the situation, these victories needed to be consolidated. A three-phase plan was developed:

Phase 1: The capture of Port Moresby on the New Guinea side of the Coral Sea, and Tulagi, the capital of the Solomon Islands, further out to the east.

Phase 2: The capture of Midway to bring on an engagement and the annihilation of Adm. Nimitz's Pacific Fleet aircraft carriers.

Phase 3: The seizure of the New Caledonia, Fiji, and Samoa Islands to cut off American air and sea lines of communications to Australia.[9]

The plan to eliminate the American "dagger pointed at the heart of Japan," which the U.S. Pearl Harbor–based aircraft carriers represented, appeared reasonable.[10] Phase 2's destruction of the aircraft carriers could enable the seizing of the Pearl Harbor base, with its valuable dry docks, maintenance shops, and oil storage facilities. Pearl Harbor could serve as a key forward-positioned outpost to secure the North Pacific approaches to Japan.[11] FRUPAC was about to play as the proverbial fly in the IJN's ointment.

Rochefort's efforts to break the 5-Number Code (later renamed JN-25 by ONI) were producing significant results through a combination of decodes and traffic analysis. On April 1, he noted in his daily CIS report that the IJN was reorganizing. Three days later, there were indications of IJN operations against the Solomons, New Britain, and Port Moresby.

For the next week or so, the FAF, consisting of the *Akagi, Soryu, Hiryu, Shokaku,* and *Zuikaku* aircraft carriers, was still operating in the Indian Ocean. But things began to change significantly on April 15, when Rochefort estimated that the IJN would initiate operations beginning on April 21 against Port Moresby and Tulagi.[12]

By this time the situation in the Pacific looked bleak, and Roosevelt took action to give the Americans a psychological boost. On April 18, Col. Jimmy Doolittle and his flight of 16 B-25 Army Air Corps bombers, launched from the newly commissioned aircraft carrier *Hornet*, flew in over the IJN's naval base at Tokyo Bay, dropping bombs on Tokyo. While the damage caused was relatively minimal, the psychological impact for both the Americans and the Japanese was enormous. The Japanese were in a state of shock.

The attack pointedly gave notice to Japan that it was now vulnerable to aerial attack. How had this happened? It appeared logical to the IJN Naval General Staff that the planes had been launched from the aircraft carriers based at Pearl Harbor. The IJN initiated a frantic weeklong search for the navy's carriers out to the east of Tokyo. FRUPAC noted that the FAF was being recalled from the Indian Ocean. The destruction of the American carriers would now become the IJN's most important operational priority.[13]

FRUPAC noted in its April 26 CIS report that a major change in the radio call signs had taken place, indicating that operations were about to be initiated from Japan's Rabaul Naval Base to points east and south. While the impending offensive now appeared aimed at the Solomon and Gilbert Islands, Rochefort's April 30 report designated Port Moresby as the target. Reports of May 3 and 4 placed the FAF's former Carrier Division Five (*Zuikaku* and *Shokaku*) along with the *Shoho* (misidentified in the CIS as "*Ryukaku*") as now operating in the vicinity of Rabaul in support of the offensive aimed toward points south.[14]

On May 7, Rochefort's CIS report advanced the possibility of IJN raids against Oahu, Hawaii, and even Alaska. This was supported by a May 8 report that noted that a conference of key IJN commanders was to take place in the vicinity of Kagoshima in the "near future." This, and the fact that there were sufficient Japanese naval forces available to support strike operations in the North Pacific as well as in the South, was disturbing.[15]

While Rochefort was making his reports to Nimitz, the Battle of the Coral Sea was taking place on May 7–8, pitting several IJN carriers against Vice Adm. Fletcher's carriers. The *Lexington* was sunk, and the *Yorktown* needed extensive repairs. The IJN's *Shoho* was sunk, and the *Zuikaku* and *Shokaku* were damaged enough to take them out of action for some months. The battle ended in a draw.

FRUPAC noted in its May 9 CIS report that the intended occupation of Port Moresby had been postponed indefinitely and that several IJN ships had been withdrawn from the region. Port Moresby had been saved. Three days later, it was reported that the *Akagi, Kaga, Soryu*, and *Hiryu* were located in the Yokosuka-Sasebo area. Something big was in the offing.[16]

Yamamoto's new strategy was to seize the inadequately protected Midway Island, the western outpost of the Hawaiian Island defenses, 1,000 miles away from Oahu, and use it as bait to draw what was left of the Pacific Fleet's aircraft carriers out from Pearl Harbor, luring them into a trap where they would be overwhelmed by a superior IJN force of up to eight aircraft carriers. But with the *Zuikaku* and the *Shokaku* out of commission, Yamamoto was reduced to six carriers.

To split the American forces as they attempted to reinforce Midway, an attack would be made on the Aleutian Islands in the North Pacific, using two of the IJN's smallest carriers.[17] Yamamoto would pit four of Vice Adm. Nagumo's original FAF Pearl Harbor Strike Force carriers, the *Akagi*, *Kaga*, *Hiryu*, and *Soryu*, along with some battleships, cruisers, destroyers, and submarines, against the U.S. Navy's two surviving carriers.

Yamamoto recalled all his carriers from the distant parts of the Japan's newly founded empire. Even the Battle for the Coral Sea and the conquest of Port Moresby were curtailed to give top priority to the upcoming Battle of Midway. Yamamoto knew only the destruction of the U.S. Pacific Fleet's carriers would give Japan a chance to win the war.[18] What Yamamoto did not know was that Rochefort's FRUPAC team at HYPO was ferreting out the essentials of his strategy.

On May 14, for the first time, a pending operation known to FRUPAC as the KING campaign was identified. While there were various components to the campaign, the occupation of Midway appeared to be a primary one. The IJN's Second Fleet was assembling in the vicinity of Saipan (north of Guam and out to the southwest of Midway). Aircraft carriers, battleships, cruisers, and submarines were forming up. A day later, on May 15, Rochefort's CIS report stated: "There can no longer be any doubt that the enemy is preparing for an offensive against U.S. territory. It is known that an attempt will be made to occupy Midway and points in the Aleutians. What action will be taken against the Hawaiian Islands is as yet unknown." The report continued, "the general move will start from Japan somewhere around 20 May."[19]

Rochefort's FRUPAC reported on May 18 that the two IJN operations were going to take place simultaneously. One, an attack from the Kurils directly into the Aleutians, would involve a complete carrier division (two carriers). The other one would involve the Second Fleet, operating to the south and eastward of Tokyo with a focus on the Hawaiian area.[20] The former FAF commander, Vice Adm. Nagumo, was now back on the *Akagi*, in charge of Carrier Divisions 1 and 2. The same report estimated that the operations most probably would try to target and occupy Dutch Harbor and Midway.[21]

The Aleutian-bound force was expected to leave Japan on May 25 or 26; and the Midway-bound force would leave Saipan some days later. That action could take place as early as June 1. By May 27, it was noted that the carriers had not been heard from and were now assumed to be operating under radio listening silence. The May 28 CIS report predicted that the initial attack on Midway would be by carrier-based aircraft on June 3 or 4 (local time), with an actual occupation planned for the night of June 5.[22] Most important for Nimitz was the CIS report of May 31: "The Midway striking force will include *at least* the following major units: Car Divs ONE and TWO (4CV [4 carriers])."[23]

Nimitz, although aware of the Japanese interest in Midway, had committed the *Lexington* and *Yorktown* to do battle in the Coral Sea in order to blunt the Japanese advance toward the South Pacific. The *Hornet* and *Enterprise* were also initially directed as reinforcements to engage in the Coral Sea operations. On May 17, an abrupt change of mission took place: they were all called back to their Pearl Harbor base. What had happened between May 14 and 16 to cause Nimitz to change his mind? Not only did Nimitz have Layton's intelligence briefings, based on Rochefort's FRUPAC-derived signal intelligence CIS reports, but Rochefort and his astute colleague, Jasper Holmes, had concocted a clever ruse, which caused the Japanese to inadvertently verify Midway as their primary target for invasion in the North Pacific.

The Japanese had been using a series of two- and three-letter code words for precise communications identification of geographic locations of operational interest, such as MO for Port Moresby in New Guinea during the Coral Sea campaign, and AF, probably signifying Midway Island. Now, the Midway Naval Base was directed via a coded navy radio transmission to send a plaintext language message to the Commandant, 14th Naval District in Hawaii, stating that the Midway distillation plant had broken and that fresh water was urgently needed, because there was only a two-week supply left. The 14th Naval District was to reply that water barges under tow would be dispatched as soon as possible. As expected, Japanese radio intercept stations supporting Yamamoto's Midway operation monitored the plaintext "water message" and duly reported it in their own daily signals intercept reports: "AF is short of water."[24] Nimitz needed no more proof than that: Midway was the IJN's primary invasion target!

With advance knowledge in late May that the IJN's Midway Strike Force would include four carriers, Nimitz organized his carriers into two task forces that would operate as a combined force under the command of Rear Adm. Frank J. Fletcher. Fletcher would command Task Force (TF) 17, which included the carrier *Yorktown* and two fast cruisers. Rear Adm. Raymond A. Spruance would command Task Force (TF) 16, which included the carriers *Enterprise* and *Hornet*, as well as four cruisers. In a June 2 updating CIS report, Rochefort laid out the general order of battle for Yamamoto's IJN commands:

CINC Combined Fleet in supreme command

CINC Second Fleet in command of invasion forces in Midway area

CINC First Air Fleet in command of striking forces (Midway)

CINC Fifth Fleet in command of striking and invasion forces North

CINC Eleventh Air Fleet shore-based air striking forces (both areas)

CINC Submarine Force in charge of observation

The initial attack on Midway was expected to take place the next day, June 3.[25] Due to FRUPAC's radio intelligence analysis, Nimitz knew the composition of his targets, the date their operations would commence, their debarkation points, and their approximate rendezvous areas. He also knew about the plan to station a submarine cordon to interdict U.S. Navy forces moving directly between Hawaii and Midway (1,135 nautical miles to the west of Pearl Harbor) and a planned seaplane reconnaissance of Oahu itself.[26]

By June 3, Japanese air attacks had taken place on Dutch Harbor, a possible attempt to divert U.S. Navy interests to the Aleutian Islands, well to the north of Midway. Over the next 24 hours, both Midway and FRUPAC intercept stations went on "double search watches." Rochefort, at his Mid-Pacific radio intercept and RDF network, was taking no chances. But it was Lt. Taylor, formerly of CAST and now in Melbourne, Australia, who made the code recovery that revealed June 4 as the date the Battle of Midway would begin.[27]

Assuming that the IJN would approach Midway from the northwest, much as it had done for its attack on Pearl Harbor, Nimitz ordered Fletcher to rendezvous his carriers at Point Luck, a position some 350 miles northeast of Midway Island between 0400 and 0800 hours on June 4. The Nimitz-Fletcher plan was to engage the IJN's four carriers from an unexpected direction, flying into the attack from the northeast, with Fletcher's 112 Douglas SBD Dauntless dive-bombers and 42 TBD Devastator torpedo bombers leading the way.[28] The plan was an *identical copy* of Adm. Kimmel's 2M1 surprise attack strategy for ambushing the IJN in the North Pacific in late November 1941.

Fletcher did not initially realize it at the time, but he had closed to a position just 200 miles from Nagumo's four carriers. Shortly after sunrise, at about 0600 hours on June 4, a Catalina long-range PBY flying boat conducting a reconnaissance mission out to the north of Midway called in a position report on two of Nagumo's carriers. A few minutes later, Fletcher ordered Spruance to move into the attack against the Japanese admiral's flank. Here was a great opportunity to surprise the Japanese. Spruance turned his TF 16 into an intercepting course, to close the distance on the unsuspecting IJN carriers.

By 0630 hours, Nagumo's dive-bombers and fighters, from all four of his carriers, were carrying out their own aerial attacks on Midway Island in

The Douglas SBD Dauntless dive-bomber was the U.S. Navy's premier ship killer in World War II, sinking three Japanese navy aircraft carriers in six minutes at the Battle of Midway, June 4, 1942. All three carriers took part in the Pearl Harbor attack. (U.S. Navy)

preparation for the amphibious invasion.[29] At 0700 hours, the *Hornet* was ordered to conduct a torpedo bomber attack against the Japanese carriers. All the *Hornet*'s Torpedo 8 planes were shot down by IJN antiaircraft fire. At 0917, Nagumo, now aware that the American carriers were nearby, changed course to avoid further attacks. This maneuver caused the *Hornet* to lose contact with the Japanese carriers, which took it out of action for the rest of the battle. Fletcher and Spruance now directed their dive-bombers from the *Yorktown* and *Enterprise* into the fray.

At about 0955, *Yorktown*'s and *Enterprise*'s SBD Dauntless dive-bombers spotted part of the *Akagi*'s battle group. The lethal Douglas SBD Dauntless dive-bombers carried an array of bombs. *Enterprise* sent out 15 planes, each carrying a single 1,000-pound bomb, six planes each carrying a 500-pound bomb, and a dozen planes each carrying not only a 500-pound bomb but also two 100-pound bombs. The *Yorktown*'s SBD aerial attack was somewhat smaller in numbers but equally well armed.

Five minutes later, in the distance, the *Akagi*, *Kaga*, and finally the *Soryu* were sighted. While most of the *Enterprise*'s SBDs concentrated on the

Kaga, a few peeled off from the formation to carry out a strike on the *Akagi*. The *Yorktown*'s formation of dive-bombers focused on *Soryu*. At approximately 1020 hours, the SBDs, having gained their attack positions of about 20,000 feet above the IJN carriers, rolled into their dives, coming in at a 70-degree angle. Launched from 1,500 to 2,000 feet above the Japanese carriers, the bombs came hurtling down. Since the IJN's carriers did not have radar to provide last-minute early warning, the surprise was complete.[30]

The battle was intense. The first wave of SBDs missed the *Kaga* completely, but the ensuing waves made four hits. A 500-pound bomb with a split-second delay fuse struck the *Kaga* in the middle of the planes parked aft and penetrated its wooden deck. At five-second intervals, four 500-pound and three 1,000-pound bombs also struck home. The *Kaga* was engulfed in flames. A similar fate awaited the *Akagi*. It suffered a catastrophic hit from a 1,000-pound bomb that landed center square on its flight deck, penetrating the hangar deck immediately below. Men on that deck had been in the process of loading planes with bombs, torpedoes, and fuel. Raging fires broke out, and the ensuing secondary explosions reduced Nagumo's flag ship to a burning hulk.

While the *Enterprise* was carrying out its attacks, 17 SBDs from the *Yorktown* went to work on the *Soryu*, attacking from several directions. Several 1,000-pound bombs scored direct hits, one on the *Soryu*'s forward elevator, another amidships, and a third directly into the engine room aft, setting the carrier ablaze. *Soryu* met the same fate as the other IJN carriers.

In just *five to six minutes*, from roughly 1020 to 1026 hours on the morning of June 4, three of the IJN's most important fleet aircraft carriers were destroyed. While impressive, these death blows were not the end of the battle.[31] Nagumo ordered the *Hiryu* to find and destroy the U.S. carriers. The *Hiryu* tracked some of the *Enterprise* and *Yorktown* planes back to their carriers.

Results came in around noon time: the *Hiryu*'s dive and torpedo bombers launched strikes against Fletcher's *Yorktown* as it was trying to recover its planes from its battle with the *Soryu*. Slowed by a number of bomb hits, the *Yorktown* could not maneuver fast enough to dodge a follow-on aerial torpedo attack. Struck by a number of bombs from air strikes above and two air-launched torpedoes that hit her below the water line, the *Yorktown* began to list. It was the beginning of the end. Surviving crews and planes were transferred over to the *Enterprise*. Spruance, undaunted, launched an attack on the *Hiryu* in the late afternoon, coming out of the east at 1600 hours. A combination of 11 SBDs from the *Enterprise*, plus 14 transferred from the *Yorktown*, found their target. The *Hiryu* took four SBD dive-bomber hits, setting it on fire. It, too, was now mortally wounded.[32] By the end of the day on June 5, all four of Nagumo's First Air Fleet carriers, all part of the attack on Pearl Harbor, were now at the bottom of the Pacific. With their naval power broken, Yamamoto and Nagumo now beat a hasty retreat back to Japan's home waters.

The Battle of Midway is one of the most decisive naval defeats in history. Japan never recovered from the loss of not only four of its most important aircraft carriers but also several hundred planes and highly trained pilots who, even if they were in the air during the battles, had no place to land except in the vast open stretches of the North Pacific. Jasper Holmes commented on the Midway battles shortly after the end of World War II: "Without radio intelligence it would have been impossible to have achieved the concentration of force and tactical surprise that made the victory possible."[33]

Nimitz's outnumbered 49 warships were able to ambush and defeat Yamamoto's much larger force, consisting of 177 ships. The combination of accurate and timely intelligence, in conjunction with well-trained and well-led U.S. Navy aviators and their massed aircraft carriers under the command of aggressive and highly capable commanders, enabled a smaller U.S. Navy force to defeat an Imperial Japanese Navy force twice its size. In this stunning defeat, the carriers *Enterprise* and *Yorktown* alone and their planes were the key battle implements that determined the outcome of the Battle of Midway.

The Battle of Midway should never have taken place on June 4, 1942. It should have taken place six months earlier, on or around December 7, 1941, along the North Pacific approaches into Pearl Harbor. It was Kimmel's plan; he should have been allowed to use it to defend his men and his ships. Kimmel should not have been set up to "take it on the chin."

FIGHTING OUTNUMBERED AND WINNING II: KIMMEL AT PEARL HARBOR—PLAN 2M1

The feasibility of Adm. Kimmel conducting a successful ambush of the IJN's First Air Fleet six-carrier Strike Force along the northern approaches into Pearl Harbor, during the first week of December 1941, would have to be predicated on several factors coming together in a synergistic manner: an aggressive, preemptive military strike policy on the part of the Roosevelt administration to defend America's national interest in the North Pacific, full exploitation and sharing with operational fleet commanders the administration's naval and political intelligence assets then available in Washington, DC; Station CAST in the Philippines; and Station HYPO in Hawaii; and, finally, the timely massing of all possible aircraft carrier assets in support of Adm. Kimmel's proactive 2M1 battle plan for defending the Pearl Harbor naval base at Oahu, Hawaii, against raiding IJN aircraft carriers.

The definitive first alert to the possibility of a Japanese attack on Pearl Harbor came from the American ambassador to Japan, Joseph Grew. In his January 27, 1941, cable to the State Department, shown to Roosevelt and Navy CNO Adm. Harold Stark, Grew stated he had received a multi-sourced report indicating that in the event of "trouble breaking out between the United States and Japan, the Japanese intend to make a surprise attack against Pearl Harbor with all of their strength and employing all of their equipment."[34]

Released on May 26, 1941, by the Office of the Chief of Naval Operations, Rainbow 5 (WPL-46) took into consideration the earlier United States–British Staff Conversations (ABC-1) in regard to anticipated Japanese moves in the South Pacific, as well as other parts of the Pacific. The U.S. Navy's general tasks for the Pacific Fleet included:

(Item: 2202.a.2) "Raid Axis forces and sea communications in the Pacific and Far East areas."

(Item: 2202.a.4) "Prevent the extension in the Western Hemisphere of ... Asiatic military power, and support the defense of the territory of the Associated Powers [British and Dutch] in the Far East area." More specifically, the Pacific Fleet (Adm. Kimmel in command) was to carry out this task.

(Item: 3212.g) "Protect the sea communications ... by destroying enemy raiding Forces," a most important task for Kimmel to carry out.

(Item: 3212.h) "Prevent the extension of enemy military power into the Western Hemisphere by destroying hostile expeditions. ..." A further delineation (Paragraph 9a) stated: "The Hawaiian coastal frontier consists of Oahu, and all of the land and sea area required for the defense of Oahu. The coastal zone extends to a distance of 500 miles from all the Hawaiian Islands."[35]

Rear Adm. Richmond K. Turner, the war plans officer for the U.S. Navy, stated at a Pearl Harbor inquiry: "If the Japanese fleet came within 500 miles of Hawaii ... we were justified in calling that an overt act and attack them." Adm. Claude C. Bloch, the commandant, 14th Naval District (Hawaii), who was also designated the commander, Hawaiian naval coastal frontier, and in charge of the naval local defense forces for Oahu, interpreted War Plan 46 as having the Pacific Fleet available to protect U.S. interests in the area east of the 180 meridian, which would include Midway Island at its westernmost extension and also be in a position from which raiding operations could be projected.[36] As far as the navy was concerned, it now had an appropriate war plan for Kimmel's Pacific Fleet.

Once the Dutch refused to grant Tokyo oil concessions in the Nether-lands East Indies at the end of July 1941, the Japanese military leadership had no option but to go to war. It was *the* great turning point in Japanese-American relations.[37] In terms of Pearl Harbor and its Pacific Fleet Naval Base, there were key indicators taking place from the beginning of January 1941, even before Ambassador Grew passed on his report about the possi-bility of a Japanese surprise attack on Pearl Harbor. A coded (J-17 Tsu code) cable, dated January 6, 1941, from Honolulu to Tokyo, intercepted in San Francisco, was decoded by Naval Intelligence in Washington on Janu-ary 10. The Japanese operative, Okuda, reported in detail about Pearl Harbor: 5 battleships, 5 heavy cruisers, 9 light cruisers, 37 destroyers, 5 destroyer tenders, and 2 heavy cruisers in dry dock. He thought that one battleship or a cruiser was outside of the harbor.[38]

With the decoded intelligence messages from Tadashi Morimura in Hawaii to his Tokyo office, sent throughout most of 1941, including coded target grid maps of U.S. Navy ships at Pearl Harbor, Roosevelt, Knox, Stark, and Turner knew that Pearl Harbor was being set up as a primary IJN target.[39]

Here was the opportunity for Washington to turn Pearl Harbor into a baited trap. What Roosevelt was thinking was expressed in a September 23 letter to Kimmel from Stark: "At the present time the President has issued shooting orders only for the Atlantic and the Southeast Pacific sub-area." In the letter, Stark quoted Article 723 from the U.S. Navy's Regulations:

> The right of self-preservation, however, is a right. . . . In no case shall force be exercised in time of peace otherwise than as an application of the right of self-preservation as above defined. It must be used only as a last resort.[40]

A defensive preemptive attack policy served as the legal basis for Kim-mel's reconnaissance in force, Exercise 191, in late November 1941 in the North Pacific. The exercise was aborted. The office of the CNO and pri-mary naval staff officers in Washington, DC, "were all in agreement that the principal naval effort should be made in the Pacific."[41]

The Pacific Fleet and the other elements in the navy in the latter part of 1941 were fully mobilized for wartime operations. This is an important point, since mobilization has always been recognized as one of the key pre-liminary steps to be taken, prior to going to war. Kimmel usually had at least one and sometimes two of his fleet task forces undergoing intensive training in the waters extending out from Pearl Harbor to the east and south.[42] All he needed was a presidential decision to preemptively defend Pearl Harbor.

In conjunction with the Pearl Harbor ship location reports being sent by the Japanese consulate in Honolulu to Tokyo, there were decision points that could have spurred strategic and operational planning for an effective preemptive defense of Pearl Harbor by the Roosevelt administration. On October 15, the Japanese plans for the conquest of Southeastern Asia were confirmed by ONI. By October 28, the Japanese consuls were directing the evacuation of Japanese nationals from the Dutch East Indies, Malaya, the Philippines, Hawaii, America, and Europe. During the first week of November, it was reported that the internal situation inside Japan had become desperate, due to the impact of the American embargos.[43] The Japanese senior political-military leadership was beginning to crack under the pressure. As ONI's Art McCollum and U.S. Ambassador Joseph Grew had pointed out, national honor was at stake.

If any of the above decision points had been acted upon by Roosevelt and Stark, Kimmel would have had at his command at least four and possibly five aircraft carriers to meet and defeat any IJN thrust toward Pearl Harbor. The *Enterprise* and *Lexington* at Pearl Harbor, the *Saratoga* based at San Diego, the *Yorktown* based at Norfolk, and the *Wasp* based at Guantanamo Bay, Cuba, could have easily been dispatched to a secret rendezvous position in the North Pacific.

The carriers could have joined Kimmel's aircraft carrier task forces, giving the admiral up to five attack carriers. The *Yorktown* and *Wasp* would have had to go through the Panama Canal at night and make the 4,600-mile voyage northwestward to their designated secret rendezvous point; this would have taken about a month. Had Stark taken these actions, they would have fit in well and supported what Gen. Marshall told a press conference at the War Department Building in Washington on November 15, 1941: "We are preparing an offensive war against Japan." Marshall went on to say: "For two months we have been moving troops and planes into the Philippines, and the movements are continuing."[44]

If Adm. Hart and Gen. MacArthur in the Philippines were worth reinforcing, why not Adm. Kimmel at Pearl Harbor? The threat to Pearl Harbor could only come from the IJN's carriers. Defeating the threat meant destroying IJN carriers, as OPNAV in Washington knew.[45]

Planning for a preemptive ambush defense of Pearl Harbor made sense and should have begun in October 1941. While opinion polls taken in October indicated that 43 percent of Americans believed that no action should be taken against Japan unless Japan attacked American territories, 34 percent believed that Japan had "already gone far enough."[46] Long-smoldering anti-Japanese hostility existed; there was little public or congressional opposition to a declaration of war against Japan in the event of actual conflict.[47]

Since U.S. Naval Intelligence played such a key role in the success of the Battle of Midway, it is important to consider what might have been, or better stated, what *should* have been the intelligence support Kimmel would have needed to make a preemptive strike against Nagumo's FAF Strike Force. Kimmel should have been provided a PURPLE Code machine to enable him, as the *primary* U.S. Navy Fleet commander in the Pacific, to keep track of Tokyo's diplomatic message traffic. Cdr. Rochefort's brilliant, hand-picked group of cryptologists should have been given top priority in July 1941 to break the IJN's operational code. Rochefort's HYPO would have read the early November 1941 Japanese Honolulu consulates' grid-targeting reports, disclosing Japan's intention to attack Pearl Harbor.

Kimmel should have been allowed to conduct a preemptive defense of Pearl Harbor. He, Rochefort, and Layton (his intelligence officers), should have been apprised by the 14th Naval District (Honolulu) and the 12th Naval District (San Francisco) of the SS *Lurline*'s and the Globe and Press Wireless station's RDF tracking reports of IJN movements in the North Pacific to points north of Pearl Harbor during the first few days of December 1941.

Finally, McCollum should have been allowed to contact Lt. Cdr. Edwin Layton, the Pacific Fleet's intelligence officer at Pearl Harbor. This would have enabled both Layton and Kimmel to have a key Washington, DC, naval intelligence officer's perspective as to what was happening in the Pacific.

The logical form of attack on an incoming IJN Strike Force would have been a surprise ambush, using Pearl Harbor as bait. Kimmel's 2M1 attack strategy would have done just that. Kimmel envisioned a circling maneuver by his carriers around and somewhat behind the IJN Strike Force headed south toward Oahu. Due to the flying range of the Japanese planes, Kimmel and his Pacific Fleet staff knew that any IJN carrier strike coming from the north would have to be launched within about 230 miles of its Pearl Harbor target. This narrowed the focus of the attack zone. As long as Kimmel's forces were to the east or the northeast of the IJN carriers, the chances of achieving surprise were assured. By attacking at a favorable time and place, and in an unexpected manner, the great sea battle that both sides had anticipated would have taken place under conditions of maximum advantage for Kimmel.

Ordering all planes into the air at daylight on a continuing basis on the chance that they just might intercept an incoming aerial attack would undoubtedly have alarmed the civilian population in Honolulu.[48] In addition, the battleships would have had to remain in their normal anchorages. The seemingly unprepared bait was supremely important, since Nagumo, on finding out that the U.S. Fleet's battleships had fully deployed from Pearl Harbor, would most likely have terminated his attack and turned back toward Japan. Only Kimmel's Pacific Fleet senior commanders and Stark's CNO office in Washington would have had to know about the ambush plan's details. The Japanese would have remained in the dark until the first U.S. Navy bombs and torpedoes were dropped on Nagumo's carriers.[49]

Given that there was a battle strategy (2M1) and bait for the ambush, it can be speculated how Kimmel might have organized his fleet to successfully take on a major portion of the IJN's carriers:

Division One: *Lexington* and *Saratoga*

Carrier Division Two: *Enterprise* and *Yorktown*

Carrier Division Three: *Ranger* and *Wasp*

But by mid-1941 the *Yorktown, Wasp,* and *Ranger* had been transferred into the Atlantic, leaving the *Enterprise, Lexington,* and *Saratoga* in the Pacific. The carrier task forces were always escorted by the relatively fast-moving cruisers and destroyers (30-knot speed), as the much slower battleships (18-knot speed) would only serve as maneuver impediments.[50]

Because of the relatively close-in nature of Kimmel's 2M1 attack strategy for engaging the IJN at less than 500 miles to the north of Oahu, there was no need for an extended long-distance transpacific refueling capability. The Pearl Harbor Base Force had at its disposal some 11 tankers, which could maintain speeds from 12 to 18 knots; they could easily be kept within range at selected rendezvous points. All the tankers were equipped for refueling ships at sea. Rounding out the support systems for the fleet were one hospital ship, two repair ships, and two fleet salvage tugs.[51]

With access to intelligence reports, Kimmel would have had more than enough time to react to Nagumo's movements. Kimmel's 2M1 ambush strategy would have used a forward deployment staging area, or waiting positions, preliminary to launching his carriers into the attack from the northeast against the left flank of the IJN carrier Strike Force. Just some six months later, this is exactly what Nimitz and the U.S. Navy did at the Battle of Midway. In Nimitz's case, the Point Luck site located northeast of Midway served a similar purpose for Fletcher and Spruance.[52] Kimmel's four carriers would have engaged Nagumo's six carriers with 144 dive-bombers and 72 torpedo bombers, considerably more than what the navy employed at Midway.[53]

The first alert of the IJN's Strike Force would have enabled Kimmel to make a stealthy tactical approach, closing the range on the unsuspecting IJN carriers and then launching full deck-loads of air strikes before they could respond. This was a state of the art security measure that the navy had been gradually integrating into its fleets throughout 1941.[54]

The big question for Kimmel was *when* the IJN attack would commence. The logical probability was that the IJN force would arrive just before dawn, maximizing their chances of surprise. On December 7, 1941, nautical morning light began at 5:35 a.m., or some 55 minutes before sunrise at 6:30. This would allow just enough light to begin launching carrier aircraft.[55] And this is exactly what Vice Adm. Nagumo did. At around 7:00 a.m., December 6, with the last refueling now complete, the Strike Force turned southeastward, reaching a designated approach point now some 650 miles due north of Oahu. That night, after turning straight south (180 degrees) at 20-knot speed and directly on course for Oahu, the Strike Force made its final dash to its aircraft launch point, 230 miles due north of Pearl Harbor.[56]

At 6:30 a.m. (Hawaii time), Nagumo's first wave of 183 attacking planes began taking off. The first bomb struck its target at 7:55.[57] With the six carriers' decks now cleared, the second wave of attack planes were positioned for the second launch. At 7:45, 167 planes would begin their own hour-long flight to Pearl Harbor.[58]

If one adds the initial two hours that the first IJN Pearl Harbor attack wave needed and its additional hour-long return flight back to its carriers (three hours), plus the hour-long return flight for the second wave, and at least another hour for the second wave, a total of four hours and some minutes would have passed. Kimmel would have had a good three- or four-hour window in which all six of Nagumo's carriers would have been vulnerable to aerial attack.

Once Nagumo's 348 planes had completed their bombing runs, they would have been out of ammunition. They would be at the mercy of Kimmel's squadrons—a highly vulnerable situation and almost identical to what Nagumo experienced six months later at Midway, where he lost three carriers within a period of just six minutes.

If Kimmel had been allowed to put his 2M1 plan into action, the impact would have greatly undermined the success of Japan's future operations in the South Pacific. Raids into the Indian Ocean area in the early part of 1942 would probably not have taken place. Kimmel's potential ambush victory, much like the navy's actual victory in the Battle of Midway, would have spelled the death knell of the Imperial Japanese Navy (IJN) and doomed it to defeat.

The initial great naval battle at the commencement of World War II in the Pacific would have been a resounding American victory instead of the dismal defeat that it was. Aggressive commanders, such as Kimmel and Halsey, and valiant sailors would have met the IJN in the near North Pacific in a manner true to the U.S Navy's high seas, offensive battle tradition. At the strategic level, Kimmel's ambush of the IJN north of Pearl Harbor would have produced the overt act that the president so much desired for a declaration of war against Japan by the U.S. Congress.

Hitler would have then declared war on the United States. Roosevelt's goal in terms of Nazi Germany would have been reached, but it would also *not* have required Adm. Kimmel and the navy's Pacific Fleet to "take it on the chin," as ONI's Arthur McCollum so candidly stated in his oral history memoir. With victory at sea denied, Kimmel now becomes a hapless victim of the fickle finger of historical fate, which would see the good admiral relegated to the role of Pearl Harbor's primary scapegoat.

Epilogue

With the attack on Pearl Harbor coming as a startling surprise and the outpouring of rage, Americans demanded to know how such a catastrophic attack could have taken place. Who was responsible? The public wanted heads to roll and indeed, heads did roll! Adm. Husband E. Kimmel and Lt. Gen. Walter C. Short immediately became Pearl Harbor's scapegoats.

On December 11, 1941, Vice Adm. Leigh Noyes ordered Laurance Safford's OP-20-G, as well as other staff sections within OPNAV, to take action in regards to the Pearl Harbor attack: "If you have got any notes or anything in writing, destroy them because somebody might see them and start something which you don't intend."[1]

At the direction of Secretary of the Navy James Forrestal and Secretary of War Henry Stimson (U.S. Army), two investigations got underway: first, the Navy Court of Inquiry (July 14–October 19, 1944), under Adm. (ret) Orin J. Murfin, and second, the Army Pearl Harbor Board (July 20–October 20, 1944), under Lt. Gen. George Grunert. These two boards focused on Kimmel and Short. It was *only* in these two hearings that Kimmel and Short were allowed to cross-examine and challenge the accusations and testimonies arrayed against them.

As Capt. Laurance Safford was preparing to testify at the hearings, he became aware that *none* of the vital, secret Japanese diplomatic and military intercepts had been transmitted to Kimmel from OPNAV during the six months leading up to the Pearl Harbor attack. Outraged that all the efforts of his OP-20-G intercepts had been for naught in terms of protecting the U.S. Pacific Fleet, Safford weighed in heavily at the Navy Court of Inquiry hearings.[2]

In an explosive turn of events, when it became clear that they had been deprived of key information by army and navy leaders in Washington, both Kimmel and Short were *absolved* of dereliction of duty. Yet, their demotions in rank remained in place. Of considerable importance was the fact that for the first time, incriminatory fingers were now being pointed in the direction of both Gen. George C. Marshall and Adm. Herald R. Stark. The highest levels of national leadership were now vividly in the spotlight, which could become embarrassing to the Roosevelt administration.

The verdict rendered by the Navy Court of Inquiry, which exonerated Adm. Kimmel, was abruptly reversed by Navy Secretary James Forrestal. In turn, the Army Board that had censured Gen. Marshall now found its own verdicts questioned and reversed by Army Secretary of War Stimson. In each case, the service secretaries were seriously concerned, if not alarmed, that the blame for the success of Adm. Nagumo's attack had been shifted away from Hawaii's local commanders and directed at their higher ranking superiors in Washington.

On November 6, 1944, Navy CNO Adm. Ernest J. King wrote a critical endorsement to the Navy Court of Inquiry's report, stating: "The derelictions on the part of Admiral Stark and Admiral Kimmel were faults of omission rather than faults of commission. In the case in question, they indicate lack of the superior judgment necessary for exercising command commensurate with their rank and their assigned duties, rather than culpable inefficiency."[3]

The Navy Court of Inquiry did render the opinion that

the Constitutional requirement that, prior to a declaration of war by the Congress, no blow may be struck until after a hostile attack has been delivered prevented the Commander-in-Chief, Pacific Fleet, from taking offensive action as a means of defense in the event of Japanese vessels or planes appearing in the Hawaiian area, and that it imposes upon him the responsibility of avoiding taking any action which might be construed as an overt act.[4]

The new rules of engagement for the Pacific Fleet had been established in Stark's November 28, 1941, "overt act" message: Kimmel would just have to "take it on the chin." But that was not all, as at the earlier Hart Investigation Cdr. Edwin Layton had testified: "I did not feel we were well informed on what the Japs were doing and I felt that we [Adm. Kimmel and himself] were operating in the dark."[5]

Forrestal then issued an administrative judgment at the end of the Hewitt Inquiry: on August 29, 1945, he directed that both Adm. Kimmel and Adm. Stark "shall not hold any position in the United States Navy which requires the exercise of superior judgment."[6]

Simple, direct, a fait accompli—this meant that Adm. Kimmel's cause, no matter how strong, would be to no avail. Adm. Ernest J. King stated that signals intelligence personnel "must not testify directly or indirectly" on anything "which was obtained by cryptanalysis."[7]

When reading the various testimonies in the hearings, one becomes aware that the personnel conducting the interviews did not know enough about the splendid arrangement's missions, techniques, and systems of reports to ask cogent questions or to follow up on testimony, which required further amplification in terms of important Japanese signal intelligence information, detailed in documents available to ONI.[8]

While the Navy Court of Inquiry was convened in early 1944, ostensibly to thrash out the extent of Adm. Kimmel's culpability for the events at Pearl Harbor, it actually revealed a great deal about Stark's role. It rendered the first damaging opinions on Stark's performance of duty:

> Admiral Kimmel was not informed of the substance of certain Japanese messages inquiring as to disposition of ships inside Pearl Harbor, which indicated a Japanese interest in Pearl Harbor as a possible target.[9]

Other critical failures on the part of Adm. Stark were noted and the Court began to see a pattern: "Admiral Kimmel was not informed of the State Department's note of 26 November to the [sic] Japanese—a definite step toward breaking relations."[10] The "note" was Secretary of State Hull's ultimatum to Tokyo that, among other things, stated that Japan would have to withdraw from China and recognize Chinese sovereignty as an independent country. This information, along with the initial Washington-monitored Winds setup message and then, a few days later, the execute message announcing that Japan was going to go to war against the United States, was also not received by Kimmel.[11]

The final "nail" in Stark's leadership coffin was rendered by the Navy Court: "Admiral Stark failed to appreciate the significance of the '1:00 p.m. message' received on the morning of 7 December, although the implications were appreciated by at least one of his subordinates." As such, "with due appreciation of its significance, it *might* have reached Admiral Kimmel in time to enable him to make some last minute preparations that would have enhanced the ability of the ships in Pearl Harbor to meet the Japanese air attack."[12]

While the Navy Court of Inquiry was conducting its investigation in 1944, the Army Pearl Harbor Board was conducting its own parallel investigation, chaired by Lt. Gen. George Grunert. The primary focus of Grunert's Board was Walter C. Short, the former commanding general of the Hawaiian Department who was responsible for the defense of Pearl Harbor in the air and on the ground.[13]

As the Board investigated deeper and deeper into the alleged culpability of Short, they found that Short's alleged failings stemmed from chief of staff of the U.S. Army Gen. George C. Marshall's own actions or inactions. Marshall failed in four particulars. The first one:

> To keep the Commanding General of the Hawaiian Department fully advised of the growing tenseness of the Japanese situation which indicated an increasing necessity for better preparations for war, of which information he [Marshall] had an abundance and Short had little.[14]

Along this line, Marshall did not relay to Short the most important comment he made during his November 15, 1941, press conference with the major news media and wire services, that war with Japan would break out during the "first ten days of December."

No message traffic from the army's Station FIVE in Hawaii (which intercepted and copied the J-19 and Pak-2 low-grade messages exchanged between Tokyo and its Honolulu consulate) was ever decoded and translated in Hawaii.

The nature of all these dozens of intercepts, including the critically revealing "Bomb Plot" messages, was never revealed to Short or Kimmel; they were simply decoded, translated, read, and filed away in the army or navy headquarters in Washington. The tragic irony of this is that the Bomb Plot messages in particular, intercepted in September and October in Honolulu, indicated Japan's stealth attack on Pearl Harbor. Had these messages been given to Short and Kimmel, this would undoubtedly have resulted in the defense of Pearl Harbor.

The army's operations manual of the day stated: "From adequate and timely military intelligence the commander is able to draw logical conclusions concerning enemy lines of action. Military intelligence is thus an essential factor in the estimate of the situation and in the conduct of operations."[15]

The Board noted a second Marshall failure:

> To send additional instructions to the Commanding General of the Hawaiian Department on November 28, 1941, when evidently he failed to realize the import of General Short's reply of November 27th, which indicated

clearly that General Short had misunderstood and misconstrued the message of 27 November (#472) and had not adequately alerted his command for war.[16]

In essence, the November 27, 1941, message from Marshall dictated orders and rules of engagement from Roosevelt to Short: "If hostilities cannot, repeat cannot, be avoided the United States desires that Japan commit the first overt act." The message then went on to say, "You are directed to undertake such reconnaissance and other measures as you deem necessary but these measures should be carried out so as not, repeat not, to alarm civil population or disclose intent."[17]

As a result, Short opted instead for a low-level alert status involving a sabotage espionage watch. He sent a terse reply to Marshall: "Department alerted to prevent sabotage. Liaison with Navy."[18] Marshall, having sent out his November 27 message, followed it up the next day with #482, another allegedly "clarifying message" to Short, issued in his name by U.S. Army Adj. Gen. Emory Adams: "Critical situation demands that all precautions be taken immediately against subversive activities." It went on to say, "Initiate forthwith all additional measures to provide for protection of your establishments, property, and equipment against sabotage . . . avoiding unnecessary publicity and alarm."

Given the large number of Japanese living in Hawaii, countersabotage measures became the name of the game, and Short very much took this to heart as his top defensive priority, replying to Marshall on November 29: "Full precautions are being taken against subversive activities."[19] The lack of any further response from Marshall satisfied Short that his preparations for the defense of Oahu were correct. That meant that his Army Air Corps aircraft were bunched up, wing tip to wing tip, and ammunition placed under lock and key for easier guarding against sabotage. What he could not know was that his low-level, antisabotage alert status was exactly in accordance with what the overt act strategy had specified and what Marshall wanted in terms of not disclosing intent. It was only when the first bombs began to drop in the early morning of December 7 that Walter Short realized that something had gone terribly wrong.

The Board noted a third Marshall failure:

> To investigate and determine the state of readiness of the Hawaiian Command between November 27 and December 7, 1941, despite the impending threat of war.[20]

Short had repeatedly asked for more planes and antiaircraft weapons for the defense of the Pearl Harbor area. Marshall testified that as far as he was concerned, his November 27 message contained all the information concerning the Japanese and the necessary instructions that Short needed to accomplish his mission.[21]

The Board noted that Marshall's fourth and final failure was:

To get to General Short on the evening of December 6th and the early morning of December 7th, the critical information indicating an almost immediate break with Japan, though there was ample time to have accomplished this.[22]

For Marshall, the fastest means would have been by telephone, using the transpacific line. The navy also had a radio-telephone system for transmissions to key commands throughout the Pacific. This system was offered to Marshall. But he declined, opting to send the War Department's warning at 11:52 (6:22 in Honolulu) by the slowest possible electronic system, Western Union teletype land lines between Washington and San Francisco. Classified as "routine" instead of "urgent" precedence, it was passed on via RCA radio in San Francisco to Honolulu. By the time Marshall had sent his message out, Nagumo's first wave of attacking aircraft were already beginning to take off from the Strike Force's six carriers. Marshall's message did not reach Short and Kimmel until noon on December 7, four hours after the Japanese had completed their attack.[23]

From Stimson's point of view, it was senseless to cashier Marshall and possibly disrupt the strategic direction of the war. Only history could now pronounce a final judgment on George C. Marshall. In the end, a U.S. Senate investigation on May 25, 1999, rendered its own judgment, stating that both Husband E. Kimmel and Walter C. Short "were denied vital intelligence that was available in Washington." This was part of the Senate's nonbinding resolution that exonerated Kimmel and Short, saying they had "competently and professionally" done their duty. The Senate did not restore the two men to their wartime rankings, which the Senate often does in these cases. Sen. Strom Thurmond, R-SC, called Husband Kimmel and Walter Short "the last final victims of Pearl Harbor."[24]

The one other senior army commander in the Pacific who was involved in the overt act strategy's defense debacle of American territory was Lt. Gen. Douglas MacArthur. No formal inquiry or investigation would ever address MacArthur's indecisiveness in the Philippines at the outbreak of war. MacArthur had immense advantages over Short—a PURPLE decoding machine on station, plus access to the MAGIC code-breaking capacities from both army and navy sources, all of which were denied Pearl Harbor. Even though MacArthur's U.S. Army Forces Far East (USAFFE) headquarters was some 9,000 miles away from Washington, DC, he was kept up to date as to what was happening, down to the last moment before Nagumo's attack took place.

As it was, MacArthur was operating under the same restrictions as Short and Kimmel at Hawaii. President Franklin D. Roosevelt's war warning and concurrent rules of engagement orders message to MacArthur was sent out from Stimson's War Department on November 27, 1941, stating in part: "If hostilities cannot, repeat cannot, be avoided the United States desires that Japan commit the first overt act."

Like his counterparts in Hawaii, MacArthur was backed into a corner and locked into a course of action that did not give him any initiative until the Japanese made a hostile act against him. Thus, he had refused Brereton permission to even conduct high altitude aerial reconnaissance photo missions over southern Formosa, for fear that this might compromise the spirit of his orders to await an overt act. MacArthur could not know it at the time but he, like Kimmel, was about to "take it on the chin."[25]

MacArthur's failure to immediately attack the nearby Japanese airbases played a major role in the loss of the Philippines as a useful forward base for nearly the whole war, as well as contributing to the immense loss of civilian life under Japanese occupation. It was one thing to lose some squadrons of fighters and bombers, but it was another to lose an entire army (some 140,000 American and Filipino troops) and a potential forward operations base just to the south of Japan so early in the war.

Be that as it may, Douglas MacArthur would escape any reprimand for his inept conduct in the Philippines and even be promoted to a four-star general just 10 days after his air force, operating under his orders, had been rendered combat ineffective. A few months later, he would receive America's highest award for courage under fire, the Congressional Medal of Honor, and after that, would be given a full joint-service command in the Southwest Pacific—an amazing amount of rewards and promotions for just following orders as the key player responsible for the unmitigated Philippine disaster.

Kimmel and Short had also followed orders, but their fate was to be relieved of duty, demoted, and cashiered from their respective services. They had become the scapegoats of Pearl Harbor. Kimmel and Short were expendable; MacArthur was not. America was in need of heroes at this point in the war, as Roosevelt fully realized. MacArthur was so popular that in some circles, he was being considered as a possible candidate for president of the United States in the November 1944 elections. A politically astute and cagey Roosevelt may have felt that keeping MacArthur on duty and occupied in a full command for the rest of the war was the politically smart thing to do. It is safe to say that very few generals in history ever profited so handsomely from catastrophic failure as did Roosevelt's senior army commander in the Philippines.

Franklin D. Roosevelt, despite all the evidence presented at the army and navy hearings, escaped condemnation for his actions. Since baiting the Japanese into an overt act at Pearl Harbor was Roosevelt's strategy for going to the war against Nazi Germany, it would have made more sense to lure the IJN into a baited, ambushed trap in the North Pacific. This would have readily fulfilled the president's overt act strategy of bringing about a militant act on the part of the Japanese against the Americans. Unfortunately, this was not done. For this reason, I would charge Roosevelt as being derelict in the performance of his duty as the commander-in-chief for not coordinating an ambush of the IJN in the North Pacific.

As McCollum, ONI's foremost Japanese intelligence expert, summed up the situation immediately after the Pearl Harbor attack: "We sent a message out to Admiral Kimmel and told him exactly what we thought he'd been hit with. . . . But the attack . . . as we all know now and *knew then here in Washington* that it came in from just where it did come in—*from the north* [author emphasis]."[26]

As Franklin D. Roosevelt once said: "In politics, nothing happens by accident. If it happens, you can bet it was planned that way." Above all else, Roosevelt kept his "eye on the ball." America's survival was *the* vital interest that had to be protected. He engineered a situation that would enable him to defeat Nazi Germany's atomic bomb project. Through the astute application of deception and guile, he successfully baited Adolf Hitler into declaring war on the United States, as a primary catalyst to arouse a reluctant America to go to war in Europe. In so doing, he doomed the Nazi dictator to defeat.

As Sun Tzu, the Chinese military analyst of 500 BCE, stated: "All warfare is based on deception. Hold out baits to entice the enemy. Feign disorder and crush him!" Had Roosevelt not adhered to this basic concept in the Pacific and had America not gone to war in Europe in 1941, the end result might well have been catastrophic for the United States. With the atomic bomb in Hitler's hands, America could well have lost its treasured freedoms and sovereignty as a constitutional democracy. Likewise, there would not have been a Greatest Generation, as World War II veterans are now being called.

Roosevelt's 1939 decision to defeat Adolf Hitler not only quashed the Nazi atomic bomb project, it also propelled the United States to become the greatest military power in world history. But there was a cost to this, and it was born by the Greatest Generation.

An appropriate anecdote will do here as the finale. At a NATO gathering of its senior staff members sometime during the Cold War, a quarter of a century after the end of World War II, a French admiral complained, "Since NATO is located here in Europe, why is it that we always have to speak English in order to please the Americans?"

A U.S. Navy admiral shot back, "We speak English here at NATO because the Americans and the British planned it that way . . . otherwise, we would all be speaking German!"

APPENDIX A

Lieutenant Commander Arthur McCollum's 8-Point Memorandum (October 7, 1940)

OP-16-F-2   ONI   7 October 1940

MEMORANDUM FOR THE DIRECTOR

SUBJECT: Estimate of the Situation in the Pacific and Recommendations for Action by the United States

1. The United States today finds herself confronted by a hostile Germany and Italy in Europe and by an equally hostile Japan in the Orient. Russia, the great land link between these two groups of hostile powers, is at present neutral, but in all probability favorably inclined towards the Axis powers, and her favorable attitude towards these powers may be expected to increase in direct proportion to increasing success in their prosecution of the war in Europe. Germany and Italy have been successful in war on the continent of Europe and all of Europe is either under their military control

or has been forced into subservience. Only the British Empire is actively opposing by war the growing world dominance of Germany and Italy and their satellites.

2. The United States at first remained coolly aloof from the conflict in Europe and there is considerable evidence to support the view that Germany and Italy attempted by every method within their power to foster a continuation of American indifference to the outcome of the struggle in Europe. Paradoxically, every success of German and Italian arms has led to further increases in United States sympathy for and material support of the British Empire, until at the present time the United States government stands committed to a policy of rendering every support short of war with the chances rapidly increasing that the United States will become a full fledged ally of the British Empire in the very near future. The final failure of German and Italian diplomacy to keep the United States in the role of a disinterested spectator has forced them to adopt the policy of developing threats to U.S. security in other spheres of the world, notably by the threat of revolutions in South and Central America by Axis-dominated groups and by the stimulation of Japan to further aggressions and threats in the Far East in the hope that by these means the United States would become so confused in thought and fearful of her own immediate security as to cause her to become so preoccupied in purely defensive preparations as to virtually preclude U.S. aid to Great Britain in any form. As a result of this policy, Germany and Italy have lately concluded a military alliance with Japan directed against the United States. If the published terms of this treaty and the pointed utterances of German, Italian and Japanese leaders can be believed, and there seems no ground on which to doubt either, the three totalitarian powers agree to make war on the United States, should she come to the assistance of England, or should she attempt to forcibly interfere with Japan's aims in the Orient and, furthermore, Germany and Italy expressly reserve the right to determine whether American aid to Britain, short of war, is a cause for war or not after they have succeeded in defeating England. In other words, after England has been disposed of her enemies will decide whether or not to immediately proceed with an attack on the United States. Due to geographic conditions, neither Germany nor Italy are in a position to offer any material aid to Japan. Japan, on the contrary, can be of much help to both Germany and Italy by threatening and possibly even attacking British dominions and supply routes from Australia, India and the Dutch East Indies, thus materially weakening Britain's position in opposition to the Axis powers in Europe. In exchange for this service, Japan receives a free hand to seize all of Asia that she can find it possible to grab, with the added promise that Germany and Italy will do all in their power to keep U.S. attention so attracted as to prevent the United

States from taking positive aggressive action against Japan. Here again we have another example of the Axis-Japanese diplomacy which is aimed at keeping American power immobilized, and by threats and alarms to so confuse American thought as to preclude prompt decisive action by the United States in either sphere of action. It cannot be emphasized too strongly that the last thing desired by either the Axis powers in Europe or by Japan in the Far East is prompt, warlike action by the United States in either theatre of operations.

3. An examination of the situation in Europe leads to the conclusion that there is little that we can do now, immediately to help Britain that is not already being done. We have no trained army to send to the assistance of England, nor will we have for at least a year. We are now trying to increase the flow of materials to England and to bolster the defense of England in every practicable way and this aid will undoubtedly be increased. On the other hand, there is little that Germany or Italy can do against us as long as England continues in the war and her navy maintains control of the Atlantic. The one danger to our position lies in the possible early defeat of the British Empire with the British Fleet falling intact into the hands of the Axis powers. The possibility of such an event occurring would be materially lessened were we actually allied in war with the British or at the very least were taking active measures to relieve the pressure on Britain in other spheres of action. To sum up: the threat to our security in the Atlantic remains small so long as the British Fleet remains dominant in that ocean and friendly to the United States.

4. In the Pacific, Japan by virtue of her alliance with Germany and Italy is a definite threat to the security of the British Empire and once the British Empire is gone the power of Japan-Germany and Italy is to be directed against the United States. A powerful land attack by Germany and Italy through the Balkans and North Africa against the Suez Canal with a Japanese threat or attack on Singapore would have very serious results for the British Empire. Could Japan be diverted or neutralized, the fruits of a successful attack on the Suez Canal could not be as far-reaching and beneficial to the Axis powers as if such a success was also accompanied by the virtual elimination of British sea power from the Indian Ocean, thus opening up a European supply route for Japan and a sea route for Eastern raw materials to reach Germany and Italy, Japan must be diverted if the British and American blockade of Europe and possibly Japan is to remain even partially in effect.

5. While as pointed out in Paragraph (3) there is little that the United States can do to immediately retrieve the situation in Europe, the United

States is able to effectively nullify Japanese aggressive action, and do it without lessening U.S. material assistance to Great Britain.

6. An examination of Japan's present position as opposed to the United States reveals a situation as follows:

ADVANTAGES

1. Geographically strong position of Japanese Islands.
2. A highly centralized strong capable government.
3. Rigid control of economy on a war basis.
4. A people inured to hardship and war.
5. A powerful army.
6. A skillful navy about 2/3 the strength of the U.S. Navy.
7. Some stocks of raw materials.
8. Weather until April rendering direct sea operations in the vicinity of Japan difficult.

DISADVANTAGES

1. A million and a half men engaged in an exhausting war on the Asiatic Continent.
2. Domestic economy and food supply severely straightened.
3. A serious lack of sources of raw materials for war. Notably oil, iron and cotton.
4. Totally cut off from supplies from Europe.
5. Dependent upon distant overseas routes for essential supplies.
6. Incapable of increasing manufacture and supply of war materials without free access to U.S. or European markets.
7. Major cities and industrial centers extremely vulnerable to air attack.

7. In the Pacific the United States possesses a very strong defensive position and a navy and naval air force at present in that ocean capable of long distance offensive operation. There are certain other factors which at the present time are strongly in our favor, viz:

A. Philippine Islands still held by the United States.
B. Friendly and possibly allied government in control of the Dutch East Indies.

C. British still hold Hong Kong and Singapore and are favorable to us.

D. Important Chinese armies are still in the field in China against Japan.

E. A small U.S. Naval Force capable of seriously threatening Japan's southern supply routes already in the theatre of operations.

F. A considerable Dutch naval force is in the Orient that would be of value if allied to U.S.

8. A consideration of the foregoing leads to the conclusion that prompt aggressive naval action against Japan by the United States would render Japan incapable of affording any help to Germany and Italy in their attack on England and that Japan itself would be faced with a situation in which her navy could be forced to fight on most unfavorable terms or accept fairly early collapse of the country through the force of blockade. A prompt and early declaration of war after entering into suitable arrangements with England and Holland, would be most effective in bringing about the early collapse of Japan and thus eliminating our enemy in the pacific before Germany and Italy could strike at us effectively. Furthermore, elimination of Japan must surely strengthen Britain's position against Germany and Italy and, in addition, such action would increase the confidence and support of all nations who tend to be friendly towards us.

9. It is not believed that in the present state of political opinion the United States government is capable of declaring war against Japan without more ado; and it is barely possible that vigorous action on our part might lead the Japanese to modify their attitude. Therefore, the following course of action is suggested:

A. Make an arrangement with Britain for the use of British bases in the Pacific, particularly Singapore.

B. Make an arrangement with Holland for the use of base facilities and acquisition of supplies in the Dutch East Indies.

C. Give all possible aid to the Chinese government of Chiang-Kai-Shek.

D. Send a division of long range heavy cruisers to the Orient, Philippines, or Singapore.

E. Send two divisions of submarines to the Orient.

F. Keep the main strength of the U.S. fleet now in the Pacific in the vicinity of the Hawaiian Islands.

G. Insist that the Dutch refuse to grant Japanese demands for undue economic concessions, particularly oil.

H. Completely embargo all U.S. trade with Japan, in collaboration with a similar embargo imposed by the British Empire.

10. If by these means Japan could be led to commit an overt act of war, so much the better. At all events we must be fully prepared to accept the threat of war.

A. H. McCollum

SUMMARY

1. The United States is faced by a hostile combination of powers in both the Atlantic and Pacific.
2. British naval control of the Atlantic prevents hostile action against the United States in this area.
3. Japan's growing hostility presents an attempt to open sea communications between Japan and the Mediterranean by an attack on the British lines of communication in the Indian Ocean.
4. Japan must be diverted if British opposition in Europe is to remain effective.
5. The United States naval forces now in the Pacific are capable of so containing and harassing Japan as to nullify her assistance to Germany and Italy.
6. It is to the interest of the United States to eliminate Japan's threat in the Pacific at the earliest opportunity by taking prompt and aggressive action against Japan.
7. In the absence of United States ability to take the political offensive, additional naval force should be sent to the orient and agreements entered into with Holland and England that would serve as an effective check against Japanese encroachments in South-eastern Asia.

COMMENT BY CAPTAIN KNOX

It is unquestionably to our general interest that Britain be not licked—just now she has a stalemate and probably can't do better. We ought to make it certain that she at least gets a stalemate. For this she will probably need from us substantial further destroyers and air reinforcements to England. We should not precipitate anything in the Orient that should hamper our ability to do this—so long as probability continues.

If England remains stable, Japan will be cautious in the Orient. Hence our assistance to England in the Atlantic is also protection to her and us in the Orient.

However, I concur in your courses of action we must be ready on both sides and probably strong enough to care for both.
D.W.K.

Re your #6:—no reason for battleships not visiting west coast in bunches.

Source: Memo from Lieutenant Commander Arthur McCollum of the Office of Naval Intelligence to Navy Captains Walter Anderson and Dudley Knox. October 7, 1940. NARA II, RG 38, Office of Naval Intelligence, Foreign Intelligence Branch Office, Far East OP-16-F-2 File (1940–1945), Box 2.[1]

---

[1] Photocopy of this classified document is held in author's files.

APPENDIX B

Pearl Harbor Original Target Grid Bomb Plot Messages (September 24 and 29, 1941)

Intercepted by Station S (SAIL near Seattle), this was the original Tokyo-initiated message (#83) that was decoded (J-19) and then translated on October 9, 1941. It laid out a target grid system that covered the principal anchorages of the U.S. Pacific Fleet at Pearl Harbor, Hawaii.

Intercepted by Mackay Radio (denoted as "X"), the J-19 coded message was then photographed by navy officials and then decoded and translated on October 10, 1941. It provided a more detailed target grid system than was originally requested (#83) by Tokyo.

From: Tokyo (Toyoda)
To: Honolulu
September 24, 1941
J-19
#83
Strictly secret.

Henceforth, we would like to have you make reports concerning vessels along the following lines insofar as possible:

1. The waters (of Pearl Harbor) are to be divided roughly into five sub-areas. (We have no objections to your abbreviating as much as you like.)

Area A. Waters between Ford Island and the Arsenal.

Area B. Waters adjacent to the Island south and west of Ford Island. (This area is on the opposite side of the Island from Area A.)

Area C. East Loch.

Area D. Middle Loch.

Area E. West Loch and the communicating water routes.

2. With regard to warships and aircraft carriers, we would like to have you report on those at anchor, (these are not so important) tied up at wharves, buoys and in locks. (Designate types and classes briefly. If possible we would like to have you make mention of the fact when there are two or more vessels along side the same wharf.)

ARMY 23260 Trans. 10/9/41 (S)

From: Honolulu (Kita)
To: Washington
29 September 1941
(J19)
Circular #041
Honolulu to Tokyo #178
Re your #083*
(Strictly secret.)

The following codes will be used hereafter to designate the location of vessels:
1. Repair dock in Navy Yard (The repair basin referred to in my message to Washington #48**): KS.
2. Navy dock in the Navy Yard (The Ten Ten Pier): KT.
3. Moorings in the vicinity of Ford Island: FV.
4. Alongside in Ford Island: FG. (East and west sides will be differentiated by A and B respectively.
Relayed to Washington, San Francisco.

*Not available.
**Available, dated 21 August.

JD-1: 5730 23312 (D) Navy Trans. 10–10–41 (X)

Source: *Pearl Harbor Attack*. Hearings before the Joint Committee on the Investigation of the Pearl Harbor Attack. 79th Congress, First Session. Part 37. Washington, DC: Government Printing Office, 1946, 646, 663–664.[2]

---

[2] Photocopy of this classified document is held in author's files.

Notes

To avoid excessive repetition, certain references will be abbreviated:

National Archives and Records Administration (NARA)

Naval Cryptologic Veterans Association (NCVA)

Pearl Harbor Attack Hearings (PHAH)

Philippines Liaison Office (PHLO)

Records Group (RG)

Special Research History (SRH)

INTRODUCTION

1. Paraphrased from the *Report of the Joint Committee on the Investigation of the Pearl Harbor Attack*, Senate Document No. 244, 79th Congress, 253.

2. Typical reports that one would expect to find in the archives include station monthly reports, station radio direction finding (RDF) reports, radio intercept shift chronology reports of Imperial Japanese Navy radio call signs and related ship identifications, radio shift supervisor reports, radio intercept operator logs, translated individual message sheets, RDF tracking charts and communications summaries, and statistical radio call sign lists with related RDF bearings from inputting intercept stations.

3. Clausewitz, *Vom Kriege (On War)*, 810–811.

4. Henry L. Stimson, *Diary* entry of Tuesday, November 25, 1941, 48–49, Yale University Microfilm Library, Reel 7, Volume 36; copy author's file and PHAH, Part 11, 5194.

CHAPTER 1

1. Herring, *From Colony to Superpower*, 212–313.

2. Kennedy, *The Rise and Fall of the Great Powers*, 208. See also Richard Story, *Japan and the Decline of the West in Asia, 1894–1943* (London: MacMillan, 1979).

3. *Encyclopedia Britannica*, vol. 15, 193 and 237–238; Beasley, *Meiji Restoration*, 122–123.

4. Beasley, *Meiji Restoration*, 407, 411–413.

5. Beasley, *Meiji Restoration*, 124–125, and Kennedy, *Rise and Fall of the Great Powers*, 206–208.

6. Beasley, *Meiji Restoration*, 247; *Encyclopedia Britannica*, vol. 15, 213; Kennedy, *Rise and Fall of the Great Powers*, 208.

7. Mahan, *Influence of Sea Power Upon History*, 287–288; Asada, *Culture Shock and Japanese-American Relations*, 53–54. See also Asada, *From Mahan to Pearl Harbor*, 3–17.

8. Herring, *From Colony to Superpower*, 317; Wolff, *Little Brown Brother*, 19, 58, and 79.

9. *Encyclopedia Britannica*, vol. 15, 194 and 213.

10. Kennedy, *Rise and Fall of the Great Powers*, 208–209; Potter, *Yamamoto*, 11–12. Note that formal Japanese names traditionally begin with the family name first.

11. Yoshihara and Holmes, "Japanese Maritime Thought: If Not Mahan, Who?" 23–27, 30, and 48 fn. 27; *Encyclopedia Britannica*, vol. 25, 595–597; Russo-Japanese War Research Society, "Sato Tetsutaro" (July 18, 2011), 1–3, http://semanticsscholar.org/382c/2f2da85b8447c82b7a92db5ba891e.pdf; Potter, *Yamamoto*, 32–33.

12. Toland, *The Rising Sun*, 62; Kennedy, *Rise and Fall of the Great Powers*, 287.

13. Aldcroft, *From Versailles to Wall Street*, 37–38; Kennedy, *Rise and Fall of the Great Powers*, 207 and 299.

14. Aldcroft, *From Versailles to Wall Street*, 67; Toland, *The Rising Sun*, 3–4.

15. Herring, *From Colony to Superpower*, 452–453; Miller, *Bankrupting the Enemy*, 134–135.

16. Agawa, *The Reluctant Admiral*, 26–27 and 32–33; Herring, *From Colony to Superpower*, 454–455 and 467.

17. Allen, *A Short Economic History of Japan*, 141; Kennedy, *Rise and Fall of the Great Powers*, 296.

18. Agawa, *The Reluctant Admiral*, 91; Kennedy, *Rise and Fall of the Great Powers*, 300–301.

19. Agawa, *The Reluctant Admiral*, 79 and 87–89; Potter, *Yamamoto*, 18 and 30.

20. Kennedy, *Rise and Fall of the Great Powers*, 301.

21. Agawa, *The Reluctant Admiral*, 92; Potter, *Yamamoto*, 31.

22. Kennedy, *Rise and Fall of the Great Powers*, 301.

23. Agawa, *The Reluctant Admiral*, 104.

24. Agawa, *The Reluctant Admiral*, 104; Kennedy, *Rise and Fall of the Great Powers*, 301.

25. Toland, *The Rising Sun*, 25–26.

26. Kennedy, *Rise and Fall of the Great Powers*, 301.

27. Kennedy, *Rise and Fall of the Great Powers*, 298; Spector, *Eagle Against The Sun*, 35 and 37.

28. Kennedy, *Rise and Fall of the Great Powers*, 329.

29. Stimson and Bundy, *On Active Service in Peace and War*, 243–244.

30. Kennedy, *Rise and Fall of the Great Powers*, 333–335.

31. Kennedy, *Rise and Fall of the Great Powers*, 302; Toland, *The Rising Sun*, 52.

32. Toland, *The Rising Sun*, 60; Kennedy, *Rise and Fall of the Great Powers*, 302.

33. Rochefort, *Reminiscences of Captain Joseph J. Rochefort*, 66. Note: This is a National Security Agency–directed revised edition of Rochefort's 1973 *Oral History* version.

34. Barnhart, *Japan Prepares for Total War*, 166.

35. Kennedy, *Rise and Fall of the Great Powers*, 337; Toland, *The Rising Sun*, 63.

36. Kennedy, *Rise and Fall of the Great Powers*, 302–303; Toland, *The Rising Sun*, 67.

37. Kennedy, *Rise and Fall of the Great Powers*, 302; Toland, *The Rising Sun*, 68.

38. Miller, *Bankrupting the Enemy*, 135; Toland, *The Rising Sun*, 68 and 71. It should be noted that in 1938 the average intake of 2,180 calories per day per capita in Japan ranked well below the 3,150 calories inside the United States and the 2,800 to 3,100 calories per day in Western Europe.

39. Toland, *The Rising Sun*, 72.

40. Toland, *The Rising Sun*, 86; Agawa, *The Reluctant Admiral*, 186.

41. Barnhart, *Japan Prepares for Total War*, 174.

42. "Dutch East Indies," *Life* (January 22, 1940), 55.

43. Barnhart, *Japan Prepares for Total War*, 102–103 and 144–145.

44. Toland, *The Rising Sun*, 172 and 180.

45. Barnhart, *Japan Prepares for Total War*, 166, Table 9.1; Vat, *The Pacific Campaign*, 102.

46. Toland, *The Rising Sun*, 173–174.

47. Vat, *The Pacific Campaign*, 68.

48. Toland, *The Rising Sun*, 75.

49. Naval Analysis Division, *Campaigns of the Pacific War*, 3.

50. Agawa, *The Reluctant Admiral*, 195.

CHAPTER 2

1. Herring, *From Colony to Superpower*, 322; Kennedy, *The Rise and Fall of the Great Powers*, 246; Stephanson, *Manifest Destiny*, 88, 90, and 94; Wolf, *Little Brown Brother*, 173.

2. Wolf, *From Colony to Superpower*, x–xi, 17, 19, 100, 252–253, 294, 306–307, 318, 358, and 363. The Krag-Jorgenson rifle was the standard-issue .30 caliber infantry weapon used by the U.S. Army in the Philippines.

3. Herring, *From Colony to Superpower*, 320.

4. Herring, *From Colony to Superpower*, 303; Kennedy, *Rise and Fall of the Great Powers*, 246–247.

5. *Encyclopedia Britannica*, vol. 13, 87: In 1908 there were a reported 72,000 Japanese and some 35,000 native Hawaiians living in the Hawaiian Islands; Herring, *From Colony to Superpower*, 349 and 356.

6. Miller, *War Plan Orange*, 33.

7. Miller, *War Plan Orange*, 33–34.

8. Kennedy, *Rise and Fall of the Great Powers*, 201.

9. Lee, "Marconi's Transatlantic Triumph," 81 and 83.

10. Foster and Demerseman, "Radio Direction Finding and Huff-Duff," 99.

11. Lee, "Marconi's Transatlantic Triumph," 83 and 89; Stephenson, "The Marconi Wireless Telegraph Apparatus in R.M.S. *Titanic*," 99–100.

12. Lee, "Radio Spies," 15–16.

13. Moreau, "The Military Communications Explosion, 1914–1918," 135.

14. Lee, "America's Wireless Spies," 21–23, 26, 28, and 30.

15. Hanyek, "Radio Intelligence on the Mexican Border, 1916–1918," 8–9; Lee, "America's Wireless Spies," 31–38. Lee's article depicts a number of photos of the types of radio signal intercept trucks and their equipment.

16. West, *The SIGINT Secrets*, 66 and 68.

17. Lee, "Radio Spies," 12–13.

18. Lee, "Radio Spies," 13; Moreau, "The Military Communications Explosion, 1914–1918," 147; West, *The SIGINT Secrets*, 56, 76, and 78.

19. West, *The SIGINT Secrets*, 56–57 and 70–72.

20. Lee, "America's Wireless Spies," 25 and 29; see also Tuchman, *The Zimmermann Telegram*.

21. Layton, Pineau, and Costello, *And I Was There*, 28.

22. Howeth, *History of Communications-Electronics in the United States Navy*, 264; SRH 149, Safford, "A Brief History of Communications Intelligence in the United States," 1 and 4.

23. Lee, "Radio Spies," 20.

24. Kennedy, *Rise and Fall of the Great Powers*, 287 and 299.

25. Miller, *War Plan Orange*, 25–26, 83, 92, 96, 118, 129, 143, 155–157, and 165.

26. Layton, Pineau, and Costello, *And I Was There*, 27.

27. Yardley, *The American Black Chamber*, 165–171 and 122; *Identification of Japanese Radio-Telegraph Signals* (Washington, DC: Federal Communications Commission Engineering Department), November 1, 1941.

28. Layton, Pineau, and Costello, *And I Was There*, 31; SRH 305, Safford, "The Undeclared War History of R.I.," 1 and 3.

29. Layton, Pineau, and Costello, *And I Was There*, 60; SRH 305, Safford, "The Undeclared War History of R.I.," 5; SRH 149, Safford, "A Brief History of Communications Intelligence in the United States," 6.

30. Layton, Pineau, and Costello, *And I Was There*, 56; "RIP-5 Underwood Typewriter," Safford-Underwood November 26 and December 10, 1924, correspondence, NARA II (College Park, Maryland), RG 38, Crane files, Box 2.

31. SRH 305, Safford, "The Undeclared War History of R.I.," 1; Stinnett, *Day of Deceit*, 335, fn 33.

32. Stinnett, *Day of Deceit*, 22, 49, and 79; NARA II, RG 38, Crane Files, Box 29 (*RIP73A*) and Box 41 (*RIP80*).

33. Stinnett, *Day of Deceit*, 74; Layton, Pineau, and Costello, *And I Was There*, 33.

34. Layton, Pineau, and Costello, *And I Was There*, 31–32.

35. *Webster's New World Dictionary*, 355–356.

36. Prados, *Combined Fleet Decoded*, 74; Sebag-Montefiore, *Enigma: The Battle for the Code*, 322.

37. Phillips and Dickey, "Reorganization of the OTRG," 22; SRH 149, Safford, "A Brief History of Communications Intelligence in the United States," 9.

38. Snyder and Bragaw, *Achievement in Radio*, 172–173.

39. West, *The SIGINT Secrets*, 30.

40. SRH 305, Safford, "The Undeclared War History of R.I.," 1–5.

41. Layton, Pineau, and Costello, *And I Was There*, 34.

42. SRH 305, Safford, "The Undeclared War History of R.I.," 7.

43. SRH 305, Safford, "The Undeclared War History of R.I.," 8.

44. SRH 305, Safford, "The Undeclared War History of R.I.," 8–9.

45. SRH 305, Safford, "The Undeclared War History of R.I.," 10.

46. SRH 305, Safford, "The Undeclared War History of R.I.," 6.

47. Layton, Pineau, and Costello, *And I Was There*, 27.

48. SRH 149, Safford, "A Brief History of Communications Intelligence in the United States," 6.

49. SRH 149, Safford, "A Brief History of Communications Intelligence in the United States," 8.

50. SRH 149, Safford, "A Brief History of Communications Intelligence in the United States," 10–11.

51. Layton, Pineau, and Costello, *And I Was There*, 45–46.

52. Bashe, Johnson, Palmer, and Pugh, *IBM'S Early Computers*, 10–13 and 18–21; "IBM 405 Electric Punched Card Accounting Machine," https://www.ibm.com/ibm/history/exhibits/vintage/vintage_4506VV4006.html; Pugh, "Responding to the Great Depression," in *Building IBM*.

53. Layton, Pineau, and Costello, *And I Was There*, 46.

54. SRH 149, Safford, "A Brief History of Communications Intelligence in the United States," 28.

55. Devours and Kruh, *Machine Cryptography and Modern Cryptanalysis*, 225; Kullback, *Statistical Methods in Cryptanalysis*, 1–2, 4, 24, 48, 81, 123, and 145.

56. SRH 305, Safford, "The Undeclared War History of R.I.," 11–13; SRH 149, Safford, "A Brief History of Communications Intelligence in the United States," 9.

57. Prados, *Combined Fleet Decoded*, 45–46.

58. SRH 305, Safford, "The Undeclared War History of R.I.," 14–15.

59. SRH 305, Safford, "The Undeclared War History of R.I.," 15–17.

60. SRH 305, Safford, "The Undeclared War History of R.I.," 16 and 18–19.

61. SRH 305, Safford, "The Undeclared War History of R.I.," 19.

62. Miller, *War Plan Orange*, 173 and 180.

63. SRH 149, Safford, "A Brief History of Communications Intelligence in the United States"; SRH 149, Wenger, "The Evolution of the Navy's Cryptologic Organization."

64. SRH 149, Safford, "A Brief History of Communications Intelligence in the United States," 4–5.

65. NCVA *Cryptolog* II, no. 5 (August 1981), 2; John P. Sinnott, *Patent and Trademark Dept., American Standard Inc.* (New York: 40 West 40th Street).

66. Teletype printer circuit systems; telepage printer systems (TPS); radiograms; telegrams; 1/2-inch automatic tape recorders; Boehme

3/8-inch tape recorders; RAB and model RAS receivers; MC-1000 HF receivers; TAW, TCR, and TBK-11 radio transmitters; teletypewriter machines in lieu of TWX services; and "telepage circuit" machines. Howeth, *History of Communications-Electronics in the United States Navy*, 539.

67. Stinnett, *Day of Deceit*, 351–352, fn 20; Pekelney, "Electronic Cipher Machine (ECM) Mark II"; Pekelney, "What Is the SIGABA-ECM Mark II and Why It Was Important?"

68. SRH 197: IBM Operations and OP-20-G Organization and Activities, 66; SRH 149, Safford, "A Brief History of Communications Intelligence in the United States," 4; Stinnett, *Day of Deceit*, 68.

69. Calder, *How to Read a Nautical Chart*, 12-1; *Webster's New World Dictionary*, 634. See also Keen, *Wireless Direction Finding*.

70. Miller, *War Plan Orange*, 48–49 and 51.

71. Miller, *War Plan Orange*, 201 and 213–214.

72. Devours and Kruh, *Machine Cryptography and Modern Cryptanalysis*, 11, 212, and 216.

73. Devours and Kruh, *Machine Cryptography and Modern Cryptanalysis*, 227; Kahn, *The Code Breakers*, 18–19 and 22–23.

74. Kahn, *The Code Breakers*, 4 and 576; Devours and Kruh, *Machine Cryptography and Modern Cryptanalysis*, 232–233 and 245; SRH 149, Safford, "A Brief History of Communications Intelligence in the United States," 6–7 and 8–10.

75. Miller, *War Plan Orange*, 215, 217, and 225–226.

76. Budiansky, *Battle of Wits*, 216; SRH 149, Safford, "A Brief History of Communications Intelligence in the United States," 12; Stinnett, *Day of Deceit*, 75.

77. NARA II, RG 38, Inactive Stations, Box 15 (2000/1) NSRS Philippines "Genser" message file.

78. NARA II, RG 38, Crane Files, Box 29 (*RIP73A*) and Box 41 (*RIP80*).

79. To begin the coding process, the navy cryptologist merely selected the kana random number and then added the additive code group number, but without making any carries:

Example:	random basic book number:	26306
	additive code group number:	59702
	add without carries:	75008

Each message was supposed to depict at its beginning and at its end the precise entry point five-digit number in the additive book. To reverse the process to get back to the basic code book number, the cryptologist stripped out the additive number and looked up the kana number in the basic book. It was not an easy task. The IBM Type 405 tabulating and card-sorter machines helped immeasurably, so that by December 1940, the initial 5-Num version of Code Book D could be reasonably read. After a message was punched into a card, the Type 405 machines could strip out the key additive, find the proper place in the additive deck to strip off the text additives, and then print the base code groups of the message. Budiansky, *Battle of Wits*, 17; Holmes, *Double-Edged Secrets*, 54–55.

80. "Memorandum" for OP-20-G (January 1, 1943) and *Chronology JN25 to August 1942*, NARA II, RG 38, Crane Files: Box 31 (*RIP74D*) and Box 41 (*RIP80*).

81. R. E. Ingersoll, secret serial no. 081420 (4 October 1940), Office of the Chief of Naval Operations (CNO), NARA II, RG 457, Box 1358 (NR 4166 "Commander Correspondence 1941").

82. Holmes, *Double-Edged Secrets*, 23.

83. SRH 149, Safford, "A Brief History of Communications Intelligence in the United States," 6 and 16; Phillips and Dickey, "Reorganization of the OTRG," 11; George E. Welker, "Memorandum of July 15, 1942," NARA II, RG 38, Crane Files, Box 2 (*RIP5*); PHAH, Part 5, 2213.

CHAPTER 3

1. PHAH, Part 5, 2213.

2. PHAH, Part 36, 18.

3. "Key Personnel Listing, Office of CNO, 1 April 1940," NARA II, RG 457, Box 579 (NR1404), Box 1358 (NR 4166), and Box 1419 (NR 4640); PHAH, Part 32, Appendix B: 276: "Organization and Personnel, Navy Department, December 7, 1941"; SRH 149, Safford, "A Brief History of Communications Intelligence in the United States," 5–6.

4. Simpson, *Admiral Harold R. Stark*, 1.

5. PHAH, Part 32, 540–541; PHAH, Part 33, 889–890; PHAH, Part 36, 29; "Organization of Naval Intelligence Sources of Information," NARA II, RG 457, Box 579 (NR 1404).

6. PHAH, Part 32, 352; OP-16-F-2: "Japan Navy Organization Fleets," NARA Laguna Niguel (now Riverside), RG 181, A8-5, Box 81, as an example report.

7. McCollum, *Reminiscences of Rear Admiral Arthur H. McCollum*, 245; PHAH, Part 36, 13; Layton, Pineau, and Costello, *And I Was There*, 39–40; FBI Archive (Washington, DC) Report 62-33413-766, all of which show that McCollum also interfaced with J. Edgar Hoover, Director of the Federal Bureau of Investigation (FBI).

8. McCollum, *Reminiscences of Rear Admiral Arthur H. McCollum*, 248–250, 307, 328, 333, and 386; PHAH, Part 16, 2294–2295; PHAH, Part 36, 13–15.

9. McCollum, *Reminiscences of Rear Admiral Arthur H. McCollum*, 246 and 251; PHAH, Part 36, 18.

10. Layton, Pineau, and Costello, *And I Was There*, 20.

11. McCollum, *Reminiscences of Rear Admiral Arthur H. McCollum*, 304.

12. PHAH, Part 26, 437–438; Layton, Pineau, and Costello, *And I Was There*, 20.

13. PHAH, Part 26, 438; Rear Adm. Glover, "Dispatch April 18, 1946," NARA II, RG 38, CNO CSNG Library, Box 118 (5750).

14. McCollum, *Reminiscences of Rear Admiral Arthur H. McCollum*, 327–328.

15. McCollum, *Reminiscences of Rear Admiral Arthur H. McCollum*, 309 and 329–330.

16. McCollum, *Reminiscences of Rear Admiral Arthur H. McCollum*, 310–311.

17. "The Organization of Naval Intelligence in General," 60–61, NARA II, RG 457, Box 579 (1504); "Intercept Station," NARA II, RG 38, CNO CSG Library, Box 113; SRH 197: IBM Operations and OP-20-G Organization and Activities, "Personnel," 81; Layton, Pineau, and Costello, *And I Was There*, 57; PHAH Part 33, 769; PHAH, Part 36, 60.

18. RDF equipment during 1941 consisted of the DT-1 and DT-2 HF direction finders of navy design and construction, which had evolved from the World War I navy RDF operations conducted along the coast of France. "D/F-in-1940 Matter," NARA II, RG 38, Inactive Stations, Box 14 (5750); "OP-20-GX Progress and Accomplishments during the Period 1 January 1941 to December 1943," NARA II, RG 38, CSNG Lib., Box 113; SRH 149, Safford, "A Brief History of Communications Intelligence in the United States" ("Pacific Intercept"), 69; McCollum, *Reminiscences of Rear Admiral Arthur H. McCollum*, 279.

19. J. M. Lietwiler, "Organization of OP-20-G in December 1941," NARA II, RG 38, Office of CNO, CNSG Lib., Box 113; Stinnett, *Day of Deceit*, 22.

20. SRH 459: "Organization of Naval Intelligence," 60; "Intercept Stations," NARA II, RG 38, CNO-CNSG Lib., Box 113; Rochefort, *Reminiscences of Captain Joseph J. Rochefort*, 135.

21. SRH 197: IBM Operations and OP-20-G Organization and Activities, 81.

22. J. M. Lietwiler, "Organization of OP-20-G in December 1941," NARA II, RG 38, Office of CNO, CNSG Lib., Box 113; Prados, *Combined Fleet Decoded*, 81.

23. Prados, *Combined Fleet Decoded*, 78–79 and 81–82.

24. Type 405 Alphabetical Accounting Machines maintained by OP-20-G had as integral parts 80 subtraction counters, 88 type bars, 80/80 speed, 20 control positions equipped with a digital selector, an alphabetical summary punching device, and finally a Type 921 Automatic Carriage. If this was not enough, there were other component machines that rounded

out a complete system. Used with great success were the Type 75 Card-Counting Horizontal Sorter, Model 1, equipped with a Multiple Column Selector; a Type 35 Alphabetical Duplicating Printing Punch; and a Type 513 Summary Punching Reproducer with 45 columns for attachment to the Type 405 machine. "Statistical Machinery for Cryptographic Work," NARA II, RG 457, Box 1126 (IBM Operations).

25. Layton, Pineau, and Costello, *And I Was There*, 5.

26. PHAH, Part 33, 848; NARA II, RG 38, Office of CNO, CNSG Lib., Box 113.

27. PHAH, Part 33, 850; Albert Pelletier, NCVA *Cryptolog* (Spring 1987), 5; J. M. Lietwiler, "Organization of OP-20-G in December 1941," NARA II, RG 38, Office of CNO, CNSG Lib., Box 113.

28. McCollum, *Reminiscences of Rear Admiral Arthur H. McCollum*, 275.

29. Devours and Kruh, *Machine Cryptography and Modern Cryptanalysis*, 78–79.

30. PHAH, Part 33, 863–864; McCollum, *Reminiscences of Rear Admiral Arthur H. McCollum*, 136.

31. "Interview with Ralph T. Briggs," Office of Naval Intelligence (Washington, DC, January 13, 1977) and "Interview" (Ralph Briggs) by Mrs. Percy L. Greaves (Las Vegas, August 14, 1988). Briggs served with Station M as an intercept operator during the latter half of 1941.

32. Office of Chief of Naval Operations, "Establishment of Naval Coastal Frontiers" (July 1, 1941), NARA Seattle, RG 181, 13th Naval District–15, District Plans Office 1919–1948, A16-1, Box 10; NARA Seattle, RG 181, 13th Naval District Plan 0-7, Annex D (April 1941), Box 1, DNC 8 and DNC 1.

33. Included the following stations: Naval Air and RDF Station, Sitka (AE); Naval Intercept/RDF Station, Bainbridge Island (SAIL) or Fort Ward (Washington); Point St. George (TARE) near Crescent City, California; Farallon Islands (FOX), California; and Point Arguello and Imperial Beach (ITEM) near San Diego. Staff HQ, 13th Naval District "Operating Instructions, Strategic Direction Finder Operations" (Seattle, October 1941), NARA II, RG 38, CNO CNSG Library, Boxes 121–122 (3270).

34. Staff HQ, 13th Naval District "Operating Instructions, Strategic Direction Finder Operations" (Seattle, October 1941), NARA II, RG 38, CNO CNSG Library, Boxes 121–122 (3270).

35. Ingersoll, "Bearings on Japanese Merchant Ships" (Washington, DC, April 2, 1941), NARA San Bruno, RG 181, Office of the 12th Naval District, Commandant, General Correspondence, Boxes 4 and 5, Compartment 3105.

36. Ingersoll, "Bearings on Japanese Merchant Ships" (Washington, DC, April 2, 1941), NARA San Bruno, RG 181, Office of the 12th Naval District, Commandant, General Correspondence, Boxes 4 and 5, Compartment

3105; NARA Laguna Niguel (now Riverside), RG 181, Commandant 11th Naval District, Secret C-76 (April 4, 1940), Box 19671; NARA Seattle, RG 181, 13th Naval District, Commandant's Office, Central Subj. Files 1938– 1941, Box 1, A6-2(1).

37. NARA Laguna Niguel (now Riverside), RG 181, 11th Naval District "Communications" (San Diego, April 24, 1941) A6/A6-2, Chief of Staff Operations, Box 56.

38. Elfendah, "Bainbridge Island Waves," 10.

39. Stations such as those at Point St. George (Station T or TARE) and Imperial Beach (Station I or ITEM) sent their RDF reports directly to SAIL's Plotting Center by TWX. The RDF capability included two Model DT and DY Intermediate–High-Frequency Receivers and one Low-Frequency Receiver. Another 11 Type RAA, RAB, and RAS high-frequency receivers performed the radio intercept functions at the station. The two systems were supported by some 60 operators, sometimes including advanced level students. "GX File Copy," NARA II, RG 38, Inactive Stations, Box 79 (3220/1), Seattle, October 27, 1941; "Naval Air Station Sitka, Alaska," 3 and 4, NARA Seattle, RG 181, 13th Naval District Plan 0-7, Annex A.

40. Station S, November and December 1941, "Radio Intelligence Report" (Bainbridge Island, December 3, 1941), 14, NARA Seattle, RG 181, Box 1, Folder A6-3, Station S.

41. "Foreign Ships—Movement of," NARA San Bruno, RG 181, File A8-2/A2-12/16 (Pearl Harbor, January 14, 1941).

42. Station S had five tape recorders, one Ediphone sound recorder, two diversity banks with three signal receivers each, as well as seven high-frequency receivers and one low-frequency receiver. A large array of antenna systems focused on various ranges of megacycles and related degree angles. These included two diversity antenna systems, four rhombic antenna systems, five single doublet antennas, one double antenna, and finally six triple doublet systems. "Station S, December 1941," NARA II, RG 38, Inactive Stations, Box 79; "TWX Service Between Intercept Stations and Navy Department," NARA II, RG 457, Box 1358, Commander Correspondence (Washington, DC, March 5, 1941); PHAH, Part 8, 3560.

43. "Radio Intelligence Report for Month Ending November 30, 1941," NARA Seattle, RG 181, Box 1, Folder A6-3, Seattle, December 1, 1941; "W/T Organization," August 2, 1941, NARA Seattle, RG 181, 13th Naval District Secret Log, A8(4), District Communications Office 1934–1941, Entry 50; NARA Seattle, Central Subject File (Entry 501), District Communications Office, 13th Naval District, Box 1, Folder A6-3, Seattle, December 1, 1941; NARA II, RG 38, Inactive Stations, Box 22.

44. "Establishment of Direct Wire and Radio Communication etc.," NARA San Bruno, RG 181, COM 13, File EF A16-13-39; "W/T

Organization," August 2, 1941, NARA Seattle, RG 181, 13th Naval District Secret Log, A-8(4), District Communications Office 1934–1941, Entry 50.

45. Tate's equipment consisted of one model DY High-Frequency Direction Finder, one model RAS-1 High-Frequency Receiver, one intermediate frequency direction finder, and some 11 RAA, RAB, RAS, and RAU receivers. Urgent dispatches were sent by radio; the more routine reporting was accomplished through airmail and phonograph recordings that were sent on a weekly basis to the 13th Naval District at Seattle. Tate was supported by five radio intercept and RDF personnel. "Radio Intelligence Reports for November and December 1941," NARA Seattle, RG 181 Central Subject Files, 1934–1945, Entry 50, 13th Naval District, Box 7, Folder A8-4; NARA Seattle, RG 181, 13th Naval District Plan 0-7, Annex A, 7g; "Other Stations in the Alaska Area during World War II," NCVA *Cryptolog Special Edition* (1991), 27.

46. "Oral History Interview: Robert Ogg" (1983), SRH 255, Dudley Knox Library (Monterey, CA), 3, 14, 19, 21, 24, 33, 35, 42, 46–49, and 50; NARA San Bruno, RG 181, P16-3/A8(3).

47. PHAH, Part 36, 64. It should be noted that Rear Admiral W. S. Anderson, Director Naval Intelligence (DNI) in Washington, DC, developed a uniform, type district intelligence organization and diagram, dated December 5, 1939. Special instructions for the various districts' "Intelligence Branch" state that each would maintain a chart "plot . . . of enemy forces for ready reference." It went on to state that the information for the plot was to come from all possible sources, including any source "under D.N.I. or not." (NARA San Bruno, RG 181, A-3-1/ND 14 Staff HQ, Central Correspondence 1938–1942, Box 18, Compartment 3108).

48. "Intercept Station 'T'," NCVA *Cryptolog* (Winter 1992), 15; "Personnel Assigned," NARA San Bruno, 12th Naval District Commandant's Coded Admin. Records, Boxes 112–127, Compartment 3089; "West Coast High Frequency Direction Finder Net," NARA II, RG 38, Inactive Stations, Box 14; NARA San Bruno, RG 181, File A6-2/A-6(21), Office of the Commandant, HQ 12th Naval District, Box 286.

49. "Personnel Assigned," NARA San Bruno, RG 181, mm/P16-3/NR(4), 12th Naval District Commandant's Coded Admin. Records (September 10, 1941), Boxes 112–127, Compartment 3089; "Communications Intelligence Organization," NARA II, RG 457, Box 1419.

50. PHAH, Part 16, 2295.

51. *Oakland Tribune*, July 13, 1999.

52. "Luke McNamee" (July 23, 2013), http://digital-commons.usnwc.edu/nwc-review/vol66/iss3 and author notes from interview with Patty McNamee, granddaughter of Luke McNamee, at NARA Seattle, July 24, 2013.

53. "Transoceanic Radio Telegraph Circuits," NARA II, RG 38, Inactive Stations, Boxes 76 and 157; "Station H Statistical Section Call List HYOO

8," NARA II, RG 457, Box 1315 (NR 3934), Folder "Codes and Ciphers of Japan," August 31, 1941; Laurance Safford letter to Percy Greaves, "Symbols on Translations," May 15, 1962, FDR Library, Toland Papers, Box 123.

54. Stinnett, *Day of Deceit*, 192; NARA Laguna Niguel (now Riverside), RG 181, Box 196741, 11th Naval District, Secret Serial C-76, April 4, 1940; PHAH, Part 35, 441–454; PHAH, Part 37, 1094; Robert Dollar Papers: Bang mss 69/113c, cartons 71, 72, and 75–77, vol. 45–47 (Bancroft Library, Berkeley, California); Press Wireless Papers, Press Wireless #1, 68/2 and press Wireless #2, 63/3 (San Francisco State University Research Center).

55. Layton, Pineau, and Costello, *And I Was There*, 50.

56. ITEM was well equipped with one each DT, DY, and DK RDF systems, three RAS receivers, and two transmitters (TBK-11 and TAX-1). Letters to OP-20-G (Safford), dated October 27 and November 24, 1941: IB 24-41C (Imperial Beach) and ND 11/S67 (11th Naval District, San Diego) respectively, NARA II, RG 38, Inactive Stations, Box 14.

57. Hoyt, "Navy Radio Imperial Beach," 9; "TINA Method of Matching Characteristics of Individual Wireless Operators (Radio Finger Printing) 1941," NARA II, RG 457, Box 1435 (NR 4806).

58. Hoyt, "History of USN Radio Point Arguello," 1; "High Frequency Radio Direction Finder Stations," NARA II, Command Correspondence 1941, OP-20-G (June 28, 1940), RG 457, Box 1358 (NR 4166).

59. "Mid-Pacific Strategic High Frequency Direction Finder Net, Organization," Commandant 14th Naval District, August 21, 1940, NARA II, RG 38, CNO CNSG Library, Box 197.

60. "Organization Fourteenth Naval District," NARA San Bruno, RG 181, Office of the Commandant 14th Naval District, A8-2, Box 1; "Joint Defense Operating Plan," NARA San Bruno, RG 181, A-16 and A-16/A7-3, 14th Naval District Commander Special Interest, Box 1; PHAH, Part 36, 329.

61. T. Emanuel letter, July 23, 1941, NARA San Bruno, RG 181, 12th Naval District General Correspondence, Office of Commandant, A6-1 (DCO-14), Box 4 of 6; "Personnel Recommendations Communications Intelligence Activities" (June 4, 1940), NARA San Bruno, RG 181, General Correspondence Office of the Commandant, Box 4 of 6; NARA II, RG 457, SRH Vol. 1, 376.

62. Type 405 with an 80 counter system, including 1 alphabetic summary punch device with 20 positions of control. In addition, there were obtained a Type 80 Sorter that was capable of sorting 400 IBM data cards per minute, a Type 513 Summary Punch Reproducer, a Type 77 Collator, a Type 55 Alphabetic Duplicating printing punch, and some 600,000 IBM Tabulating Cards of various types for recording data. "Statistical Machinery for Cryptographic Work" (OP-20-GY, July 23, 1937; July 18, 1940; and November 7, 1940), NARA II, RG 457, Box 1126; NARA San Bruno, RG 181, entry 47, 14th Naval District, Box 6.

63. "Camera-Oscillograph—Study of U.S. Fleet Radio Emissions," Commandant 14th Naval District, A16-3/A7-2/FPXXI, May 24, 1940, NARA II, RG 38, Office of CNO, CNSG Library, Box 197; NARA II, RG 38, Inactive Stations, Box 83 (3225/1).

64. High-Frequency—RAO-RAS 1—30 megacycles range focused on the IJN's radio communications systems and the XR1 and RAA 10–100 kilocycles lower ranges of frequencies. Related recording equipment involved some 6 Recorders Type 4-G, 12 Tape Pullers Type 4-F, 6 Line Amplifiers, 6 Tape Reels Type 7-H, and 6 Tape Bridges Type 1-K. Receiving equipment involved the RCA diversity, model RAE-1, and the General Electric model RAE, which could receive continuous wave signals at speeds of 1,000 words per minute. In addition there were the Boehme High-Speed Ink Recorder, Type 4-G, and its Tape Puller models 2-F and 4-F, which enabled it to receive at speeds from 15 to 575 words per minute. For exchanging daily and weekly plots of RDF data and ship locations with the 12th and 13th Naval Districts, as well as OP-20-G in Washington, the 14th Naval District utilized the navy's ECM-coded COPEK circuit for urgent dispatches. For lower priority intelligence reports, the U.S. postal airmail service was generally utilized. Station HYPO also relayed intercepted IJN 5-Num operational signals (even though they could not be deciphered) via the navy's ECM systems. These priority intercepts were usually reenciphered before being transmitted as an additional security measure against possible compromise of the system; otherwise they, too, were sent by airmail. Also utilized was the TESTM circuit for exchanging RDF data with Station CAST in the Philippines, as well as OP-20-GX. Safford to Dyer letter, May 9, 1940, "Communications Intelligence Stations, Fourteenth Naval District, Materiel Requirements"; September 24, 1940; January 17 and February 21, 1941 (14th Naval District reports), NARA II, RG 457, Box 1626.

65. "High Speed Operation of Radio Circuits," 14th Naval District, NARA San Bruno, RG 181, A-6-2(2)/(433); "Radio Direction Finding Bearings," 12th and 13th Naval Districts, NARA San Bruno, RG 181, A6-2; Layton, Pineau, and Costello, *And I Was There*, 139.

66. Pekelney, "Electronic Cipher Machine (ECM) Mark II"; Pekelney, "What Is the SIGABA-ECM Mark II And Why It Was Important?"

67. Layton, Pineau, and Costello, *And I Was There*, 95; PHAH, Part 32, 98, 141, and 358.

68. Rochefort, *Oral History*, 105 and 151; PHAH, Part 8, 3560.

69. "Current Employment of Personnel," Rochefort reports of September 22 and November 15, 1941, NARA II, RG 38, Inactive Stations, Box 81; Carlson, *Joe Rochefort's War*, 99; SRH 355: Capt. J. S. Holtwick, Naval Security Group History, 427–429.

70. "Combat Intelligence Unit, Establishment of," NARA San Bruno, RG 181, Communication Staff Special Interest, A8-2, Box 1 (Compartment 3114).

71. NARA II, RG 38, Inactive Stations, Box 23; PHAH, Part 32, 216.

72. PHAH, Part 32, 358 and 360; NARA II, RG 38, Inactive Stations, Box 23; Layton, Pineau, and Costello, *And I Was There*, 58.

73. J. J. Rochefort, "Current Employment of Personnel Pearl Harbor Unit, 15 November 1941," NARA II, RG 38, Inactive Stations, Box 81; Holmes, *Double-Edged Secrets*, 57; Spector, *Eagle Against The Sun*, 154.

74. "Station H. Statistical Call List, 31 August 1941," NARA II, RG 457, Box 1315 (NR 7934) "Codes and Ciphers of Japan—HYOO 8."

75. "Station H Status of Personnel," July 12, 1941, NCVA *Cryptolog* (Spring 2001), 10; NARA II, RG 38, Inactive Stations, Box 81; Stinnett, *Day of Deceit*, 54–55.

76. NARA II, RG 38, Inactive Stations, Box 81.

77. NCVA *Cryptolog Special Edition—Dutch Harbor* (1991); see also U.S. Marine Corps study of November 22, 1940, NARA Seattle, RG 181, Box 14, 13th Naval District Central Subject Files 1892–1948, NA 34-Q8/53-1//PSNS 13, NA50; NARA Seattle, RG 181, Box 1, 13th Naval District Plans 1932–1948, DNC 8 and DNC 7.

78. In addition to the DT high-frequency direction finder, King also had two Type RAS search receivers, a typewriter, a LM frequency meter, and an electronic cipher machine (ECM). "High Frequency D/F Radio Intelligence Report," NARA Seattle, RG 181, 13th Naval District Communications Office, Box 4, A8-2; NCVA *Cryptolog Special Edition—Dutch Harbor* (1991), 6–7; "HF D/F-Radio Intelligence Reports (Dutch Harbor)" (2 pages), NARA San Bruno, RG 181, 12th Naval District Communications, A6-2.

79. NCVA *Cryptolog* (Spring 1985), 3; "U.S. Naval Communications Supplementary Activity Vaitogi [VICTOR], Samoa," 1 and 6–9, NARA II, RG 38, CNO-CNSG Library, Box 195, SRH 180.

80. "U.S. Naval Communications Supplementary Activity Vaitogi [VICTOR], Samoa," 1 and 6–9, NARA II, RG 38, CNO-CNSG Library, Box 195, SRH 180.

81. NCVA *Cryptolog* (Summer NFI), 15; Miller, *War Plan Orange*, 101.

82. "Radio Intelligence Service, Development of," NARA II, RG 38, Inactive Stations, Box 18.

83. "Intercept Station 'C'," NCVA *Cryptolog* (Summer 1992), 4–5.

84. "Intercept Station 'C'," NCVA *Cryptolog* (Summer 1992), 6, 11, and 16; NARA II, RG 457, Box 949 (NR 2792); Winslow, *The Fleet the Gods Forgot*, 10.

85. NARA II, RG 38, Inactive Stations, Box 22; Stinnett, *Day of Deceit*, 310–312.

86. NCVA *Cryptolog Special Edition* (Summer 1992), 10.

87. NARA II, RG 38, CNO-CNSG Library, Box 113; PHAH, Part 38, 45.

88. NARA II, *SRH180*, RG 457, Box 949, 51 and 53–55; PHAH, Part 36, 61; PHAH, Part 38, 45–47.

89. NARA II, RG 38, Office of CNO, CNSG Library, Box 176; PHAH, Part 36, 61.

90. NARA II, RG 38, Inactive Stations, Boxes 16 and 18; RG 457, Box 949; Stinnett, *Day of Deceit*, photo section between pages 208–209.

91. "COMINT History of Guam," NARA II, RG 38, Office of the CNO, CNSG Library, Boxes 196–197, 1, C-1 and C-2.

92. A total of 16 pieces of signal intercept receiving equipment were utilized, consisting of various types of RAA, RAS-1, RAO, XR, NC, and RME receivers. The receivers were supported by a 650-foot-high "tilted" antenna on 39 kHz for Tokyo interceptions, a 500-foot-high "tilted" antenna on 125 kHz also for Tokyo interceptions, a 175-foot vertical antenna for low-frequency interceptions, a half-wave doublet cut for 4075 kHz interceptions, and a diamond cut for 8440 kHz interceptions. NARA II, RG 38, Office of the CNO, CNSG Library, Boxes 196–197, 2, 14–16, 22–23, and A-1; NCVA *Newsletter* (July 1982), 3.

93. "Libugon Hill Naval Radio Station [BAKER]," NCVA *Cryptolog Guam Special Issue* (Fall 1993 11.

94. Miller, *War Plan Orange*, 70–71; NCVA *Newsletter* (July 1982), 3.

95. Wilford, "Watching the North Pacific," 133–134; Aldrich, *Intelligence and the War against Japan*, 22–26 and 36; Stinnett, *Day of Deceit*, 289.

96. Lt. Cdr. A. McCollum/Capt. A. G. Kirk, Director ONI, "Proposed Joint Instruction Regarding Cooperation with British Intelligence in the Far East," July 8, 1941, and Secretary of Navy Frank Knox, "Letter to Secretary of State," Serial No. 038513, November 8, 1941, NARA II, RG 457, Box 1358 (NR 4166); PHAH, Part 36, 61.

97. Lt. Cdr. A. McCollum/Capt. A. G. Kirk, Director ONI, "Proposed Joint Instruction Regarding Cooperation with British Intelligence in the Far East," July 8, 1941, and Secretary of Navy Frank Knox, "Letter to Secretary of State," Serial No. 038513, November 8, 1941, NARA II, RG 457, Box 1358 (NR 4166); PHAH, Part 36, 61.

98. McCollum, *Reminiscences of Rear Admiral Arthur H. McCollum*, 354–355.

99. Thorpe, *East Wind, Rain*, 37.

100. Layton, Pineau, and Costello, *And I Was There*, 206; Thorpe, *East Wind, Rain*, 51 and 53; Aldrich, *Intelligence and the War against Japan*, 81; Lt. Cdr. A. McCollum/Capt. A. G. Kirk, Director ONI, "Proposed Joint Instruction Regarding Cooperation with British Intelligence in the Far East," July 8, 1941, and Secretary of Navy Frank Knox, "Letter to Secretary of State," Serial No. 038513, November 8, 1941, NARA II, RG 457, Box 1358 (NR 4166).

101. "Military Attaché Report 5725" and "Detection N.E.I." from COIS Singapore to Navy Department (T.O.O. 05130/27), NARA II, RG 38, Inactive Stations, Box 54.

102. Leutze, *A Different Kind of Victory*, 199; NARA II, RG 457, Box 792 (NR 2222); Thorpe, *East Wind, Rain*, 53.

103. Stinnett, *Day of Deceit*, 331, fn 6; "Johan Everhard Meijer Ranneft" (February 5, 2012).

104. Stinnett, *Day of Deceit*, 40–41.

105. NARA II, RG 457, Box 1419 (NR 4640).

CHAPTER 4

1. Burns, *Roosevelt, The Lion and the Fox*.
2. Sherwood, *Roosevelt and Hopkins*, 364.
3. Kennedy, *The Rise and Fall of the Great Powers*, 329.
4. Kennedy, *The Rise and Fall of the Great Powers*, 285.
5. Crowley, *Japan's Quest for Autonomy*, 159.
6. Carlson, *Joe Rochefort's War*, 56.
7. Carlson, *Joe Rochefort's War*, 56. In the code book, each word or code group was represented by five numbers of the coded text. Example: 12345, meaning "Tokyo." For a military term, the five numbers were frequently followed by an X. Example: 54321X, meaning IJN ship *Akagi*. The other was an *additive* code book. It was utilized to confuse a code breaker with meaningless "additives" selected from a separate table or book of other five-digit numbers, which were then added arithmetically to each basic five-digit code cipher. Example: one could take a number 63982, representing a battleship, from the primary code book, and add 12345 as the additive or superencryption to form the number 75227. This would then be transmitted via radio as part of the original coded message consisting of a variety of other similarly formed five-number combinations.
8. Henry Stimson, *Diary* entry of January 25, 1932, Yale University Microfilm Library; Stimson and Bundy, *On Active Service in Peace and War*, 243–244.
9. Kennedy, *Rise and Fall of the Great Powers*, 334.
10. Howarth, *Fighting Ships of the Rising Sun*, 185.
11. Howarth, *Fighting Ships of the Rising Sun*, 188 and 194.
12. Kennedy, *Rise and Fall of the Great Powers*, 283; Potter, *Yamamoto*, 33.
13. Grew, *Ten Years in Japan*, 185–188.
14. Crowley, *Japan's Quest for Autonomy*, 299–300.
15. Blair, *Silent Victory*, 64; Kennedy, *Rise and Fall of the Great Powers*, 296.
16. Gallup, *The Gallup Poll Vol. I*, 46.
17. Crowley, *Japan's Quest for Autonomy*, 308–309 and 319.
18. Crowley, *Japan's Quest for Autonomy*, 377 and 396–397.

19. Toland, *The Rising Sun*, 57.

20. Thompson, *A Time for War*, 76–80.

21. Thompson, *A Time for War*, 100, 108 and 150.

22. Gallup, poll of October 6–11, 1937, *The Gallup Poll Vol. I*, 90.

23. Grew, *Ten Years in Japan*, 270–271.

24. Grew, *Ten Years in Japan*, 121.

25. Toland, *The Rising Sun*, fn on 55–56; Kennedy, *Rise and Fall of the Great Powers*, 330; Simpson, *Admiral Harold R. Stark*, 13.

26. Gallup, *The Gallup Poll Vol. I*, 84.

27. Chang, *The Rape of Nanking*, 144–147.

28. *Vinson Act* of May 17, 1938, https://govtrackus.s3.amazonaws.com /legislink/pdf/stat/52/STATUTE-52-Pg401.pdf; Simpson, *Admiral Harold R. Stark*, 25; Kennedy, *Rise and Fall of the Great Powers*, 296 and 331; Miller, *War Plan Orange*, 251.

29. Kennedy, *Rise and Fall of the Great Powers*, 302.

30. Kennedy, *Rise and Fall of the Great Powers*, 304, 309, and 330.

31. Kennedy, *Rise and Fall of the Great Powers*, 200–201.

32. Gallup, "Japan June 16," poll of May 20–25, 1939, *The Gallup Poll Vol. I*, 159; Herring, *From Colony to Superpower*, 530.

33. *New York Herald Tribune*, December 21, 1939; *New York Times*, November 30, 1940.

34. Simpson, *Admiral Harold R. Stark*, 9; Richardson, *On the Treadmill to Pearl Harbor*, 156–157.

35. Richardson, *On the Treadmill to Pearl Harbor*, 160.

36. Gallup, "European War," poll of September 18, *The Gallup Poll Vol. I*, 180.

37. Isaacson, *Einstein*, 407 and 471–472; Wigner, "Leo Szilard," 337–347.

38. Isaacson, *Einstein*, 472–475.

39. DeGroot, *The Bomb*, 23; Isaacson, *Einstein*, 275–276; Ambrose, *Rise to Globalism*, 3–4; Perkins, *The Roosevelt I Knew*, 164. Note: Author copy of Einstein letter to FDR courtesy of Franklin D. Roosevelt Presidential Library at Hyde Park, New York.

40. Isaacson, *Einstein*, 477.

41. *Report of National Defense Research Committee* (July 16, 1941), FDR Library, Secretary File, Box 2.

42. Brown and MacDonald, *The Secret History of the Atomic Bomb*, 31; Davis, *FDR: The War President*, 304–335; Hewlett and Anderson, *History of the United States Atomic Energy Commission*, 37–39 and 41.

43. Davis, *FDR: The War President*, 310; Hewlett and Anderson, *History of the United States Atomic Energy Commission*, 44–45.

44. Brown and MacDonald, *The Secret History of the Atomic Bomb*, xviii.

45. Kennedy, *Rise and Fall of the Great Powers*, 340.

46. Gallup, "European War," poll of May 29, 1940, *The Gallup Poll Vol. I*, 226.

47. Churchill, *The Second World War, Vol. 2, Their Finest Hour*, 24–25.

48. Churchill, *The Second World War, Vol. 2, Their Finest Hour*, 56–57.

49. Perkins, *The Roosevelt I Knew*, 19.

50. Simpson, *Admiral Harold R. Stark*, 39–40; Richardson, *On the Treadmill to Pearl Harbor*, 433.

51. Kennedy, *Rise and Fall of the Great Powers*, 331.

52. Gallup, *The Gallup Poll Vol. I*, 225.

53. Churchill, *The Second World War, Vol. 2, Their Finest Hour*, 142.

54. Feis, *The Road to Pearl Harbor*, 41.

55. Miller, *War Plan Orange*, 5; "Strategic Materials Desired [by Japan] from East Indies," Naval Attaché Report (Tokyo) to ONI, June 20, 1940, FDR Library, Secretary File, Box 66; "1937 Japanese/French Shipments of Iron Ore from New Caledonia," Intelligence Report, ONI Serial No. 208-31, File 407-100, Commandant's Office, 14th Naval District, NARA II, RG 457, Box 598.

56. Herring, *From Colony to Superpower*, 539.

57. Naval Attaché Report (Tokyo) No. 132 (August 2, 1940) and No. 137 (September 6, 1940) to Office of Naval Intelligence, FDR Library, Secretary File, Box 68 (Tokyo Vol. II).

58. McCollum, *Reminiscences of Rear Admiral Arthur H. McCollum*, 104.

59. *Japanese-German-Italian Agreement*, Report No. 167, U.S. Embassy Tokyo, October 1, 1940, FDR Library, Secretary File, Box 82; PHAH, Part 6, 2852.

60. Herring, *From Colony to Superpower*, 531.

61. Miller, *Bankrupting the Enemy*, 92–93.

62. "Japanese Plans to Seize the Dutch East Indies," ONI (F-2) Memorandum (October 16, 1940), FDR Library, Secretary File, Box 58.

63. Kennedy, *Rise and Fall of the Great Powers*, 341.

64. Israel, *War Diary of Breckenridge Long*, 129.

65. Layton, Pineau, and Costello, *And I Was There*, 39; McCollum, *Reminiscences of Rear Admiral Arthur H. McCollum*.

66. Potter, *Yamamoto*, 103–104.

67. McCollum, *Reminiscences of Rear Admiral Arthur H. McCollum*, 104.

68. ONI OP-16-F report: "Naval Situations—Information Summary" (January 17, 1941), 12, NARA II, RG 313, JICPOA, Box 27.

69. "Dutch East Indies," *Life* (January 22, 1940); Van Mook, *The Netherlands Indies and Japan*.

70. Van Mook, *The Netherlands Indies and Japan*; "Oil Industry in Dutch East Indies" (May 13, 1930), NARA II, RG 38, CNO Records, Box 1;

"Netherlands East Indies Field Monograph 1939–46," NARA II, RG 38, CNO Records, Box 3, 83.

71. Miller, *Bankrupting the Enemy*, ix–x.

72. PHAH, Part 36, 18 and 64. See also Appendix A, this volume.

73. Gallup, poll of June 9, 1940, 227, and poll of July 7, 1940, 231, *The Gallup Poll Vol. I*.

74. See McCollum's Memorandum in Appendix A, this volume; Gallup, *The Gallup Poll Vol. I*, 246.

75. Howarth, *Fighting Ships of the Rising Sun*, 234; PHAH, Part 1, 261.

76. Simpson, *Admiral Harold R. Stark*, 56; PHAH, Part 1, 262 and 265–266.

77. Richardson, *On the Treadmill to Pearl Harbor*, 427; PHAH, Part 1, 266.

78. Richardson, *On the Treadmill to Pearl Harbor*, 435.

79. Layton, Pineau, and Costello, *And I Was There*, 54.

80. Admiral H. R. Stark, Memorandum for the Secretary (November 12, 1941), FDR library, Secretary File, Boxes 4 and 59; Miller, *War Plan Orange*, 270; Simpson, *Admiral Harold R. Stark*, 66–67.

81. Tugwell, *The Democratic Roosevelt*, 560; Herring, *From Colony to Superpower*, 524–525.

82. Gallup, *The Gallup Poll Vol. I*, 250.

83. Churchill, *The Second World War, Vol. 2, Their Finest Hour*, 560–556.

84. Churchill, *The Second World War, Vol. 2, Their Finest Hour*, 568–569; Perkins, *The Roosevelt I Knew*, 352–353.

85. Churchill, *The Second World War, Vol. 3, The Grand Alliance*, 20; and Sherwood, *Roosevelt and Hopkins*, 249.

86. Churchill, *The Second World War, Vol. 3, The Grand Alliance*, 20.

87. Grew, *Ten Years in Japan*, 368; PHAH, Part 2, 2582; PHAH, Part 14, 1042 (full text).

88. "Rumored Japanese Attack on Pearl Harbor," McCollum to Kimmel, OP-16-F2, Serial No. 09716, January 31, 1941 (dispatched February 1, 1941), NARA II, RG 80, PHLO, Office of the CNO, Box 4; Potter, *Yamamoto*, 56–57.

89. Potter, *Yamamoto*, 56–57.

90. Miller, *War Plan Orange*, 271.

91. Miller, *War Plan Orange*, 272.

92. Morison, *The Battle of the Atlantic*, 38–52.

93. Miller, *War Plan Orange*, 271.

94. Gallup, poll of February 24, 1941, *The Gallup Poll Vol. I*, 266.

95. Simpson, *Admiral Harold R. Stark*, 101–102; PHAH, Part 16, 2150; PHAH, Part 33, 1203–1204; Richardson, *On the Treadmill to Pearl Harbor*, 427.

96. PHAH, Part 33, 1199.

97. PHAH, Part 26, 339–340; PHAH, Part 35, 431; PHAH, Part 37, 1026.

98. Stinnett, *Day of Deceit*, 323, fn 15.

99. Stinnett, *Day of Deceit*, 323, fn 15–17.

100. NARA II, RG 457, Box 1358, CNO to CINCAF (February 7, 1941).

101. Israel, *War Diary of Breckenridge Long*, 132.

102. Toland, *The Rising Sun*, 145.

103. "Memorandum for Secretary of Navy" (September 30, 1941), FDR Library, Secretary File, FDR Correspondence for September 1941.

104. "Japan-Soviet Neutrality Pact," Naval Attaché Report (Tokyo), April 16, 1941, Serial No. 55, Intelligence Division, Office of Naval Operations, FDR Library, Secretary File, Boxes 62 and 82; Kennedy, *Rise and Fall of the Great Powers*, 142.

105. "Memorandum for the Under Secretary of the Navy: British Shipping Situation, March 16, 1941," NARA II, RG 38, Inactive Stations (ONI, March 27, 1941), copy author's files.

106. "Naval Situations—Great Britain" (January 17, 1941), Office of Naval Intelligence Report, NARA II, RG 313, JICPOA, Box 27; FDR Library, Secretary File, Box 59.

107. "Unlimited National Emergency," retransmission to all Navy personnel by SECNAV (27 May 1941), NARA Laguna Niguel (now Riverside), RG 181, A-14, Box 1.

108. Gallup, "European War," Survey #239-K, poll of June 29, 1941, *The Gallup Poll Vol. I*, 286.

109. NARA Laguna Niguel (now Riverside), RG 181, 11th Naval District, A-9, Secretary of the Navy, Box 81.

110. "15,000 Plane Program etc.," NARA Laguna Niguel (now Riverside), RG 181, Box 41, CNO OP-12A-drc. Serial 010212.

111. "Biennial Report of the Chief of Staff, July 1, 1941," in *War Department: Report of the Secretary of War to the President, 1941* (Washington, DC: Government Printing Office, 1941), 55–56.

112. Sherwood, *Roosevelt and Hopkins*, 357; NARA II, RG 457, NSA P-10, Box 38.

113. PHAH, Part 12, Exhibit No. 1, 1–2.

114. PHAH, Part 12, 2–3 (PURPLE #255).

115. PHAH, Part 12, 3–4.

116. PHAH, Part 12, 4–6 (PURPLE #406 and 545).

117. Miller, *Bankrupting the Enemy*, 172–174.

118. "Memorandum," July 3, 1941, NARA San Bruno, RG 181, OP-16-F-2, COM 14, Confidential File; PHAH, Part 17, 2601.

119. Secretary of the Treasury, Reports of July 5 and 8 and November 19, 1941, FDR Library, Secretary File (Treasury), Box 78.

120. Miller, *Bankrupting the Enemy*, 174 and 178; Ickes, *Secret Diary of Harold L. Ickes*, Vol. II, 390.

121. Department of Treasury, "Exports of Petroleum Products 1941," FDR Library, Secretary File, Box 78.

122. Howarth, *Fighting Ships of the Rising Sun*, 250; Miller, *Bankrupting the Enemy*, 170, 187, 189, and 242.

123. "Welles-Nomura Memorandum" (July 24, 1941), FDR Library, Secretary File, Box 43.

124. Miller, *Bankrupting the Enemy*, 241.

125. Miller, *Bankrupting the Enemy*, 1–2.

126. Miller, *Bankrupting the Enemy*, 198–203.

127. Miller, *Bankrupting the Enemy*, 166; Kennedy, *Rise and Fall of the Great Powers*, 343.

128. Barnhart, *Japan Prepares for Total War*, 255.

129. Kennedy, *Rise and Fall of the Great Powers*, 303; Vat, *The Pacific Campaign*, 104; PHAH, Part 20, 4393.

130. "Third Konoye Cabinet," Naval Attaché (Tokyo) Intelligence Report, Serial 79-41 (July 29, 1941), NARA II, RG 80, PHLO, Box 55.

131. Miller, *Bankrupting the Enemy*, 257.

132. PHAH, Part 12, 9 (PURPLE #433).

133. "Japanese Naval Oil Storage," Naval Attaché Report (Tokyo) No. 71 (June 27, 1941), FDR Library, Secretary File, Box 66; Report (Item) 6-3-94, FDR Library, Secretary File, Box 67; Howarth, *Fighting Ships of the Rising Sun*, 254; Kennedy, *Rise and Fall of the Great Powers*, 302.

134. A. G. Kirk, director of naval intelligence, "Fortnightly Summary of Current National Situations" (ONI, August 1, 1941), NARA II, RG 313, Box 27; "Intelligence Report: Japan Political Estimate, August 20, 1941," OP-16-F-2, ONI NARA San Bruno, RG 181, 14th Naval District Staff HQ, General Correspondence 1935–42, Box 33, Compartment 3108.

135. FDR Library, Secretary File, Box 67, Item G-3-95, July 1941; PHAH, Part 6, 2629; PHAH, Part 31, 3218; PHAH, Part 34, 186.

136. NARA II, RG 38, CNSG Library, Office of CNO, August 14, 1941, Box 149.

137. A. G. Kirk, director of naval intelligence, "Fortnightly Summary of Current National Situation" (ONI, August 15, 1941), Copy No. 2, NARA II, RG 313, JICPOA, Box 27.

138. Rochefort, *Reminiscences of Captain Joseph J. Rochefort*, 65.

139. Layton, Pineau, and Costello, *And I Was There*, 131–133; Franklin Roosevelt and Winston S. Churchill, "Proposed Declaration [Atlantic Charter]," August 12, 1941, FDR Library, Roosevelt Papers for August 1941. This is copy 1 of the typewritten, black and red ink–corrected Atlantic Charter that was eventually released in final form to the public.

140. Layton, Pineau, and Costello, *And I Was There*, 134.

141. Weintraub, *Long Day's Journey into War*, 301; Churchill, *The Second World War, Vol. 3, The Grand Alliance*, 593.

142. PHAH, Part 12, 17.

143. Letter, August 8, 1941, 13th Naval district Liaison Officer, NARA Seattle, RG 181, A8-2/EF 37. See also RG 181, Box 1, 13th Naval District Communications Office, Log A-8(1), Entry 50.

144. Henry L. Stimson, *Diary* entry of August 19, 1941, 37, Yale University Microfilm Library, Reel 7, Volume 35.

145. Henry L. Stimson, *Diary* entry of August 19, 1941, 20, Yale University Microfilm Library, Reel 7, Volume 35.

146. Gallup, "Japan" Question 13, poll of September 7, 1941, *The Gallup Poll Vol. I*, 296.

147. Simpson, *Admiral Harold R. Stark*, 93; Sherwood, *Roosevelt and Hopkins*, 365.

148. Morison, *The Battle of the Atlantic*, 79–81.

149. Herring, *From Colony to Superpower*, 533–534; Simpson, *Admiral Harold R. Stark*, 90.

150. Stark to Kimmel letter, September 23, 1941, PHAH Part 33, 1168; Simpson, *Admiral Harold R. Stark*, 94.

151. Morison, *The Battle of the Atlantic*, 92–93; and Herring, *From Colony to Superpower*, 534.

152. Herring, *From Colony to Superpower*, 534; Gallup, "European War," Question #6, poll of October 3, 1941, *The Gallup Poll Vol. I*, 299.

153. PHAH, Part 33, 1175.

154. Wedemeyer, *Wedemeyer Reports!*, 34, 65, 74–75; *Chicago Tribune*, December 4, 1941; John Toland taped interview of Wedemeyer, FDR Library, SRT 84-3-43 (CD).

155. Wedemeyer, *Wedemeyer Reports!*, 19–20, 34, and 65–66.

156. Wedemeyer, *Wedemeyer Reports!*, 34.

157. Rosenman, *Working with Roosevelt*, 303.

158. Kennedy, *Rise and Fall of the Great Powers*, 353 and 355.

159. Grew, *Ten Years in Japan*, 439–440.

160. Sherwood, *Roosevelt and Hopkins*, 356.

161. PHAH, Part 12, 261.

162. PHAH, Part 12, 262; "Japanese Espionage at Hawaii," NARA II, RG 38, CNO-CNSG Library, Box 164.

163. Tolley, *Cruise of the Lanikai*, 32–33.

164. PHAH, Part 20, 4468; Usher Book listing of the Sarnoff visit and White House luncheon with Roosevelt, FDR Library, October 14, 1941.

165. PHAH, Part 23, 686.

166. PHAH, Part 33, 1171.

167. PHAH, Part 33, 1171–1172.

168. PHAH, Part 33, 1238.

169. Office of Naval Intelligence (ONI), "Fortnightly Summary of Current National Situation" (October 15, 1941), NARA II, RG 313, JICPOA, Box 27.

170. Office of Naval Intelligence (ONI), "Fortnightly Summary of Current National Situation" (November 1, 1941), NARA II, ARG 313, JICPOA, Box 27.

171. PHAH, Part 12, 72–73; Sherwood, *Roosevelt and Hopkins*, 356.

172. Henry L. Stimson, *Diary* entry of October 16, 1941, 136–137, Yale University Microfilm Library, Reel 7, Volume 35.

173. Ickes, *Secret Diary of Harold L. Ickes*, Vol. III, 630.

174. PHAH, Part 12, 100; PHAH, Part 33, 736.

175. Hull, *Memoirs of Cordell Hull*, Vol. 2, 1056–1062.

176. Grew, *Ten Years in Japan*, 470; PHAH, Part 2, 680, which quotes Grew's comments on Japanese attitudes and psyche: "National suicide not only possible, but probable." (November 3, 1941, message to Cordell Hull).

177. PHAH, Part 11, 5420; Henry L. Stimson, *Diary* entry of November 6–7, 1941, Yale University Microfilm Library, Reel 7, Volume 36.

178. Henry L. Stimson, *Diary* entry of November 7, 1941, Yale University Microfilm Library, Reel 7, Volume 36; PHAH, Part 5, 2121.

179. PURPLE intercept of November 25, 1941, PHAH, Part 12, 130.

CHAPTER 5

1. SRH 149, Safford, "A Brief History of Communications Intelligence in the United States," 6.

2. National Bureau of Standards, *Radio Transmission Handbook*, 2–7; NARA Laguna Niguel (now Riverside), RG 181, A6-2(1), Box 17.

3. National Bureau of Standards, *Radio Transmission Handbook*, 8–9 and 12–16.

4. Robert Stinnett, e-mail to author September 25, 2008; Stinnett, *Day of Deceit*, 54–56; NARA II, RG 457, Boxes 1315, 1470, and 1473.

5. R. E. Ingersoll, *Japanese Naval Code Systems*, Secret Serial 081420 of October 4, 1940, NARA II, RG 38, Office of the CNO-CNSG Library, Box 13; SRH 149, Safford, "A Brief History of Communications Intelligence in the United States," 13.

6. SRH 149, Safford, "A Brief History of Communications Intelligence in the United States," 13; NARA II, RG 457, NSA P-10, Box 38.

7. R. E. Ingersoll, *Japanese Naval Code Systems*, Secret Serial 081420 of October 4, 1940, NARA II, RG 38, Office of the CNO-CNSG Library, Box 13.

8. Laurence Safford to Joseph Wenger letter, September 10, 1940, NARA II, RG 38, Inactive Stations (NSG), Box 6.

9. Pelletier, "My Life with JN-25," 3 and 5.

10. Rusbridger, "JN-25, the NSA, and Pearl Harbor," 4; NARA II, RG 457, SRH 355, 398.

11. Aldrich, *Intelligence and the War against Japan*, 77.

12. Carlson, *Joe Rochefort's War*, 120.

13. Rochefort, *Reminiscences of Captain Joseph J. Rochefort*, 99; Layton, Pineau, and Costello, *And I Was There*, 64; PHAH, Part 8, 3560.

14. Rochefort, *Reminiscences of Captain Joseph J. Rochefort*, 121; NARA II, RG 38, Inactive Stations, Box 54; PHAH, Part 36, 61.

15. SRH 149, Safford, "A Brief History of Communications Intelligence in the United States," 13; Carlson, *Joe Rochefort's War*, 121.

16. "Chronology of Japanese Naval Codes (JN 25 Series)," NARA II, RG 457, Box 1419; SRH 355, Part 1, 398, NARA II, RG 457, Box 108.

17. Kahn, *Seizing The Enigma*, 11–12.

18. U-33 in February 1940, Shiff-26 in April 1940, Krebs trawler in March 1941, U-110 in May 1941, and the Lauenburg weather ship in July 1941. Sebag-Montefiore, *Enigma: The Battle for the Code*, 59, 69, 73–74, 76, 119, 140, 143–144, 151, 161–162, 312–320, 329, and 390–391; Budiansky, *Battle of Wits*, 23–25.

19. Gladwin, "Alan M. Turing's Critique," 50–54; Hanyek, "Still Desperately Seeking Miss Agnes," 23; Safford to Greaves letter, May 15, 1962, FDR Library, John Toland Papers, Box 123.

20. Carlson, *Joe Rochefort's War*, 206–207; Layton, Pineau, and Costello, *And I Was There*, 358; Prados, *Combined Fleet Decoded*, 74; Rochefort, *Oral History*, 128–130.

21. SRH 149, Safford, "A Brief History of Communications Intelligence in the United States," 14.

22. CINCAF to CNO, March 5, 1941, NARA II, RG 38, Inactive Stations, Box 54.

23. 16th Naval District to CNO Fabian letter, May 5, 1941, NARA II, RG 38, Inactive Stations, Boxes 15 and 18.

24. SRH 305, Safford, "The Undeclared War History of R.I.," 22–24, NARA II, RG 38, CNSG Library, Box 196; Laurance Safford, NCVA *Cryptolog Supplement* (Summer 1987), A-13-1–15; PHAH, Part 33, 848 and 852–853.

25. Spector, *Eagle Against The Sun*, 11; PHAH, Part 33, 855, and 863–864; West, *The SIGINT Secrets*, 205.

26. Layton, Pineau, and Costello, *And I Was There*, 91; SRH 305, Safford, "The Undeclared War History of R.I.," 23.

27. PHAH, Part 35, 441–456; PHAH, Part 36, 62 and 64; SRH 149, Safford, "A Brief History of Communications Intelligence in the United States," 15.

28. PHAH, Part 23, 686.

29. Myers, "Key Role of Japanese Cryptolinguists in WW II COMINT," 2; Departments of the Army and the Air Force, *Fundamentals of Traffic Analysis (Radio-Telegraph)*, 24; "Traffic Analysis," 2–3, NARA II, RG 457, Boxes 549 (NR 1404) and 938 (NR 2719).

30. NSA, *History of Crypto Operations*, NARA II, RG 457, Box 806, 1–5; NARA II, RG 38, Inactive Stations, Box 84.

31. Departments of the Army and the Air Force, *Fundamentals of Traffic Analysis (Radio-Telegraph)*, 8.

32. NARA II, RG 457, Box 1435; NARA II, RG 38, Inactive Stations, Box 84.

33. NARA II, RG 38, RIP44, 17-9 and 17-17.

34. Departments of the Army and the Air Force, *Fundamentals of Traffic Analysis (Radio-Telegraph)*, 3–15; Prados, *Combined Fleet Decoded*, 75; Spector, *Eagle Against The Sun*, 14–15.

35. There were three types of radio call signs in use for the IJN's warships: an *administrative* two kana + number (example: HE YO 6); a *tactical* or *secret* number + two kana (example: 8 YU NA); and a three kana (example: HO MO SA) for major land bases and ports. NARA II, RG 457, Boxes 1284, 1315, 1470, and 1473; NARA II, RG 38, Inactive Stations (NSG), Box 18.

36. NARA II, RG 457, Boxes 1284, 1315, 1470, and 1473; NARA II, RG 38, Inactive Stations (NSG), Box 18.

37. NARA II, RG 457, Boxes 1284, 1315, and 1470–1473.

38. Rochefort, *Oral History*, 127–128 and 133; Prados, *Combined Fleet Decoded*, 79 and 80–81.

39. Rochefort, *Oral History*, 127–130; 14th Naval District, IBM punchcard example submitted to OP-20-GY, October 12, 1939, NARA II, RG 457, Box 953.

40. "IBM Operations," NARA II, RG 457, Box 1126, 1–13 (note: pages 2–13 not numbered)

41. Keen, *Wireless Direction Finding*, 32–35, 40–41, and 256–259; "Direction Finding Bearings," NARA Laguna Niguel (now Riverside), RG 181, Box 54, Commandant, 11th Naval District, CF 30, January–December 1941; "Bearings Report," NARA Seattle, RG 181, A6-2, Box 9, 13th Naval District, Serial NO. 784; SRH 211, "Japanese Radio Communications and Radio Intelligence," January 1, 1945, NARA II, RG 457, Box 83; Aldrich, *Intelligence and the War against Japan*, 75, fn. 5,

42. *ModelDY-2* (Washington, DC: Radio Laboratory, Navy Yard, April 1941), NARA II, RG 457, Box 1129, 3 and plates 1C and 9.

43. Departments of the Army and the Air Force, *Fundamentals of Traffic Analysis (Radio-Telegraph)*, 43–44; NARA II, RG 38, Inactive Stations, Boxes 117, 145, and 164; Keen, *Wireless Direction Finding*, 258–259 and 564–565; Calder, *How to Read a Nautical Chart*, 12-1 and 12-2.

44. NARA II, RG 38, Inactive Stations, Box 14; Tom Warren, NCVA *Cryptolog* (July 1981), 5.

45. NARA II, RG 38, Inactive Stations, Box 14.

46. "Far East Y Organization," NARA II, RG 38, Inactive Stations, Box 54; West, *The SIGINT Secrets*, 248; Aldrich, *Intelligence and the War*

against Japan, 37; SRH 149, Safford, "A Brief History of Communications Intelligence in the United States," 4.

47. SRH 149, Safford, "A Brief History of Communications Intelligence in the United States," 16; NARA II, RG 38, Inactive Stations, Box 18; NARA II, RG 457, Box 1358, Commander's Correspondence Serial 230820, May 16, 1941.

48. "CAST Monthly Report," NARA II, RG 38, Inactive Stations (NSG), Boxes 15 through 18.

49. Miller, *War Plan Orange,* 61–62; Blair, *Silent Victory,* 89; "Employment of Me and Equipment" (June, September, and October 1941), NARA II, RG 38, Inactive Stations, Boxes 15 and 16.

50. PURPLE #433 (July 25, 1941), PHAH, Part 12, 316.

51. Whitlock, "The Silent War against the Japanese Navy," 4–5.

52. NARA II, RG 38, Inactive Stations, Box 15.

53. NARA II, RG 38, Inactive Stations, Box 15; John Lietwiler to R. L. Densford letter, October 6, 1941, NARA II, RG 38, Inactive Stations, Box 18.

54. Prados, *Combined Fleet Decoded,* 214; Whitlock, "Station 'C' Corregidor As I Recall It," 19.

55. CAST TESTM (RDF) reports for October 4 and 8, 1941, including both hard copy IJN ship listings by radio call sign and bearings with initials "TGH" (Lt. Thomas Glendon Hoover) and coded TESTM Station C copy, NARA II, RG 38, Inactive Stations, Box 18.

56. "Station 'C' Monthly Report, Part III Direction Finding," NARA II, RG 38, Inactive Stations, Box 18 (3270/1 Philippines), 193–236; NARA II, RG 38, Box 370/2/23/7.

57. SRH 406, NARA II, RG 38, Inactive Stations, 9.

58. TEST(M) for December 4, 1941, Station CAST, NARA II, RG 38, Inactive Stations, Box 18.

59. NARA II, RG 38, Inactive Stations, Box 196.

60. Aldrich, *Intelligence and the War against Japan,* 36–38, 75, 80–81; "Far East Y Organization," NARA II, RG 38, Inactive Stations, Box 54, 1 and 14.

61. Layton, Pineau, and Costello, *And I Was There,* 206; Leutze, *A Different Kind of Victory,* 199.

62. Lietwiler to Parke letter, November 16, 1941, NARA II, RG 38, Inactive Stations, Box 15.

63. SRH 406, NARA II, RG 38, Inactive Stations.

64. Leutze, *A Different Kind of Victory,* 199; Winslow, *The Fleet the Gods Forgot,* 1, 8–9, and 23–24.

65. NARA Laguna Niguel (now Riverside), RG 181, Box 741, Commandant 11th Naval District, Secret Serial C-76 (April 4, 1940); Safford to Greaves letter, May 15, 1962, FDR Library, John Toland Papers, Box 123.

66. Farago, *The Broken Seal,* 392–395.

67. "Japanese Raiders and Potential Armed Merchant Cruisers" (April 4, 1941), NARA San Bruno, RG 181, 12th Naval District, Office of Commandant, General Correspondence, Box 4 (Compartment 3105); Prados, *Combined Fleet Decoded*, 595.

68. NARA San Bruno, RG 181, Commander-in-Chief File No. A16/059, Correspondence (January 14, 1940).

69. NARA II, RG 38, CNO-CNSG Library, Box 149; McCollum, *Reminiscences of Rear Admiral Arthur H. McCollum*, 317.

70. PHAH, Parts 36–38, Hewitt Inquiry 70, Document 38; NARA II, RG 80, Box 41.

71. Carlson, *Joe Rochefort's War*, 135; "Subject: Tracking Japanese Merchant Ships" and Enclosure: Photostat Great Sailing Chart of North Pacific for period July 12–25 inclusive, NARA II, RG 313, Box 48, 14th Naval District, A 6-2/ADCO, Z-2033, July 28, 1941.

72. "Japanese Merchant Ship Locations," reports of July 9, 16, 23, and 30, 1941, NARA San Bruno, RG 181, 12th Naval District, Commandant's File, V4006, Box 13 (Compartment 3089).

73. Pelletier, "My Life with JN-25."

74. Layton, Pineau, and Costello, *And I Was There*, 471–472.

75. Ernest E. Wolcott, District Communications Officer, 13th Naval District (Seattle) to Lt. Cdr. George W. Welker, OPNAV, Navy Building, Washington, DC, letter, November 1941, NARA II, RG 38, Inactive Stations, Boxes 121–122.

76. NARA San Bruno, RG 181, 12th Naval District Commandant's File QS1/EF(8), 1941, V4006 Box 13 (Compartment 3089); Station S Monthly Report #803 for November 1941, NARA Seattle, RG 181, Central Subject Files 1934–1945, Entry 50, 13th Naval District, Box 1, Folder A6-3; Commander North West Sea Frontier, 13th Naval District, A9-6/F31-CI; NARA II, RG 457, Box 1315; PHAH, Part 32, 541.

77. Bainbridge Island to CNO TWX reports for November 3, 7 and 9, 1941, NARA II, RG 38, Inactive Stations, Box 80.

78. Layton, Pineau, and Costello, *And I Was There*, 92; PHAH, Part 32, 358; Potter, *Yamamoto*, 54–55.

79. Layton, Pineau, and Costello, *And I Was There*, 125.

80. Rochefort, *Oral History*, 111.

81. Duane Whitlock, letter, November 23, 1985, NCVA *Cryptolog* (Spring 1986).

82. NARA San Bruno, 14th Naval District Commandant's File, RG 181, Box 4, Compartment 3108; NARA II, RG 38, Inactive Stations, Box 81; Holmes, *Double-Edged Secrets*, 62; PHAH, Part 35, 46.

83. Layton, Pineau, and Costello, *And I Was There*, 77–78, 94, and 119–120; PHAH, Part 2, 811–813; PHAH, Part 10, 4697 and 4846; PHAH, Part 36, 320.

84. Blair, *Silent Victory*, 88.

85. Layton, Pineau, and Costello, *And I Was There*, 92–93; Carlson, *Joe Rochefort's War*, 98–99; Rochefort, *Oral History*, 114–115 and 127; PHAH, Part 35, 46.

86. Evans and Peattie, *Kaigun*, 360.

87. NARA II, RG 38, Box 149, *Hewitt Inquiry*, Parts 36–38, Exhibit 70, Document 40, 299.

88. NARA II, RG 38, Box 149, *Hewitt Inquiry*, Parts 36–38, Exhibit 70, Document 40, 299.

89. Layton, Pineau, and Costello, *And I Was There*, 119.

90. PHAH, Part 35, 46; Evans and Peattie, *Kaigun*, 111; Layton, Pineau, and Costello, *And I Was There*, 124 and 126–127; Mayfield report of July 29, 1941, NARA San Bruno, RG 181, Box 27, Compartment 3108, 14th Naval District, A-8-2, General Correspondence.

91. Layton, Pineau, and Costello, *And I Was There*, 128.

92. "Memorandum: Combat Intelligence Unit; Establishment of," August 15, 1941, NARA San Bruno, RG 181, Box 1, Compartment 3114, Communications Staff Special Interests (A8-2).

93. Carlson, *Joe Rochefort's War*, 100; Rochefort, *Oral History*, 157–158; "Pearl Harbor Unit—Current Employment of Personnel," NARA II, RG 38, Inactive Stations, Box 81, September 22, 1941; Holmes, *Double-Edged Secrets*, 4, 15–16, and 18–19.

94. "Station H Statistical Section Call List August 31, 1941 (HYOO 8)," NARA II, RG 457, Box 1315, 260–261.

95. "Station H Statistical Section Call List August 31, 1941 (HYOO 8)," NARA II, RG 457, Box 1315, 260–261; "Great Circle Chart, North America-Far East;" author's own "Great Circle Sailing Chart of the North Pacific Ocean" (NIMA Ref. NO. WOPZP56, 1973).

96. "Station H Statistical Section Call List August 31, 1941 (HYOO 8)," NARA II, RG 457, Box 1315, 260–261.

97. "Pearl Harbor Unit—Current Employment of Personnel, September 22, 1941, NARA II, RG 38, Inactive Stations, Box 81.

98. "Pearl Harbor Unit—Current Employment of Personnel, September 22, 1941, NARA II, RG 38, Inactive Stations, Box 81; PHAH, Part 8, 3560.

99. "Station H Statistical Section Radi Organization List," September 23, 1941, NARA II, RG 457, NSA Historical Crypto Collection, Box 1376; Carlson, *Joe Rochefort's War*, 115 and 122; "Combat Intelligence Plot, Utilization of, " September 23, 1941, NARA II, RG 80, PHLO, Box 41, Fourteenth Naval District A4-3/14ND/CI serial Z-2048 (Note: mentions plots to be made on "8 x 10 Chart of the Pacific, and are to be entered on cards [IBM] for future reference").

100. PHAH, Part 10, 4831; PHAH, Part 26, 42, and 44; Rochefort, *Oral History*, 146–148; Layton, Pineau, and Costello, *And I Was There*, 183.

101. NARA Seattle, RG 181, COM 14, Secret Serial Z-2051, October 8, 1941, and COM 13, A6-2 file; Communications Summary (COMSUM), July 15, 1941, NARA II, RG 80, PHLO, Box 41.

102. NARA II, RG 38, Inactive Stations, Box 113. For one of the best commentaries and analyses of Japan's espionage effort against the U.S. Pacific Fleet at Pearl Harbor see Stinnett, *Day of Deceit*, 83–118.

103. Weintraub, *Long Day's Journey into War*, 12; Layton, Pineau, and Costello, *And I Was There*, 146.

104. Prados, *Combined Fleet Decoded*, 151–153.

105. PHAH, Part 12, 261: For the complete J-19 Code, September 24, 1941, Tokyo to Honolulu "bomb plot message" as transcribed and translated on October 9, 1941, see NARA II, RG 38, CNO CNSG, Box 113 (copy author's file) and Appendix B this volume.

106. PHAH, Part 12, 262: For the complete J-19 Code, September 29, 1941, Honolulu (Kita) to Tokyo bomb plot message with amplified Pearl Harbor grid code coordinates, see NARA II, RG 38, CNO CNSG, Box 113 (copy author's file) and Appendix B this volume.

107. Layton, Pineau, and Costello, *And I Was There*, 131.

108. Layton, Pineau, and Costello, *And I Was There*, 164.

109. PHAH, Part 36, 64.

110. PHAH, Exhibits, Part 17, 2570–2600; PHAH, Part 33, 946 (Exhibit No. 4-WPL-46).

111. Toland, *Infamy*, 57–60 and 63; Layton, Pineau, and Costello, *And I Was There*, 166; Prados, *Combined Fleet Decoded*, 166; NARA II, RG 457, Box 579 (Kirk-Wilkinson letters); PHAH, Part 4, 1841–1842 and 1849.

112. PHAH, Part 10, 4697–4698; PHAH, Part 36, 320.

113. Toland, *Infamy*, 105–106; Layton, Pineau, and Costello, *And I Was There*, 165.

114. Carlson, *Joe Rochefort's War*, 155.

115. PHAH, Part 23, 686; Layton, Pineau, and Costello, *And I Was There*, 132 and 167; Agawa, *The Reluctant Admiral*, 251.

116. *Usher Book*, October 14, 1941, FDR Library; PHAH, Part 20, 4468; Japanese Honolulu Consulate's message log book, PHAH, Part 35, 430ff.; PHAH, Part 36, 64.

117. "Interrogation Report No. 10: Captain Minoru Genda, Pearl Harbor Attack," NARA II, RG 38, CNSG Library, Box 167, 1; Toland, *The Rising Sun*, 178 and 185; Vat, *The Pacific Campaign*, 120–121; Prados, *Combined Fleet Decoded*, 111, 114, 129, and 137.

118. Potter, *Yamamoto*, 66 and 68.

119. Station H intercept operators can be identified by their initials appearing on the messages as part of the time of intercept (TOI) data: "XT"—RM2 J. Howard, "DX"—RM2 E. Disharoon, "RX"—RM2 R. Finley,

"JR"—RM2 J. Randle, "SG"—S. Gramblin, etc. Station H "Status of Personnel," NARA II, RG 38, Inactive Stations, Box 84.

120. NARA II, RG 457, Boxes 139–144, Serials 078, 410, 490, 502, and 504; Potter, *Yamamoto*, 64.

121. NARA II, RG 457, Boxes 139–144, Serials 10800 and 11500.

122. NARA II, RG 457, Boxes 139–144, Serials 337, 506, and 702.

123. NARA II, RG 457, Boxes 139–144, Serials 026, 068, 269, 312, 414, 726, and 830.

124. NARA II, RG 457, Boxes 139–144, Serial nfi.; Layton, Pineau, and Costello, *And I Was There*, 112.

125. NARA II, RG 457, Boxes 139–144, Serial 26823.

126. NARA II, RG 457, Box 1470; Layton, Pineau, and Costello, *And I Was There*, 173.

127. PHAH, Part 6, 2517.

128. PHAH, Part 6, 2516.

129. PHAH, Part 12, 100; PHAH, Part 32, 129; PHAH, Part 33, 736.

130. NARA II, RG 80, PHLO, Box 41; Layton, Pineau, and Costello, *And I Was There*, 55 and 111–112; Combat Intelligence Unit (CIU), 14th Naval District, *Traffic Intelligence Summary* (*TIS*), Part I (July16–December 31, 1941), *SRMN-012*, Dudley Knox Library, Naval Post Graduate School, Monterey, California, 196.

131. Combat Intelligence Unit (CIU), 14th Naval District, *Traffic Intelligence Summary* (*TIS*), Part I, COMSUM, November 6, 1941, 199.

132. "Organization of the Japanese Fleets," NARA II, RG 313, Box 2, OP-16-F-2, ONI Serial #54-41, October 30, 1941.

133. Naval Analysis Division, *Campaigns of the Pacific War*, Appendix 14, "Japanese Dispatches Ordering Commencement of Hostilities," 49–50.

134. Navy Department translations of pages 1–2 and 152 from *Combined Fleet Operations Orders 1 and 2*, dated November 5 and 7, 1941, respectively, found on the sunken IJN heavy cruiser *Nachi* in Manila Bay in April 1945, NARA II, RG 38, CNSG, Box 167.

135. *Memorandum* for Admiral Edwards, Order No. 1, September 28, 1945, NARA II, RG 38, CNSG, Box 167.

136. Naval Analysis Division, *Campaigns of the Pacific War*, Appendix 14.

137. "Station H Status of Personnel," July 12, 1941, NARA II, RG 38, Inactive Stations, Box 84; Stinnett, *Day of Deceit*, 51: note full page reproduction of actual translation of message intercept in spring of 1946.

138. NARA II, RG 457, Boxes 139–144, Serials: 054, 111, 123, 174, 395, 514, 564, 604, 633, 636, 687, 792, 795, and 803.

139. Holmes, *Double-Edged Secrets*, 81.

140. "Weekly Summary—Far East," Serial #56-41, November 1, 1941, OP-16-F-2, ONI intelligence report, NARA II, FG 313, Box 27.

141. Robert Stinnett, *IJNSMS Vol. I* (Oakland Park, California), 49, 56–57, 69, 73, 83, and 89; see also Rochefort, "Communications Intelligence Summary," on WI WI message transmissions, November 13, 1941, NARA II, RG 80, PHLO, Box 41.

142. Minoru Genda, "Pearl Harbor Attack," *Interrogation Report No. 10*, Naval Technical Mission, November 28, 1945, NARA II, PHLO, Box 4; Potter, *Yamamoto*, 39.

143. PHAH, Part 13, 713–717; Carlson, *Joe Rochefort's War*, 137.

144. PHAH, Part 1, 185 and 238; Goldstein and Dillon, *Pearl Harbor Papers*, 143; See also Station S, December 1941 Monthly Report: "Direction Finder Characteristic of Enemy Transmissions," NARA Seattle, RG 181, Box 6, 13th Naval District Secret Log, A6-3–A8-3, 12-A.

145. "Radio Deception," 5, NARA Seattle, RG 181, Station AE, December 1941; Rochefort, *Oral History*, 157.

146. Robert Stinnett, *IJNSMS Vol. I* (Oakland Park, California), 66, 83, and 89–90.

147. Robert Stinnett, *IJNSMS Vol. I* (Oakland Park, California), 66–67, 83, and 89.

148. Robert Stinnett, *IJNSMS Vol. I* (Oakland Park, California), 70; Goldstein and Dillon, *Pearl Harbor Papers*, 16 and 174–176.

149. Carlson, *Joe Rochefort's War*, 138.

150. Carlson, *Joe Rochefort's War*, 138.

151. PHAH, Part 15, 1878–1879; McCollum, *Reminiscences of Rear Admiral Arthur H. McCollum*, "Memorandum: Japanese Fleet Locations."

152. Layton, Pineau, and Costello, *And I Was There*, 183 and 185.

153. Layton, Pineau, and Costello, *And I Was There*, 174; Carlson, *Joe Rochefort's War*, 132; NARA II, RG 80, Philippines Liaison Office (PHLO), Box 41; PHAH, Part 26, 4680.

154. Robert Sherrod, Memorandum for David W. Hulburd, Jr., "Subject: General Marshall's Conference Today," November 15, 1941.

155. Robert Sherrod, Memorandum for David W. Hulburd, Jr., "Subject: General Marshall's Conference Today," November 15, 1941; Sherrod, *I Can Tell It Now*, 39–45.

CHAPTER 6

1. PHAH, Part 26, 48; Records of CNO—Plans and Orders: CINCPAC, Confidential A-4–3/FFU(1), NARA II, RG 38, Box 19, (NND 968133); CINCPAC Order 37-44 (November 5, 1941), copy in author's file; NARA II, RG 38, CNO CSNG Library, Box 149; "U.S. Pacific Fleet Employment Schedule (October–December 1941)," NARA II, RG 80, PHLO, Box 3; King and Whitehill, *Fleet Admiral King*, 281–282; Carlson, *Joe Rochefort's War*, 90. It

should be noted that CNO Stark had informed Admiral Kimmel on several occasions in 1941 to employ some of his ships to the northward of Hawaii in order to detect approaching Japanese raiders (PHAH, Part 4, 2015).

2. PHAH, Part 33, 1169.

3. "Organization of the U.S. Pacific Fleet" (September 11, 1941), NARA II, RG 80, PHLO, Box 3.

4. "CINCPAC Operations Order No. 37-41, Annex A, Part I," NARA II, *op. cit.* See also "CINCPAC Order, 37-41" (November 5, 1941), Confidential A-4-3/FF 12[1], Serial 0181, NARA II, RG 313.

5. NARA II, *op. cit. Annex A, Part II (Exercise191)*; *Pacific Fleet Tactical Bulletin No. 3-41: Battle Plan 2M1*, NARA Laguna Niguel (now Riverside), RG 181, CO PACPLT 1941, CF 18c, Box 37, 1 and 2.

6. *Lexington* aircraft carrier "Deck Log," Sunday, November 23 (8 a.m.), NARA II, RG 24, Box 5510; "North Pacific Ocean Hawaii to French Frigate Shoals," *NOAA* Chart #19007, NARA II, RG 370, in which the Prokofiev Seamount is clearly depicted.

7. PHAH, Part 5, 2488; PHAH, Part 6, 2517; PHAH, Part 33, 1173–1174; NARA II, RG 38, Inactive Stations, CNO Papers, Box 62; NARA II, RG 313, file A-16-3, Exercise 191. It should be noted that Admiral Kimmel had discussed the vulnerabilities of Pearl Harbor as a Pacific Fleet base with both CNO Stark and Roosevelt in the spring of 1941, informing them that "the only real answer to an attack was not to have the Fleet in port" (PHAH, Part 6, 2619).

8. Vice Admiral W. Halsey Order No. 112–41, NARA II, RG 313.

9. Goldstein and Dillon, *Pearl Harbor Papers*, 37; PHAH, Part 15, 1882–1883; McCollum, OP-16-F-2, "Memorandum: Japanese Fleet Locations"; Carlson, *Joe Rochefort's War*, 139; "Interrogation Report," November 22, 1945 (Captain Minoru Genda) NARA II, RG 38, CNSG Library, 1.

10. PURPLE #812, November 22, 1941, PHAH, Part 33, 877 and 1365.

11. Henry L. Stimson, *Diary* entry of November 25, 1941, 48–49, Yale University Microfilm Library, Reel 7, Volume 36, copy author's file; PHAH, Part 11, 5421.

12. PHAH, Part 11, 5194.

13. PHAH, Part 11, 49.

14. NARA II, RG 38. CSNG Library, Box 196; PHAH, Part 33, 1366.

15. PURPLE #1189, PHAH, Part 33, 1369–1370; "Hull's Final Deal," NARA II, RG 80, PHLO, Box 6.

16. NARA II, RG 80, PHLO, General Records Navy, Box 53; PHAH, Part 33, 702 and 1177.

17. PHAH, Part 33, 1286.

18. PHAH, Part 32, 404.

19. PHAH, Part 6, 2519; PHAH, Part 32, 108; NARA II, RG 80, PHLO, Box 41.

20. NARA II, RG 80, PHLO, Box 41.

21. PHAH, Part 11, 5422 and 5433.

22. PHAH, Part 11, 5423.

23. NARA II, RG 38, CNSG Library, Box 161; PHAH, Part 4, 1328.

24. PHAH, Part 3, 1310; PHAH, Part 11, 5424; PHAH, Part 14, 1328.

25. PHAH, Part 39, 85.

26. NARA II, RG 38, Box 161.

27. Lt. Gen. Short realized that coast artillery and antiaircraft artillery were located in and around Honolulu itself. To have gone on a "high level" alert would have meant army troops manning their guns and moving ammunition into ready racks for immediate loading in preparation to fire under the gaze of any Americans and Japanese living or passing by in the area. In addition, it was estimated that the Japanese consulate maintained an espionage network of some 80 agents. Ultimately, as an antisabotage defense solution, Short located some 475 army and navy aircraft together in groups under guard at their respective airfields. PHAH, Part 7, 2985; PHAH, Part 32, 408; PHAH, Part 35, 524 and 555–557; "Naval Attaché Intelligence report No. 61," April 25, 1941, NARA II, RG 313, Box 2.

28. NARA II, RG 38, CNSG Library, Box 161. See also Robert Shivers's FBI report, *Honolulu Star Bulletin Edition* (Home) for December 6, 1957, 1–8, Column 1, FDR Library, Toland Papers, Box 133.

29. NARA II, RG 38, CNO-NSC Library, Box 167; PHAH, Part 7, 3015–3016. Short took the precautions as directed by Marshall, but only after the attack had taken place did he realize in mid-December that it became clear "there was not a single attempt made to sabotage any of these essential utilities on the morning of December 7" ("The Lack of Sabotage at Pearl Harbor," report of February 9, 1942, PHAH, Part 35, 337–338.

30. NARA II, RG 38, Box 164; RG 80, General Records Navy, PHLO, Box 53; PHAH, Part 33, 1176.

31. NARA II, RG 38, Box 164; PHAH, Part 32, 564.

32. PHAH, Part 22, 526; PHAH, Part 32, 289, 403, and 615; PHAH, Part 35, 52–62.

33. NARA II, RG 38, CNO CNSG Library, Boxes 113, 149, 164, and 183; see also cable messages from Tokyo to Honolulu for September 24; November 18, 20 and 28; and December 2 and 6, 1941. Note: torpedo nets were not requested for Pearl Harbor, since the maximum harbor depth was no more than 46 feet and it was thought that aerial torpedoes needed at least 75 feet to enter the water to stabilize themselves before continuing on to their targets. As such, it was thought that Pearl Harbor was immune to any form of aerial torpedo attack. (PHAH, Part 26, 67–70; PHAH, Part 32, 405; PHAH, Part 33, 1386; PHAH, Part 35, 583–590.)

34. PHAH, Part 32, 330.

35. PHAH, Part 36, 224–225.

36. Toland, *Infamy*, 62–63; Layton, Pineau, and Costello, *And I Was There*, 139–140.

37. Weintraub, *Long Day's Journey into War*, 88.

38. Naval Analysis Division, *Campaigns of the Pacific War*, Appendix 14, 50; Note: The Survey may have had access to the actual IJN message intercepts (Yamamoto's message series intercepts for the November 1941 period have not been released to the public from the U.S. government agencies concerned). Paraphrased versions of these messages can be seen in PHAH, Part 13, 415–417. The reader needs to keep in mind that November 26 is the Tokyo date/time, but, due to the international dateline that begins in Guam, the date is November 25 in Hawaii and Washington, DC. The time of 6:00 a.m., November 26, in Tokyo is 12:30 p.m., November 25, at Pearl Harbor, just as December 7 at Pearl Harbor is December 8 in Tokyo. See also Vice Admiral Homer N. Wallin, *Pearl Harbor*, 86.

39. McCollum, *Reminiscences of Rear Admiral Arthur H. McCollum*, 442–443.

40. Goldstein and Dillon, *Pearl Harbor Papers*, 187; Prange, Goldstein, and Dillon, *At Dawn We Slept*, 416.

41. Agawa, *The Reluctant Admiral*, 243 and 250; McCollum, *Reminiscences of Rear Admiral Arthur H. McCollum*, 443; Potter, *Yamamoto*, 79; Toland, *The Rising Sun*, 179.

42. Prados, *Combined Fleet Decoded*, 73 and 75; Holmes, *Double-Edged Secrets*, 28. Note: some documents claim as many as 30 I-Class submarines were included in the Shimizu Force.

43. Agawa, *The Reluctant Admiral*, 250.

44. Captain Takahisa Amagai (IJN) *AITG Report* #2 (5–6 October 1945), NARA II, RG 80, PHLO, Box 49.

45. *Kyokuto Maru* (call sign unk.), *Toohoo Maru* (TU FU 759), *Tooei Maru* (NE U 459), *Shinkoku Maru* (call sign unk.), *Nippon Maru* (SA WA 559), *Kuroshio Maru* (TE TU 459), *Kokuyo Maru* (RI TE 559), *Kenyoo Maru* (TA HA 4). November 9, 1941, U.S. Navy Intercept (NFI), NARA II, RG 457, Box 727.

46. Prados, *Combined Fleet Decoded*, 156; NARA II, RG 457, Box 727; see map in Goldstein and Dillon, *Pearl Harbor Papers*, 97.

47. Goldstein and Dillon, *Pearl Harbor Papers*, 177–178.

48. *Combined Fleet Desord #11*, 0950/25, November 1941, NARA II, RG 457, Boxes 146 and 728.

49. "Station H, Status of Personnel, November 1941," NARA II, RG 38, Inactive Stations, Box 84.

50. 1800/27 November 1941, HA FU 6 Tokyo Radio, NARA II, RG 38, CNSG Library, Box 183; NARA II, RG 457, Box 728; PHAH, Part 4, 1944.

51. NARA II, RG 38, Office of the CNO, CNSG Library, Box 49.

52. PHAH, Part 12, 317, Exhibit No. 3.

53. PHAH, Part 4, 1942.

54. NARA II, RG 38, Office of CNO, CNSG Library, Box 149; NARA II, RG 80, General Records Navy, PHLO, Box 53; PHAH, Part 4, 1944.

55. See weather reports for November 27, 28, and 30 and December 1, 1941, NARA II, RG 38, CNSG Library, Box 183.

56. Goldstein and Dillon, *Pearl Harbor Papers*, 183–185; PHAH, Part 13, 516; PHAH, Part 36, 36 and 515; 14th Naval District (HYPO) CIS for November 30, 1941, NARA II, RG 38, Inactive Stations, Box 3; NARA II, RG 80, PHLO, Box 4; NARA II, RG 457, Box 598; Layton, Pineau, and Costello, *And I Was There*, 174. The reader may wonder why there are no apparent official RDF reports concerning this series of IJN radio transmission. It should be noted here, that beginning with some of the October issues of Rochefort's CIS reports, the RDF section for each day's summary has been crudely cut off, apparently in an attempt to deny the Pearl Harbor Attack Hearings access to this otherwise critical information. In addition, the monthly Station H (HYPO) IBM statistical radio call sign and RDF bearings listings for the November (HYOO 9) and December (HYOO 10) monthly printouts covering both the mid-Pacific and West Coast Communications Intercept network of both military and commercial intercept/RDF stations (several hundred pages or more in length) are completely missing from the national archives.

57. Goldstein and Dillon, *Pearl Harbor Papers*, 186, 188, 208, and 281; PHAH, Part 13, 516.

58. NARA II, RG 457, SRN 117687, Box 147. It is interesting to note that in the NARA San Bruno Archive, RG 181, COM 14, the National Bureau of Standards (NBS) issued a report for December 1941–February 1942, indicating that on November 28–December 1 there would be a North Pacific storm of a category 8 (extremely violent) on a scale of 0 to 9. See also Bureau of Standards *Handbook*, NARA Laguna Niguel (now Riverside), RG 181, Box 196506 for solar storm activity on November 28–December 1, 1941.

59. November 19, 1941, Confidential QS/A-4-3(4), 12th Naval District, Office of the Commandant, NARA San Bruno, RG 181, Box 5 (of 6)—V40006, Compartment 3105; Grogan, "Record for Posterity," 1, 3–4, and 8, copy in author's file.

60. Grogan, "Record for Posterity," 2–3.

61. Grogan, "Record for Posterity," 3.

62. Leslie Grogan 1967 interview with Ladislas Farago, *The Broken Seal*, 385–386; Grogan, "Record for Posterity," 3; Naval Analysis Division, *Campaigns of the Pacific War*, Appendix 14.

63. Grogan, "Record for Posterity," 1; Carlson, *Joe Rochefort's War*, 160.

64. Grogan, "Record for Posterity," 8; PHAH, Part 35, 453; PHAH, Part 38, 167.

65. PHAH, Part 10, 4908.

66. SRH 255: Oral History Interview with Mr. Robert D. Ogg (1983), Monterey, California, Dudley Knox Library, 35, 37–40, and 48; see also SRH 255, NARA II, RG 38, CNS CSNG, Box 197.

67. Robert Ogg, "Nautical Tracking Chart of Pearl Harbor Strike Force Route Across the North Pacific" (1987), courtesy of Robert Stinnett, copy in author's file.

68. IJN Call List HYOO 10, December 1, 1941, to April 9, 1942, NARA II, RG 457, Boxes 1284 and 1470; note that there is an original copy and bits and pieces of several carbon copies of HYOO 10 distributed between the two boxes; copies in author's file.

69. Toland, *Infamy*, 295; "Antiaircraft Action Summary—World War II" (U.S. Fleet Information Bulletin No. 29, October 1945), 6–7, NARA Pacific Alaska Region (Seattle), RG 181, Commandant's Office Central Subject File 1940–1950, Box 13, FF 1 A16-3(1), Entry PSNS-3. Note: "The 40mm developed into the most effective weapon in the fleet." It was credited with shooting down one-third (33 percent) of all Japanese planes attempting to directly attack U.S. Navy ships in the Pacific.

70. Ranneft, *Dagboek van Schout-bij-Nacht J. E. Meijer Ranneft*, 39, original Dutch photocopy with official English translation (1995), copy in author's file courtesy of Robert Stinnett; PHAH, Part 26, 388; PHAH, Part 36, 19.

CHAPTER 7

1. Aldrich, *Intelligence and the War against Japan*, 89.

2. PHAH, Part 12, 165 (PURPLE #812).

3. Simpson, *Admiral Harold R. Stark*, 107.

4. PHAH, Part 33, 1370.

5. NARA II, RG 457, NSA P10, Box 38; PHAH, Part 33, 770: PHAH, Part 36, 67; PHAH, Part 37, 682; See also SRH 305, Safford, "The Undeclared War History of R.I.," 29, NARA II, RG 38, CSNG Library, Box 196; a copy of the original intercept and translation (RG 457, NSA P-10 in Box 38) in author file.

6. NARA II, RG 80, PHLO, Box 6, Berlin to Tokyo (PURPLE #1393, Part III), November 29, 1941, 202.

7. PHAH, Part 12, 202, and 229.

8. NARA II, RG 38, Box 164; PHAH, Part 36, 37; SRH 305, Safford, "The Undeclared War History of R.I.," 22–23 and 26.

9. Manchester, *The Glory and The Dream*, 308; Note: December 8 is the Tokyo dateline for December 7 in Hawaii and Washington, DC.

10. Blair, *Silent Victory*, 81.

11. Blair, *Silent Victory*, 81–83.

12. Leutze, *A Different Kind of Victory*, 216; Naval Intelligence Division, Office of CNO, Serial/Report 160, September 27, 1941, FDR Library, Secretary File, Box 66.

13. Blair, *Silent Victory*, 85; James, "The Other Pearl Harbor," in *No End Save Victory*, 145; Potter, *Yamamoto*, 216; NARA II, RG 80, PHLO, General Records Dept. Navy, Boxes 41 and 55: W. T. Holmes, "JICPPOA" (1947), 39, NARA II, RG 38, Inactive Stations, Box 83.

14. PHAH, Part 33, 911.

15. SRH 305, Safford, "The Undeclared War History of R.I.," 21.

16. NARA II, RG 80, PHLO, Box 53; PHAH, Part 20, 4473–4476, FDR Library, Secretary File, Box 59.

17. NARA II, RG 80, PHLO, Box 41.

18. PHAH, Part 14, 1251; PHAH, Part 33, 1361; NARA II, RG 80, PHLO, Box 41; "Intelligence Report British Empire Army-Navy-Air, Serial 52-41" from U.S. Naval Observer, Singapore, NARA II, RG 313, Box 2. It is worth noting that the Military Intelligence Division of the War Department under Brig. Gen. Sherman Miles was reporting on November 27 that there were 70,000 IJA troops in southern Indochina, along with 132 tanks, 230 artillery pieces, over 1,000 trucks, and some 5,000 collapsible rubber boats. See PHAH, Part 14, 1366–1368, FDR Library, Secretary File, Box 82.

19. Gallup, Survey #252-K, released November 22, 1941, *The Gallup Poll Vol. I*; Perkins, *The Roosevelt I Knew*, 380.

20. Brands, *Traitor to His Class*, 108.

21. PHAH, Part 9, 4252–4254; PHAH, Part 16, 2163. It should be noted that Station VICTOR in the South Pacific, during the two weeks leading up to the December 7, 1941, outbreak of the war, took upwards of some 500 RDF bearings on IJN troop transports, supply vessels, and other types of warships, all moving back and forth from Japan's home islands to Formosa, Hainan, and French Indochina. See NARA II, RG 38, Crane Inactive Stations, Box 69, for daily reports with RDF bearings.

22. PHAH, Part 2, 955; PHAH, Part 14, 1207. Note that Rear Adm. Turner testified later on that Capt. R. M. Brainard, a member of his staff, drafted the message at the direction of Roosevelt (PHAH, Part 4, 2044).

23. PHAH, Part 9, 4252–4253; PHAH, Part 11, 5427; Morton, *Fall of the Philippines*, 47; Leutze, *A Different Kind of Victory*, 223.

24. Tolley, *Cruise of the Lanikai*, 269; Winslow, *The Fleet the Gods Forgot*, 251 and 254.

25. Layton, Pineau, and Costello, *And I Was There*, 248; Tolley, *Cruise of the Lanikai*, 269; Winslow, *The Fleet the Gods Forgot*, 257–258.

26. McCollum, *Reminiscences of Rear Admiral Arthur H. McCollum*, 403; PHAH, Part 33, 889–890; PHAH, Part 36, 26.

27. PHAH, Part 32, 352.

28. PHAH, Part 33, 1390.

29. McCollum, *Reminiscences of Rear Admiral Arthur H. McCollum*, 332–333; McCollum, (OP-16-F2) "Memorandum for the Director" (December 1, 1941), NARA II, RG 80, PHLO, Boxes 4 and 6.

30. McCollum, (OP-16-F2) "Memorandum for the Director" (December 1, 1941), NARA II, RG 80, PHLO, Boxes 4 and 6; PHAH, Part 15, 1896; PHAH, Part 36, 18–19.

31. PHAH, Part 32, 381–382.

32. PHAH, Part 33, 880; PHAH, Part 36, 18; Ranneft, *Dagboek van Schout-bij-Nacht J. E. Meijer Ranneft*, 39.

33. "Daily Information Summary—OP-12, Far East," December 1, 1941, NARA II, RG 80, PHLO, Box 4.

34. PHAH, Part 33, 877.

35. McCollum, *Reminiscences of Rear Admiral Arthur H. McCollum*, 383–384 and 387–388; PHAH, Part 12, 209 (PURPLE #2444) and 215 (PURPLE #867); SRH 305, Safford, "The Undeclared War History of R.I.," 27.

36. NARA II, RG 457, NSA CNSG, Box 144.

37. JN 25 B Intercept, Serial 676, NARA II, RG 457, NSA CNSG, Box 144 (copy author file); Station H, July 12, 1941, "Status of Personnel," 14th Naval District, RG 38, Inactive Stations, Box 84 (copy in author file); SRH 305, Safford, "The Undeclared War History of R.I.," 21; Safford to Percy Greaves Jr. letter, April 10, 1963, Laurance F. Safford Collection, Accession No. 1357, Box 1, Greaves Folder, American Heritage Center, University of Wyoming.

38. Capt. L. F. Safford, "Statement Regarding Winds Message" (Washington, DC: Department of the Navy—Naval History and Heritage Command, 1946), 2–7; SRH 305, Safford, "The Undeclared War History of R.I.," 29; Station S (SAIL) Monthly Report for December 1941, "Communications Data," 7, NARA II, RG 38, Inactive Stations, Box 79; Federal Communications certification of August 18, 1941, NARA II, RG 38, Box 113; PHAH, Part 10, 4700; PHAH, Part 33, 771; Tokyo Circular #2353, November 19, 1941, 10, NARA II, RG 457, NSA, Box 38.

39. Capt. L. F. Safford, "Statement Regarding Winds Message" (Washington, DC: Department of the Navy—Naval History and Heritage Command, 1946), 1, 10–17, and 20; PHAH, Part 3, 1317–1318; PHAH, Part 8, 3579–3591; PHAH, Part 14, 1409; PHAH, Part 39, 223–226. On the Friday before December 7, the DOI placed the Far East (F-2) Section on a 24-hour continuous watch to be stood by all the senior officers involved in the processing, evaluation, and dissemination of intelligence. Pressure was now building up among the OPNAV staff.

40. PHAH, Part 32, 252; NARA II, RG 80, PHLO, Boxes 54 and 55.

41. PHAH, Part 32, 131.

42. PHAH, Part 33, 770 and 773; Toland, *Infamy*, 346.

43. PHAH, Part 8, 3588–3591; PHAH, Part 26, 392; PHAH, Part 33, 774 and 777.

44. PHAH, Part 3, 1343–1344; PHAH, Part 26, 393–394; PHAH, Part 32, 22; PHAH, Part 33, 774–775; PHAH, Part 36, 18–19; McCollum, *Reminiscences of Rear Admiral Arthur H. McCollum*, 87.

45. CAVITE (CAST) December 4 RDF bearings taken on Japanese home island radio signals simulating, in part, the *Akagi* aircraft carrier radio call signs (8 YUNA, HE HO 7, and YU NE 8), NARA II, RG 38, NSG Inactive Stations, Box 15; Beatty, "Another Version of What Started War with Japan," 49; OP-16 (December 5, 1941), "Memorandum for the President: O.N.I. Estimate of Japanese Forces in Indo-China and Adjacent Areas," NARA II, RG 80, PHLO, Box 6. Note: Rear Adm. Turner testified at a Pearl Harbor investigation hearing, "I intended that if the Japanese fleet came within somewhere around 500 miles of Hawaii that we were justified in considering that an overt act and attacking them" (PHAH, Part 4, 2046).

46. OP-16, "Memorandum for the President: O.N.I. Estimate of Japanese Forces in Indo-China and Adjacent Areas," December 5, 1941, NARA II, RG 80, PHLO, Box 6; "Oil Map of Netherlands East Indies," NARA II, RG 38, CNO Records, NEI 1939–1946, Box 3; OP-16 "ONI Estimate for the President," December 5, 1941; Ranneft, *Dagboek van Schout-bij-Nacht J. E. Meijer Ranneft*, 39.

47. Ranneft, *Dagboek van Schout-bij-Nacht J. E. Meijer Ranneft*, diary entry 2–12–1941, 39.

48. Robert E. Israel to John Toland letter, May 10, 1982, with attached message log of 1:05 a.m., December 6, 1941, FDR Library, John Toland Papers, Box 133 (copy in author file); "Organization Chart, Pacific Northern Coastal Frontier," November 13, 1941, Memorandum, A16-1(49)(E1-2), prepared by Laurence Bennett, District Plans Officer, NARA Seattle, RG 181, Box 10, 13th Naval District–15(53), District Plans Office 1919–1947, A16-1 (44–55); "Strength and Composition of Garrisons for Defense of Naval Bases in Alaska," March 21, 1941, 2, Unalaska (Dutch Harbor), NARA Seattle, RG 181, 13th Naval District Planning office, Central Subject Files 1919–1947, A16-1 (1–3), Box 1, 13 ND-15(53). It should be noted that Israel was a U.S. Army captain on duty with the 1st Battalion, 37th Infantry Battalion Headquarters located at Dutch Harbor and, by chance, kept the message locked in his personal trunk until he brought it out for a 1982 reunion with his fellow soldiers. Ultimately, when made aware of John Toland's research for *Infamy*, he then passed it on to that author.

49. Chart #1500 "Table of distances from Dutch Harbor to important points," NARA Seattle, RG 181, 13th Naval District, Central Subject Files 1892–1948, Box 14, NA 34-QB/53-1//PSNS 13, NA 50.

50. Station KING, "HF D/F Radio Intelligence Report," Operations, December 1, 1941–January 1, 1942, dated January 5, 1942, NARA Seattle, RG 181, 13th Naval District, Classified Files (Secret), A6-3 thru A8-3, Box 6; SRH 255: Oral History Interview with Mr. Robert D. Ogg (1983), 37–39, 46, and 48. Note that the 12th Naval District was using the highly respected 1938 book *Wireless Direction Finding* by Ronald Keen for training its personnel in how to conduct RDF chart plotting and tracking; copy examined by author at NARA San Bruno, RG 181, Naval District 11/N8-6/A 10, Serial RS 347 and 12th Naval District A10-3(1). See also PHAH, Part 36, 62, where Laurance Safford of OP-20-G complained that some of the West Coast naval districts are using untrained amateurs to track IJN warships, forgetting that the so-called amateurs had tracked a considerable number of the Japanese merchant marine ships as they were being recalled across the Pacific in order to mass in the home islands, as an official part of the splendid arrangement.

51. CAST COPEK, Serial 041502, COMSIXTEEN to OPNAV, December 4, 1941, NARA II, RG 80, PHLO, Box 54; Rusbridger and Nave, *Betrayal at Pearl Harbor*, 145–146. At Pearl Harbor Commander Ed Layton and Adm. Husband Kimmel noted that the IJN's change in radio call signs after only one month in service indicated that "operations on a large scale" were about to take place (PHAH, Part 36, 128).

52. Wilford, "Watching the North Pacific," 131.

53. Boner Fellers to Admiral Husband E. Kimmel letter, March 6, 1967, FDR Library, John Toland Papers, Container/Box 117; Toland, *The Rising Sun*, 214–215; Sherwood, *Roosevelt and Hopkins*, 420.

54. PHAH, Part 6, 2521; see also CINCAF and SPENAV London reports to OPNAV, December 6, 1941, NARA II, RG 80, PHLO, Box 54; NARA II, RG 38, CNO CNSG Library, Box 161.

55. PHAH, Part 10, 5082–5083; PHAH, Part 14, 1412; Leutze, *A Different Kind of Victory*, 225–228.

56. Winslow, *The Fleet the Gods Forgot*, 44–45; PHAH, Part 15, 1783; PHAH, Part 20, 4515; PHAH, Part 36, 231; NARA II, RG 38, CSNG Library, Box 164; NARA II, RG 80, PHLO, Boxes 6 and 54; NARA II, RG 313, Box 28; FDR Library, Secretary File, Box 59.

57. NARA II, RG 38, Inactive Stations, Box 17.

58. PHAH, Part 33, 1176–1179; OPNAV, December 3, 1941, Serial 031855, NARA II, RG 38, CNS Library, Box 164; NAVATT Singapore, Circular No. 12-87, NARA II, RG 80, PHLO, Box 54; OP-16-F-2, December 6, 1941, Serial 74-41, NARA II, RG 313, Box 28.

59. CINCAF to OPNAV, December 7, 1941 (Japan dateline), Serial 070329, five-part message signed Thomas C. Hart and Tom S. V. Phillips, NARA II, RG 80 PHLO, Box 54.

60. Agawa, *The Reluctant Admiral*, 250–252 and 254; Goldstein and Dillon, *Pearl Harbor Papers*, 155.

61. Potter, *Yamamoto*, 94; 179; Minoru Genda, "Interrogation Report 10," November 28, 1945, NARA II, RG 80, PHLO, Box 4.

62. Goldstein and Dillon, *Pearl Harbor Papers*, 226; Potter, *Yamamoto*, 87–88.

63. CINCPAC to CNO, "Defense of Outlying Bases," December 2, 1941, NARA San Bruno, RG 181, Communications Special Staff Interest, A 16-1/ EG 61 (1940–1941), Box 1 (Compartment 3114): PHAH, Part 17, 2479; PHAH, Part 26, 321–322.

64. PHAH, Part 26, 322–324.

65. Deck Log USS *Lexington*, December 5, 1941, "*Lexington* November– December 1941 Deck Log," NARA, RG 24, Records of Bureau of Naval Personnel, Box 5510; CINCPAC Mailgram 040237 December 1941 to COMTASKFOR 3, NARA II, RG 80, PHLO, Box 54; Layton, Pineau, and Costello, *And I Was There*, 216: PHAH Part 14, 1328. Note also the U.S. Navy Court of Inquiry challenge to Admiral Stark's decision to send Admiral Kimmel's carriers out on a plane transfer operation when the situation was every day becoming more and more critical. PHAH, Part 32, 530.

66. PHAH, Part 10, 4694; PHAH, Part 28, 870; PHAH, Part 36, 33; Carlson, *Joe Rochefort's War*, 140; Holmes, *Double-Edged Secrets*, 26.

67. Holmes, *Double-Edged Secrets*, 27; PHAH, Part 26, 59; PHAH, Part 32, 605; NARA II, RG 80, PHLO, Box 54; Station H *Chronology*, November 21, 1941, NARA II, RG 38, Box 83; Station H *Chronology*, December 4, 1941, NARA II, RG 38, Box 4; Station H *Chronology*, December 6, 1941, NARA II, RG 38, Box 10.

68. Layton, Pineau, and Costello, *And I Was There*, 18, 52, 229–230, and 525; COMSUM 14th Naval District, November 25, 1941, NARA II, RG 80, PHLO, Box 41; PHAH, Part 6, 2523; PHAH, Part 32, 582; PHAH, Part 36, 127–128.

69. Lambert and Polmar, *Defenseless*, 67; Layton, Pineau, and Costello, *And I Was There*, 223–224; Rochefort, *Reminiscences of Captain Joseph J. Rochefort*, 165; PHAH, Part 6, 2532–2534; PHAH, Part 32, 126 and 236; PHAH, Part 36, 455–456; NARA II, RG 80, PHLO, Box 54.

70. PHAH, Part 32, 334–335; PHAH, Part 33, 1348; PHAH, Part 36, 536.

71. PHAH, Part 36, 537; Lambert and Polmar, *Defenseless*, 74; Note: Newton's delivery of Marine fighter aircraft would ultimately be cancelled due to the Pearl Harbor attack (PHAH, Part 26, 344 and 536).

72. PHAH, Part 32, 237, 291, 340, 536, and 589; PHAH, Part 33, 834 and 920; Carlson, *Joe Rochefort's War*, 180; Rochefort, *Reminiscences of Captain Joseph J. Rochefort*, 160–162.

73. PHAH, Part 32, 253.

74. Stimson, Henry Lewis, *Diary*, vol. II (New Haven: Yale University Press, 1953), p. 80; Commander Cato Glover, Navy Operations Watch

Officer Log, December 6–7, 1941: introduced as part of Congressional Pearl Harbor Investigation, April 18, 1946, NARA II, RG 38, CNO CNSG Library, Box 118.

75. Station S (SAIL), "Radio Intelligence Report," December 1941, NARA II, RG 38, Crane Inactive Stations, Box 70; PHAH, Part 33, 762–763; PHAH, Part 36, 73.

76. PHAH, Part 9, 4512; PHAH, Part 14, 1414–1415; PHAH, Part 33, 763–766 and 1380; Kahn, *The Code Breakers*, 49.

77. PHAH, Part 8, 3443 and 3556–3557; PHAH, Part 9, 3983; PHAH, Part 33, 783; PHAH, Part 39, 228.

78. PHAH, Part 10, 4660–4664.

79. "Information from Documentary Evidence on Messages No. 901, 902, 907 and 910," NARA II, RG 80, PHLO, Box 14; PHAH, Part 9, 3997; PHAH, Part 33, 1384; PHAH, Part 37, 699; McCollum, *Reminiscences of Rear Admiral Arthur H. McCollum*, 789.

80. PHAH, Part 4, 1766–1768; PHAH, Part 8, 3910; PHAH, Part 33, 780 and 1385; PHAH, Part 36, 25–26 and 84; PHAH, Part 37, 700; McCollum, *Reminiscences of Rear Admiral Arthur H. McCollum*, 406–409, 411, and 413.

81. PHAH, Part 32, 416 and 428; PHAH, Part 33, 780 and 1385; McCollum, *Reminiscences of Rear Admiral Arthur H. McCollum*, 411.

82. Honolulu-Tokyo, December 6, 1941, PA-K2 diplomatic code, NARA II, RG 38, CNO CSNG Library, Box 164.

83. "Striking Force Action Summary #1, 12/171100," NARA II, RG 38, CSNG Library, Box 183.

84. "Burning of Secret and Confidential Codes and Ciphers by Japanese Embassy," NARA II, RG 80, PHLO, Box 6; NARA II, RG 457, NSA P-10, Box 38; PHAH, Part 32, 416; PHAH, Part 33, 818.

85. PHAH, part 33, 781 and 859.

86. Sherman Miles Memorandum, "Sunday Morning, December 7, 1941," December 15, 1941, and attached General Marshall's cable and transmission log data, December 15, 1941, NARA II, RG 80, PHLO, Box 5; PHAH, Part 32, 63, 136, 354, and 545; PHAH, Part 39, 95; Kahn, *The Code Breakers*, 554–555; McCollum, *Reminiscences of Rear Admiral Arthur H. McCollum*, 412–413; Stinnett, *Day of Deceit*, 301 (full typed copy and dispatch data).

87. McCollum, *Reminiscences of Rear Admiral Arthur H. McCollum*, 413.

88. PHAH, Part 32, 254.

89. Frank Knox, "Report by the Secretary of the Navy to the President December 14, 1941," FDR Library, Secretary File, Box 59; Agawa, *The Reluctant Admiral*, 255 and 259. Note that in NARA II, RG 38, CSNG Library, Box 167, and RG 80, PHLO, Box 4, Captain Minoru Genda,

Nagumo's Air Operations Officer, contends in his November 28, 1945, interrogation report "Pearl Harbor Attack" that there were 331 aircraft participating in the attack, a 22-plane difference from Agawa's 353-plane total.

90. Morton, *Fall of the Philippines*, 82–84; Manchester, *American Caesar*, 28–212; James, *The Years of MacArthur*, 10; Prados, *Combined Fleet Decoded*, 208.

91. Sherwood, *Roosevelt and Hopkins*, 431.

92. *Stimson Diary, op. cit.*, p. 81; "Francis Biddle Papers," Box 1, and FDR-Churchill Messages, Box 1, vol. 3, July–December 1941, FDR Library.

93. Churchill, *The Second World War, Vol. 3, The Grand Alliance*, 606–607.

94. Sherwood, *Roosevelt and Hopkins*, 428.

95. Liddell-Hart, *Strategy*, 238, 240, 243, 247–249, and 251; Kennedy, *Rise and Fall of the Great Powers*, 332, 341, 343, 355, and 361.

96. Kennedy, *Rise and Fall of the Great Powers*, 208 and 302–303.

97. Osaka Mainichi, "Indictment against America," Newspaper article NFI, 15, NARA II, RG 181.2.3, 14th Naval District, Office of the Commandant Correspondence 1912–1957; Sherrill, *Have We a Far East Policy?*, 250.

98. Kennedy, *Rise and Fall of the Great Powers*, 350 and 353.

CHAPTER 8

1. SRH 355, vol. 1, 399, NARA II, RG 457; Layton, Pineau, and Costello, *And I Was There*, 95.

2. SRH 149, Safford, "A Brief History of Communications Intelligence in the United States" (NSA SRH 149, March 1952), NARA II, RG 38, CSNG Library, Box 196.

3. SRH 020, W. J. Holmes, "Narrative of the Combat Intelligence Center, Joint Intelligence Center, Pacific Ocean Areas," U.S. Pacific Fleet, December 8, 1945, NARA II, RG 80, Box 41; Forest Baird, "The Dungeon" a speech presented 12 July 2002 (David Aiken, 13 July 2002).

4. HYPO/14th Naval District Communications Intelligence Summary (CIS), December 9, 1941, NARA II, RG 80, PHLO, Box 41; NARA II, RG 38, Inactive Stations, Box 3.

5. "Corregidor Unit Contribution Before Evacuation," *RIP87Z*, 204, NARA II, RG 38, Inactive Stations, Box 16; Kahn, *The Code Breakers*, 562–563; Layton, Pineau, and Costello, *And I Was There*, 340; OPNAV message 170350, December 16, 1941, NARA II, RG 38, Office of CNO, NSG Library, copy provided author by Robert Stinnett.

6. HYPO's IBM tabulating machines now began the process of transferring the code groups from the intercepts into the punch cards, requiring

up to 100 cards per intercepted message. Within a few months, hundreds of thousands of cards were being processed each week. Layton, Pineau, and Costello, *And I Was There*, 358; Rochefort, *Reminiscences of Captain Joseph J. Rochefort*, 111.

7. "Personnel Evacuated from Corregidor," NARA II, RG 457, Box 949.

8. Kahn, *The Code Breakers*, 568; Hoyt, *Japan's War*, 290; Symonds, *The Battle of Midway*, 139, 143, and 146–148; Agawa, *The Reluctant Admiral*, 307.

9. SRH 230, Henry F. Schorreck, *The Role of COMINT in the Battle of Midway*, (1983), 2, NARA II, RG 457.

10. Potter, *Yamamoto*, 34.

11. McCollum, *Reminiscences of Rear Admiral Arthur H. McCollum*, 417.

12. "Communications Intelligence Summaries" (CIS) with comments by CINCPAC War Plans/Fleet Intelligence Section, Part III, April 1–June 30, 1942, Combat Intelligence Unit (HYPO), 14th Naval District (Monterey, CA: Dudley Knox Library, Naval Postgraduate School), 3, 32, 44, 77, and 102. Note that by early April 1942 the CIU (HYPO) had recovered some 25,000 text additives of the 5-Number Code (JN-25), which greatly facilitated decryption efforts ("General History of OP-20-3-GYP," 23, NARA II, RG 38, Box 116, file 5750/199).

13. SRH 230, Henry F. Schorreck, *The Role of COMINT in the Battle of Midway*, (1983), 1–2, NARA II, RG 457; "Communications Intelligence Summaries" (CIS) with comments by CINCPAC War Plans/Fleet Intelligence Section, Part III, April 1–June 30, 1942, Combat Intelligence Unit (HYPO), 14th Naval District (Monterey, CA: Dudley Knox Library, Naval Postgraduate School), 126–127, 163, and 168.

14. "Communications Intelligence Summaries" (CIS) with comments by CINCPAC War Plans/Fleet Intelligence Section, Part III, April 1–June 30, 1942, Combat Intelligence Unit (HYPO), 14th Naval District (Monterey, CA: Dudley Knox Library, Naval Postgraduate School), 183, 203, 231–233, and 237.

15. "Communications Intelligence Summaries" (CIS) with comments by CINCPAC War Plans/Fleet Intelligence Section, Part III, April 1–June 30, 1942, Combat Intelligence Unit (HYPO), 14th Naval District (Monterey, CA: Dudley Knox Library, Naval Postgraduate School), 271 and 365.

16. "Communications Intelligence Summaries" (CIS) with comments by CINCPAC War Plans/Fleet Intelligence Section, Part III, April 1–June 30, 1942, Combat Intelligence Unit (HYPO), 14th Naval District (Monterey, CA: Dudley Knox Library, Naval Postgraduate School), 277 and 301.

17. SRH 230, Henry F. Schorreck, *The Role of COMINT in the Battle of Midway*, (1983), 2, NARA II, RG 457.

18. SRH 230, Henry F. Schorreck, *The Role of COMINT in the Battle of Midway*, (1983), 2, NARA II, RG 457.

19. "Communications Intelligence Summaries" (CIS) with comments by CINCPAC War Plans/Fleet Intelligence Section, Part III, April 1–June 30, 1942, Combat Intelligence Unit (HYPO), 14th Naval District (Monterey, CA: Dudley Knox Library, Naval Postgraduate School), 317 and 326.

20. "Communications Intelligence Summaries" (CIS) with comments by CINCPAC War Plans/Fleet Intelligence Section, Part III, April 1–June 30, 1942, Combat Intelligence Unit (HYPO), 14th Naval District (Monterey, CA: Dudley Knox Library, Naval Postgraduate School), 346–347.

21. "Communications Intelligence Summaries" (CIS) with comments by CINCPAC War Plans/Fleet Intelligence Section, Part III, April 1–June 30, 1942, Combat Intelligence Unit (HYPO), 14th Naval District (Monterey, CA: Dudley Knox Library, Naval Postgraduate School), 358 and 360.

22. "Communications Intelligence Summaries" (CIS) with comments by CINCPAC War Plans/Fleet Intelligence Section, Part III, April 1–June 30, 1942, Combat Intelligence Unit (HYPO), 14th Naval District (Monterey, CA: Dudley Knox Library, Naval Postgraduate School), 377, 391, 423, 429, 438, and 436.

23. "Communications Intelligence Summaries" (CIS) with comments by CINCPAC War Plans/Fleet Intelligence Section, Part III, April 1–June 30, 1942, Combat Intelligence Unit (HYPO), 14th Naval District (Monterey, CA: Dudley Knox Library, Naval Postgraduate School), 458.

24. Nelson, "The Codebreaker and the Battle of Midway," 21; SRH 230, Henry F. Schorreck, *The Role of COMINT in the Battle of Midway*, (1983), 6, NARA II, RG 457.

25. "Communications Intelligence Summaries" (CIS) with comments by CINCPAC War Plans/Fleet Intelligence Section, Part III, April 1–June 30, 1942, Combat Intelligence Unit (HYPO), 14th Naval District (Monterey, CA: Dudley Knox Library, Naval Postgraduate School), 469.

26. SRH 230, Henry F. Schorreck, *The Role of COMINT in the Battle of Midway*, (1983), 9, NARA II, RG 457.

27. "Communications Intelligence Summaries" (CIS) with comments by CINCPAC War Plans/Fleet Intelligence Section, Part III, April 1–June 30, 1942, Combat Intelligence Unit (HYPO), 14th Naval District (Monterey, CA: Dudley Knox Library, Naval Postgraduate School), 484–485 and 487; Duane Whitlock, "The Rochefort Medal: Rebuttal," NCVA *Cryptolog* (1985).

28. Symonds, *The Battle of Midway*, 200; Boyne, *Clash of Titans*, 181.

29. Boyne, *Shattered Sword*, 184–187.

30. Boyne, *Shattered Sword*, 190; Symonds, *The Battle of Midway*, 52 and 301.

31. Toll, *Pacific Crucible*, 426 and 429–434; Symonds, *The Battle of Midway*, 302–306; Boyne, *Shattered Sword*, 190: See also Moore, *Pacific Payback*, 235 (Chapter 10: "Five Minutes of Glory").

32. Boyne, *Shattered Sword*, 192–193; Toll, *Pacific Crucible*, 453–454.

33. SRH 020, W. J. Holmes, "Narrative of the Combat Intelligence Center, Joint Intelligence Center, Pacific Ocean Areas," U.S. Pacific Fleet, December 8, 1945, 3, NARA II, RG 80, Box 41.

34. PHAH, Part 33, 1390.

35. PHAH, Part 33, 926, 931, 933, 938, and 972.

36. PHAH, Part 26, 183.

37. "Memorandum for the Chief of Naval Operations, Items 4 and 5," 3, NARA II, RG 38, CNO CNSG Library, Box 149.

38. PHAH, Part 12, 255.

39. PHAH, Part 9, 4196.

40. PHAH, Part 33, 1168.

41. PHAH, Part 23, 686; PHAH, Part 26, 265–266.

42. PHAH, Part 32, 546; Layton, Pineau, and Costello, *And I Was There*, 136–137.

43. PHAH, Part 26, 390.

44. Thompson, *A Time for War*, 345; Miller, *War Plan Orange*, 45–46; Symonds, *The Battle of Midway*, 370.

45. OPNAV to Kimmel, December 8, 1941, NARA II, RG 80, PHLO, Box 54; NARA II, RG 457, CNO Naval Security Group, Box 143.

46. Simon, *Public Opinion in America: 1936–1970*, 125 and 137.

47. Alan Barth to Ferdinand Kuhn Jr., "Editorial Opinion on Foreign Affairs: Eyes on the Orient," *Newsletter*, November 28, 1941, 1 and 2, NARA FDR Library, Secretary File, Treasury Department (Morgenthau File), Box 80.

48. PHAH, Part 32, 290 and 669.

49. PHAH, Part 32, 531.

50. Each carrier carried a uniformly similar assortment of planes called an "air group." Besides a group command plane in the form of a single scout bomber, the remaining planes were divided into two SBD Dauntless dive-bombing squadrons (18 planes each), one torpedo squadron (18 planes), and one fighter squadron (18 planes). NARA Seattle, RG 181, Box 40, FF 1, A 3-1 (3 of 4), Commandant's Office, Central Subject File 1925–1942; Richardson, *On the Treadmill to Pearl Harbor*, 477–484. By September the Saratoga had been upgraded to reflect on SBD Dauntless Dive Bomber squadrons. See also "Organization of U.S. Pacific Fleet," September 11, 1941, NARA II, RG 80, PHLO, Box 3.

51. PHAH, Part 32, 587.

52. Miller, *War Plan Orange*, 305.

53. NARA Seattle, RG 181, Box 40, FF 1, A 3-1 (3 of 4), Commandant's Office, Central Subject File 1925–1942.

54. PHAH, Part 26, 347–348 and 375–376; "Radar-Installations in Ships," FDR Library, Secretary File, Box 59.

55. PHAH, Part 5, 2439; PHAH, Part 13, 517.

56. Goldstein and Dillon, *Pearl Harbor Papers*, 97, 190, 191, 203, 221, and 259; PHAH, Part 13, 516.

57. Goldstein and Dillon, *Pearl Harbor Papers*, 259–260.

58. Goldstein and Dillon, *Pearl Harbor Papers*, 193 and 302.

EPILOGUE

1. PHAH, Part 8, 3571; PHAH, Part 10, 4739.

2. Toland, *Infamy*, 55.

3. Navy Court of Inquiry, Admiral Ernest King's November 6, 1944, "Endorsement," PHAH, Parts 32 and 33.

4. PHAH, Part 39, 397.

5. PHAH, Part 26, 325.

6. PHAH, Part 39, 708.

7. "Memorandum for the Secretary of the Navy," NARA II, RG 80, PHLO, Box 6, COMINCH File M FF 1/A6-3, Serial 8313, Ref. Presidential Directive of August 28, 1945, "Concerning Information on Cryptanalysis."

8. Key reports would have included daily radio intercept log sheets from Stations CAST and HYPO and the integrated monthly reports involving the IJN's radio call sign and radio direction finder (RDF) intercepts recorded by Station H (HYPO), the West Coast Communications Intelligence network, the mid-Pacific network, and even the Western Pacific network.

9. PHAH, Parts 32 and 33, Navy Court of Inquiry, Admiral Ernest King's November 6, 1944, "Endorsement," 22.

10. PHAH, Parts 32 and 33, Navy Court of Inquiry, Admiral Ernest King's November 6, 1944, "Endorsement," 21.

11. PHAH, Parts 32 and 33, Navy Court of Inquiry, Admiral Ernest King's November 6, 1944, "Endorsement," 22.

12. PHAH, Parts 32 and 33, Navy Court of Inquiry, Admiral Ernest King's November 6, 1944, "Endorsement," 22.

13. PHAH, Part 32, 148.

14. PHAH, Part 3, 1469.

15. PHAH, Part 7, 2961.

16. PHAH, Part 3, 1469.

17. PHAH, Part 32, 187 and 564.

18. PHAH, Part 7, 2985–2986; PHAH, Part 32, 187 and 203.

19. These last four messages can be found in the *Walter Short Papers* at the Hoover Institution Archives, Stanford University; PHAH, Part 32, 187–191.

20. PHAH, Part 3, 1469.

21. PHAH, Part 3, 1469.

22. PHAH, Part 3, 1469.

23. PHAH, Part 2, 813 and 934; PHAH, Part 3, 1213; PHAH, Part 10, 1469; PHAH, Part 29, 2403–2404; PHAH, Part 39, 95.

24. *New York Times*, Section A-26 (May 26, 1999).

25. Manchester, *American Caesar*, 200 and 205–212. MacArthur's USAFFE Command consisted of the 5th Fighter Interceptor Command and the 5th Bomber Command, as well as 12 full infantry divisions. (PHAH, Part 11, 5320 and 5338.)

26. McCollum, *Reminiscences of Rear Admiral Arthur H. McCollum*, 422, author's emphasis in italics. It should be noted that the JCC Report of the PHAH, Part 39, 66-S, quoted Representative French B. Keefe as stating: "With full knowledge of Japan's intentions prior to the attack, Washington had one plain duty to the American people. That duty was to inform them of their peril. That was not done."

Bibliography

BOOKS

Agawa, Hiroyuki. *The Reluctant Admiral: Yamamoto and the Imperial Navy*. Tokyo: Kodansha, 1979, First English trans., New York: Kodansha, 1982.

Aldcroft, Derek H. *From Versailles to Wall Street, 1919–1929 (History of the World Economy in the Twentieth Century)*. Berkeley and Los Angeles: University of California Press, 1977.

Aldrich, Richard J. *Intelligence and the War against Japan: Britain, America and the Politics of Secret Service*. Cambridge: Cambridge University Press, 2001.

Allen, G. C. *A Short Economic History of Modern Japan, 1867–1937*. London: Alwin & Unwin, 1946.

Ambrose, Stephen E. *Rise to Globalism: American Foreign Policy Since 1938*. New York, Penguin Books, 1971.

Asada, Sadao. *Culture Shock and Japanese-American Relations.* Columbia: University of Missouri, 2007.

Asada, Sadao. *From Mahan to Pearl Harbor: The Imperial Japanese Navy and the United States.* Annapolis, MD: Naval Institute Press, 2006.

Baldwin, Hanson W. *Great Mistakes of the War.* New York: Harper & Brothers, 1950.

Barnhart, Michael A. *Japan Prepares for Total War: The Search for Economic Security, 1919–1941.* Ithaca, NY: Cornell University Press, 1987.

Bashe, Charles J., Lyle R. Johnson, John H. Palmer, and Emerson Pugh. *IBM's Early Computers.* Cambridge, MA, MIT Press, 1985.

Beach, Edward L. *Scapegoats: A Defense of Kimmel and Short at Pearl Harbor.* Annapolis, MD: Naval Institute Press, 1995.

Beard, Charles A. *Roosevelt and the Coming of the War 1941: Appearances and Realities.* New Haven, CT: Yale University Press, 1948.

Beasley, W. G. *The Meiji Restoration.* Stanford, CA: Stanford University Press, 1972.

Blair, Clay, Jr. *Silent Victory: The U.S. Submarine War against Japan.* New York: Lippincott Williams & Wilkins, 1975.

Borch, Fred, and Daniel Martinez. *Kimmel, Short, and Pearl Harbor: The Final Report Revealed.* Annapolis, MD: Naval Institute Press, 2005.

Boyne, Walter J. *Clash of Titans: World War II at Sea.* New York: Simon & Schuster, 1995.

Boyne, Walter J. *Shattered Sword: The Untold Story of the Battle of Midway.* Dulles, VA: Potomac Books, 2005.

Brands, H. W. *Traitor to His Class: The Privileged Life and Radical Presidency of Franklin Delano Roosevelt.* New York: Doubleday, 2008.

Brown, Anthony Cave, and Charles B. MacDonald. *The Secret History of the Atomic Bomb.* New York: Dial Press, 1977.

Budiansky, Stephen. *Battle of Wits: The Complete Story of Codebreaking in World War II.* New York: Free Press, 2000.

Burns, James MacGregor. *Roosevelt: The Lion and the Fox 1882–1940.* New York: Konecky & Konecky, 1984.

Calder, Nigel. *How to Read a Nautical Chart: A Complete Guide to Using and Understanding Electronic and Paper Charts.* New York: McGraw-Hill, 2012.

Carlson, Elliot. *Joe Rochefort's War: The Odyssey of the Codebreaker Who Outwitted Yamamoto at Midway.* Annapolis, MD: Naval Institute Press, 2011.

Chang, Iris. *The Rape of Nanking: The Forgotten Holocaust of World War II.* New York: Basic Books, 1997.

Churchill, Winston S., and John Keegan. *The Second World War, Vol. 1, The Gathering Storm.* Boston: Houghton Mifflin Harcourt, 1948.

Churchill, Winston S. *The Second World War, Vol. 2, Their Finest Hour.* Boston: Houghton Mifflin Harcourt, 1949.

Churchill, Winston S. *The Second World War, Vol. 3, The Grand Alliance.* Boston: Houghton Mifflin Harcourt, 1950.

Clausewitz, Carl von. *Vom Krieg.* Regensburg, Germany: Hofenberg, 1991. English edition: *On War,* Michael Howard and Peter Paret, eds. and trans., Princeton, NJ: Princeton University Press, 1984.

Costello, John. *Days of Infamy. Macarthur, Roosevelt, Churchill—The Shocking Truth Revealed: How Their Secret Deals and Strategic Blunders Caused Disasters at Pearl Harbor.* New York: Pocket Books, 1994.

Crowley, James B. *Japan's Quest for Autonomy: National Security and Foreign Policy, 1930–1938.* Princeton, NJ: Princeton University Press, 1966.

Davis, Kenneth S. *FDR: The War President, 1940–1943, A History.* New York: Random House, 2000.

DeGroot, Gerald. *The Bomb: A Life.* Cambridge, MA: Harvard University Press, 2005.

Devours, Cipher A., and Louis Kruh. *Machine Cryptography and Modern Cryptanalysis.* Norwood, MA: Artech House, 1985.

Encyclopedia Britannica, 11th ed. Cambridge: Cambridge University Press, 1911.

Evans, David C., and Mark K. Peattie. *Kaigun: Strategy, Tactics, and Technology in the Imperial Japanese Navy, 1887–1941.* Annapolis, MD: Naval Institute Press, 1997.

Farago, Ladislas. *The Broken Seal: "Operation Magic" and the Secret Road to Pearl Harbor.* New York: Random House, 1967.

Feis, Herbert. *Road to Pearl Harbor: The Coming of the War between the United States and Japan.* Princeton, NJ: Princeton University Press, 1950.

Fuchida, Mitsuo, and David C. Evans, eds. *The Japanese Navy in World War II: In the Words of Former Japanese Naval Officers.* Annapolis, MD: Naval Institute Press, 1969.

Gailey, Harry A. *War in the Pacific: From Pearl Harbor to Tokyo Bay.* New York: Ballantine, 1997.

Gallup, George H. *The Gallup Poll, Volume One 1935–1948.* New York, Random House, 1972.

Goldstein, Donald M., and Katherine V. Dillon, eds. *The Pearl Harbor Papers: Inside the Japanese Plans.* London, Brassey's, 1993.

Grew, Joseph C. *Ten Years in Japan.* Westport, CT: Praeger, 1944.

Hanyok, Robert J., and David P. Mowry. *West Wind Clear: Cryptology and the Winds Message Controversy—A Documentary History.* Fort George Meade, MD: National Security Agency, 2008.

Herring, George C. *From Colony to Superpower: U.S. Foreign Relations Since 1776*. Oxford: Oxford University Press, 2008.

Hewlett, Richard G., and Oscar E. Anderson Jr. *A History of the United States Atomic Energy Commission, Volume I, The New World 1939/1946*. Philadelphia: University of Pennsylvania Press, 1970.

Holmes, W. J. *Double-Edged Secrets: U.S. Naval Intelligence Operations in the Pacific During World War II*. Annapolis, MD: Naval Institute Press, 1979.

Howarth, Stephen. *The Fighting Ships of the Rising Sun: The Drama of the Imperial Japanese Navy, 1895–1945*. New York: Atheneum, 1983.

Howeth, Linwood S. *History of Communications-Electronics in the United States Navy*. Annapolis, MD: Naval Institute Press, 1963.

Hoyt, Edwin P. *Japan's War: The Great Pacific Conflict*. New York: McGraw-Hill, 1986.

Hull, Cordell. *The Memoirs of Cordell Hull*. New York: Macmillan, 1948.

Ickes, Harold L. *The Secret Diary of Harold L. Ickes, Volume III: The Lowering Clouds, 1939–1941*. New York: Simon & Schuster, 1954.

Isaacson, Walter. *Einstein: His Life and Universe*. New York: Simon & Schuster, 2007.

Israel, Fred L., ed. *The War Diary of Breckinridge Long: Selections from the Years 1939–1944*. Lincoln: University of Nebraska Press, 1966.

James, Clayton D. *No End Save Victory*. New York: G. P. Putnam's Sons, 2001.

James, Clayton D. *The Years of MacArthur*, vol. II. Boston: Houghton-Mifflin, 1975.

Kahn, David. *The Codebreakers: The Comprehensive History of Secret Communication from Ancient Times to the Internet, Revised and Updated*. New York: Scribner, 1996.

Kahn, David. *Seizing the Enigma: The Race to Break the German U-Boats Codes, 1939–1943*. Boston: Houghton Mifflin Harcourt, 1991.

Keen, Roland. *Wireless Direction Finding*. London: Iliffe & Sons Ltd., Dorset House; Enlarged 3rd edition, 1938.

Kennedy, Paul. *The Rise and Fall of the Great Powers: Economic Change and Military Conflict from 1500 to 2000*. New York: Vintage, 1987.

King, Ernest J., and Walter Muir Whitehill. *Fleet Admiral King: A Naval Record*. New York: W. W. Norton, 1952.

Kullback, Solomon. *Statistical Methods in Cryptanalysis*. Washington, DC: Government Printing Office, 1938 [Paperback: Walnut Creek, CA: Aegean Park Press, 1976].

Lambert, John W., and Norman Polmar. *Defenseless: Command Failure at Pearl Harbor*. New York: Zenith, 2003.

Layton, Edwin T., Roger Pineau, and John Costello. *And I Was There: Pearl Harbor and Midway—Breaking the Secrets*. New York: William Morrow, 1985.

Leutze, James. *A Different Kind of Victory: A Biography of Admiral Thomas C. Hart.* Annapolis, MD: Naval Institute Press, 1981.

Liddell Hart, Basil Henry. *Strategy: The Classic Book on Military Strategy,* 2nd Revised ed. New York: Plume, 1991.

Mahan, Alfred Thayer. *The Influence of Sea Power upon History: 1660–1783.* Gretna, LA: Pelican, 2003. [Boston: Little, Brown and Company, 1890].

Manchester, William. *American Caesar: Douglas MacArthur 1880–1964.* Boston: Little, Brown and Company, 1978.

Manchester, William. *The Glory and the Dream: A Narrative History of America 1932–1972, Vol. 1.* Boston: Little, Brown and Company, 1974.

Marshall, George, C. *The Papers of George Catlett Marshall, Volume 2, "We Cannot Delay" July 1, 1939–December 6, 1941.* Baltimore, MD: Johns Hopkins University Press, 1986.

Marshall, Jonathan. *To Have and Have Not: Southeast Asian Raw Materials and the Origins of the Pacific War.* Berkeley: University of California Press, 1995.

Miller, Edward S. *Bankrupting the Enemy: The U.S. Financial Siege of Japan Before Pearl Harbor.* Annapolis, MD: Naval Institute Press, 2007.

Miller, Edward S. *War Plan Orange: The U.S. Strategy to Defeat Japan, 1897–1945.* Annapolis, MD: Naval Institute Press, 1991.

Moore, Stephen L. *Pacific Payback.* New York: NAL Caliber/Penguin Group, 2014.

Morison, Samuel E. *The Battle of the Atlantic, September 1939–May 1943.* Boston: Little, Brown and Company, 1947.

Morton, Louis. *The Fall of the Philippines.* Washington, DC: Government Printing Office, 1953.

Okins, Elliott E. *To Spy or Not to Spy.* Chula Vista, CA: Pateo, 1985.

Parker, Frederick D. *Pearl Harbor Revisited: United States Navy Communications Intelligence, 1924–1941.* Fort George Meade, MD: National Security Agency, 2013.

Parshall, Jonathan, and Anthony Tully. *Shattered Sword: The Untold Story of the Battle of Midway.* Dulles, VA: Potomac Books, 2005.

Perkins, Frances. *The Roosevelt I Knew.* New York: Viking, 1946.

Potter, John Deane. *Yamamoto: The Man Who Menaced America.* New York: Viking, 1965.

Prados, John. *Combined Fleet Decoded: The Secret History of American Intelligence and the Japanese Navy in World War II.* New York: Random House, 1995.

Prange, Gordon W., with Donald M. Goldstein and Katherine V. Dillon. *At Dawn We Slept: The Untold Story of Pearl Harbor.* New York: Penguin Books, 1981.

Preston, Diana. *Lusitania: An Epic Tragedy*. New York: Bloomsbury, 2002.

Pugh, Emerson W. *Building IBM: Shaping an Industry and Its Technology*. Cambridge, MA: MIT Press, 1995.

Rhodes, Richard. *The Making of the Atomic Bomb*. New York: Simon & Schuster, 1986.

Richardson, James O., as told to George C. Dyer. *On the Treadmill to Pearl Harbor: Memoirs of Admiral James O. Richardson*. Washington, DC: Government Printing Office, 1974.

Rosenman, Samuel I. *Working with Roosevelt*. New York: Harper & Brothers, 1952.

Rusbridger, James, and Eric Nave. *Betrayal at Pearl Harbor: How Churchill Lured Roosevelt into Pearl Harbor*. New York: Simon & Schuster, 1991.

Sebag-Montefiore, Hugh. *Enigma: The Battle for the Code*. New York: John Wiley & Sons, 2004.

Sherrill, Charles Hitchcock. *Have We a Far East Policy?* New York: Charles Scribner, 1920.

Sherrod, Robert. *I Can Tell It Now*, ed. David Brown and Richard Bruner. New York: E. P. Dutton, 1964.

Sherwood, Robert E. *Roosevelt and Hopkins: An Intimate History*. New York: Grosset & Dunlop, 1948.

Simon, Rita James. *Public Opinion in America,1936–1970*. Urbana-Champaign: University of Illinois Press, 1974.

Simpson, B. Mitchell III. *Admiral Harold R. Stark: Architect of Victory 1939–1945*. Columbia: University of South Carolina Press, 1989.

Snyder, Wilbert F., and Charles L. Bragaw. *Achievement in Radio: Seventy Years of Radio Science, Technology, Standards and Measurement at the National Bureau of Standards*. Boulder, CO: U.S. Department of Commerce,1986.

Spector, Ronald H. *Eagle Against the Sun: The American War with Japan*. New York: Free Press, 1985.

Spector, Ronald H. *Listening to the Enemy: Key Documents on the Role of Communications Intelligence in the War with Japan*. Lanham, MD: Rowman & Littlefield, 1997.

Stephanson, Anders. *Manifest Destiny: American Expansion and the Empire of Right*. New York: Hill & Wang, 1996.

Stimson, Henry L., and McGeorge Bundy. *On Active Service in Peace and War*. New York: Hippocrene Books, 1971.

Stinnett, Robert B. *Day of Deceit: The Truth About FDR and Pearl Harbor*. New York: Free Press, 1999.

Strunk, Mildred, and Hadley Cantril, eds. *Public Opinion 1935–1946*. Princeton, NJ: Princeton University Press, 1951.

Symonds, Craig L. *The Battle of Midway*. New York: Oxford University Press, 2011.

Thompson, Robert Smith. *A Time for War: Franklin Delano Roosevelt and the Path to Pearl Harbor.* New York: Prentice Hall, 1991.

Thorpe, Elliott R. *East Wind, Rain: A Chief of Counter-intelligence Remembers Peace and War in the Pacific.* Boston: Gambit, 1969.

Toland, John. *Infamy: Pearl Harbor and Its Aftermath.* New York: Doubleday, 1982.

Toland, John. *The Rising Sun: The Decline and Fall of the Japanese Empire, 1936–1945.* New York: Random House, 1970.

Toll, Ian W. *Pacific Crucible: War at Sea in the Pacific, 1941–1942.* New York: W. W. Norton, 2011.

Tolley, Kemp. *Cruise of the Lanikai: Incitement to War.* Annapolis, MD: Naval Institute Press, 1973.

Tuchman, Barbara. *The Zimmermann Telegram: America Enters the War, 1917–1918.* New York: Random House, 1958.

Tugwell, Rexford G. *The Democratic Roosevelt: A Biography of Franklin D. Roosevelt.* New York: Doubleday, 1957.

Van der Vat, Daniel. *The Pacific Campaign: World War II: The U.S.–Japanese Naval War, 1941–1945.* New York: Simon & Schuster, 1991.

Van Mook, H. J. *The Netherlands, Indies and Japan: Their Relations 1940–1941.* London: Routledge, 2010.

Wallin, Homer N. *Pearl Harbor: Why, How, Fleet Salvage, and Final Appraisal.* Washington, DC: Naval History Division, 1968.

Webster's New World Dictionary, College Edition. New York: World Publishing Company, 1955.

Wedemeyer, Albert C. *Wedemeyer Reports!,* New York: Henry Holt, 1958.

Weintraub, Stanley. *Long Day's Journey into War: December 7, 1941.* New York: Dutton, 1991.

West, Nigel (pseudonym for Rupert William Simon Allason). *The SIGINT Secrets: The Signals Intelligence War 1900 to Today including the Persecution of Gordon Welchman.* New York: William Morrow, 1988.

Wigner, Eugene. "Leo Szilard." *Biographical Memoirs of the National Academy of Sciences, Vol. XL.* Washington, DC: National Academy of Sciences, 1969.

Wilford, Timothy. *Pearl Harbor Redefined: U.S.N. Radio Intelligence in 1941.* Lanham, MD: University Press of America, 2001.

Winslow, W. G. *The Fleet the Gods Forgot: The U.S. Asiatic Fleet in World War II.* Annapolis, MD: Naval Institute Press, 1989.

Wolff, Leon. *Little Brown Brother: How the United States Purchased and Pacified the Philippine Islands at the Century's Turn.* New York: History Book Club, 1960.

Yardley, Herbert O. *The American Black Chamber.* Annapolis, MD: Naval Institute Press, 1931.

ORAL HISTORIES AND DIARIES

Biard, Forrest. *Oral History Collection*. Denton: University of North Texas, 1992.

Briggs, Ralph T., by Bettina B. Greaves. Interview, Las Vegas, 1988.

Kirk, Alan Goodrich. *The Reminiscences of Alan Goodrich Kirk*. New York: Naval Historical Foundation, 1962.

McCollum, Arthur H. *Reminiscences of Rear Admiral Arthur H. McCollum*. Annapolis, MD: Naval Historical Foundation, 1973.

Ranneft, Johan. *Dagboek van Schout-bij-Nacht J. E. Meijer Ranneft*. The Hague: Institute for Maritime History, Ministry of Defense, 1952.

Rochefort, Joseph. *Oral History*. Annapolis, MD: Naval Historical Foundation, 1969.

Rochefort, Joseph. *The Reminiscences of Captain Joseph J. Rochefort*. Annapolis, MD: Naval Historical Foundation, 1983.

Stimson, Henry Lewis. *Diaries* (microfilm). Yale University Microfilm Library, New Haven, CT.

Vol. 35 Microfilm Reel 7: 20, 25, 37, and 136–137; Reel 7: October 16, 1941; Vol. 36: Reel 7: November 7, 1941, 48–49.

ARTICLES AND CHAPTERS

Barth, Alan. Editorial Opinion—"Eyes on the Orient." Newsletter, Office of the Secretary of the Treasury, November 28, 1941.

Beatty, Frank. "Another Version of What Started War with Japan." *U.S. News and World Report*, May 28, 1954.

Bristol, Horace, photographer. "Dutch East Indies." *Life* 8, no. 4 (January 22, 1940).

Elfendah, Gerald. "Bainbridge Island Waves." *Cryptolog* (Fall 1997).

Foster, Richard C., and Pierre Demerseman. "Radio Direction Finding and Huff-Duff." *AWA Review* 8 (2000).

Gladwin, Leo A. "Alan M. Turing's Critique of Running Short Cribs on the U.S. Navy Bombe." *Cryptolog* (January 2003).

Hanyek, Bob. "Radio Intelligence on the Mexican Border, 1916–1918." *Cryptolog* (Winter 1997).

Hanyek, Bob. "Still Desperately Seeking Miss Agnes." *Cryptolog* (Fall 1997).

Hoyt, Frederick G. "History of USN Radio Point Arguello." *Cryptolog* (Summer 1995).

Hoyt, Frederick G. "Navy Radio Imperial Beach." *Cryptolog* (May 1995).

Jacobsen, Philip H. "Radio Silence and Radio Deception Secrecy Insurance for the Pearl Harbor." *Intelligence and National Security* 19, no. 4 (Winter, 2004).

Lee, Bartholomew. "America's Wireless Spies." *AWA Review* 5 (1990).

Lee, Bartholomew. "Marconi's Transatlantic Triumph." *AWA Review* 8 (May 1977).

Lee, Bartholomew. "Radio Spies: Episodes in the Ether Wars." *AWA Review* 15 (2002).

Moreau, Louise. "The Military Communications Explosion, 1914–1918." *AWA Review* 6 (1991).

Myers, Larry. "Key Role of Japanese Cryptolinguists in WW II CIMINT." *Cryptolog* (Fall 1995).

Nelson, Lars Erik. "The Codebreaker and the Battle of Midway." *Cryptolog* (Fall 1986).

Pekelney, Rich. "Electronic Cipher Machine (ECM) Mark II." https://mari time.org>tech>ecm2.

Pekelney, Rich. "What Is the SIGABA-ECM Mark II And Why It Was Important?" www.jproc.ca/crypto/ecm2.html.

Pelletier, Al. "My Life with JN-25." *Cryptolog* (Summer 1992).

Phillips, Pearly L., and Elmer Dickey. "Reorganization of the OTRG." *Cryptolog* (Fall, 1982).

Rusbridger, James. "JN-25, the NSA, and Pearl Harbor." *Cryptolog,* Summer 1992).

Sherrod, Robert. "Secret Conference with General Marshall," Memorandum for Editor David W. Hulburd, Jr. *Time,* November 15, 1941.

Stephenson, Parks. "The Marconi Wireless Telegraph Apparatus in R.M.S. *Titanic* Confirmed by Observations of the Wreck." *AWA Review* 15 (2002).

U.S. Fleet. *Information Bulletin* #29, "Antiaircraft Action Summary—World War II," October 1945.

Whitlock, Duane. "The Silent War against the Japanese Navy." *Naval War College Review* 48, no. 4 (Autumn 1995).

Whitlock, Duane. "Station C Corregidor As I Recall It." *Cryptolog Special* (Summer 1992).

Wilford, Timothy. "Watching the North Pacific: British and Commonwealth Intelligence Before Pearl Harbor." *Intelligence and National Security* 17, no. 4 (2002).

Yoshihara, Toshi, and James R. Holmes. "Japanese Maritime Thought: If Not Mahan, Who?" *Naval War College Review* 59, no. 3 (Summer 2006).

GOVERNMENT PUBLICATIONS

Knox, Frank. "Report of the Commission Appointed by The President," 1942, FDR Library.

National Bureau of Standards. *Radio Transmission Handbook*. Washington, DC, 1942.

Naval Analysis Division. *The Campaigns of the Pacific War—United States Strategic Bombing Survey (Pacific)*, Washington, DC, 1946.

Pearl Harbor Attack Hearings, the Joint Committee on the Investigation of the Pearl Harbor Attack, 79th Congress—39 Volumes (Parts), Washington, DC, U.S. Government Printing Office:

Roberts Commission: December 18, 1941–January 23, 1942 (Parts 22–25)

Hart Investigation: February 12–June 15, 1944 (Part 26)

Army Pearl Harbor Board: July 20–October 20, 1944 (Parts 27–31)

Navy Court of Inquiry: July 24–October 10, 1944 (Parts 32–33)

Clark Investigation: August 4–September 20, 1944 (Part 34)

Clausen Investigation: January 24–September 12, 1945 (Part 35)

Hewitt Inquiry: May 14–July 11, 1945 (Parts 36–38)

Joint Congressional Committee: November 15, 1945–May 31, 1946 (Parts 1–21 and 40)

Multiple Hearings Reports, Findings, and Conclusions: (Part 39)

Wenger, Joseph N. "The Evolution of the Navy's Cryptographic Organization," SRMN-084, Navy Department Library, Washington, DC.

NATIONAL ARCHIVES AND RESEARCH ADMINISTRATION (NARA)

Archives II, Textual Archives Services Division, Modern Military Records Branch (MMRB), College Park, Maryland

Note: NARA II (the MMRB) maintains a system of finding aids to assist the researcher in locating documents of interest. The MMRB withdraws from time to time various documents for "national security reasons" and substitutes withdrawal notices in their place.

Record Group 24: Records of Bureau of Naval Personnel: Ship Logs ("Deck Log")

Record Group 38: Chief of Naval Operations files, 1940–1941; Office of Naval Intelligence files

Admiral Kimmel papers:

Crane Files: Contains many of the Registered Intelligence Publications (RIPs) and information on the evolution of U.S. Naval Intelligence

Crane Inactive Stations: Covers most of the 17 U.S. Navy intercept and tracking stations that made up the "splendid arrangement" and formed part of the West Coast, Mid-Pacific, and Western Pacific Strategic radio direction finder nets; information on British Far East intelligence operations included. Note: John M. Lietwiler (CAST) letter of November 16, 1941, to L. W. Parke of OP-20-GY

(Navy Department) and others in Box 15. Some military attaché (Tokyo) reports can be found. Station H radio intercept daily chronologies can be found, as well as other station intelligence reports.

Crane Office of the CNO, CNSG Library: Reports from various stations, offices, and Pearl Harbor Attack Hearings. Information on mid-Pacific RDF network can be found. Note Arthur McCollum's "Memorandum for the Director" of October 7, 1940 (aka McCollum's Action Proposal) located in Box 6. Also includes some RDF (OP-20-GX) material and J-19 Code espionage efforts of IJN at Pearl Harbor during 1941. See also interrogation reports (Capt. Minoru Genda) of IJN Strike Force participants and Honolulu-Tokyo diplomatic message traffic concerning espionage at Pearl Harbor and oil production data and maps of Dutch East Indies.

Record Group 80 (Pearl Harbor Liaison Office—PHLO): General records navy and assorted intelligence reports and RDF chart plots, including intelligence reports by U.S. Naval Attaché at Singapore. Note: Lt. Cmdr. A. H. McCollum's February 1, 1941, response to Ambassador Joseph Grew's intelligence report of the Japanese possibly planning an attack on Pearl Harbor: "Subject: Rumored Japanese attack on Pearl Harbor" in Box 4 and W. J. Holmes "Narrative of the Combat Intelligence Center, Pacific Ocean Areas" SRH 020 in Box 41; details on U.S. Pacific Fleet employment schedule, orders and organization and Secretary of State Hull's final ultimatum to Tokyo; Berlin to Tokyo PURPLE messages 1941; Admiral Tom Hart and his U.S. Asiatic Fleet; Station H daily communications reports can be found; Some PHAH investigative reports covering PURPLE diplomatic messages are available; "Narrative of the Combat Intelligence Center, Joint Intelligence Center, Pacific Ocean Areas" by W. J. Holmes available as SRH 020; Some OPNAV/CNO directives and orders found here.

Record Group 313: Records of Naval Operating Forces and Adm. Kimmel's CINCPAC order to conduct operations (Exercise 191) in the near-North Pacific in November 1941, as well as Vice Adm. Halsey's orders in December 1941; as well as U.S. Naval Observer reports from Singapore for 1941.

Record Group 370: Pacific Ocean Maps, including North Pacific and points north of Hawaii.

Record Group 457: Contains documents released by National Security Agency (NSA); Some documents have been partially redacted (censored); includes Imperial Japanese Navy messages; codes and ciphers, radio intercept log sheets, radio direction finding data, IBM operations to include Station HYPO printouts for August–October 1941 (HYOO 8 in Boxes 1378 and 1470), November 1941

(HYOO 9 in Boxes 1315 and 1470), and December 1941 (HYOO 10 in Boxes 1284 and 1298). Includes IJN tactical radio call signs for administration and training and actual operations, as well as key personnel listings and organization of Navy Department; Adm. Kimmel papers and commander's correspondence, including interview with Roosevelt; Special Research Histories (SRH) reports:

SRH 149: Safford, L. F., "The Evolution of the Navy's Cryptologic Organization," and Wenger, J. N., "A Brief History of Communications Intelligence in the United States"

SRH 180: Station CAST Technical Upgrades

SRH 197: IBM Operations and OP-20-G Organization and Activities

SRH 211: "Japanese Radio Communications and Radio Intelligence," January 1, 1945

SRH 230: Schorreck, Henry F., "The Role of COMINT in the Battle of Midway"

SRH 250: Hurt, John, "A Version of the Japanese Problem"

SRH 255: Oral History Interview with Mr. Robert D. Ogg (1983)

SRH 305: Safford, L. F., "The Undeclared War History of R.I." (1943)

SRH 355: Capt. J. S. Holtwick, Naval Security Group History

SRH 459: "Organization of Naval Intelligence"

Archives II: Cartographic Branch: Nautical Charts
North Pacific Ocean

Note: "Pilot Chart of the North Pacific Ocean Eastern Part" (Chart 527), "North Pacific Ocean Middle Part" (Chart 528), and "North Pacific Ocean Western Part" (Chart 529), and others.

NARA Franklin D. Roosevelt Presidential Library,
Hyde Park, New York (FDR Library)

Contains a number of files involving Roosevelt (Safe Files and Map Room Papers), the Usher Books that chronicle selected daily White House visitors, as well as the John Toland Papers and the Diary of Adolf A. Berle Jr. Tapes and transcripts on Robert D. Ogg and Rear Adm. Johan E. R. Ranneft are available, as are those concerning Rear Adm. Kemp Tolley; Letter from Robert Israel to John Toland, May 10, 1982, with December 6, 1941, radio report message about IJN "southeast of Dutch Harbor." Also on hand are John Toland's papers, correspondence, and interviews with Ralph T. Briggs and Bonner Fellers and Arthur McCollum's letter to A. A. Hoehling, March 7, 1962.

NARA Laguna Niguel (now Riverside), California

Uses the RG 181 Navy filing system for organizing its archives. Documents concerning Station H and Adm. Kimmel's abortive ambush maneuver Battle Plan 2M1 of November 21, 1941, can be found. The A-6 intelligence files contain information from other naval districts that are not otherwise found in other archives. Radio direction finding (RDF) bearings reports can be found, as well as Adm. Kimmel's "Battle Plan 2M1." All files labeled SECRET and CONFIDENTIAL are useful. The 11th Naval District's communications intelligence files are located here. The researcher needs to examine *all* RG 181 listings and files in order to cover the West Coast archives.

NARA Pacific Region at San Bruno, California

This archive uses the RG 181 filing system and its A-6 intelligence file, which covers the 12th and 13th Naval Districts (San Francisco and Seattle respectively), as well as the 14th Naval District (Hawaii and Central Pacific) and the 16th Naval District (Philippines). Documents are filed in Hollinger and cardboard boxes. Some tracking data reports on Japanese merchant ship locations for mid- to late 1941. Some information can also be found on the commercial radio and cable companies that formed part of the navy's West Coast Communications Intelligence Network and the U.S. Pacific Fleet's organization in 1941. The Port Director's file contains a federal withdrawal notice from sometime in the 1970s for the missing SS *Lurline* Radio Log. North Pacific weather reports and storm predictions by the National Bureau of Standards can be found here.

NARA Pacific—Alaska Region in Seattle, Washington

This archive contains some data and reports on Dutch Harbor and Sitka, Territory of Alaska, intercept and tracking stations, as well as the Bainbridge Island 13th Naval District and related Canadian intelligence and communications networks. Information on the establishment of the Naval Coastal Frontier can be found here. Again, the RG 181 filing system is used.

MISCELLANEOUS

Combat Intelligence Unit Fourteenth Naval District, Communications Intelligence Summaries, Parts I and III in Dudley Knox Library, Naval Postgraduate School, Monterey, CA.

Departments of the Army and the Air Force, *Fundamentals of Traffic Analysis (Radio-Telegraph)* (TM32-250/AFM 100-80). Washington, DC: U.S. Government Printing Office, 1948.

Great Circle Sailing Chart of the North Pacific Ocean (#56). 1973 Edition. NIMA Ref. Number WOPZP56 and Tracking Chart No. 16 North Pacific HO5405-16, 1943.

Grogan, Leslie E. "Record for Posterity" (Matson Line). San Francisco (December 10, 1941).

Sherrod, Robert L. Memorandum for David W. Hulburd, Jr., "Subject: General Marshall's Conference Today," November 15, 1941 (with additional comment appended August 29, 1945), George C. Marshall Foundation, https://www.marshallfoundation.org/library/digital-archive/robert-l-sherrod-memorandum-for-david-w-hulburd-jr/.

Index

About the Author

Sewall Menzel, PhD, is a political-military analyst and scholar with a degree in history from The Citadel and a doctorate in international relations from the University of Miami (Coral Gables). A graduate of the Army War College with extensive studies in military strategy, he is the author of several books, including *Bullets vs. Ballots*; *Dictators, Drugs and Revolution*; and the award-winning *Cobs, Pieces of Eight and Treasure Coins*. Currently an adjunct professor with the Department of Political Science at Florida Atlantic University, he teaches the courses American Foreign Policy, Military Strategy and Policy, and War and Peace. During his 25-year military career as a decorated U.S. Army officer, he served on General Creighton Abrams' wartime Joint General Staff (Saigon) working in its J-2 (Intelligence) directorate. Further service saw him working two assignments with the Army General Staff at the Pentagon and then later as a Defense Intelligence Agency U.S. naval attaché in Latin America.